Reading Drama

AN ANTHOLOGY OF

PLAYS

Reading Drama

AN ANTHOLOGY OF

PLAYS

ROBERT DIYANNI

Pace University, Pleasantville

Macmillan/McGraw-Hill School Publishing Company

Project Editor: Charles Roebuck
Production Supervisor: Diane K. Lindeman
Cover Design: DanielsDesign Inc., New York

Text Development, Design, and Production: Keim Publishing, New York
Designer: Claudia DePolo

1 2 3 4 5 6 7 8 9 0   DOCDOC   8 9 4 3 2 1 0 9

ISBN 0-07-537505-2

For Robert M. Dell

Author's Acknowledgments

For encouraging me to undertake this project, and for supporting me generously and graciously, I would like to thank Charles Roebuck and Gerry Gabianelli. For her expert work on the Teacher's Guide to *Reading Drama*, with its wealth of practical classroom applications, I would like to thank Judith A. Stanford of Rivier College, who, like me, has also taught high school students. To Bob Dell, I owe a debt of gratitude far beyond what my affectionate dedication of this book can convey. He has long been a model of the dedicated teacher, and he continues to be a source of inspiration.

PREFACE

Reading Drama is a textbook. No attempt has been made to disguise that fact. But it is a textbook that offers many hours of reading pleasure because it contains plays that, quite simply, are enjoyable to read. Some are humorous, others serious, still others both surprising and thought provoking. Some are unforgettable. The plays were chosen because they are well crafted and wide ranging in vision. They are written in a wide variety of styles and voices, and they reflect varying perspectives. Some are long and complex, others are short and more accessible. Classic plays, such as *The Tragedy of Macbeth,* balance contemporary works, such as *True West,* by playwrights whose reputations are still growing. Plays by women complement others by men; plays by American writers stand alongside those by playwrights from other countries.

This book is designed to prepare you to read drama thoughtfully and perceptively. Chapter One, Reading and Responding, provides an overview of the reading process. It describes what you do as you read, and it explains how you can improve your ability to interpret and evaluate plays. Chapter Two, Elements of Drama, identifies and explains basic characteristics of drama, such as dialogue and imagery, character and conflict, symbolism and irony, plot and structure, and setting and staging. The critical vocabulary introduced in this chapter will enable you to discuss plays and analyze them carefully and well.

An appendix—Writing About Drama—has also been included. It contains guidelines for the various stages of writing, including making notes, drafting, organizing, and revising. The appendix also suggests general topics for papers. A glossary has been included to provide a convenient way to check the meaning of critical terms.

An ability to read perceptively, with understanding, is one sign of an educated person. An ability to read appreciatively, with enjoyment, is a source of lifelong pleasure. *Reading Drama* can bring you both.

Robert DiYanni

CONTENTS

PART ONE   INTRODUCTION TO DRAMA

Chapter One   Reading and Responding   3

  The Pleasures of Drama   3

  Reading   6

    Isabella Augusta Persse, Lady Gregory

    The Rising of the Moon   7

  Interpreting   19

  Evaluating   22

Chapter Two   Elements of Drama   26

  Plot and Structure   26

  Character and Conflict   30

  Dialogue and Monologue   32

  Setting and Staging   37

  Symbolism and Irony   44

  Thought and Theme   47

  Genre and Convention   49

PART TWO   ANTHOLOGY OF PLAYS

  Sophocles

    Antigonê   61

  William Shakespeare

    The Tragedy of Macbeth   98

  Molière

    The Doctor in Spite of Himself   180

  Henrik Ibsen

    An Enemy of the People   214

  August Strindberg

    The Stronger   303

Anton Chekhov
    A Marriage Proposal   309
William Butler Yeats
    Purgatory   322
John Millington Synge
    Riders to the Sea   329
Susan Glaspell
    Trifles   341
Tennessee Williams
    The Glass Menagerie   356
Eugène Ionesco
    The Gap   420
Arthur Miller
    A View from the Bridge   428
Lorraine Hansberry
    A Raisin in the Sun   486
Sam Shepard
    True West   578

Appendix   **Writing About Drama**   634
Glossary   651

PART ONE

Introduction to Drama

CHAPTER ONE

Reading and Responding

The Pleasures of Drama

Drama, unlike the other literary genres, is meant to be performed on a stage. A play is written to be brought to life in the theater. Much of the pleasure drama brings us arises from the way the language of the play's script comes alive in the speech of living actors. These actors are, of course, real people who represent fictional, or imaginary, characters. Part of our pleasure involves watching actors dramatically enact the "lives" of the characters they portray. We enjoy the way they walk and talk, the way they interact with other characters, even their facial expressions and bodily gestures. For even the smallest gesture, such as the lowering of a hand, or the slightest facial movement, such as the raising of an eyebrow, can contribute to our sense of the play's human experience.

When we either read or view drama, we are aware, even if only implicitly, of its major characteristics, or features. The first of these is its representational quality. Drama is a *mimetic* art, one that imitates or represents human life and experience. A large part of the pleasure drama brings us, in fact, reflects its ability to show us aspects of human life meaningfully enacted. Drama is also an *active* art in which actors portraying characters say and do things to one another. Actors are agents, or doers, who make things happen through speech and bodily action. In addition, drama is an *im-*

mediate art, one that represents action that occurs in the play's present. This is so even when a play's subject is historical, that is, even when its dramatic action concerns the past. A play can bring the feeling of the past to life right before us. Our experience of drama is one of watching events *as* they occur. We are firsthand witnesses of present-tense actions rather than auditors who simply hear about events later from a narrator at second hand.

One additional and critically important feature of drama derives from its mimetic, active, and immediate qualities: its *interactive nature*. Plays represent human action mainly through the interaction of characters. The action of plays is based on interaction, for dramatic characters respond and relate to one another. They engage one another in dialogue and action, in speech and visual displays. Such character interaction is the heart of drama: it is the spring of plot, the source of meaning, and the central reason for our pleasure in dramatic experience.

Drama is interactive in still another way. Unlike fiction and poetry, which are largely verbal arts (though poetry is also allied with music or song), drama is a *composite* art—one that makes use of many of the other arts. Painting and architecture are used in the design and creation of stage sets and in the way stage and actors are lighted or kept in shadow. Music and other sound effects may be used to suggest feelings, to build tension, or to create mood and atmosphere. Sculpture and dance are suggested by the way characters are positioned on stage and by their movements around it. Drama is a complex art that involves a dynamic interaction of many visual and aural elements. In viewing drama and in reading it, we need to be as alert as possible, keeping our eyes and ears, as well as our minds, open.

Our pleasure in drama, then, arises from the cumulative impact of a multitude of impressions both visual and aural. Makeup and costume, lighting and sound, speech and action, posture and gesture, movement and expression—all work together to bring plays to life, to imbue them with meaning and feeling, and most importantly to create a distinctive theatrical experience for the audience. It is this experience we attempt to capture when we read drama, knowing all the while that reading a play is not the same as sitting in a crowded theater watching it enacted on a stage. To compensate for this fact, we try to read drama imaginatively as if we were watching it. We attempt to read drama theatrically.

But what does it mean to read a play theatrically? How do we imaginatively reconstruct a play in our minds? Essentially, we translate the script we read into a mental performance that we imagine. By attending to the demonstrable implications of the words on the page, we can imagine how they might be dramatized on the stage. We learn to look not only at what a play's words mean, but also at what they suggest about the behavior, movements, gestures, and feelings of the characters who say them. We learn to listen for the effect those words have on the other characters. We try to imagine how the words might be uttered — loudly or softly, swiftly or slowly, gently or threateningly, graciously or sarcastically, to suggest just a few possibilities. We imagine where the characters are positioned relative to one another, how close or far apart they are. We imagine the manner of their walk, the style of their physical gestures, and the subtlest alteration of their voices and facial expressions. These details, coupled with the costumes of the characters, the scenery on stage, and the sound effects, all contribute to the richness of our imaginative reenactment of a play. The better we can imagine such elements, the better we will absorb the atmosphere and feeling of the play, and the more complete and theatrical our experience of it will be.

There are several ways to learn to read plays theatrically. By reading patiently and deliberately, we can train ourselves to be attentive not only to the literal meanings of dialogue but also to the implications of its sound, accent, and rhythm. Reading aloud, perhaps with other students in small groups, can be helpful. And it can often be enlightening to talk with others about our mental reconstructions of scenes.

In the process of learning to read the plays in this book theatrically, we will also attend to the fullest expression of their literary meaning. Drama is literature as well as theater, for, like poetry and fiction, drama is an art of language. While drama entertains us with its representation of life, it offers provocative ideas about the life it portrays, and it provides an imaginative extension of its possibilities.

To say all this is to claim a great deal for drama. The true test of just how well these claims are met will be the degree to which you truly enjoy (in the broadest and deepest senses of the word) the plays included in this book. As a way of helping you toward both an understanding of the plays and an enriched experience in reading them, we include in this chapter an approach to drama that stresses three things: your experience of a play; your interpretation of its ideas; and your evaluation both of its artistic merit and of the social, cultural, and moral values it presents. Our discussion will thus be arranged in three parts, each devoted to a different aspect of the process of reading drama, and each based on a consideration of one of the following questions:

1. What feelings does the play evoke? Or alternatively: How am I affected by this play? How do I feel as I read it?
2. What ideas does the play express? Or alternatively: What sense do I make of it?
3. What values does the play endorse and how effectively does it endorse them? Or alternatively: What do I think about the beliefs, attitudes, and values it displays and the way that it displays them?

We will call these three aspects of the reading process reading, interpreting, and evaluating. By *reading* we mean primarily our subjective experience of the play; by *interpreting* we mean the process of analysis we engage in to understand the play; by *evaluating* we mean our estimation of the attitudes it conveys and the values it endorses as well as our assessment of its effectiveness in expressing those attitudes and values. All three aspects of reading drama can be used in measuring the extent to which any play moves or touches us, stimulates us to think, feel, wonder, and imagine.

Reading

When we read a play, something happens to us. We experience the play both intellectually and emotionally. This experience involves our feelings about the play's characters and their situation, and it includes our desire to see how the dramatic action works out in the end. At this *reading* stage, our primary concern is with this personal and subjective involvement in the play. Instead of immediately asking ourselves what the play means, we consider what it does to us, how it affects us—and why. To examine this dimension of our experience of drama, we will read the opening section of the following one-act play.

ISABELLA AUGUSTA PERSSE,
LADY GREGORY

The Rising of the Moon

Characters

POLICEMAN B   SERGEANT
POLICEMAN X   MAN

Scene *Side of a quay in a seaport town. Some posts and chains. A large barrel. Enter three policemen. Moonlight.*
SERGEANT, *who is older than the others, crosses the stage to right and looks down steps. The others put down a pastepot and unroll a bundle of placards.*

POLICEMAN B: I think this would be a good place to put up a notice. (*He points to barrel.*)
POLICEMAN X: Better ask him. (*Calls to* SERGEANT) Will this be a good place for a placard? (*No answer.*)
POLICEMAN B: Will we put up a notice here on the barrel? (*No answer.*)
SERGEANT: There's a flight of steps here that leads to the water. This is a place that should be minded well. If he got down here, his friends might have a boat to meet him; they might send it in here from outside.

POLICEMAN B: Would the barrel be a good place to put a notice up?

SERGEANT: It might; you can put it there.

They paste the notice up.

SERGEANT *(reading it)*: Dark hair—dark eyes, smooth face, height five feet five—there's not much to take hold of in that—It's a pity I had no chance of seeing him before he broke out of gaol. They say he's a wonder, that it's he makes all the plans for the whole organization. There isn't another man in Ireland would have broken gaol the way he did. He must have some friends among the gaolers.

POLICEMAN B: A hundred pounds is little enough for the Government to offer for him. You may be sure any man in the force that takes him will get promotion.

SERGEANT: I'll mind this place myself. I wouldn't wonder at all if he came this way. He might come slipping along there *(points to side of quay),* and his friends might be waiting for him there *(points down steps),* and once he got away it's little chance we'd have of finding him; it's maybe under a load of kelp he'd be in a fishing boat, and not one to help a married man that wants it to the reward.

POLICEMAN X: And if we get him itself, nothing but abuse on our heads for it from the people, and maybe from our own relations.

SERGEANT: Well, we have to do our duty in the force. Haven't we the whole country depending on us to keep law and order? It's those that are down would be up and those that are up would be down, if it wasn't for us. Well, hurry on, you have plenty of other places to placard yet, and come back here then to me. You can take the lantern. Don't be too long now. It's very lonesome here with nothing but the moon.

POLICEMAN B: It's a pity we can't stop with you. The Government should have brought more police into the town, with *him* in gaol, and at assize time too. Well, good luck to your watch. *(They go out.)*

SERGEANT *(walks up and down once or twice and looks at placard)*: A hundred pounds and promotion sure. There must be a great deal of spending in a hundred pounds. It's a pity some honest man not to be the better of that.

A ragged man appears at left and tries to slip past. SERGEANT *suddenly turns.*

We have read too little of the play to discuss its meaning, but enough to have our curiosity aroused about the action to follow. In thinking about our experience in reading any literary work, plays in particular, we should attend to our moment-by-moment response to what we are given.

First we see the play's title, *The Rising of the Moon.* Almost immediately we realize that the action occurs at night under "moonlight." Before a word of dialogue is spoken, we begin wondering about the importance of this detail. And we are already being affected by the way the moon's light falls on our mental stage. We must imagine the sea just beyond the steps of the quay; and we must imagine the Sergeant and assisting policemen pasting up their notices, one of which they affix to a barrel.

We quickly see who is in charge by the questions and answers exchanged among the Sergeant and his men. But we notice something else as well: that the Sergeant seems preoccupied, more anxious and concerned than the two policemen. We notice, too, how none of these characters is named, how each of them is identified simply by his role. Although the stage directions don't tell us how the men are dressed, we might imagine them in uniform, since they are on a duty mission.

If we read slowly and deliberately, we will notice how much pointing occurs in this opening, with Policeman B pointing to the barrel and the Sergeant pointing to the side of the quay and to the steps. The parenthetical stage directions that describe these actions help us to visualize the scene and the action. By clearly visualizing these specifics from the start, we will be in a better position to relate them to details of action that follow.

We will also notice how the Sergeant's attitude toward the escaped criminal mixes admiration and fear with a sense of duty. His little speech after reading the placard provides us with the important fact that the Sergeant has never actually seen the escapee. But it also suggests his sense of amazement at what the criminal has accomplished. From this we gain our impression of the escaped man, an impression reinforced by the large reward offered for his capture and by Policeman B's assertion that whoever captures him will be promoted.

In reading that the Sergeant wants to take his position at the quay alone, we may think that he anticipates the reward and possible promotion for himself. Interestingly, his assistants express concern that capturing the escaped man will make them unpopular with "the people" and with their own family relations. We may be surprised at this point to discover that "the people" wouldn't want this criminal captured, and we may be further surprised by the attitude of the Sergeant's subordinates. In response, the Sergeant simply emphasizes their duty in keeping law and order.

Very likely this opening excerpt has aroused our curiosity about the escaped man and about his anticipated arrival and confrontation with the police. We may wonder how the Sergeant (and possibly his men) will respond to his appearance. In short, we want to see what will happen.

Here, then, is the remainder of this short, one-act play.

SERGEANT: Where are you going?

MAN: I'm a poor ballad-singer, your honor. I thought to sell some of these *(holds out bundle of ballads)* to the sailors. *(He goes on.)*

SERGEANT: Stop! Didn't I tell you to stop? You can't go on there.

MAN: Oh, very well. It's a hard thing to be poor. All the world's against the poor!

SERGEANT: Who are you?

MAN: You'd be as wise as myself if I told you, but I don't mind. I'm one Jimmy Walsh, a ballad-singer.

SERGEANT: Jimmy Walsh? I don't know that name.

MAN: Ah, sure, they know it well enough in Ennis. Were you ever in Ennis, Sergeant?

SERGEANT: What brought you here?

MAN: Sure, it's to the assizes I came, thinking I might make a few shillings here or there. It's in the one train with the judges I came.

SERGEANT: Well, if you came so far, you may as well go farther, for you'll walk out of this.

MAN: I will, I will; I'll just go on where I was going. *(Goes toward steps.)*

SERGEANT: Come back from those steps; no one has leave to pass down them tonight.

MAN: I'll just sit on the top of the steps till I see will some sailor buy a ballad off me that would give me my supper. They do be late going back to the ship. It's often I saw them in Cork carried down the quay in a hand-cart.

SERGEANT: Move on, I tell you. I won't have any one lingering about the quay tonight.

MAN: Well, I'll go. It's the poor have the hard life! Maybe yourself might like one, Sergeant. Here's a good sheet now. *(Turns one over)* "Content and a pipe"—that's not much. "The Peeler and the Goat"—you wouldn't like that. "Johnny Hart"—that's a lovely song.

SERGEANT: Move on.

MAN: Ah, wait till you hear it.

Sings.

> There was a rich farmer's daughter lived near the town of Ross;
> She courted a Highland soldier, his name was Johnny Hart;
> Says the mother to her daughter, "I'll go distracted mad
> If you marry that Highland soldier dressed up in Highland
> plaid."

SERGEANT: Stop that noise.

(MAN *wraps up his ballads and shuffles toward the steps.)*

SERGEANT: Where are you going?

MAN: Sure you told me to be going, and I am going.

SERGEANT: Don't be a fool. I didn't tell you to go that way; I told you to go back to the town.

MAN: Back to the town, is it?

SERGEANT *(taking him by the shoulder and shoving him before him)*: Here, I'll show you the way. Be off with you. What are you stopping for?

MAN *(who has been keeping his eye on the notice, points to it)*: I think I know what you're waiting for, Sergeant.

SERGEANT: What's that to you?

MAN: And I know well the man you're waiting for—I know him well—I'll be going. *(He shuffles on.)*

SERGEANT: You know him? Come back here. What sort is he?

MAN: Come back is it, Sergeant? Do you want to have me killed?

SERGEANT: Why do you say that?

MAN: Never mind. I'm going. I wouldn't be in your shoes if the reward was ten times as much. *(Goes on off stage to left)* Not if it was ten times as much.

SERGEANT *(rushing after him)*: Come back here, come back. *(Drags him back)* What sort is he? Where did you see him?

MAN: I saw him in my own place, in the County Clare. I tell you you wouldn't like to be looking at him. You'd be afraid to be in the one place with him. There isn't a weapon he doesn't know the use of, and as to strength, his muscles are as hard as that board. *(Slaps barrel.)*

SERGEANT: Is he as bad as that?

MAN: He is then.

SERGEANT: Do you tell me so?

MAN: There was a poor man in our place, a sergeant from Ballyvaughan.—It was with a lump of stone he did it.

SERGEANT: I never heard of that.

MAN: And you wouldn't, Sergeant. It's not everything that happens gets into the papers. And there was a policeman in plain clothes, too . . . It is in Limerick he was. . . . It was after the time of the attack on the police barrack at Kilmallock. . . . Moonlight . . . just like this . . . waterside. . . . Nothing was known for certain.

SERGEANT: Do you say so? It's a terrible county to belong to.

MAN: That's so, indeed! You might be standing there, looking out that way, thinking you saw him coming up this side of the quay *(points),* and he might be coming up this other side *(points),* and he'd be on you before you knew where you were.

SERGEANT: It's a whole troop of police they ought to put here to stop a man like that.

MAN: But if you'd like me to stop with you, I could be looking down this side. I could be sitting up here on this barrel.

SERGEANT: And you know him well, too?

MAN: I'd know him a mile off, Sergeant.

SERGEANT: But you wouldn't want to share the reward?

MAN: Is it a poor man like me, that has to be going the roads and singing in fairs, to have the name on him that he took a reward? But you don't want me. I'll be safer in the town.

SERGEANT: Well, you can stop.

MAN *(getting up on barrel)*: All right, Sergeant. I wonder, now, you're not tired out, Sergeant, walking up and down the way you are.

SERGEANT: If I'm tired I'm used to it.

MAN: You might have hard work before you tonight yet. Take it easy while you can. There's plenty of room up here on the barrel, and you see farther when you're higher up.

SERGEANT: Maybe so. *(Gets up beside him on barrel, facing right. They sit back to back, looking different ways.)* You made me feel a bit queer with the way you talked.

MAN: Give me a match, Sergeant *(he gives it and MAN lights pipe)*; take a draw yourself? It'll quiet you. Wait now till I give you a light, but you needn't turn round. Don't take your eye off the quay for the life of you.

SERGEANT: Never fear, I won't. *(Lights pipe. They both smoke.)* Indeed it's a hard thing to be in the force, out at night and no thanks for it, for all the danger we're in. And it's little we get but abuse from the people, and no choice but to obey our orders, and never asked when a man is sent into danger, if you are a married man with a family.

MAN *(sings)*:

As through the hills I walked to view the hills and shamrock plain,
I stood awhile where nature smiles to view the rocks and streams,
On a matron fair I fixed my eyes beneath a fertile vale,
As she sang her song it was on the wrong of poor old Granuaile.

SERGEANT: Stop that; that's no song to be singing in these times.

MAN: Ah, Sergeant, I was only singing to keep my heart up. It sinks when I think of him. To think of us two sitting here, and he creeping up the quay, maybe, to get to us.

SERGEANT: Are you keeping a good lookout?

MAN: I am; and for no reward too. Amn't I the foolish man? But when I saw a man in trouble, I never could help trying to get him out of it. What's that? Did something hit me? *(Rubs his heart.)*

SERGEANT *(patting him on the shoulder)*: You will get your reward in heaven.

MAN: I know that, I know that, Sergeant, but life is precious.

SERGEANT: Well, you can sing if it gives you more courage.

MAN (*sings*):

> Her head was bare, her hands and feet with iron bands were
> bound,
> Her pensive strain and plaintive wail mingles with the evening
> gale,
> And the song she sang with mournful air, I am old Granuaile.
> Her lips so sweet that monarchs kissed . . .

SERGEANT: That's not it. . . . "Her gown she wore was stained with gore." . . . That's it—you missed that.

MAN: You're right, Sergeant, so it is; I missed it. (*Repeats line*) But to think of a man like you knowing a song like that.

SERGEANT: There's many a thing a man might know and might not have any wish for.

MAN: Now, I daresay, Sergeant, in your youth, you used to be sitting up on a wall, the way you are sitting up on this barrel now, and the other lads beside you, and you singing "Granuaile"? . . .

SERGEANT: I did then.

MAN: And the "Shan Bhean Bhocht"? . . .

SERGEANT: I did then.

MAN: And the "Green on the Cape"?

SERGEANT: That was one of them.

MAN: And maybe the man you are watching for tonight used to be sitting on the wall, when he was young, and singing those same songs. . . . It's a queer world.

SERGEANT: Whisht! . . . I think I see something coming. . . . It's only a dog.

MAN: And isn't it a queer world? . . . Maybe it's one of the boys you used to be singing with that time you will be arresting today or tomorrow, and sending into the dock.

SERGEANT: That's true indeed.

MAN: And maybe one night, after you had been singing, if the other boys had told you some plan they had, some plan to free the country, you might have joined with them . . . and maybe it is you might be in trouble now.

SERGEANT: Well, who knows but I might? I had a great spirit in those days.

MAN: It's a queer world, Sergeant, and it's little any mother knows when she sees her child creeping on the floor what might happen to it before it has gone through its life, or who will be who in the end.

SERGEANT: That's a queer thought now, and a true thought. Wait now till I think it out. . . . If it wasn't for the sense I have, and for my wife and family, and for me joining the force the time I did, it might be myself now would be after breaking gaol and hiding in the dark, and it might be him that's hiding in the dark and that got out of gaol would be sitting up where I am on this barrel. . . . And it might be myself would be creeping up trying to make my escape from himself, and it might be himself would be keeping the law, and myself would be breaking it, and myself would be trying maybe to put a bullet in his head, or to take up a lump of a stone the way you said he did . . . no, that myself did. . . . Oh! *(Gasps. After a pause)* What's that? *(Grasps* MAN's *arm.)*

MAN *(jumps off barrel and listens, looking out over water)*: It's nothing, Sergeant.

SERGEANT: I thought it might be a boat. I had a notion there might be friends of his coming about the quays with a boat.

MAN: Sergeant, I am thinking it was with the people you were, and not with the law you were, when you were a young man.

SERGEANT: Well, if I was foolish then, that time's gone.

MAN: Maybe, Sergeant, it comes into your head sometimes, in spite of your belt and your tunic, that it might have been as well for you to have followed Granuaile.

SERGEANT: It's no business of yours what I think.

MAN: Maybe, Sergeant, you'll be on the side of the country yet.

SERGEANT *(gets off barrel)*: Don't talk to me like that. I have my duties and I know them. *(Looks round)* That was a boat; I hear the oars. *(Goes to the steps and looks down.)*

MAN *(sings)*:

O, then, tell me, Shawn O'Farrell,
   Where the gathering is to be.
In the old spot by the river
   Right well known to you and me!

SERGEANT: Stop that! Stop that, I tell you!

MAN *(sings louder)*:

> One word more, for signal token,
>   Whistle up the marching tune,
> With your pike upon your shoulder,
>   At the Rising of the Moon.

SERGEANT: If you don't stop that, I'll arrest you.

A whistle from below answers, repeating the air.

SERGEANT: That's a signal. *(Stands between him and steps)* You must not pass this way. . . . Step farther back. . . . Who are you? You are no ballad-singer.

MAN: You needn't ask who I am; that placard will tell you. *(Points to placard.)*

SERGEANT: You are the man I am looking for.

MAN *(takes off hat and wig.* SERGEANT *seizes them)*: I am. There's a hundred pounds on my head. There is a friend of mine below in a boat. He knows a safe place to bring me to.

SERGEANT *(looking still at hat and wig)*: It's a pity! It's a pity. You deceived me. You deceived me well.

MAN: I am a friend of Granuaile. There is a hundred pounds on my head.

SERGEANT: It's a pity, it's a pity!

MAN: Will you let me pass, or must I make you let me?

SERGEANT: I am in the force. I will not let you pass.

MAN: I thought to do it with my tongue. *(Puts hand in breast)* What is that?

(Voice of POLICEMAN X *outside.)* Here, this is where we left him.

SERGEANT: It's my comrades coming.

MAN: You won't betray me . . . the friend of Granuaile. *(Slips behind barrel.)*

(Voice of POLICEMAN B.*)* That was the last of the placards.

POLICEMAN X *(as they come in)*: If he makes his escape it won't be unknown he'll make it.

*(*SERGEANT *puts hat and wig behind his back.)*

POLICEMAN B: Did any one come this way?

SERGEANT *(after a pause)*: No one.

POLICEMAN B: No one at all?

SERGEANT: No one at all.

POLICEMAN B: We had no orders to go back to the station; we can stop along with you.

SERGEANT: I don't want you. There is nothing for you to do here.

POLICEMAN B: You bade us to come back here and keep watch with you.

SERGEANT: I'd sooner be alone. Would any man come this way and you making all that talk? It is better the place to be quiet.

POLICEMAN B: Well, we'll leave you the lantern anyhow. *(Hands it to him.)*

SERGEANT: I don't want it. Bring it with you.

POLICEMAN B: You might want it. There are clouds coming up and you have the darkness of the night before you yet. I'll leave it over here on the barrel. *(Goes to barrel.)*

SERGEANT: Bring it with you I tell you. No more talk.

POLICEMAN B: Well, I thought it might be a comfort to you. I often think when I have it in my hand and can be flashing it about into every dark corner *(doing so)* that it's the same as being beside the fire at home, and the bits of bogwood blazing up now and again. *(Flashes it about, now on the barrel, now on the* SERGEANT.*)*

SERGEANT *(furious)*: Be off the two of you, yourselves and your lantern!

They go out. MAN *comes from behind barrel. He and* SERGEANT *stand looking at one another.*

SERGEANT: What are you waiting for?

MAN: For my hat, of course, and my wig. You wouldn't wish me to get my death of cold?

SERGEANT *gives them.*

MAN *(going toward steps)*: Well, good night, comrade, and thank you. You did me a good turn tonight, and I'm obliged to you. Maybe I'll be able to do as much for you when the small rise up and the big fall down . . . when we all change places at the Rising *(waves his hand and disappears)* of the Moon.

SERGEANT *(turning his back to audience and reading placard)*: A hundred pounds reward! A hundred pounds! *(Turns toward audience)* I wonder, now, am I as great a fool as I think I am?

How do we describe our experience in reading *The Rising of the Moon?* If the play has engaged our attention, why has it done so? If not, to what do we attribute our lack of interest? Assuming that we were interested enough to become involved in the action, we can then consider our emotional reactions as we were reading. At what points did we feel the strongest pull to continue? At what points was our emotional involvement most intense? What was our reaction to the Sergeant's speech about exchanging places with the criminal? How did we respond to the Sergeant's moment of recognizing the criminal? To his complicity in helping him escape? To his final question at the end of the play?

Our response to these and other details of dialogue and action constitute our experience of the play. This experience may be affected by our social and political views, as well as by our gender, our age, and our race or ethnicity. Our experience in reading *The Rising of the Moon* will also be affected by our previous experience with attending or reading other plays. And it may be further affected by our knowledge of Irish literary history and our experience with additional plays by Lady Gregory or with other literary works with concerns similar to those displayed in *The Rising of the Moon.* Thus, although much of our sense of the play will overlap with the experience of other readers, most readers will not experience the play in exactly the same way.

Let us single out a few moments for a consideration of our experience and response. For instance, let's consider our reaction when policemen B and X return while the ballad-singer hides behind the barrel. During this climactic moment, we experience tension as we wonder whether the Sergeant will turn the Man in. Another highly charged moment occurs when the Sergeant corrects the ballad-singer's omission of a line from the song about Granuaile, apparently a revolutionary song about England's political domination of Ireland. Even if we know little about the history of this period, we have the sense that this is a revolutionary song because when the ballad-singer began to sing it, the Sergeant cut him off sharply, saying, "Stop that; that's no song to be singing in these times." So, very likely this moment of correction gave us pause. We may have stopped reading for a moment not only to reflect on the significance of the action but also to feel its emotional resonance. In other words, although that moment certainly can be analyzed for an intellectual meaning and related to the play's meaning as a whole, it is also a wonderfully theatrical moment. Something surprising happens onstage, something we can both see and hear. It affects us emotionally before we make sense of it intellectually.

A critical element in our experience of the play is our response to its ending. At the very least we should have an aesthetic sense of completeness or closure, a sense that the play has ended or culminated rather than simply stopped. But we will also have a sense of satisfaction (or dissatisfaction) at the way the play's action has been resolved. All these responses to the play as an imitation of human action coupled with our imagining of its theatrical elements constitute our experience of the play. This subjective dimension is what we attend to at this reading stage.

Interpreting

When we interpret a play, we explain it to ourselves. We make sense of it. If reading is viewed primarily as a subjective experience in which we satisfy our personal needs as readers, then *interpreting* directs us to more objective considerations. When we interpret a play, we concern ourselves less with how it affects us and how it makes us feel than with what it means or suggests. Interpretation, in short, aims at understanding; it relies on our intellectual comprehension and rational understanding rather than on our emotional response.

The act of interpreting involves essentially four things: observing, connecting, inferring, and concluding. To understand a play, we first need to observe its details. For example, we notice the articles and decor of its stage setting; we watch the actions of its characters; we listen to dialogue and monologue; we absorb the effects of lighting, stage props, and sound effects. As we do these things, we begin formulating a sense of the play's situation, focus, and point. We arrive at this formulation, however tentative it may be, largely by making connections among the many details we observe. On the basis of these connections we make inferences or interpretive hypotheses about their significance. Finally, we come to some kind of provisional conclusion about the play's meaning based on our observations, connections, and inferences.

Our acts of interpretation are continuous as we read. That is, the four interpretive actions of observing, connecting, inferring, and concluding occur together, sometimes simultaneously, and not in a series of neatly separate sequential stages. We don't delay making inferences, for example, until after we have made and connected all our observations. Instead, we develop tentative conclusions *as* we read and observe, *while* we make connections and develop inferences. We may change and adjust our inferences and provisional conclusions both *during* our reading of a play and *afterward* as we think back over its details. We also do not separate this intellectual process from our subjective reactions and emotional responses. Although they have been separated here for convenience, the way we actually read a play combines emotional response and intellectual analysis.

Whether you were aware of it or not, you were performing this complex act of reading-interpreting when you read *The Rising of the Moon*. Our discussion of important moments of the play was based partly on an implicit interpretation. For even though we focused our discussion of reading on aspects of our experience of the play's script, the only way to make sense of that experience is to make some sense of the action of the play. In doing so we were beginning the work of interpretation.

Read *The Rising of the Moon* again slowly and deliberately, noticing as much as you can about its language and its action. List a series of details about each, establish connections among related details, and on the basis of those connections develop a set of inferences implied by the characters' speeches and interactions. Then provide a brief and tentative interpretation or explanation of one possible meaning of the play.

One way to begin following through on this interpretive exercise would be to work first with a single scene, such as the section from the entrance of the ballad-singer to the point where the Sergeant takes him by the shoulders and tells him to leave (pages 9, 10–11). Or look at the scene that begins at that point and ends with the Sergeant's reversing his order and allowing the Man instead to remain with him (pages 11–12). The point is to concentrate on a section of the play and begin looking closely at its action and listening carefully to its language. We will illustrate this by focusing on the section (or scene) beginning with the Sergeant's grasping the Man's arm and the Man's jumping off the barrel to the point where the two policemen return (pages 15–16).

What happens in this section? The most important event, of course, is the revelation of the man's identity. But let's consider the details, the action and reaction, the speeches and gestures that surround that important moment of revelation.

We might observe first of all that, as with the policemen, the characters are identified generically rather than individually. That is, rather than being given particular, individualizing names, they are referred to as "Sergeant" and "Man." (The name, Jimmy Walsh, that the ballad-singer gives, is, of course, a fabrication.) The generic names may suggest that the situation the two men find themselves in should be generalized to include not only specifically Irish social inequalities but problems of political and social conflict elsewhere as well. An even broader interpretation of the central characters' generic names can be made: the Sergeant represents the law; the Man represents the people the law attempts to keep in their place. This play's symbolic quality makes its situation applicable to other times and places besides those explicitly indicated.

Much of the initial dialogue of this section centers on the Man's attempt to persuade the Sergeant that, even though he represents the law, he really sides with the people. Notice how the Man's more voluble speech contrasts with the Sergeant's brusqueness. When the Man suggests that the Sergeant may well have been a follower of Granuaile just as he is, the Sergeant curtly dismisses the idea. The sharpness of this and other of the Sergeant's replies suggest that the Man has touched a nerve — the Sergeant probably agrees with what the Man says. The Sergeant's overly emphatic denial reinforces our suspicion that he sympathizes with the Man. And when the Sergeant says, "It's a pity, it's a pity," we could interpret this to mean a number of things: 1) that it is too bad that the Man must be arrested, but the Sergeant has his duty to perform, and that's that; 2) that it is a pity that the Sergeant is put in this difficult position; 3) that it is a shame that a man the Sergeant seems to like has to be on the opposite side of the law; 4) that it is too bad that the Sergeant never followed through on his youthful idealism to follow Granuaile. This line, "it's a pity," in fact, has been uttered earlier, in the opening scene, by both the Sergeant and one of the policemen. Echoing here at a climactic moment, it is endowed with a rich resonance of meanings.

Even though this scene does not bring the play to its conclusion, it does serve to point to the significant crisis at its heart. This is the decision the Sergeant must make as the scene ends and his companions return. The Man puts the Sergeant's decision in terms of betrayal, categorically affirming (rather than questioning) that the Sergeant, friend of Granuaile that he is, will not betray him. And, of course, he doesn't, which leads us to ask more or less the same question the Sergeant himself asks at the end of the play: Why does the Sergeant act as he does? What principles motivated his action? And what does the play seem to suggest about that motivation? In pointing up and answering questions like these, we incline toward an interpretation of the play overall.

In reaching an interpretation of this section of the play, of the play as a whole, or indeed of any play, we should be concerned less with finding the *right* answer than with arriving at a satisfying explanation. Some interpretations, nonetheless, will be more satisfying than others; they will be more convincing, largely because they take into account more of the play's details. Other interpretations, while perhaps not as convincing, may be valuable for the intellectual stimulation they provide. Still others may strain credibility to the breaking point. Because we invariably bring different experiences to our reading of plays, we will each see different things in them. Through conversation and discussion we can debate the merits of those viewpoints while sharpening and enriching our understanding of plays.

Evaluating

An *evaluation* is essentially a judgment, an opinion about a play formulated as a conclusion. We may agree or disagree with the attitude toward law and order expressed by the Sergeant. We may accept or reject the Man's claim that the Sergeant would really like to support the revolution and that to turn the Man in would be a betrayal. And we may approve or disapprove of the Sergeant's decision to let the Man go. However we evaluate these aspects of the play, we invariably measure them on a scale of our own values.

Evaluating is partly an unconscious process. We are not always aware, except perhaps in a vaguely general way, why we respond to something as we do. We may know that we like or dislike it without bothering much to think about why. We sometimes accept particular ideas, events, experiences, or works of art, and reject others almost instinctively, even automatically. Even though part of our evaluation of a play is unconscious, we can make it more deliberate and more fully conscious. We simply need to ask ourselves how we respond to the values the work supports and why we respond as we do. By asking these questions, we should be able to consider our own values more clearly and to discuss more fairly and sensibly why we agree or disagree with the values displayed in the play.

When we evaluate a play, we appraise it according to our own unique combination of cultural, moral, and aesthetic values. Our cultural values derive from our lives as members of families and societies. Our moral values reflect our ethical norms—what we consider to be good or evil, right or wrong. Our aesthetic values concern what we see as beautiful or ugly, well-made or ill-made. Over time, through education and experience, our values may change. A play we once valued for what it reveals about human experience or for its moral perspective may mean little to us later. Conversely, a play that we once found uninteresting or disappointing we may later find to be powerfully engaging.

Our personal response to any play's values is closely tied to our interpretation of it. Evaluation depends upon interpretation; our judgment of a play's values (and perhaps of its value as a literary work or theatrical performance as well) depends on how well we understand it. Our evaluation, moreover, may be linked to our initial experience of the play, with our first impressions and pre-critical, preanalytical reactions. If our reaction is unsympathetic to the play as a whole or to the values it seems to display, we may be reluctant to change both our interpretation and our evaluation, even when we discover convincing evidence to warrant a reconsideration of both.

Consider *The Rising of the Moon* from the standpoint of evaluation. What values animate the two major characters? What is the Sergeant's attitude toward the men he supervises? Toward the law he enforces? Toward the people he serves? What is the Man's attitude toward the law? Toward the Sergeant as a representative of the law? Toward the Sergeant as a man? Asking questions like these and considering the values—social, cultural, and moral—that underlie them lead us most often to the heart of many plays.

We have already referred, implicitly, at least, to the values and ideals that govern the behavior of the Man and the Sergeant. The heart of the play is the conflict between the two sets of values represented by the two men. The ballad-singer represents a revolutionary ideal that espouses the cause of Ireland's freedom from England; the Sergeant represents the law and order that would prevent any revolutionary upheaval in society. Alternatively, we may see the conflict as occurring within the Sergeant himself, with one part of him siding with the social values of law and order and another part of him siding with the poor and oppressed. We may wonder to what extent the Sergeant resents the authority he espouses and enacts, and to what extent he resents people like the Man in the play who cause him to reenact the conflict of loyalties he feels torn between. Here is where our own political attitudes, social dispositions, even moral beliefs, influence our judgment about the values the play seems to endorse.

The Rising of the Moon suggests that the Sergeant is not a fool in ignoring his responsibility to uphold the law by arresting the Man. Depending on our values, however, the opposite conclusion can be stated. In one sense, of course, the Sergeant is a fool, since he wastes an opportunity to gain a promotion and to collect a sizable financial reward. In another sense, however, he is no fool at all, since he knows exactly what he is doing and why. He values the Man and his cause more than his own good fortune; he values his own diminished but still living idealism more than the glory he would gain by arresting the Man. Although he wonders aloud whether he has done the right thing, his wondering rests on practical rather than moral grounds. Morally, he feels vindicated. It is only in the realm of practical considerations that there is room for debate.

Your evaluation of the Sergeant's decision, action, and motivation may differ from this view. If so, it is most likely linked with a different interpretation of the play's dialogue and action as well as a contrasting set of social, political, and moral values.

Of the kinds of evaluations we make when reading drama, those about a play's aesthetic qualities are hardest to discuss. Aesthetic responses are difficult to describe because they involve our feelings and perceptions, especially our subjective personal impressions about what we find pleasing. They also involve our expectations about what we think a play should be, as well as our prior experience in reading or attending plays. Our aesthetic responses, moreover, are complicated still further by our tendency to react quickly and decisively to what we like and dislike, often without knowing why we respond as we do.

Admittedly, if we lack experience in reading and viewing drama, judgments about a play's values and considerations of its aesthetic merit need to be made with caution. But we must begin somewhere, since evaluation is inevitable. We cannot avoid judging the plays we read any more than we can avoid judging the people we meet. The process is natural.

How we develop our aesthetic responses to plays depends partly on letting the informed and sensitive responses of other experienced readers guide and enrich our own perceptions. These other readers may be classmates or teachers. They may also be critics who have written articles and books about the plays we read. Their understanding of drama can deepen and enrich our own. Besides learning directly from what critics say about particular plays, we can also learn how to discuss literary and dramatic works in general. The best drama critics, for example, provide models we can emulate, while the worst can at least show us what to avoid. Our goal in reading, interpreting, and evaluating drama—and also in listening to the views of other readers—is to develop a sense of literary tact, the kind of balanced judgment that comes with experience in reading and living coupled with thoughtful reflection on both. There are no shortcuts or simple formulas for developing such evaluative competence and confidence. They come with practice in attentive reading and viewing of many plays, with a patient consideration of their language and action and with a willingness to reflect on our responses to them. Above all, understanding, appreciation, and enjoyment of drama are achieved by devotion, effort, and repeated acts of thoughtful attention.

CHAPTER TWO

Elements of Drama

In Chapter One we discussed an approach to reading plays based on three aspects of responding to dramatic texts: reading, interpreting, and evaluating. In this chapter we offer a critical vocabulary for discussing drama. Besides introducing the language of drama, Chapter Two explains how to interpret plays by analyzing their elements: plot and structure, character and conflict, dialogue and monologue, setting and staging, symbolism and irony, thought and theme, genre and convention. Although we will discuss these elements individually, this is strictly a matter of convenience. No dramatic element exists in isolation. Plays are unified, complex networks of action and reference that we analyze piecemeal only to understand better how they create meaning and embody feeling.

Plot and Structure

One of the reasons we read plays is to discover what happens, to see how particular consequences result from specific, observable actions. We become engaged by a play's story line and remain held by its twists and turns until the playwright resolves it. The details of action, or incidents, in a well-organized play form a unified structure. This unified structure of a play's incidents is called its *plot*.

It is important to realize that a dramatic plot is not merely a series of haphazardly occurring events. It is, rather, a carefully arranged series of related incidents. The incidents of the plot, that is, must be connected in such a way that one directly results from another. And, of course, the playwright shapes and arranges the incidents of the plot to do precisely these things.

Besides being unified, a good plot will also be economical. By this we mean that all the incidents of the play contribute to its cumulative effect, its overall meaning and impression. No actions included in the play are extraneous or unnecessary. The economy of a play's plot distinguishes it from everyday life, in which a multitude of minor actions mingle indiscriminately with significant related incidents. Dramatists combine and integrate the actions of their plays in meaningful ways.

We can describe the plot of many plays by using the following diagram:

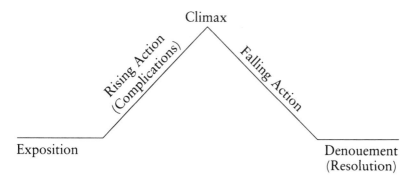

The *exposition* of a play presents background necessary for the development of the plot. The *rising action* includes the separate incidents that "complicate" the plot and build toward its most dramatic moment. These incidents often involve conflicts either between characters or within them, conflicts that lead to a crisis. The point of crisis toward which the play's action builds is called its *climax*. Following this high point of intensity in the play is the *falling action*, in which there is a relaxation of emotional intensity and a gradual resolution of the various strands of the plot in the play's *denouement* (a French word that refers to the untying of a knot).

Whether playwrights use this traditional plot structure or vary the formula, they control our expectations about what is happening through their arrangement of incidents. They decide when to present information and when to withhold it, when to speed up action and when to slow it down, when to arouse our curiosity and when to satisfy it. By the arrangement of incidents a dramatist may create suspense, evoke laughter, cause anxiety, or elicit surprise. One of our main sources of pleasure in the plot, in fact, is surprise. Often surprise follows suspense, thus fulfilling our need to find out what happens. Sometimes we are shown something we didn't expect; sometimes the surprise lies in seeing *how* something will happen even when we may know *what* will happen.

In considering our expectations and response to the developing action of a play, we approach the concept of plot less as a schematic diagram of a play's completed action and more as an evolving series of experiences we undergo as we read or view it. For, as we learned in Chapter One, our emotional experience in reading a play is an important aspect of the play's meaning for us. And this experience is designed by the playwright as he or she structures the incidents of the plot, largely by keeping us guessing about something, keeping before us as we read a series of temporarily unanswered questions. To find answers to those questions, we continue reading.

Playwrights arrange incidents of their plots to create particular effects, especially to evoke emotional responses from the audience. This is one aspect of their dramatic art. After we have undergone the experiences dramatists have invented, we can stand back, so to speak, and analyze the dramatic effects more objectively. In doing so, we focus attention on aspects of artistic design. For example, a dramatist may prepare for a major revelation late in a play by presenting smaller, less dramatic scenes earlier that lead up to it. Or the playwright may interpose a comic scene between two scenes of tragic resonance.

These examples suggest that we can appreciate the literary and theatrical care lavished by dramatists on their plays. In developing our appreciation for the artistry of drama, we invariably develop along with it our capacity for aesthetic response, that is, our ability to see and appreciate the beauty and elegance of a play's artistic design overall.

We can be alert for some details of a play's structure even as we read it for the first time. Repeated elements and recurring details—of action and gesture, of dialogue and description—should draw our attention. Repetition signals important connections and relationships in the play, relationships between characters, connections among ideas. We can look for shifts in plot direction because they are often signaled by such visual or aural clues as a change of scene or the appearance of additional characters. They may be indicated by alterations in the play's language, especially in shifts between prose and verse, shifts between long monologues and quick conversational exchanges, or shifts from the use of literal to metaphoric language. And they may also be indicated by changes in the *tempo,* or rate of speed at which scenes proceed.

We can illustrate some of these ideas about plot and structure by turning back to reconsider Lady Gregory's *The Rising of the Moon.* This a tightly organized play whose action centers initially on the appearance of the wanted man and then on the Sergeant's crisis of conscience. The exposition begins the play and ends with the departure of the two policemen. The first major incident occurs with the appearance of the ragged man, the ballad-singer. This incident inaugurates the play's rising action, which becomes intensified as the Sergeant learns that the ballad-singer knows the wanted man and that the wanted man is dangerous. Additional incidents complicate the action as the Sergeant reveals that he is familiar with many revolutionary songs. After that, the playwright slows down the tempo of the play both to provide her audience with an insight into how the positions of the two men might have been reversed and to increase suspense as we wonder what will happen. Three incidents, one right after another, mark the play's climax: the Man reveals that he is the criminal the Sergeant seeks, the policemen return, and the Sergeant chooses to hide the Man's hat and wig. The falling action, though brief (consisting simply of the Sergeant's dismissing the two policemen), is still suspenseful since when Policeman B swings around his lantern, he could catch the fugitive as well as his Sergeant red-handed. The denouement is equally brief: it includes the final conversation of the Man and the Sergeant, followed by the Sergeant's concluding question.

Such a description reveals the plot's unity and economy. Additional structural details in *The Rising of the Moon* include the repetition of words and phrases, such as the Sergeant's "It's a pity," and the repetition of gestures, such as the pointing of both the Sergeant and the Man. The repeated utterance invites consideration of its meaning. The repeated gesture indicates a connection between the Sergeant and the Man.

Character and Conflict

If we read plays for their plots—to find out what happens—we also read them to discover the fates of their characters. We become interested in dramatic characters for varying, even contradictory reasons. They may remind us in some ways of ourselves; they may appeal to us because they differ from us. They may represent alternative directions we might have taken, alternative decisions we might have made. They represent people caught in the changing conditions of circumstance.

Characters bring plays to life. First and last we attend to characters: to how they look and what their appearance tells us about them; to what they say and what their manner of saying it expresses; to what they do and how their actions reveal who they are and what they stand for. We may come to know them and respond to them in almost the same way we come to know and respond to actual people, all the while realizing that characters are imaginative constructions, literary imitations of human beings. Even though characters in plays are not real people, their human dimension is often impossible to ignore, since actors portray them and playwrights typically endow them with human qualities. Nonetheless, it is helpful to remember the distinction between dramatic characters and actual people so that we do not expect characters always to behave realistically, and so we do not expect playwrights to tell us more about them than we need to know.

Characters in drama can be classified as major and minor, static and dynamic, flat and round. A *major character* is an important figure at the center of the play's action and meaning. A major character is sometimes called a *protagonist*, whose conflict with an *antagonist* sparks the play's central conflict. Supporting the major character or characters are one or more secondary figures, or *minor characters*, whose function is partly to illuminate the major characters. Minor characters are often *static*, or unchanging: they remain essentially the same throughout the play. *Dynamic characters*, on the other hand, exhibit some kind of change—of attitude, of purpose, of behavior. Another way of describing static and dynamic characters is as flat and round characters: *flat characters* reveal only a single dimension, and their behavior and speech are predictable; *round characters* are more individualized, reveal more than one aspect of their human nature, and are not completely predictable in behavior or speech.

In the same way that a play's plot must be unified, so a character must be coherent. This means that all aspects of the character must work together to suggest a focused and unified whole. Our sense of the identity and personality of characters is derived essentially from four things: 1) their actions—what they do; 2) their words—what they say and how they say it; 3) their physical attributes—what they look like; 4) the responses of other characters to them—what others say or do about them. If these aspects all work together, we should be able to gain a good sense of who characters are and what they are like.

Drama lives in the encounter of characters; its action is often interaction and its interaction frequently involves conflict. Dramatic characters come together and affect each other, making things happen by coming into conflict. In fact, drama is essentially the creation, development, and resolution of conflicts between and within characters. For it is in conflict that characters reveal themselves, advance the plot, and dramatize the meanings of plays.

Conflict in drama typically occurs between characters whose ideals, goals, and values differ in significant ways. In *The Rising of the Moon* such a conflict exists between the Sergeant and the ballad-singer. As we have noted earlier, this external conflict parallels an internal conflict within the Sergeant himself. The Sergeant debates with himself whether to follow his impulse to allow the ballad-singer to escape or to observe his duty to capture him. This inner conflict, in turn, mirrors the larger conflict between the social forces the two men represent—the people versus the law.

Let us consider our approach to character and conflict further by looking more closely at the characters in *The Rising of the Moon*. The two policemen are clearly minor characters, necessary primarily for the plot, though they also serve to reveal the character of the Sergeant. In the first scene, for example, we notice how differently the Sergeant responds from his men. Policemen B and

X seem more casual, less concerned about the danger of the situation and more concerned with the details of finding places to post the placards. The Sergeant is shown to be more experienced at the job and more aware of what is at stake.

More important, however, is the relationship that develops between the Sergeant, the protagonist, and the Man, the antagonist. As it turns out, neither is what he seems to be. The Sergeant does not uphold the law and arrest the Man; the Man does not live up to his reputation as a dangerous killer. Both have opportunities to act within their expected roles, but neither does. Each surprises the other; both surprise us and perhaps themselves as well. The conflict between them thus remains a potential, or theoretical conflict. Although their suggested conflict is imminent, and potentially dangerous to both, it never develops into an actual, demonstrable, physical conflict. In fact, their potential conflict dissolves into something more like comradeship, its opposite.

The seed of this transformation is contained in the Sergeant's musings about fate, which serve as a significant revelation of his character. He imagines his life having turned out differently, with himself as a hunted criminal and the fugitive as a policeman hunting him. The Sergeant sees the connection rather than the distinction betwen himself and the revolutionary. This perception leads him to a radically different sense of his responsibility toward the Man and toward their countrymen. In a small way the Sergeant helps to bring about the Man's prediction that "the small [will] rise up and the big fall down," largely because a part of the Sergeant believes this should occur. The Sergeant is thus shown to be a more complex man than he seems initially—though his practical, orthodox side appears with his final question: "I wonder, now, am I as great a fool as I think I am?"

Dialogue and Monologue

This discussion of character and conflict brings us to a critical aspect of dramatic characters—their speech, or dialogue. (Although generally we use the word "dialogue" to refer to all the speech of a play, strictly speaking, *dialogue* involves two speakers and *monologue* involves one.) An important dramatic convention is the use of soliloquy to express a character's state of mind. A *soliloquy* is a speech given by a character when alone on stage. A kind of thinking out loud, its purpose is to reveal the character's thoughts and feelings. Soliloquies should be distinguished from *asides*, which are comments made directly to the audience in the presence of other characters, but without those other characters hearing what is said. Unlike a soliloquy, an aside is usually just a brief remark.

Dialogue is more than simply the words characters utter. It is also itself action, since characters' words have the power to affect other characters and the audience. Words in drama do things, affect change, initiate events. Through his words (and song), the escaped man in *The Rising of the Moon* convinces the Sergeant not to betray him. Through her words, Lady Macbeth propels Macbeth into murdering Duncan, the Scottish king.

Dialogue, moreover, is an important index of a character's personality. This is true not only in what characters say about themselves and each other, but in their manner or way of expressing what they have to say. Lady Gregory's Sergeant is forceful, authoritative, even peremptory in dialogue with his two police subordinates. And he sounds brusque and dismissive at first in dialogue with the ballad-singer. But the harshness and brusqueness evaporate in the following, more meditative, speech:

> If it wasn't for the sense I have, and for my wife and family, and for me joining the force the time I did, it might be myself now would be after breaking gaol and hiding in the dark, and it might be him that's hiding in the dark and that got out of gaol would be sitting up where I am on this barrel. . . . And it might be myself would be creeping up trying to make my escape from himself, and it might be himself would be keeping the law, and myself would be breaking it, and myself would be trying maybe to put a bullet in his head, or to take up a lump of a stone the way you said he did . . . no, that myself did. . . .

What the Sergeant says here is clear enough: he could picture himself in the other man's shoes. But his manner of saying it—in a long sentence strung together with numerous "ands"—is equally revealing. It shows a more sympathetic and understanding man, one who is not as predictable and single-minded as his police subordinates. The ongoing quality of the sentence simulates the ongoing nature of his thought. The neat balances of "him" and "I" suggest that the Sergeant acknowledges a kinship with the "other" seemingly different but ultimately similar man. The Sergeant's little speech implies that he sees that they are more alike than different.

This concern with characters' language is crucial, whether we watch plays in the theater or imagine them performed in the theaters of our minds. We need to develop our auditory imagination, our sense of how speech sounds as it is uttered, really to hear it or to imagine how it might be spoken. Listen to the beginning of Macbeth's famous speech, made upon learning of his wife's death. Attend especially to its rhythm:

> Tomorrow, and tomorrow, and tomorrow
> Creeps in this petty pace from day to day,
> To the last syllable of recorded time;
> And all our yesterdays have lighted fools
> The way to dusty death.

The slow, deliberate, even dragging rhythm accentuates what the words themselves indicate: the slowness of time. The words also suggest the state of the speaker's mind—a boredom and frustration at this slowness, captured most notably with the verb "Creeps," the phrases "petty pace" and "day to day," and the repeated "tomorrow." Beyond these, however, is the way key words are stressed in utterance: "tomorrow," "creeps," "last," "time," "all," "fools," and "death."

Another related aspect of dialogue is an equally important indicator of characters' attitudes and feelings: *imagery*, or the comparisons we find in their speech, usually within a play's longer speeches. Consider this additional example from *Macbeth*, which follows directly from the lines just quoted. Macbeth's speech continues:

> . . . Out, Out, brief candle!
> Life's but a walking shadow, a poor player
> That struts and frets his hour upon the stage
> And then is heard no more. It is a tale
> Told by an idiot, full of sound and fury
> Signifying nothing.

Shakespeare reveals Macbeth's state of mind by using a series of comparisons (metaphors in this case), each of which describes "Life." First, the brevity of life is emphasized as it is compared with a candle, which can be snuffed out. Second comes the comparison of life with a shadow, an insubstantial reflection of the real thing. This is followed immediately by the more elaborate comparison of life with the situation of an actor. Literally, an actor portrays a character whose life is confined to the duration (an hour or two) of a given play. Shakespeare's image resonates to suggest that in a way "[a]ll the world's a stage," that we are all just actors who strut proudly through life full of confidence and optimism one moment, while the next worrying anxiously as we fret over the lost opportunities and brutal realities we may be powerless to change. And then, quite simply, we die.

The most powerful and frightening comparison is reserved for last. Life, Macbeth says, is an idiot's story, filled with noise and much wild action. But ultimately, it means nothing. And the reason is because death ends it all. Because it has a final, often untimely, end, life is reduced to the incoherence of idiocy and the absurdity of meaninglessness. Shakespeare uses powerful imagery to express this sense of nihilism, that existence is useless. He ends the speech with the all-important word "nothing."

Two other aspects of dialogue that affect our response to characters are voice and tempo. In listening to a speech in the theater or in reading it (preferably aloud) ourselves, we should attend to the following characteristics: stress, or accent; speed, or pace; strength, or power; pitch, or elevation of voice; and silence, or pauses. How would you read the speeches quoted earlier? What words or syllables should be stressed? At what tempo should the lines be spoken? Should the tempo change anywhere? Why? How loudly or softly should the lines be read? In how high or low a voice? And where and for how long should there be pauses?

These aspects of dialogue and character are admittedly much harder to discern in a silent reading of a play. Some would contend that they are impossible to hear. But with an imaginative effort and a willingness to read aloud on occasion, we can begin to hear how much meaning and feeling dialogue conveys. Better yet, we can go to the theater and hear the drama for ourselves.

In the meantime, let us consider how these aspects of speech would sound in a reading of the following brief scene from *Mac-*

beth. This time we will listen to a dialogue rather than a monologue. Pay close attention to how the tempo of the dialogue quickly increases, then shifts to a higher pitch of intensity with Macbeth's talk of murder, then slows with Macbeth's famous speech about sleep—until Lady Macbeth cuts him off with a question, seizing the scene by sheer force of will.

The scene occurs just after Macbeth has murdered the king.

MACBETH: I have done the deed. Didst thou not hear a noise?
LADY MACBETH: I heard the owl scream and the crickets cry.
Did not you speak?
MACBETH: When?
LADY MACBETH: Now.
MACBETH: As I descended?
LADY MACBETH: Ay.
MACBETH: Hark!
Who lies i' th' second chamber?
LADY MACBETH: Donalbain.
MACBETH: This is a sorry sight.
LADY MACBETH: A foolish thought, to say a sorry sight.
MACBETH: There's one did laugh in 's sleep, and one cried
    "Murder!"
That they did wake each other. I stood and heard them.
But they did say their prayers, and addressed them
Again to sleep.
LADY MACBETH: There are two lodged together.
MACBETH: One cried "God bless us!"' and "Amen" the other,
As they had seen me with these hangman's hands:
List'ning their fear, I could not say "Amen,"
When they did say "God bless us!"
LADY MACBETH: Consider it not so deeply.
MACBETH: But wherefore could not I pronounce "Amen"?
I had most need of blessing, and "Amen"
Stuck in my throat.
LADY MACBETH: These deeds must not be thought
After these ways; so, it will make us mad.
MACBETH: Methought I heard a voice cry "Sleep no more!
Macbeth does murder sleep"—the innocent sleep,
Sleep that knits up the raveled sleave of care,

The death of each day's life, sore labor's bath,
Balm of hurt minds, great nature's second course,
Chief nourisher in life's feast——

LADY MACBETH:　　　　　　　What do you mean?

MACBETH: Still it cried "Sleep no more!" to all the house:
"Glamis hath murdered sleep, and therefor Cawdor
Shall sleep no more: Macbeth shall sleep no more."

LADY MACBETH: Who was it that thus cried? Why, worthy Thane,
You do unbend your noble strength, to think
So brainsickly of things. Go get some water,
And wash this filthy witness from your hand.
Why did you bring these daggers from the place?
They must lie there: go carry them, and smear
The sleepy grooms with blood.

MACBETH:　　　　　　　　　I'll go no more.
I am afraid to think what I have done;
Look on 't again I dare not.

LADY MACBETH:　　　　　Infirm of purpose!
Give me the daggers. The sleeping and the dead
Are but as pictures. 'Tis the eye of childhood
That fears a painted devil. If he do bleed,
I'll gild the faces of the grooms withal,
For it must seem their guilt.

Exit. Knock within.

We have introduced this scene to alert you to the way dramatists can alter the tempo of dialogue. The scene should also be analyzed, of course, for what it reveals about the character of Macbeth and Lady Macbeth. Their dialogue, moreover, is more than mere talk. In coming after the murder of King Duncan and before Lady Macbeth's plan to frame the grooms, by smearing them with blood while they sleep, their dialogue both describes action and exhibits it. Dialogue, in this instance, becomes action.

Setting and Staging

The action of a play, like that of any fictional work, occurs in a particular place and time. We call this spatial and temporal location its *setting*. Some plays are set approximately in the times and places of their composition—Henrik Ibsen's *An Enemy of the People*, for example, or Sam Shepard's *True West*. The setting for Lady Gregory's *The Rising of the Moon* closely approximates the temporal and spatial context of its author's time—Ireland in the nineteenth century. More often than not, however, a play's setting departs significantly from the time and place of its composition. The immediate world of a playwright is not often directly represented in the environment and milieu in which he or she sets a particular play. This does not mean, however, that there cannot be important connections between the playwright's immediate milieu and the possibly very different time and place of the play's action. Sometimes, in fact, particularly in political plays (and often in Shakespeare), historical events of earlier times reflect social and political situations of the playwright's own time. Shakespeare's London is clearly not the world depicted in *Macbeth*. Yet the issue of the divine right of kings and the honor accorded monarchy, both central to the play, were taken seriously in sixteenth-century London. The important thing, though, is not the literal identity of a playwright's milieu with that of a given play, but rather the impression the setting makes on us, what it contributes to our understanding and experience of the play.

When we attend a play (and when we read one), the first thing we see is the stage set, the physical objects that suggest the world of the play. The stage set is usually indicated by the playwright, though the degree of detail and the specificity of this rendering vary from one playwright to another and from one literary period to another. Consider the stage directions for setting that begin *The Rising of the Moon:*

Scene *Side of a quay in a seaport town. Some posts and chains. A large barrel. Enter three policemen. Moonlight.*

Clearly this is a simple and highly generalized set. We are given just a few basic objects and some moonlight, nothing more. Yet the objects, simple as they are, nonetheless establish the elemental world of the play. It will be a play, this set suggests, and a world, in which a rich collection of "things" is not important. Far more important is a basic human conflict, seen more clearly and represented more intensely in a sparse, uncluttered setting.

The set for the opening scene of *Macbeth* is similarly uncluttered and general. It reads:

SCENE I   *An open place.*

Thunder and lightning. Enter THREE WITCHES.

Although this too is a direct, brief, and "natural" setting, the atmosphere it creates differs radically from the setting of *The Rising of the Moon*. Shakespeare's setting for the opening scene of *Macbeth* conveys a sense of mysteriousness. The storm is more than an everyday storm. The witches' appearance endows it with a supernatural and sinister quality. And although the world of this scene is not the world of the entire play, its starkness and mystery establish an ominous atmosphere of disorder that affects subsequent scenes.

The sets for both of these plays leave room for directors and stage managers to decide just how to represent the worlds called for. There is less room for such decisions, however, in plays with very explicit directions for stage sets. Consider, for example, this set from the opening scene of Bernard Shaw's *Pygmalion:*

> *London at 11:15 p.m. Torrents of heavy summer rain. Cab whistles blowing frantically in all directions. Pedestrians running for shelter into the portico of St. Paul's church (not Wren's cathedral but Inigo Jones's church in Covent Garden vegetable market), among them a lady and her daughter in evening dress. All are peering out gloomily at the rain, except one man with his back turned to the rest, wholly preoccupied with a notebook in which he is writing.*
>
> *The church clock strikes the first quarter.*

Shaw's set is considerably more specific than our previous examples, though it functions in much the same general way—by providing a sense of the play's physical environment and an indication of its symbolic values. The important element here is the "evening dress" of the "lady and her daughter," suggesting, of course, wealth, privilege, and social standing, a central concern of the play.

One last point about setting. Although one-act plays typically employ a single stage set, multi-act dramas change sets, sometimes many times. (*Macbeth* is an example.) In a long play such as this, it is important to notice such changes of scene and setting, and to consider what the varied sets contribute to our experience and understanding of the play.

The setting of a play is one element of its *staging*, or the spectacle a play presents in performance. Staging in general refers to all the visual and aural details of a play. It includes the positions of actors onstage (sometimes referred to as *blocking);* their postures, gestures, movements, and expressions *(stage business);* the scenic background; the props and costumes; the lighting and sound effects. Though some of these details may be called for specifically in the script, decisions about staging are often left to the play's director.

We can illustrate these aspects of staging by considering *The Rising of the Moon* once again. The first thing we might notice about the characters is their physical appearance, especially their dress. The policemen should be distinguishable from their Sergeant, perhaps by an emblem or badge the superior officer wears. The greater visual distinction, however, is that between the Sergeant and the "ragged" man. Very likely in casting these roles, one would make the Sergeant the bigger, stronger, better fed of the two. On appearance alone, most likely, our sympathy will lie with the escaped man.

The props include the placards that the two policemen are putting up. These posters are important as much for what they omit as for what they contain. They omit, for example, a picture of the man being sought; and they also omit the details of the man's criminal exploits. Like the policemen who post them, the placards are matter-of-fact. The barrel on which they paste one of the placards is the central prop of the play. Its importance stems from two crucial actions that involve it—the Sergeant sits on it back to back with the man he seeks, and the Man hides behind it upon the return of the two policemen. Because of its importance, the barrel would most likely be placed center stage. Finally, and also important, are the Man's hat and wig—his simple disguise, which the Sergeant hides behind his back while dismissing the two policemen.

The positions of the characters onstage and their postures and gestures are not always specifically indicated in the stage directions and script. Occasionally they are, however, as when the Sergeant "crosses the stage to right and looks down steps." The Sergeant is also specifically directed to take the Man's shoulder and shove him. Later the Sergeant and the ragged man echo each other's actions visually when they point to the water. Such movements and gestures are important not only because they advance the plot, but also because they direct us to the play's central concerns and imply aspects of its meaning. We noted earlier how the pointing reinforces the connection between the Sergeant and the Man established in the Sergeant's speech about the possibility of each of them being in the other's place.

The lighting of the play is important as well. The quality of the lighting indicated by "moonlight" suggests literally a shadowy light from a distance. Its effect should be to increase the play's suspense and drama.

Sound, too, is important. There is the sound of the policemen's talk as they return, which is accentuated by the sparseness of the setting and the time—late at night. There is the sound of a boat being rowed—heard by both the Man and the Sergeant—a sound that precipitates the play's climax. There is also the whistle the Man's friends use as a signal as they approach the quay. And there is the sound of singing, which functions both to advance the plot and to highlight one of the central issues of the play. Notice, for example, how the songs are ballads about Irish nationalist heroes. And, of course, remember that when the ballad-singer omits a line from one ballad, the Sergeant supplies it, indicating still another way in which he, the Man, and the common people are joined together.

We can consider a bit further what sound effects can contribute to a play. We listen to the end of one scene and the beginning of another, joined by the sound of knocking at the gate. This excerpt from *Macbeth* follows directly upon the dialogue we quoted earlier, in which Macbeth reveals his phantasmagoric imagination and his confused state of mind after the murder. (Remember that he imagines hearing voices that say "Macbeth does murder sleep." He has trouble, it seems, distinguishing between real voices and imaginary ones.)

MACBETH: Whence is that knocking?
   How is 't with me, when every noise appalls me?
   What hands are here? Ha! They pluck out mine eyes!
   Will all great Neptune's ocean wash this blood
   Clean from my hand? No; this my hand will rather
   The multitudinous seas incarnadine,
   Making the green one red.

Enter LADY MACBETH.

LADY MACBETH: My hands are of your color, but I shame
   To wear a heart so white. *(Knock.)* I hear a knocking
   At the south entry. Retire we to our chamber.
   A little water clears us of this deed:
   How easy is it then! Your constancy
   Hath left you unattended. *(Knock.)* Hark! more knocking.
   Get on your nightgown, lest occasion call us
   And show us to be watchers. Be not lost
   So poorly in your thoughts.
MACBETH: To know my deed, 'twere best not know myself.
   (Knock.)
   Wake Duncan with thy knocking! I would thou couldst!

Exeunt. (They leave the stage.)

SCENE III   *Macbeth's Castle.*

Enter a PORTER. *Knocking within.*

PORTER: Here's a knocking indeed! If a man were porter of hell
   gate, he should have old turning the key. *(Knock.)* Knock,
   knock, knock! Who's there, i' th' name of Beelzebub! Here's a
   farmer, that hanged himself on th' expectation of plenty. Come
   in time! Have napkins enow about you; here you'll sweat for 't.
   (Knock.) Knock, knock! Who's there, in th' other devil's name?

Faith, here's an equivocator, that could swear in both the scales against either scale; who committed treason enough for God's sake, yet could not equivocate to heaven. O, come in, equivocator. *(Knock.)* Knock, knock, knock! Who's there? Faith, here's an English tailor come hither for stealing out of a French hose: come in, tailor. Here you may roast your goose. *(Knock.)* Knock, knock; never at quiet! What are you? But this place is too cold for hell. I'll devil-porter it no further. I had thought to have let in some of all professions that go the primrose way to th' everlasting bonfire. *(Knock.)* Anon, anon! *(Opens an entrance.)* I pray you, remember the porter.

What can we say about all this knocking, both the insistent knocking at the gate and the repeated references to it by Macbeth and the Porter? First, of course, the knocking means something very different to Macbeth from what it does to the Porter. The Porter seems almost to make a game of talking about the knocking while he goes to answer it. This provides a kind of comic relief after the tremendous tension built up during and immediately following the scene of the murder. Yet Shakespeare also uses the knocking to stretch the waiting time for the audience, increasing our suspense at just who is knocking, awaiting entrance to the castle. The knocking becomes a symbolic echo for a similar pounding of Macbeth's heart while at the same time representing the real, everyday, matter-of-fact world insistently returning and breaking into the intensely felt but wild imaginings of Macbeth. (Remember that he had trouble distinguishing what he sees from what he imagines, such as the hands he thinks are attempting to tear out his eyes.) Macbeth wishes he could undo the deed and expresses that wish with a reference to the knocking that under normal circumstances would waken Duncan, who now sleeps the profound sleep of death. Finally, the knocking in this scene possesses a dramatic structure that builds to a climax and then falls off; it is part of a larger dramatic movement that prepares for the eventual arousal of the people in the castle and the discovery of the murdered king, which is signaled by the clang of a bell that shatters the nocturnal silence.

A playwright's stage directions will sometimes help us see and hear things such as these as we read. But with or without stage directions, we need to use our aural as well as our visual imagination. An increased imaginative alertness to the sights and sounds of a play, though no substitute for a dramatic performance, can nonetheless help us approximate the experience. It can also enhance our appreciation of the dramatist's craftsmanship and increase our understanding of the play.

Symbolism and Irony

In our discussion of the staging of *The Rising of the Moon*, and in our observations about its dialogue and conflict, we touched briefly and implicitly on two additional aspects of drama: symbolism and irony. A *symbol* can be defined simply as any object or action that means more than itself, that represents something beyond its literal self. Objects, actions, clothing, gestures, dialogue—all may have symbolic meaning. A rose, for example, might represent beauty, love, or transience (or all three). A tree might represent a family's roots and branches. A soaring bird might stand for freedom. Light might symbolize hope or knowledge or life. These symbolic associations, however, are not necessary or automatic, since the meaning of any symbol is controlled by its context and function in a particular dramatic scene.

How, then, do we know if a particular detail is symbolic? How do we decide whether to leap beyond the literal dialogue or action into a symbolic interpretation? There are no simple or absolute rules about this. Like an interpretive connection we make in reading, the decision to view something as symbolic depends partly on our skill in reading and partly on whether the dramatic context invites and rewards a symbolic interpretation. The following questions can be used to guide our thinking about literary symbols:

1. Is the object, action, gesture, or dialogue important to the play? Is it described in detail? Does it occur more than once, or does it occur at a climactic or significant moment?

2. Does the play seem to warrant our granting its details more significance than their immediate literal meaning? Why?

3. Does a symbolic interpretation make sense? Does it account for the literal details without either ignoring or distorting them?

Even in considering such questions there will be occasions when we are not certain that a particular object, action, or utterance is symbolic. And there will be times when, though we are fairly confident *that* we are dealing with a symbol, we are not confident about *what* it represents. Such uncertainty is due largely to the nature of interpretation, which is an art rather than a science. Interpretive uncertainty is also due to the differences in complexity and the variability with which dramatists use symbols. And it is further complicated by the fact that most complex symbols resist definitive explanation.

Consider, for example, the symbolic force of the revolutionary songs the ballad-singer sings in the *The Rising of the Moon*. At the end of the play he sings a song about "The Rising of the Moon." What does the moon's rising stand for in the context of the play's action? Consider also the symbolic importance of the scene in which the Sergeant and the ballad-singer sit back-to-back on the barrel, looking out in opposite directions. To what extent does this action symbolize their differences of attitude, belief, and perspective? And when they jump together off the barrel, can this be construed as a symbolic representation of their decision to overlook their differences?

Irony is not so much an element of a fictional text as a pervasive quality in it. Irony may appear in plays in three basic ways: in their language, in their incidents, or in their point of view. In whatever forms it emerges, though, *irony* almost always involves a contrast or discrepancy between what is said and what is meant or between what happens and what is expected to happen.

Verbal irony refers to saying the opposite of what is meant. When someone says, "That was a brilliant remark," and we know that it was anything but brilliant, we understand the speaker's ironic intention. In such a relatively simple instance there is usually no problem in perceiving irony. In more complex situations, however, the identification of an action or a remark as ironic can be much more complicated. Consider, for instance, the ending of *The Rising of the Moon*. After the Sergeant has let the ballad-singer escape, he asks himself whether he was a fool in doing so. The Sergeant's question is ironic, since once we accept his action and understand the sympathy that motivates it, we do not expect him to express such doubts concerning it. Moreover, his words seem to indicate the opposite of what they actually say, with our understanding being that he is not a fool at all.

Another type of irony plays may contain is *irony of circumstance* (sometimes called *irony of situation*), in which a playwright creates a discrepancy between what characters think is the case and what actually is the case. You will find examples of irony of circumstance in many of the plays in this anthology, including *Antigonê*, *Macbeth*, *The Doctor in Spite of Himself*, *The Stronger*, *Trifles*, *The Gap*, and *True West*. Irony of circumstance also appears forcefully in *The Rising of the Moon*, since what we expect to happen is actually not what happens at all; the opposite, in fact, is what occurs. It initially appears that the Sergeant is out to capture the fugitive, but he abandons his opportunity to do so. It appears that the fugitive is dangerous and will act to protect himself, but he instead persuades with his language and song. And it appears that these two men have really nothing in common, but it turns out they have very much in common, most importantly their shared sense of idealism. In these and other ways the action of the play creates ironic situations that form the heart of its dramatic action.

The final type of irony found in plays is called dramatic irony. *Dramatic irony* involves a discrepancy between what characters know and what readers or viewers know. Playwrights often let us know things that their characters do not. We know, for example, that the ballad-singer is the man the Sergeant seeks even though for a while the Sergeant does not know it. And we know that the ballad-singer is hiding behind a barrel nearby while the Sergeant dismisses his two police assistants near the end of the play. Our knowledge of these things increases our pleasure in the play's situation and action. And it enhances our appreciation of the dramatist's skill in structuring the play's action to create such ironic situations.

When a dramatist's work is pervaded by ironies in these various forms, we may characterize such pervasiveness as an *ironic point of view*. The persistent use of irony can also be called an *ironic vision*. A play like Sophocles' *Antigonê* is informed by an ironic vision, as is Sophocles' work overall. In such works, the dramatist's ironic vision infuses the plot, controls the dialogue, and surfaces repeatedly in its other dramatic elements.

Thought and Theme

From examining the various elements of a play we derive a sense of its significance and meaning. We use the word *theme* to designate the main idea or point of a play stated as a generalization. Although it is a common exercise to attempt to identify a central idea or set of ideas from a play, or from any literary work, we should be aware of the limitations in doing so.

First, we should distinguish the ideas that may appear *in* a play from the idea *of* a play. The meaning of a play—its central, governing, or animating idea—is rarely identifiable as an explicit social, political, or philosophical idea manifest in the dialogue. Rather, a play's theme is almost always implicit, bound up with and derivable from the play's structure, character interactions, dialogue, and staging. One of the dangers of reading drama without attending sufficiently to its theatrical dimension is that we may reduce its meaning to a single, unnecessarily simplified and overly generalized statement of idea. Yet this poses a paradox. Since the theme of a play grows out of the relationships among its concrete details, any statement of it that omits significant aspects of a play's dramatic elements will inevitably represent a limitation and a distortion of the play's meaning. At the same time, because formulating the theme of a play involves abstracting from it a generalizable idea, theme inevitably moves away from the very details of character and action that give the play its life. So, any statement of theme, in fact, inevitably only approximates a play's meaning rather than fully characterizing or embodying it. Even when we speak of multiple themes (as we should, since plays often suggest a multiplicity of ideas), we are still concerned only with the intellectual aspect of meaning. And as we have suggested earlier, a play's meaning encompasses emotional apprehension as well as intellectual comprehension.

As readers of drama, we tend to reach for a theme as a way of organizing our responses to a play, as a way of coming to terms with what it implies about how human beings live. At times we emphasize our personal responses, our emotional reactions to what the play dramatizes. At times we seize an intellectual response based on observations of its action and inferences drawn from connections we establish from among its details. At times we look at what the play is; at times we feel what the play does. Both are important aspects of its meaning. For the meaning of any play is ultimately more than any statement of theme, any series of words and sentences that we employ to describe it. Our experience, our moment-by-moment engagement with the play on stage or page, constitutes its meaning for us.

But there is more even than this to the meaning of any play. For it is not only our intellectual comprehension and emotional apprehension of the play as we read or watch it that matters. We also remember the play after seeing or reading it. And in this remembering, we remake it, reconstruct it, and often "see" aspects of it we overlooked during our moment-by-moment encounter. A play's meaning is not always readily and completely available to us even as we complete our encounter with it. We can return to a play for second and subsequent encounters and understand it differently after repeated readings or viewings. A play's meaning, then, is almost always provisional, tentative, temporary. Its meaning changes as we change. Its meaning includes its way of affecting us, not once and for all, but again and again in different ways.

Does this mean that we should abandon our attempts to state a play's theme(s)? Not necessarily. But we should certainly avoid thinking of theme as somehow hidden in the dialogue for us to ferret out. And we should be aware that to reduce the play's thought to a satisfactorily inclusive statement of theme is no easy matter. At best such statements offer approximations of any play's meaning, which, again at best, can clarify and illuminate our experience of drama and of life. At worst, statements of theme oversimplify plays, distorting their significance and impoverishing our experience.

As far as possible, then, we should try to discuss the thought of a play in terms of its general significance, in terms of its implied idea(s). We can explore its central issues and speculate about its major concerns without insisting that it possesses a single, definitive, absolute message. Let us briefly consider the thought and theme of *The Rising of the Moon*.

First, it is a political play, occurring amid the turmoil of a beleaguered Irish populace. The historical details of the political situation are not explicitly rendered, largely because they would have been familiar to Lady Gregory's audience. But they are alluded to in references to Granuaile, who appears to be an Irish revolutionary hero. Moreover, we are meant to side with the man who fights for the cause of Granuaile and to see the justice of that revolutionary cause and its ultimate triumph over the social and political status quo. According to the Man (and the play overall), a social revolution is in the making. The play alludes to a spirit of optimistic idealism and a corresponding sense that injustice and inequity will not always prevail.

This political idea is closely associated with the crisis of conscience the Sergeant undergoes. His decision to trust his instinctive sympathy for the Man and his cause, and his impulse to act in accordance with his reawakened youthful idealism rather than to capture the criminal, are powerfully dramatized. And even though the play ends with a question, an answer is clearly implied. When the Sergeant asks, "Am I as great a fool as I think I am?" his question reminds us to understand the meaning of the play not merely as an abstract intellectual idea but as a living moment of decision. Our answers to his question may vary, though one that seems endorsed by the many interrelated details and elements of the play is "No, you're not a fool at all. In fact, you're a good man who's trying to do what you believe is right."

As we think back to the Sergeant and his crisis of conscience, to the escaped man, his ballads about Ireland, and his friends and their effort to rescue him, we begin to realize the significance of the play. Our consideration of its personal, human, and social issues and our memory of its effect on us constitute its meaning.

Genre and Convention

Genre   *Genre* refers to a literary type or kind. Fictional works, for example, may be classified as novels, short stories, romances, and novellas or short novels. Poems may be classified generally as narrative, lyric, or epic. Plays, analogously, fall under three general generic headings: tragedy, comedy, and tragicomedy. Within these broad categories are subgenres, such as the revenge tragedy, a kind of tragic play popular in the sixteenth century in which murder and bloodshed are prominent; and farce, a type of short comic play in which crude jokes and wildly exaggerated and improbable situations predominate.

Tragedy   In *Poetics*, Aristotle described *tragedy* as "an imitation of an action that is serious, complete in itself, and of a certain magnitude." This definition suggests that tragedies are solemn plays concerned with grave human actions and their consequences. The action of a tragedy is complete—it possesses a beginning, a middle, and an end in which the events grow naturally one out of another, each leading to an inevitable catastrophe, usually the downfall of the hero.

Some readers of tragedy have suggested that the catastrophe results from a *tragic flaw*, a flaw in the character of the hero. Others have contended that the hero's tragic flaw results from fate or coincidence, from circumstances beyond the hero's control. A third view proposes that tragedy results from an error of judgment committed by the hero, one that may or may not have as its source a weakness in character. Typically, tragic protagonists make mistakes: they misjudge other characters, they misinterpret events, and they confuse appearance with reality. The misfortune and catastrophes of tragedy are frequently precipitated by errors of judgment; mistaken perceptions lead to misdirected actions that eventually result in catastrophe.

Tragic heroes are grand, noble characters. They are privileged, exalted personages who have earned their high repute and status by heroic exploit, by intelligence, or by their inherent nobility. Their tragedy resides in a fall from glory that crushes not only the tragic hero himself but other related characters as well. Greek tragedy, typically, involves the destruction and downfall of a whole house or family, reaching across generations. The catastrophe of Shakespearean tragedy is usually not as extensive.

An essential element of the tragic hero's experience is a *recognition* of what has happened to him. Frequently this takes the form of the hero's discovering something previously unknown or something he knew but misconstrued. The tragic hero's recognition (or discovery) is often allied with a reversal of his expectations. Once the reversal and discovery occur, tragic plots move swiftly to their conclusions.

We may consider why, amid such suffering and catastrophe, tragedies are not depressing. Perhaps it is because tragedy provides the audience with a *catharsis*: the pity and fear aroused in the audience are purged, or released, so that the audience experiences a cleansing of those emotions and a sense of relief that the action is over. Perhaps tragedy represents for us the ultimate downfall we will all experience in death: we watch in fascination and awe a dramatic reminder of our own inevitable mortality. Or perhaps we are somehow exalted in witnessing the high human aspiration and the noble conception of human character embodied in tragic heroes.

Comedy Some of the same dramatic elements we find in tragedy occur in comedy as well. Discovery scenes and consequent reversals of fortune, for example, occur in both. So too do misperceptions and errors of judgment, exhibitions of human weakness and failure. But in comedy the reversals and errors lead not to calamity, as they do in tragedy, but to prosperity and happiness. Comic heroes are usually ordinary people; they are less grand, less noble than tragic protagonists. Moreover, comic characters are frequently one-dimensional to the extent that many are stereotypes: the braggart, for example, or the hypocrite, the unfaithful wife, the cuckold, the ardent young lovers.

If comic characters are frequently predictable in their behavior, comic plots are not: they thrive on the surprise of the unexpected, and on improbability. Cinderella stories like these are the staples of comedy: an impoverished student inherits a fortune; a beggar turns out to be a prince; a wife (or husband or child) presumed dead turns up alive and well; the war (between nations, classes, families, the sexes) ends, the two sides are reconciled and everybody lives happily ever after. To these large-scale improbabilities we can add smaller-scale incongruities. But whether the incongruities of comedy exist between a character's speech and actions, between what we expect the characters to be and what they show themselves to be, or between how they think of themselves and how we see them, things work out in the end.

The happy endings of comedies are not always happy for all the characters involved. This marks one of the significant differences between the two major types of comedy: satiric and romantic comedy. Though much of what we have said so far about comedy applies to both types, it applies more extensively to romantic than to satiric comedy, or satire. *Satire* exposes human folly, criticizes human conduct, and aims to correct it. Ridiculing the weaknesses of human nature, satiric comedy shows us the low level to which human behavior can sink. Although things may work out well in the end for most of the characters, a satire may contain some harsh moments.

Romantic comedy, on the other hand, portrays characters gently, even generously; its spirit is more tolerant; and its tone, more genial. Whatever adversities the heroes and heroines of romantic comedy must overcome, the tone is typically devoid of rancor and bitterness. The humor of romantic comedy is more sympathetic than corrective, and it intends more to entertain than to instruct, to delight than to ridicule.

Because of such differences, our approaches to reading satire and romance should be different. When we read satiric comedies, we should identify the object of the dramatist's criticism and determine why the behavior of certain characters is objectionable. In reading romantic comedies, we are invited simply to enjoy the raveling and unraveling of plot as the protagonists are led to the inevitable happy ending.

These distinctions, however, are useful only as they help us gauge a play's prevailing characteristics. They should serve as guidelines to prevailing tendencies rather than as rigid descriptions of dramatic types. Frequently romantic comedies may contain elements of satire; and satiric comedies, elements of romance.

Tragicomedy Many modern plays mix not just modes of comedy, but elements of comedy and tragedy as well. These works are not so easy to classify. In fact, it's often less important to decide whether a play is predominantly comic or tragic, romantic or satiric, than to acknowledge its mixture of modes and to respond fully to the characters or situations it dramatizes. Such plays are often designated *tragicomedies* to identify their mode. Some twentieth-century dramatists have found that tragicomedy is more suitable for representing a complex, uncertain, and often irrational world than either tragedy or comedy alone.

Convention *Conventions* are essentially the rules or characteristic features of a genre. In drama, for example, when a character speaks directly to the audience in a manner suggesting that other characters present onstage do not hear him or her, we accept this as a convention. It is a theatrical device that allows us to learn what a particular character is thinking without the other characters knowing this. We know, of course, that the other actors can actually hear the spoken words, but we agree to ignore this fact because observing the convention of the aside (or the soliloquy, to cite another example) provides playwrights with an efficient way to advance their dramatic plot.

Theatrical conventions are not hard-and-fast rules set in stone never to be altered. In fact, theatrical conventions can and do change. Thus, although it was once a convention for characters to wear masks (in ancient performances of Greek tragedy) and although women's roles were assumed by boys in Elizabethan drama, these conventions are no longer generally adhered to. The history of drama in large part is a history of changing theatrical conventions. The main characteristics of Western drama from ancient Greece to our own time reveal many such changes.

Greek Drama   Greek plays were performed in huge outdoor amphitheaters capable of seating upwards of fourteen thousand people. Members of the audience were seated in tiers that sloped up hillsides where the theaters were built; the hills echoed the sound of the actors' voices. The actors wore masks that amplified their voices in the manner of megaphones. The masks were large, and with the elevated shoes sometimes worn by the actors, they projected the characters as larger-than-life figures. The masks and elevated shoes restricted what the actors could do and what the dramatist could expect of them. Subtle nuances of voice, of facial expression, and of gesture were impossible. The playwright's language rather than his stage business conveyed nuances of meaning and feeling.

The plays were performed on an elevated platform. Behind the acting area was a scene building *(skene)* that functioned both as dressing room and as a simple scenic background, and below the stage was the *orchestra,* or dancing place for the chorus. Standing between the actors and the audience, the *chorus* represented the common or communal viewpoint. Its leader, the *choragos,* sometimes engaged the chorus in dialogue with the other characters, and sometimes the choragos engaged in dialogue with the chorus itself.

An important function of the chorus was to mark the divisions between the scenes of a play, when the chorus would dance and chant poetry. Lyric rather than dramatic in form, these choral interludes sometimes commented on the action, sometimes generalized from it. They remained in Greek drama as vestiges of its origins in religious ritual. For modern readers these choric interludes pace the play, affording respite from the gradually intensifying action, and allowing time to ponder its implications.

The scenes of Greek plays usually consist of two characters. Sometimes there is a third character, usually acting as an observer who occasionally comments on the debate occurring between the other two characters. Sometimes most of a scene is given over to a debate between two characters, as, for example, in Scene III of *Antigonê,* with Haimon challenging Creon, his father. Some scenes contain several debates. Scene II of *Antigonê,* for example, includes debates between Creon-Antigonê, Antigonê-Ismenê, Ismenê-Creon, and Creon-Choragos. The debates typically begin with leisurely speeches in which each character sets forth a position. The speeches are followed by rapid-fire dialogue *(stichomythia)* that brings the characters' antagonisms to a climax. This pattern is repeated throughout the play in something like a theme with variations, each scene usually developing a conflict. The accumulation of conflicts advances the action, leading to the inevitable tragic catastrophe.

Elizabethan Drama   The drama of Shakespeare's time, the Elizabethan Age (1558–1604), shares some features with Greek drama. Like Greek dramatists, Elizabethan playwrights wrote both comedies and tragedies, but the Elizabethans extended the possibilities of each genre. They wrote, for example, domestic tragedies, tragedies of character, and revenge tragedies; they contributed comedies of manners and comedies of humors to the earlier romantic and satiric comedies. As in the Greek theater, props were few, scenery was simple, and dialogue often indicated changes of locale and time. Also, Elizabethan plays, like Greek dramas, were written in verse rather than prose.

Unlike the large Greek amphitheaters, which could seat thousands, an Elizabethan playhouse such as the Globe, where many of Shakespeare's plays were staged, had a much smaller seating capacity. The Globe, for example, could accommodate about twenty-three hundred people, including roughly eight hundred "groundlings," who, exposed to the elements, stood around the stage. The stage itself projected from an inside wall into their midst. More prosperous spectators sat in one of the three stories that nearly encircled the stage. The vastly smaller size and seating capacity of the Elizabethan theater and the projection of its stage made for a greater intimacy between actors and audience. Though actors still had to project their voices and exaggerate their gestures, they could be heard and seen without the aid of large megaphonic masks and elevated shoes. Elizabethan actors could modulate their voices and vary their pitch, stress, and intonation in ways not suited to the Greek stage. They could also make greater and more subtle use of facial expression and of gesture to enforce their greater verbal and vocal flexibility.

Neoclassical Drama   Perhaps the first thing to say about the neo-classical French theater of Molière (1622–1673), is that its conventions were inspired by the classical drama of Greece and Rome. Hence the term *neoclassical* to describe it. Like its ancient antecedents, the seventeenth-century French theater observed what Aristotle described as the *unities:* the unity of time, a stipulation that a play's action be confined to a twenty-four-hour period; the unity of place, a single setting; and the unity of action, a single plot. Plays that violated the unities were thought to be crude and inelegant by Molière's educated audience, which consisted largely of courtiers, aristocrats, and well-to-do merchants. His plays sometimes reflected the ideas and upheld the values popular among these classes; sometimes they satirized them. In either case, the good manners, wit, and common sense of Molière's comedy mirrored his world and suited his audience.

The neoclassical stage differed from those of Shakespeare and Sophocles. Molière's was an indoor theater with a picture-frame stage. The proscenium arch with its curtain separated audience from actors. Molière's plays were enacted on a box stage, which represented a room with a missing fourth wall, allowing the audience to look in on the action. Though the scenery was not elaborate, it was painted and it served as a backdrop for the action. Candles and lanterns illuminated both the actors and the audience.

Costume tended toward the elaborate and ornate, as in Elizabethan drama. On both the Elizabethan and neoclassical stages, actors were ordinarily costumed in contemporary dress that was appropriate to the social status of the characters (except, of course, when the play was historical). A major difference between neoclassical and earlier drama was that female actresses assumed women's roles, enabling playwrights to include more extensive, more frequent, and more realistic love scenes than had been possible previously (since boys had assumed women's roles in Shakespeare's time). As in the earlier eras of drama, however, language still did much of the work, so that even though the intimacy of the French neoclassical playhouse—with a capacity to seat perhaps four hundred spectators—allowed for refinements of facial and physical gesture, action remained subordinate to dialogue.

Modern Realistic and Absurdist Drama   The representation of everyday life in literature is called *realism*. Concerned with the average, the commonplace, the ordinary, realism employs theatrical conventions to create the illusion of everyday life. With realistic drama came the depiction of subjects close to the lives of middle-class people: work, marriage, and family life. From this standpoint, Arthur Miller's *A View from the Bridge* and Henrik Ibsen's *An Enemy of the People* are more realistic than Shakespeare's *Macbeth*, which, in turn, is more realistic than Sophocles' *Antigonê*. Though each of these plays possesses a true-to-life quality, each operates according to different theatrical conventions. Royal personages, gods, military heroes, and exalted language are absent from Miller's and Ibsen's plays as modern dramatists turned to an approximation of the daily life of the lower and middle classes.

Many conventions of realistic theater are designed to create and sustain the illusion that the audience is watching a slice of domestic life. The set is often a three-walled room with an open fourth wall into which the audience peers to view and overhear the action. Dialogue approximates the idiom of everyday discourse—polished, to be sure, but designed especially to sound like speech rather than poetry. Plots, though they are highly contrived, seem to turn on a series of causally related actions. Subjects come not from mythology or history, but from the concerns of ordinary life.

One of the most noteworthy developments in theater following the rise of realism has been the emergence of the theater of the absurd in the second half of the twentieth century. *Absurdist drama,* as it is called, is nonrealistic, even antirealistic. Absurdist playwrights reject the conventions of realism, substituting well-contrived plots with storyless action; they replace believable characters of psychological complexity with barely recognizable figures; and for witty repartee and grand speeches they offer incoherent ramblings and disconnected dialogue.

Why such an about-face, why such a rejection of realistic theatrical conventions? Primarily because ways of perceiving reality had changed so radically that realistic dramatic conventions were inadequate to the task of representing reality as dramatists of the absurd envisioned it. Absurdist dramatists reject the implications that lie behind realistic conventions; they object, for example, to the idea that characters can be understood or that plot should be ordered. For them, people are not understandable, and life is disorderly and chaotic. Absurdist writers attempt to dramatize these and other conceptions in plays that depict experience as meaningless and existence as purposeless; they portray human beings as irrational, pathetic figures, helpless against life's chaos. For the absurdist, humans are uprooted, cut off from their historical context, dispossessed of religious certainty, alienated from their social and physical environment, and unable to communicate with others.

Martin Esslin, a leading drama critic and expert on absurdist drama, has noted that the word *absurd* when used with reference to the theater of the absurd does not mean "ridiculous," but "out of harmony" (*The Theater of the Absurd,* Doubleday, 1969). Modern individuals, according to the absurdist dramatists, are out of tune with nature, with other human beings, and with themselves. This sense of being at odds with life thwarts their happiness and robs their lives of meaning.

Esslin has also recognized that dramatists of the absurd, like Eugene Ionesco, have moved beyond arguing about the absurdity of the human condition to present that condition in concrete dramatic terms of the theater. When dramatists of the absurd, thus, violate the rules of conventional drama, they do so because they see that strategy as the most effective way to illustrate the conditions of modern experience.

PART TWO

Anthology of
Plays

SOPHOCLES

Antigonê

An English Version by Dudley Fitts and Robert Fitzgerald

Characters

ANTIGONÊ   TEIRESIAS
ISMENÊ   A SENTRY
EURYDICÊ   A MESSENGER
CREON   CHORUS
HAIMON

Scene *Before the palace of* CREON, *King of Thebes. A central double door, and two lateral doors. A platform extends the length of the façade, and from this platform three steps lead down into the "orchestra," or chorus-ground.*

Time *Dawn of the day after the repulse of the Argive army from the assault on Thebes.*

PROLOGUE

ANTIGONÊ *and* ISMENÊ *enter from the central door of the palace.*

ANTIGONÊ: Ismenê, dear sister,
  You would think that we had already suffered enough
  For the curse on Oedipus.

³**Oedipus,** *former King of Thebes, father of Antigonê and Ismenê, and of Polyneicês and Eteoclês, their brothers. Oedipus unwittingly killed his father, Laïos, and married his mother, Iocastê. When he learned what he had done, he blinded himself and left Thebes. Eteoclês and Polyneicês quarreled; Polyneicês was defeated but returned to assault Thebes. Both brothers were killed in the battle; Creon ordered that Polyneicês remain unburied.*

I cannot imagine any grief
That you and I have not gone through. And now—
Have they told you of the new decree of our King Creon?

ISMENÊ: I have heard nothing: I know
That two sisters lost two brothers, a double death
In a single hour; and I know that the Argive army
Fled in the night; but beyond this, nothing.

ANTIGONÊ: I thought so. And that is why I wanted you
To come out here with me. There is something we must do.

ISMENÊ: Why do you speak so strangely?

ANTIGONÊ: Listen, Ismenê:
Creon buried our brother Eteoclês
With military honors, gave him a soldier's funeral,
And it was right that he should; but Polyneicês,
Who fought as bravely and died as miserably,—
They say that Creon has sworn
No one shall bury him, no one mourn for him,
But his body must lie in the fields, a sweet treasure
For carrion birds to find as they search for food.
That is what they say, and our good Creon is coming here
To announce it publicly; and the penalty—
Stoning to death in the public square!

                                   There it is,
And now you can prove what you are:
A true sister, or a traitor to your family.

ISMENÊ: Antigonê, you are mad! What could I possibly do?

ANTIGONÊ: You must decide whether you will help me or not.

ISMENÊ: I do not understand you. Help you in what?

ANTIGONÊ: Ismenê, I am going to bury him. Will you come?

ISMENÊ: Bury him! You have just said the new law forbids it.

ANTIGONÊ: He is my brother. And he is your brother, too.

ISMENÊ: But think of the danger! Think what Creon will do!

ANTIGONÊ: Creon is not strong enough to stand in my way.

ISMENÊ: Ah sister!
Oedipus died, everyone hating him
For what his own search brought to light, his eyes
Ripped out by his own hand; and Iocastê died,
His mother and wife at once: she twisted the cords
That strangled her life; and our two brothers died,

Each killed by the other's sword. And we are left:
But oh, Antigonê,
Think how much more terrible than these
Our own death would be if we should go against Creon 45
And do what he had forbidden! We are only women,
We cannot fight with men, Antigonê!
The law is strong, we must give in to the law
In this thing, and in worse. I beg the Dead
To forgive me, but I am helpless: I must yield 50
To those in authority. And I think it is dangerous business
To be always meddling.
ANTIGONÊ: If that is what you think,
I should not want you, even if you asked to come.
You have made your choice, you can be what you want to be.
But I will bury him; and if I must die, 55
I say that this crime is holy: I shall lie down
With him in death, and I shall be as dear
To him as he to me.
            It is the dead,
Not the living, who make the longest demands:
We die for ever . . .
            You may do as you like, 60
Since apparently the laws of the gods mean nothing to you.
ISMENÊ: They mean a great deal to me; but I have no strength
To break laws that were made for the public good.
ANTIGONÊ: That must be your excuse, I suppose. But as for me,
I will bury the brother I love.
ISMENÊ: Antigonê, 65
I am so afraid for you!
ANTIGONÊ: You need not be:
You have yourself to consider, after all.
ISMENÊ: But no one must hear of this, you must tell no one!
I will keep it a secret, I promise!
ANTIGONÊ: O tell it! Tell everyone!
Think how they'll hate you when it all comes out 70
If they learn that you knew about it all the time!
ISMENÊ: So fiery! You should be cold with fear.
ANTIGONÊ: Perhaps. But I am doing only what I must.
ISMENÊ: But can you do it? I say that you cannot.

ANTIGONÊ: Very well: when my strength gives out,
    I shall do no more.   75
ISMENÊ: Impossible things should not be tried at all.
ANTIGONÊ: Go away, Ismenê:
    I shall be hating you soon, and the dead will too,
    For your words are hateful. Leave me my foolish plan:
    I am not afraid of the danger; if it means death,   80
    It will not be the worst of deaths—death without honor.
ISMENÊ: Go then, if you feel that you must.
    You are unwise,
    But a loyal friend indeed to those who love you.

Exit into the palace. ANTIGONÊ *goes off, left. Enter the* CHORUS.

PÁRODOS

Strophe 1

CHORUS: Now the long blade of the sun, lying
    Level east to west, touches with glory
    Thebes of the Seven Gates. Open, unlidded
    Eye of golden day! O marching light
    Across the eddy and rush of Dircê's stream,   5
    Striking the white shields of the enemy
    Thrown headlong backward from the blaze of morning!
CHORAGOS: Polyneicês their commander
    Roused them with windy phrases,
    He the wild eagle screaming   10
    Insults above our land,
    His wings their shields of snow,
    His crest their marshalled helms.

Antistrophe 1

CHORUS: Against our seven gates in a yawning ring
    The famished spears came onward in the night;   15

---

⁵**Dircê's stream** *river near Thebes*
⁸**Choragos** *leader of the chorus*

But before his jaws were sated with our blood,
Or pinefire took the garland of our towers,
He was thrown back; and as he turned, great Thebes—
No tender victim for his noisy power—
Rose like a dragon behind him, shouting war.   20

CHORAGOS: For God hates utterly
  The bray of bragging tongues;
  And when he beheld their smiling,
  Their swagger of golden helms,
  The frown of his thunder blasted   25
  Their first man from our walls.

Strophe 2

CHORUS: We heard his shout of triumph high in the air
  Turn to a scream; far out in a flaming arc
  He fell with his windy torch, and the earth struck him.
  And others storming in turn no less than his   30
  Found shock of death in the dusty joy of battle.
CHORAGOS: Seven captains at seven gates
  Yielded their clanging arms to the god
  That bends the battle-line and breaks it.
  These two only, brothers in blood,   35
  Face to face in matchless rage,
  Mirroring each the other's death,
  Clashed in long combat.

Antistrophe 2

CHORUS: But now in the beautiful morning of victory
  Let Thebes of the many chariots sing for joy!   40
  With hearts for dancing we'll take leave of war:
  Our temples shall be sweet with hymns of praise,
  And the long nights shall echo with our chorus.

Scene I

CHORAGOS: But now at last our new King is coming:
Creon of Thebes, Menoikeus' son.
In this auspicious dawn of his reign
What are the new complexities
That shifting Fate has woven for him?   5
What is his counsel? Why has he summoned
The old men to hear him?

Enter CREON *from the palace, center. He addresses the* CHORUS *from the top step.*

CREON: Gentlemen: I have the honor to inform you that our Ship of State, which recent storms have threatened to destroy, has come safely to harbor at last, guided by the merciful wisdom 10 of Heaven. I have summoned you here this morning because I know that I can depend upon you: your devotion to King Laïos was absolute; you never hesitated in your duty to our late ruler Oedipus; and when Oedipus died, your loyalty was transferred to his children. Unfortunately, as you know, his two 15 sons, the princes Eteoclês and Polyneicês, have killed each other in battle; and I, as the next in blood, have succeeded to the full power of the throne.

I am aware, of course, that no Ruler can expect complete loyalty from his subjects until he has been tested in office. 20 Nevertheless, I say to you at the very outset that I have nothing but contempt for the kind of Governor who is afraid, for whatever reason, to follow the course that he knows is best for the State; and as for the man who sets private friendship above the public welfare,—I have no use for him, either. I call 25 God to witness that if I saw my country headed for ruin, I should not be afraid to speak out plainly; and I need hardly remind you that I would never have any dealings with an enemy of the people. No one values friendship more highly than I; but we must remember that friends made at the risk of wrecking 30 our Ship are not real friends at all.

These are my principles, at any rate, and that is why I have made the following decision concerning the sons of Oedipus: Eteoclês, who died as a man should die, fighting for his country,

66

is to be buried with full military honors, with all the ceremony 35
that is usual when the greatest heroes die; but his brother
Polyneicês, who broke his exile to come back with fire and sword
against his native city and the shrines of his fathers' gods, whose
one idea was to spill the blood of his blood and sell his own
people into slavery—Polyneicês, I say, is to have no burial: no 40
man is to touch him or say the least prayer for him; he shall lie
on the plain, unburied; and the birds and the scavenging dogs
can do with him whatever they like.

    This is my command, and you can see the wisdom behind it.
As long as I am King, no traitor is going to be honored with 45
the loyal man. But whoever shows by word and deed that he is
on the side of the State,—he shall have my respect while he is
living and my reverence when he is dead.

CHORAGOS: If that is your will, Creon son of Menoikeus,
    You have the right to enforce it: we are yours. 50
CREON: That is my will. Take care that you do your part.
CHORAGOS: We are old men: let the younger ones carry it out.
CREON: I do not mean that: the sentries have been appointed.
CHORAGOS: Then what is it that you would have us do?
CREON: You will give no support to whoever breaks this law. 55
CHORAGOS: Only a crazy man is in love with death!
CREON: And death it is; yet money talks, and the wisest
    Have sometimes been known to count a few coins too many.

Enter SENTRY *from left.*

SENTRY: I'll not say that I'm out of breath from running, King,
    because every time I stopped to think about what I have to 60
tell you, I felt like going back. And all the time a voice kept
saying, "You fool, don't you know you're walking straight into
trouble?"; and then another voice: "Yes, but if you let somebody
else get the news to Creon first, it will be even worse than that
for you!" But good sense won out, at least I hope it was good 65
sense, and here I am with a story that makes no sense at all; but
I'll tell it anyhow, because, as they say, what's going to happen's
going to happen and—
CREON: Come to the point. What have you to say?
SENTRY: I did not do it. I did not see who did it. You must not
    punish me for what someone else has done. 70

CREON: A comprehensive defense! More effective, perhaps,
　If I knew its purpose. Come: what is it?
SENTRY: A dreadful thing . . . I don't know how to put it—
CREON: Out with it!
SENTRY:　　　　　　Well, then;
　The dead man—
　　　　　　Polyneicês—

Pause. The SENTRY *is overcome, fumbles for words.* CREON *waits impasssively.*

　　　　　　　　out there—
　　　　　　　　　　someone,—　　　　　　　　75
　New dust on the slimy flesh!

Pause. No sign from CREON.

　Someone has given it burial that way, and
　Gone . . .

Long pause. CREON *finally speaks with deadly control.*

CREON: And the man who dared do this?
SENTRY:　　　　　　　　I swear I
　Do not know! You must believe me!　　　　　80
　　Listen:
　The ground was dry, not a sign of digging, no,
　Not a wheeltrack in the dust, no trace of anyone.
　It was when they relieved us this morning: and one of them,
　The corporal, pointed to it.
　　　　　　　There it was,
　The strangest—
　　　　　　Look:　　　　　　　　　　85
　The body, just mounded over with light dust: you see?
　Not buried really, but as if they'd covered it
　Just enough for the ghost's peace. And no sign
　Of dogs or any wild animal that had been there.
　And then what a scene there was! Every man of us　　　90
　Accusing the other: we all proved the other man did it,
　We all had proof that we could not have done it.
　We were ready to take hot iron in our hands,
　Walk through fire, swear by all the gods,
　It was not I!　　　　　　　　　　95
　I do not know who it was, but it was not I!

CREON's *rage has been mounting steadily, but the* SENTRY *is too intent upon his story to notice it.*

And then, when this came to nothing, someone said
A thing that silenced us and made us stare
Down at the ground: you had to be told the news,
And one of us had to do it! We threw the dice,   100
And the bad luck fell to me. So here I am,
No happier to be here than you are to have me:
Nobody likes the man who brings bad news.

CHORAGOS: I have been wondering, King: can it be that the gods
    have done this?

CREON *(furiously)*: Stop!   105
Must you doddering wrecks
Go out of your heads entirely? "The gods"!
Intolerable!
The gods favor this corpse? Why? How had he served them?
Tried to loot their temples, burn their images,   110
Yes, and the whole State, and its laws with it!
Is it your senile opinion that the gods love to honor bad men?
A pious thought!—
               No, from the very beginning
There have been those who have whispered together,
Stiff-necked anarchists, putting their heads together,   115
Scheming against me in alleys. These are the men,
And they have bribed my own guard to do this thing.
(Sententiously.) Money!
There's nothing in the world so demoralizing as money.
Down go your cities,   120
Homes gone, men gone, honest hearts corrupted,
Crookedness of all kinds, and all for money!
            (To SENTRY.*)*
                    But you—!
I swear by God and by the throne of God,
The man who has done this thing shall pay for it!
Find that man, bring him here to me, or your death   125
Will be the least of your problems: I'll string you up
Alive, and there will be certain ways to make you
Discover your employer before you die;

And the process may teach you a lesson you seem to
    have missed:
The dearest profit is sometimes all too dear: 130
That depends on the source. Do you understand me?
A fortune won is often misfortune.
SENTRY: King, may I speak?
CREON: Your very voice distresses me.
SENTRY: Are you sure that it is my voice, and not your conscience?
CREON: By God, he wants to analyze me now! 135
SENTRY: It is not what I say, but what has been done, that hurts
    you.
CREON: You talk too much.
SENTRY: Maybe; but I've done nothing.
CREON: Sold your soul for some silver: that's all you've done.
SENTRY: How dreadful it is when the right judge judges wrong!
CREON: Your figures of speech 140
    May entertain you now; but unless you bring me the man,
    You will get little profit from them in the end.

Exit CREON *into the palace.*

SENTRY: "Bring me the man"—!
    I'd like nothing better than bringing him the man!
    But bring him or not, you have seen the last of me here. 145
    At any rate, I am safe!

Exit SENTRY.

ODE I

Strophe 1

CHORUS: Numberless are the world's wonders, but none
    More wonderful than man; the stormgray sea
    Yields to his prows, the huge crests bear him high;
    Earth, holy and inexhaustible, is graven
    With shining furrows where his plows have gone 5
    Year after year, the timeless labor of stallions.

Antistrophe 1

The lightboned birds and beasts that cling to cover,
The lithe fish lighting their reaches of dim water,
All are taken, tamed in the net of his mind;
The lion on the hill, the wild horse windy-maned,   10
Resign to him; and his blunt yoke has broken
The sultry shoulders of the mountain bull.

Strophe 2

Words also, and thought as rapid as air,
He fashions to his good use; statecraft is his,
And his the skill that deflects the arrows of snow,   15
The spears of winter rain: from every wind
He has made himself secure—from all but one:
In the late wind of death he cannot stand.

Antistrophe 2

O clear intelligence, force beyond all measure!
O fate of man, working both good and evil!   20
When the laws are kept, how proudly his city stands!
When the laws are broken, what of his city then?
Never may the anárchic man find rest at my hearth,
Never be it said that my thoughts are his thoughts.

Scene II

Reenter SENTRY *leading* ANTIGONÊ.

CHORAGOS: What does this mean? Surely this captive woman
  Is the Princess, Antigonê. Why should she be taken?
SENTRY: Here is the one who did it! We caught her
  In the very act of burying him—Where is Creon?
CHORAGOS: Just coming from the house.

Enter CREON, *center.*

CREON: What has happened?   5

71

Why have you come back so soon?

SENTRY *(expansively)*:   O King,
 A man should never be too sure of anything:
 I would have sworn
 That you'd not see me here again: your anger
 Frightened me so, and the things you threatened me with;   10
 But how could I tell then
 That I'd be able to solve the case so soon?
 No dice-throwing this time: I was only too glad to come!
 Here is this woman. She is the guilty one:
 We found her trying to bury him.   15
 Take her, then; question her; judge her as you will.
 I am through with the whole thing now, and glad of it.

CREON: But this is Antigonê! Why have you brought her here?

SENTRY: She was burying him, I tell you!

CREON *(severely)*:   Is this the truth?

SENTRY: I saw her with my own eyes. Can I say more?   20

CREON: The details: come, tell me quickly!

SENTRY: It was like this:
 After those terrible threats of yours, King,
 We went back and brushed the dust away from the body.
 The flesh was soft by now, and stinking,
 So we sat on a hill to windward and kept guard.   25
 No napping this time! We kept each other awake.
 But nothing happened until the white round sun
 Whirled in the center of the round sky over us:
 Then, suddenly,
 A storm of dust roared up from the earth, and the sky   30
 Went out, the plain vanished with all its trees
 In the stinging dark. We closed our eyes and endured it.
 The whirlwind lasted a long time, but it passed;
 And then we looked, and there was Antigonê!
 I have seen   35
 A mother bird come back to a stripped nest, heard
 Her crying bitterly a broken note or two
 For the young ones stolen. Just so, when this girl
 Found the bare corpse, and all her love's work wasted,
 She wept, and cried on heaven to damn the hands   40
 That had done this thing.

                              And then she brought more dust
And sprinkled wine three times for her brother's ghost.
We ran and took her at once. She was not afraid,
Not even when we charged her with what she had done.
She denied nothing.
                         And this was a comfort to me,   45
And some uneasiness: for it is a good thing
To escape from death, but it is no great pleasure
To bring death to a friend.
                              Yet I always say
There is nothing so comfortable as your own safe skin!
CREON *(slowly, dangerously)*: And you, Antigonê,   50
     You with your head hanging,—do you confess this thing?
ANTIGONÊ: I do. I deny nothing.
CREON *(to* SENTRY*)*:   You may go.

Exit SENTRY.

(To ANTIGONÊ.*)* Tell me, tell me briefly:
Had you heard my proclamation touching this matter?
ANTIGONÊ: It was public. Could I help hearing it?   55
CREON: And yet you dared defy the law.
ANTIGONÊ: I dared.
     It was not God's proclamation. That final Justice
     That rules the world below makes no such laws.

     Your edict, King, was strong,
     But all your strength is weakness itself against   60
     The immortal unrecorded laws of God.
     They are not merely now: they were, and shall be,
     Operative for ever, beyond man utterly.

     I knew I must die, even without your decree:
     I am only mortal. And if I must die   65
     Now, before it is my time to die,
     Surely this is no hardship: can anyone
     Living, as I live, with evil all about me,
     Think Death less than a friend? This death of mine
     Is of no importance; but if I had left my brother   70
     Lying in death unburied, I should have suffered.

73

Now I do not.
                    You smile at me. Ah Creon,
Think me a fool, if you like; but it may well be
That a fool convicts me of folly.
CHORAGOS: Like father, like daughter: both headstrong,
    deaf to reason!   75
She has never learned to yield.
CREON: She has much to learn.
    The inflexible heart breaks first, the toughest iron
    Cracks first, and the wildest horses bend their necks
    At the pull of the smallest curb.
                              Pride? In a slave?
    This girl is guilty of a double insolence,   80
    Breaking the given laws and boasting of it.
    Who is the man here,
    She or I, if this crime goes unpunished?
    Sister's child, or more than sister's child,
    Or closer yet in blood—she and her sister   85
    Win bitter death for this!

(*To* SERVANTS.)
                              Go, some of you,
    Arrest Ismenê. I accuse her equally.
    Bring her: you will find her sniffling in the house there.

    Her mind's a traitor: crimes kept in the dark
    Cry for light, and the guardian brain shudders;   90
    But how much worse than this
    Is brazen boasting of barefaced anarchy!
ANTIGONÊ: Creon, what more do you want than my death?
CREON: Nothing.
    That gives me everything.
ANTIGONÊ: Then I beg you: kill me.
    This talking is a great weariness: your words   9
    Are distasteful to me, and I am sure that mine
    Seem so to you. And yet they should not seem so:
    I should have praise and honor for what I have done.
    All these men here would praise me
    Were their lips not frozen shut with fear of you.   10
    (*Bitterly.*) Ah the good fortune of kings,

Licensed to say and do whatever they please!
CREON: You are alone here in that opinion.
ANTIGONÊ: No, they are with me. But they keep their tongues in
  leash.
CREON: Maybe. But you are guilty, and they are not.   105
ANTIGONÊ: There is no guilt in reverence for the dead.
CREON: But Eteoclês—was he not your brother too?
ANTIGONÊ: My brother too.
CREON: And you insult his memory?
ANTIGONÊ *(softly)*: The dead man would not say that I insult it.
CREON: He would: for you honor a traitor as much as him.   110
ANTIGONÊ: His own brother, traitor or not, and equal in blood.
CREON: He made war on his country. Eteoclês defended it.
ANTIGONÊ: Nevertheless, there are honors due all the dead.
CREON: But not the same for the wicked as for the just.
ANTIGONÊ: Ah Creon, Creon,   115
  Which of us can say what the gods hold wicked?
CREON: An enemy is an enemy, even dead.
ANTIGONÊ: It is my nature to join in love, not hate.
CREON *(finally losing patience)*: Go join them then; if you must
    have your love,
  Find it in hell!   120
CHORAGOS: But see, Ismenê comes:

Enter ISMENÊ, *guarded.*

  Those tears are sisterly, the cloud
  That shadows her eyes rains down gentle sorrow.
CREON: You too, Ismenê,
  Snake in my ordered house, sucking my blood   125
  Stealthily—and all the time I never knew
  That these two sisters were aiming at my throne!
                                                        Ismenê,
  Do you confess your share in this crime, or deny it?
  Answer me.
ISMENÊ: Yes, if she will let me say so. I am guilty.   130
ANTIGONÊ *(coldly)*: No, Ismenê. You have no right to say so.
  You would not help me, and I will not have you help me.
ISMENÊ: But now I know what you meant; and I am here
  To join you, to take my share of punishment.

ANTIGONÊ: The dead man and the gods who rule the dead   135
 Know whose act this was. Words are not friends.
ISMENÊ: Do you refuse me, Antigonê? I want to die with you:
 I too have a duty that I must discharge to the dead.
ANTIGONÊ: You shall not lessen my death by sharing it.
ISMENÊ: What do I care for life when you are dead?   140
ANTIGONÊ: Ask Creon. You're always hanging on his opinions.
ISMENÊ: You are laughing at me. Why, Antigonê?
ANTIGONÊ: It's a joyless laughter, Ismenê.
ISMENÊ: But can I do nothing?
ANTIGONÊ: Yes. Save yourself. I shall not envy you.
 There are those who will praise you; I shall have honor, too.   145
ISMENÊ: But we are equally guilty!
ANTIGONÊ: No more, Ismenê.
 You are alive, but I belong to Death.
CREON *(to the* CHORUS*)*: Gentlemen, I beg you to observe
 these girls:
 One has just now lost her mind; the other,
 It seems, has never had a mind at all.   150
ISMENÊ: Grief teaches the steadiest minds to waver, King.
CREON: Yours certainly did, when you assumed guilt with the guilty!
ISMENÊ: But how could I go on living without her?
CREON: You are.
 She is already dead.
ISMENÊ: But your own son's bride!
CREON: There are places enough for him to push his plow.   155
 I want no wicked women for my sons!
ISMENÊ: O dearest Haimon, how your father wrongs you!
CREON: I've had enough of your childish talk of marriage!
CHORAGOS: Do you really intend to steal this girl from your son?
CREON: No; Death will do that for me.
CHORAGOS: Then she must die?   160
CREON *(ironically)*: You dazzle me.
        —But enough of this talk!
 (To GUARDS.*)* You, there, take them away and guard them well:
 For they are but women, and even brave men run
 When they see Death coming.

Exeunt ISMENÊ, ANTIGONÊ, *and* GUARDS.

ODE II

Strophe 1

CHORUS: Fortunate is the man who has never tasted God's
   vengeance!
   Where once the anger of heaven has struck, that house is shaken
   For ever: damnation rises behind each child
   Like a wave cresting out of the black northeast,
   When the long darkness under sea roars up   5
   And bursts drumming death upon the windwhipped sand.

Antistrophe 1

   I have seen this gathering sorrow from time long past
   Loom upon Oedipus' children: generation from generation
   Takes the compulsive rage of the enemy god.
   So lately this last flower of Oedipus' line   10
   Drank the sunlight! but now a passionate word
   And a handful of dust have closed up all its beauty.

Strope 2

   What mortal arrogance
   Transcends the wrath of Zeus?
   Sleep cannot lull him nor the effortless long months   15
   Of the timeless gods: but he is young for ever,
   And his house is the shining day of high Olympos.
      All that is and shall be,
      And all the past, is his.
   No pride on earth is free of the curse of heaven.   20

Antistrophe 2

   The straying dreams of men
      May bring them ghosts of joy:
   But as they drowse, the waking embers burn them;
   Or they walk with fixed eyes, as blind men walk.
   But the ancient wisdom speaks for our own time: 25
      Fate works most for woe
      With Folly's fairest show.
   Man's little pleasure is the spring of sorrow.

Scene III

CHORAGOS: But here is Haimon, King, the last of all your sons.
Is it grief for Antigonê that brings him here,
And bitterness at being robbed of his bride?

Enter HAIMON.

CREON: We shall soon see, and no need of diviners.

            —Son,

You have heard my final judgment on that girl: 5
Have you come here hating me, or have you come
With deference and with love, whatever I do?
HAIMON: I am your son, father. You are my guide.
You make things clear for me, and I obey you.
No marriage means more to me than your continuing wisdom. 10
CREON: Good. That is the way to behave: subordinate
Everything else, my son, to your father's will.
This is what a man prays for, that he may get
Sons attentive and dutiful in his house,
Each one hating his father's enemies,   15
Honoring his father's friends. But if his sons
Fail him, if they turn out unprofitably,
What has he fathered but trouble for himself
And amusement for the malicious?

          So you are right

Not to lose your head over this woman.   20
Your pleasure with her would soon grow cold, Haimon,
And then you'd have a hellcat in bed and elsewhere.
Let her find her husband in Hell!
Of all the people in this city, only she
Has had contempt for my law and broken it.   25

Do you want me to show myself weak before the people?
Or to break my sworn word? No, and I will not.
The woman dies.
I suppose she'll plead "family ties." Well, let her.
If I permit my own family to rebel,   30
How shall I earn the world's obedience?
Show me the man who keeps his house in hand,

He's fit for public authority.
                              I'll have no dealings
With lawbreakers, critics of the government:
Whoever is chosen to govern should be obeyed—   35
Must be obeyed, in all things, great and small,
Just and unjust! O Haimon,
The man who knows how to obey, and that man only,
Knows how to give commands when the time comes.
You can depend on him, no matter how fast   40
The spears come: he's a good soldier, he'll stick it out.

Anarchy, anarchy! Show me a greater evil!
This is why cities tumble and the great houses rain down,
This is what scatters armies!
No, no: good lives are made so by discipline.   45
We keep the laws then, and the lawmakers,
And no woman shall seduce us. If we must lose,
Let's lose to a man, at least! Is a woman stronger than we?
CHORAGOS: Unless time has rusted my wits,
What you say, King, is said with point and dignity.   50
HAIMON (*boyishly earnest*): Father:
Reason is God's crowning gift to man, and you are right
To warn me against losing mine. I cannot say—
I hope that I shall never want to say!—that you
Have reasoned badly. Yet there are other men   55
Who can reason, too; and their opinions might be helpful.
You are not in a position to know everything
That people say or do, or what they feel:
Your temper terrifies—everyone
Will tell you only what you like to hear.   60
But I, at any rate, can listen; and I have heard them
Muttering and whispering in the dark about this girl.
They say no woman has ever, so unreasonably,
Died so shameful a death for a generous act:
"She covered her brother's body. Is this indecent?   65
She kept him from dogs and vultures. Is this a crime?
Death?—She should have all the honor that we can give her!"

This is the way they talk out there in the city.

You must believe me:
Nothing is closer to me than your happiness.   70
What could be closer? Must not any son
Value his father's fortune as his father does his?
I beg you, do not be unchangeable:
Do not believe that you alone can be right.
The man who thinks that,   75
The man who maintains that only he has the power
To reason correctly, the gift to speak, the soul—
A man like that, when you know him, turns out empty.

It is not reason never to yield to reason!

In flood time you can see how some trees bend,   80
And because they bend, even their twigs are safe,
While stubborn trees are torn up, roots and all.
And the same thing happens in sailing:
Make your sheet fast, never slacken,—and over you go,
Head over heels and under: and there's your voyage.   85
Forget you are angry! Let yourself be moved!
I know I am young; but please let me say this:
The ideal condition
Would be, I admit, that men should be right by instinct;
But since we are all too likely to go astray,   90
The reasonable thing is to learn from those who can teach.
CHORAGOS: You will do well to listen to him, King,
    If what he says is sensible. And you, Haimon,
    Must listen to your father.—Both speak well.
CREON: You consider it right for a man of my years and experience   95
    To go to school to a boy?
HAIMON: It is not right
    If I am wrong. But if I am young, and right,
    What does my age matter?
CREON: You think it right to stand up for an anarchist?
HAIMON: Not at all. I pay no respect to criminals.   100
CREON: Then she is not a criminal?
HAIMON: The City would deny it, to a man.
CREON: And the City proposes to teach me how to rule?
HAIMON: Ah. Who is it that's talking like a boy now?

CREON: My voice is the one voice giving orders in this City!   105
HAIMON: It is no City if it takes orders from one voice.
CREON: The State is the King!
HAIMON: Yes, if the State is a desert.

Pause.

CREON: This boy, it seems, has sold out to a woman.
HAIMON: If you are a woman: my concern is only for you.
CREON: So? Your "concern"! In a public brawl with your father!   110
HAIMON: How about you, in a public brawl with justice?
CREON: With justice, when all that I do is within my rights?
HAIMON: You have no right to trample on God's right.
CREON *(completely out of control)*: Fool, adolescent fool! Taken
    in by a woman!
HAIMON: You'll never see me taken in by anything vile.   115
CREON: Every word you say is for her!
HAIMON *(quietly, darkly)*:   And for you.
    And for me. And for the gods under the earth.
CREON: You'll never marry her while she lives.
HAIMON: Then she must die.—But her death will cause another.
CREON: Another?   120
    Have you lost your senses? Is this an open threat?
HAIMON: There is no threat in speaking to emptiness.
CREON: I swear you'll regret this superior tone of yours!
    You are the empty one!
HAIMON: If you were not my father, I'd say
    you were perverse.   125
CREON: You girlstruck fool, don't play at words with me!
HAIMON: I am sorry. You prefer silence.
CREON: Now, by God—!
    I swear, by all the gods in heaven above us,
    You'll watch it, I swear you shall!

(*To the* SERVANTS.)

                    Bring her out!
    Bring the woman out! Let her die before his eyes!   130
    Here, this instant, with her bridegroom beside her!
HAIMON: Not here, no; she will not die here, King.
    And you will never see my face again.

Go on raving as long as you've a friend to endure you.

Exit HAIMON.

CHORAGOS: Gone, gone.
   Creon, a young man in a rage is dangerous!   135
CREON: Let him do, or dream to do, more than a man can.
   He shall not save these girls from death.
CHORAGOS: These girls?
   You have sentenced them both?
CREON: No, you are right.
   I will not kill the one whose hands are clean.   140
CHORAGOS: But Antigonê?
CREON *(somberly)*:   I will carry her far away
   Out there in the wilderness, and lock her
   Living in a vault of stone. She shall have food,
   As the custom is, to absolve the State of her death.
   And there let her pray to the gods of hell: 145
   They are her only gods:
   Perhaps they will show her an escape from death,
   Or she may learn,
              though late,
   That piety shown the dead is pity in vain.

Exit CREON.

ODE III

Strophe

CHORUS: Love, unconquerable
   Waster of rich men, keeper
   Of warm lights and all-night vigil
   In the soft face of a girl:
   Sea-wanderer, forest-visitor!   5

Even the pure Immortals cannot escape you,
And mortal man, in his one day's dusk,
Trembles before your glory.

Antistrophe

Surely you swerve upon ruin
The just man's consenting heart,   10
As here you have made bright anger
Strike between father and son—
And none has conquered but Love!
A girl's glánce wórking the will of heaven:
Pleasure to her alone who mocks us,   15
Merciless Aphroditê.

SCENE IV

CHORAGOS *(as* ANTIGONÊ *enters guarded)*: But I can no longer
    stand in awe of this,
Nor, seeing what I see, keep back my tears.
Here is Antigonê, passing to that chamber
Where all find sleep at last.

Strophe 1

ANTIGONÊ: Look upon me, friends, and pity me   5
    Turning back at the night's edge to say
    Good-by to the sun that shines for me no longer;
    Now sleepy Death
    Summons me down to Acheron, that cold shore:
    There is no bridesong there, nor any music.   10
CHORUS: Yet not unpraised, not without a kind of honor,
    You walk at last into the underworld;
    Untouched by sickness, broken by no sword.
    What woman has ever found your way to death?

[16]**Aphroditê** *goddess of love*
[9]**Acheron** *a river of the underworld*

Antistrophe 1

ANTIGONÊ: How often I have heard the story of Niobê,   15
  Tantalos' wretched daughter, how the stone
  Clung fast about her, ivy-close: and they say
  The rain falls endlessly
  And sifting soft snow; her tears are never done.
  I feel the loneliness of her death in mine.   20
CHORUS: But she was born of heaven, and you
  Are woman, woman-born. If her death is yours,
  A mortal woman's, is this not for you
  Glory in our world and in the world beyond?

Strophe 2

ANTIGONÊ: You laugh at me. Ah, friends, friends,   25
  Can you not wait until I am dead? O Thebes,
  O men many-charioted, in love with Fortune,
  Dear springs of Dircê, sacred Theban grove,
  Be witnesses for me, denied all pity,
  Unjustly judged! and think a word of love   30
  For her whose path turns
  Under dark earth, where there are no more tears.
CHORUS: You have passed beyond human daring and come at last
  Into a place of stone where Justice sits.
  I cannot tell   35
  What shape of your father's guilt appears in this.

Antistrophe 2

ANTIGONÊ: You have touched it at last: that bridal bed
  Unspeakable, horror of son and mother mingling:
  Their crime, infection of all our family!
  O Oedipus, father and brother!   40
  Your marriage strikes from the grave to murder mine.
  I have been a stranger here in my own land:
  All my life
  The blasphemy of my birth has followed me.
CHORUS: Reverence is a virtue, but strength   45

Lives in established law: that must prevail.
You have made your choice,
Your death is the doing of your conscious hand.

Epode

ANTIGONÊ: Then let me go, since all your words are bitter,
And the very light of the sun is cold to me.   50
Lead me to my vigil, where I must have
Neither love nor lamentation; no song, but silence.

CREON *interrupts impatiently.*

CREON: If dirges and planned lamentations could put off death,
Men would be singing for ever.

(*To the* SERVANTS.)

                          Take her, go!
You know your orders; take her to the vault   55
And leave her alone there. And if she lives or dies,
That's her affair, not ours: our hands are clean.

ANTIGONÊ: O tomb, vaulted bride-bed in eternal rock,
Soon I shall be with my own again
Where Persephonê welcomes the thin ghosts underground: 60
And I shall see my father again, and you, mother,
And dearest Polyneicês—
                          dearest indeed
To me, since it was my hand
That washed him clean and poured the ritual wine:
And my reward is death before my time!   65

And yet, as men's hearts know, I have done no wrong,
I have not sinned before God. Or if I have,
I shall know the truth in death. But if the guilt
Lies upon Creon who judged me, then, I pray,
May his punishment equal my own.
CHORAGOS: O passionate heart,   70
Unyielding, tormented still by the same winds!
CREON: Her guards shall have good cause to regret their delaying.

---

[60]Persephonê *queen of the underworld*

ANTIGONÊ: Ah! That voice is like the voice of death!
CREON: I can give you no reason to think you are mistaken.
ANTIGONÊ: Thebes, and you my fathers' gods,   75
  And rulers of Thebes, you see me now, the last
  Unhappy daughter of a line of kings,
  Your kings, led away to death. You will remember
  What things I suffer, and at what men's hands,
  Because I would not transgress the laws of heaven.   80
  (To the GUARDS, *simply.)* Come: let us wait no longer.
Exit ANTIGONÊ, *left, guarded.*

ODE IV

Strophe 1

CHORUS: All Danaê's beauty was locked away
  In a brazen cell where the sunlight could not come:
  A small room still as any grave, enclosed her.
  Yet she was a princess too,
  And Zeus in a rain of gold poured love upon her.   5
  O child, child,
  No power in wealth or war
  Or tough sea-blackened ships
  Can prevail against untiring Destiny!

Antistrophe 1

  And Dryas' son also, that furious king,   10
  Bore the god's prisoning anger for his pride:
  Sealed up by Dionysos in deaf stone,
  His madness died among echoes.
  So at the last he learned what dreadful power
  His tongue had mocked: 15
  For he had profaned the revels,
  And fired the wrath of the nine
  Implacable Sisters that love the sound of the flute.

[10]**Dryas' son** *Lycurgus, King of Thrace*
[18]**Implacable Sisters** *the Muses*

Strophe 2

And old men tell a half-remembered tale
Of horror where a dark ledge splits the sea   20
And a double surf beats on the gráy shóres:
How a king's new woman, sick
With hatred for the queen he had imprisoned,
Ripped out his two sons' eyes with her bloody hands
While grinning Arês watched the shuttle plunge   25
Four times: four blind wounds crying for revenge,

Antistrophe 2

Crying, tears and blood mingled. — Piteously born,
Those sons whose mother was of heavenly birth!
Her father was the god of the North Wind
And she was cradled by gales,   30
She raced with young colts on the glittering hills
And walked untrammeled in the open light:
But in her marriage deathless Fate found means
To build a tomb like yours for all her joy.

Scene V

Enter blind TEIRESIAS, *led by a boy. The opening speeches of*
TEIRESIAS *should be in singsong contrast to the realistic lines of*
CREON.

TEIRESIAS: This is the way the blind man comes, Princes, Princes,
   Lock-step, two heads lit by the eyes of one.
CREON: What new thing have you to tell us, old Teiresias?
TEIRESIAS: I have much to tell you: listen to the prophet, Creon.
CREON: I am not aware that I have ever failed to listen.   5
TEIRESIAS: Then you have done wisely, King, and ruled well.

---

[22]**king's new woman** *Eidothea, second wife of King Phineas, blinded her stepsons
after the King had imprisoned their mother in a cave.*
[25]**Arês** *god of war*

CREON: I admit my debt to you. But what have you to say?
TEIRESIAS: This, Creon: you stand once more on the edge of fate.
CREON: What do you mean? Your words are a kind of dread.
TEIRESIAS: Listen, Creon: 10
    I was sitting in my chair of augury, at the place
    Where the birds gather about me. They were all a-chatter,
    As is their habit, when suddenly I heard
    A strange note in their jangling, a scream, a
    Whirring fury; I knew that they were fighting,   15
    Tearing each other, dying
    In a whirlwind of wings clashing. And I was afraid.
    I began the rites of burnt-offering at the altar,
    But Hephaistos failed me: instead of bright flame,
    There was only the sputtering slime of the fat thigh-flesh   20
    Melting: the entrails dissolved in gray smoke,
    The bare bone burst from the welter. And no blaze!

    This was a sign from heaven. My boy described it,
    Seeing for me as I see for others.

    I tell you, Creon, yourself have brought   25
    This new calamity upon us. Our hearths and altars
    Are stained with the corruption of dogs and carrion birds
    That glut themselves on the corpse of Oedipus' son.
    The gods are deaf when we pray to them, their fire
    Recoils from our offering, their birds of omen   30
    Have no cry of comfort, for they are gorged
    With the thick blood of the dead.
                                    O my son,
    These are no trifles! Think: all men make mistakes,
    But a good man yields when he knows his course is wrong,
    And repairs the evil. The only crime is pride.   35

    Give in to the dead man, then: do not fight with a corpse—
    What glory is it to kill a man who is dead?
    Think, I beg you:
    It is for your own good that I speak as I do.

---

[19]Hephaistos *god of fire*

You should be able to yield for your own good. 40
CREON: It seems that prophets have made me their
  especial province.
  All my life long
  I have been a kind of butt for the dull arrows
  Of doddering fortune-tellers!
               No, Teiresias:
  If your birds—if the great eagles of God himself 45
  Should carry him stinking bit by bit to heaven,
  I would not yield. I am not afraid of pollution:
  No man can defile the gods.
              Do what you will,
  Go into business, make money, speculate
  In India gold or that synthetic gold from Sardis, 50
  Get rich otherwise than by my consent to bury him.
  Teiresias, it is a sorry thing when a wise man
  Sells his wisdom, lets out his words for hire!
TEIRESIAS: Ah Creon! Is there no man left in the world—
CREON: To do what?—Come, let's have the aphorism! 55
TEIRESIAS: No man who knows that wisdom outweighs
  any wealth?
CREON: As surely as bribes are baser than any baseness.
TEIRESIAS: You are sick, Creon! You are deathly sick!
CREON: As you say: it is not my place to challenge a prophet.
TEIRESIAS: Yet you have said my prophecy is for sale. 60
CREON: The generation of prophets has always loved gold.
TEIRESIAS: The generation of kings has always loved brass.
CREON: You forget yourself! You are speaking to your King.
TEIRESIAS: I know it. You are a king because of me.
CREON: You have a certain skill; but you have sold out. 65
TEIRESIAS: King, you will drive me to words that—
CREON: Say them, say them!
  Only remember: I will not pay you for them.
TEIRESIAS: No, you will find them too costly.
CREON: No doubt. Speak:
  Whatever you say, you will not change my will.
TEIRESIAS: Then take this, and take it to heart! 70
  The time is not far off when you shall pay back
  Corpse for corpse, flesh of your own flesh.

You have thrust the child of this world into living night,
You have kept from the gods below the child that is theirs:
The one in a grave before her death, the other,   75
Dead, denied the grave. This is your crime:
And the Furies and the dark gods of Hell
Are swift with terrible punishment for you.

Do you want to buy me now, Creon?
Not many days,
And your house will be full of men and women weeping,   80
And curses will be hurled at you from far
Cities grieving for sons unburied, left to rot
Before the walls of Thebes.

These are my arrows, Creon: they are all for you.

(To BOY.*)* But come, child: lead me home.   85
Let him waste his fine anger upon younger men.
Maybe he will learn at last
To control a wiser tongue in a better head.

Exit TEIRESIAS.

CHORAGOS: The old man has gone, King, but his words
    Remain to plague us. I am old, too,   90
    But I cannot remember that he was ever false.
CREON: That is true. . . . It troubles me.
    Oh it is hard to give in! but it is worse
    To risk everything for stubborn pride.
CHORAGOS: Creon: take my advice.
CREON: What shall I do?   95
CHORAGOS: Go quickly: free Antigonê from her vault
    And build a tomb for the body of Polyneicês.
CREON: You would have me do this!
CHORAGOS: Creon, yes!
    And it must be done at once: God moves
    Swiftly to cancel the folly of stubborn men.   100
CREON: It is hard to deny the heart! But I
    Will do it: I will not fight with destiny.
CHORAGOS: You must go yourself, you cannot leave it to others.

CREON: I will go.
         —Bring axes, servants:
Come with me to the tomb. I buried her. I   105
Will set her free.
              Oh quickly!
My mind misgives—
The laws of the gods are mighty, and a man must serve them
To the last day of his life!

Exit CREON.

PAEAN[†]

Strophe 1

CHORAGOS: God of many names
CHORUS: O Iacchos
                          son
  of Kadmeian Sémelê
              O born of the Thunder!
Guardian of the West
              Regent
  of Eleusis' plain
          O Prince of maenad Thebes
and the Dragon Field by rippling Ismenós.   5

Antistrophe 1

CHORAGOS: God of many names
CHORUS: the flame of torches
  flares on our hills
          the nymphs of Iacchos

[†]**Paean** *a hymn*
[1]**Iacchos** *Bacchos or Dionysos, god of wine and revelry*
[2]**Sémelê** *mother of Iacchos, consort of Zeus*
[4]**maenad** *female worshipper, attendant of Iacchos*
[5]**Ismenós** *a river near Thebes where, according to legend, dragon's teeth were sown from which sprang the ancestors of Thebes*

dance at the spring of Castalia
from the vine-close mountain
                              come ah come in ivy:
Evohé evohé! sings through the streets of Thebes   10

Strophe 2

CHORAGOS: God of many names
CHORUS: Iacchos of Thebes
  heavenly Child
                  of Sémelê bride of the Thunderer!
  The shadow of plague is upon us:
                                    come
  with clement feet
                      oh come from Parnasos
  down the long slopes
                        across the lamenting water   15

Antistrophe 2

CHORAGOS: Iô Fire! Chorister of the throbbing stars!
  O purest among the voices of the night!
  Thou son of God, blaze for us!
CHORUS: Come with choric rapture of circling Maenads
  Who cry *Iô Iacche!*
                        God of many names!   20

EXODOS

Enter MESSENGER *from left.*

MESSENGER: Men of the line of Kadmos, you who live
  Near Amphion's citadel,
                            I cannot say

---

[8]**Castalia** *a spring on Mount Parnasos*
[1]**Kadmos** *sowed the dragon's teeth; founded Thebes*
[2]**Amphion's citadel** *Amphion's lyre playing charmed stones to form a wall around Thebes*

Of any condition of human life "This is fixed,
This is clearly good, or bad." Fate raises up,
And Fate casts down the happy and unhappy alike: 5
No man can foretell his Fate.
                    Take the case of Creon:
Creon was happy once, as I count happiness:
Victorious in battle, sole governor of the land,
Fortunate father of children nobly born.
And now it has all gone from him! Who can say   10
That a man is still alive when his life's joy fails?
He is a walking dead man. Grant him rich,
Let him live like a king in his great house:
If his pleasure is gone, I would not give
So much as the shadow of smoke for all he owns.   15

CHORAGOS: Your words hint at sorrow: what is your news
    for us?

MESSENGER: They are dead. The living are guilty of their death.

CHORAGOS: Who is guilty? Who is dead? Speak!

MESSENGER: Haimon.
    Haimon is dead; and the hand that killed him
    Is his own hand.

CHORAGOS: His father's? or his own?   20

MESSENGER: His own, driven mad by the murder his father
    had done.

CHORAGOS: Teiresias, Teiresias, how clearly you saw it all!

MESSENGER: This is my news: you must draw what conclusions
    you can from it.

CHORAGOS: But look: Eurydicê, our Queen:
    Has she overheard us?   25

Enter EURYDICÊ *from the palace, center.*

EURYDICÊ: I have heard something, friends:
    As I was unlocking the gate of Pallas' shrine,
    For I needed her help today, I heard a voice
    Telling of some new sorrow. And I fainted
    There at the temple with all my maidens about me.   30
    But speak again: whatever it is, I can bear it:
    Grief and I are no strangers.

MESSENGER: Dearest Lady,

93

I will tell you plainly all that I have seen.
I shall not try to comfort you: what is the use,
Since comfort could lie only in what is not true?   35
The truth is always best.

     I went with Creon
To the outer plain where Polyneicês was lying,
No friend to pity him, his body shredded by dogs.
We made our prayers in that place to Hecatê
And Pluto, that they would be merciful. And we bathed   40
The corpse with holy water, and we brought
Fresh-broken branches to burn what was left of it,
And upon the urn we heaped up a towering barrow
Of the earth of his own land.

      When we were done, we ran
To the vault where Antigonê lay on her couch of stone.   45
One of the servants had gone ahead,
And while he was yet far off he heard a voice
Grieving within the chamber, and he came back
And told Creon. And as the King went closer,
The air was full of wailing, the words lost,   50
And he begged us to make all haste. "Am I a prophet?"
He said, weeping, "And must I walk this road,
The saddest of all that I have gone before?
My son's voice calls me on. Oh quickly, quickly!
Look through the crevice there, and tell me   55
If it is Haimon, or some deception of the gods!"

We obeyed; and in the cavern's farthest corner
We saw her lying:
She had made a noose of her fine linen veil
And hanged herself. Haimon lay beside her,   60
His arms about her waist, lamenting her,
His love lost under ground, crying out
That his father had stolen her away from him.

When Creon saw him the tears rushed to his eyes
And he called to him: "What have you done, child?

---

³⁹**Hecatê** *goddess of sorcery*

Speak to me. 65
What are you thinking that makes your eyes so strange?
O my son, my son, I come to you on my knees!"
But Haimon spat in his face. He said not a word,
Staring—
        And suddenly drew his sword
And lunged. Creon shrank back, the blade missed; and the boy, 70
Desperate against himself, drove it half its length
Into his own side, and fell. And as he died
He gathered Antigonê close in his arms again,
Choking, his blood bright red on her white cheek.
And now he lies dead with the dead, and she is his 75
At last, his bride in the house of the dead.

Exit EURYDICÊ *into the palace.*

CHORAGOS: She has left us without a word. What can this mean?
MESSENGER: It troubles me, too; yet she knows what is best,
    Her grief is too great for public lamentation,
    And doubtless she has gone to her chamber to weep 80
    For her dead son, leading her maidens in his dirge.

Pause.

CHORAGOS: It may be so: but I fear this deep silence.
MESSENGER: I will see what she is doing. I will go in.

Exit MESSENGER *into the palace.*

ENTER CREON *with attendants, bearing* HAIMON'S *body.*

CHORAGOS: But here is the king himself: oh look at him,
    Bearing his own damnation in his arms. 85
CREON: Nothing you say can touch me any more.
    My own blind heart has brought me
    From darkness to final darkness. Here you see
    The father murdering, the murdered son—
    And all my civic wisdom! 90

    Haimon my son, so young, so young to die,
    I was the fool, not you; and you died for me.
CHORAGOS: That is the truth; but you were late in learning it.
CREON: This truth is hard to bear. Surely a god
    Has crushed me beneath the hugest weight of heaven, 95

And driven me headlong a barbaric way
To trample out the thing I held most dear.

The pains that men will take to come to pain!

Enter MESSENGER *from the palace.*

MESSENGER: The burden you carry in your hands is heavy,
But it is not all: you will find more in your house.   10
CREON: What burden worse than this shall I find there?
MESSENGER: The Queen is dead.
CREON: O port of death, deaf world,
Is there no pity for me? And you, Angel of evil,
I was dead, and your words are death again.   10
Is it true, boy? Can it be true?
Is my wife dead? Has death bred death?
MESSENGER: You can see for yourself.

The doors are opened and the body of EURYDICÊ *is disclosed within.*

CREON: Oh pity!
All true, all true, and more than I can bear!   11
O my wife, my son!
MESSENGER: She stood before the altar, and her heart
Welcomed the knife her own hand guided,
And a great cry burst from her lips for Megareus dead,
And for Haimon dead, her sons; and her last breath   1
Was a curse for their father, the murderer of her sons.
And she fell, and the dark flowed in through her closing eyes.
CREON: O God, I am sick with fear.
Are there no swords here? Has no one a blow for me?
MESSENGER: Her curse is upon you for the deaths of both.   1
CREON: It is right that it should be. I alone am guilty.
I know it, and I say it. Lead me in,
Quickly, friends.
I have neither life nor substance. Lead me in.
CHORAGOS: You are right, if there can be right in so much wrong. 1
The briefest way is best in a world of sorrow.
CREON: Let it come,
Let death come quickly, and be kind to me.
I would not ever see the sun again.

CHORAGOS: All that will come when it will; but we, meanwhile,   130
  Have much to do. Leave the future to itself.
CREON: All my heart was in that prayer!
CHORAGOS: Then do not pray any more: the sky is deaf.
CREON: Lead me away. I have been rash and foolish.
  I have killed my son and my wife.   135
  I look for comfort; my comfort lies here dead.
  Whatever my hands have touched has come to nothing.
  Fate has brought all my pride to a thought of dust.

As CREON *is being led into the house, the* CHORAGOS *advances and speaks directly to the audience.*

CHORAGOS: There is no happiness where there is no wisdom;
  No wisdom but in submission to the gods.   140
  Big words are always punished,
  And proud men in old age learn to be wise.

WILLIAM SHAKESPEARE

The Tragedy of Macbeth

Characters

DUNCAN, *King of Scotland*

MALCOLM
DONALBAIN } *his sons*

MACBETH
BANQUO
MACDUFF
LENNOX
ROSS } *noblemen of Scotland*
MENTEITH
ANGUS
CAITHNESS

FLEANCE, *son to* BANQUO

SIWARD, *Earl of Northumberland, general of the English forces*

YOUNG SIWARD, *his son*

SEYTON, *an officer attending on* MACBETH

SON TO MACDUFF

AN ENGLISH DOCTOR

A SCOTTISH DOCTOR

A PORTER

AN OLD MAN

THREE MURDERERS

LADY MACBETH

LADY MACDUFF

A GENTLEWOMAN *attending on* LADY MACBETH

HECATE

WITCHES
APPARITIONS
LORDS, OFFICERS, SOLDIERS, ATTENDANTS, *and* MESSENGERS

Scene   *Scotland; England*

ACT I

SCENE I   *An open place.*

Thunder and lightning. Enter THREE WITCHES.

FIRST WITCH: When shall we three meet again?
  In thunder, lightning, or in rain?
SECOND WITCH: When the hurlyburly's done,
  When the battle's lost and won.
THIRD WITCH: That will be ere the set of sun.   5
FIRST WITCH: Where the place?
SECOND WITCH: Upon the heath.
THIRD WITCH: There to meet with Macbeth.
FIRST WITCH: I come, Graymalkin.
SECOND WITCH: Paddock calls.
THIRD WITCH: Anon!
ALL: Fair is foul, and foul is fair.   10
  Hover through the fog and filthy air.

Exeunt.

SCENE II   *A camp.*

Alarum within. Enter KING (DUNCAN), MALCOLM, DONALBAIN,
LENNOX, *with* ATTENDANTS, *meeting a bleeding* CAPTAIN.

KING: What bloody man is that? He can report,
  As seemeth by his plight, of the revolt

---

⁸**Graymalkin** *(the witch's attendant spirit, a gray cat)*   ⁹**Paddock** *toad;* **Anon** *at once*

The newest state.

MALCOLM: This is the sergeant
Who like a good and hardy soldier fought
'Gainst my captivity. Hail, brave friend!   5
Say to the king the knowledge of the broil
As thou didst leave it.

CAPTAIN: Doubtful it stood,
As two spent swimmers, that do cling together
And choke their art. The merciless Macdonwald—
Worthy to be a rebel for to that   10
The multiplying villainies of nature
Do swarm upon him—from the Western Isles
Of kerns and gallowglasses is supplied;
And Fortune, on his damnèd quarrel smiling,
Showed like a rebel's whore: but all's too weak: 15
For brave Macbeth—well he deserves that name—
Disdaining Fortune, with his brandished steel,
Which smoked with bloody execution,
Like valor's minion carved out his passage
Till he faced the slave;   20
Which nev'r shook hands, nor bade farewell to him,
Till he unseamed him from the nave to th' chops,
And fixed his head upon our battlements.

KING: O valiant cousin! Worthy gentleman!

CAPTAIN: As whence the sun 'gins his reflection   25
Shipwracking storms and direful thunders break,
So from that spring whence comfort seemed to come
Discomfort swells. Mark, King of Scotland, mark:
No sooner justice had, with valor armed,
Compelled these skipping kerns to trust their heels   30
But the Norweyan lord, surveying vantage,
With furbished arms and new supplies of men,

---

⁶broil *quarrel*   ⁹choke their art *hamper each other's doings*
¹²Western Isles *Hebrides*   ¹³Of kerns and gallowglasses *with lightly armed Irish
foot soldiers and heavily armed ones*   ¹⁴damnèd quarrel *accursed cause*
¹⁵Showed like a rebel's whore *i.e., falsely appeared to favor Macdonwald*
¹⁹minion *(trisyllabic) favorite*   ²²nave to th' chops *navel to the jaws*
²⁵reflection *(four syllables; the ending—ion here and often elsewhere in the play—is
disyllabic)*   ³¹surveying vantage *seeing an opportunity*

Began a fresh assault.
KING: Dismayed not this
Our captains, Macbeth and Banquo?
CAPTAIN: Yes;
As sparrows eagles, or the hare the lion.   35
If I say sooth, I must report they were
As cannons overcharged with double cracks;
So they doubly redoubled strokes upon the foe.
Except they meant to bathe in reeking wounds,
Or memorize another Golgotha,   40
I cannot tell—
But I am faint; my gashes cry for help.
KING: So well thy words become thee as thy wounds;
They smack of honor both. Go get him surgeons.

Exit CAPTAIN, *attended.*

Enter ROSS *and* ANGUS.

Who comes here?
MALCOLM: The worthy Thane of Ross.   45
LENNOX: What a haste looks through his eyes! So should he look
That seems to speak things strange.
ROSS: God save the king!
KING: Whence cam'st thou, worthy Thane?
ROSS: From Fife, great King;
Where the Norweyan banners flout the sky
And fan our people cold.   50
Norway himself, with terrible numbers,
Assisted by that most disloyal traitor
The Thane of Cawdor, began a dismal conflict;
Till that Bellona's bridegroom, lapped in proof,
Confronted him with self-comparisons,   55
Point against point, rebellious arm 'gainst arm,

[36]**sooth** *truth*   [37]**cracks** *explosives*   [39]**Except** *unless*
[40]**memorize another Golgotha** *make the place as memorable as Golgotha, "the place of the skull"*   [45]**Thane** *a Scottish title of nobility*   [47]**seems to** *seems about to*
[51]**Norway** *the King of Norway*   [53]**dismal** *threatening*   [54]**Bellona's ... proof** *the mate of the goddess of war, clad in tested (proved) armor*
[55]**self-comparisons** *counter-movements*

Curbing his lavish spirit: and, to conclude,
The victory fell on us.

KING: Great happiness!

ROSS: That now
Sweno, the Norways' king, craves composition;
Nor would we deign him burial of his men   60
Till he disbursèd, at Saint Colme's Inch,
Ten thousand dollars to our general use.

KING: No more that Thane of Cawdor shall deceive
Our bosom interest: go pronounce his present death,
And with his former title greet Macbeth.   65

ROSS: I'll see it done.

KING: What he hath lost, noble Macbeth hath won.

Exeunt.

SCENE III *A heath.*

Thunder. Enter the THREE WITCHES.

FIRST WITCH: Where hast thou been, sister?

SECOND WITCH: Killing swine.

THIRD WITCH: Sister, where thou?

FIRST WITCH: A sailor's wife had chestnuts in her lap,
And mounched, and mounched, and mounched.   5
    "Give me," quoth I.
"Aroint thee, witch!" the rump-fed ronyon cries.
Her husband's to Aleppo gone, master o' th' Tiger:
But in a sieve I'll thither sail,
And, like a rat without a tail,
I'll do, I'll do, and I'll do.   10

SECOND WITCH: I'll give thee a wind.

FIRST WITCH: Th' art kind.

---

⁵⁷lavish *insolent*   ⁵⁹composition *terms of peace*   ⁶¹Inch *island*   ⁶²dollars *here, it is Spanish and Dutch currency*   ⁶⁴Our bosom interest *my (plural of royalty) heart's trust;* present *immediate*   ⁶Aroint thee *begone;* rump-fed ronyon *fat-rumped, scabby creature*

THIRD WITCH: And I another.
FIRST WITCH: I myself have all the other;
  And the very ports they blow,   15
  All the quarters that they know
  I' th' shipman's card.
  I'll drain him dry as hay:
  Sleep shall neither night nor day
  Hang upon his penthouse lid;   20
  He shall live a man forbid:
  Weary sev'nights nine times nine
  Shall he dwindle, peak, and pine:
  Though his bark cannot be lost,
  Yet it shall be tempest-tossed.   25
  Look what I have.
SECOND WITCH: Show me, show me.
FIRST WITCH: Here I have a pilot's thumb,
  Wracked as homeward he did come.

Drum within.

THIRD WITCH: A drum, a drum!   30
  Macbeth doth come.
ALL: The weïrd sisters, hand in hand,
  Posters of the sea and land,
  Thus do go about, about:
  Thrice to thine, and thrice to mine,   35
  And thrice again, to make up nine.
  Peace! The charm's wound up.

Enter MACBETH *and* BANQUO.

MACBETH: So foul and fair a day I have not seen.
BANQUO: How far is 't called to Forres? What are these
  So withered, and so wild in their attire,
  That look not like th' inhabitants o' th' earth,   40
  And yet are on 't? Live you, or are you aught

---

[15]**ports they blow** *harbors to which the winds blow (?)*   [17]**card** *compass card*
[20]**penthouse lid** *eyelid (the figure is of a lean-to)*   [21]**forbid** *cursed*   [23]**peak** *waste away*   [32]**weïrd** *destiny-serving (?)*   [33]**Posters** *swift travelers*

That man may question? You seem to understand me,
By each at once her choppy finger laying
Upon her skinny lips. You should be women,　　　　　　　　45
And yet your beards forbid me to interpret
That you are so.
MACBETH:　　　　　　Speak, if you can: what are you?
FIRST WITCH: All hail, Macbeth! Hail to thee, Thane of Glamis!
SECOND WITCH: All hail, Macbeth! Hail to thee, Thane
　　of Cawdor!
THIRD WITCH: All hail, Macbeth, that shalt be King hereafter!　　50
BANQUO: Good sir, why do you start, and seem to fear
　　Things that do sound so fair? I' th' name of truth,
　　Are ye fantastical, or that indeed
　　Which outwardly ye show? My noble partner
　　You greet with present grace and great prediction　　55
　　Of noble having and of royal hope,
　　That he seems rapt withal: to me you speak not.
　　If you can look into the seeds of time,
　　And say which grain will grow and which will not,
　　Speak then to me, who neither beg nor fear　　60
　　Your favors nor your hate.
FIRST WITCH: Hail!
SECOND WITCH: Hail!
THIRD WITCH: Hail!
FIRST WITCH: Lesser than Macbeth, and greater.　　65
SECOND WITCH: Not so happy, yet much happier.
THIRD WITCH: Thou shalt get kings, though thou be none.
　　So all hail, Macbeth and Banquo!
FIRST WITCH: Banquo and Macbeth, all hail!
MACBETH: Stay, you imperfect speakers, tell me more:　　70
　　By Sinel's death I know I am Thane of Glamis;
　　But how of Cawdor? The Thane of Cawdor lives,
　　A prosperous gentleman; and to be King
　　Stands not within the prospect of belief,
　　No more than to be Cawdor. Say from whence　　7

---

[43]question *talk to*　　[44]choppy *chapped*　　[53]fantastical *imaginary*　　[55]grace *honor*
[56]having *possession*　　[57]rapt withal *entranced by it*　　[66]happy *fortunate*
[67]get *beget*　　[70]imperfect *incomplete*　　[71]Sinel *(Macbeth's father)*

You owe this strange intelligence? Or why
Upon this blasted heath you stop our way
With such prophetic greeting? Speak, I charge you.

WITCHES *vanish.*

BANQUO: The earth hath bubbles as the water has,
    And these are of them. Whither are they vanished?   80
MACBETH: Into the air, and what seemed corporal melted
    As breath into the wind. Would they had stayed!
BANQUO: Were such things here as we do speak about?
    Or have we eaten on the insane root
    That takes the reason prisoner?   85
MACBETH: Your children shall be kings.
BANQUO: You shall be King.
MACBETH: And Thane of Cawdor too. Went it not so?
BANQUO: To th' selfsame tune and words. Who's here?

Enter ROSS *and* ANGUS.

ROSS: The King hath happily received, Macbeth,
    The news of thy success; and when he reads   90
    Thy personal venture in the rebels' fight,
    His wonders and his praises do contend
    Which should be thine or his. Silenced with that,
    In viewing o'er the rest o' th' selfsame day,
    He finds thee in the stout Norweyan ranks,   95
    Nothing afeard of what thyself didst make,
    Strange images of death. As thick as tale
    Came post with post, and every one did bear
    Thy praises in his kingdom's great defense,
    And poured them down before him.
ANGUS: We are sent   100
    To give thee, from our royal master, thanks;
    Only to herald thee into his sight,
    Not pay thee.

---

[76]owe *own, have;* intelligence *information*   [81]corporal *corporeal*
[84]insane *insanity-producing*   [90]reads *considers*
[92–93]His wonders ... his *i.e., Duncan's speechless admiration, appropriate to him,*
contends with his desire to praise you (?)   [97–98]As thick ... post *as fast as could be*
counted came messenger after messenger

ROSS: And for an earnest of a greater honor,
    He bade me, from him, call thee Thane of Cawdor; 105
    In which addition, hail, most worthy Thane!
    For it is thine.
BANQUO: What, can the devil speak true?
MACBETH: The Thane of Cawdor lives: why do you dress me
    In borrowed robes?
ANGUS: Who was the thane lives yet,
    But under heavy judgment bears that life 110
    Which he deserves to lose. Whether he was combined
    With those of Norway, or did line the rebel
    With hidden help and vantage, or that with both
    He labored in his country's wrack, I know not;
    But treasons capital, confessed and proved, 11
    Have overthrown him.
MACBETH *(Aside)*:   Glamis, and Thane of Cawdor:
    The greatest is behind *(To* ROSS *and* ANGUS*)* Thanks
       for your pains.
    (Aside to BANQUO*)* Do you not hope your children
       shall be kings,
    When those that gave the Thane of Cawdor to me
    Promised no less to them?
BANQUO *(Aside to* MACBETH*)*: That, trusted home, 12
    Might yet enkindle you unto the crown,
    Besides the Thane of Cawdor. But 'tis strange:
    And oftentimes, to win us to our harm,
    The instruments of darkness tell us truths,
    Win us with honest trifles, to betray 's 12
    In deepest consequence.
    Cousins, a word, I pray you.
MACBETH *(Aside)*:   Two truths are told
    As happy prologues to the swelling act
    Of the imperial theme.—I thank you, gentlemen.—
    (Aside) This supernatural soliciting 13

---

[104]earnest *pledge*   [106]addition *title*   [111]combined *allied*   [112]line *support*
[113]vantage *opportunity*   [114]wrack *ruin*   [117]behind *i.e., to follow*   [120]home *all the way*   [126]In deepest consequence *in the most significant sequel*
[127]Cousins *i.e., fellow noblemen*   [128]swelling *stately*   [130]soliciting *inviting*

Cannot be ill, cannot be good. If ill,
Why hath it given me earnest of success,
Commencing in a truth? I am Thane of Cawdor:
If good, why do I yield to that suggestion
Whose horrid image doth unfix my hair   135
And make my seated heart knock at my ribs,
Against the use of nature? Present fears
Are less than horrible imaginings.
My thought, whose murder yet is but fantastical,
Shakes so my single state of man that function   140
Is smothered in surmise, and nothing is
But what is not.
BANQUO: Look, how our partner's rapt.
MACBETH *(Aside)*: If chance will have me King, why, chance
   may crown me,
Without my stir.
BANQUO: New honors come upon him,
   Like our strange garments, cleave not to their mold   145
   But with the aid of use.
MACBETH: *(Aside)*:   Come what come may,
   Time and the hour runs through the roughest day.
BANQUO: Worthy Macbeth, we stay upon your leisure.
MACBETH: Give me your favor. My dull brain was wrought
   With things forgotten. Kind gentlemen, your pains   150
   Are registered where every day I turn
   The leaf to read them. Let us toward the King.
   (Aside to BANQUO*)* Think upon what hath chanced, and
      at more time,
   The interim having weighed it, let us speak
   Our free hearts each to other.
BANQUO: Very gladly.   155
MACBETH: Till then, enough. Come, friends.
Exeunt.

---

[136]seated *fixed*   [137]**Against the use of nature** *contrary to my natural way*
[139]fantastical *imaginary*   [140]single *unaided, weak (or "entire"?)*   [145]strange *new*
[148]**stay upon your leisure** *await your convenience*   [149]favor *pardon*
[154]**The interim having weighed it** *i.e., when we have had time to think*
[155]**Our free hearts** *our minds freely*

SCENE IV *Forres. The palace.*

Flourish.[†] *Enter* KING (DUNCAN), LENNOX, MALCOLM,
DONALBAIN, *and* ATTENDANTS.

KING: Is execution done on Cawdor? Are not
  Those in commission yet returned?
MALCOLM: My liege,
  They are not yet come back. But I have spoke
  With one that saw him die, who did report
  That very frankly he confessed his treasons,   5
  Implored your Highness' pardon and set forth
  A deep repentance: nothing in his life
  Became him like the leaving it. He died
  As one that had been studied in his death,
  To throw away the dearest thing he owed   10
  As 'twere a careless trifle.
KING: There's no art
  To find the mind's construction in the face:
  He was a gentleman on whom I built
  An absolute trust.

Enter MACBETH, BANQUO, ROSS, *and* ANGUS.

              O worthiest cousin!
  The sin of my ingratitude even now   15
  Was heavy on me: thou art so far before,
  That swiftest wing of recompense is slow
  To overtake thee. Would thou hadst less deserved,
  That the proportion both of thanks and payment
  Might have been mine! Only I have left to say,   20
  More is thy due than more than all can pay.
MACBETH: The service and the loyalty I owe,
  In doing it, pays itself. Your Highness' part
  Is to receive our duties: and our duties
  Are to your throne and state children and servants; 25
  Which do but what they should, by doing every thing

[†]**Flourish** *fanfare*   [2]**in commission** *i.e., commissioned to oversee the execution*
[9]**studied** *rehearsed*   [10]**owed** *owned*   [11]**careless** *uncared-for*
[19]**proportion** *preponderance*   [23]**pays itself** *is its own reward*

Safe toward your love and honor.
KING: Welcome hither.
  I have begun to plant thee, and will labor
  To make thee full of growing. Noble Banquo,
  That hast no less deserved, nor must be known   30
  No less to have done so, let me enfold thee
  And hold thee to my heart.
BANQUO: There if I grow,
  The harvest is your own.
KING: My plenteous joys,
  Wanton in fullness, seek to hide themselves
  In drops of sorrow. Sons, kinsmen, thanes,   35
  And you whose places are the nearest, know,
  We will establish our estate upon
  Our eldest, Malcolm, whom we name hereafter
  The Prince of Cumberland: which honor must
  Not unaccompanied invest him only,   40
  But signs of nobleness, like stars, shall shine
  On all deservers. From hence to Inverness,
  And bind us further to you.
MACBETH: The rest is labor, which is not used for you.
  I'll be myself the harbinger, and make joyful   45
  The hearing of my wife with your approach;
  So, humbly take my leave.
KING: My worthy Cawdor!
MACBETH *(Aside)*: The Prince of Cumberland! That is a step
  On which I must fall down, or else o'erleap,
  For in my way it lies. Stars, hide your fires;   50
  Let not light see my black and deep desires:
  The eye wink at the hand, yet let that be
  Which the eye fears, when it is done, to see.

Exit.

KING: True, worthy Banquo; he is full so valiant,

---

²⁷**Safe toward** *safeguarding (?)*   ³⁴**Wanton** *unrestrained*
³⁷**establish our estate** *settle the succession*   ⁴⁴**The rest . . . you** *i.e., repose is
laborious when not employed for you*   ⁵²**wink at the hand** *i.e., be blind to the
hand's deed*

And in his commendations I am fed;   55
It is a banquet to me. Let's after him,
Whose care is gone before to bid us welcome.
It is a peerless kinsman.

Flourish. Exeunt.

SCENE V *Inverness.* MACBETH's *castle.*

Enter MACBETH's *wife, alone, with a letter.*

LADY MACBETH *(Reads)*: "They met me in the day of success; and
I have learned by the perfect'st report they have more in them
than mortal knowledge. When I burned in desire to question
them further, they made themselves air, into which they
vanished. Whiles I stood rapt in the wonder of it, came missives   5
from the King, who all-hailed me 'Thane of Cawdor'; by which
title, before, these weïrd sisters saluted me, and referred me to
the coming on of time, with 'Hail, King that shalt be!' This have
I thought good to deliver thee, my dearest partner of greatness,
that thou mightst not lose the dues of rejoicing, by being   10
ignorant of what greatness is promised thee. Lay it to thy heart,
and farewell."

Glamis thou art, and Cawdor, and shalt be
What thou art promised. Yet do I fear thy nature;
It is too full o' th' milk of human kindness   15
To catch the nearest way. Thou wouldst be great,
Art not without ambition, but without
The illness should attend it. What thou wouldst highly,
That wouldst thou holily; wouldst not play false,
And yet wouldst wrongly win. Thou'dst have, great Glamis,   20
That which cries "Thus thou must do" if thou have it;
And that which rather thou dost fear to do

---

⁵⁵**his commendations** *commendations of him*   ⁵**missives** *messengers*
⁹**deliver thee** *report to you*   ¹⁵**milk of human kindness** *i.e., gentle quality of human
nature*   ¹⁸**illness** *wickedness*

Than wishest should be undone. Hie thee hither,
That I may pour my spirits in thine ear,
And chastise with the valor of my tongue   25
All that impedes thee from the golden round
Which fate and metaphysical aid doth seem
To have thee crowned withal.

Enter MESSENGER.

                         What is your tidings?

MESSENGER: The King comes here tonight.

LADY MACBETH: Thou'rt mad to say it!
Is not thy master with him, who, were 't so,   30
Would have informed for preparation?

MESSENGER: So please you, it is true. Our thane is coming.
One of my fellows had the speed of him,
Who, almost dead for breath, had scarcely more
Than would make up his message.

LADY MACBETH: Give him tending;   35
He brings great news.

Exit MESSENGER.

                   The raven himself is hoarse
That croaks the fatal entrance of Duncan
Under my battlements. Come, you spirits
That tend on mortal thoughts, unsex me here,
And fill me, from the crown to the toe, top-full   40
Of direst cruelty! Make thick my blood,
Stop up th' access and passage to remorse,
That no compunctious visitings of nature
Shake my fell purpose, nor keep peace between
Th' effect and it! Come to my woman's breasts,   45
And take my milk for gall, you murd'ring ministers,
Wherever in your sightless substances
You wait on nature's mischief! Come, thick night,

---

[26]round *crown*   [27]metaphysical *supernatural*   [28]withal *with*
[33]had the speed of him *outdistanced him*   [39]mortal *deadly*
[42]remorse *compassion*   [43]compunctious visitings of nature *natural feelings of compassion*   [44]fell *savage*   [45]effect *fulfillment*   [46]for *in exchange for;* ministers *agents*   [47]sightless *invisible*   [48]wait on *assist*

And pall thee in the dunnest smoke of hell,
That my keen knife see not the wound it makes, 50
Nor heaven peep through the blanket of the dark,
To cry "Hold, hold!"

Enter MACBETH.

Great Glamis! Worthy Cawdor!
Greater than both, by the all-hail hereafter!
Thy letters have transported me beyond
This ignorant present, and I feel now 55
The future in the instant.

MACBETH: My dearest love,
Duncan comes here tonight.

LADY MACBETH: And when goes hence?

MACBETH: Tomorrow, as he purposes.

LADY MACBETH: O, never
Shall sun that morrow see!
Your face, my Thane, is as a book where men 60
May read strange matters. To beguile the time,
Look like the time; bear welcome in your eye,
Your hand, your tongue: look like th' innocent flower,
But be the serpent under 't. He that's coming
Must be provided for: and you shall put 65
This night's great business into my dispatch;
Which shall to all our nights and days to come
Give solely sovereign sway and masterdom.

MACBETH: We will speak further.

LADY MACBETH: Only look up clear.
To alter favor ever is to fear. 70
Leave all the rest to me.

Exeunt.

---

[49]**pall** *enshroud;* **dunnest** *darkest* [53]**all-hail hereafter** *the third all-hail (?) the all-hail of the future (?)* [55]**ignorant** *unknowing* [56]**instant** *present*
[61]**To beguile the time** *i.e., to deceive people of the day* [66]**dispatch** *management*
[69]**look up clear** *appear undisturbed* [70]**To alter ... fear** *to show a disturbed face is dangerous*

SCENE VI *Before* MACBETH's *castle.*

Hautboys† and torches. Enter KING *(*DUNCAN*)*, MALCOLM,
DONALBAIN, BANQUO, LENNOX, MACDUFF, ROSS, ANGUS,
and ATTENDANTS.

KING: This castle hath a pleasant seat; the air
  Nimbly and sweetly recommends itself
  Unto our gentle senses.
BANQUO: This guest of summer,
  The temple-haunting martlet, does approve
  By his loved mansionry that the heaven's breath   5
  Smells wooingly here. No jutty, frieze,
  Buttress, nor coign of vantage, but this bird
  Hath made his pendent bed and procreant cradle.
  Where they most breed and haunt, I have observed
  The air is delicate.

Enter LADY MACBETH.

KING: See, see, our honored hostess!   10
  The love that follows us sometimes is our trouble,
  Which still we thank as love. Herein I teach you
  How you shall bid God 'ield us for your pains
  And thank us for your trouble.
LADY MACBETH: All our service
  In every point twice done, and then done double,   15
  Were poor and single business to contend
  Against those honors deep and broad wherewith
  Your Majesty loads our house: for those of old,
  And the late dignities heaped up to them,
  We rest your hermits.
KING: Where's the Thane of Cawdor?   20
  We coursed him at the heels, and had a purpose

---

†Hautboys *oboes* ¹seat *site* ³gentle *soothed* ⁴temple-haunting martlet *martin
(swift) nesting in churches* ⁵mansionry *nests* ⁶jutty *projection*
⁷coign of vantage *advantageous corner* ⁸procreant *breeding* ⁹haunt *visit*
¹¹⁻¹²The love . . . love *the love offered me sometimes inconveniences me, but still I
value it as love* ¹³'ield *reward* ¹⁶single business *feeble service*
²⁰your hermits *dependents bound to pray for you* ²¹coursed *pursued*

To be his purveyor: but he rides well,
And his great love, sharp as his spur, hath holp him
To his home before us. Fair and noble hostess,
We are your guest tonight.

LADY MACBETH: Your servants ever   25
Have theirs, themselves, and what is theirs, in compt,
To make their audit at your Highness' pleasure,
Still to return your own.

KING: Give me your hand.
Conduct me to mine host: we love him highly,
And shall continue our graces towards him.   30
By your leave, hostess.

Exeunt.

SCENE VII MACBETH's *castle.*

Hautboys. Torches. Enter a SEWER,[†] *and diverse* SERVANTS *with dishes and services over the stage. Then enter* MACBETH.

MACBETH: If it were done when 'tis done, then 'twere well
It were done quickly. If th' assassination
Could trammel up the consequence, and catch,
With his surcease, success; that but this blow
Might be the be-all and the end-all—here,   5
But here, upon this bank and shoal of time,
We'd jump the life to come. But in these cases
We still have judgment here; that we but teach
Bloody instructions, which, being taught, return
To plague th' inventor: this even-handed justice   10
Commends th' ingredients of our poisoned chalice

[22]purveyor *advance-supply officer*   [23]holp *helped*   [26]Have theirs . . . compt *have their dependents, themselves, and their possessions in trust*   [28]Still *always*
[†]Sewer *chief butler*   [1]done *over and done with*   [3]trammel up *catch in a net*
[4]his surcease *Duncan's death (?) the consequence's cessation (?);* success *what follows*   [7]jump *risk*   [8]still *always*   [10]even-handed *impartial*
[11]Commends *offers*

To our own lips. He's here in double trust:
First, as I am his kinsman and his subject,
Strong both against the deed; then, as his host,
Who should against his murderer shut the door, 15
Not bear the knife myself. Besides, this Duncan
Hath borne his faculties so meek, hath been
So clear in his great office, that his virtues
Will plead like angels trumpet-tongued against
The deep damnation of his taking-off; 20
And pity, like a naked newborn babe,
Striding the blast, or heaven's cherubin horsed
Upon the sightless couriers of the air,
Shall blow the horrid deed in every eye,
That tears shall drown the wind. I have no spur 25
To prick the sides of my intent, but only
Vaulting ambition, which o'erleaps itself
And falls on th' other——

Enter LADY MACBETH.

                  How now! What news?
LADY MACBETH: He has almost supped. Why have you
    left the chamber?
MACBETH: Hath he asked for me?
LADY MACBETH: Know you not he has? 30
MACBETH: We will proceed no further in this business:
    He hath honored me of late, and I have bought
    Golden opinions from all sorts of people,
    Which would be worn now in their newest gloss,
    Not cast aside so soon.
LADY MACBETH: Was the hope drunk 35
    Wherein you dressed yourself? Hath it slept since?
    And wakes it now, to look so green and pale
    At what it did so freely? From this time
    Such I account thy love. Art thou afeard
    To be the same in thine own act and valor 40
    As thou art in desire? Wouldst thou have that

---

[17]faculties *powers*   [18]clear *spotless*   [22]Striding *bestriding*
[23]sightless couriers *invisible coursers (i.e., the winds)*   [25]That *so that*
[32]bought *acquired*   [37]green *sickly*

Which thou esteem'st the ornament of life,
And live a coward in thine own esteem,
Letting "I dare not" wait upon "I would,"
Like the poor cat i' th' adage?

MACBETH: Prithee, peace!   45
I dare do all that may become a man;
Who dares do more is none.

LADY MACBETH: What beast was 't then
That made you break this enterprise to me?
When you durst do it, then you were a man;
And to be more than what you were, you would   50
Be so much more the man. Nor time nor place
Did then adhere, and yet you would make both.
They have made themselves, and that their fitness now
Does unmake you. I have given suck, and know
How tender 'tis to love the babe that milks me: 55
I would, while it was smiling in my face,
Have plucked my nipple from his boneless gums,
And dashed the brains out, had I so sworn as you
Have done to this.

MACBETH: If we should fail?

LADY MACBETH: We fail?
But screw your courage to the sticking-place,   60
And we'll not fail. When Duncan is asleep—
Whereto the rather shall his day's hard journey
Soundly invite him—his two chamberlains
Will I with wine and wassail so convince,
That memory, the warder of the brain,   65
Shall be a fume, and the receipt of reason
A limbeck only: when in swinish sleep
Their drenchèd natures lies as in a death,
What cannot you and I perform upon
Th' unguarded Duncan, what not put upon   70

---

⁴⁴wait upon *follow*   ⁴⁵cat *(who wants to fish but fears to wet its paws)*
⁴⁸break *broach*   ⁵²adhere *suit*   ⁵³that their *their very*   ⁶⁰But *only;* sticking-
place *notch (holding a bowstring of a taut crossbow)*   ⁶⁴wassail *carousing;*
convince *overpower*   ⁶⁵warder *guard*   ⁶⁶⁻⁶⁷receipt ... only *i.e., the receptacle*
(receipt), *which should collect the distillate of thought—reason—will be a mere*
vessel (limbeck) *of undistilled liquids*   ⁶⁸lies *lie*

His spongy officers, who shall bear the guilt
Of our great quell?

MACBETH: Bring forth men-children only;
For thy undaunted mettle should compose
Nothing but males. Will it not be received,
When we have marked with blood those sleepy two   75
Of his own chamber, and used their very daggers,
That they have done 't?

LADY MACBETH: Who dares receive it other,
As we shall make our griefs and clamor roar
Upon his death?

MACBETH: I am settled, and bend up
Each corporal agent to this terrible feat.   80
Away, and mock the time with fairest show:
False face must hide what the false heart doth know.

Exeunt.

ACT II

SCENE I *Inverness. Court of* MACBETH'S *castle.*

Enter BANQUO, *and* FLEANCE, *with a torch before him.*

BANQUO: How goes the night, boy?
FLEANCE: The moon is down; I have not heard the clock.
BANQUO: And she goes down at twelve.
FLEANCE: I tak't, 'tis later, sir.
BANQUO: Hold, take my sword. There's husbandry in heaven.
Their candles are all out. Take thee that too.   5
A heavy summons lies like lead upon me,
And yet I would not sleep. Merciful powers,
Restrain in me the cursèd thoughts that nature
Gives way to in repose!

---

[71]**spongy** *sodden*   [72]**quell** *killing*   [73]**mettle** *substance*   [77]**other** *otherwise*
[81]**mock the time** *beguile the world*   [4]**husbandry** *frugality*   [6]**summons** *call (to sleep)*

Enter MACBETH, *and a* SERVANT *with a torch.*

                           Give me my sword!

Who's there?   10

MACBETH: A friend.

BANQUO: What, sir, not yet at rest? The King's a-bed:

   He hath been in unusual pleasure, and

   Sent forth great largess to your offices:

   This diamond he greets your wife withal,   15

   By the name of most kind hostess; and shut up

   In measureless content.

MACBETH: Being unprepared,

   Our will became the servant to defect,

   Which else should free have wrought.

BANQUO: All's well.

   I dreamt last night of the three weïrd sisters: 20

   To you they have showed some truth.

MACBETH: I think not of them.

   Yet, when we can entreat an hour to serve,

   We would spend it in some words upon that business,

   If you would grant the time.

BANQUO: At your kind'st leisure.

MACBETH: If you shall cleave to my consent, when 'tis,   25

   It shall make honor for you.

BANQUO: So I lose none

   In seeking to augment it, but still keep

   My bosom franchised and allegiance clear,

   I shall be counseled.

MACBETH: Good repose the while!

BANQUO: Thanks, sir. The like to you!   30

Exit BANQUO *with* FLEANCE.

MACBETH: Go bid thy mistress, when my drink is ready,

   She strike upon the bell. Get thee to bed.

Exit SERVANT.

---

[14]**largess to your offices** *gifts to your servants' quarters*   [16]**shut up** *concluded*
[18]**Our . . . defect** *our good will was hampered by our deficient preparations*
[25]**cleave . . . 'tis** *join my cause, when the time comes*   [26]**So** *provided that*
[28]**franchised** *free (from guilt);* **clear** *spotless*

Is this a dagger which I see before me,
The handle toward my hand? Come, let me clutch thee.
I have thee not, and yet I see thee still.   35
Art thou not, fatal vision, sensible
To feeling as to sight, or art thou but
A dagger of the mind, a false creation,
Proceeding from the heat-oppressèd brain?
I see thee yet, in form as palpable   40
As this which now I draw.
Thou marshal'st me the way that I was going;
And such an instrument I was to use.
Mine eyes are made the fools o' th' other senses,
Or else worth all the rest. I see thee still;   45
And on thy blade and dudgeon gouts of blood,
Which was not so before. There's no such thing.
It is the bloody business which informs
Thus to mine eyes. Now o'er the one half-world
Nature seems dead, and wicked dreams abuse   50
The curtained sleep; witchcraft celebrates
Pale Hecate's offerings; and withered murder,
Alarumed by his sentinel, the wolf,
Whose howl's his watch, thus with his stealthy pace,
With Tarquin's ravishing strides, towards his design   55
Moves like a ghost. Thou sure and firm-set earth,
Hear not my steps, which way they walk, for fear
Thy very stones prate of my whereabout,
And take the present horror from the time,
Which now suits with it. Whiles I threat, he lives: 60
Words to the heat of deeds too cold breath gives.

A bell rings.

I go, and it is done: the bell invites me.

---

[36]**sensible** *perceptible*   [46]**dudgeon** *wooden hilt;* **gouts** *large drops*
[48]**informs** *gives shape (?)*   [50]**abuse** *deceive*   [52]**Hecate's offerings** *offerings to Hecate (goddess of sorcery)*   [53]**Alarumed** *called to action*   [55]**Tarquin** *(Roman tyrant who ravished Lucrece)*   [59–60]**take ... it** *remove (by noise) the horrible silence attendant on this moment and suitable to it (?)*

Hear it not, Duncan, for it is a knell
That summons thee to heaven, or to hell.

Exit.

Scene II macbeth's *castle.*

Enter LADY MACBETH.

LADY MACBETH: That which hath made them drunk hath
   made me bold;
  What hath quenched them hath given me fire. Hark! Peace!
  It was the owl that shrieked, the fatal bellman,
  Which gives the stern'st good-night. He is about it.
  The doors are open, and the surfeited grooms   5
  Do mock their charge with snores. I have drugged their possets,
  That death and nature do contend about them,
  Whether they live or die.
MACBETH *(Within)*:   Who's there? What, ho?
LADY MACBETH: Alack, I am afraid they have awaked
  And 'tis not done! Th' attempt and not the deed   10
  Confounds us. Hark! I laid their daggers ready;
  He could not miss 'em. Had he not resembled
  My father as he slept, I had done 't.

Enter MACBETH.

                   My husband!
MACBETH: I have done the deed. Didst thou not hear a noise?
LADY MACBETH: I heard the owl scream and the crickets cry.   15
  Did not you speak?
MACBETH: When?
LADY MACBETH: Now.
MACBETH: As I descended?
LADY MACBETH: Ay.
MACBETH: Hark!

[3-4] **bellman . . . good-night** *i.e., the owl's call, portending death, is like the town crier's call to a condemned man*   [6] **possets** *bedtime drinks*   [7] **nature** *natural vitality*   [11] **Confounds** *ruins*

Who lies i' th' second chamber?

LADY MACBETH: Donalbain.

MACBETH: This is a sorry sight.   20

LADY MACBETH: A foolish thought, to say a sorry sight.

MACBETH: There's one did laugh in 's sleep, and one cried
    "Murder!"
    That they did wake each other. I stood and heard them.
    But they did say their prayers, and addressed them
    Again to sleep.

LADY MACBETH: There are two lodged together.   25

MACBETH: One cried "God bless us!" and "Amen" the other,
    As they had seen me with these hangman's hands:
    List'ning their fear, I could not say "Amen,"
    When they did say "God bless us!"

LADY MACBETH: Consider it not so deeply.

MACBETH: But wherefore could not I pronounce "Amen"?   30
    I had most need of blessing, and "Amen"
    Stuck in my throat.

LADY MACBETH: These deeds must not be thought
    After these ways; so, it will make us mad.

MACBETH: Methought I heard a voice cry "Sleep no more!
    Macbeth does murder sleep"—the innocent sleep,   35
    Sleep that knits up the raveled sleave of care,
    The death of each day's life, sore labor's bath,
    Balm of hurt minds, great nature's second course,
    Chief nourisher in life's feast——

LADY MACBETH: What do you mean?

MACBETH: Still it cried "Sleep no more!" to all the house: 40
    "Glamis hath murdered sleep, and therefore Cawdor
    Shall sleep no more: Macbeth shall sleep no more."

LADY MACBETH: Who was it that thus cried? Why, worthy Thane,
    You do unbend your noble strength, to think
    So brainsickly of things. Go get some water,   45
    And wash this filthy witness from your hand.

---

[20]sorry *miserable*   [27]hangman's *executioner's (i.e., bloody)*
[36]knits up the raveled sleave *straightens out the tangled skein*
[38]second course *i.e., sleep (the less substantial first course is food)*
[44]unbend *relax*   [46]witness *evidence*

Why did you bring these daggers from the place?
They must lie there: go carry them, and smear
The sleepy grooms with blood.

MACBETH: I'll go no more.
I am afraid to think what I have done;   50
Look on 't again I dare not.

LADY MACBETH: Infirm of purpose!
Give me the daggers. The sleeping and the dead
Are but as pictures. 'Tis the eye of childhood
That fears a painted devil. If he do bleed,
I'll gild the faces of the grooms withal,   55
For it must seem their guilt.

Exit. Knock within.

MACBETH: Whence is that knocking?
How is 't with me, when every noise appalls me?
What hands are here? Ha! They pluck out mine eyes!
Will all great Neptune's ocean wash this blood
Clean from my hand? No; this my hand will rather   60
The multitudinous seas incarnadine,
Making the green one red.

Enter LADY MACBETH.

LADY MACBETH: My hands are of your color, but I shame
To wear a heart so white. *(Knock.)* I hear a knocking
At the south entry. Retire we to our chamber.   65
A little water clears us of this deed:
How easy is it then! Your constancy
Hath left you unattended. *(Knock.)* Hark! more knocking.
Get on your nightgown, lest occasion call us
And show us to be watchers. Be not lost   70
So poorly in your thoughts.

---

[54]**painted** *depicted*   [55]**gild** *paint*   [61]**incarnadine** *redden*
[62]**the green one red** *(perhaps "the green one" means "the ocean," but perhaps "one"
here means "totally," "uniformly")*   [67–68]**Your . . . unattended** *your firmness has
deserted you*   [69]**nightgown** *dressing-gown*   [70]**watchers** *i.e., up late*
[71]**poorly** *weakly*

MACBETH: To know my deed, 'twere best not know myself.
(Knock.)
Wake Duncan with thy knocking! I would thou couldst!
Exeunt.

SCENE III MACBETH's *castle.*

Enter a PORTER. *Knocking within.*

PORTER: Here's a knocking indeed! If a man were porter of hell
gate, he should have old turning the key. *(Knock.)* Knock,
knock, knock! Who's there, i' th' name of Beelzebub? Here's a
farmer, that hanged himself on th' expectation of plenty. Come
in time! Have napkins enow about you; here you'll sweat for 't. 5
(Knock.) Knock, knock! Who's there, in th' other devil's name?
Faith, here's an equivocator, that could swear in both the scales
against either scale; who committed treason enough for God's
sake, yet could not equivocate to heaven. O, come in, equivocator. *(Knock.)* Knock, knock, knock! Who's there? Faith, here's 10
an English tailor come hither for stealing out of a French hose:
come in, tailor. Here you may roast your goose. *(Knock.)* Knock,
knock; never at quiet! What are you? But this place is too cold
for hell. I'll devil-porter it no further. I had thought to have let
in some of all professions that go the primrose way to th' 15
everlasting bonfire. *(Knock.)* Anon, anon! *(Opens an entrance.)*
I pray you, remember the porter.

Enter MACDUFF *and* LENNOX.

MACDUFF: Was it so late, friend, ere you went to bed,
That you do lie so late?
PORTER: Faith, sir, we were carousing till the second cock: and 20
drink, sir, is a great provoker of three things.

---

²**old** *colloquial for having a high old time*   ⁴**farmer ... plenty** *(the farmer hoarded
so he could later sell high, but when it looked as though there would be a crop
surplus, he hanged himself)*   ⁵**enow** *enough*   ⁷**equivocator** *i.e., Jesuit (who
allegedly employed deceptive speech to further God's ends)*   ¹¹**French hose** *tight-
fitting hose*   ¹²**goose** *pressing iron*   ²⁰**second cock** *(about 3 A.M.)*

MACDUFF: What three things does drink especially provoke?

PORTER: Marry, sir, nose-painting, sleep, and urine. Lechery, sir, it provokes and unprovokes; it provokes the desire, but it takes away the performance: therefore much drink may be said to be 25 an equivocator with lechery: it makes him and it mars him; it sets him on and it takes him off; it persuades him and disheartens him; makes him stand to and not stand to; in conclusion, equivocates him in a sleep, and giving him the lie, leaves him.

MACDUFF: I believe drink gave thee the lie last night. 30

PORTER: That it did, sir, i' the very throat on me: but I requited him for his lie, and, I think, being too strong for him, though he took up my legs sometime, yet I make a shift to cast him.

MACDUFF: Is thy master stirring?

Enter MACBETH.

Our knocking has awakened him; here he comes. 35

LENNOX: Good morrow, noble sir.

MACBETH: Good morrow, both.

MACDUFF: Is the king stirring, worthy Thane?

MACBETH: Not yet.

MACDUFF: He did command me to call timely on him:
I have almost slipped the hour.

MACBETH: I'll bring you to him.

MACDUFF: I know this is a joyful trouble to you; 40
But yet 'tis one.

MACBETH: The labor we delight in physics pain.
This is the door.

MACDUFF: I'll make so bold to call,
For 'tis my limited service.

Exit MACDUFF.

LENNOX: Goes the king hence today?

MACBETH: He does: he did appoint so. 45

LENNOX: The night has been unruly. Where we lay,
Our chimneys were blown down, and, as they say,

---

[30]**gave thee the lie** *called you a liar (with a pun on "stretched you out")*
[33]**cast** *(with a pun on "cast," meaning "vomit")*   [38]**timely** *early*
[39]**slipped** *let slip*   [42]**The labor . . . pain** *labor that gives us pleasure cures discomfort*   [44]**limited service** *appointed duty*

Lamentings heard i' th' air, strange screams of death,
And prophesying with accents terrible
Of dire combustion and confused events   50
New hatched to th' woeful time: the obscure bird
Clamored the livelong night. Some say, the earth
Was feverous and did shake.
MACBETH: 'Twas a rough night.
LENNOX: My young remembrance cannot parallel
A fellow to it.   55

Enter MACDUFF.

MACDUFF: O horror, horror, horror! Tongue nor heart
Cannot conceive nor name thee.
MACBETH *and* LENNOX: What's the matter?
MACDUFF: Confusion now hath made his masterpiece.
Most sacrilegious murder hath broke ope
The Lord's anointed temple, and stole thence   60
The life o' th' building.
MACBETH: What is 't you say? The life?
LENNOX: Mean you his Majesty?
MACDUFF: Approach the chamber, and destroy your sight
With a new Gorgon: do not bid me speak;
See, and then speak yourselves. Awake, awake!   65

Exeunt MACBETH *and* LENNOX.

Ring the alarum bell. Murder and Treason!
Banquo and Donalbain! Malcolm! Awake!
Shake off this downy sleep, death's counterfeit,
And look on death itself! Up, up, and see
The great doom's image! Malcolm! Banquo!   70
As from your graves rise up, and walk like sprites,
To countenance this horror. Ring the bell.

Bell rings. Enter LADY MACBETH.

LADY MACBETH: What's the business,
That such a hideous trumpet calls to parley

---

⁵⁰combustion *tumult*   ⁵¹obscure bird *bird of darkness, i.e., the owl*
⁵⁸Confusion *destruction*   ⁶⁴Gorgon *(creature capable of turning beholders to*
stone)   ⁶⁸counterfeit *imitation*   ⁷⁰great doom's image *likeness of Judgment Day*
⁷¹sprites *spirits*   ⁷²countenance *be in keeping with*

The sleepers of the house? Speak, speak!

MACDUFF: O gentle lady,   75
  'Tis not for you to hear what I can speak:
  The repetition, in a woman's ear,
  Would murder as it fell.

Enter BANQUO.

                O Banquo, Banquo!
  Our royal master's murdered.

LADY MACBETH: Woe, alas!
  What, in our house?

BANQUO: Too cruel anywhere.   80
  Dear Duff, I prithee, contradict thyself,
  And say it is not so.

Enter MACBETH, LENNOX, *and* ROSS.

MACBETH: Had I but died an hour before this chance,
  I had lived a blessèd time; for from this instant
  There's nothing serious in mortality: 8.
  All is but toys. Renown and grace is dead,
  The wine of life is drawn, and the mere lees
  Is left this vault to brag of.

Enter MALCOLM *and* DONALBAIN.

DONALBAIN: What is amiss?

MACBETH: You are, and do not know 't.
  The spring, the head, the fountain of your blood   9
  Is stopped; the very source of it is stopped.

MACDUFF: Your royal father's murdered.

MALCOLM: O, by whom?

LENNOX: Those of his chamber, as it seemed, had done 't:
  Their hands and faces were all badged with blood;
  So were their daggers, which unwiped we found   9
  Upon their pillows. They stared, and were distracted.
  No man's life was to be trusted with them.

MACBETH: O, yet I do repent me of my fury,
  That I did kill them.

---

[77] **repetition** *report*   [85] **serious in mortality** *worthwhile in mortal life*   [86] **toys** *trifles*
[87] **lees** *dregs*   [88] **vault** *(1) wine vault (2) earth, with the sky as roof (?)*
[94] **badged** *marked*

MACDUFF: Wherefore did you so?

MACBETH: Who can be wise, amazed, temp'rate and furious,   100
    Loyal and neutral, in a moment? No man.
    The expedition of my violent love
    Outrun the pauser, reason. Here lay Duncan,
    His silver skin laced with his golden blood,
    And his gashed stabs looked like a breach in nature   105
    For ruin's wasteful entrance: there, the murderers,
    Steeped in the colors of their trade, their daggers
    Unmannerly breeched with gore. Who could refrain,
    That had a heart to love, and in that heart
    Courage to make 's love known?

LADY MACBETH: Help me hence, ho!   110

MACDUFF: Look to the lady.

MALCOLM (*Aside to* DONALBAIN): Why do we hold our tongues,
    That most may claim this argument for ours?

DONALBAIN (*Aside to* MALCOLM): What should be spoken here,
    Where our fate, hid in an auger-hole,   115
    May rush, and seize us? Let's away:
    Our tears are not yet brewed.

MALCOLM (*Aside to* DONALBAIN): Nor our strong sorrow
    Upon the foot of motion.

BANQUO: Look to the lady.

LADY MACBETH *is carried out.*

    And when we have our naked frailties hid,   120
    That suffer in exposure, let us meet
    And question this most bloody piece of work,
    To know it further. Fears and scruples shake us.
    In the great hand of God I stand, and thence
    Against the undivulged pretense I fight   125

---

[100]amazed *bewildered*   [102]expedition *haste*   [108]**Unmannerly breeched with gore** *covered with unseemly breeches of blood;* **refrain** *check oneself*   [111]**Look to** *look after*   [113]**That most . . . ours?** *who are the most concerned with this topic*   [115]**auger-hole** *i.e., unsuspected place*   [117–119]**Our tears . . . motion** *i.e., we have not yet had time for tears nor to express our sorrows in action (?)*   [120]**naked frailties hid** *poor bodies clothed*   [122]**question** *discuss*   [123]**scruples** *suspicions*   [125]**undivulged pretense** *hidden purpose*

Of treasonous malice.

MACDUFF: And so do I.

ALL: So all.

MACBETH: Let's briefly put on manly readiness,
   And meet i' th' hall together.

ALL: Well contented.

Exeunt all but MALCOLM *and* DONALBAIN.

MALCOLM: What will you do? Let's not consort with them.
   To show an unfelt sorrow is an office   130
   Which the false man does easy. I'll to England.

DONALBAIN: To Ireland, I; our separated fortune
   Shall keep us both the safer. Where we are
   There's daggers in men's smiles; the near in blood,
   The nearer bloody.

MALCOLM: This murderous shaft that's shot   135
   Hath not yet lighted, and our safest way
   Is to avoid the aim. Therefore to horse;
   And let us not be dainty of leave-taking,
   But shift away. There's warrant in that theft
   Which steals itself when there's no mercy left.   140

Exeunt.

SCENE IV   *Outside* MACBETH's *castle.*

Enter ROSS *with an* OLD MAN.

OLD MAN: Threescore and ten I can remember well:
   Within the volume of which time I have seen
   Hours dreadful and things strange, but this sore night
   Hath trifled former knowings.

ROSS: Ha, good father,
   Thou seest the heavens, as troubled with man's act,   5

---

[127]**briefly** *quickly*   [130]**office** *function*   [138]**dainty of** *fussy about*
[139]**warrant** *justification*   [140]**steals itself** *steals oneself away*   [3]**sore** *grievous*
[4]**trifled former knowings** *made trifles of former experiences*

Threatens his bloody stage. By th' clock 'tis day,
And yet dark night strangles the traveling lamp:
Is 't night's predominance, or the day's shame,
That darkness does the face of earth entomb,
When living light should kiss it?
OLD MAN: 'Tis unnatural,   10
   Even like the deed that's done. On Tuesday last
   A falcon, tow'ring in her pride of place,
   Was by a mousing owl hawked at and killed.
ROSS: And Duncan's horses—a thing most strange and certain—
   Beauteous and swift, the minions of their race,   15
   Turned wild in nature, broke their stalls, flung out,
   Contending 'gainst obedience, as they would make
   War with mankind.
OLD MAN: 'Tis said they eat each other.
ROSS: They did so, to th' amazement of mine eyes,
   That looked upon 't.
Enter MACDUFF.
                              Here comes the good Macduff.   20
   How goes the world, sir, now?
MACDUFF: Why, see you not?
ROSS: Is 't known who did this more than bloody deed?
MACDUFF: Those that Macbeth hath slain.
ROSS: Alas, the day!
   What good could they pretend?
MACDUFF: They were suborned:
   Malcolm and Donalbain, the king's two sons,   25
   Are stol'n away and fled, which puts upon them
   Suspicion of the deed.
ROSS: 'Gainst nature still.
   Thriftless ambition, that will ravin up
   Thine own life's means! Then 'tis most like
   The sovereignty will fall upon Macbeth.   30
MACDUFF: He is already named, and gone to Scone

---

[7]**traveling lamp** *i.e., the sun*   [8]**predominance** *astrological supremacy*
[12]**tow'ring . . . place** *soaring at her summit*   [13]**mousing** *i.e., normally mouse-eating*
[15]**minions** *darlings*   [16]**flung out** *lunged wildly*   [18]**eat** *ate*   [24]**pretend** *hope for;*
suborned *bribed*   [28]**Thriftless** *wasteful;* **ravin up** *greedily devour*
[31]**named** *selected*

To be invested.

ROSS: Where is Duncan's body?

MACDUFF: Carried to Colmekill,
  The sacred storehouse of his predecessors
  And guardian of their bones.

ROSS: Will you to Scone?   35

MACDUFF: No, cousin, I'll to Fife.

ROSS: Well, I will thither.

MACDUFF: Well, may you see things well done there.
    Adieu,
  Lest our old robes sit easier than our new!

ROSS: Farewell, father.

OLD MAN: God's benison go with you, and with those   40
  That would make good of bad, and friends of foes!

Exeunt omnes.

ACT III

SCENE I *Forres. The palace.*

Enter BANQUO.

BANQUO: Thou hast it now: King, Cawdor, Glamis, all,
  As the weïrd women promised, and I fear
  Thou play'dst most foully for 't. Yet it was said
  It should not stand in thy posterity,
  But that myself should be the root and father   5
  Of many kings. If there come truth from them—
  As upon thee, Macbeth, their speeches shine—
  Why, by the verities on thee made good,
  May they not be my oracles as well
  And set me up in hope? But hush, no more!   10

---

³²**invested** *installed as king*   ⁴⁰**benison** *blessing*   ⁴**stand** *continue*

Sennet[†] sounded. Enter MACBETH *as King,* LADY MACBETH, LENNOX, ROSS, LORDS, *and* ATTENDANTS

MACBETH: Here's our chief guest.
LADY MACBETH: If he had been forgotten,
  It had been as a gap in our great feast,
  And all-thing becoming.
MACBETH: Tonight we hold a solemn supper, sir,
  And I'll request your presence.
BANQUO: Let your Highness   15
  Command upon me, to the which my duties
  Are with a most indissoluble tie
  For ever knit.
MACBETH: Ride you this afternoon?
BANQUO: Ay, my good lord.
MACBETH: We should have else desired your good advice   20
  (Which still hath been both grave and prosperous)
  In this day's council; but we'll take tomorrow.
  Is 't far you ride?
BANQUO: As far, my lord, as will fill up the time
  'Twixt this and supper. Go not my horse the better,   25
  I must become a borrower of the night
  For a dark hour or twain.
MACBETH: Fail not our feast.
BANQUO: My lord, I will not.
MACBETH: We hear our bloody cousins are bestowed
  In England and in Ireland, not confessing   30
  Their cruel parricide, filling their hearers
  With strange invention. But of that tomorrow,
  When therewithal we shall have cause of state
  Craving us jointly. Hie you to horse. Adieu,
  'Till you return at night. Goes Fleance with you?   35
BANQUO: Ay, my good lord: our time does call upon 's.
MACBETH: I wish your horses swift and sure of foot,

[†]**Sennet** *trumpet call*   ¹³**all-thing** *altogether*   ¹⁴**solemn** *ceremonious*
²¹**still** *always;* **grave and prosperous** *weighty and profitable*   ²⁵**Go ... better** *unless my horse goes better than I expect*   ²⁹**are bestowed** *have taken refuge*
³²**invention** *lies*   ^{33–34}**cause ... jointly** *matters of state demanding our joint attention*

And so I do commend you to their backs.
Farewell.

Exit BANQUO.

Let every man be master of his time   40
Till seven at night. To make society
The sweeter welcome, we will keep ourself
'Till supper-time alone. While then, God be with you!

Exeunt LORDS *and all but* MACBETH *and a* SERVANT.

Sirrah, a word with you: attend those men
Our pleasure?   45
ATTENDANT: They are, my lord, without the palace gate.
MACBETH: Bring them before us.

Exit SERVANT.

To be thus is nothing, but to be safely thus —
Our fears in Banquo stick deep,
And in his royalty of nature reigns that   50
Which would be feared. 'Tis much he dares;
And, to that dauntless temper of his mind,
He hath a wisdom that doth guide his valor
To act in safety. There is none but he
Whose being I do fear: and under him   55
My genius is rebuked as it is said
Mark Antony's was by Cæsar. He chid the sisters,
When first they put the name of King upon me,
And bade them speak to him; then prophetlike
They hailed him father to a line of kings.   60
Upon my head they placed a fruitless crown
And put a barren scepter in my gripe,
Thence to be wrenched with an unlineal hand,
No son of mine succeeding. If 't be so,
For Banquo's issue have I filed my mind;   65
For them the gracious Duncan have I murdered;
Put rancors in the vessel of my peace

---

⁴³**While** *until*   ⁴⁴**Sirrah** *(common address to an inferior)*; **attend** *await*
⁴⁶**without** *outside*   ⁴⁸**but** *unless*   ⁴⁹**in** *about*   ⁵¹**would** *must*
⁵²**to** *added to*; **temper** *quality*   ⁵⁶**genius is rebuked** *guardian spirit is cowed*
⁶²**gripe** *grasp*   ⁶⁵**filed** *defiled*   ⁶⁷**rancors** *bitter enmities*

Only for them, and mine eternal jewel
Given to the common enemy of man,
To make them kings, the seeds of Banquo kings!   70
Rather than so, come, fate, into the list,
And champion me to th' utterance! Who's there?

Enter SERVANT *and* TWO MURDERERS.

Now go to the door, and stay there till we call.

Exit SERVANT.

Was it not yesterday we spoke together?
MURDERERS: It was, so please your Highness.
MACBETH: Well then, now   75
   Have you considered of my speeches? Know
   That it was he in the times past, which held you
   So under fortune, which you thought had been
   Our innocent self: this I made good to you
   In our last conference; passed in probation with you,   80
   How you were borne in hand, how crossed; the instruments,
   Who wrought with them, and all things else that might
   To half a soul and to a notion crazed
   Say "Thus did Banquo."
FIRST MURDERER: You made it known to us.
MACBETH: I did so; and went further, which is now   85
   Our point of second meeting. Do you find
   Your patience so predominant in your nature,
   That you can let this go? Are you so gospeled,
   To pray for this good man and for his issue,
   Whose heavy hand hath bowed you to the grave   90
   And beggared yours for ever?
FIRST MURDERER: We are men, my liege.
MACBETH: Ay, in the catalogue ye go for men;
   As hounds and greyhounds, mongrels, spaniels, curs,

[68]**eternal jewel** *i.e., soul*   [69]**common enemy of man** *i.e., the Devil*   [71]**list** *lists, arena for combat*   [72]**champion me to th' utterance** *fight against me to the death*   [77-78]**held . . . fortune** *kept you from good fortune (?)*   [80]**passed in probation** *reviewed the proofs*   [81]**borne in hand** *deceived;* **crossed** *thwarted;* **instruments** *tools*   [83]**half a soul** *a halfwit;* **notion** *mind*   [88]**gospeled** *i.e., made meek by the gospel*   [92]**go for** *pass as*

Shoughs, water-rugs and demi-wolves, are clept
All by the name of dogs: the valued file   95
Distinguishes the swift, the slow, the subtle,
The housekeeper, the hunter, every one
According to the gift which bounteous nature
Hath in him closed, whereby he does receive
Particular addition, from the bill   100
That writes them all alike: and so of men.
Now if you have a station in the file,
Not i' th' worst rank of manhood, say 't,
And I will put that business in your bosoms
Whose execution takes your enemy off,   105
Grapples you to the heart and love of us,
Who wear our health but sickly in his life,
Which in his death were perfect.
SECOND MURDERER: I am one, my liege,
    Whom the vile blows and buffets of the world
    Hath so incensed that I am reckless what   110
    I do to spite the world.
FIRST MURDERER: And I another
    So weary with disasters, tugged with fortune,
    That I would set my life on any chance,
    To mend it or be rid on 't.
MACBETH: Both of you
    Know Banquo was your enemy.
BOTH MURDERERS: True, my lord.   115
MACBETH: So is he mine, and in such bloody distance
    That every minute of his being thrusts
    Against my near'st of life: and though I could
    With barefaced power sweep him from my sight
    And bid my will avouch it, yet I must not,   120
    For certain friends that are both his and mine,
    Whose loves I may not drop, but wail his fall

---

⁹⁴Shoughs, water-rugs *shaggy dogs, long-haired dogs;* clept *called*
⁹⁵valued file *classification by valuable traits*   ⁹⁷housekeeper *watchdog*
⁹⁹closed *enclosed*   ¹⁰⁰Particular . . . bill *special distinction in opposition to the list*
¹⁰⁷wear . . . life *have only imperfect health while he lives*   ¹¹³set *risk*
¹¹⁶distance *quarrel*   ¹¹⁸near'st of life *most vital spot*   ¹²⁰avouch *justify*
¹²¹For *because of*   ¹²²wail his fall *bewail his death*

Who I myself struck down: and thence it is
That I to your assistance do make love,
Masking the business from the common eye   125
For sundry weighty reasons.
SECOND MURDERER: We shall, my lord,
  Perform what you command us.
FIRST MURDERER: Though our lives——
MACBETH: Your spirits shine through you. Within this
    hour at most
  I will advise you where to plant yourselves,
  Acquaint you with the perfect spy o' th' time,   130
  The moment on 't; for 't must be done tonight,
  And something from the palace; always thought
  That I require a clearness: and with him—
  To leave no rubs nor botches in the work—
  Fleance his son, that keeps him company,   135
  Whose absence is no less material to me
  Than is his father's, must embrace the fate
  Of that dark hour. Resolve yourselves apart:
  I'll come to you anon.
MURDERERS: We are resolved, my lord.
MACBETH: I'll call upon you straight. Abide within.   140
  It is concluded: Banquo, thy soul's flight,
  If it find heaven, must find it out tonight.
Exeunt.

SCENE II *The palace.*

Enter LADY MACBETH *and a* SERVANT.

LADY MACBETH: Is Banquo gone from court?
SERVANT: Ay, madam, but returns again tonight.

---

[130]**perfect spy** *exact information (?) ("spy" literally means "observation"; apparently*
Macbeth already has the Third Murderer in mind)   [131]**on 't** *of it*
[132]**something** *some distance;* **thought** *remembered*   [133]**clearness** *freedom from*
suspicion   [134]**rubs** *flaws*   [138]**Resolve yourselves apart** *decide by yourselves*
[140]**straight** *immediately*

LADY MACBETH: Say to the King, I would attend his leisure
  For a few words.
SERVANT: Madam, I will.

Exit.

LADY MACBETH: Nought's had, all's spent,
  Where our desire is got without content: 5
  'Tis safer to be that which we destroy
  Than by destruction dwell in doubtful joy.

Enter MACBETH.

  How now, my lord! Why do you keep alone,
  Of sorriest fancies your companions making,
  Using those thoughts which should indeed have died   10
  With them they think on? Things without all remedy
  Should be without regard: what's done is done.
MACBETH: We have scorched the snake, not killed it:
  She'll close and be herself, whilst our poor malice
  Remains in danger of her former tooth.   15
  But let the frame of things disjoint, both the worlds suffer,
  Ere we will eat our meal in fear, and sleep
  In the affliction of these terrible dreams
  That shake us nightly: better be with the dead,
  Whom we, to gain our peace, have sent to peace,   20
  Than on the torture of the mind to lie
  In restless ecstasy. Duncan is in his grave;
  After life's fitful fever he sleeps well.
  Treason has done his worst: nor steel, nor poison,
  Malice domestic, foreign levy, nothing,   25
  Can touch him further.
LADY MACBETH: Come on.
  Gentle my lord, sleek o'er your rugged looks;
  Be bright and jovial among your guests tonight.
MACBETH: So shall I, love; and so, I pray, be you:

---

[9]sorriest *most despicable*   [11]without *beyond*   [13]scorched *slashed, scored*
[14]close *heal;* poor malice *feeble enmity*   [16]frame . . . disjoint *universe collapse;*
both the worlds *heaven and earth* (?)   [21]torture *i.e., rack*   [22]ecstasy *frenzy*
[24]his *its*   [25]Malice domestic *civil war*   [27]sleek *smooth;* rugged *furrowed*

Let your remembrance apply to Banquo; 30
Present him eminence, both with eye and tongue:
Unsafe the while, that we must lave
Our honors in these flattering streams
And make our faces vizards to our hearts,
Disguising what they are.

LADY MACBETH: You must leave this. 35

MACBETH: O, full of scorpions is my mind, dear wife!
Thou know'st that Banquo, and his Fleance, lives.

LADY MACBETH: But in them nature's copy's not eterne.

MACBETH: There's comfort yet; they are assailable.
Then be thou jocund. Ere the bat hath flown 40
His cloistered flight, ere to black Hecate's summons
The shard-borne beetle with his drowsy hums
Hath rung night's yawning peal, there shall be done
A deed of dreadful note.

LADY MACBETH: What's to be done?

MACBETH: Be innocent of the knowledge, dearest chuck, 45
Till thou applaud the deed. Come, seeling night,
Scarf up the tender eye of pitiful day,
And with thy bloody and invisible hand
Cancel and tear to pieces that great bond
Which keeps me pale! Light thickens, and the crow 50
Makes wing to th' rooky wood.
Good things of day begin to droop and drowse,
Whiles night's black agents to their preys do rouse.
Thou marvel'st at my words: but hold thee still;
Things bad begun make strong themselves by ill: 55
So, prithee, go with me.

Exeunt.

---

[30]Let . . . Banquo *focus your thoughts on Banquo*   [31]Present him eminence *honor him*   [32]Unsafe . . . lave *i.e., you and I are unsafe because we must dip*   [34]vizards *masks*   [38]nature's copy *nature's lease (?) imitation (i.e., a son) made by nature (?)*   [42]shard-borne *borne on scaly wings (?) dung-bred (?)*   [45]chuck *chick (term of endearment)*   [46]seeling *eye-closing*   [47]Scarf up *blindfold*   [49]bond *i.e., between Banquo and fate (?) Banquo's lease on life (?) Macbeth's link to humanity (?)*   [51]rooky *full of rooks*

Scene III *Near the palace.*

Enter THREE MURDERERS.

FIRST MURDERER: But who did bid thee join with us?

THIRD MURDERER: Macbeth.

SECOND MURDERER: He needs not our mistrust; since he delivers
   Our offices and what we have to do
   To the direction just.

FIRST MURDERER: Then stand with us.
   The west yet glimmers with some streaks of day.   5
   Now spurs the lated traveler apace
   To gain the timely inn, and near approaches
   The subject of our watch.

THIRD MURDERER: Hark! I hear horses.

BANQUO *(Within)*: Give us a light there, ho!

SECOND MURDERER: Then 'tis he. The rest
   That are within the note of expectation   10
   Already are i' th' court.

FIRST MURDERER: His horses go about.

THIRD MURDERER: Almost a mile: but he does usually—
   So all men do—from hence to th' palace gate
   Make it their walk.

Enter BANQUO *and* FLEANCE, *with a torch.*

SECOND MURDERER: A light, a light!

THIRD MURDERER: 'Tis he.

FIRST MURDERER: Stand to 't.   15

BANQUO: It will be rain tonight.

FIRST MURDERER: Let it come down.

They set upon BANQUO.

BANQUO: O, treachery! Fly, good Fleance, fly, fly, fly!

Exit FLEANCE.

  Thou mayst revenge. O slave! *(Dies.)*

THIRD MURDERER: Who did strike out the light?

---

²⁻⁴**He needs . . . just** *we need not mistrust him (i.e., the Third Murderer) since he describes our duties according to exact directions*   ⁶**lated** *belated*
¹⁰**within the note of expectation** *on the list of expected guests*

FIRST MURDERER: Was 't not the way?
THIRD MURDERER: There's but one down; the son is fled.   20
SECOND MURDERER: We have lost best half of our affair.
FIRST MURDERER: Well, let's away and say how much is done.
Exeunt.

SCENE IV *The palace.*

Banquet prepared. Enter MACBETH, LADY MACBETH, ROSS,
LENNOX, LORDS, *and* ATTENDANTS.

MACBETH: You know your own degrees; sit down:
  At first and last, the hearty welcome.
LORDS: Thanks to your Majesty.
MACBETH: Ourself will mingle with society
  And play the humble host.   5
  Our hostess keeps her state, but in best time
  We will require her welcome.
LADY MACBETH: Pronounce it for me, sir, to all our friends,
  For my heart speaks they are welcome.

Enter FIRST MURDERER.

MACBETH: See, they encounter thee with their hearts' thanks.   10
  Both sides are even: here I'll sit i' th' midst:
  Be large in mirth; anon we'll drink a measure
  The table round. *(Goes to* MURDERER*)* There's blood upon thy
    face.
MURDERER: 'Tis Banquo's then.
MACBETH: 'Tis better thee without than he within.   15
  Is he dispatched?
MURDERER: My lord, his throat is cut; that I did for him.
MACBETH: Thou art the best o' th' cutthroats.
  Yet he's good that did the like for Fleance;
  If thou didst it, thou art the nonpareil.   20

---

[19]**way** *i.e., thing to do*   [1]**degrees** *ranks*   [4]**society** *the company*
[6]**keeps her state** *remains seated in her chair of state*   [7]**require** *request*
[12]**measure** *goblet*   [15]**thee without than he within** *outside you than inside him*

MURDERER: Most royal sir, Fleance is 'scaped.

MACBETH *(Aside):* Then comes my fit again: I had else been perfect,
　Whole as the marble, founded as the rock,
　As broad and general as the casing air:
　But now I am cabined, cribbed, confined, bound in　　　　　25
　To saucy doubts and fears.—But Banquo's safe?

MURDERER: Ay, my good lord: safe in a ditch he bides,
　With twenty trenchèd gashes on his head,
　The least a death to nature.

MACBETH:　　　　　　　　　　Thanks for that.
　(Aside) There the grown serpent lies; the worm that's fled　　　30
　Hath nature that in time will venom breed,
　No teeth for th' present. Get thee gone. Tomorrow
　We'll hear ourselves again.

Exit MURDERER.

LADY MACBETH:　　　　　　　My royal lord,
　You do not give the cheer. The feast is sold
　That is not often vouched, while 'tis a-making,　　　　　35
　'Tis given with welcome. To feed were best at home;
　From thence, the sauce to meat is ceremony;
　Meeting were bare without it.

Enter the GHOST OF BANQUO, *and sits in* MACBETH's *place.*

MACBETH:　　　　　　　　　Sweet remembrancer!
　Now good digestion wait on appetite,
　And health on both!

LENNOX:　　　　　　　May 't please your Highness sit.　　　　　40

MACBETH: Here had we now our country's honor roofed,
　Were the graced person of our Banquo present—
　Who may I rather challenge for unkindness
　Than pity for mischance!

---

²³founded *firmly based*　²⁴broad . . . casing *unconfined as the surrounding*
²⁵cribbed *penned up*　²⁶saucy *insolent*　²⁸trenchèd *trenchlike*　³⁰worm *serpent*
³³hear ourselves *talk it over*　³⁴the cheer *a sense of cordiality*
³⁴⁻³⁶The feast . . . home *i.e., the feast seems sold (not given) during which the host fails to welcome the guests. Mere eating is best done at home*　³⁷meat *food*
³⁸remembrancer *reminder*　⁴¹our country's honor roofed *our nobility under one roof*　⁴³⁻⁴⁴Who . . . mischance *whom I hope I may reprove because he is unkind rather than pity because he has encountered an accident*

ROSS: His absence, sir,
    Lays blame upon his promise. Please 't your Highness   45
    To grace us with your royal company?
MACBETH: The table's full.
LENNOX: Here is a place reserved, sir.
MACBETH: Where?
LENNOX: Here, my good lord. What is 't that moves
    your Highness?
MACBETH: Which of you have done this?
LORDS: What, my good lord?   50
MACBETH: Thou canst not say I did it. Never shake
    Thy gory locks at me.
ROSS: Gentlemen, rise, his Highness is not well.
LADY MACBETH: Sit, worthy friends. My lord is often thus,
    And hath been from his youth. Pray you, keep seat.   55
    The fit is momentary; upon a thought
    He will again be well. If much you note him,
    You shall offend him and extend his passion.
    Feed, and regard him not.—Are you a man?
MACBETH: Ay, and a bold one, that dare look on that   60
    Which might appall the devil.
LADY MACBETH: O proper stuff!
    This is the very painting of your fear.
    This is the air-drawn dagger which, you said,
    Led you to Duncan. O, these flaws and starts,
    Impostors to true fear, would well become   65
    A woman's story at a winter's fire,
    Authorized by her grandam. Shame itself!
    Why do you make such faces? When all's done,
    You look but on a stool.
MACBETH: Prithee, see there!
    Behold! Look! Lo! How say you?   70
    Why, what care I? If thou canst nod, speak too.
    If charnel houses and our graves must send

---

[56] **upon a thought** *as quick as thought*   [58] **extend his passion** *lengthen his fit*
[64] **flaws** *gusts, outburst*   [65] **to** *compared with*   [67] **Authorized** *vouched for*
[72] **charnel houses** *vaults containing bones*

Those that we bury back, our monuments
Shall be the maws of kites.

Exit GHOST.

LADY MACBETH: What, quite unmanned in folly?

MACBETH: If I stand here, I saw him.

LADY MACBETH: Fie, for shame!   75

MACBETH: Blood hath been shed ere now, i' th' olden time,
Ere humane statute purged the gentle weal;
Ay, and since too, murders have been performed
Too terrible for the ear. The times has been
That, when the brains were out, the man would die,   80
And there an end; but now they rise again,
With twenty mortal murders on their crowns,
And push us from our stools. This is more strange
Than such a murder is.

LADY MACBETH: My worthy lord,
Your noble friends do lack you.

MACBETH: I do forget.   85
Do not muse at me, my most worthy friends;
I have a strange infirmity, which is nothing
To those that know me. Come, love and health to all!
Then I'll sit down. Give me some wine, fill full.

Enter GHOST.

I drink to th' general joy o' th' whole table,   90
And to our dear friend Banquo, whom we miss;
Would he were here! To all and him we thirst,
And all to all.

LORDS: Our duties, and the pledge.

MACBETH: Avaunt! and quit my sight! Let the earth hide thee!
Thy bones are marrowless, thy blood is cold;   95
Thou hast no speculation in those eyes
Which thou dost glare with.

LADY MACBETH: Think of this, good peers,

[73-74]**our ... kites** *our tombs shall be the bellies of rapacious birds*
[77]**purged the gentle weal** *i.e., cleansed the state and made it gentle*
[82]**mortal ... crowns** *deadly wounds on their heads*   [92]**thirst** *desire to drink*
[93]**all to all** *everything to everybody (?) let everybody drink to everybody (?)*
[96]**speculation** *sight*

But as a thing of custom; 'tis no other.
Only it spoils the pleasure of the time.
MACBETH: What man dare, I dare.   100
    Approach thou like the rugged Russian bear,
    The armed rhinoceros, or th' Hyrcan tiger;
    Take any shape but that, and my firm nerves
    Shall never tremble. Or be alive again,
    And dare me to the desert with thy sword.   105
    If trembling I inhabit then, protest me
    The baby of a girl. Hence, horrible shadow!
    Unreal mock'ry, hence!
Exit GHOST.
                                Why, so: being gone,
    I am a man again. Pray you, sit still.
LADY MACBETH: You have displaced the mirth, broke the   110
    good meeting,
    With most admired disorder.
MACBETH: Can such things be,
    And overcome us like a summer's cloud,
    Without our special wonder? You make me strange
    Even to the disposition that I owe,
    When now I think you can behold such sights,   115
    And keep the natural ruby of your cheeks,
    When mine is blanched with fear.
ROSS: What sights, my lord?
LADY MACBETH: I pray you, speak not: he grows worse and worse;
    Question enrages him: at once, good night.
    Stand not upon the order of your going,   120
    But go at once.
LENNOX: Good night; and better health
    Attend his Majesty!
LADY MACBETH: A kind good night to all!
Exeunt LORDS.
MACBETH: It will have blood, they say: blood will have blood.

---

[102]**Hyrcan** *of Hyrcania (near the Caspian Sea)*   [103]**nerves** *sinews*   [105]**the desert**
a lonely place   [106-07]**If ... girl** *if then I tremble, proclaim me a baby girl*
[112]**overcome us** *come over us*   [113-14]**You ... owe** *i.e., you make me wonder what
my nature is*   [120]**Stand ... going** *do not insist on departing in your order of rank*

143

Stones have been known to move and trees to speak;
Augures and understood relations have 125
By maggot-pies and choughs and rooks brought forth
The secret'st man of blood. What is the night?
LADY MACBETH: Almost at odds with morning, which is which.
MACBETH: How say'st thou, that Macduff denies his person
  At our great bidding?
LADY MACBETH: Did you send to him, sir? 130
MACBETH: I hear it by the way, but I will send:
  There's not a one of them but in his house
  I keep a servant fee'd. I will tomorrow,
  And betimes I will, to the weïrd sisters:
  More shall they speak, for now I am bent to know 135
  By the worst means the worst. For mine own good
  All causes shall give way. I am in blood
  Stepped in so far that, should I wade no more,
  Returning were as tedious as go o'er.
  Strange things I have in head that will to hand, 140
  Which must be acted ere they may be scanned.
LADY MACBETH: You lack the season of all natures, sleep.
MACBETH: Come, we'll to sleep. My strange and self-abuse
  Is the initiate fear that wants hard use.
  We are yet but young in deed. 145
Exeunt.

SCENE V   *A Witches' haunt.*

Thunder. Enter the THREE WITCHES, *meeting* HECATE.

FIRST WITCH: Why, how now, Hecate! you look angerly.
HECATE: Have I not reason, beldams as you are,

125Augures and understood relations *auguries and comprehended reports*
126By . . . forth *by magpies, choughs, and rooks (telltale birds) revealed*
127What is the night *What time of night is it?*   128at odds *striving*
131by the way *incidentally*   133fee'd *i.e., paid to spy*   134betimes *quickly*
135bent *determined*   137causes *considerations*   141may be scanned *can be examined*   142season of all natures *seasoning (preservative) of all living creatures*
144initiate . . . use *beginner's fear that lacks hardening practice*   2beldams *hags*

Saucy and overbold? How did you dare
To trade and traffic with Macbeth
In riddles and affairs of death;   5
And I, the mistress of your charms,
The close contriver of all harms,
Was never called to bear my part,
Or show the glory of our art?
And, which is worse, all you have done   10
Hath been but for a wayward son,
Spiteful and wrathful; who, as other do,
Loves for his own ends, not for you.
But make amends now: get you gone,
And at the pit of Acheron   15
Meet me i' th' morning: thither he
Will come to know his destiny.
Your vessels and your spells provide,
Your charms and everything beside.
I am for th' air: this night I'll spend   20
Unto a dismal and a fatal end:
Great business must be wrought ere noon.
Upon the corner of the moon
There hangs a vap'rous drop profound;
I'll catch it ere it come to ground: 25
And that distilled by magic sleights
Shall raise such artificial sprites
As by the strength of their illusion
Shall draw him on to his confusion.
He shall spurn fate, scorn death, and bear   30
His hopes 'bove wisdom, grace, and fear:
And you all know security
Is mortals' chiefest enemy.
Music and a song.
Hark! I am called; my little spirit, see,
Sits in a foggy cloud and stays for me.   35
Exit.

---

[7]**close contriver** *secret inventor*   [15]**Acheron** *(river of Hades)*   [24]**profound** *heavy*
[26]**sleights** *arts*   [27]**artificial sprites** *spirits created by magic arts (?) artful (cunning)*
spirits (?)   [29]**confusion** *ruin*   [32]**security** *overconfidence*

Sing within, "Come away, come away," &c.
FIRST WITCH: Come, let's make haste; she'll soon be back again.
Exeunt.

SCENE VI *The palace.*

Enter LENNOX *and another* LORD.

LENNOX: My former speeches have but hit your thoughts,
    Which can interpret farther. Only I say
    Things have been strangely borne. The gracious Duncan
    Was pitied of Macbeth: marry, he was dead.
    And the right-valiant Banquo walked too late;   5
    Whom, you may say, if 't please you, Fleance killed,
    For Fleance fled. Men must not walk too late.
    Who cannot want the thought, how monstrous
    It was for Malcolm and for Donalbain
    To kill their gracious father? Damnèd fact!   10
    How it did grieve Macbeth! Did he not straight,
    In pious rage, the two delinquents tear,
    That were the slaves of drink and thralls of sleep?
    Was not that nobly done? Ay, and wisely too;
    For 'twould have angered any heart alive   15
    To hear the men deny 't. So that I say
    He has borne all things well: and I do think
    That, had he Duncan's sons under his key—
    As, an 't please heaven, he shall not—they should find
    What 'twere to kill a father. So should Fleance.   20
    But, peace! for from broad words, and 'cause he failed
    His presence at the tyrant's feast, I hear,
    Macduff lives in disgrace. Sir, can you tell
    Where he bestows himself?

[1]**My . . . thoughts** *i.e., my recent words have only coincided with what you have in your mind*   [3]**borne** *managed*   [8]**cannot want the thought** *can fail to think*   [10]**fact** *evil deed*   [13]**thralls** *slaves*   [17]**borne** *managed*   [19]**an 't** *if it*   [21]**for from broad words** *because of frank talk*

LORD: The son of Duncan
  From whom this tyrant holds the due of birth,   25
  Lives in the English court, and is received
  Of the most pious Edward with such grace
  That the malevolence of fortune nothing
  Takes from his high respect. Thither Macduff
  Is gone to pray the holy King, upon his aid   30
  To wake Northumberland and warlike Siward;
  That by the help of these, with Him above
  To ratify the work, we may again
  Give to our tables meat, sleep to our nights,
  Free from our feasts and banquets bloody knives,   35
  Do faithful homage and receive free honors:
  All which we pine for now. And this report
  Hath so exasperate the King that he
  Prepares for some attempt of war.
LENNOX: Sent he to Macduff?
LORD: He did: and with an absolute "Sir, not I,"   40
  The cloudy messenger turns me his back,
  And hums, as who should say "You'll rue the time
  That clogs me with this answer."
LENNOX: And that well might
  Advise him to a caution, t' hold what distance
  His wisdom can provide. Some holy angel   45
  Fly to the court of England and unfold
  His message ere he come, that a swift blessing
  May soon return to this our suffering country
  Under a hand accursed!
LORD: I'll send my prayers with him.
Exeunt.

---

[25]**due of birth** *birthright*   [27]**Edward** *Edward the Confessor (reigned 1042–1066)*
[28–29]**nothing . . . respect** *does not diminish the high respect in which he is held*
[30]**upon his aid** *to aid him (Malcolm)*   [31]**To wake Northumberland** *i.e., to arouse the people in an English county near Scotland*   [36]**free** *freely granted*
[41]**cloudy** *disturbed*   [43]**clogs** *burdens*

ACT IV

SCENE I *A Witches' haunt.*

Thunder. Enter the THREE WITCHES.

FIRST WITCH: Thrice the brinded cat hath mewed.
SECOND WITCH: Thrice and once the hedge-pig whined.
THIRD WITCH: Harpier cries. 'Tis time, 'tis time.
FIRST WITCH: Round about the caldron go:
  In the poisoned entrails throw.   5
  Toad, that under cold stone
  Days and nights has thirty-one
  Swelt'red venom sleeping got,
  Boil thou first i' th' charmèd pot.
ALL: Double, double, toil and trouble;   10
  Fire burn and caldron bubble.
SECOND WITCH: Fillet of a fenny snake,
  In the caldron boil and bake;
  Eye of newt and toe of frog,
  Wool of bat and tongue of dog,   15
  Adder's fork and blindworm's sting,
  Lizard's leg and howlet's wing,
  For a charm of pow'rful trouble,
  Like a hell-broth boil and bubble.
ALL: Double, double, toil and trouble;   20
  Fire burn and caldron bubble.
THIRD WITCH: Scale of dragon, tooth of wolf,
  Witch's mummy, maw and gulf
  Of the ravined salt-sea shark,
  Root of hemlock digged i' th' dark,   25
  Liver of blaspheming Jew,
  Gall of goat, and slips of yew

---

[1]brinded *brindled*   [2]hedge-pig *hedgehog*   [3]Harpier *an attendant spirit, like
Graymalkin and Paddock in Act I, Scene I*   [8]Swelt'red venom sleeping got
venom sweated out while sleeping   [12]Fillet *slice; fenny from a swamp*
[16]fork *forked tongue;* blindworm *a legless lizard*   [17]howlet *owlet*
[23]Witch's mummy *mummified flesh of a witch;* maw and gulf *stomach and gullet*
[24]ravined *ravenous*

Slivered in the moon's eclipse,
Nose of Turk and Tartar's lips,
Finger of birth-strangled babe   30
Ditch-delivered by a drab
Make the gruel thick and slab:
Add thereto a tiger's chaudron,
For th' ingredience of our caldron.
ALL: Double, double, toil and trouble;   35
  Fire burn and caldron bubble.
SECOND WITCH: Cool it with a baboon's blood,
  Then the charm is firm and good.

Enter HECATE *and the other* THREE WITCHES.

HECATE: O, well done! I commend your pains;
  And every one shall share i' th' gains: 40
  And now about the caldron sing,
  Like elves and fairies in a ring,
  Enchanting all that you put in.

Music and a song: "Black Spirits," &c.
Exeunt HECATE *and the other* THREE WITCHES.

SECOND WITCH: By the pricking of my thumbs,
  Something wicked this way comes: 45
  Open, locks,
  Whoever knocks!

Enter MACBETH.

MACBETH: How now, you secret, black, and midnight hags!
  What is 't you do?
ALL: A deed without a name.
MACBETH: I conjure you, by that which you profess,   50
  Howe'er you come to know it, answer me:
  Though you untie the winds and let them fight
  Against the churches; though the yesty waves
  Confound and swallow navigation up;
  Though bladed corn be lodged and trees blown down;   55
  Though castles topple on their warders' heads;

---

³¹**Ditch-delivered by a drab** *born in a ditch of a harlot*   ³²**slab** *viscous*
³³**chaudron** *entrails*   ⁵³**yesty** *foamy*   ⁵⁴**Confound** *destroy*
⁵⁵**bladed corn be lodged** *grain in the ear be beaten down*

Though palaces and pyramids do slope
Their heads to their foundations; though the treasure
Of nature's germens tumble all together,
Even till destruction sicken, answer me   60
To what I ask you.

FIRST WITCH: Speak.

SECOND WITCH: Demand.

THIRD WITCH: We'll answer.

FIRST WITCH: Say, if th' hadst rather hear it from our mouths,
Or from our masters?

MACBETH: Call 'em, let me see 'em.

FIRST WITCH: Pour in sow's blood, that hath eaten
Her nine farrow; grease that's sweaten   65
From the murderer's gibbet throw
Into the flame.

ALL: Come, high or low,
Thyself and office deftly show!

Thunder. FIRST APPARITION: *an Armed Head.*

MACBETH: Tell me, thou unknown power——

FIRST WITCH: He knows thy thought:
Hear his speech, but say thou nought.   70

FIRST APPARITION: Macbeth! Macbeth! Macbeth! Beware
    Macduff!
Beware the Thane of Fife. Dismiss me: enough.

He descends.

MACBETH: Whate'er thou art, for thy good caution thanks:
Thou hast harped my fear aright. But one word more——

FIRST WITCH: He will not be commanded. Here's another,   75
More potent than the first.

Thunder. SECOND APPARITION: *a Bloody Child.*

SECOND APPARITION: Macbeth! Macbeth! Macbeth!

MACBETH: Had I three ears, I'd hear thee.

SECOND APPARITION: Be bloody, bold, and resolute! Laugh to
    scorn

---

[57]slope *bend*   [59]nature's germens *seeds of all life*   [60]sicken *i.e., sicken at its own
work*   [65]farrow *young pigs;* sweaten *sweated*   [68]office *function*   [74]harped *hit
upon, struck the note of*

The pow'r of man, for none of woman born   80
  Shall harm Macbeth.

Descends.

MACBETH: Then live, Macduff: what need I fear of thee?
  But yet I'll make assurance double sure,
  And take a bond of fate. Thou shalt not live;
  That I may tell pale-hearted fear it lies,   85
  And sleep in spite of thunder.

Thunder. THIRD APPARITION: *a Child Crowned, with a tree in his hand.*

                         What is this,
  That rises like the issue of a king,
  And wears upon his baby-brow the round
  And top of sovereignty?

ALL: Listen, but speak not to 't.

THIRD APPARITION: Be lion-mettled, proud, and take no care   90
  Who chafes, who frets, or where conspirers are:
  Macbeth shall never vanquished be until
  Great Birnam Wood to high Dunsinane Hill
  Shall come against him.

Descends.

MACBETH: That will never be.
  Who can impress the forest, bid the tree   95
  Unfix his earth-bound root? Sweet bodements, good!
  Rebellious dead, rise never, till the Wood
  Of Birnam rise, and our high-placed Macbeth
  Shall live the lease of nature, pay his breath
  To time and mortal custom. Yet my heart   100
  Throbs to know one thing. Tell me, if your art
  Can tell so much: shall Banquo's issue ever
  Reign in this kingdom?

---

[84]**take a bond of fate** *get a guarantee from fate (i.e., he will kill Macduff and thus will compel fate to keep its word)*   [87]**issue** *offspring*   [88–89]**round/And top of sovereignty** *i.e., crown*   [95]**impress** *conscript*   [96]**bodements** *prophecies*   [97]**Rebellious dead** *(perhaps a reference to Banquo; but perhaps a misprint for "rebellion's head")*   [99]**lease of nature** *natural lifespan*   [100]**mortal custom** *natural death*

ALL: Seek to know no more.

MACBETH: I will be satisfied. Deny me this,
 And an eternal curse fall on you! Let me know.   105
 Why sinks that caldron? And what noise is this?

Hautboys.

FIRST WITCH: Show!
SECOND WITCH: Show!
THIRD WITCH: Show!
ALL: Show his eyes, and grieve his heart;   110
 Come like shadows, so depart!

A show of eight KINGS *and* BANQUO, *last* KING *with a glass† in his hand.*

MACBETH: Thou art too like the spirit of Banquo. Down!
 Thy crown does sear mine eyelids. And thy hair,
 Thou other gold-bound brow, is like the first.
 A third is like the former. Filthy hags!   115
 Why do you show me this? A fourth! Start, eyes!
 What, will the line stretch out to th' crack of doom?
 Another yet! A seventh! I'll see no more.
 And yet the eighth appears, who bears a glass
 Which shows me many more; and some I see   120
 That twofold balls and treble scepters carry:
 Horrible sight! Now I see 'tis true;
 For the blood-boltered Banquo smiles upon me,
 And points at them for his. What, is this so?

FIRST WITCH: Ay, sir, all this is so. But why   125
 Stands Macbeth thus amazedly?
 Come, sisters, cheer we up his sprites,
 And show the best of our delights:
 I'll charm the air to give a sound,
 While you perform your antic round,   130
 That this great king may kindly say
 Our duties did his welcome pay.

---

[104]satisfied *i.e., fully informed*   [106]noise *music*   †glass *mirror*   [116]Start *i.e.,
from the sockets*   [117]crack of doom *blast (of a trumpet?)*   [121]twofold balls and
treble scepters *(coronation emblems)*   [123]blood-boltered *matted with blood*
[127]sprites *spirits*   [130]antic round *grotesque circular dance*

Music. THE WITCHES *dance, and vanish.*

MACBETH: Where are they? Gone? Let this pernicious hour
   Stand aye accursèd in the calendar!
   Come in, without there!

Enter LENNOX.

LENNOX: What's your Grace's will?   135
MACBETH: Saw you the weïrd sisters?
LENNOX: No, my lord.
MACBETH: Came they not by you?
LENNOX: No indeed, my lord.
MACBETH: Infected be the air whereon they ride,
   And damned all those that trust them! I did hear
   The galloping of horse. Who was 't came by?   140
LENNOX: 'Tis two or three, my lord, that bring you word
   Macduff is fled to England.
MACBETH: Fled to England?
LENNOX: Ay, my good lord.
MACBETH *(Aside)*: Time, thou anticipat'st my dread exploits.
   The flighty purpose never is o'ertook   145
   Unless the deed go with it. From this moment
   The very firstlings of my heart shall be
   The firstlings of my hand. And even now,
   To crown my thoughts with acts, be it thought and done:
   The castle of Macduff I will surprise;   150
   Seize upon Fife; give to th' edge o' th' sword
   His wife, his babes, and all unfortunate souls
   That trace him in his line. No boasting like a fool;
   This deed I'll do before this purpose cool:
   But no more sights!—Where are these gentlemen?   155
   Come, bring me where they are.

Exeunt.

---

[140]horse *horses (or "horsemen")*   [144]anticipat'st *foretold*   [145-46]The flighty . . . it
the fleeting plan is never fulfilled unless an action accompanies it   [147]firstlings of
my heart *i.e., first thoughts, impulses*   [150]surprise *attack suddenly*   [153]trace him
in his line *are of his lineage*

Enter MACDUFF'S WIFE, *her* SON, *and* ROSS.

LADY MACDUFF: What had he done, to make him fly the land?
ROSS: You must have patience, madam.
LADY MACDUFF: He had none:
　His flight was madness. When our actions do not,
　Our fears do make us traitors.
ROSS: You know not
　Whether it was his wisdom or his fear.   5
LADY MACDUFF: Wisdom! To leave his wife, to leave his babes,
　His mansion and his titles, in a place
　From whence himself does fly? He loves us not;
　He wants the natural touch: for the poor wren,
　The most diminutive of birds, will fight,   10
　Her young ones in her nest, against the owl.
　All is the fear and nothing is the love;
　As little is the wisdom, where the flight
　So runs against all reason.
ROSS: My dearest coz,
　I pray you, school yourself. But, for your husband,   15
　He is noble, wise, judicious, and best knows
　The fits o' th' season. I dare not speak much further:
　But cruel are the times, when we are traitors
　And do not know ourselves; when we hold rumor
　From what we fear, yet know not what we fear,   20
　But float upon a wild and violent sea
　Each way and move. I take my leave of you.
　Shall not be long but I'll be here again.
　Things at the worst will cease, or else climb upward
　To what they were before. My pretty cousin,   25
　Blessing upon you!
LADY MACDUFF: Fathered he is, and yet he's fatherless.
ROSS: I am so much a fool, should I stay longer,

---

[7]titles *possessions*　[9]wants the natural touch *i.e., lacks natural affection for his*
wife and children　[14]coz *cousin*　[15]school *control*　[17]fits o' th' season *disorders*
of the time　[19-20]hold rumor . . . fear *believe rumors because we fear*
[24]cease *i.e., cease worrying*

It would be my disgrace and your discomfort.
I take my leave at once.

Exit ROSS.

LADY MACDUFF: Sirrah, your father's dead: 30
  And what will you do now? How will you live?
SON: As birds do, mother.
LADY MACDUFF: What, with worms and flies?
SON: With what I get, I mean; and so do they.
LADY MACDUFF: Poor bird! thou'dst never fear the net nor lime,
  The pitfall nor the gin.   35
SON: Why should I, mother? Poor birds they are not set for.
  My father is not dead, for all your saying.
LADY MACDUFF: Yes, he is dead: how wilt thou do for a father?
SON: Nay, how will you do for a husband?
LADY MACDUFF: Why, I can buy me twenty at any market.   40
SON: Then you'll buy 'em to sell again.
LADY MACDUFF: Thou speak'st with all thy wit, and yet, i' faith,
  With wit enough for thee.
SON: Was my father a traitor, mother?
LADY MACDUFF: Ay, that he was.   45
SON: What is a traitor?
LADY MACDUFF: Why, one that swears and lies.
SON: And be all traitors that do so?
LADY MACDUFF: Every one that does so is a traitor, and must be
  hanged.   50
SON: And must they all be hanged that swear and lie?
LADY MACDUFF: Every one.
SON: Who must hang them?
LADY MACDUFF: Why, the honest men.
SON: Then the liars and swearers are fools; for there are liars   55
  and swearers enow to beat the honest men and hang up them.
LADY MACDUFF: Now, God help thee, poor monkey! But how wilt
  thou do for a father?

---

[29]**It would be my disgrace** *i.e., I would weep*   [30]**Sirrah** *(here an affectionate
address to a child)*   [34]**lime** *bird-lime (smeared on branches to catch birds)*
[35]**gin** *trap*   [41]**sell** *betray*   [43]**for thee** *i.e., for a child*   [47]**swears and lies** *i.e., takes
an oath and breaks it*   [56]**enow** *enough*

SON: If he were dead, you'd weep for him. If you would not,
    it were a good sign that I should quickly have a new father.   60
LADY MACDUFF: Poor prattler, how thou talk'st!

Enter a MESSENGER.

MESSENGER: Bless you, fair dame! I am not to you known,
    Though in your state of honor I am perfect.
    I doubt some danger does approach you nearly:
    If you will take a homely man's advice,   65
    Be not found here; hence, with your little ones.
    To fright you thus, methinks I am too savage;
    To do worse to you were fell cruelty,
    Which is too nigh your person. Heaven preserve you!
    I dare abide no longer.

Exit MESSENGER.

LADY MACDUFF: Whither should I fly?   70
    I have done no harm. But I remember now
    I am in this earthly world, where to do harm
    Is often laudable, to do good sometime
    Accounted dangerous folly. Why then, alas,
    Do I put up that womanly defense,   75
    To say I have done no harm?—What are these faces?

Enter MURDERERS.

MURDERER: Where is your husband?
LADY MACDUFF: I hope, in no place so unsanctified
    Where such as thou mayst find him.
MURDERER: He's a traitor.
SON: Thou li'st, thou shag-eared villain!
MURDERER: What, you egg!   80
(Stabbing him.)
    Young fry of treachery!
SON: He has killed me, mother:
    Run away, I pray you!
(Dies.)

Exit LADY MACDUFF, *crying* "Murder!" *followed by* MURDERERS.

---

[63]in . . . perfect *I am fully informed of your honorable rank*   [64]doubt *fear*
[65]homely *plain*   [68]fell *fierce;*   [80]shag-eared *hairy-eared (?), with shaggy hair hanging over the ears (?)*   [81]fry *spawn*

SCENE III   *England. Before the King's palace.*

Enter MALCOLM *and* MACDUFF.

MALCOLM: Let us seek out some desolate shade, and there
  Weep our sad bosoms empty.

MACDUFF: Let us rather
  Hold fast, the mortal sword, and like good men
  Bestride our down-fall'n birthdom. Each new morn
  New widows howl, new orphans cry, new sorrows   5
  Strike heaven on the face, that it resounds
  As if it felt with Scotland and yelled out
  Like syllable of dolor.

MALCOLM: What I believe, I'll wail;
  What know, believe; and what I can redress,
  As I shall find the time to friend, I will.   10
  What you have spoke, it may be so perchance.
  This tyrant, whose sole name blisters our tongues,
  Was once thought honest: you have loved him well;
  He hath not touched you yet. I am young; but something
  You may deserve of him through me; and wisdom   15
  To offer up a weak, poor, innocent lamb
  T' appease an angry god.

MACDUFF: I am not treacherous.

MALCOLM: But Macbeth is.
  A good and virtuous nature may recoil
  In an imperial charge. But I shall crave your pardon;   20
  That which you are, my thoughts cannot transpose:
  Angels are bright still, though the brightest fell:
  Though all things foul would wear the brows of grace,
  Yet grace must still look so.

MACDUFF: I have lost my hopes.

MALCOLM: Perchance even there where I did find my doubts.   25
  Why in that rawness left you wife and child,

---

³mortal *deadly*   ⁴Bestride our down-fall'n birthdom *protectively stand over our
native land*   ⁶that *so that*   ⁸Like syllable of dolor *similar sound of grief*
¹⁰to friend *friendly, propitious*   ¹²sole *very*   ¹³honest *good*   ¹⁵deserve of him
through me *i.e., earn by betraying me to Macbeth;* wisdom *it may be wise*
¹⁹⁻²⁰recoil/In *give way*   ²¹transpose *transform*   ²²the brightest *i.e., Lucifer*
²³would wear *desire to wear*   ²⁴so *i.e., like itself*   ²⁶rawness *unprotected
condition*

157

Those precious motives, those strong knots of love,
Without leave-taking? I pray you,
Let not my jealousies be your dishonors,
But mine own safeties. You may be rightly just   30
Whatever I shall think.
MACDUFF: Bleed, bleed, poor country:
Great tyranny, lay thou thy basis sure,
For goodness dare not check thee: wear thou thy wrongs;
The title is affeered. Fare thee well, lord:
I would not be the villain that thou think'st   35
For the whole space that's in the tyrant's grasp
And the rich East to boot.
MALCOLM: Be not offended:
I speak not as in absolute fear of you.
I think our country sinks beneath the yoke;
It weeps, it bleeds, and each new day a gash   40
Is added to her wounds. I think withal
There would be hands uplifted in my right;
And here from gracious England have I offer
Of goodly thousands: but, for all this,
When I shall tread upon the tyrant's head,   45
Or wear it on my sword, yet my poor country
Shall have more vices than it had before,
More suffer, and more sundry ways than ever,
By him that shall succeed.
MACDUFF: What should he be?
MALCOLM: It is myself I mean, in whom I know   50
All the particulars of vice so grafted
That, when they shall be opened, black Macbeth
Will seem as pure as snow, and the poor state
Esteem him as a lamb, being compared
With my confineless harms.
MACDUFF: Not in the legions   55
Of horrid hell can come a devil more damned

---

²⁹jealousies *suspicions*   ³⁰rightly just *perfectly honorable*   ³²basis *foundation*
³³check *restrain*   ³⁴affeered *legally confirmed*   ⁴¹withal *moreover*
⁴²in my right *on behalf of my claim*   ⁴³England *i.e., the King of England*
⁴⁴for *despite*   ⁵¹particulars *special kinds;* grafted *engrafted*   ⁵²opened *in bloom,
i.e., revealed*   ⁵⁵confineless harms *unbounded evils*

In evils to top Macbeth.

MALCOLM: I grant him bloody,
Luxurious, avaricious, false, deceitful,
Sudden, malicious, smacking of every sin
That has a name: but there's no bottom, none,   60
In my voluptuousness: your wives, your daughters,
Your matrons and your maids, could not fill up
The cistern of my lust, and my desire
All continent impediments would o'erbear,
That did oppose my will. Better Macbeth   65
Than such an one to reign.

MACDUFF: Boundless intemperance
In nature is a tyranny; it hath been
Th' untimely emptying of the happy throne,
And fall of many kings. But fear not yet
To take upon you what is yours: you may   70
Convey your pleasures in a spacious plenty,
And yet seem cold, the time you may so hoodwink.
We have willing dames enough. There cannot be
That vulture in you, to devour so many
As will to greatness dedicate themselves,   75
Finding it so inclined.

MALCOLM: With this there grows
In my most ill-composed affection such
A stanchless avarice that, were I King,
I should cut off the nobles for their lands,
Desire his jewels and this other's house: 80
And my more-having would be as a sauce
To make me hunger more, that I should forge
Quarrels unjust against the good and loyal,
Destroying them for wealth.

MACDUFF: This avarice
Sticks deeper, grows with more pernicious root   85
Than summer-seeming lust, and it hath been

---

[58]**Luxurious** *lecherous*   [59]**Sudden** *violent*   [61]**voluptuousness** *lust*
[64]**continent** *restraining*   [67]**In nature** *in man's nature*   [71]**Convey** *secretly manage*
[72]**time** *age, i.e., people*   [77]**ill-composed affection** *evilly compounded character*
[78]**stanchless** *never-ending*   [86]**summer-seeming** *befitting summer, i.e., youthful (?)*
transitory (?)

The sword of our slain kings. Yet do not fear.
Scotland hath foisons to fill up your will
Of your mere own. All these are portable,
With other graces weighed.   90

MALCOLM: But I have none: the king-becoming graces,
As justice, verity, temp'rance, stableness,
Bounty, perseverance, mercy, lowliness,
Devotion, patience, courage, fortitude,
I have no relish of them, but abound   95
In the division of each several crime,
Acting it many ways. Nay, had I pow'r, I should
Pour the sweet milk of concord into hell,
Uproar the universal peace, confound
All unity on earth.

MACDUFF: O Scotland, Scotland!   100

MALCOLM: If such a one be fit to govern, speak:
I am as I have spoken.

MACDUFF: Fit to govern!
No, not to live. O nation miserable!
With an untitled tyrant bloody-sceptered,
When shalt thou see thy wholesome days again,   105
Since that the truest issue of thy throne
By his own interdiction stands accursed,
And does blaspheme his breed? Thy royal father
Was a most sainted king: the queen that bore thee,
Oft'ner upon her knees than on her feet,   110
Died every day she lived. Fare thee well!
These evils thou repeat'st upon thyself
Hath banished me from Scotland. O my breast,
Thy hope ends here!

MALCOLM: Macduff, this noble passion,
Child of integrity, hath from my soul   11.

---

[87]**sword of our slain kings** *i.e., the cause of death to our kings*   [88-89]**foisons . . .
own** *enough abundance of your own to satisfy your covetousness*   [95]**relish of** *taste
for (?) trace of (?)*   [96]**division of each several crime** *variations of each kind of
crime*   [99]**Uproar** *put into a tumult*   [107]**interdiction** *curse, exclusion*
[108]**breed** *ancestry*   [111]**Died** *i.e., prepared for heaven*

Wiped the black scruples, reconciled my thoughts
To thy good truth and honor. Devilish Macbeth
By many of these trains hath sought to win me
Into his power; and modest wisdom plucks me
From over-credulous haste: but God above   120
Deal between thee and me! For even now
I put myself to thy direction, and
Unspeak mine own detraction; here abjure
The taints and blames I laid upon myself,
For strangers to my nature. I am yet   125
Unknown to woman, never was forsworn,
Scarcely have coveted what was mine own,
At no time broke my faith, would not betray
The devil to his fellow, and delight
No less in truth than life. My first false speaking   130
Was this upon myself. What I am truly,
Is thine and my poor country's to command:
Whither indeed, before thy here-approach,
Old Siward, with ten thousand warlike men,
Already at a point, was setting forth.   135
Now we'll together, and the chance of goodness
Be like our warranted quarrel! Why are you silent?
MACDUFF: Such welcome and unwelcome things at once
   'Tis hard to reconcile.

Enter a DOCTOR.

MALCOLM: Well, more anon. Comes the King forth, I pray you?   140
DOCTOR: Ay, sir. There are a crew of wretched souls
   That stay his cure: their malady convinces
   The great assay of art; but at his touch,
   Such sanctity hath heaven given his hand,
   They presently amend.
MALCOLM: I thank you, doctor.   145

Exit DOCTOR.

---

[116]scruples *suspicions*   [118]trains *plots*   [119]modest wisdom *i.e., prudence*
[122]to *under*   [125]For *as*   [135]at a point *prepared*
[136–37]the chance . . . quarrel *i.e., may our chance of success equal the justice of our cause*   [142]stay *await*   [142–43]convinces/The great assay of art *i.e., defies the efforts of medical science*   [145]presently amend *immediately recover*

MACDUFF: What's the disease he means?

MALCOLM: 'Tis called the evil:
A most miraculous work in this good King,
Which often since my here-remain in England
I have seen him do. How he solicits heaven,
Himself best knows: but strangely-visited people,   150
All swoll'n and ulcerous, pitiful to the eye,
The mere despair of surgery, he cures,
Hanging a golden stamp about their necks,
Put on with holy prayers: and 'tis spoken,
To the succeeding royalty he leaves   155
The healing benediction. With this strange virtue
He hath a heavenly gift of prophecy,
And sundry blessings hang about his throne
That speak him full of grace.

Enter ROSS.

MACDUFF: See, who comes here?

MALCOLM: My countryman; but yet I know him not.   160

MACDUFF: My ever gentle cousin, welcome hither.

MALCOLM: I know him now: good God, betimes remove
The means that makes us strangers!

ROSS: Sir, amen.

MACDUFF: Stands Scotland where it did?

ROSS: Alas, poor country!
Almost afraid to know itself! It cannot   165
Be called our mother but our grave, where nothing
But who knows nothing is once seen to smile;
Where sighs and groans, and shrieks that rent the air,
Are made, not marked; where violent sorrow seems
A modern ecstasy. The dead man's knell   170
Is there scarce asked for who, and good men's lives
Expire before the flowers in their caps,
Dying or ere they sicken.

---

[146]evil *(scrofula, called "the king's evil" because it could allegedly be cured by the
king's touch)*   [150]strangely-visited *oddly afflicted*   [152]mere *utter*   [153]stamp *coin*
[156]virtue *power*   [159]speak *proclaim*   [161]gentle *noble*   [162]betimes *quickly*
[166]nothing *no one*   [169]marked *noticed*   [170]modern ecstasy *i.e., ordinary emotion*

MACDUFF: O, relation
  Too nice, and yet too true!
MALCOLM: What's the newest grief?
ROSS: That of an hour's age doth hiss the speaker;   175
  Each minute teems a new one.
MACDUFF: How does my wife?
ROSS: Why, well.
MACDUFF: And all my children?
ROSS: Well too.
MACDUFF: The tyrant has not battered at their peace?
ROSS: No; they were well at peace when I did leave 'em.
MACDUFF: Be not a niggard of your speech: how goes 't?   180
ROSS: When I came hither to transport the tidings,
  Which I have heavily borne, there ran a rumor
  Of many worthy fellows that were out;
  Which was to my belief witnessed the rather,
  For that I saw the tyrant's power afoot.   185
  Now is the time of help. Your eye in Scotland
  Would create soldiers, make our women fight,
  To doff their dire distresses.
MALCOLM: Be 't their comfort
  We are coming thither. Gracious England hath
  Lent us good Siward and ten thousand men;   190
  An older and a better soldier none
  That Christendom gives out.
ROSS: Would I could answer
  This comfort with the like! But I have words
  That would be howled out in the desert air,
  Where hearing should not latch them.
MACDUFF: What concern they? 195
  The general cause or is it a fee-grief
  Due to some single breast?
ROSS: No mind that's honest

[173–74]relation/Too nice *tale too accurate*   [175]That . . . speaker *i.e., the report of the grief of an hour ago is hissed as stale news*   [176]teems *gives birth to*
[182]heavily *sadly*   [183]out *i.e., up in arms*   [184]witnessed *attested*   [185]power *army*
[192]gives out *reports*   [194]would *should*   [195]latch *catch*   [196–97]fee-grief/Due to some single breast *i.e., a personal grief belonging to an individual*

But in it shares some woe, though the main part
Pertains to you alone.

MACDUFF: If it be mine,
 Keep it not from me, quickly let me have it.   200

ROSS: Let not your ears despise my tongue for ever,
 Which shall possess them with the heaviest sound
 That ever yet they heard.

MACDUFF: Humh! I guess at it.

ROSS: Your castle is surprised; your wife and babes
 Savagely slaughtered. To relate the manner,   205
 Were, on the quarry of these murdered deer,
 To add the death of you.

MALCOLM: Merciful heaven!
 What, man! Ne'er pull your hat upon your brows;
 Give sorrow words. The grief that does not speak
 Whispers the o'er-fraught heart, and bids it break. 210

MACDUFF: My children too?

ROSS: Wife, children, servants, all
 That could be found.

MACDUFF: And I must be from thence!
 My wife killed too?

ROSS: I have said.

MALCOLM: Be comforted.
 Let's make us med'cines of our great revenge,
 To cure this deadly grief.   215

MACDUFF: He has no children. All my pretty ones?
 Did you say all? O hell-kite! All?
 What, all my pretty chickens and their dam
 At one fell swoop?

MALCOLM: Dispute it like a man.

MACDUFF: I shall do so;   220
 But I must also feel it as a man.
 I cannot but remember such things were,
 That were most precious to me. Did heaven look on,
 And would not take their part? Sinful Macduff,
 They were all struck for thee! Naught that I am, 225

[204]**surprised** *suddenly attacked* [206]**quarry** *heap of slaughtered game*
[210]**Whispers the o'er-fraught heart** *whispers to the overburdened heart*
[217]**hell-kite** *hellish bird of prey* [220]**Dispute** *counter* [225]**Naught** *wicked*

Not for their own demerits but for mine
Fell slaughter on their souls. Heaven rest them now!
MALCOLM: Be this the whetstone of your sword. Let grief
  Convert to anger; blunt not the heart, enrage it.
MACDUFF: O, I could play the woman with mine eyes,   230
  And braggart with my tongue! But, gentle heavens,
  Cut short all intermission; front to front
  Bring thou this fiend of Scotland and myself;
  Within my sword's length set him. If he 'scape,
  Heaven forgive him too!
MALCOLM: This time goes manly.   235
  Come, go we to the King. Our power is ready;
  Our lack is nothing but our leave. Macbeth
  Is ripe for shaking, and the pow'rs above
  Put on their instruments. Receive what cheer you may.
  The night is long that never finds the day.   240
Exeunt.

ACT V

Scene I   *Dunsinane. In the castle.*

Enter a DOCTOR OF PHYSIC *and a* WAITING-GENTLEWOMAN.

DOCTOR: I have two nights watched with you, but can perceive
  no truth in your report. When was it she last walked?
GENTLEWOMAN: Since his Majesty went into the field, I have seen
  her rise from her bed, throw her nightgown upon her, unlock
  her closet, take forth paper, fold it, write upon 't, read it,   5
  afterwards seal it, and again return to bed; yet all this while in
  a most fast sleep.
DOCTOR: A great perturbation in nature, to receive at once the
  benefit of sleep and do the effects of watching! In this slumb'ry

---

[232]intermission *interval;* front to front *forehead to forehead, i.e., face to face*
[237]Our lack is nothing but our leave *i.e., we need only to take our leave*
[239]Put on their instruments *arm themselves (?) urge us, their agents, onward (?)*
[9]effects of watching *deeds of one awake*

agitation, besides her walking and other actual performances, 10
what, at any time, have you heard her say?

GENTLEWOMAN: That, sir, which I will not report after her.

DOCTOR: You may to me, and 'tis most meet you should.

GENTLEWOMAN: Neither to you nor anyone, having no witness to
confirm my speech. 15

Enter LADY MACBETH, *with a taper.*

Lo you, here she comes! This is her very guise, and, upon my
life, fast asleep! Observe her; stand close.

DOCTOR: How came she by that light?

GENTLEWOMAN: Why, it stood by her. She has light by her
continually. 'Tis her command. 20

DOCTOR: You see, her eyes are open.

GENTLEWOMAN: Ay, but their sense are shut.

DOCTOR: What is it she does now? Look, how she rubs her hands.

GENTLEWOMAN: It is an accustomed action with her, to seem thus
washing her hands: I have known her continue in this a quarter 25
of an hour.

LADY MACBETH: Yet here's a spot.

DOCTOR: Hark! she speaks. I will set down what comes from her,
to satisfy my remembrance the more strongly.

LADY MACBETH: Out, damned spot! Out, I say! One: two: why, 30
then 'tis time to do 't. Hell is murky. Fie, my lord, fie! A soldier,
and afeard? What need we fear who knows it, when none can
call our pow'r to accompt? Yet who would have thought the
old man to have had so much blood in him?

DOCTOR: Do you mark that? 35

LADY MACBETH: The Thane of Fife had a wife. Where is she now?
What, will these hands ne'er be clean? No more o' that, my lord,
no more o' that! You mar all with this starting.

DOCTOR: Go to, go to! You have known what you should not.

GENTLEWOMAN: She has spoke what she should not, I am sure of 40
that. Heaven knows what she has known.

LADY MACBETH: Here's the smell of the blood still. All the
perfumes of Arabia will not sweeten this little hand. Oh, oh, oh!

---

[10]actual performances *deeds*   [13]meet *suitable*   [16]guise *custom*   [17]close *hidden*
[22]sense *i.e., powers of sight*   [29]satisfy *confirm*   [33]to accompt *into account*
[39]Go to *(an exclamation)*

DOCTOR: What a sigh is there! The heart is sorely charged.

GENTLEWOMAN: I would not have such a heart in my bosom for 45
the dignity of the whole body.

DOCTOR: Well, well, well——

GENTLEWOMAN: Pray God it be, sir.

DOCTOR: This disease is beyond my practice. Yet I have known
those which have walked in their sleep who have died holily in 50
their beds.

LADY MACBETH: Wash your hands; put on your nightgown; look
not so pale! I tell you yet again, Banquo's buried. He cannot
come out on 's grave.

DOCTOR: Even so? 55

LADY MACBETH: To bed, to bed! There's knocking at the gate.
Come, come, come, come, give me your hand! What's done
cannot be undone. To bed, to bed, to bed!

Exit LADY MACBETH.

DOCTOR: Will she go now to bed?

GENTLEWOMAN: Directly. 60

DOCTOR: Foul whisp'rings are abroad. Unnatural deeds
Do breed unnatural troubles. Infected minds
To their deaf pillows will discharge their secrets.
More needs she the divine than the physician.
God, God forgive us all! Look after her; 65
Remove from her the means of all annoyance,
And still keep eyes upon her. So good night.
My mind she has mated and amazed my sight:
I think, but dare not speak.

GENTLEWOMAN: Good night, good doctor.

Exeunt.

SCENE II   *The country near Dunsinane.*

Drum and colors. Enter MENTEITH, CAITHNESS, ANGUS, LENNOX,
SOLDIERS.

MENTEITH: The English pow'r is near, led on by Malcolm,

---

⁴⁴charged *burdened*   ⁴⁶dignity *worth, rank*   ⁴⁹practice *professional skill*
⁵⁴on 's *of his*   ⁶⁶annoyance *injury*   ⁶⁷still *continuously*   ⁶⁸mated *baffled*
¹pow'r *army*

His uncle Siward and the good Macduff.
Revenges burn in them; for their dear causes
Would to the bleeding and the grim alarm
Excite the mortified man.

ANGUS: Near Birnam Wood
Shall we well meet them; that way are they coming.

CAITHNESS: Who knows if Donalbain be with his brother?

LENNOX: For certain, sir, he is not. I have a file
Of all the gentry: there is Siward's son,
And many unrough youths that even now
Protest their first of manhood.

MENTEITH: What does the tyrant?

CAITHNESS: Great Dunsinane he strongly fortifies.
Some say he's mad; others, that lesser hate him,
Do call it valiant fury: but, for certain,
He cannot buckle his distempered cause
Within the belt of rule.

ANGUS: Now does he feel
His secret murders sticking on his hands;
Now minutely revolts upbraid his faith-breach.
Those he commands move only in command,
Nothing in love. Now does he feel his title
Hang loose about him, like a giant's robe
Upon a dwarfish thief.

MENTEITH: Who then shall blame
His pestered senses to recoil and start,
When all that is within him does condemn
Itself for being there?

CAITHNESS: Well, march we on,
To give obedience where 'tis truly owed.
Meet we the med'cine of the sickly weal,

---

³dear *heartfelt*   ⁴⁻⁵Would . . . man *i.e., would incite a dead man (or "a paralyzed man") to join the bloody and grim call to battle*   ⁸file *list*   ¹⁰unrough *i.e., beardless*   ¹¹Protest *assert*   ¹⁵distempered *swollen by dropsy*   ¹⁶rule *self-control*   ¹⁸minutely revolts upbraid *rebellions every minute rebuke*
²³pestered *tormented*   ²⁷med'cine *i.e., Malcolm;* weal *commonwealth*

And with him pour we, in our country's purge,
Each drop of us.

LENNOX: Or so much as it needs
  To dew the sovereign flower and drown the weeds.   30
  Make we our march towards Birnam.

Exeunt, marching.

SCENE III *Dunsinane. In the castle.*

Enter MACBETH, DOCTOR, *and* ATTENDANTS.

MACBETH: Bring me no more reports; let them fly all!
  Till Birnam Wood remove to Dunsinane
  I cannot taint with fear. What's the boy Malcolm?
  Was he not born of woman? The spirits that know
  All mortal consequences have pronounced me thus: 5
  "Fear not, Macbeth; no man that's born of woman
  Shall e'er have power upon thee." Then fly, false thanes,
  And mingle with the English epicures.
  The mind I sway by and the heart I bear
  Shall never sag with doubt nor shake with fear.   10

Enter SERVANT.

  The devil damn thee black, thou cream-faced loon!
  Where got'st thou that goose look?
SERVANT: There is ten thousand——
MACBETH: Geese, villain?
SERVANT: Soldiers, sir.
MACBETH: Go prick thy face and over-red thy fear,
  Thou lily-livered boy. What soldiers, patch?   15
  Death of thy soul! Those linen cheeks of thine

---

[29]**Each drop of us** *i.e., every last drop of our blood (?)*   [30]**dew** *bedew, water
(and thus make grow);* **sovereign** *(1) royal (2) remedial*   [3]**taint** *become infected*
[5]**mortal consequences** *future human events*   [9]**sway** *move*   [11]**loon** *fool*
[14]**over-red** *cover with red*   [15]**patch** *fool*   [16]**of** *upon;* **linen** *i.e., pale*

Are counselors to fear. What soldiers, whey-face?
SERVANT: The English force, so please you.
MACBETH: Take thy face hence. (*Exit* SERVANT.)
                                    Seyton!—I am sick at heart,
When I behold—Seyton, I say!—This push   20
Will cheer me ever, or disseat me now.
I have lived long enough. My way of life
Is fall'n into the sear, the yellow leaf,
And that which should accompany old age,
As honor, love, obedience, troops of friends,   25
I must not look to have; but, in their stead,
Curses not loud but deep, mouth-honor, breath,
Which the poor heart would fain deny, and dare not.
Seyton!

Enter SEYTON.

SEYTON: What's your gracious pleasure?
MACBETH: What news more?   30
SEYTON: All is confirmed, my lord, which was reported.
MACBETH: I'll fight, till from my bones my flesh be hacked.
  Give me my armor.
SEYTON: 'Tis not needed yet.
MACBETH: I'll put it on.
  Send out moe horses, skirr the country round.   35
  Hang those that talk of fear. Give me mine armor.
  How does your patient, doctor?
DOCTOR: Not so sick, my lord,
  As she is troubled with thick-coming fancies
  That keep her from her rest.
MACBETH: Cure her of that.
  Canst thou not minister to a mind diseased,   40
  Pluck from the memory a rooted sorrow,
  Raze out the written troubles of the brain,
  And with some sweet oblivious antidote
  Cleanse the stuffed bosom of that perilous stuff
  Which weighs upon the heart?

---

[20]**push** *effort*   [21]**disseat** *i.e., unthrone (with wordplay on "cheer," pronounced*
"chair")   [23]**sear** *withered*   [35]**moe** *more;* **skirr** *scour*   [42]**Raze out** *erase*
[43]**oblivious** *causing forgetfulness*

DOCTOR: Therein the patient   45
   Must minister to himself.
MACBETH: Throw physic to the dogs, I'll none of it.
   Come, put mine armor on. Give me my staff.
   Seyton, send out.—Doctor, the thanes fly from me.—
   Come, sir, dispatch. If thou couldst, doctor, cast   50
   The water of my land, find her disease
   And purge it to a sound and pristine health,
   I would applaud thee to the very echo,
   That should applaud again.—Pull 't off, I say.—
   What rhubarb, senna, or what purgative drug,   55
   Would scour these English hence? Hear'st thou of them?
DOCTOR: Ay, my good lord; your royal preparation
   Makes us hear something.
MACBETH: Bring it after me.
   I will not be afraid of death and bane
   Till Birnam Forest come to Dunsinane.   60
DOCTOR: *(Aside):* Were I from Dunsinane away and clear,
   Profit again should hardly draw me here.
Exeunt.

SCENE IV *Country near Birnam Wood.*

Drum and colors. Enter MALCOLM, SIWARD, MACDUFF, SIWARD's
SON, MENTEITH, CAITHNESS, ANGUS, *and* SOLDIERS, *marching.*

MALCOLM: Cousins, I hope the days are near at hand
   That chambers will be safe.
MENTEITH: We doubt it nothing.
SIWARD: What wood is this before us?
MENTEITH: The Wood of Birnam.
MALCOLM: Let every soldier hew him down a bough
   And bear 't before him. Thereby shall we shadow   5

---

[47]physic *medical science*   [50]dispatch *hurry*   [50-51]cast/The water *analyze the urine*   [58]it *i.e., the armor*   [59]bane *destruction*   [2]That chambers will be safe *i.e., that a man will be safe in his bedroom;* nothing *not at all*

The numbers of our host, and make discovery
Err in report of us.

SOLDIERS: It shall be done.

SIWARD: We learn no other but the confident tyrant
Keeps still in Dunsinane, and will endure
Our setting down before 't.

MALCOLM: 'Tis his main hope,   10
For where there is advantage to be given
Both more and less have given him the revolt,
And none serve with him but constrainèd things
Whose hearts are absent too.

MACDUFF: Let our just censures
Attend the true event, and put we on   15
Industrious soldiership.

SIWARD: The time approaches,
That will with due decision make us know
What we shall say we have and what we owe.
Thoughts speculative their unsure hopes relate,
But certain issue strokes must arbitrate: 20
Towards which advance the war.

Exeunt, marching.

SCENE V   *Dunsinane. Within the castle.*

Enter MACBETH, SEYTON, *and* SOLDIERS, *with drum and colors.*

MACBETH: Hang out our banners on the outward walls.
The cry is still "They come!" Our castle's strength
Will laugh a siege to scorn. Here let them lie
Till famine and the ague eat them up.
Were they not forced with those that should be ours,   5

---

⁶discovery *reconnaisance*   ⁸no other but *nothing but that*   ⁹endure *allow*
¹¹advantage to be given *afforded an opportunity*   ¹²more and less *high and low*
¹⁴⁻¹⁵just censures/Attend the true event *true judgment awaits the actual outcome*
¹⁸owe *own (the contrast is between "what we shall say we have" and "what we
shall really have")*   ²⁰certain issue strokes must arbitrate *the definite outcome must
be decided by battle*   ²¹war *army*   ⁴ague *fever*   ⁵forced *reinforced*

We might have met them dareful, beard to beard,
And beat them backward home.

A cry within of women.

What is that noise?

SEYTON: It is the cry of women, my good lord. *(Exit.)*
MACBETH: I have almost forgot the taste of fears:
　　The time has been, my senses would have cooled　　　　10
　　To hear a night-shriek, and my fell of hair
　　Would at a dismal treatise rouse and stir
　　As life were in 't. I have supped full with horrors.
　　Direness, familiar to my slaughterous thoughts,
　　Cannot once start me.
　　(Enter SEYTON.*)*

Wherefore was that cry?　　　　15

SEYTON: The Queen, my lord, is dead.
MACBETH: She should have died hereafter;
　　There would have been a time for such a word.
　　Tomorrow, and tomorrow, and tomorrow
　　Creeps in this petty pace from day to day,　　　　20
　　To the last syllable of recorded time;
　　And all our yesterdays have lighted fools
　　The way to dusty death. Out, out, brief candle!
　　Life's but a walking shadow, a poor player
　　That struts and frets his hour upon the stage　　　　25
　　And then is heard no more. It is a tale
　　Told by an idiot, full of sound and fury
　　Signifying nothing.
　　(Enter a MESSENGER.*)*
　　Thou com'st to use thy tongue; thy story quickly!

MESSENGER: Gracious my lord,　　　　30
　　I should report that which I say I saw,
　　But know not how to do 't.
MACBETH:　　　　　　　　Well, say, sir.
MESSENGER: As I did stand my watch upon the hill,
　　I looked toward Birnam, and anon, methought,
　　The wood began to move.

---

⁶**met them dareful** *i.e., met them in the battlefield boldly*　　¹¹**fell** *pelt*
¹²**treatise** *story*　　¹⁵**start** *startle*　　¹⁷**should** *inevitably would (?)*　　¹⁸**word** *message*

MACBETH: <div style="text-align:center">Liar and slave!</div> 35

MESSENGER: Let me endure your wrath, if 't be not so.
  Within this three mile may you see it coming;
  I say a moving grove.

MACBETH: If thou speak'st false,
  Upon the next tree shalt thou hang alive,
  Till famine cling thee. If thy speech be sooth, 40
  I care not if thou dost for me as much.
  I pull in resolution, and begin
  To doubt th' equivocation of the fiend
  That lies like truth: "Fear not, till Birnam Wood
  Do come to Dunsinane!" And now a wood 45
  Comes toward Dunsinane. Arm, arm, and out!
  If this which he avouches does appear,
  There is nor flying hence nor tarrying here.
  I 'gin to be aweary of the sun,
  And wish th' estate o' th' world were now undone. 50
  Ring the alarum bell! Blow wind, come wrack!
  At least we'll die with harness on our back.

Exeunt.

SCENE VI *Dunsinane. Before the castle.*

Drum and colors. Enter MALCOLM, SIWARD, MACDUFF, *and their army, with boughs.*

MALCOLM: Now near enough. Your leavy screens throw down,
  And show like those you are. You, worthy uncle,
  Shall, with my cousin, your right noble son,
  Lead our first battle. Worthy Macduff and we
  Shall take upon 's what else remains to do, 5
  According to our order.

---

⁴⁰cling *wither;* sooth *truth*   ⁴²pull in resolution *restrain confidence*
⁴³doubt *suspect*   ⁴⁷avouches *asserts*   ⁵⁰th' estate *the orderly condition*
⁵²harness *armor*   ¹leavy *leafy*   ⁴battle *battalion;* we *(Malcolm uses the royal "we")*   ⁶order *plan*

SIWARD: Fare you well.
  Do we but find the tyrant's power tonight,
  Let us be beaten, if we cannot fight.
MACDUFF: Make all our trumpets speak; give them all breath,
  Those clamorous harbingers of blood and death. 10

Exeunt. Alarums continued.

SCENE VII *Another part of the field.*

Enter MACBETH.

MACBETH: They have tied me to a stake; I cannot fly,
  But bearlike I must fight the course. What's he
  That was not born of woman? Such a one
  Am I to fear, or none.

Enter YOUNG SIWARD.

YOUNG SIWARD: What is thy name?
MACBETH: Thou'lt be afraid to hear it. 5
YOUNG SIWARD: No; though thou call'st thyself a hotter name
  Than any is in hell.
MACBETH: My name's Macbeth.
YOUNG SIWARD: The devil himself could not pronounce a title
  More hateful to mine ear.
MACBETH: No, nor more fearful.
YOUNG SIWARD: Thou liest, abhorrèd tyrant; with my sword 10
  I'll prove the lie thou speak'st.

Fight, and YOUNG SIWARD *slain.*

MACBETH: Thou wast born of woman.
  But swords I smile at, weapons laugh to scorn,
  Brandished by man that's of a woman born.

Exit.

Alarums. Enter MACDUFF.

MACDUFF: That way the noise is. Tyrant, show thy face!

----

[7]**Do we** *if we do;* **power** *forces*   [2]**course** *bout, round (he has in mind an attack of dogs or men upon a bear chained to a stake)*

If thou be'st slain and with no stroke of mine,   15
My wife and children's ghosts will haunt me still.
I cannot strike at wretched kerns, whose arms
Are hired to bear their staves. Either thou, Macbeth,
Or else my sword, with an unbattered edge,
I sheathe again undeeded. There thou shouldst be;   20
By this great clatter, one of greatest note
Seems bruited. Let me find him, Fortune!
And more I beg not.

Exit. Alarums.

Enter MALCOLM *and* SIWARD.

SIWARD: This way, my lord. The castle's gently rend'red:
The tyrant's people on both sides do fight;   25
The noble thanes do bravely in the war;
The day almost itself professes yours,
And little is to do.
MALCOLM: We have met with foes
That strike beside us.
SIWARD: Enter, sir, the castle.

Exeunt. Alarum.

SCENE VIII   *Another part of the field.*

Enter MACBETH.

MACBETH: Why should I play the Roman fool, and die
On mine own sword? Whiles I see lives, the gashes
Do better upon them.

Enter MACDUFF.

MACDUFF: Turn, hell-hound, turn!

---

[17]kerns *foot soldiers (contemptuous)*   [18]staves *spears*   [20]undeeded *i.e., having done nothing*   [22]bruited *reported*   [24]gently rend'red *surrendered without a struggle*   [27]itself professes *declares itself*   [29]beside us *i.e., deliberately miss us (?) as our comrades (?)*   [2]Whiles I see lives *so long as I see living men*

MACBETH: Of all men else I have avoided thee.
But get thee back! My soul is too much charged 5
With blood of thine already.
MACDUFF: I have no words:
My voice is in my sword, thou bloodier villain
Than terms can give thee out!

Fight. Alarum.

MACBETH: Thou losest labor:
As easy mayst thou the intrenchant air
With thy keen sword impress as make me bleed: 10
Let fall thy blade on vulnerable crests;
I bear a charmèd life, which must not yield
To one of woman born.
MACDUFF: Despair thy charm,
And let the angel whom thou still hast served
Tell thee, Macduff was from his mother's womb 15
Untimely ripped.
MACBETH: Accursèd be that tongue that tells me so,
For it hath cowed my better part of man!
And be these juggling fiends no more believed,
That palter with us in a double sense; 20
That keep the word of promise to our ear,
And break it to our hope. I'll not fight with thee.
MACDUFF: Then yield thee, coward,
And live to be the show and gaze o' th' time:
We'll have thee, as our rarer monsters are, 25
Painted upon a pole, and underwrit,
"Here may you see the tyrant."
MACBETH: I will not yield,
To kiss the ground before young Malcolm's feet,
And to be baited with the rabble's curse.
Though Birnam Wood be come to Dunsinane, 30

---

⁵**charged** *burdened*   ⁸**terms can give thee out** *words can describe you*
⁹**intrenchant** *incapable of being cut*   ¹⁰**impress** *make an impression on*
¹³**Despair** *despair of*   ¹⁴**angel** *i.e., fallen angel, fiend*   ¹⁸**better part of man**
manly spirit   ²⁰**palter** *equivocate*   ²⁴**gaze o' th' time** *spectacle of the age*
²⁵**monsters** *freaks*   ²⁶**Painted upon a pole** *i.e., pictured on a banner set by a*
showman's booth   ²⁹**baited** *assailed (like a bear by dogs)*

And thou opposed, being of no woman born,
Yet I will try the last. Before my body
I throw my warlike shield. Lay on, Macduff;
And damned be him that first cries "Hold, enough!"

Exeunt, fighting. Alarums. (Reenter fighting, and MACBETH
slain.) Exit MACDUFF, *with* MACBETH. *Retreat and flourish.*
Enter, with drum and colors, MALCOLM, SIWARD, ROSS, THANES,
and SOLDIERS.

MALCOLM: I would the friends we miss were safe arrived.   35
SIWARD: Some must go off; and yet, by these I see,
  So great a day as this is cheaply bought.
MALCOLM: Macduff is missing, and your noble son.
ROSS: Your son, my lord, has paid a soldier's debt:
  He only lived but till he was a man;   40
  The which no sooner had his prowess confirmed
  In the unshrinking station where he fought,
  But like a man he died.
SIWARD: Then he is dead?
ROSS: Ay, and brought off the field. Your cause of sorrow
  Must not be measured by his worth, for then   45
  It hath no end.
SIWARD: Had he his hurts before?
ROSS: Ay, on the front.
SIWARD: Why then, God's soldier be he!
  Had I as many sons as I have hairs,
  I would not wish them to a fairer death:
  And so his knell is knolled.
MALCOLM: He's worth more sorrow,   50
  And that I'll spend for him.
SIWARD: He's worth no more:
  They say he parted well and paid his score:
  And so God be with him! Here comes newer comfort.

Enter MACDUFF, *with* MACBETH's *head.*

MACDUFF: Hail, King! for so thou art: behold, where stands

---

[36]**go off** *die (theatrical metaphor)*   [42]**unshrinking station** *i.e., place at which he
stood firmly*   [52]**parted well and paid his score** *departed well and settled his account*

Th' usurper's cursèd head. The time is free.　　　　55
I see thee compassed with thy kingdom's pearl,
That speak my salutation in their minds,
Whose voices I desire aloud with mine:
Hail, King of Scotland!
ALL:　　　　　　　　　Hail, King of Scotland!
MALCOLM: We shall not spend a large expense of time　　60
Before we reckon with your several loves,
And make us even with you. My thanes and kinsmen,
Henceforth be earls, the first that ever Scotland
In such an honor named. What's more to do,
Which would be planted newly with the time—　　65
As calling home our exiled friends abroad
That fled the snares of watchful tyranny,
Producing forth the cruel ministers
Of this dead butcher and his fiendlike queen,
Who, as 'tis thought, by self and violent hands　　70
Took off her life—this, and what needful else
That calls upon us, by the grace of Grace
We will perform in measure, time, and place:
So thanks to all at once and to each one,
Whom we invite to see us crowned at Scone.　　75

Flourish. Exeunt Omnes.

---

[55]**The time is free** *the world is liberated*　　[56]**compassed** *surrounded*
[61]**reckon with your several loves** *reward the devotion of each of you*
[64–65]**What's more . . . time** *i.e., what else must be done which should be newly established in this age*　[68]**ministers** *agents*　[70]**self and violent** *her own violent*
[72]**calls upon us** *demands my attention*　[73]**in measure, time, and place** *fittingly, at the appropriate time and place*

MOLIÈRE

The Doctor in Spite of Himself

Characters

SGANARELLE, *husband of* MARTINE
MARTINE, *wife of* SGANARELLE
MONSIEUR ROBERT, *neighbor of* SGANARELLE
VALÈRE, *servant of* GÉRONTE
LUCAS, *husband of* JACQUELINE
GÉRONTE, *father of* LUCINDE
JACQUELINE, *wet-nurse at Géronte's and wife of* LUCAS
LUCINDE, *daughter of* GÉRONTE
LÉANDRE, *in love with* LUCINDE
THIBAUT, *a peasant, father of* PERRIN
PERRIN, *a peasant, son of* THIBAUT

ACT I

A clearing. The houses of SGANARELLE *and* MONSIEUR ROBERT *may be seen through the trees.*

SCENE I   SGANARELLE, MARTINE (*who enter quarreling*)

SGANARELLE: No, I tell you I won't do anything of the sort, and I'm the one to say and be the master.
MARTINE: And *I* tell *you* that I want you to live to suit me, and I didn't marry you to put up with your carryings-on.
SGANARELLE: Oh, what a weary business it is to have a wife, and how right Aristotle is when he says a wife is worse than a demon!
MARTINE: Just listen to that smart fellow with his half-wit Aristotle!

SGANARELLE: Yes, a smart fellow. Just find me a woodcutter who knows how to reason about things, like me, who served a famous doctor for six years, and who as a youngster knew his elementary Latin book by heart.

MARTINE: A plague on the crazy fool!

SGANARELLE: A plague on the slut!

MARTINE: Cursed be the day when I went and said yes!

SGANARELLE: Cursed be the hornified notary who had me sign my own ruin!

MARTINE: Really, it's a fine thing for you to complain of that affair! Should you let a single moment go by without thanking Heaven for having me for your wife? And did you deserve to marry a person like me?

SGANARELLE: Oh, yes, you did me too much honor, and I had reason to congratulate myself on our wedding night! Oh, my Lord! Don't get me started on that! I'd have a few things to say . . .

MARTINE: What? What would you say?

SGANARELLE: Let it go at that; let's drop that subject. Enough that we know what we know, and that you were very lucky to find me.

MARTINE: What do you mean, lucky to find you? A man who drags me down to the poorhouse, a debauchee, a traitor, who eats up everything I own?

SGANARELLE: That's a lie: I drink part of it.

MARTINE: Who sells, piece by piece, everything in the house.

SGANARELLE: That's living on our means.

MARTINE: Who's taken even my bed from under me.

SGANARELLE: You'll get up all the earlier in the morning.

MARTINE: In short, who doesn't leave a stick of furniture in the whole house.

SGANARELLE: All the easier to move out.

MARTINE: And who does nothing but gamble and drink from morning to night.

SGANARELLE: That's so I won't get bored.

MARTINE: And what do you expect me to do with my family in the meantime?

SGANARELLE: Whatever you like.

MARTINE: I have four poor little children on my hands.

SGANARELLE: Set them on the floor.

MARTINE: Who are constantly asking me for bread.

SGANARELLE: Give them the whip. When I've had plenty to eat and drink, I want everyone in my house to have his fill.

MARTINE: And you, you drunkard, do you expect things to go on forever like this?

SGANARELLE: My good wife, let's go easy, if you please.

MARTINE: And me to endure your insolence and debauchery to all eternity?

SGANARELLE: Let's not get excited, my good wife.

MARTINE: And that I can't find a way to make you do your duty?

SGANARELLE: My good wife, you know that my soul isn't very patient and my arm is pretty good.

MARTINE: You make me laugh with your threats.

SGANARELLE: My good little wife, my love, you're itching for trouble, as usual.

MARTINE: I'll show you I'm not afraid of you.

SGANARELLE: My dear better half, you're asking for something.

MARTINE: Do you think your words frighten me?

SGANARELLE: Sweet object of my eternal vows, I'll box your ears.

MARTINE: Drunkard that you are!

SGANARELLE: I'll beat you.

MARTINE: Wine-sack!

SGANARELLE: I'll wallop you.

MARTINE: Wretch!

SGANARELLE: I'll tan your hide.

MARTINE: Traitor, wiseacre, deceiver, coward, scoundrel, gallows-bird, beggar, good-for-nothing, rascal, villain, thief . . .

SGANARELLE: *(takes a stick and beats her)*: Ah! So you want it, eh?

MARTINE: Oh, oh, oh, oh!

SGANARELLE: That's the right way to pacify you.

SCENE II MONSIEUR ROBERT, SGANARELLE, MARTINE

MONSIEUR ROBERT: Hey there, hey there, hey there! Fie! What's this? What infamy! Confound the rascal for beating his wife that way!

MARTINE *(arms akimbo, forces* MONSIEUR ROBERT *back as she talks, and finally gives him a slap)*: And as for me, I want him to beat me.

MONSIEUR ROBERT: Oh! Then with all my heart, I consent.

MARTINE: What are you meddling for?

MONSIEUR ROBERT: I'm wrong.

MARTINE: Is it any business of yours?

MONSIEUR ROBERT: You're right.

MARTINE: Just look at this meddler, trying to keep husbands from beating their wives.

MONSIEUR ROBERT: I take it all back.

MARTINE: What have you got to do with it?

MONSIEUR ROBERT: Nothing.

MARTINE: Have you any right to poke your nose in?

MONSIEUR ROBERT: No.

MARTINE: Mind your own business.

MONSIEUR ROBERT: I won't say another word.

MARTINE: I like to be beaten.

MONSIEUR ROBERT: All right.

MARTINE: It's no skin off your nose.

MONSIEUR ROBERT: That's true.

MARTINE: And you're a fool to come butting in where it's none of your business. *(Slaps* MONSIEUR ROBERT. *He turns toward* SGANARELLE, *who likewise forces him back as he talks, threatening him with the same stick and finally beating and routing him with it.)*

MONSIEUR ROBERT: Neighbor, I beg your pardon with all my heart. Go on, beat your wife and thrash her to your heart's content; I'll help you if you want.

SGANARELLE: Me, I don't want to.

MONSIEUR ROBERT: Oh well, that's another matter.

SGANARELLE: I want to beat her if I want to; and I don't want to beat her if I don't want to.

MONSIEUR ROBERT: Very well.

SGANARELLE: She's my wife, not yours.

MONSIEUR ROBERT: Undoubtedly.

SGANARELLE: I don't take orders from you.

MONSIEUR ROBERT: Agreed.

SGANARELLE: I don't need any help from you.

MONSIEUR ROBERT: That's fine with me.

SGANARELLE: And you're a meddler to interfere in other people's affairs. Learn that Cicero says that you mustn't put the bark between the tree and your finger. *(Beats* MONSIEUR ROBERT *and drives him offstage, then returns to his wife and clasps her hand.)* Well now, let's us two make peace. Shake on it.

MARTINE: Oh yes! After beating me that way!

SGANARELLE: That's nothing. Shake.

MARTINE: I will not.

SGANARELLE: Eh?

MARTINE: No.

SGANARELLE: My little wife!

MARTINE: No sir.

SGANARELLE: Come on, I say.

MARTINE: I won't do anything of the kind.

SGANARELLE: Come, come, come.

MARTINE: No, I want to be angry.

SGANARELLE: Fie! It's nothing. Come on, come on.

MARTINE: Let me be.

SGANARELLE: Shake, I say.

MARTINE: You've treated me too badly.

SGANARELLE: All right then, I ask your pardon: give me your hand.

MARTINE: I forgive you; *(aside)* but you'll pay for it.

SGANARELLE: You're crazy to pay any attention to that: those little things are necessary from time to time for a good friendship; and five or six cudgel-blows between people in love only whet their affection. There now, I'm off to the woods, and I promise you more than a hundred bundles of kindling wood today.

SCENE III   MARTINE *(alone)*

MARTINE: All right, whatever face I put on, I'm not forgetting my resentment; and I'm burning inside to find ways to punish you for the beatings you give me. I know very well that a wife always has in hand means of taking revenge on a husband; but that's too delicate a punishment for my gallowsbird. I want a vengeance that he'll feel a bit more; and that would be no satisfaction for the offense I've received.

Scene IV   VALÈRE, LUCAS, MARTINE

LUCAS: Doggone it! We sure both tooken on one heck of a job; and me, I don't know what I'm gonna come up with.

VALÈRE: Well, what do you expect as the wet-nurse's husband? We have to obey our master; and then we both have an interest in the health of the mistress, his daughter; and no doubt her marriage, put off by her illness, would be worth some kind of present to us. Horace, who is generous, has the best chances of anyone to win her hand; and although she has shown a fondness for a certain Léandre, you know very well that her father has never consented to accept him as a son-in-law.

MARTINE *(musing, aside)*: Can't I think up some scheme to get revenge?

LUCAS: But what kind of wild idea has the master tooken into his head, now that the doctors have used up all their Latin?

VALÈRE: You sometimes find, by looking hard, what you don't find at first; and often in simple places . . .

MARTINE: Yes, I must get revenge, whatever the price; that beating sticks in my crop, I can't swallow it, and . . . *(She says all this still musing, not noticing the two men, so that when she turns around she bumps into them.)* Oh! Gentlemen, I beg your pardon; I didn't see you, and I was trying to think of something that's bothering me.

VALÈRE: Everyone has his problems in this world, and we too are looking for something we would very much like to find.

MARTINE: Would it be anything I might help you with?

VALÈRE: It just might. We're trying to find some able man, some special doctor, who might give some relief to our master's daughter, ill with a disease that has suddenly taken away the use of her tongue. Several doctors have already exhausted all their learning on her; but you sometimes find people with wonderful secrets, with certain special remedies, who can very often do what the others couldn't; and that's what we're looking for.

MARTINE *(aside)*: Oh! What a wonderful scheme Heaven inspires me with to get revenge on my gallowsbird! *(Aloud)* You couldn't have come to a better place to find what you're looking for; and we have a man here, the most marvelous man in the world for hopeless illnesses.

VALÈRE: And, pray, where can we find him?

MARTINE: You'll find him right now in that little clearing over there, spending his time cutting wood.

LUCAS: A doctor cutting wood?

VALÈRE: Spending his time gathering herbs, do you mean?

MARTINE: No, he's an extraordinary man who enjoys that—strange, fantastic, crotchety—you'd never take him for what he is. He goes around dressed in an eccentric way, sometimes affects ignorance, keeps his knowledge hidden, and every day avoids nothing so much as exercising the marvelous talents Heaven has given him for medicine.

VALÈRE: It's an amazing thing that all great men always have some caprice, some little grain of folly mingled with their learning.

MARTINE: This one's mania is beyond all belief, for it sometimes goes to the point of his wanting to be beaten before he'll acknowledge his capacity; and I'm telling you you'll never get the better of him, he'll never admit he's a doctor, if he's in that mood, unless you each take a stick and beat him into confessing in the end what he'll hide from you at first. That's what *we* do when we need him.

VALÈRE: That's a strange mania!

MARTINE: That's true; but afterward, you'll see he does wonders.

VALÈRE: What's his name?

MARTINE: His name is Sganarelle, but he's easy to recognize. He's a man with a big black beard, wearing a ruff and a green and yellow coat.

LUCAS: A green and yaller coat? So he's a parrot doctor?[1]

VALÈRE: But is it really true that he's as skillful as you say?

MARTINE: What? He's a man who works miracles. Six months ago a woman was abandoned by all the other doctors. They thought she'd been dead for a good six hours, and were getting ready to bury her, when they forced the man we're talking about to come. After he'd looked her over, he put a little drop of something or other in her mouth, and that very moment she got up out of bed and right away started walking around her room as if nothing had happened.

LUCAS: Ah!

---

[1] In Molière's time, doctors always wore black robes.

VALÈRE: It must have been a drop of elixir of gold.

MARTINE: That might well be. Then again, not three weeks ago a youngster twelve years old fell down from the top of the steeple and broke his head, arms, and legs on the pavement. They had no sooner brought our man in than he rubbed the boy's whole body with a certain ointment he knows how to make; and right away the boy got up on his feet and ran off to play marbles.

LUCAS: Ah!

VALÈRE: That man must have a universal cure.

MARTINE: Who doubts it?

LUCAS: By jingo, that's sure the man we need. Let's go get him quick.

VALÈRE: We thank you for the favor you're doing us.

MARTINE: But anyway, be sure to remember what I warned you about.

LUCAS: Tarnation! Leave it to us. If a beating is all it takes, she's our cow.

VALÈRE: That certainly was a lucky encounter for us; and for my part, I'm very hopeful about it.

Scene V   SGANARELLE, VALÈRE, LUCAS

SGANARELLE *(enters singing, bottle in hand)*: La, la, la!

VALÈRE: I hear someone singing and cutting wood.

SGANARELLE: La, la, la . . . ! My word, that's enough work for a while. Let's take a little breather. *(Drinks)* That wood is salty as the devil. *(Sings)*

> Sweet glug-glug,
> How I love thee!
> Sweet glug-glug
> Of my little jug!
> But everybody would think me too smug
> If you were as full as you can be.
> Just never be empty, that's my plea.
> Come, sweet, let me give you a hug.

(Speaks again) Come on, good Lord, we mustn't breed melancholy.

VALÈRE: There's the man himself.

LUCAS: I think you're right, and we done stumbled right onto him.

VALÈRE: Let's get a closer look.

SGANARELLE *(seeing them, looks at them, turning first toward one then toward the other, and lowers his voice)*: Ah! my little hussy! How I love you, my little jug!

But everybody . . . would think . . . me . . . too smug,
If . . .

What the devil! What do these people want?

VALÈRE: That's the one, no doubt about it.

LUCAS: That's him, his spit an' image, just like they prescribed him to us.

SGANARELLE *(aside)*: They're looking at me and consulting. What can they have in mind? *(He puts his bottle on the ground. As* VALÈRE *bows to greet him,* SGANARELLE *thinks he is reaching down to take his bottle away, and so puts it on the other side of him. When* LUCAS *bows in turn, he picks it up again and clutches it to his belly, with much other byplay.)*

VALÈRE: Sir, isn't your name Sganarelle?

SGANARELLE: How's that?

VALÈRE: I'm asking you if you're not the man named Sganarelle?

SGANARELLE *(turning toward* VALÈRE, *then toward* LUCAS*)*: Yes and no, depending on what you want with him.

VALÈRE: All we want is to pay him all the civilities we can.

SGANARELLE: In that case, my name *is* Sganarelle.

VALÈRE: Sir, we are delighted to see you. We have been addressed to you for something we're looking for; and we come to implore your aid, which we need.

SGANARELLE: If it's something, sirs, connected with my little line of business, I am all ready to serve you.

VALÈRE: Sir, you are too kind. But sir, put on your hat, please; the sun might give you trouble.

LUCAS: Slap it on, sir.

SGANARELLE *(aside)*: These are very ceremonious people.

VALÈRE: Sir, you must not find it strange that we should come to you. Able men are always sought out, and we are well informed about your capability.

SGANARELLE: It is true, gentlemen, that I'm the best man in the world for cutting kindling wood.

VALÈRE: Ah, sir . . . !

SGANARELLE: I spare no pains, and cut it in such a way that it's above criticism.

VALÈRE: Sir, that's not the point.

SGANARELLE: But also I sell it at a hundred and ten sous for a hundred bundles.

VALÈRE: Let's not talk about that, if you please.

SGANARELLE: I promise you I can't let it go for less.

VALÈRE: Sir, we know how things stand.

SGANARELLE: If you know how things stand, you know that that's what I sell them for.

VALÈRE: Sir, you're joking when . . .

SGANARELLE: I'm not joking, I can't take anything off for it.

VALÈRE: Let's talk in other terms, please.

SGANARELLE: You can find it for less elsewhere: there's kindling and kindling; but as for what I cut . . .

VALÈRE: What? Sir, let's drop this subject.

SGANARELLE: I swear you couldn't get it for a penny less.

VALÈRE: Fie now!

SGANARELLE: No, on my conscience, that's what you'll pay. I'm speaking sincerely, and I'm not the man to overcharge.

VALÈRE: Sir, must a person like you waste his time on these crude pretenses and stoop to speaking like this? Must such a learned man, a famous doctor like yourself, try to disguise himself in the eyes of the world and keep his fine talents buried?

SGANARELLE *(aside)*: He's crazy.

VALÈRE: Please, sir, don't dissimulate with us.

SGANARELLE: What?

LUCAS: All this here fiddle-faddle don't do no good; we knows what we knows.

SGANARELLE: What about it? What are you trying to tell me? Whom do you take me for?

VALÈRE: For what you are: for a great doctor.

SGANARELLE: Doctor yourself: I'm not one and I've never been one.

VALÈRE *(aside)*: That's his madness gripping him. *(Aloud)* Sir, please don't deny things any longer; and pray let's not come to regrettable extremes.

SGANARELLE: To what?

VALÈRE: To certain things that we would be sorry for.

SGANARELLE: Good Lord! Come to whatever you like. I'm no doctor, and I don't know what you're trying to tell me.

VALÈRE (*aside*): I can certainly see we'll have to use the remedy. (*Aloud*) Once more, sir, I beg you to admit what you are.

LUCAS: Dad bust it! No more messin' around; confess franklike that you're a doctor.

SGANARELLE: I'm getting mad.

VALÈRE: Why deny what everyone knows?

LUCAS: Why all this fuss and feathers? And what good does that done you?

SGANARELLE: Gentlemen, I tell you in one word as well as in two thousand: *I'm not a doctor.*

VALÈRE: You're not a doctor?

SGANARELLE: No.

LUCAS: You ain't no doc?

SGANARELLE: No, I tell you.

VALÈRE: Since you insist, we'll have to go ahead.

They each take a stick and beat him.

SGANARELLE: Oh, oh, oh! Gentlemen, I'm whatever you like.

VALÈRE: Why, sir, do you force us to this violence?

LUCAS: Why do you give us the botherment of beating you?

VALÈRE: I assure you that I could not regret it more.

LUCAS: By jeepers, I'm sorry about it, honest.

SGANARELLE: What the devil is this, gentlemen? I ask you, is it a joke, or are you both crazy, to insist I'm a doctor?

VALÈRE: What? You still won't give in, and you deny you're a doctor?

SGANARELLE: Devil take me if I am!

LUCAS: It ain't true that you're a doc?

SGANARELLE: No, plague take me! (*They start beating him again.*) Oh, oh! Well, gentlemen, since you insist, I'm a doctor, I'm a doctor; an apothecary too, if you see fit. I'd rather consent to anything than get myself beaten to death.

VALÈRE: Ah! That's fine, sir; I'm delighted to find you in a reasonable mood.

LUCAS: You fair cram my heart with joy when I see you talk thataway.

VALÈRE: I beg your pardon with all my heart.

LUCAS: I begs your excuse for the liberty I done tooken.

SGANARELLE *(aside)*: Well now! Suppose I'm the one that's mistaken? Could I have become a doctor without noticing it?

VALÈRE: Sir, you won't regret showing us what you are; and you'll certainly be satisfied with your treatment.

SGANARELLE: But, gentlemen, aren't you making a mistake yourselves? Is it quite certain that I'm a doctor?

LUCAS: Yup, by jiminy!

SGANARELLE: Honestly?

VALÈRE: Beyond a doubt.

SGANARELLE: Devil take me if I knew it!

VALÈRE: What? You're the ablest doctor in the world.

SGANARELLE: Aha!

LUCAS: A doc which has cureded I don't know how many maladies.

SGANARELLE: My Lord!

VALÈRE: A woman had been taken for dead six hours before; she was ready to be buried, when, with a drop of something or other, you brought her back to life and set her walking around the room right away.

SGANARELLE: I'll be darned!

LUCAS: A little boy twelve years old left himself fall from the top of a steeple, from which he got his head, legs, and arms busted; and you, with some kind of ointment or other, you fixed him so he gets right up on his feet and goes off to play marbles.

SGANARELLE: The devil you say!

VALÈRE: In short, sir, you will have every satisfaction with us; and you'll earn whatever you like if you'll let us take you where we mean to.

SGANARELLE: I'll earn whatever I like?

VALÈRE: Yes.

SGANARELLE: Oh! I'm a doctor, there's no denying it. I'd forgotten, but now I remember. What's the problem? Where do we have to go?

VALÈRE: We'll take you. The problem is to go see a girl who's lost her speech.

SGANARELLE: My word! I haven't found it.

VALÈRE: He likes his little joke. Let's go, sir.

SGANARELLE: Without a doctor's gown?

VALÈRE: We'll get one.

SGANARELLE *(presenting his bottle to* VALÈRE*):* Hold that, you: that's where I put my potions. *(Turning toward* LUCAS *and spitting on the ground.)* You, step on that; doctor's orders.

LUCAS: Land's sakes! That's a doctor I like. I reckon he'll do all right, 'cause he's a real comic.[2]

ACT II

A room in Géronte's house

SCENE I   GÉRONTE, VALÈRE, LUCAS, JACQUELINE

VALÈRE: Yes, sir, I think you'll be satisfied; and we've brought you the greatest doctor in the world.

LUCAS: Oh, gee whillikins! You gotta pull up the ladder after that one, and all the rest ain't good enough to take off his shoon.

VALÈRE: He's a man who has performed wonderful cures.

LUCAS: As has cureded some folk as were dead.

VALÈRE: He's a bit capricious, as I've told you; and sometimes he has moments when his mind wanders and he doesn't seem what he really is.

LUCAS: Yup, he likes to clown; and sometimes you'd say, with no offense, that he'd been hit on the head with an axe.

VALÈRE: But underneath it, he's all learning, and very often he says quite lofty things.

LUCAS: When he gets to it, he talks right straight out just like he was reading out of a book.

VALÈRE: His reputation has already spread hereabouts, and everybody is coming to see him.

GÉRONTE: I'm dying to meet him. Bring him to me quick.

VALÈRE: I'll go and get him.

JACQUELINE: Land's sakes, sir, this'un'll do just what the others

---

[2]Some have taken this remark as Molière's own disgruntled comment on the mediocre success of *The Misanthrope*.

done. I reckon it'll be just the same old stuff; and the bestest med'cine anyone could slip your daughter, if you're asking me, would be a good handsome husband she had a hankering for.

GÉRONTE: Well now! My good wet-nurse, you certainly meddle in lots of things.

LUCAS: Be quiet, Jacqueline, keep to your housework: you ain't the one to stick your nose in there.

JACQUELINE: I told you before and I'll tell you some more that all these here doctors won't do nothing more for her than plain branch water, that your daughter needs something mighty different from rhubarb and senna, and that a husband is the kind of poultice that'll cure all a girl's troubles.

GÉRONTE: Is she in condition now for anyone to want to take her on, with the infirmity she has? And when I was minded to have her married, didn't she oppose my will?

JACQUELINE: I should think she did: you was wanting to pass her a man she don't love. Why didn't you take that Monsieur Léandre that she had a soft spot for? She would've been real obedient; and I'm gonna bet you he'd take her just like she is, if you'd give her to him.

GÉRONTE: That Léandre is not what she needs; he's not well off like the other.

JACQUELINE: He's got such a rich uncle, and he's his heir.

GÉRONTE: All this property to come is just so much nonsense to me. There's nothing like what you've got; and you run a big risk of fooling yourself when you count on what someone else is keeping for you. Death doesn't always keep her ears open to the wishes and prayers of their honors the heirs; and you can grow a long set of teeth when you're waiting for someone's death so as to have a livelihood.

JACQUELINE: Anyway I've always heard that in marriage, as elsewhere, happiness counts more than riches. The pas and mas, they have that goldarned custom of always asking "How much has he got?" and "How much has she got?" and neighbor Peter married off his daughter Simonette to fat Thomas 'cause he had a quarter vineyard more than young Robin, which she'd set her heart on; and now, poor critter, it's turned her yellow as a quince, and she hasn't got her property in all the time since.

That's a fine example for *you*, sir. All we got in this world is our pleasure; and I'd rather give my daughter a good husband which she liked than all the revenues in Beauce.

GÉRONTE: Plague take it, Madame Nurse, how you do spit it out! Be quiet, please; you're getting too involved and you're heating up your milk.

LUCAS *(by mistake, tapping* GÉRONTE *on the chest instead of* JACQUELINE*)*: Gosh darn it! Shut up, you're just a meddler. The master don't have no use for your speeches, and he knows what he's got to do. You see to nursing the child you're nurse to, and don't give us none of your big ideas. The master is his daughter's father, and he's good enough and wise enough to see what she needs.

GÉRONTE: Easy! Oh! Easy!

LUCAS: Sir, I want to mortify her a bit, and teach her the *re*spect she owes you.

GÉRONTE: Yes, but those gestures aren't necessary.

SCENE II VALÈRE, SGANARELLE, GÉRONTE, LUCAS, JACQUELINE

VALÈRE: Sir, prepare yourself. Here comes our doctor.

GÉRONTE: Sir, I'm delighted to have you in my house, and we need you badly.

SGANARELLE *(in a doctor's gown, with a sharply pointed hat)*: Hippocrates says . . . that we should both put our hats on.

GÉRONTE: Hippocrates says that?

SGANARELLE: Yes.

GÉRONTE: In what chapter, if you please?

SGANARELLE: In his chapter on hats.

GÉRONTE: Since Hippocrates says it, we must do it.

SGANARELLE: Sir Doctor, since I have heard the wonderful things . . .

GÉRONTE: Whom are you speaking to, pray?

SGANARELLE: You.

GÉRONTE: I'm not a doctor.

SGANARELLE: You're not a doctor?

GÉRONTE: No, really.

SGANARELLE *(takes a stick and beats him just as he himself was beaten)*: You really mean it?

GÉRONTE: I really mean it. Oh, oh, oh!

SGANARELLE: You're a doctor now. I never got any other license.

GÉRONTE: What the devil kind of a man have you brought me?

VALÈRE: I told you he was a joker of a doctor.

GÉRONTE: Yes, but I'd send him packing with his jokes.

LUCAS: Don't pay no attention to that, sir: that's just for a laugh.

GÉRONTE: I don't like that kind of a laugh.

SGANARELLE: Sir, I ask your pardon for the liberty I took.

GÉRONTE: Your servant, sir.

SGANARELLE: I'm sorry . . .

GÉRONTE: That's nothing.

SGANARELLE: For the cudgeling . . .

GÉRONTE: No harm done.

SGANARELLE: That I had the honor of giving you.

GÉRONTE: Let's say no more about it. Sir, I have a daughter who has caught a strange disease.

SGANARELLE: Sir, I'm delighted that your daughter needs me; and I wish with all my heart that you and your whole family needed me too, just to show you how much I want to serve you.

GÉRONTE: I am obliged to you for those sentiments.

SGANARELLE: I assure you that I'm speaking straight from the heart.

GÉRONTE: You do me too much honor.

SGANARELLE: What's your daughter's name?

GÉRONTE: Lucinde.

SGANARELLE: Lucinde! Oh, what a fine name to prescribe for! Lucinde![3]

GÉRONTE: I'll just go and have a look to see what she's doing.

SGANARELLE: Who's that big buxom woman?

GÉRONTE: She's the wet-nurse of a little baby of mine.

SGANARELLE: Plague take it! That's a pretty piece of goods! Ah, nurse, charming nurse, my medicine is the very humble slave of your nurseship, and I'd certainly like to be the lucky little doll

---

[3]Here a theatrical tradition has Sganarelle decline the name: Lucindus, Lucinda, Lucindum.

who sucked the milk *(puts his hand on her breast)* of your good graces. All my remedies, all my learning, all my capacity is at your service, and . . .

LUCAS: With your pummission, Mister Doctor, leave my wife be, I beg you.

SGANARELLE: What? Is she your wife?

LUCAS: Yes.

SGANARELLE *(makes as if to embrace* LUCAS, *then, turning toward the nurse, embraces her)*: Oh! really! I didn't know that, and I'm delighted for the sake of you both.

LUCAS *(pulling him away)*: Easy now, please.

SGANARELLE: I assure you I'm delighted that you're united. I congratulate her *(he again makes as if to embrace* LUCAS, *and, passing under his arms, throws himself on* JACQUELINE's *neck)* on having a husband like you; and you, I congratulate you on having a wife as beautiful, modest, and well-built as she is.

LUCAS *(pulling him away again)*: Hey! Goldarn it! Not so much compliment, I ask you now.

SGANARELLE: Don't you want me to rejoice with you at such a fine assembly?

LUCAS: With me, all you like; but with my wife, let's skip these kind of formalities.

SGANARELLE: I take part in the happiness of you both alike; and *(same business as before)* if I embrace you to attest my joy to you, I embrace her as well to attest my joy to her too.

LUCAS *(pulling him away once more)*: Oh! Dad blast it, Mister Doctor, what a lot of fiddle-faddle!

SCENE III   SGANARELLE, GÉRONTE, LUCAS, JACQUELINE

GÉRONTE: Sir, they're going to bring my daughter to you. She'll be here right away.

SGANARELLE: I await her sir, and all medicine with me.

GÉRONTE: Where is it?

SGANARELLE *(tapping his forehead)*: In there.

GÉRONTE: Very good.

SGANARELLE *(trying to touch the nurse's breasts)*: But since I am interested in your whole family, I must take a small sample of your nurse's milk, and inspect her bosom.

LUCAS *(pulling him away and spinning him around)*: Nah, nah, I don't want no truck with that.

SGANARELLE: It's the doctor's job to examine nurses' breasts.

LUCAS: Job nor no job, I'm your servant.

SGANARELLE: Do you really have the audacity to set yourself up against the doctor? Begone!

LUCAS: The heck with that!

SGANARELLE *(looking at him askance)*: I'll give you the fever.

JACQUELINE *(taking LUCAS by the arm and spinning him around)*: That's right, get out of there. Ain't I big enough to defend myself if he does something to me as a person hadn't ought?

LUCAS: Well, me, I don't want him a-feeling you.

SGANARELLE: Fie! The peasant! He's jealous of his wife!

GÉRONTE: Here is my daughter.

SCENE IV   LUCINDE, VALÈRE, GÉRONTE, LUCAS, SGANARELLE, JACQUELINE

SGANARELLE: Is this the patient?

GÉRONTE: Yes, she's the only daughter I have, and I'd be heart-broken if she were to die.

SGANARELLE: She'd better not! She mustn't die except on doctor's orders.

GÉRONTE: Come, come, a chair![4]

SGANARELLE: That's not such a bad-looking patient, and I maintain that a really healthy man would make out all right with her.

GÉRONTE: You've made her laugh, sir.

SGANARELLE: That's fine. When the doctor makes the patient laugh, that's the best possible sign. Well! What's the problem? What's wrong with you? Where does it hurt?

---

[4]Chairs were relatively rare luxuries in Molière's France. By ordering a regular chair, not a folding stool, Géronte shows his respect for the learned doctor.

LUCINDE *(answers in sign language, putting her hand to her mouth, her head, and under her chin)*: Hah, heeh, hoh, hah.

SGANARELLE: Eh? What's that you say?

LUCINDE *(same gestures as before)*: Hah, heeh, hoh, hah, hah, heeh, hoh.

SGANARELLE: What?

LUCINDE: Hah, heeh, hoh.

SGANARELLE *(imitating her)*: Hah, heeh, hoh, hah, hah: I don't understand you. What the devil kind of language is that?

GÉRONTE: Sir, that's her illness. She's been struck dumb, and up to now no one has been able to learn the reason why; and it's an accident that has put off her marriage.

SGANARELLE: And why so?

GÉRONTE: The man she is to marry wants to wait until she's cured to make things final.

SGANARELLE: And who is the fool that doesn't want his wife to be dumb? Would God mine had that disease! I'd be the last one to want to cure her.

GÉRONTE: Anyway, sir, we beg you to make every effort to relieve her of her trouble.

SGANARELLE: Oh! Don't worry. Tell me now, does this trouble bother her a lot?

GÉRONTE: Yes, sir.

SGANARELLE: Very good. Does she feel great pains?

GÉRONTE: Very great.

SGANARELLE: That's just fine. Does she go—you know where?

GÉRONTE: Yes.

SGANARELLE: Copiously?

GÉRONTE: I don't know anything about that.

SGANARELLE: Does she achieve laudable results?

GÉRONTE: I'm no expert in those matters.

SGANARELLE *(turning to the patient)*: Give me your arm. That pulse shows your daughter is dumb.

GÉRONTE: Why yes, sir, that's her trouble! You found it the very first thing.

SGANARELLE: Aha!

JACQUELINE: Just lookit how he guessed her illness!

SGANARELLE: We great doctors, we know things right away. An ignorant one would have been embarrassed and would have gone and told you "It's this" or "It's that"; but *I* hit the mark on the first shot, and I inform you that your daughter is dumb.

GÉRONTE: Yes; but I wish you could tell me what it comes from.

SGANARELLE: Nothing easier: it comes from the fact that she has lost her speech.

GÉRONTE: Very good; but the reason, please, why she has lost her speech?

SGANARELLE: All our best authors will tell you that it's the stoppage of the action of her tongue.

GÉRONTE: But still, what are your views about this stoppage of the action of her tongue?

SGANARELLE: Aristotle, on that subject, says ... some very fine things.

GÉRONTE: I believe it.

SGANARELLE: Oh! He was a great man!

GÉRONTE: No doubt.

SGANARELLE *(raising his forearm)*: An utterly great man: a man who was greater than I by all of that! So, to get back to our reasoning, I hold that this stoppage of the action of her tongue is caused by certain humors, which among us scholars we call peccant humors: peccant, that is to say ... peccant humors; because the vapors formed by the exhalations of the influences arising in the region where the maladies lie, when they come ... so to speak ... to ... Do you understand Latin?

GÉRONTE: Not in the least.

SGANARELLE *(getting up in astonishment)*: You don't understand Latin?

GÉRONTE: No.

SGANARELLE *(assuming various comical poses)*: *Cabricias arci thuram, catalamus, singulariter, nominativo haec Musa,* "the Muse," *bonus, bona, bonum, Deus sanctus, estne oratio latinas? Etiam,* "yes." *Quare,* "why?" *Quia substantivo et adjectivum concordat in generi, numerum, et casus.*[5]

GÉRONTE: Oh! Why did I never study?

JACQUELINE: Land! That's an able man!

---

[5]Traditionally, as Sganarelle winds up this hodge-podge of gibberish and elementary Latin phrases with the word *casus* ("case," or "fall"), he throws himself back in his chair too hard, and falls over in it on his back. He remains in this position during the next two remarks.

LUCAS: Yup, that's so purty I can't make out a word of it.

SGANARELLE: Now when these vapors I'm speaking of come to pass from the left side, where the liver is, to the right side, where the heart is, it happens that the lungs, which in Latin we call *armyan,* having communication with the brain, which in Greek we call *nasmus,* by means of the vena cava, which in Hebrew we call *cubile,*[6] on its way encounters the said vapors, which fill the ventricles of the omoplate; and because the said vapors— follow this reasoning closely, I beg you—and because the said vapors have a certain malignity ... Listen to this carefully, I conjure you.

GÉRONTE: Yes.

SGANARELLE: Have a certain malignity, which is caused ... Be attentive, please.

GÉRONTE: I am.

SGANARELLE: Which is caused by the acridity of the humors engendered in the concavity of the diaphragm, it happens that these vapors ... *Ossabandus, nequeys, nequer, potarinum, quipsa milus.* That's exactly what is making your daughter dumb.

JACQUELINE: Oh! That man of ourn! Ain't that well said?

LUCAS: Why ain't *my* tongue that slick?

GÉRONTE: No one could reason any better, no doubt about it. There's just one thing that surprised me: the location of the liver and the heart. It seems to me that you place them otherwise than they are; that the heart is on the left side and the liver on the right side.

SGANARELLE: Yes, it used to be that way; but we have changed all that, and now we practice medicine in a completely new way.

GÉRONTE: That's something I didn't know, and I beg your pardon for my ignorance.

SGANARELLE: No harm done, and you're not obliged to be as able as we are.

GÉRONTE: To be sure. But, sir, what do you think needs to be done for this illness?

SGANARELLE: What I think needs to be done?

GÉRONTE: Yes.

---

[6]These are all invented names, except that *cubile* is Latin for *bed.*

SGANARELLE: My advice is to put her back in bed and have her take, as a remedy, a lot of bread steeped in wine.

GÉRONTE: And why that, sir?

SGANARELLE: Because in bread and wine mixed together there is a sympathetic virtue that makes people speak. Haven't you noticed that they don't give anything else to parrots, and that they learn to speak by eating that?

GÉRONTE: That's true. Oh, what a great man! Quick, lots of bread and wine!

SGANARELLE: I'll come back toward evening and see how she is. *(To the nurse)* Hold on, you. Sir, here is a nurse to whom I must administer a few little remedies.

JACQUELINE: Who? Me? I couldn't be in better health.

SGANARELLE: Too bad, nurse, too bad. Such good health is alarming, and it won't be a bad thing to give you a friendly little bloodletting, a little dulcifying enema.

GÉRONTE: But, sir, that's a fashion I don't understand. Why should we go and be bled when we haven't any illness?

SGANARELLE: No matter, it's a salutary fashion; and just as we drink on account of the thirst to come, so we must have ourselves bled on account of the illness to come.

JACQUELINE *(starting to go off)*: My Lord! The heck with that, and I don't want to make my body into a drugstore.

SGANARELLE: You are resistant to remedies, but we'll manage to bring you to reason.

Exit JACQUELINE.

(To GÉRONTE*)* I bid you good day.

GÉRONTE: Wait a bit, please.

SGANARELLE: What do you want to do?

GÉRONTE: Give you some money, sir.

SGANARELLE *(holding out his hand behind, beneath his gown, while* GÉRONTE *opens his purse)*: I won't take any, sir.

GÉRONTE: Sir . . .

SGANARELLE: Not at all.

GÉRONTE: Just a moment.

SGANARELLE: By no means.

GÉRONTE: Please!

SGANARELLE: You're joking.

GÉRONTE: That's that.

SGANARELLE: I'll do nothing of the sort.

GÉRONTE: Eh?

SGANARELLE: Money is no motive to me.

GÉRONTE: I believe it.

SGANARELLE *(after taking the money)*: Is this good weight?

GÉRONTE: Yes, sir.

SGANARELLE: I'm not a mercenary doctor.

GÉRONTE: I'm well aware of it.

SGANARELLE: I'm not ruled by self-interest.

GÉRONTE: I have no such idea.

SCENE V SGANARELLE, LÉANDRE

SGANARELLE *(looking at his money)*: My word! That's not too bad; and if only . . .

LÉANDRE: Sir, I've been waiting for you a long time, and I come to implore your assistance.

SGANARELLE *(taking his wrist)*: That's a very bad pulse.

LÉANDRE: I'm not sick, sir, and that's not why I've come to see you.

SGANARELLE: If you're not sick, why the devil don't you say so?

LÉANDRE: No. To put the whole thing in a word, my name is Léandre, and I'm in love with Lucinde, whom you've just examined; and since, because of her father's bad disposition, I'm denied all access to her, I'm venturing to beg you to serve my love, and give me a chance to carry out a scheme I've thought up to say a word or two to her on which my happiness and my life depend absolutely.

SGANARELLE *(feigning anger)*: Whom do you take me for? How can you dare come up and ask me to serve you in your love, and try to degrade the dignity of a doctor to this type of employment?

LÉANDRE: Sir, don't make so much noise.

SGANARELLE: *I* want to make noise. You're an impertinent young man.

LÉANDRE: Ah! Gently, sir.

SGANARELLE: A dunderhead.

LÉANDRE: Please!

SGANARELLE: I'll teach you that I'm not the kind of man for that, and that it's the height of insolence . . .

LÉANDRE *(pulling out a purse and giving it to him)*: Sir . . .

SGANARELLE: To want to use me . . . I'm not speaking about you, for you're a gentleman, and I would be delighted to do you a service; but there are some impertinent people in the world who come and take people for what they're not; and I admit that makes me angry.

LÉANDRE: I ask your pardon, sir, for the liberty that . . .

SGANARELLE: Don't be silly. What's the problem?

LÉANDRE: You shall know, then, sir, that this illness that you want to cure is make-believe. The doctors have reasoned in due form about it, and have not failed to say that it came, some say from the brain, some from the intestines, some from the spleen, some from the liver; but it is certain that love is the real cause of it, and that Lucinde hit upon this illness only to deliver herself from a threatened marriage. But, for fear we may be seen together, let's get out of here, and as we walk I'll tell you what I would like from you.

SGANARELLE: Let's go, sir: you've given me an inconceivable fondness for your love; and unless I'm no doctor, either the patient will die or else she'll be yours.

ACT III

Géronte's garden

SCENE I SGANARELLE, LÉANDRE

LÉANDRE: It seems to me I don't look bad this way as an apothecary; and since the father has scarcely ever seen me, this change of costume and wig may well succeed, I think, in disguising me to his eyes.

SGANARELLE: No doubt about it.

LÉANDRE: All I could wish would be to know five or six big medical terms to adorn my speech and make me seem like a learned man.

SGANARELLE: Come, come, all that is unnecessary: the costume is enough, and I know no more about it than you.

LÉANDRE: What?

SGANARELLE: Devil take me if I know anything about medicine! You're a good sort, and I'm willing to confide in you, just as you are confiding in me.

LÉANDRE: What? You're not really . . . ?

SGANARELLE: No, I tell you: they made me a doctor in spite of me. I had never bothered my head about being that learned; and all my studies went only up to seventh grade. I don't know what put this idea into their heads; but when I saw that they absolutely insisted on my being a doctor, I decided to be one, at the expense of whom it may concern. However, you'd never believe how the mistaken idea has gotten around, and how everybody is hell-bent on thinking me a learned man. They come looking for me from all directions; and if things keep on this way, I believe I'll stick to medicine all my life. I think it's the best trade of all; for whether you do well or badly, you're always paid just the same. Bad work never comes back onto our backs, and we cut the material we work on as we please. A cobbler making shoes could never botch a piece of leather without paying for the broken crockery; but in this work we can botch a man without its costing us anything. The blunders are never ours, and it's always the fault of the person who dies. In short, the best part of this profession is that there's a decency, an unparalleled discretion, among the dead; and you never see one of them complaining of the doctor who killed him.

LÉANDRE: It's true that dead men are very decent folk on that score.

SGANARELLE *(seeing some men coming toward him)*: There are some people who look as though they were coming to consult me. Go ahead and wait for me near your sweetheart's house.

Scene II THIBAUT, PERRIN, SGANARELLE

THIBAUT: Sir, we done come to see you, my son Perrin and me.

SGANARELLE: What's the matter?

THIBAUT: His poor mother, her name is Perrette, is sick in bed these six months now.

SGANARELLE *(holding out his hand to receive money)*: And what do you expect me to do about it?

THIBAUT: We'd like, sir, for you to slip us some kind of funny business for to cure her.

SGANARELLE: I'll have to see what she's sick of.

THIBAUT: She's sick of a proxy, sir.

SGANARELLE: Of a proxy?

THIBAUT: Yes, that is to say she's all swelled up all over; and they say it's a whole lot of seriosities she's got inside her, and that her liver, her belly, or her spleen, whatever you want to call it, 'stead of making blood don't make nothing but water. Every other day she has a quotigian fever, with pains and lassitules in the muskles of her legs. You can hear in her throat phleg-ums like to choke her; and sometimes she gets tooken with syncopations and compulsions till I think she done passed away. In our village we got a 'pothecary, all respect to him, who's given her I don't know how many kinds of stuff; and it costs me more'n a dozen good crowns in enemas, no offense, and beverages he had her take, in jacinth confusions and cordial portions. But all that stuff, like the feller said, was just a kind of salve that didn't make her no better nor no worse. He wanted to slip her one certain drug that they call hermetic wine; but me, frankly, I got scared that would send her to join her ancestors; and they do say those big doctors are killing off I don't know how many people with that there invention.[7]

SGANARELLE *(still holding out his hand and signaling with it for money)*: Let's get to the point, my friend, let's get to the point.

THIBAUT: The fact is, sir, that we done come to ask you to tell us what we should do.

SGANARELLE: I don't understand you at all.

---

[7]A big medical controversy of the time concerned the value of emetic wine, which contained antimony.

PERRIN: Sir, my mother is sick; and here be two crowns that we've brung you so you'll give us some cure.

SGANARELLE: Oh! Now *you*, I understand you. Here's a lad who speaks clearly and explains himself properly. You say that your mother is ill with dropsy, that her whole body is swollen, that she has a fever and pains in her legs, and that she is sometimes seized with syncopes and convulsions, that is to say, fainting spells?

PERRIN: Oh, yes, sir, that's exactly it.

SGANARELLE: I understood you right away. You have a father who doesn't know what he's talking about. Now you're asking me for a remedy?

PERRIN: Yes, sir.

SGANARELLE: A remedy to cure her?

PERRIN: That's what we got in mind.

SGANARELLE: Look, here's a piece of cheese that you must have her take.

PERRIN: Cheese, sir?

SGANARELLE: Yes, it's a specially prepared cheese containing gold, coral, pearls, and lots of other precious things.

PERRIN: Sir, we be much obliged to you; and we'll have her take this right away.

SGANARELLE: Go ahead. If she dies, don't fail to give her the best burial you can.

SCENE III   JACQUELINE, SGANARELLE; LUCAS *(backstage)*

SGANARELLE: Here's that beautiful nurse. Ah, nurse of my heart, I'm delighted that we meet again, and the sight of you is the rhubarb, cassia, and senna that purge my soul of all its melancholy!

JACQUELINE: Well I swan, Mister Doctor, you say that too purty for me, and I don't understand none of your Latin.

SGANARELLE: Fall ill, nurse, I beg you; fall ill for my sake: it would give me all the pleasure in the world to cure you.

JACQUELINE: I'm your servant, sir: I'd much rather not have no one cure me.

SGANARELLE: How sorry I am for you, fair nurse, for having a jealous, troublesome husband like the one you have!

JACQUELINE: What would you have me do, sir? It's a penance for my sins. Where the goat is tied, that's where she's got to graze.

SGANARELLE: What? A clod like that! A man who's always watching you, and won't let anyone talk to you!

JACQUELINE: Mercy me, you ain't seen nothin' yet, and that's only a little sample of his bad humor.

SGANARELLE: Is it possible? And can a man have a soul so base as to mistreat a person like you? Ah, lovely nurse, I know people, and not far from here either, who would think themselves happy just to kiss the little tips of your footsies! Why must so lovely a person have fallen into such hands, and must a mere animal, a brute, a lout, a fool . . . ? Pardon me, nurse, if I speak in this way of your husband.

JACQUELINE: Oh, sir, I know good and well he deserves all them names.

SGANARELLE: Yes, nurse, he certainly does deserve them; and he would also deserve to have you plant a certain decoration on his head, to punish him for his suspicions.

JACQUELINE: It's quite true that if I was only thinking about him, he might drive me to some strange carryings-on.

SGANARELLE: My word! It wouldn't be a bad idea for you to take vengeance on him with someone else. He's a man, I tell you, who really deserves that; and if I were fortunate enough, beautiful nurse, to be chosen to . . . (*At this point they both notice* LUCAS, *who was in back of them all the time listening to their talk. They go off in opposite directions, the doctor with comical byplay*).

Scene IV GÉRONTE, LUCAS

GÉRONTE: Hey there, Lucas! Haven't you seen our doctor around?

LUCAS: Yup, tarnation take it! I seen him, and my wife too.

GÉRONTE: Then where can he be?

LUCAS: I dunno, but I wish he'd go to the devil in hell.

GÉRONTE: Go take a look and see what my daughter is doing.

Scene V   SGANARELLE, LÉANDRE, GÉRONTE

GÉRONTE: Ah, sir! I was just asking where you were.

SGANARELLE: I was busy in your courtyard—expelling the super-fluity of my potations. How is the patient?

GÉRONTE: A little worse since taking your prescription.

SGANARELLE: Very good: that's a sign that it's working.

GÉRONTE: Yes; but as it works, I'm afraid it will choke her.

SGANARELLE: Don't worry; I have remedies that make light of everything, and I'll wait for her in her death agony.

GÉRONTE: Who's this man you're bringing with you?

SGANARELLE (*gesturing like an apothecary giving an enema*): He's . . .

GÉRONTE: What?

SGANARELLE: The one . . .

GÉRONTE: Eh?

SGANARELLE: Who . . .

GÉRONTE: I understand.

SGANARELLE: Your daughter will need him.

Scene VI   JACQUELINE, LUCINDE, GÉRONTE, LÉANDRE, SGANARELLE

JACQUELINE: Sir, here's your daughter as wants to take a little walk.

SGANARELLE: That will do her good. Mister Apothecary, go along and take her pulse a bit so that I can discuss her illness with you presently. (*At this point he draws* GÉRONTE *to one side of the stage, and, passing one arm over his shoulders, puts his hand under his chin and turns him back toward himself whenever* GÉRONTE *tries to watch what his daughter and the apothecary are doing together.*) Sir, it's a great and subtle question among the learned whether women are easier to cure than men. I beg you to listen to this, if you please. Some say no, others say yes; and *I* say yes and no: inasmuch as the incongruity of the opaque humors that are found in the natural temperament of women, is the reason why the brutish part always tries to gain power

over the sensitive part, we see that the inequality of their opinions depends on the oblique movement of the moon's circle; and
since the sun, which darts its rays over the concavity of the earth,
finds . . .

LUCINDE: No, I'm utterly incapable of changing my feelings.

GÉRONTE: That's my daughter speaking! Oh, what wonderful virtue in that remedy! Oh, what an admirable doctor! How obliged
I am to you for this marvelous cure! And what can I do for you
after such a service?

SGANARELLE *(walking around the stage and wiping his brow)*:
That's an illness that gave me a lot of trouble!

LUCINDE: Yes, father, I've recovered my speech; but I've recovered it to tell you that I shall never have any other husband than Léandre, and that there's no use your trying to give
me Horace.

GÉRONTE: But . . .

LUCINDE: Nothing can shake my resolution.

GÉRONTE: What . . . ?

LUCINDE: All your fine objections will be in vain.

GÉRONTE: If . . .

LUCINDE: All your arguments will be no use.

GÉRONTE: I . . .

LUCINDE: It's a thing I'm determined on.

GÉRONTE: But . . .

LUCINDE: There is no paternal authority that can force me to
marry in spite of myself.

GÉRONTE: I've . . .

LUCINDE: All your efforts will not avail.

GÉRONTE: He . . .

LUCINDE: My heart could never submit to this tyranny.

GÉRONTE: There . . .

LUCINDE: And I'll cast myself into a convent rather than marry a
man I don't love.

GÉRONTE: But . . .

LUCINDE *(in a deafening voice)*: No. By no means. Nothing doing.
You're wasting your time. I won't do anything of the sort. That's
settled.

GÉRONTE: Oh! What a rush of words! There's no way to resist it.
Sir, I beg you to make her dumb again.

SGANARELLE: That's impossible for me. All I can do for your service is to make you deaf, if you want.

GÉRONTE: Many thanks! *(To* LUCINDE *)* Then do you think . . . ?

LUCINDE: No. All your reasons will make no impression on my soul.

GÉRONTE: You shall marry Horace this very evening.

LUCINDE: I'll sooner marry death.

SGANARELLE: Good Lord! Stop, let me medicate this affair. Her illness still grips her, and I know the remedy we must apply.

GÉRONTE: Is it possible, sir, that you can also cure this illness of the mind?

SGANARELLE: Yes. Leave it to me, I have remedies for everything, and our apothecary will serve us for this cure. *(Calls the apothecary.)* One word. You see that ardor she has for this Léandre is completely contrary to her father's will, that there is no time to lose, that the humors are very inflamed, and that it is necessary to find a remedy promptly for this ailment, which could get worse with delay. For my part, I see only one, which is a dose of purgative flight, which you will combine properly with two drams of matrimonium in pill form. She may make some difficulty about taking this remedy; but since you are an able man at your trade, it's up to you to persuade her and make her swallow the dose as best you can. Go along and get her to take a little turn around the garden, so as to prepare the humors, while I talk to her father here; but above all don't waste time. The remedy, quickly, the one specific remedy!

SCENE VII GÉRONTE, SGANARELLE

GÉRONTE: What are those drugs, sir, that you just mentioned? It seems to me I've never heard of them.

SGANARELLE: They are drugs used in great emergencies.

GÉRONTE: Did you ever see such insolence as hers?

SGANARELLE: Daughters are sometimes a little headstrong.

GÉRONTE: You wouldn't believe how crazy she is about this Léandre.

SGANARELLE: The heat of the blood does this to young minds.

GÉRONTE: For my part, ever since I discovered the violence of this love, I've managed to keep my daughter always locked up.

SGANARELLE: You've done wisely.

GÉRONTE: And I've kept them from having any communication together.

SGANARELLE: Very good.

GÉRONTE: Some folly would have resulted if I'd allowed them to see each other.

SGANARELLE: No doubt.

GÉRONTE: And I think she'd have been just the girl to run off with him.

SGANARELLE: That's prudent reasoning.

GÉRONTE: I've been warned that he's making every effort to speak to her.

SGANARELLE: What a clown!

GÉRONTE: But he'll be wasting his time.

SGANARELLE: Ha, ha!

GÉRONTE: And I'll keep him from seeing her, all right.

SGANARELLE: He's not dealing with a dolt, and you know tricks of the game that he doesn't. Smarter than you is no fool.

SCENE VIII   LUCAS, GÉRONTE, SGANARELLE

LUCAS: Dad blast it, sir, here's a lot of ruckus: your daughter's done run off with her Léandre. The 'pothecary, that was him; and Mister Doctor here's the one as pufformed that fine operation.

GÉRONTE: What? Assassinate me in that way! Here, get a policeman! Don't let him get out. Ah, traitor! I'll have the law on you.

LUCAS: Hah! By jingo, Mister Doctor, you'll be hung: just don't move outa there.

SCENE IX   MARTINE, SGANARELLE, LUCAS

MARTINE: Oh, Good Lord! What a time I've had finding this house! Tell me, what's the news of the doctor I provided for you?

LUCAS: Here he be. Gonna be hung.

MARTINE: What? My husband hanged? Alas! What's he done?

LUCAS: He fixed it for our master's daughter to get run away with.

MARTINE: Alas! My dear husband, is it really true they're going to hang you?

SGANARELLE: As you see. Oh!

MARTINE: Must you let yourself die in the presence of all these people?

SGANARELLE: What do you expect me to do about it?

MARTINE: At least if you'd finished cutting our wood, I'd have some consolation.

SGANARELLE: Get out of here, you're breaking my heart.

MARTINE: No, I mean to stay to give you courage in the face of death, and I won't leave you until I see you hanged.

SGANARELLE: Oh!

SCENE X GÉRONTE, SGANARELLE, MARTINE, LUCAS

GÉRONTE: The constable will be here soon, and they'll put you in a place where they'll be answerable for you to me.

SGANARELLE *(hat in hand)*: Alas! Can't this be changed to a modest cudgeling?

GÉRONTE: No, no, justice will take its course . . . But what's this I see?

SCENE XI LÉANDRE, LUCINDE, JACQUELINE, LUCAS, GÉRONTE, SGANARELLE, MARTINE

LÉANDRE: Sir, I come to reveal Léandre to you and restore Lucinde to your power. We both intended to run away and get married; but this plan has given way to a more honorable procedure. I do not aim to steal your daughter from you, and it is only from your hands that I wish to receive her. I will tell you this, sir: I have just received letters informing me that my uncle has died and that I am heir to all his property.

GÉRONTE: Sir, I have the highest consideration for your virtues, and I give you my daughter with the greatest pleasure in the world.

SGANARELLE: That was a close shave for medicine!

MARTINE: Since you're not going to be hanged, you can thank me for being a doctor; for I'm the one who procured you that honor.

SGANARELLE: Yes, you're the one who procured me quite a beating.

LÉANDRE: The result is too fine for you to harbor resentment.

SGANARELLE: All right: I forgive you for the beatings in consideration of the dignity you've raised me to; but prepare henceforth to live in the greatest respect with a man of my consequence, and bear in mind that the wrath of a doctor is more to be feared than anyone can ever believe.

HENRIK IBSEN

An Enemy of the People

Characters

DR. THOMAS STOCKMANN, *staff physician at the municipal baths*
MRS. STOCKMANN, *his wife*
PETRA, *their daughter, a teacher*
EILIF
MORTEN } *their sons, aged 12 and 10*
PETER STOCKMANN, *the doctor's older brother, mayor, police chief, chairman of the board of the municipal baths, etc.*
MORTEN KIIL, *master tanner;* MRS. STOCKMANN's *foster-father*
HOVSTAD, *editor of the* People's Courier
BILLING, *his assistant on the paper*
CAPTAIN HORSTER
ASLAKSEN, *a printer*
PARTICIPANTS IN A PUBLIC MEETING: *men of all social ranks, several women, and a gang of schoolboys*

Scene *The action takes place in a coastal town in southern Norway.*

ACT I

Evening. DR. STOCKMANN's *living room, simply but attractively furnished and decorated. In the side wall to the right are two doors, the farther one leading out to the hall, and the nearer into the* DOCTOR's *study. In the facing wall, directly opposite the hall door, is a door to the family's living quarters. At the middle of this wall stands the stove; closer in the foreground, a sofa with a mirror above it, and in front of these, an oval table covered by a cloth.*

On the table a lamp, shaded and lit. In the back wall, an open door to the dining room. The table is set for dinner within, with a lit lamp on it.

BILLING, *napkin under his chin, sits at the table inside.* MRS. STOCKMANN *is standing by the table, passing him a plate with a large slice of roast beef. The other places at the table are empty; the settings are in disorder, as after a meal.*

MRS. STOCKMANN: Well, if you come an hour late, Mr. Billing, then you have to accept cold food.

BILLING *(eating)*: It tastes simply marvelous—just perfect.

MRS. STOCKMANN: Because you know how precise my husband is about keeping his regular mealtime—

BILLING: Doesn't bother me in the least. In fact, I really think food tastes best to me when I can eat like this, alone and undisturbed.

MRS. STOCKMANN: Yes, well—just so you enjoy it— *(Turns, listening, toward the hall door.)* Now that must be Hovstad coming.

BILLING: Probably.

PETER STOCKMANN *enters, wearing an overcoat and the official hat of his mayor's office. He carries a walking stick.*

MAYOR STOCKMANN: A most pleasant good evening, my dear Katherine.

MRS. STOCKMANN *(comes into the living room)*: Why, good evening! So it's you? How nice that you stopped up to see us.

MAYOR STOCKMANN: I was just passing by, so— *(With a glance toward the dining room.)* Ah, but it seems you have company already.

MRS. STOCKMANN *(somewhat embarrassed)*: No, no—he was quite unexpected. *(Hurriedly.)* Won't you step in and join him for a bite?

MAYOR STOCKMANN: I? No, thank you. Good heavens, hot food at night! Not with *my* digestion.

MRS. STOCKMANN: Oh, but just this once—

MAYOR STOCKMANN: No, really, that's kind of you; but I'll stick to my bread and butter and tea. It's healthier in the long run—and a bit more economical, too.

MRS. STOCKMANN *(smiling)*: Now you mustn't think that Thomas and I live so lavishly, either.

MAYOR STOCKMANN: Not *you*, Katherine. *That* never crossed my mind. *(Points toward the* DOCTOR's *study.)* I suppose he isn't home?

MRS. STOCKMANN: No, he went for a little walk after dinner—he and the boys.

MAYOR STOCKMANN: How healthy is that, I wonder? *(Listening.)* That ought to be him.

MRS. STOCKMANN: No, I don't think it is. *(A knock at the door.)* Come in!

HOVSTAD *enters from the hall.*

MRS. STOCKMANN: Ah, so it's Mr. Hovstad—

HOVSTAD: Yes, you'll have to excuse me, but I got held up at the printer's. Good evening, Mr. Mayor.

MAYOR STOCKMANN *(bowing rather stiffly)*: Mr. Hovstad. Here on business, I suppose?

HOVSTAD: Partly. It's about something going in the paper.

MAYOR STOCKMANN: I'm not surprised. I hear my brother's become a very active contributor to the *People's Courier*.

HOVSTAD: Yes, he deigns to write for the *Courier* whenever he has a little plain speaking to do about this and that.

MRS. STOCKMANN *(to* HOVSTAD*)*: But won't you—? *(Points toward the dining room.)*

MAYOR STOCKMANN: Oh, well now, I can hardly blame him for writing for the sort of readers who'd give him the best reception. And of course, personally, you know, I haven't the least cause for any ill will toward your paper, Mr. Hovstad.

HOVSTAD: No, I wouldn't think so.

MAYOR STOCKMANN: On the whole, there's a fine spirit of tolerance in this town of ours—a remarkable public spirit. And that stems, of course, from our having a great common concern that binds us all together—a concern that involves to the same high degree every right-minded citizen—

HOVSTAD: The spa, yes.

MAYOR STOCKMANN: Exactly. We have our great, new, magnificent installation, the spa. Mark my words, Mr. Hovstad—these baths will become the very life-principle of our town. Unquestionably!

MRS. STOCKMANN: That's what Thomas says, too.

MAYOR STOCKMANN: Why, it's simply extraordinary the way this place has revived in the past two years! People here have some money again. There's life, excitement! Land and property values are rising every day.

HOVSTAD: And unemployment's down.

MAYOR STOCKMANN: Yes, that too. The taxes for public welfare have been cut by a comfortable margin for the propertied classes, and will be still more if we can only have a really good summer this year—hordes of visitors—masses of invalids who can give the baths a reputation.

HOVSTAD: And that's the prospect, I hear.

MAYOR STOCKMANN: The outlook is very auspicious. Every day, inquiries coming in about accommodations and the like.

HOVSTAD: Well, then the doctor's article ought to be quite timely.

MAYOR STOCKMANN: Has he been writing something again?

HOVSTAD: This is something he wrote last winter: a recommendation of the baths, and a report on the health-promoting character of the life here. But I held the article back at the time.

MAYOR STOCKMANN: There was a flaw in it somewhere, I suppose?

HOVSTAD: No, that's not it. I thought it was better to wait till now, in the spring, when people start planning their summer vacations—

MAYOR STOCKMANN: Quite right. Absolutely right, Mr. Hovstad.

MRS. STOCKMANN: Yes, Thomas spares nothing when the baths are involved.

MAYOR STOCKMANN: Well, he *is* on the staff, after all.

HOVSTAD: Yes, and then he's the one, too, who really originated the idea.

MAYOR STOCKMANN: He *did?* Really? Yes, I do occasionally hear that certain people hold that opinion. But I still had an impression that *I* also played some modest part in this enterprise.

MRS. STOCKMANN: Yes, Thomas says that always.

HOVSTAD: No one denies that, Mr. Mayor. You got the thing moving and put it into practical reality—we all know that. I only meant that the idea came from the doctor first.

MAYOR STOCKMANN: Yes, my brother's had more than enough ideas in his time, I'm afraid. But when there's something to be done, it's another sort of man that's called for, Mr. Hovstad. And I really had thought that, at least here, in this house—

MRS. STOCKMANN: But, my dear Peter—

HOVSTAD: Sir, how can you possibly think—?

MRS. STOCKMANN: Mr. Hovstad, do go in and take some refreshment. My husband's sure to be back any moment.

HOVSTAD: Thank you; just a bite, maybe. *(He goes into the dining room.)*

MAYOR STOCKMANN *(dropping his voice)*: It's curious with these people of peasant stock: they never can learn any tact.

MRS. STOCKMANN: But why let that bother you? It's not worth it. Can't you and Thomas share the honor, like brothers?

MAYOR STOCKMANN: Yes, it would seem so; but it isn't everyone who can be satisfied with his share, apparently.

MRS. STOCKMANN: Oh, nonsense! You and Thomas get along splendidly together. *(Listening.)* There, now I think we have him. *(Goes over and opens the hall door.)*

DR. STOCKMANN *(laughing and raising commotion outside)*: Look, Katherine—you've got another guest here. Isn't this a treat, eh? There we are, Captain Horster; hang your coat up on the peg. Oh, that's right—you don't wear a coat. Imagine, Katherine, I met him on the street, and he almost didn't want to come up.

CAPTAIN HORSTER *enters and greets* MRS. STOCKMANN. DR. STOCKMANN *appears in the doorway.*

In you go, boys. They're ravenous all over again! Come on, Captain Horster; now you're going to have some roast beef—

He propels HORSTER *into the dining room;* EILIF *and* MORTEN *follow after.*

MRS. STOCKMANN: But, Thomas, don't you see—?

DR. STOCKMANN *(turning by the door)*: Oh, it's you, Peter! *(Goes over to shake hands.)* Well, this *is* a pleasure.

MAYOR STOCKMANN: I'm afraid I have to be going in just a moment—

DR. STOCKMANN: Rubbish! There's hot toddy on the table now, any minute. You haven't forgotten the toddy, Katherine?

MRS. STOCKMANN: Of course not. The water's boiling. *(She goes into the dining room.)*

MAYOR STOCKMANN: Toddy, too—!

DR. STOCKMANN: Yes, have a seat, so we can get comfortable.

MAYOR STOCKMANN: Thank you, I never take part in toddy parties.

DR. STOCKMANN: But this isn't a party.

MAYOR STOCKMANN: Well, it looks to me— *(Glancing toward the dining room.)* It's astonishing how they put all that food away.

DR. STOCKMANN *(rubbing his hands)*: Yes, isn't it wonderful to watch young people eat? Endless appetites—just as it ought to be! They've got to have food—for strength! They're the ones who'll put a kick in the future, Peter.

MAYOR STOCKMANN: May I ask what, here, needs a "kick put in it," in your manner of speaking?

DR. STOCKMANN: Well, you better ask the young ones that—when the time comes. We don't see it, of course. Naturally. A pair of old fogies like you and me—

MAYOR STOCKMANN: Now really! That's a very peculiar term—

DR. STOCKMANN: Oh, you mustn't take things so literally with me, Peter. Because you know, I've been feeling so buoyant and happy. I can't tell you how lucky I feel to be part of this life that's budding and bursting out everywhere. What an amazing age we live in! It's as if a whole new world were rising around us.

MAYOR STOCKMANN: You really believe that?

DR. STOCKMANN: Of course you can't see it as well as I can. You've lived in the midst of it all your life, and that dulls the impression. But I, who've been stuck all these many years in my little limbo up north, hardly ever seeing a stranger with a fresh idea to share—to me, it's as if I'd been plunked down in the middle of a swarming metropolis.

MAYOR STOCKMANN: Hm—metropolis—

DR. STOCKMANN: Oh, I'm well aware this is small scale compared with a lot of other places. But there's life here—a promise, an immensity of things to work and fight for; and *that's* what's important. *(Calls.)* Katherine, didn't the mailman come?

MRS. STOCKMANN *(from the dining room)*: No, not today.

DR. STOCKMANN: And then to make a good living, Peter! That's something you learn to appreciate when you've been getting along, as we have, on starvation wages—

MAYOR STOCKMANN: Oh, come—

DR. STOCKMANN: You can just imagine how tight things were for us up there, yes, many times. And now we can live like kings!

Today, for instance, we had roast beef for dinner, and we had some more for supper. Don't you want a piece? Or, anyway, let me show it to you. Come here—

MAYOR STOCKMANN: No, definitely not—

DR. STOCKMANN: Well, then come over here. Look, we bought a new tablecloth.

MAYOR STOCKMANN: Yes, so I noticed.

DR. STOCKMANN: And we got a lampshade. See? It's all out of Katherine's savings. And it makes the room so cozy, don't you think? Just stand right here—no, no, no, not there. Just—so! Look, how the light concentrates there where it falls. Really, I find that quite elegant. Don't you?

MAYOR STOCKMANN: Yes, if you can allow yourself luxuries like that—

DR. STOCKMANN: Oh yes. I can allow myself that. Katherine says I'm now earning almost as much as we spend.

MAYOR STOCKMANN: Almost—!

DR. STOCKMANN: But a man of science ought to live with a little style. I'm sure the average district judge spends more in a year than I do.

MAYOR STOCKMANN: Yes, I expect so! A district judge, a superior magistrate—

DR. STOCKMANN: Well, an ordinary businessman then. That kind of man spends a lot more—

MAYOR STOCKMANN: It's a matter of circumstances.

DR. STOCKMANN: In any case, I honestly don't waste anything on luxuries, Peter. But I don't feel I can deny myself the gratification of having people in. You see, I need that. Having been shut out for so long—for me it's a necessity of life to spend time with high-spirited, bold young people, with adventurous minds and a wealth of energy—and that's what they are, all of them sitting and savoring their food in there. I wish you knew Hovstad a bit better—

MAYOR STOCKMANN: Yes, come to think of it, Hovstad told me he'll be printing another of your articles.

DR. STOCKMANN: Of *my* articles?

MAYOR STOCKMANN: Yes, about the baths. Something you wrote last winter.

DR. STOCKMANN: Oh yes, that! No, I don't want that in right now.

MAYOR STOCKMANN: No? It strikes me this is just the opportune time.

DR. STOCKMANN: Yes, you might be right—under ordinary circumstances— *(He paces about the room.)*

MAYOR STOCKMANN *(following him with his eyes)*: What's extraordinary about the circumstances now?

DR. STOCKMANN: *(stops)*: Peter, I swear, at this moment I can't tell you—anyway, not this evening. There could be something quite extraordinary about the circumstances—or it might be nothing at all. It could well be that it's just imagination.

MAYOR STOCKMANN: I have to confess, it sounds very mysterious. Is anything wrong? Something I'm excluded from? I would assume that I, as chairman of the board of the municipal baths—

DR. STOCKMANN: And I would assume that—oh, come on, Peter, let's not fly at each other like this.

MAYOR STOCKMANN: Heaven forbid! I'm not in the habit of flying at people, as you put it. But I most definitely must insist that all necessary steps be taken and carried out in a businesslike manner by the legally constituted authorities. I can't condone any sly or underhanded activities.

DR. STOCKMANN: When have I ever been sly or underhanded?

MAYOR STOCKMANN: You have an inveterate tendency to go your own way, in any case. And in a well-ordered society, that's nearly as inexcusable. The individual has to learn to subordinate himself to the whole—or, I should say, to those authorities charged with the common good.

DR. STOCKMANN: Possibly. But what in thunder does that have to do with me?

MAYOR STOCKMANN: Because, my dear Thomas, it's this you seem never to want to learn. But watch out; someday you're going to pay for it—sooner or later. Now I've told you. Good-bye.

DR. STOCKMANN: Are you stark, raving mad? You're completely on the wrong track—

MAYOR STOCKMANN: That's not my custom. And now, if I may excuse myself— *(With a bow toward the dining room.)* Good night, Katherine. Good night, gentlemen. *(Goes out.)*

MRS. STOCKMANN *(coming into the living room)*: He's gone?

DR. STOCKMANN: Yes, and in a foul humor.

MRS. STOCKMANN: Oh, Thomas dear, what did you do to him this time?

DR. STOCKMANN: Nothing at all. He can't demand that I settle accounts with him before the time comes.

MRS. STOCKMANN: What accounts do you have to settle with him?

DR. STOCKMANN: Hm, don't ask me, Katherine. It's odd that the mailman hasn't come.

HOVSTAD, BILLING, *and* HORSTER *have risen from the table and come into the living room.* EILIF *and* MORTEN *follow after a moment.*

BILLING *(stretching his arms)*: Ah, a meal like that and, ye gods, you feel like a new man!

HOVSTAD: The mayor wasn't in his best spirits tonight.

DR. STOCKMANN: It's his stomach; he has bad digestion.

HOVSTAD: I'm sure it was mainly us from the *Courier* he couldn't digest.

MRS. STOCKMANN: You were getting on rather well with him, I thought.

HOVSTAD: Oh yes, but it's nothing more than an armistice.

BILLING: That's it! That's the word for it.

DR. STOCKMANN: We have to remember, Peter's a lonely man. Poor fellow, he has no home to give him comfort—just business, business. And all that damn weak tea he's always sloshing down. Well, now, pull up your chairs to the table, boys! Katherine, don't we get any toddy?

MRS. STOCKMANN *(going toward the dining room)*: I'm just bringing it.

DR. STOCKMANN: And you sit here on the sofa by me, Captain Horster. A rare guest like you—please, sit down, everyone.

The men seat themselves at the table. MRS. STOCKMANN *comes back with a tray, holding a hotplate, glasses, decanters, and the like.*

MRS. STOCKMANN: There now. This is arrack, and here's rum, and cognac. So just help yourselves.

DR. STOCKMANN *(taking a glass)*: Oh, I think we'll manage! *(While the toddy is mixed.)* And let's have the cigars. Eilif, I'm sure you know where the box is. And, Morten, you can fetch my pipe. *(The boys go into the room on the right.)* I have a suspicion that Eilif sneaks a cigar now and then—but I play innocent. *(Calls.)* And my smoking cap too, Morten! Katherine, can't you tell him where I left it? Ah, he's got it! *(The boys bring in the various items.)* Help yourselves, everybody. I'll stick to my pipe. This one's taken me through a lot of dirty weather on my rounds up north. *(Clinking glasses.)* Skoal! Ah, it's a lot better sitting here, snug and warm.

MRS. STOCKMANN *(sits and starts knitting)*: Are you sailing soon, Captain Horster?

HORSTER: I think we'll be ready by next week.

MRS. STOCKMANN: And you'll be going to America then?

HORSTER: That's the intention, yes.

BILLING: But then you can't vote in the new town election.

HORSTER: There's an election coming up?

BILLING: Didn't you know?

HORSTER: No, I don't bother with such things.

BILLING: But you *are* concerned about public affairs, aren't you?

HORSTER: No, I don't understand them.

BILLING: Even so, a person at least ought to vote.

HORSTER: People who don't understand, too?

BILLING: Understand? What do you mean by that? Society's like a ship: all hands have to stand to the wheel.

HORSTER: Maybe on land; but at sea it wouldn't work too well.

HOVSTAD: It's remarkable how most sailors are so little concerned with what happens on land.

BILLING: Very strange.

DR. STOCKMANN: Sailors are like birds of passage: north, south, wherever they are is home. But it's why the rest of us have to be all the more effective, Mr. Hovstad. Anything of general interest in tomorrow's *Courier?*

HOVSTAD: No local items. But I was thinking of running your article the day after tomorrow—

DR. STOCKMANN: Hell's bells, that article! No, listen, you'll have to wait on that.

HOVSTAD: Oh? We have so much space right now, and it seems like the opportune moment—

DR. STOCKMANN: Yes, yes, you're probably right; but you'll have to wait all the same—

PETRA, *wearing a hat and coat, comes in from the hall, with a stack of exercise books under her arm.*

PETRA: Good evening.

DR. STOCKMANN: That's you, Petra? Good evening.

Greetings all around. PETRA *takes off her hat and coat and leaves them, with the books, on a chair by the door.*

PETRA: And here you all sit partying while I'm out slaving away.

DR. STOCKMANN: Well, now it's your party, too.

BILLING: Can I fix you a little drink?

PETRA *(coming to the table)*: Thanks, I'll do it myself. You always make it too strong. Oh, Father, by the way, I have a letter for you. *(Goes over to the chair where her things are.)*

DR. STOCKMANN: A letter! Who from?

PETRA *(searching in her coat pocket)*: I got it from the mailman as I was just going out—

DR. STOCKMANN *(gets up and goes toward her)*: And you don't bring it till now!

PETRA: I really hadn't the time to run up again. Here it is.

DR. STOCKMANN *(seizing the letter)*: Let me see, let me see, child. *(Looks at the envelope.)* Yes, that's it—!

MRS. STOCKMANN: Is *this* the one you've been so impatient for?

DR. STOCKMANN: Exactly. I must take it straight in and—where can I find a light, Katherine? Is there no lamp in my room again?

MRS. STOCKMANN: The lamp is lit and standing on your desk.

DR. STOCKMANN: Good, good. Excuse me a minute— *(Goes into his study to the right.)*

PETRA: Mother, what do you suppose that is?

MRS. STOCKMANN: I don't know. These last days he's been asking constantly about the mailman.

BILLING: Most likely some patient out of town—

PETRA: Poor Father, he's taking on too much work. *(Mixing a drink.)* Ooh, this'll be good!

HOVSTAD: Were you teaching night school again today?

PETRA *(sipping her glass)*: Two hours.

BILLING: And four hours mornings at the Institute—

PETRA *(sitting by the door)*: Five hours.

MRS. STOCKMANN: And papers to correct in the evening, I see.

PETRA: A whole batch, yes.

HORSTER: It looks like you take on your own full share.

PETRA: Yes, but that's fine. You feel so delectably tired afterward.

BILLING: You like that?

PETRA: Yes. Then you sleep so well.

MORTEN: You must be horribly wicked, Petra.

PETRA: Wicked?

MORTEN: Yes, when you work so hard. Mr. Rørland says that work is a punishment for our sins.

EILIF *(snorts)*: Pah, how stupid you are, to believe that stuff.

MRS. STOCKMANN: Now, now, Eilif!

BILLING *(laughing)*: Oh, marvelous!

HOVSTAD: You'd rather not work so hard, Morten?

MORTEN: No, I wouldn't.

HOVSTAD: Yes, but what do you want to be in life?

MORTEN: Best of all, I want to be a Viking.

EILIF: But then you'd have to be a pagan.

MORTEN: Well, so then I'll be a pagan!

BILLING: I'm with you, Morten! Exactly what I say!

MRS. STOCKMANN *(making signals)*: No, you don't really, Mr. Billing.

BILLING: Ye gods, yes—! I *am* a pagan, and proud of it. Just wait, we'll all be pagans soon.

MORTEN: And can we then do anything we want?

BILLING: Well, you see, Morten—

MRS. STOCKMANN: Now, in you go, boys, both of you. I'm sure you've got homework for tomorrow.

EILIF: *I* could stay a little longer—

MRS. STOCKMANN: Oh no, you can't. The two of you, out!

The boys say good night and go into the room to the left.

HOVSTAD: Do you really think it could hurt the boys to hear these things?

MRS. STOCKMANN: Well, I don't know. But I don't like it.

PETRA: Oh, Mother, I think you're just being silly.

MRS. STOCKMANN: Yes, that's possible; but I don't like it—not here at home.

PETRA: Oh, there's so much hypocrisy, both at home and in school. At home we have to keep quiet, and in school we have to stand there and lie to the children.

HORSTER: You have to lie?

PETRA: Yes, don't you know, we have to teach them all kinds of things we don't believe in ourselves?

BILLING: Yes, that's for certain.

PETRA: If I only had the means, then I'd start a school myself, and things would be different there.

BILLING: Pah, the means—!

HORSTER: Well, if that's your idea, Miss Stockmann, I'll gladly provide you the facilities. My father's old place has been standing nearly empty; there's a huge dining room on the ground floor—

PETRA *(laughing)*: Oh, thank you! But nothing'll come of it, I'm sure.

HOVSTAD: No, I think Miss Petra's more apt to go in for journalism. Incidentally, have you had time to look over that English story you promised to translate for us?

PETRA: No, not yet. But I'll get it to you in time.

DR. STOCKMANN *comes in from his study, the open letter in his hand.*

DR. STOCKMANN *(waving the letter)*: Well, let me tell you, here's news for the town!

BILLING: News?

MRS. STOCKMANN: What sort of news?

DR. STOCKMANN: A great discovery, Katherine!

HOVSTAD: Really?

MRS. STOCKMANN: That you've made?

DR. STOCKMANN: My own, yes. *(Pacing back and forth.)* Now let them come around the way they do, saying it's just whims and wild fantasies. But they better watch out! *(With a laugh.)* They're going to watch out, I think!

PETRA: But, Father, tell what it is!

DR. STOCKMANN: Yes, all right, just give me time, and you'll learn everything. If I only had Peter here now! There you see how we human beings can go around, passing judgments as blind as moles—

HOVSTAD: What do you mean by that, Doctor?

DR. STOCKMANN *(stops by the table)*: It's the general opinion, isn't it, that our town is a healthy place?

HOVSTAD: Why, of course.

DR. STOCKMANN: A most outstandingly healthy place, as a matter of fact—a place to be glowingly recommended to sick and well alike—

MRS. STOCKMANN: But, Thomas, dear—

DR. STOCKMANN: And recommend it we have, and praised it to the skies. I've written endlessly in the *Courier* and in pamphlets—

HOVSTAD: All right, so?

DR. STOCKMANN: This establishment, the baths, that's been called the "main artery" of the town, and its "nerve center," and— who the hell knows what else—

BILLING: "The pulsating heart of our town" I once, in a moment of exuberance, went so far as to—

DR. STOCKMANN: Oh yes, that too. But do you know what they are in reality, these great, splendid, celebrated baths that have cost such a lot of money—you know what they are?

HOVSTAD: No, what are they?

MRS. STOCKMANN: What?

DR. STOCKMANN: The whole setup's a pesthole.

PETRA: The baths, Father!

MRS. STOCKMANN *(simultaneously)*: Our baths!

HOVSTAD *(likewise)*: But, Doctor—

BILLING: Simply incredible!

DR. STOCKMANN: It's a whited sepulcher, the whole establishment—poisoned, you hear me! A health hazard in the worst way. All that pollution up at Mølledal—all that reeking waste from the mill—it's seeped into the pipes feeding the pump-room; and the same damn poisonous slop's been draining out on the beach as well.

HORSTER: You mean in the bathing area?

DR. STOCKMANN: Exactly.

HOVSTAD: How can you be so certain of all this, Doctor?

DR. STOCKMANN: I've investigated the facts as scrupulously as possible. Oh, I've had suspicions for quite a while. Last year there were a number of unusual cases among the visitors here—typhoid and gastritis—

MRS. STOCKMANN: That's right, there were.

DR. STOCKMANN: At the time we assumed the visitors had brought their maladies with them. But later, over the past winter, I began having second thoughts; so I set out to analyze the water with the best means available.

MRS. STOCKMANN: So *that's* what you've been so involved in!

DR. STOCKMANN: Yes, involved—you can well say that, Katherine. But here, of course, I lacked the necessary scientific equipment, so I sent samples of both the drinking water and the seawater to the university for a strict laboratory analysis.

HOVSTAD: And this you've just gotten?

DR. STOCKMANN *(showing the letter)*: This is it! There's irrefutable proof of the presence of decayed organic matter in the water—millions of bacteria. It's positively injurious to health, for either internal or external use.

MRS. STOCKMANN: What a godsend that you found out in time!

DR. STOCKMANN: You can say that again.

HOVSTAD: And what do you plan to do now, Doctor?

DR. STOCKMANN: To see things set to rights, of course.

HOVSTAD: Can that be done?

DR. STOCKMANN: It's got to be. Otherwise, the baths are totally useless—ruined. But there's no need for that. I'm quite clear about what actions have to be taken.

MRS. STOCKMANN: But, Thomas dear, why have you made such a secret of all this?

DR. STOCKMANN: Maybe I should have run out in the streets, blabbering about it before I had sure proof. No thanks, I'm not that crazy.

PETRA: But to us at home—

DR. STOCKMANN: Not to one living soul! But tomorrow you can run over to the Badger—

MRS. STOCKMANN: Really, Thomas—!

DR. STOCKMANN: All right then, your grandfather. Yes, this'll stand the old boy on his ear. He's always thought I'm a bit unhinged—oh yes, and a lot more think the same, I'm aware. But now these good people are going to find out—! *(Walks about, rubbing his hands.)* What a stir this'll make in town, Katherine! You can't imagine. The whole water system has to be relaid.

HOVSTAD *(rising)*: The whole water system—?

DR. STOCKMANN: Well, obviously. The intake's too low; it's got to be placed much higher up.

PETRA: So you were right, after all.

DR. STOCKMANN: Ah, you remember that, Petra? I wrote a protest when they were just starting construction. But nobody would listen to me then. Well, now you can bet I'll pour on the heat—yes, because naturally I've written a report for the board of directors. It's been lying in my drawer a whole week; I've just been waiting for this. *(Waving the letter.)* But now it'll be sent right off. *(Goes into his study and returns with a sheaf of papers.)* See here! Four closely written pages! And a covering letter. A newspaper, Katherine—something to wrap this in! Good, that's it. Give it to—to—*(Stamps his foot.)*—what the hell's her name? The maid! Well, give it to her and tell her to take it straight to the mayor.

MRS. STOCKMANN *takes the packet and goes out through the dining room.*

PETRA: What do you think Uncle Peter will say, Father?

DR. STOCKMANN: What should he say? Undoubtedly he has to be glad that a fact of such importance is brought to light.

HOVSTAD: May I have permission to run a little item on your discovery in the *Courier?*

DR. STOCKMANN: I'd be most gratified if you would.

HOVSTAD: The public should hear about this, and the sooner the better.

DR. STOCKMANN: Absolutely.

MRS. STOCKMANN *(returning)*: She's gone with it.

BILLING: So help me, Doctor, you're the foremost citizen of this town!

DR. STOCKMANN *(walks about, looking pleased)*: Oh, come on—really, I haven't done anything more than my duty. I've been a lucky treasure-hunter, and that's it. All the same—

BILLING: Hovstad, don't you think this town owes Doctor Stockmann a parade?

HOVSTAD: I'll come out for it, in any case.

BILLING: And I'll put it up to Aslaksen.

DR. STOCKMANN: No, my dear friends, please—forget all this nonsense. I don't want any ceremonies. And if the board tries to vote me a raise in salary, I won't take it. Katherine, I'm telling you this—I won't take it.

MRS. STOCKMANN: That's only right, Thomas.

PETRA *(raising her glass)*: Skoal, Father!

HOVSTAD *and* BILLING: Skoal, skoal, Doctor!

HORSTER *(clinking glasses with him)*: May this bring you nothing but joy.

DR. STOCKMANN: Thank you. Dear friends, thank you! My heart is so full of happiness—! Ah, what a blessing it is to feel that you've done some service for your own home town and your fellow citizens. Hurrah, Katherine!

He wraps both hands around her neck and whirls about the room with her; she screams and struggles against him. Laughter, applause, and cheers for the DOCTOR. *The* BOYS *poke their heads in at the door.*

ACT II

The DOCTOR's *living room. The dining-room door is closed. It is morning.* MRS. STOCKMANN, *with a sealed letter in her hand, enters from the dining room, goes across to the door of the* DOCTOR's *study, and peers inside.*

MRS. STOCKMANN: Are you in, Thomas?

DR. STOCKMANN *(from within)*: Yes, I just got back. *(Entering)* Is there something?

MRS. STOCKMANN: Letter from your brother. *(Hands it to him.)*

DR. STOCKMANN: Ah, let's see. *(Opens the envelope and reads.)* "The enclosed manuscript is returned herewith—" *(Reads on in an undertone.)* Hm—

MRS. STOCKMANN: What does he say?

DR. STOCKMANN: *(slips the papers in his pocket)*: Only that he'll be stopping up around noon sometime.

MRS. STOCKMANN: You *must* remember not to go out, then.

DR. STOCKMANN: Oh, that's no problem. I've finished my calls for the morning.

MRS. STOCKMANN: I'm terribly curious to know how he takes it.

DR. STOCKMANN: You'll see, he's not going to like it that I made the discovery, and he didn't.

MRS. STOCKMANN: Yes, doesn't that worry you?

DR. STOCKMANN: Oh, basically he'll be pleased, you can imagine. All the same—Peter's so damned nervous that somebody besides himself might do this town a little good.

MRS. STOCKMANN: But, you know what, Thomas—that's why you ought to be nice and share the honors with him. Couldn't it get around that he was the one who put you on the track—?

DR. STOCKMANN: Fine, as far as I'm concerned. If I can just get this thing cleared up—

Old MORTEN KIIL *sticks in his head at the hall door, looks about inquisitively, and shakes with silent laughter.*

MORTEN KIIL *(slyly)*: Is is—is it true?

MRS. STOCKMANN *(moving toward him)*: Father—it's you!

DR. STOCKMANN: Why, Father-in-law, good morning, good morning!

MRS. STOCKMANN: Oh, but aren't you coming in?

MORTEN KIIL: Yes, if it's true—if not, I'm leaving—

DR. STOCKMANN: If what's true?

MORTEN KIIL: This wild story about the waterworks. Is that true?

DR. STOCKMANN: Of course it's true. But how did *you* hear about it?

MORTEN KIIL *(entering)*: Petra flew in on her way to school—

DR. STOCKMANN: Oh, did she?

MORTEN KIIL: Oh yes, and she told me. I thought she was just making a fool of me; but that isn't like Petra, either.

DR. STOCKMANN: You don't mean that!

MORTEN KIIL: Oh, you can't trust anybody. You can be made a fool of before you know it. It really is true, though?

DR. STOCKMANN: Yes, irrefutably. Now, please, have a seat, Father. *(Pressing him down onto the sofa.)* Isn't this a real piece of luck for the town?

MORTEN KIIL *(stifling his laughter)*: Luck for the town?

DR. STOCKMANN: Yes, that I made this discovery in the nick of time—

MORTEN KIIL *(as before)*: Yes, yes, yes! But I'd never have dreamed that you'd play your monkeyshines on your own brother.

DR. STOCKMANN: Monkeyshines!

MRS. STOCKMANN: But, Father—

MORTEN KIIL (*rests his hands and chin on the handle of his cane and winks slyly at the* DOCTOR): How was it now? You're saying that some animals got loose in the waterpipes?

DR. STOCKMANN: Yes, bacteria.

MORTEN KIIL: And there are lots of those animals in there, Petra said. A huge crowd of them.

DR. STOCKMANN: Up in the millions, most likely.

MORTEN KIIL: But no one can see them—wasn't that it?

DR. STOCKMANN: You can't *see* them, of course not.

MORTEN KIIL (*chuckling to himself*): Damned if this isn't the best one you've pulled off yet.

DR. STOCKMANN: What do you mean?

MORTEN KIIL: But you'll never get the mayor believing anything like that.

DR. STOCKMANN: Well, we'll see.

MORTEN KIIL: You think he's that crazy?

DR. STOCKMANN: I hope the whole town will be that crazy.

MORTEN KIIL: The whole town! Yes, that's not impossible. It'd serve them right—and show them up. They think they're so much smarter than us old boys. They hounded me out of the town council. That's right, I'm telling you, like a dog they hounded me out, they did. But now they're going to get it. You just go on and lay your monkeyshines on them, Stockmann.

DR. STOCKMANN: Yes, but—

MORTEN KIIL: Make monkeys out of them, I say. (*Getting up.*) If you can work it so the mayor and his cronies get their ears pinned back, right then and there I'll donate a hundred crowns to the poor.

DR. STOCKMANN: You're very generous.

MORTEN KIIL: Yes, of course I've got little enough to spare, you understand. But if you can do that, I'll remember the poor next Christmas with a good fifty crowns.

HOVSTAD *comes in from the hall.*

HOVSTAD: Good morning! (*Stopping.*) Oh, excuse me—

DR. STOCKMANN: No, come in, come in.

MORTEN KIIL (*chuckling again*): Him! Is he in on this too?

HOVSTAD: What do you mean?

DR. STOCKMANN: Why, of course he is.

MORTEN KIIL: I might have guessed it. It's going into the paper. You're really the limit, Stockmann. Well, now you two get together; I'm leaving.

DR. STOCKMANN: No, stay a while, Father.

MORTEN KIIL: No, I'm leaving. And scheme up all the monkeyshines you can. You damn well aren't going to lose by it!

He goes, accompanied by MRS. STOCKMANN.

DR. STOCKMANN *(laughing)*: What do you think—the old man doesn't believe a word of this about the water system.

HOVSTAD: Oh, was it *that*—?

DR. STOCKMANN: Yes, that's what we were talking about. And I suppose you're here for the same.

HOVSTAD: That's right. Do you have just a moment, Doctor?

DR. STOCKMANN: As long as you like.

HOVSTAD: Have you heard anything from the mayor?

DR. STOCKMANN: Not yet. He's stopping by later.

HOVSTAD: I've been thinking a good deal about this business since last evening.

DR. STOCKMANN: Oh?

HOVSTAD: For you, as a doctor and a scientist, this condition in the water system is something all to itself. I mean, it hasn't occurred to you that it's interrelated with a lot of other things.

DR. STOCKMANN: How so? Here, let's sit down. No, on the sofa there.

HOVSTAD *sits on the sofa, and* STOCKMANN *in an armchair on the other side of the table.*

DR. STOCKMANN: Well? You were thinking—?

HOVSTAD: You said yesterday that the polluted water came from impurities in the soil.

DR. STOCKMANN: Yes, beyond any doubt it comes from that poisoned swamp up at Mølledal.

HOVSTAD: If you'll pardon me, Doctor, I think it comes from another swamp altogether.

DR. STOCKMANN: What sort?

HOVSTAD: The swamp where our whole community lies rotting.

DR. STOCKMANN: What the deuce is that supposed to mean, Mr. Hovstad?

HOVSTAD: Little by little every activity in this town has passed into the hands of a little clique of politicians —

DR. STOCKMANN: Come on now, they're not all of them politicians.

HOVSTAD: No, but those who aren't politicians are their friends and camp followers. All the rich in town, and the old established names — they're the powers that rule our lives.

DR. STOCKMANN: Yes, but then those people have a great deal of competence and vision.

HOVSTAD: Did they show competence and vision when they laid the water mains where they are now?

DR. STOCKMANN: No, of course that was an enormous piece of stupidity. But that'll be straightened out now.

HOVSTAD: You think it'll go so smoothly?

DR. STOCKMANN: Smoothly or not — it's going to go through.

HOVSTAD: Yes, if the press steps in.

DR. STOCKMANN: That won't be necessary, really. I'm positive that my brother —

HOVSTAD: Excuse me, Doctor; but I'm telling you that I plan to take this matter up.

DR. STOCKMANN: In the paper?

HOVSTAD: Yes. When I took over the *Courier*, it was my intention to break up that ring of pig-headed reactionaries who hold all the power.

DR. STOCKMANN: But you've told me yourself what the outcome was: you nearly wrecked the paper over them.

HOVSTAD: Yes, that time we had to back down, it's true. There was some risk that the baths might never have been constructed if those men had fallen. But now we have the baths, and the high and mighty are expendable now.

DR. STOCKMANN: Expendable, yes; but we still owe them a great debt.

HOVSTAD: And we'll acknowledge that, in all fairness. But a journalist of my radical leanings can't let an opportunity like this go by. The myth of the infallibility of the ruling class has to be shattered. It has to be rooted out, like any other superstition.

DR. STOCKMANN: I fully agree with you there, Mr. Hovstad. If it's a superstition, then out with it!

HOVSTAD: Of course I'm rather loath to involve the mayor, since he *is* your brother. But certainly you believe as I do, that the truth comes before anything else.

DR. STOCKMANN: No question of that. *(In an outburst.)* Yes, but—but—!

HOVSTAD: You mustn't think badly of me. I'm no more self-seeking or power-hungry than most people.

DR. STOCKMANN: But—whoever said you were?

HOVSTAD: I come from a poor family, as you know; and I've had ample opportunity to observe what the most pressing need is among the lower classes. Doctor, it's to play some part in directing our public life. That's the thing that develops skills and knowledge and self-respect—

DR. STOCKMANN: I understand absolutely—

HOVSTAD: Yes—and so I think a journalist is terribly remiss if he neglects the least opportunity for the liberation of the powerless, oppressed masses. Oh, I know—those on top are going to label this agitation, among other things; but they can say what they please. So long as my conscience is clear, then—

DR. STOCKMANN: That's it, yes! That's it, Mr. Hovstad. But all the same—damn it—! *(A knock at the door.)* Come in!

ASLAKSEN, *the printer, appears at the hall door. He is plainly but respectably dressed in black, with a white, somewhat wrinkled cravat; he holds gloves and a high silk hat in his hand.*

ASLAKSEN *(bowing)*: Pardon me, Doctor, for intruding like this—

DR. STOCKMANN *(rises)*: Well, now—it's Mr. Aslaksen!

ASLAKSEN: That's right, Doctor.

HOVSTAD *(getting up)*: Were you looking for me, Aslaksen?

ASLAKSEN: No, I didn't think to meet you here. No, it was the doctor himself—

DR. STOCKMANN: Well, what can I do for you?

ASLAKSEN: Is it true, what I heard from Mr. Billing, that you're of a mind to get us a better water system?

DR. STOCKMANN: Yes, for the baths.

ASLAKSEN: Of course; I understand. Well, then I'm here to say, I'm throwing my full support behind you in this.

HOVSTAD *(to the* DOCTOR*)*: You see!

ASLAKSEN: Because it might just come in handy to have us small businessmen in back of you. We make up pretty much of a solid majority in this town—that is, when we *choose* to. And it's always good to have the majority with you, Doctor.

DR. STOCKMANN: That's undoubtedly true. But I can hardly believe that any special measures are going to be needed here. With something as clear-cut as this, it would seem to me—

ASLAKSEN: Oh, it could be a good thing all the same. Because I know these local authorities. The ones that run things don't take too kindly to propositions coming from the outside. And so I was thinking it wouldn't be out of the way if we staged a little demonstration.

HOVSTAD: That's the idea.

DR. STOCKMANN: You say, a demonstration? Just how would you plan to demonstrate?

ASLAKSEN: Naturally with great moderation, Doctor. I always make every effort for moderation. Because moderation is a citizen's chief virtue—in *my* opinion, anyway.

DR. STOCKMANN: You're certainly well known for it, Mr. Aslaksen.

ASLAKSEN: Yes, I think that's not too much to say. And this question of the water system, it's immensely important to us little businessmen. The baths show every sign of becoming like a miniature gold mine for this town. It's the baths that'll give us all a living, and especially us home owners. That's why we want to support this operation in every possible way. And since I'm now chairman of the Home Owners Council—

DR. STOCKMANN: Yes—?

ASLAKSEN: And since, moreover, I'm a representative of the Temperance Union—you knew, Doctor, did you not, that I am a temperance worker?

DR. STOCKMANN: Yes, that follows.

ASLAKSEN: Well—so it's quite obvious that I come in contact with a wide variety of people. And since I'm known for being a sober, law-abiding citizen, as you yourself said, Doctor, I've acquired a certain influence in this town—just a little position of power—if I may say so myself.

DR. STOCKMANN: I'm well aware of that, Mr. Aslaksen.

ASLAKSEN: So you see—it would be a small matter for me to work up a tribute, in a pinch.

DR. STOCKMANN: A tribute?

ASLAKSEN: Yes, a kind of tribute of thanks from the townspeople to you, for having advanced such a vital interest for the community. It goes without saying that it's got to be phrased with all due moderation, so it doesn't offend the authorities, or anyone else in power. And if we just watch ourselves *there,* then I don't think anyone will object, do you?

HOVSTAD: So, even if they didn't like it too well—

ASLAKSEN: No, no, no! No affronts to the authorities, Mr. Hovstad. No collisions with people so much involved in our lives. I've had enough of that in my time; and no good ever comes of it, either. But a citizen's sober and honest opinions are not to be scorned by any man.

DR. STOCKMANN *(shaking his hand)*: My dear Mr. Aslaksen, I can't tell you how deeply it pleases me to find so much sympathy among my fellow citizens. It makes me so happy—so happy! Listen, why not a little glass of sherry, what?

ASLAKSEN: Many thanks, but no. I never indulge in spirits.

DR. STOCKMANN: Well, then a glass of beer—what do you say to that?

ASLAKSEN: Thanks again, Doctor, but I never partake so early in the day. Just now I want to get around town and talk to some of the home owners and prepare their reactions.

DR. STOCKMANN: That's exceptionally kind of you, Mr. Aslaksen. But I simply can't get it through my head that all these measures are going to be necessary. I think the matter could very well take care of itself.

ASLAKSEN: Authorities tend to need goading, Doctor Stockmann— though, on my soul, I don't mean to be critical of them—!

HOVSTAD: We'll go after them in the paper tomorrow, Aslaksen.

ASLAKSEN: But without violence, Mr. Hovstad. Proceed in moderation, or you'll never get anywhere. You can trust my word on that, because I've gleaned my experience in the school of life. Well, then—I'll say good-bye to you, Doctor. Now you know that, in any event, we small businessmen stand behind you, like a wall. You've got the solid majority on your side, Doctor.

DR. STOCKMANN: Thank you for that, Mr. Aslaksen. *(Shaking his hand.)* Good-bye, good-bye!

ASLAKSEN: Will you be coming along to the pressroom, Mr. Hovstad?

HOVSTAD: I'll be in later. I still have a bit more to do.

ASLAKSEN: Very good.

He bows and leaves. DR. STOCKMANN *accompanies him into the hall.*

HOVSTAD *(as the* DOCTOR *re-enters)*: Well, what do you say now, Doctor? Don't you think it's about time to stir up and air out all the stale, spineless inertia in this town?

DR. STOCKMANN: You're referring to Aslaksen?

HOVSTAD: Yes, I am. He's one of them who's sunk in the swamp— good a man as he is in some other ways. He's what most of them are around here: they go along tacking and trimming from this side to that. With all their scruples and second thoughts, they never dare strike out for anything.

DR. STOCKMANN: But to me Aslaksen seemed so thoroughly well-intentioned.

HOVSTAD: There's something I value more—and that's standing your ground as a strong, self-reliant man.

DR. STOCKMANN: I agree with you there entirely.

HOVSTAD: That's why I want to take this opportunity now and see if I can't force some of these models of intention to make men of themselves for once. The worship of authority in this town has to be uprooted. This inexcusable lapse of judgment about the water system has to be driven home to every eligible voter.

DR. STOCKMANN: All right. If you think it's best for the community, then go ahead. But not before I've talked with my brother.

HOVSTAD: Meanwhile, I'm writng an editorial to have on hand. And if the mayor doesn't get after this thing—

DR. STOCKMANN: Oh, but how can you think he wouldn't?

HOVSTAD: It's quite thinkable. And, if so—?

DR. STOCKMANN: Well, then I promise you—listen—then you can print my report—complete and uncut.

HOVSTAD: May I? Your word on that?

DR. STOCKMANN *(hands him the manuscript)*: Here it is. Take it along. It can't hurt if you read it through; and you can give it back to me later.

HOVSTAD: Very good; I'll do that. Good-bye then, Doctor.

DR. STOCKMANN: Good-bye, good-bye. Yes, you'll see now, it'll all go smoothly, Mr. Hovstad. Very smoothly.

HOVSTAD: Hm—we'll see. *(He bows and goes out by the hall door.)*

DR. STOCKMANN *(goes over to the dining room and looks in)*: Katherine—! Oh, are you back, Petra?

PETRA *(entering)*: Yes, I just came from school.

MRS. STOCKMANN *(entering)*: He's still not been in?

DR. STOCKMANN: Peter? No. But I had a long talk with Hovstad. He's very much excited by the discovery I've made. Its repercussions go a lot further, apparently, than I thought at first. So he's put his paper at my disposal, if it comes to that.

MRS. STOCKMANN: Do you think it will come to that?

DR. STOCKMANN: Oh, of course not. But all the same, it's a heady feeling to know you've got the independent liberal press on your side. Yes, and guess what? I also had a visit from the chairman of the Home Owners Council.

MRS. STOCKMANN: Oh? And what did he want?

DR. STOCKMANN: To support me, as well. They'll all support me, if things get rough. Katherine—do you know what I have backing me up?

MRS. STOCKMANN: Backing you up? No, what do you have?

DR. STOCKMANN: The solid majority.

MRS. STOCKMANN: Really. And that's a good thing, is it, Thomas?

DR. STOCKMANN: Well, I should hope it's a good thing! *(Paces up and down, rubbing his hands together.)* My Lord, how gratifying it is to stand like this, joined together in brotherhood with your fellow citizens.

PETRA: And then to accomplish so much that's fine and useful, Father!

DR. STOCKMANN: And for one's own birthplace in the bargain.

MRS. STOCKMANN: There's the bell.

DR. STOCKMANN: That's got to be him. *(A knock at the door.)* Come in!

MAYOR STOCKMANN *(entering from the hall)*: Good morning.

DR. STOCKMANN: Good to see you, Peter!

MRS. STOCKMANN: Morning, Peter. How's everything with you?

MAYOR STOCKMANN: Just so-so, thank you. *(To the DOCTOR.)*

Yesterday, after office hours, I received a report from you, discussing the condition of the water at the baths.

DR. STOCKMANN: Yes. Have you read it?

MAYOR STOCKMANN: I have.

DR. STOCKMANN: What have you got to say about it?

MAYOR STOCKMANN *(glancing at the others)*: Hm—

MRS. STOCKMANN: Come along, Petra.

She and PETRA *go into the room on the left.*

MAYOR STOCKMANN *(after a moment)*: Was it necessary to press
all these investigations behind my back?

DR. STOCKMANN: Well, as long as I didn't have absolute proof,
then—

MAYOR STOCKMANN: And now you think you do?

DR. STOCKMANN: You must be convinced of that yourself.

MAYOR STOCKMANN: Is it your object to put this document before
the board of directors by way of an official recommendation?

DR. STOCKMANN: Of course. Something has to be done about this.
And fast.

MAYOR STOCKMANN: As usual, in your report you let your language get out of hand. You say, among other things, that what
we're offering our summer visitors is guaranteed poison.

DR. STOCKMANN: But, Peter, how else can you describe it? You've
got to realize—this water *is* poison for internal *or* external use!
And it's foisted on poor, suffering creatures who turn to us in
good faith and pay us exorbitant fees to gain their health back
again!

MAYOR STOCKMANN: And then you arrive at the conclusion, by
your line of reasoning, that we have to build a sewer to drain
off these so-called impurities from Mølledal, and that all the
water mains have to be relaid.

DR. STOCKMANN: Well, do you see any other way out? I don't.

MAYOR STOCKMANN: I invented a little business this morning down
at the town engineer's office. And in a half-joking way, I brought
up these proposals as something we perhaps ought to take under
advisement at some time in the future.

DR. STOCKMANN: Some time in the future!

MAYOR STOCKMANN: He smiled at my whimsical extravagance—
naturally. Have you gone to the trouble of estimating just what

these proposed changes would cost? From the information I received, the expenditure would probably run up into several hundred thousand crowns.

DR. STOCKMANN: As high as that?

MAYOR STOCKMANN: Yes. But that's not the worst. The work would extend over at least two years.

DR. STOCKMANN: Two years? Two full years?

MAYOR STOCKMANN: At the least. And meanwhile what do we do with the baths? Shut them down? Yes, we'll have to. Do you really think anyone would make the effort to come all the distance here if the rumor got out that the water was contaminated?

DR. STOCKMANN: Yes, but Peter, that's what it is.

MAYOR STOCKMANN: And then all this happens now—just now, when the baths were being recognized. Other towns in this area have the same resources for development as health resorts. Don't you think they'll leap at the chance to attract the whole flow of tourists to them? No question of it. And there we are, left stranded. We'll most likely have to abandon the whole costly enterprise; and then you'll have ruined the town you were born in.

DR. STOCKMANN: I—ruined—!

MAYOR STOCKMANN: It's through the baths alone that this town has any future to speak of. You can see that just as plain as I can.

DR. STOCKMANN: But then what do you think ought to be done?

MAYOR STOCKMANN: From your report I'm unable to persuade myself that the condition of the baths is as critical as you claim.

DR. STOCKMANN: Look, if anything, it's worse! Or it'll be that by summer, when the warm weather comes.

MAYOR STOCKMANN: Once again. I think you're exaggerating considerably. A capable doctor must know the right steps to take— he should be able to control toxic elements, and to treat them if they make their presence too obvious.

DR. STOCKMANN: And then—? What else—?

MAYOR STOCKMANN: The water system for the baths as it now stands is simply a fact and clearly has to be accepted as such. But in time the directors will more than likely agree to take under consideration to what extent—depending on the funds available—they can institute certain improvements.

DR. STOCKMANN: And you can think I'd play along with that kind of trickery!

MAYOR STOCKMANN: Trickery?

DR. STOCKMANN: Yes, it's a trick—a deception, a lie, an out-and-out crime against the public and society at large!

MAYOR STOCKMANN: As I've already observed, I've not yet persuaded myself that there's any real impending danger here.

DR. STOCKMANN: Yes, you have! There's no alternative. My report is perfectly accurate, I know that! And you're very much aware of it, Peter, but you won't admit it. You're the one who got the baths and the water system laid out where they are today; and it's *this*—it's this hellish miscalculation that you won't concede. Pah! You don't think I can see right through you?

MAYOR STOCKMANN: And even if it were true? Even if I seem a bit overanxious about my reputation, it's all for the good of the town. Without moral authority I could hardly guide and direct affairs in the way I believe serves the general welfare. For this reason—among many others—it strikes me as imperative that your report not be submitted to the board of directors. It has to be withheld for the common good. Then, later, I'll bring the matter up for discussion, and we'll do the very best we can, as quietly as possible. But nothing—not the slightest word of this catastrophe must leak out to the public.

DR. STOCKMANN: My dear Peter, there's no stopping it now.

MAYOR STOCKMANN: It must and it will be stopped.

DR. STOCKMANN: I'm telling you, it's no use. Too many people know already.

MAYOR STOCKMANN: Know already! Who? Not those fellows from the *Courier*—?

DR. STOCKMANN: Why, of course they know. The independent liberal press is going to see that you do your duty.

MAYOR STOCKMANN (*after a short pause*): You're an exceptionally thoughtless man, Thomas. Haven't you considered the consequences that can follow for you?

DR. STOCKMANN: Consequences? For me?

MAYOR STOCKMANN: For you and your family as well.

DR. STOCKMANN: What the devil does *that* mean?

MAYOR STOCKMANN: I think, over the years, I've proved a helpful and accommodating brother to you.

DR. STOCKMANN: Yes, you have, and I'm thankful to you for that.

MAYOR STOCKMANN: I'm not after thanks. Because, in part, I was forced into it—for my own sake. I always hoped I could keep you in check somewhat if I helped better your economic status.

DR. STOCKMANN: What? Just for your own sake—!

MAYOR STOCKMANN: In part, I said. It's embarrassing for a public servant when his closest relative goes and compromises himself again and again.

DR. STOCKMANN: And that's what you think I do?

MAYOR STOCKMANN: Yes, unfortunately you do, without your knowing it. You have a restless, unruly, combative nature. And then this unhappy knack of bursting into print on all kinds of likely and unlikely subjects. You're no sooner struck by an idea than right away you have to scribble a newspaper article on it, or a whole pamphlet even.

DR. STOCKMANN: Well, but isn't it a citizen's duty to inform the public if he comes on a new idea?

MAYOR STOCKMANN: Oh, the public doesn't need new ideas. The public is served best by the good, old, time-tested ideas it's always had.

DR. STOCKMANN: That's putting it plainly!

MAYOR STOCKMANN: I have to talk to you plainly for once. Up till now I've always tried to avoid that because I know how irritable you are; but now I'm telling you the truth, Thomas. You have no conception how much you injure yourself with your impetuosity. You complain about the authorities and, yes, the government; you rail against them—and insist you're being passed over and persecuted. But what can you expect—someone as troublesome as you.

DR. STOCKMANN: Ah—so I'm troublesome, too?

MAYOR STOCKMANN: Yes, Thomas, you're a very troublesome man to work with. I know from experience. You show no consideration at all. You seem to forget completely that I'm the one you can thank for your post here as staff physician at the baths—

DR. STOCKMANN: I was the inevitable choice—I and nobody else! I was the first to see that this town could become a flourishing spa; and I was the *only* one who could see it then. I stood alone fighting for that idea for years; and I wrote and wrote—

MAYOR STOCKMANN: Unquestionably. But the right moment

hadn't arrived yet. Of course you couldn't judge that from up there in the wilds. But when the opportune time came, and I— and a few others—took the matter in hand—

DR. STOCKMANN: Yes, and bungled the whole magnificent plan. Oh yes, it's really coming out now what a brilliant crew you've been!

MAYOR STOCKMANN: All that's coming out, to my mind, is your usual hunger for a good fight. You want to attack your superiors—it's your old pattern. You can't stand any authority over you; you resent anyone in a higher position and regard him as a personal enemy—and then one weapon's as good as another to use. But now I've acquainted you with the vital interests at stake here for this whole town—and, naturally, for me as well. And so I'm warning you, Thomas, I'll be adamant about the demand I am going to make of you.

DR. STOCKMANN: What demand?

MAYOR STOCKMANN: Since you've been so indiscreet as to discuss this delicate issue with outsiders, even though it should have been kept secret among the directors, it of course can't be hushed up now. All kinds of rumors will go flying around, and the maliciously inclined will dress them up with trimmings of their own. It'll therefore be necessary that you publicly deny these rumors.

DR. STOCKMANN: I! How? I don't understand.

MAYOR STOCKMANN: We can expect that, after further investigation, you'll arrive at the conclusion that things are far from being as critical or dangerous as you'd first imagined.

DR. STOCKMANN: Ah—you expect that!

MAYOR STOCKMANN: Moreover, we expect that you'll support and publicly affirm your confidence in the present directors to take thorough and conscientious measures, as necessary, to remedy any possible defects.

DR. STOCKMANN: But that's utterly out of the question for me, as long as they try to get by with patchwork. I'm telling you that, Peter; and it's my unqualified opinion—!

MAYOR STOCKMANN: As a member of the staff, you're not entitled to any personal opinions.

DR. STOCKMANN *(stunned)*: Not entitled—!

MAYOR STOCKMANN: As a staff member, I said. As a private person—why, that's another matter. But as a subordinate official at the baths, you're not entitled to express any opinions that contradict your superiors.

DR. STOCKMANN: That's going too far! I, as a doctor, a man of science, aren't entitled to—!

MAYOR STOCKMANN: What's involved here isn't a purely scientific problem. It's a mixture of both technical and economic considerations.

DR. STOCKMANN: I don't care what the hell it is! I want the freedom to express myself on any problem under the sun!

MAYOR STOCKMANN: Anything you like—except for the baths. We forbid you that.

DR. STOCKMANN *(shouting)*: You forbid—! You! A crowd of—!

MAYOR STOCKMANN: *I* forbid it—*I*, your supervisor. And when I forbid you, then you obey.

DR. STOCKMANN *(controls himself)*: Peter—if you weren't my brother—

PETRA *(flinging the door open)*: You don't have to take this, Father!

MRS. STOCKMANN *(following her)*: Petra, Petra!

MAYOR STOCKMANN: Ah, an ear to the keyhole.

MRS. STOCKMANN: You were so loud, we couldn't avoid—

PETRA: Oh, but I was there, listening.

MAYOR STOCKMANN: Well, I'm just as glad, really—

DR. STOCKMANN *(approaching him)*: You were talking to me about forbidding and obeying—?

MAYOR STOCKMANN: You forced me to adopt that tone.

DR. STOCKMANN: So you want me to stand up in public and confess I'm a liar?

MAYOR STOCKMANN: We find it absolutely essential that you make a public statement along the lines I've indicated.

DR. STOCKMANN: And what if I don't—obey?

MAYOR STOCKMANN: Then we ourselves will issue a statement to soothe the public.

DR. STOCKMANN: Very well. But then I'll attack you in print. I'll stand my ground. I'll prove that I'm right, and you're wrong. And then what will you do?

MAYOR STOCKMANN: Then I won't be able to prevent your dismissal.

DR. STOCKMANN: What—!

PETRA: Father—dismissal!

MRS. STOCKMANN: Dismissal!

MAYOR STOCKMANN: You'll be dismissed from the staff. I'll find myself obliged to see you put on immediate notice and suspended from all activities involving the baths.

DR. STOCKMANN: And you'll dare that!

MAYOR STOCKMANN: You're the one playing the daredevil.

PETRA: Uncle, this is a shameful way to treat a man like Father!

MRS. STOCKMANN: Will you please be quiet, Petra!

MAYOR STOCKMANN (*regarding* PETRA): Ah, so we've already learned to voice opinions. Yes, naturally. (*To* MRS. STOCKMANN.) Katherine, I expect you're the most sensible member of this household. Use whatever influence you have over your husband, and make him understand what effect this will have on both his family—

DR. STOCKMANN: My family concerns no one else but me.

MAYOR STOCKMANN: As I was saying, on both his family and the town he lives in.

DR. STOCKMANN: I'm the one who really wants the best for the town! I want to expose failings that'll come to light sooner or later anyway. That ought to show that I love this town.

MAYOR STOCKMANN: Yes, by setting out in blind spite to cut off our major source of revenue.

DR. STOCKMANN: That source is poisoned, man! Are you crazy! We live by marketing filth and corruption. The whole affluence of this community has its roots in a lie!

MAYOR STOCKMANN: Sheer fantasy—or something worse. Any man who could hurl such nauseating charges at his own home town must be an enemy of society.

DR. STOCKMANN (*going for him*): You dare—!

MRS. STOCKMANN (*throws herself between them*): Thomas!

PETRA (*seizing her father by the arm*): Easy, Father!

MAYOR STOCKMANN: I don't have to subject myself to violence. Now you've been warned. Just consider what you owe yourself and your family. Good-bye. (*He leaves.*)

DR. STOCKMANN (*pacing up and down*): And I have to take this treatment! In my own house, Katherine! What do you say to that!

MRS. STOCKMANN: Of course it's humiliating, Thomas—

PETRA: Oh, what I could do to Uncle—!

DR. STOCKMANN: It's my own fault. I should have faced them down long ago—shown my teeth—and bit back! Call *me* an enemy of society! So help me God, I'm not going to swallow that!

MRS. STOCKMANN: But, Thomas dear, your brother does have the power—

DR. STOCKMANN: Yes, but I'm in the right!

MRS. STOCKMANN: The right? Ah, what does it help to be in the right if you don't have any power?

PETRA: Mother, no—why do you talk like that?

DR. STOCKMANN: You mean it doesn't help in a free society to be on the side of right? Don't be absurd, Katherine. And besides— don't I have the independent liberal press to lead the way—and the solid majority behind me? There's power enough in them, I'd say!

MRS. STOCKMANN: But Thomas, for heaven's sake—surely you're not thinking of—

DR. STOCKMANN: Thinking of what?

MRS. STOCKMANN: Of setting yourself up against your brother.

DR. STOCKMANN: What in hell do you want me to do? Abandon everything that's true and right?

PETRA: Yes, I'd ask the same.

MRS. STOCKMANN: But it won't do you the least bit of good. If they won't, they won't.

DR. STOCKMANN: Oh ho, Katherine, just give me time! You'll see, I'll push this fight through to the end.

MRS. STOCKMANN: Yes, maybe you'll just push yourself out of your job—that's what you'll do.

DR. STOCKMANN: Then anyway I'll have done my duty to the people—to society. Though they call me its enemy!

MRS. STOCKMANN: And to your family, Thomas? To us at home? You think that's doing your duty to those who depend on you?

PETRA: Oh, stop always thinking of us first of all, Mother.

MRS. STOCKMANN: Yes, it's easy for *you* to talk. If need be, you can stand on your own feet. But remember the boys, Thomas. And think of yourself a little, and of me—

DR. STOCKMANN: You must be utterly mad, Katherine! If I had to

crawl like an abject coward to Peter and his damned cohorts—
do you think I'd ever know one moment's happiness for the rest
of my life?

MRS. STOCKMANN: I don't know about that. But God preserve us
from the kind of happiness we'll share if you press your defiance.
You'll be back again where you started—no position, no assured
income. I thought we'd had enough of that in the old days.
Remember that, Thomas; and think of what lies ahead.

DR. STOCKMANN *(clenching his fists and writhing in inner conflict)*:
And this is how these bureaucrats can clamp down on a plain,
honest man! It's despicable, Katherine, isn't it?

MRS. STOCKMANN: Yes, they've acted shamefully toward you, of
course. But, my Lord, there's so much injustice that people have
to bear with in this world—There are the boys, Thomas! Look
at them! What'll become of them? No, no, you wouldn't have
the heart—

As she speaks, EILIF *and* MORTEN *come in, carrying their
schoolbooks.*

DR. STOCKMANN: The boys—! *(Suddenly resolved.)* I don't care
if all the world caves in, I'm not going to lick the dust. *(He
heads for his study.)*

MRS. STOCKMANN *(following him)*: Thomas—what are you doing?

DR. STOCKMANN *(at the door)*: I want the chance to look my boys
straight in the eyes when they've grown up to be free men. *(He
goes within.)*

MRS. STOCKMANN *(bursting into tears)*: Oh, God help us all!

PETRA: Father—he's wonderful! He's not giving in.

The boys, in bewilderment, ask what has happened; PETRA *signals
them to be quiet.*

ACT III

The editorial office of the People's Courier. *At the back, left, is the entrance door; to the right in the same wall is another door, through which one can see the pressroom. In the wall to the right, a third door. At the center of the room is a large table covered with papers, newspapers, and books. In the foreground at the left a window and, next to it, a writing desk with a high stool. A couple of armchairs are drawn up by the table; several other chairs along the walls. The room is barren and cheerless, the furnishings old, the armchairs grimy and torn. In the pressroom two typesetters can be seen at work, and, beyond them, a handpress in operation.*

HOVSTAD *is seated at the desk, writing. After a moment* BILLING *enters from the right, the* DOCTOR's *manuscript in his hand.*

BILLING: Well, that's really something—!

HOVSTAD *(writing)*: Did you read it all?

BILLING *(lays the manuscript on the desk)*: I'll say I did.

HOVSTAD: He makes a pretty sharp statement, doesn't he?

BILLING: Sharp? Ye gods, it's pulverizing? Every word hits home like a sledgehammer.

HOVSTAD: Yes, but that crowd isn't going to come down at one blow.

BILLING: That's true. But then we'll keep on hitting them—blow upon blow, till their whole leadership crumbles. When I sat in there reading this, it was exactly as if I could see the revolution breaking like the dawn.

HOVSTAD *(turning)*: Shh! Don't say that so Aslaksen hears.

BILLING *(dropping his voice)*: Aslaksen's a chicken-livered coward; there's no spine in the man. But this time you'll carry your own will through, uh? Right? You'll run the doctor's article?

HOVSTAD: Yes, if only the mayor doesn't give in—

BILLING: That'd be boring as hell.

HOVSTAD: Well, fortunately, no matter what happens, we can make something out of the situation. If the mayor won't buy the doctor's proposal, then he gets the small businessmen down on his neck—the Home Owners Council and that sort. And if he does buy it, he'll fall out with a whole host of the big stockholders in the baths, the ones who've been his best supporters up to now—

BILLING: Yes, that's right; they'll have to kick in a lot of new capital—

HOVSTAD: You bet they will! And then the ring is broken, see. And day after day in the paper we'll keep drumming it into the public that the mayor's incompetent on one score after another, and that all the elective offices in town—the whole administration—ought to be placed in the hands of the liberals.

BILLING: Ye gods, that's the living truth! I see it—I can see it! We're right on the verge of a revolution!

A knock at the door.

HOVSTAD: Shh! *(Calls out.)* Come in!

DR. STOCKMANN *enters by the door at the back, left.*

HOVSTAD *(goes to meet him)*: Ah, here's the doctor. Well?

DR. STOCKMANN: Roll your presses, Mr. Hovstad!

HOVSTAD: Then it's come to that?

BILLING: Hurray!

DR. STOCKMANN: I said, roll your presses. Yes, it's come to that. But now they'll get what they're asking for. Now it's war in this town, Mr. Billing!

BILLING: War to the knife, I hope! Lay into them, Doctor!

DR. STOCKMANN: This article's only the beginning. My head's already brimming with ideas for four or five more pieces. Where do I find Aslaksen?

BILLING *(shouting into the pressroom)*: Aslaksen, come here a minute!

HOVSTAD: Four or five more pieces, you say? On the same subject?

DR. STOCKMANN: No, not by a long shot. No, they're on totally different topics. But they all originate from the water system and the sewers. One thing leads to another, you know. It's the way it is when you start patching up an old building. Precisely like that.

BILLING: Ye gods, but that's the truth. You find out you'll never be done with it till you've torn down the whole rotten structure.

ASLAKSEN *(comes in from the pressroom)*: Torn down! You don't plan to tear down the baths, Doctor?

HOVSTAD: Not at all. Don't get frightened.

DR. STOCKMANN: No, that was something else entirely. Well, what do you say about my article, Mr. Hovstad?

HOVSTAD: I think it's a pure masterpiece—

DR. STOCKMANN: Yes, isn't it—? Well, I'm most gratified, most gratified.

HOVSTAD: It's so clear and readable; you don't have to be a specialist at all to follow the argument. I daresay you'll have every reasonable man on your side.

ASLAKSEN: And all the moderates, too?

BILLING: Moderates and immoderates both—well, I mean, practically the entire town.

ASLAKSEN: Then we might take a chance on running it.

DR. STOCKMANN: Yes, I should think so!

HOVSTAD: It'll go in tomorrow morning.

DR. STOCKMANN: Good grief, it better; we can't waste a single day. Look, Mr. Aslaksen, I know what I wanted to ask you: would you give the manuscript your personal attention?

ASLAKSEN: I certainly will.

DR. STOCKMANN: Handle it like gold. No misprints; every word is vital. I'll stop back in again later; maybe I could glance over the proofs. Oh, I can't tell you how I'm dying to see this thing in print—delivered—

BILLING: Delivered—like a lightning-bolt!

DR. STOCKMANN: —addressed to the judgment of every thinking man. Ah, you can't imagine what I've been subjected to today. They've threatened me from all sides; they've tried to deprive me of my most fundamental human rights—

HOVSTAD: Of your rights!

DR. STOCKMANN: They've tried to humiliate me, and turn me into a jellyfish, and make me deny my deepest and holiest convictions for private profit.

BILLING: Ye gods, that's unforgivable.

HOVSTAD: Oh well, you have to expect anything from that crowd.

DR. STOCKMANN: But with me it's not going to work: they're going to get it, spelled out in black and white. I'm going to drop anchor right here at the *Courier* and rake them with broadsides: a fresh article every day—

ASLAKSEN: Yes, but now listen—

BILLING: Hurray! It's war—war!

DR. STOCKMANN: I'll smash them into the ground and shatter them! I'll wreck their defenses in the eyes of every fair-minded man! That's what I'll do!

ASLAKSEN: But do it temperately, Doctor. War, yes—in moderation.

BILLING: No, no! Don't spare the dynamite!

DR. STOCKMANN: *(continues, unruffled)*: Because now, you see, this isn't simply a matter of sewers and water mains anymore. No, it's the whole society that has to be purged and disinfected—

BILLING: That's the remedy!

DR. STOCKMANN: All these lunkheads in the old generation have to be dumped. And that means: no matter *who* they are! I've had such endless vistas opening up for me today. I haven't quite clarified it yet, but I'm working it out. My friends, we have to go forth and search out fresh, young standard-bearers; we have to have new commanders for all our outposts.

BILLING: Hear, hear!

DR. STOCKMANN: And if we only can stick together, everything will go off smoothly. The entire revolution will be launched as trim as a ship down the ways. Don't you think so?

HOVSTAD: For my part, I think we now have every prospect of seeing community control put right where it belongs.

ASLAKSEN: And if we just move ahead in moderation, I can't believe there's likely to be any danger.

DR. STOCKMANN: Who the hell cares about danger! Whatever I do will be done in the name of truth, for the sake of my conscience.

HOVSTAD: You're a man who deserves support, Doctor.

ASLAKSEN: Yes, that's a fact: the doctor's a true friend to the town, and a real friend to society.

BILLING: Ye gods, Aslaksen; Doctor Stockmann is the people's friend!

ASLAKSEN: I can imagine the Home Owners Council may pick that up as a slogan.

DR. STOCKMANN *(moved, pressing their hands)*: Thank you, thank you, my dear, unfailing friends—it's so heartening to hear you say these things—my esteemed brother called me something quite different. Well, I swear he's going to get it back, with interest! But now I've got to look in on a patient, poor devil. I'll stop by again, as I said. Don't forget to look out for my manuscript, Mr. Aslaksen—and, whatever you do, don't cut any exclamation points. If anything, put a few more in! Fine, fine! Good-bye till later, good-bye, good-bye!

Amid mutual farewells, he is escorted to the door and departs.

HOVSTAD: He can be an exceptionally useful man for us.

ASLAKSEN: As long as he limits himself to the baths. But if he goes further, then it wouldn't be politic to join forces with him.

HOVSTAD: Hm, that all depends—

BILLING: You're always so damn fearful, Aslaksen.

ASLAKSEN: Fearful? Yes, as far as the local authorities go, I'm fearful, Mr. Billing. Let met tell you, it's something I've learned in the school of experience. But put me in the arena of national politics, opposed to the government itself, and then you'll see if I'm fearful.

BILLING: No, you're certainly not. But that's exactly where you're so inconsistent.

ASLAKSEN: I'm a man of conscience, that's the thing. As long as you attack the government, you can't do any real damage to society. You see, the men on that level, they aren't affected— they just ride it out. But the *local* authorities, *they* can be ousted; and then you might wind up with a lot of bunglers in power, who could do enormous damage to the property owners, among others.

HOVSTAD: But how about self-government as part of a citizen's education—don't you care about that?

ASLAKSEN: When a man has material assets at stake, he can't go thinking of everything.

HOVSTAD: Then I hope I'm never burdened with material assets.

BILLING: Hear, hear!

ASLAKSEN *(smiles)*: Hm. *(Pointing at the desk.)* In that editor's chair, right there, your predecessor, Councilman Stengaard, used to sit.

BILLING *(spits)*: Pah! That renegade.

HOVSTAD: I'm no double-dealer—and I never will be.

ASLAKSEN: A politician has to keep all possibilities open, Mr. Hovstad. And you, Mr. Billing—I think you better take a reef or two in your sails, now that you've put in for a job in the town clerk's office.

BILLING I—!

HOVSTAD: *You* have, Billing?

BILLING: Yes, uh—you can damn well imagine I only did it to needle the establishment.

ASLAKSEN: Well, it's no business of mine, of course. But when I get labeled fearful and inconsistent in my stand, there's one thing I want to emphasize: my political record is available to all comers. I've never changed my position, except that I've become more moderate. My heart belongs to the people, always; but I can't deny that my reason disposes me toward the authorities— I mean, only the local ones, that is.

He goes into the pressroom.

BILLING: Shouldn't we call it quits with him, Hovstad?

HOVSTAD: You know any other printer who'll extend us credit for paper and labor costs?

BILLING: It's damnable that we don't have any capital.

HOVSTAD *(sitting at the desk)*: Yes, if we only had that—

BILLING: How about approaching Stockmann?

HOVSTAD *(leafing through some papers)*: What use would there be in that? He has nothing.

BILLING: No, but he's got a good man backing him: old Morten Kiil—the one they call the Badger.

HOVSTAD *(writing)*: How can you know for sure *he* has anything?

BILLING: Ye gods, of course he does! And some part of it has to come to the Stockmanns. He's got to make provision—at least for the children.

HOVSTAD *(half turning)*: Are you figuring on *that?*

BILLING: Figuring? I never figure on anything.

HOVSTAD: That's wise. And you'd better not figure on that job with the town, because I can promise you—you won't get it.

BILLING: Don't you think I've known that all along? There's nothing I'd welcome more than not getting it. A rejection like that really kindles your fighting spirit—it's almost like an infusion of fresh gall, and that's exactly what you need in an anthill like this, where hardly anything ever happens to really stir you up.

HOVSTAD *(continues writing)*: How true, how true.

BILLING: Well—they'll soon be hearing from *me!* Now I'll go in and write that appeal to the Home Owners Council. *(He goes into the room to the right.)*

HOVSTAD *(sits at the desk, chews the end of his pen and says slowly)*: Hm—so that's how it is. *(A knock at the door.)* Come in!

PETRA *enters by the door at the back, left.*

HOVSTAD *(getting up)*: Oh, it's you? What are you doing here?

PETRA: You'll have to excuse me—

HOVSTAD *(pulls an armchair forward)*: Won't you sit?

PETRA: No, thanks—I can't stay.

HOVSTAD: Is it something from your father that—?

PETRA: No, it's something from me. *(Takes a book out of her coat pocket.)* Here's that English story.

HOVSTAD: Why are you giving it back?

PETRA: Because I don't want to translate it.

HOVSTAD: But you promised me, definitely—

PETRA: Well, I hadn't read it then. And of course you haven't read it either.

HOVSTAD: No. You know I don't understand English; but—

PETRA: All right, that's why I wanted to tell you that you'll have to find somebody else. *(Lays the book on the table.)* This could never be used in the *Courier*.

HOVSTAD: Why not?

PETRA: It's totally opposed to everything you stand for.

HOVSTAD: Well, actually—

PETRA: You still don't understand me. It shows how a supernatural power, watching over the so-called good people of this world, arranges everything for the best in their lives—and how all the so-called wicked get their punishment.

HOVSTAD: But that's fair enough. It's exactly what the public wants.

PETRA: And do you want to be the one who feeds the public that sort of thing? You don't believe a word of it yourself. You know perfectly well things don't happen like that in reality.

HOVSTAD: You're perfectly right; but then an editor can't always do what he might prefer. You often have to bow to public opinions in lesser matters. After all, politics is the main thing in life—

for a newspaper, in any event. And if I want to lead people toward greater liberation and progress, then I mustn't scare them away. When they find a moral story like this in the back pages, they're more willing to accept what we print up front—they feel more secure.

PETRA: Oh, come! You wouldn't be so tricky and lay snares for your readers. You're not a spider.

HOVSTAD *(smiles)*: Thank you for thinking so well of me. No, it really was Billing's scheme, and not mine.

PETRA: Billing's!

HOVSTAD: Yes. At any rate, he was speaking of it just the other day. It's Billing who's been so hot about getting that story in; I don't know the book.

PETRA: But how could Billing, with his liberal attitude—?

HOVSTAD: Oh, Billing is a many-sided man. Now I hear he's out for a job in the town clerk's office.

PETRA: I don't believe it, Hovstad. How could he ever conform himself to that?

HOVSTAD: That's something you'll have to ask him.

PETRA: I never would have thought it of Billing.

HOVSTAD *(looks more sharply at her)*: You wouldn't? Does it surprise you so?

PETRA: Yes. Or maybe not, really. Oh, honestly, I don't know—

HOVSTAD: We journalists don't amount to much, Miss Stockmann.

PETRA: You actually mean that?

HOVSTAD: It's what I think sometimes.

PETRA: Yes, in your normal day-to-day existence—I can understand that well enough. But now that you're lending a hand in a great cause—

HOVSTAD: This matter of your father, you mean?

PETRA: Exactly. Now I think you must feel like a man who's more valuable than most.

HOVSTAD: Yes, I feel something of that today.

PETRA: Yes, you do, don't you? Oh, it's a glorious calling you've chosen! To pioneer the way for embattled truths and daring new insights—or simply to stand up fearlessly for a man who's been wronged—

HOVSTAD: Especially when that man who's been wronged is— hm—I don't quite know how to put it—

PETRA: When he's so direct and honest, you mean?

HOVSTAD (*in a softer voice*): No, I meant—especially when he's your father.

PETRA (*startled*): It's *that*!

HOVSTAD: Yes, Petra—Miss Petra.

PETRA: Is *that* the main thing for you? Not the issue itself? Not the truth? Not my father's compassion for life?

HOVSTAD: Why, yes—of course, that too.

PETRA: No, thanks, Mr. Hovstad; you betrayed yourself. And now I'll never trust you again, in anything.

HOVSTAD: How can you be so hard on me, when it's mostly for your own sake—?

PETRA: What I'm mad at you about is you haven't played fair with Father. You've talked to him as if the truth and the good of the community lay closest to your heart. You've made fools of both him and me. You're not the man you pretend to be. And for that I'll never forgive you—never!

HOVSTAD: You shouldn't be so bitter, Miss Petra—particularly right now.

PETRA: Why not now?

HOVSTAD: Because your father can't dispense with my help.

PETRA (*scanning him*): And you're that kind, too? So!

HOVSTAD: No, no, I'm not. I don't know what brought that on. You have to believe me.

PETRA: I know what I have to believe. Good-bye.

ASLAKSEN (*entering from the pressroom, brusquely and cryptically*): God Almighty, Hovstad— (*Sees* PETRA.) Oh, what a mess—

PETRA: There's the book; you can give it to somebody else. (*Goes toward the entrance door.*)

HOVSTAD (*following her*): But, Miss Petra—

PETRA: Good-bye. (*She leaves.*)

ASLAKSEN: Mr. Hovstad, listen!

HOVSTAD: Yes, all right, what is it?

ASLAKSEN: The mayor's out there in the pressroom.

HOVSTAD: You say, the mayor?

ASLAKSEN: Yes, he wants to talk to you. He came in the back entrance—didn't want to be seen, I guess.

HOVSTAD: What's this all about? No, wait, I'll go—

He crosses to the door of the pressroom, opens it, and beckons the MAYOR *in.*

HOVSTAD: Keep an eye out, Aslaksen, so nobody—

ASLAKSEN: I understand— *(Goes into the pressroom.)*

MAYOR STOCKMANN: I imagine you hardly expected to see me here, Mr. Hovstad.

HOVSTAD: No, I really hadn't.

MAYOR STOCKMANN *(looking about)*: You've certainly made yourself quite comfortable here. Very nice.

HOVSTAD: Oh—

MAYOR STOCKMANN: And now I come along unceremoniously and monopolize your time.

HOVSTAD: By all means, Mr. Mayor; I'm at your service. But please, let me take your things— *(Sets the* MAYOR'S *hat and stick on a chair.)* Won't you have a seat?

MAYOR STOCKMANN *(sitting at the table)*: Thank you.

HOVSTAD *likewise sits at the table.*

MAYOR STOCKMANN: I've gone through—really a most troublesome episode today, Mr. Hovstad.

HOVSTAD: Yes? Oh well, with all the cares that the mayor has—

MAYOR STOCKMANN: It involves the staff physician at the baths.

HOVSTAD: You mean, the doctor?

MAYOR STOCKMANN: He's penned a kind of report to the board of directors, alleging that the baths have certain deficiencies.

HOVSTAD: He has?

MAYOR STOCKMANN: Yes, didn't he tell you—? I thought he said—

HOVSTAD: Oh yes, that's true. He made some mention of it—

ASLAKSEN *(entering from the pressroom)*: I need to have that manuscript—

HOVSTAD *(vexed)*: Hm, it's there on the desk.

ASLAKSEN *(locating it)*: Good.

MAYOR STOCKMANN: But look—that's *it*, exactly—

ASLAKSEN: Yes, that's the doctor's article, Mr. Mayor.

HOVSTAD: Oh, is *that* what you were talking about?

MAYOR STOCKMANN: None other. What do you think of it?

HOVSTAD: I'm really no expert, and I've barely skimmed through it.

MAYOR STOCKMANN: Still, you're going to print it.

HOVSTAD: A man of his reputation I can hardly refuse—

ASLAKSEN: I have no say at all in this paper, Mr. Mayor.

MAYOR STOCKMANN: Naturally.

ASLAKSEN: I only print what's put in my hands.

MAYOR STOCKMANN: Quite properly.

ASLAKSEN: So, if you'll pardon me— *(Goes toward the press-room.)*

MAYOR STOCKMANN: No, just a minute, Mr. Aslaksen. With your permission, Mr. Hovstad—

HOVSTAD: My pleasure.

MAYOR STOCKMANN: You're a sober-minded and thoughtful man, Mr. Aslaksen.

ASLAKSEN: I'm glad Your Honor holds that opinion.

MAYOR STOCKMANN: And a man of influence in many circles.

ASLAKSEN: That's mostly among the little people.

MAYOR STOCKMANN: The small taxpayers are the great majority— here, as elsewhere.

ASLAKSEN: That's the truth.

MAYOR STOCKMANN: And I don't doubt that you know the general sentiment among most of them. Am I right?

ASLAKSEN: Yes, I daresay I do Mr. Mayor.

MAYOR STOCKMANN: Well—if there's such a worthy spirit of self-sacrifice prevailing among the town's less affluent citizens, then—

ASLAKSEN: How's that?

HOVSTAD: Self-sacrifice?

MAYOR STOCKMANN: It's a beautiful token of community spirit, an exceptionally beautiful token. I was close to saying that I wouldn't have expected it. But you know the feelings of these people far better than I.

ASLAKSEN: Yes, but, Your Honor—

MAYOR STOCKMANN: And as a matter of fact, it's no small sacrifice this town will be asked to bear.

HOVSTAD: The town?

ASLAKSEN: But I don't follow— It's the baths—!

MAYOR STOCKMANN: At a tentative estimate, the changes that our staff physician finds desirable run up to a couple of hundred thousand crowns.

ASLAKSEN: That's a lot of money, but—

MAYOR STOCKMANN: Of course it'll be necessary for us to take out a municipal loan.

HOVSTAD *(rises)*: It can't be your intention for the town to—

ASLAKSEN: Not out of property taxes! Out of the empty pockets of the home owners!

MAYOR STOCKMANN: Well, my dear Mr. Aslaksen, where else would the capital come from?

ASLAKSEN: The men who own the baths can raise it.

MAYOR STOCKMANN: The owners find themselves in no position to extend themselves further than they are already.

ASLAKSEN: Is that quite definite, Mr. Mayor?

MAYOR STOCKMANN: I've ascertained it for a fact. So if one wants all these elaborate changes, the town itself will have to pay for them.

ASLAKSEN: But hell and damnation—excuse me, sir!—but this is a totally different picture, Mr. Hovstad.

HOVSTAD: It certainly is.

MAYOR STOCKMANN: The worst part of it is that we'll be forced to shut down the baths for a two-year period.

HOVSTAD: Shut down? Completely?

ASLAKSEN: For two years!

MAYOR STOCKMANN: Yes, the work has to take that long—at the least.

ASLAKSEN: But, God Almighty, we'll never last that out, Mr. Mayor! What'll we home owners live on in the meantime?

MAYOR STOCKMANN: Unhappily, it's extremely difficult to answer that, Mr. Aslaksen. But what do you want us to do? You think we'll get a single summer visitor here if anyone goes around posing suppositions that the water is polluted, that we're living in a pesthole, that the whole town—

ASLAKSEN: And it's all just supposition?

MAYOR STOCKMANN: With the best will in the world, I haven't been able to persuade myself otherwise.

ASLAKSEN: Yes, but then its absolutely indefensible of Dr. Stockmann—begging your pardon, Mayor, but—

MAYOR STOCKMANN: It's distressingly true, what you imply, Mr. Aslaksen. I'm afraid my brother's always been a reckless man.

ASLAKSEN: And in spite of this, you want to go on supporting him, Mr. Hovstad!

HOVSTAD: But how could anyone have suspected—?

MAYOR STOCKMANN: I've drawn up a brief statement of the relevant facts, as they might appear to a disinterested observer; and I've suggested therein how any possible deficiencies might well be covered without exceeding the current budget for the baths.

HOVSTAD: Do you have this statement with you, Mr. Mayor?

MAYOR STOCKMANN *(groping in his pocket)*: Yes, I took it along just in case—

ASLAKSEN *(abruptly)*: Oh, my God, there he is!

MAYOR STOCKMANN: Who? My brother?

HOVSTAD: Where—where!

ASLAKSEN: Coming through the pressroom.

MAYOR STOCKMANN: How embarrassing! I don't want to run up against him here, and I still have things to talk to you about.

HOVSTAD *(pointing toward the door at the right)*: Step in there for a moment.

MAYOR STOCKMANN: But—?

HOVSTAD: It's just Billing in there.

ASLAKSEN: Quick, Your Honor! He's coming!

MAYOR STOCKMANN: Yes, all right, but try to get rid of him fast.

He goes out the door, right, as ASLAKSEN *opens and closes it for him.*

HOVSTAD: Look like you're doing something, Aslaksen.

He sits and starts to write. ASLAKSEN *rummages in a pile of papers on a chair to the right.*

DR. STOCKMANN *(entering from the pressroom)*: Here I am again. *(Puts down his hat and stick.)*

HOVSTAD *(writing)*: Already, Doctor? Get going on what we were talking about, Aslaksen. We can't waste time today.

DR. STOCKMANN *(to* ASLAKSEN*)*: I gather, no proofs as yet.

ASLAKSEN *(without turning)*: How could you expect that, Doctor?

DR. STOCKMANN: No, no, I'm just impatient—you have to understand. I won't have a moment's peace till I see it in print.

HOVSTAD: Hm—it's bound to be a good hour still. Don't you think so, Aslaksen?

ASLAKSEN: Yes, I'm afraid so.

DR. STOCKMANN: My dear friends, that's quite all right; I'll come back. I'll gladly come back twice, if necessary. With anything so important—the welfare of this whole town—it's no time to take it easy. *(Starts to go, then pauses and returns.)* Oh, listen—there's still something I want to mention to you.

HOVSTAD: Sorry, but couldn't we some other time—?

DR. STOCKMANN: I can say it in two seconds. It's simply this—when people read my article in the paper tomorrow and find out as well that I've spent the whole winter in seclusion, working for the good of the town—

HOVSTAD: Yes, but Doctor—

DR. STOCKMANN: I know what you'll say. You don't think it was any more than my blasted duty—ordinary civic responsibility. Well, of course; I know that just as well as you do. But my fellow townspeople, you see—bless their souls, they hold such a high regard for me—

ASLAKSEN: Yes, the people have held you in the highest regard—up till now, Doctor.

DR. STOCKMANN: Yes, and it's just the reason I'm afraid that—What I'm trying to say is this: my article, if it affects the people—especially the deprived classes—as an incitement to take the future affairs of the town into their own hands—

HOVSTAD *(getting up)*: Hm, Doctor, I don't want to mislead you—

DR. STOCKMANN: Aha—I thought there was something brewing! But I won't hear of it. So if they go preparing anything—

HOVSTAD: Such as?

DR. STOCKMANN: Oh, anything of the kind—a parade or a banquet or a testimonial award or whatever, then you promise me by all that's holy to get it quashed. And you too, Mr. Aslaksen; you hear me!

HOVSTAD: Pardon me, Doctor, but we'd better tell you the unvarnished truth right now—

MRS. STOCKMANN, *in hat and coat, comes in by the entrance door, back left.*

MRS. STOCKMANN *(seeing the* DOCTOR*)*: I thought so!

HOVSTAD *(going toward her)*: Mrs. Stockmann, you too?

DR. STOCKMANN: Katherine, what the deuce are you doing here?

MRS. STOCKMANN: You know very well what I want.

HOVSTAD: Won't you have a seat? Or perhaps—

MRS. STOCKMANN: Thanks, but don't bother. And please, don't be offended that I'm here to fetch Stockmann; because I'm the mother of three children, I want you to know.

DR. STOCKMANN: Oh, bosh! We know all that.

MRS. STOCKMANN: Well, it really doesn't seem as if you're thinking much of your wife and children these days, or else you wouldn't have gone on this way, hurling us all into perdition.

DR. STOCKMANN: Are you utterly insane, Katherine? Does a man with a wife and children have no right to proclaim the truth — no right to be an effective citizen — or to serve the town he lives in?

MRS. STOCKMANN: All those things — in moderation, Thomas!

ASLAKSEN: I agree. Moderation in all things.

MRS. STOCKMANN: That's why you wrong us terribly, Mr. Hovstad, when you inveigle my husband out of house and home and down here to make a fool of himself in this.

HOVSTAD: I don't make fools of people —

DR. STOCKMANN: Fools! Nobody fools *me!*

MRS. STOCKMANN: Oh yes, they do. I know you're the smartest man in town, but you're so very easy to fool, Thomas. *(To* HOVSTAD.*)* And just consider that he'll lose his job at the baths if you print what he's written —

ASLAKSEN: What!

HOVSTAD: Yes, but you know, Doctor —

DR. STOCKMANN *(laughing)*: Just let them try! Oh, no — they won't dare. Because, you see, I've got the solid majority behind me.

MRS. STOCKMANN: Yes, that's the trouble, exactly. An ugly lot like that behind you.

DR. STOCKMANN: Balderdash, Katherine! Go home and take care of your house and let me take care of society. How can you be so scared, when I'm so secure and happy? *(Walks up and down, rubbing his hands.)* Truth and the people will win the battle, you can count on that. Oh, I can see all the liberal-minded citizens everywhere gathering into a victorious army —! *(Stops by a chair.)* What — what the hell is *this?*

ASLAKSEN *(looking over)*: Ow-ah!

HOVSTAD *(likewise)*: Hm —!

DR. STOCKMANN: Here we see the summit of authority.

He takes the MAYOR's *hat delicately between his fingertips and holds it high.*

MRS. STOCKMANN: The mayor's hat!

DR. STOCKMANN: And here's the scepter of command, too. How in blazes—?

HOVSTAD: Well, uh—

DR. STOCKMANN: Ah, I get it! He's been here to coax you over. Ho ho, he knew right where to come. And then he caught sight of me in the pressroom. *(Explodes with laughter.)* Did he run, Mr. Aslaksen?

ASLAKSEN *(hurriedly)*: Oh yes, Doctor, he ran off.

DR. STOCKMANN: Ran away from his stick and his— My eye! Peter never runs from anything. But where the devil have you put him? Ah—inside, of course. Now you watch this, Katherine!

MRS. STOCKMANN: Thomas—please—!

ASLAKSEN: Watch yourself, Doctor!

DR. STOCKMANN *sets the* MAYOR's *hat on his head and takes his stick; he then goes over, throws open the door, and raises his hand in salute. The* MAYOR *comes in, red with anger.* BILLING *enters behind him.*

MAYOR STOCKMANN: What's the meaning of this rowdyism?

DR. STOCKMANN: Some respect, if you will, Peter. I'm the authority in town now. *(He parades up and down.)*

MRS. STOCKMANN *(nearly in tears)*: Thomas, no!

MAYOR STOCKMANN *(following him)*: Give me my hat and my stick!

DR. STOCKMANN: If you're the police chief, then I'm the mayor. I'm in charge of the whole town, see!

MAYOR STOCKMANN: I'm telling you, take off that hat. Remember, that's an insignia of office!

DR. STOCKMANN: Pah! Do you think the waking lion of the people's strength is going to be scared of a hat? Yes, because you better know: tomorrow we're making a revolution in town. You threatened me with my dismissal, but now I'm dismissing you— from all your public offices. You don't think I can? Oh yes, you'll see. I've got the ascendant forces of society on my side. Hovstad and Billing will thunder in the *People's Courier;* and Aslaksen will take the field, leading the whole Home Owners Council—

ASLAKSEN: I won't do it, Doctor.

DR. STOCKMANN: Why, of course you will—

MAYOR STOCKMANN: Ah, but perhaps, even so, Mr. Hovstad will be joining this rebellion?

HOVSTAD: No, Mr. Mayor.

ASLAKSEN: No, Mr. Hovstad isn't so crazy that he'd go and wreck both himself and the paper for the sake of a mere surmise.

DR. STOCKMANN *(looking about)*: What's going on here?

HOVSTAD: You've presented your case in a false light, Doctor; and that's why I can't support it.

BILLING: No, after what the mayor was good enough to tell me in there—

DR. STOCKMANN: False! You can leave that to me. Just print my article. I can take care of defending it.

HOVSTAD: I'm not printing it. I cannot and will not and dare not print it.

DR. STOCKMANN: You dare not? What kind of rot is that? You're the editor, aren't you? And it's the editors who run the press, I hope!

ASLAKSEN: No, it's the readers, Doctor.

MAYOR STOCKMANN: Thankfully, yes.

ASLAKSEN: It's public opinion, the informed citizens, the home owners, and all the rest—they're the ones that run the press.

DR. STOCKMANN *(comprehending)*: And all these powers I have against me?

ASLAKSEN: That's right. If your article is printed, it'll mean absolute ruin for this town.

DR. STOCKMANN: I see.

MAYOR STOCKMANN: My hat and my stick!

DR. STOCKMANN *removes the hat and sets it, along with the stick, on the table.*

MAYOR STOCKMANN *(reclaiming them both)*: That was a sudden end to your first term in office.

DR. STOCKMANN: It's not the end yet. *(To* HOVSTAD.*)* Then there's no possibility of getting my article in the *Courier?*

HOVSTAD: None whatever. Partly out of regard for your family.

MRS. STOCKMANN: Oh, never mind about this family, Mr. Hovstad.

MAYOR STOCKMANN (*takes a sheet of paper from his pocket*): For the protection of the public, it will be sufficient if this goes in. It's an authorized statement. If you will.

HOVSTAD (*taking the sheet*): Good. We'll insert it right away.

DR. STOCKMANN: But not mine! People think they can stifle me and choke off the truth! But it won't go as smooth as you think. Mr. Aslaksen, would you take my manuscript and issue it at once as a pamphlet—at my expense—under my own imprint. I'll want four hundred copies; no, five—six hundred I'll need.

ASLAKSEN: Even if you gave me its weight in gold, I couldn't put my plant to that use, Doctor. I wouldn't dare, in view of public opinion. You won't get that printed anywhere in this town.

DR. STOCKMANN: Then give it back.

HOVSTAD (*hands him the manuscript*): There.

DR. STOCKMANN (*picks up his hat and stick*): It's coming out, no matter what. I'll hold a mass meeting and read it aloud. All my fellow townspeople are going to hear the voice of truth.

MAYOR STOCKMANN: There's not an organization in town that'll rent you a hall for such a purpose.

ASLAKSEN: Not one. I'm positive of that.

BILLING: Ye gods, no!

MRS. STOCKMANN: But this is shameful. Why do they all turn against you, these men?

DR. STOCKMANN (*furiously*): I'll tell you why! It's because all the so-called men in this town are old women—like you. They all just think of their families and never the common good.

MRS. STOCKMANN (*taking his arm*): Then I'll show them a—an old woman who can be a man for once. I'm standing with you, Thomas!

DR. STOCKMANN: That was well said, Katherine. And, by God, I'll get this out! If I can't rent a hall, then I'll hire a drummer to walk the town with me, and I'll cry out the truth on every street corner.

MAYOR STOCKMANN: You're not going to act like a raving maniac!

DR. STOCKMANN: Yes, I am!

ASLAKSEN: In this whole town, you won't get one solitary man to go with you.

BILLING: Ye gods, I'll say you won't!

MRS. STOCKMANN: Don't give in, Thomas. I'll ask the boys to go with you.

DR. STOCKMANN: That's a marvelous idea!

MRS. STOCKMANN: Morten would love to do it; and Eilif—he'll go along.

DR. STOCKMANN: Yes, and Petra too! And you yourself, Katherine!

MRS. STOCKMANN: No, no, that's not for me. But I'll stand at the window and watch you; that I'll do.

DR. STOCKMANN (*throws his arms about her and kisses her*): Thanks for that! And now, gentlemen, let's try our steel. I'd just like to see if conniving hypocrisy can gag the mouth of a patriot who's out to clean up society!

He and MRS. STOCKMAN *leave by the entrance door, back left.*

MAYOR STOCKMANN (*gravely shaking his head*): Now he's driven her crazy, too.

ACT IV

A large, old-fashioned room in CAPTAIN HORSTER'S *house. Double doors, standing open at the back, lead to an anteroom. Spaced along the wall, left, are three windows. At the middle of the opposite wall a platform has been prepared, with a small table; on it are two candles, a water carafe, a glass, and a bell. The room is mainly illuminated by wall lamps between the windows. In the left foreground stands a table with candles on it, and a chair. Farther forward at the right is a door, with several chairs beside it.*

There is a large assemblage of TOWNSPEOPLE *from all levels of society. Scattered among them are a few* WOMEN *and some* SCHOOLBOYS. *More and more people gradually crowd in from the rear, until the room is full.*

A CITIZEN (*to another, as he jostles against him*): Are you here too, Lamstad?

SECOND CITIZEN: I never miss a public meeting.

THIRD CITIZEN: I hope you brought along your whistle?

SECOND CITIZEN: You bet I did. And you?

THIRD CITIZEN: Of course. Skipper Evensen has a whopping big horn he said he'd bring.

SECOND CITIZEN: He's a character, that Evensen.

Laughter among the group.

FOURTH CITIZEN *(joining them)*: Say, tell me, what's going on here tonight?

SECOND CITIZEN: It's Dr. Stockmann; he's giving a speech against the mayor.

FOURTH CITIZEN: But the mayor's his brother.

FIRST CITIZEN: What of it? The doctor isn't afraid.

THIRD CITIZEN: Yes, but he's all wrong. The *Courier* said so.

SECOND CITIZEN: Yes, he really must be this time, because nobody'll rent him a hall—neither the Home Owners Council nor the civic club.

FIRST CITIZEN: Even the hall at the baths wouldn't have him.

SECOND CITIZEN: Well, that you can imagine.

A MAN *(in another group)*: Who are we backing in this?

ANOTHER MAN *(next to him)*: Just watch Aslaksen and do what he does.

BILLING *(with a portfolio under his arm, forcing his way through the crowd)*: Excuse me, gentlemen! If you'll let me by, please? I'm covering this for the *Courier*. Thank you so much! *(He sits at the table on the left.)*

A WORKMAN: Who's he?

ANOTHER WORKMAN: You don't know *him?* That's Billing—writes for Aslaksen's paper.

CAPTAIN HORSTER *conducts* MRS. STOCKMANN *and* PETRA *in through the door to the right.* EILIF *and* MORTEN *follow.*

HORSTER: I was thinking the family could sit here. If anything should happen, you could slip out quietly.

MRS. STOCKMANN: Do you think there'll be a disturbance?

HORSTER: You never can tell—with so many people. But sit down and rest easy.

MRS. STOCKMANN *(sitting)*: How kind of you to offer Thomas this room.

HORSTER: When nobody else would, then—

PETRA *(who also has seated herself)*: And it was brave of you, too, Captain Horster.

HORSTER: Oh, I don't think it took much courage for that.

HOVSTAD *and* ASLAKSEN *make their way forward at the same time, but separately, through the crowd.*

ASLAKSEN *(moves across to* HORSTER*)*: Hasn't the doctor come yet?

HORSTER: He's waiting inside.

A flurry of activity by the doorway in back.

HOVSTAD *(to* BILLING*)*: Here's the mayor. Look!

BILLING: Ye gods, he showed up after all!

The MAYOR *proceeds quietly through the crowd, exchanging polite greetings, and then stations himself by the wall, left. After a moment* DR. STOCKMANN *enters through the door to the right. He is dressed in a black frock coat with a white tie. There is scattered, hesitant applause, which is met by subdued hissing. The room grows silent.*

DR. STOCKMANN *(in an undertone)*: How do you feel, Katherine?

MRS. STOCKMANN: Oh, I'm all right. *(Lowering her voice.)* Now, Thomas, don't fly off the handle.

DR. STOCKMANN: I can manage myself, you know that. *(Looks at his watch, then ascends the platform and bows.)* It's already a quarter past—so I'd like to begin— *(Taking his manuscript out.)*

ASLAKSEN: First, we really ought to elect a chairman.

DR. STOCKMANN: No, that's quite unnecessary.

SEVERAL VOICES *(shouting)*: Yes, yes!

MAYOR STOCKMANN: I also submit that we ought to elect a moderator.

DR. STOCKMANN: But I've called this meeting to present a lecture, Peter!

MAYOR STOCKMANN: The doctor's lecture is likely to arouse some contrary opinions.

MORE VOICES FROM THE CROWD: A chairman! A moderator!

HOVSTAD: The will of the people seems to demand a chairman.

DR. STOCKMANN *(restraining himself)*: All right, then, let the will of the people rule.

ASLAKSEN: Would the mayor agree to accept the chair?

THREE GENTLEMEN *(applauding)*: Bravo! Bravo!

MAYOR STOCKMANN: For certain self-evident reasons, I must decline. But luckily we have in our midst a man whom I think we can all accept. I'm referring to the chairman of the Home Own-ers Council, Mr. Aslaksen.

MANY VOICES: Yes, yes! Aslaksen! Hurray for Aslaksen!

DR. STOCKMANN *puts away his manuscript and leaves the platform.*

ASLAKSEN: If my fellow townspeople express their confidence in me, I cannot refuse—

Applause and shouts of approval. ASLAKSEN *mounts the platform.*

BILLING *(writing)*: So—"Mr. Aslaksen chosen by acclamation—"

ASLAKSEN: And since I'm standing here now in this role, permit me to say a few brief words. I am a man of peace and quiet who's dedicated himself to prudent moderation and to—and to moderate prudence; everyone who knows me can attest to that.

MANY VOICES: Right! You said it, Aslaksen!

ASLAKSEN: I've learned in life's school of experience that moder-ation is the most rewarding of all virtues for the citizen—

MAYOR STOCKMANN: Hear, hear!

ASLAKSEN: And, moreover, that prudence and temperance are what serve society best. Therefore, I would urge the estimable gentleman who convened this meeting that he make every effort to stay within the bounds of moderation.

A DRUNK *(near the door)*: To the Temperance Union, skoal!

A VOICE: Shut the hell up!

MANY VOICES: Sh, sh!

ASLAKSEN: No interruptions, gentlemen! Does anyone have some-thing to say?

MAYOR STOCKMANN: Mr. Chairman!

ASLAKSEN: The chair recognizes the mayor.

MAYOR STOCKMANN: Considering my close relationship, which you all know, to the present staff physician of the baths, I would very much have wished not to express myself here this evening. But my official connection with the baths, and a due regard for the crucial interests of this town, compel me to present a pro-posal. I think it safe to assume that not a single citizen here tonight would find it desirable that exaggerated and unreliable charges about the sanitary conditions of the baths should gain currency abroad.

MANY VOICES: No, no, no! Of course not! We protest!

MAYOR STOCKMANN: I therefore move that this gathering refuse to permit the staff physician to read or otherwise report on his version of the matter.

DR. STOCKMANN *(infuriated)*: Refuse permission— What's that?

MRS. STOCKMANN *(coughing)*: Hm, hm!

DR. STOCKMANN *(controls himself)*: Permission refused—all right.

MAYOR STOCKMANN: In my statement to the *People's Courier*, I've acquainted the public with the pertinent facts, so that every right-minded citizen can easily form his own judgment. You'll see there that the doctor's proposal—besides being a vote of no confidence in the leadership of this town—would actually mean afflicting our local taxpayers with a needless expenditure of at least a hundred thousand crowns.

Cries of outrage and the sound of whistles.

ASLAKSEN *(ringing the bell)*: Quiet, gentlemen! Allow me to second the mayor's proposal. It's *my* opinion, also, that the doctor's agitation has an ulterior motive. He talks about the baths, but it's a revolution he's after. He wants to put the government into different hands. No one doubts the doctor's honest intentions; Lord knows there's no divided opinion on that. I'm also a friend of self-determination by the people—as long as it doesn't hit the taxpayer too hard. But that exactly would be the case here; and it's why I'll be damned—excuse me—if I can go along with Dr. Stockmann in this. You can pay too much, even for gold; that's *my* opinion.

Lively approval from all sides.

HOVSTAD: Likewise I feel obligated to clarify my own position. Dr. Stockmann's agitation seemed at first to be winning a good deal of acceptance, and I supported it as impartially as I could. But then we began to sense that we'd let ourselves be misled by a false interpretation—

DR. STOCKMANN: False—!

HOVSTAD: A less reliable interpretation, then. The mayor's statement has proved that. I hope no one here tonight would challenge my liberal sentiments; the *Courier's* policy on our great political issues is well known to all of you. Still, I've learned from men of wisdom and experience that in purely local matters a paper ought to move with a certain caution.

ASLAKSEN: I agree perfectly.

HOVSTAD: And, in the matter in question, it's now indisputable that Dr. Stockmann has the will of the majority against him. But an editor's first and foremost responsibility—what is that, gentlemen? Isn't it to work in collaboration with his readers? Hasn't he received something on the order of an unspoken mandate to strive actively and unceasingly on behalf of those who share his beliefs? Or maybe I'm wrong in this?

MANY VOICES: No, no, no! He's right.

HOVSTAD: It's been a bitter struggle for me to break with a man in whose home I've lately been a frequent guest—a man who, until today, could bask in the undivided esteem of the community—a man whose only fault, or whose greatest fault at least, is that he follows his heart more than his head.

SOME SCATTERED VOICES: That's true! Hurray for Dr. Stockmann.

HOVSTAD: But my duty to society compelled me to break with him. And then there's another consideration that prompts me to oppose him and, if possible, to deter him from the ominous course he's chosen: namely, consideration for his family—

DR. STOCKMANN: Stick to the sewers and water mains!

HOVSTAD: —consideration for his wife and his distressed children.

MORTEN: Is that us, Mother?

MRS. STOCKMANN: Hush!

ASLAKSEN: I hereby put the mayor's proposal to a vote.

DR. STOCKMANN: Never mind that! It's not my intention to speak tonight of all that squalor in the baths. No, you're going to hear something quite different.

MAYOR STOCKMANN (*muttering*): Now what?

THE DRUNK (*from the main doorway*): I'm a taxpayer! And, therefore, so I got rights to an opinion! And I have the sotted—solid and incomprehensible opinion that—

SEVERAL VOICES: Quiet over there!

OTHERS: He's drunk! Throw him out!

The DRUNK *is ejected.*

DR. STOCKMANN: Do I have the floor?

ASLAKSEN (*ringing the bell*): Dr. Stockmann has the floor!

DR. STOCKMANN: If it had been only a few days ago that anyone had tried to gag me like this tonight—I'd have fought for my sacred human rights like a lion! But it doesn't matter to me now. Because now I have greater things to discuss.

The CROWD *presses in closer around him;* MORTEN KIIL *becomes visible among them.*

DR. STOCKMANN *(continuing)*: I've been thinking a lot these past few days—pondering so many things that finally my thoughts began running wild—

MAYOR STOCKMANN *(coughs)*: Hm—!

DR. STOCKMANN: But then I got everything in place again, and I saw the whole structure so distinctly. It's why I'm here this evening. I have great disclosures to make, my friends! I'm going to unveil a discovery to you of vastly different dimension than this trifle that our water system is polluted and that our health spa is built on a muckheap.

MANY VOICES *(shouting)*: Don't talk of the baths! We won't listen! Enough of that!

DR. STOCKMANN: I've said I'd talk about the great discovery I've made these last few days: the discovery that all the sources of our spiritual life are polluted, and that our entire community rests on a muckheap of lies.

STARTLED VOICES *(in undertones)*: What's he saying?

MAYOR STOCKMANN: Of all the insinuations—

ASLAKSEN *(his hand on the bell)*: The speaker is urged to be moderate.

DR. STOCKMANN: I've loved my birthplace as much as any man can. I was barely grown when I left here; and distance and deprivation and memory threw a kind of enchantment over the town, and the people, too.

Scattered applause and cheers.

For many years, then, I practiced in the far north, at the dead end of nowhere. When I came in contact with some of the people who lived scattered in that waste of rocks, I many times thought it would have done those poor starved creatures more good if they'd gotten a veterinary instead of someone like me.

Murmuring among the crowd.

BILLING *(setting down his pen)*: Ye gods, why I never heard such—!

HOVSTAD: That's an insult to the common man!

DR. STOCKMANN: Just a minute—! I don't think anyone could ever say that I'd forgotten my home town up there. I brooded on my egg like an eider duck; and what I hatched—was the plan for the baths.

Applause and objections.

And finally, at long last, when fate relented and allowed me to come back home—my friends, then it seemed as though I had nothing left to wish for in this world. No, I did have one wish: a fierce, insistent, burning desire to contribute to the best of my town and my people.

MAYOR STOCKMANN (*gazing into space*): It's a funny way to—hm.

DR. STOCKMANN: And so I went around, exulting in my blind happiness. But yesterday morning—no, actually it was the night before last—the eyes of my spirit were opened wide, and the first thing I saw was the consummate stupidity of the authorities—

Confusion, outcries, and laughter. MRS. STOCKMANN *coughs vigorously.*

MAYOR STOCKMANN: Mr. Chairman!

ASLAKSEN (*ringing his bell*): By the powers vested in me—!

DR. STOCKMANN: It's petty to get hung up on a word, Mr. Aslaksen! I only mean that it came to me then what a consummate mess our local leaders had made out of the baths. Our leaders are one group that, for the life of me, I can't stand. I've had enough of that breed in my days. They're like a pack of goats in a stand of new trees—they strip off everything. They get in a free man's way wherever he turns—and I really don't see why we shouldn't exterminate them like any other predator—

Tumult in the room.

MAYOR STOCKMANN: Mr. Chairman, can you let such a statement pass?

ASLAKSEN (*his hand on the bell*): Doctor—!

DR. STOCKMANN: I can't imagine why I've only now taken a really sharp look at these gentlemen, because right before my eyes almost daily I've had a superb example—my brother Peter—slow of wit and thick of head—

Laughter, commotion, and whistles. MRS. STOCKMANN *coughs repeatedly.* ASLAKSEN *vehemently rings his bell.*

THE DRUNK *(who has gotten in again)*: Are you referring to me? Yes, my name's Pettersen all right—but I'll fry in hell, before—

ANGRY VOICES: Out with that drunk! Throw him out!

Again the DRUNK *is ejected.*

MAYOR STOCKMANN: Who was that person?

A BYSTANDER: I don't know him, Your Honor.

ANOTHER: He's not from this town.

A THIRD: It must be that lumber dealer from over in— *(The rest is inaudible.)*

ASLAKSEN: The man was obviously muddled on Munich beer. Go on, Dr. Stockmann, but try to be more temperate.

DR. STOCKMANN: So then, my friends and neighbors, I'll say nothing further about our leading citizens. If, from what I've just said, anyone imagines that I'm out to get those gentlemen here this evening, then he's wrong—most emphatically wrong. Because I nourish a benign hope that all those mossbacks, those relics of a dying world of thought, are splendidly engaged in digging their own graves—they don't need a doctor's aid to speed them off the scene. And besides, *They're* not the overwhelming menace to society; *they're* not the ones most active in poisoning our spiritual life and polluting the very ground we stand on; *they're* not the most insidious enemies of truth and freedom in our society.

SHOUTS FROM ALL SIDES: Who, then! Who are they? Name them!

DR. STOCKMANN: Yes, you can bet I'll name them! Because *that's* exactly my great discovery yesterday. *(Raising his voice.)* The most insidious enemy of truth and freedom among us is the solid majority. Yes, the damned, solid, liberal majority—that's it! Now you know.

Wild turmoil in the room. Almost all those present are shouting, stamping, and whistling. Several elderly gentlemen exchange sly glances and appear to be amused. EILIF *and* MORTEN *move threateningly toward the* SCHOOLBOYS, *who are making a disturbance.* ASLAKSEN *rings his bell and calls for order. Both* HOVSTAD *and* BILLING *are talking, without being heard. Finally quiet is restored.*

ASLAKSEN: As chairman, I urge the speaker to withdraw his irresponsible comments.

DR. STOCKMANN: Not a chance, Mr. Aslaksen. It's that same majority in our community that's stripping away my freedom and trying to keep me from speaking the truth.

HOVSTAD: The majority is always right.

BILLING: And it acts for truth. Ye gods!

DR. STOCKMANN: The majority is never right. I say, never! That's one of those social lies that any free man who thinks for himself has to rebel against. Who makes up the majority in any country—the intelligent, or the stupid? I think we've got to agree that, all over this whole wide earth, the stupid are in a fearsomely overpowering majority. But I'll be damned to perdition if it's part of the eternal plan that the stupid are meant to rule the intelligent!

Commotion and outcries.

Oh yes, you can shout me down well enough, but you can't refute me. The majority has the might—unhappily—but it lacks the *right*. The right is with me, and the other few, the solitary individuals. The minority is always right.

Renewed turmoil.

HOVSTAD (*laughs*): So, in a couple of days, the doctor's turned aristocrat.

DR. STOCKMANN: I've told you I'm not going to waste any words on that wheezing, little, narrow-chested pack of reactionaries. The tide of life has already passed them by. But I'm thinking of the few, the individuals among us, who've mastered all the new truths that have been germinating. Those men are out there holding their positions like outposts, so far in the vanguard that the solid majority hasn't even begun to catch up—and *there's* where they're fighting for truths too newly born in the world's consciousness to have won any support from the majority.

HOVSTAD: Well, and now he's a revolutionist!

DR. STOCKMANN: Yes, you're damn right I am, Mr Hovstad! I'm fomenting a revolution against the lie that only the majority owns the truth. What are these truths the majority flocks around? They're the ones so ripe in age they're nearly senile.

But, gentlemen, when a truth's grown that old, it's gone a long way toward becoming a lie.

Laughter and jeers.

Oh yes, you can believe me as you please: but truths aren't at all the stubborn old Methuselahs people imagine. An ordinary, established truth lives, as a rule—let's say—some seventeen, eighteen, at the most twenty years; rarely more. But those venerable truths are always terribly thin. Even so, it's only *then* that the majority takes them up and urges them on society as wholesome spiritual food. But there isn't much nutriment in that kind of diet, I promise you; and as a doctor, I know. All these majority-truths are like last year's salt meat—like rancid, tainted pork. And there's the cause of all the moral scurvy that's raging around us.

ASLAKSEN: It strikes me that the distinguished speaker has strayed rather far from his text.

MAYOR STOCKMANN: I must agree with the chairman's opinion.

DR. STOCKMANN: You're out of your mind, Peter! I'm sticking as close to the text as I can. Because this is exactly what I'm talking about: that the masses, the crowd, this damn solid majority— that *this* is what I say is poisoning our sources of spiritual life and defiling the earth under our feet.

HOVSTAD: And the great liberal-minded majority does this because they're reasonable enough to honor only basic, well-accepted truths?

DR. STOCKMANN: Ah, my dear Mr. Hovstad, don't talk about basic truths! The truths accepted by the masses now are the ones proclaimed basic by the advance guard in our grandfathers' time. We fighters on the frontiers today, we no longer recognize them. There's only one truth that's basic in my belief: that no society can live a healthy life on the bleached bones of that kind of truth.

HOVSTAD: Instead of standing there rambling on in the blue, it might be interesting to describe some of those bleached bones we're living on.

Agreement from various quarters.

DR. STOCKMANN: Oh, I could itemize a whole slew of abominations; but to start with, I'll mention just one recognized truth that's actually a vicious lie, though Mr. Hovstad and the *Courier* and all the *Courier*'s devotees live on it.

HOVSTAD: That being—?

DR. STOCKMANN: That being the doctrine inherited from your ancestors, which you mindlessly disseminate far and wide—the doctrine that the public, the mob, the masses are the vital core of the people—in fact, that they *are* the people—and that the common man, the inert, unformed component of society, has the same right to admonish and approve, to prescribe and to govern as the few spiritually accomplished personalities.

BILLING: Well, I'll be—

HOVSTAD (*simultaneously, shouting*): Citizens, did you hear that!

ANGRY VOICES: Oh, we're not the people, uh? So, only the accomplished rule!

A WORKMAN: Out with a man who talks like that!

OTHERS: Out the door! Heave him out!

A MAN (*yells*): Evensen, blow the horn!

Deep blasts on a horn are heard; whistles and furious commotion in the room.

DR. STOCKMANN (*when the noise has subsided a bit*): Now just be reasonable! Can't you stand hearing the truth for a change? I never expected you all to agree with me on the spot. But I really did expect that Mr. Hovstad would admit I'm right, after he'd simmered down a little. Mr. Hovstad claims to be a freethinker—

STARTLED VOICES (*in undertones*): What was that? A freethinker? Hovstad a freethinker?

HOVSTAD (*loudly*): Prove it, Dr. Stockmann! When have I said that in print?

DR. STOCKMANN (*reflecting*): No, by God, you're right—you've never had the courage. Well, I don't want to put you in hot water. Let's say I'm the freethinker then. Because I'm going to demonstrate scientifically that the *Courier*'s leading you shamelessly by the nose when they say that you—the public, the masses—are the vital core of the people. You see, that's just a journalistic lie! The masses are no more than the raw material out of which a people is shaped.

Mutterings, laughter, and disquiet in the room.

Well, isn't that a fact throughout all the rest of life? What about the difference between a thoroughbred and a hybrid animal? Look at your ordinary barnyard fowl. What meat can you get off such scrawny bones? Not much! And what kind of eggs does it lay? Any competent crow or raven could furnish about the same. But now take a purebred Spanish or Japanese hen, or a fine pheasant or turkey—there's where you'll see the difference! Or again with dogs, a family we humans so closely resemble. First, think of an ordinary stray dog—I mean, one of those nasty, ragged, common mongrels that run around the streets, and spatter the walls of houses. Then set that stray alongside a poodle whose pedigree runs back through a distinguished line to a house where fine food and harmonious voices and music have been the rule. Don't you think the mentality of that poodle will have developed quite differently from the stray's? Of course it will! A young pedigreed poodle can be raised by its trainer to perform the most incredible feats. Your common mongrel couldn't learn such things if you stood him on his head.

Tumult and derision generally.

A CITIZEN *(shouting)*: Now you're making us into dogs, uh?

ANOTHER MAN: We're not animals, Doctor!

DR. STOCKMANN: Oh yes, brother, we *are* animals! We're the best animals, all in all, that any man could wish for. But there aren't many animals of quality among us. There's a terrible gap between the thoroughbreds and the mongrels in humanity. And what's amusing is that Mr. Hovstad totally agrees with me as long as we're talking of four-legged beasts—

HOVSTAD: Well, but they're a class by themselves.

DR. STOCKMANN: All right. But as soon as I extend the law to the two-legged animals, Mr. Hovstad stops cold. He doesn't dare think his own thoughts any longer, or follow his ideas to a logical conclusion. So he turns the whole doctrine upside down and declares in the *Courier* that the barnyard fowl and the mongrel dog—that *these* are the real paragons of the menagerie. But that's how it always goes as long as conformity is in your system, and you haven't worked through to a distinction of mind and spirit.

HOVSTAD: I make no claim of any kind of distinction. I was born of simple peasants, and I'm proud that my roots run deep in those masses that he despises.

NUMEROUS WOMEN: Hurray for Hovstad! Hurray, hurray!

DR. STOCKMANN: The kind of commonness I'm talking of isn't only found in the depths: it teems and swarms all around us in society—right up to the top. Just look at your own neat and tidy mayor. My brother Peter's as good a common man as any that walks on two feet—

Laughter and hisses.

MAYOR STOCKMANN: I protest against these personal allusions.

DR. STOCKMANN *(unruffled)*: —and that's not because he's descended, just as I am, from a barbarous old pirate from Pomerania or thereabouts—because so we are—

MAYOR STOCKMANN: A ridiculous fiction. I deny it!

DR. STOCKMANN: —no, he's that because he thinks what the higher-ups think and believes what they believe. The people who do that are the spiritually common men. And that's why my stately brother Peter, you see, is in fact so fearfully lacking in distinction—and consequently so narrowminded.

MAYOR STOCKMANN: Mr. Chairman—!

HOVSTAD: So you have to be distinguished to be liberal-minded in this country. That's a completely new insight.

General laughter.

DR. STOCKMANN: Yes, that's also part of my new discovery. And along with it goes the idea that broadmindedness is almost exactly the same as morality. That's why I say it's simply inexcusable of the *Courier*, day in and day out, to promote the fallacy that it's the masses, the solid majority, who stand as the guardian of tolerance and morality—and that degeneracy and corruption of all kinds are a sort of by-product of culture, filtering down to us like all the pollution filtering down to the baths from the tanneries up at Mølledal.

Turmoil and interruptions.

DR. STOCKMANN *(unfazed, laughing in his enthusiasm)*: And yet this same *Courier* can preach that the deprived masses must be raised to greater cultural opportunities. But, hell's bells—if the *Courier*'s assumption holds true, then raising the masses like that would be precisely the same as plunging them smack into depravity! But luckily it's only an old wives' tale—this inherited lie that culture demoralizes. No, it's ignorance and poverty and ugliness in life that do the devil's work! In a house that isn't aired and swept every day—my wife Katherine maintains that the floors ought to be scrubbed as well, but that's debatable—anyway—I say in a house like that, within two or three years, people lose all power for moral thought and action. Lack of oxygen dulls the conscience. And there must be a woeful dearth of oxygen in the houses of this town, it seems, if the entire solid majority can numb their consciences enough to want to build this town's prosperity on a quagmire of duplicity and lies.

ASLAKSEN: It's intolerable—such a gross attack on a whole community.

A GENTLEMAN: I move the chairman rule the speaker out of order.

FURIOUS VOICES: Yes, yes! That's right! Out of order!

DR. STOCKMANN (*vehemently*): Then I'll cry out the truth from every street corner. I'll write to newspapers in other towns! The entire country'll learn what's happened here!

HOVSTAD: It almost looks like the doctor's determined to destroy this town.

DR. STOCKMANN: Yes. I love my home town so much I'd rather destroy it than see it flourishing on a lie.

ASLAKSEN: That's putting it plain.

Tumult and whistling. MRS. STOCKMANN *coughs in vain; the* DOCTOR *no longer hears her.*

HOVSTAD (*shouting above the noise*): Any man who'd destroy a whole community must be a public enemy!

DR. STOCKMANN (*with mountng indignation*): What's the difference if a lying community gets destroyed! It ought to be razed to the ground, I say! Stamp them out like vermin, everyone who lives by lies! You'll contaminate this entire nation in the end, till the land itself deserves to be destroyed. And if it comes to that even, then I say with all my heart: let this whole land be destroyed, let its people all be stamped out!

A MAN: That's talking like a real enemy of the people!

BILLING: Ye gods, but *there's* the people's voice!

THE WHOLE CROWD (*shrieking*): Yes, yes, yes! He's an enemy of the people! He hates his country! He hates all his people!

ASLAKSEN: Both as a citizen and as a human being, I'm profoundly shaken by what I've had to listen to here. Dr. Stockmann has revealed himself in a manner beyond anything I could have dreamed. I'm afraid that I have to endorse the judgment just rendered by my worthy fellow citizens; and I propose that we ought to express this judgment in a resolution, as follows: "This meeting declares that it regards Dr. Thomas Stockmann, staff physician at the baths, to be an enemy of the people."

Tumultuous cheers and applause. Many onlookers close in around the DOCTOR, *whistling at him.* MRS. STOCKMANN *and* PETRA *have risen.* MORTEN *and* EILIF *are fighting with the other* SCHOOLBOYS, *who have also been whistling. Several grown-ups separate them.*

DR. STOCKMANN *(to the hecklers)*: Ah, you fools—I'm telling you—

ASLAKSEN *(ringing his bell)*: The doctor is out of order! A formal vote is called for; but to spare personal feelings, it ought to be a secret ballot. Do you have any blank paper, Mr. Billing?

BILLING: Here's some blue and white both—

ASLAKSEN *(leaving the platform)*: Fine. It'll go faster that way. Cut it in slips—yes, that's it. *(To the gathering.)* Blue means no, white means yes. I'll go around myself and collect the votes.

The MAYOR *leaves the room.* ASLAKSEN *and a couple of other citizens circulate through the crowd with paper slips in their hats.*

A GENTLEMAN *(to* HOVSTAD*)*: What's gotten into the doctor? How should we take this?

HOVSTAD: Well, you know how hot-headed he is.

ANOTHER GENTLEMAN *(to* BILLING*)*: Say, you've visited there off and on. Have you noticed if the man drinks?

BILLING: Ye gods, I don't know what to say. When anybody stops in, there's always toddy on the table.

A THIRD GENTLEMAN: No, I think at times he's just out of his mind.

FIRST GENTLEMAN: I wonder if there isn't a strain of insanity in the family?

BILLING: It's quite possible.

A FOURTH GENTLEMAN: No, it's pure spite, that's all. Revenge for something or other.

BILLING: He was carrying on about a raise at one time—but he never got it.

ALL THE GENTLEMEN *(as one voice)*: Ah, there's the answer!

THE DRUNK *(within the crowd)*: Let's have a blue one! And—let's have a white one, too!

CRIES: There's that drunk again! Throw him out!

MORTEN KIIL *(approaching the* DOCTOR*)*: Well, Stockmann, now you see what your monkeyshines come to?

DR. STOCKMANN: I've done my duty.

MORTEN KIIL: What was that you said about the tanneries at Mølledal?

DR. STOCKMANN: You heard it. I said all the pollution came from them.

MORTEN KIIL: From *my* tannery, too?

DR. STOCKMANN: I'm afraid your tannery's the worst of them.

MORTEN KIIL: You're going to print *that* in the papers?

DR. STOCKMANN: I'm sweeping nothing under the carpet.

MORTEN KIIL: That could cost you plenty, Stockmann. *(He leaves.)*

A FAT GENTLEMAN *(going up to* HORSTER, *without greeting the ladies)*: Well, Captain, so you lend out your house to enemies of the people?

HORSTER: I think I can dispose of my property, sir, as I see fit.

THE MAN: So you'll certainly have no objection if I do the same with mine.

HORSTER: What do you mean?

THE MAN: You'll hear from me in the morning. *(He turns and leaves.)*

PETRA *(to* HORSTER*)*: Doesn't he own your ship?

HORSTER: Yes, that was Mr. Vik.

ASLAKSEN *(ascends the platform with ballots in hand and rings for order)*: Gentlemen, let me make you acquainted with the outcome. All of the votes with one exception—

A YOUNG MAN: That's the drunk!

ASLAKSEN: All of the votes, with the exception of an intoxicated man, are in favor of this assembly of citizens declaring the staff physician of the baths, Dr. Thomas Stockmann, an enemy of the people. *(Shouts and gestures of approval.)* Long live our ancient and glorious community! *(More cheers.)* Long live our capable and effective mayor, who so loyally has suppressed the ties of family! *(Cheers.)* This meeting is adjourned. *(He descends from the platform.)*

BILLING: Long live the chairman!

THE ENTIRE CROWD: Hurray for Aslaksen!

DR. STOCKMANN: My hat and coat, Petra. Captain, have you room for several passengers to the New World?

HORSTER: For you and your family, Doctor, we'll make room.

DR. STOCKMANN *(as* PETRA *helps him on with his coat)*: Good. Come, Katherine! Come on, boys!

He takes his wife by the arm.

MRS. STOCKMANN *(dropping her voice)*: Thomas, dear, let's leave by the back way.

DR. STOCKMANN: No back ways out, Katherine. *(Raising his voice.)* You'll be hearing from the enemy of the people before he shakes this dust off his feet! I'm not as meek as one certain person; I'm not saying, "I forgive them, because they know not what they do."

ASLAKSEN *(in an outcry)*: That's a blasphemous comparison, Dr. Stockmann!

BILLING: That it is, so help me—It's a bit much for a pious man to take.

A COARSE VOICE: And then he threatened us, too!

HEATED VOICES: Let's smash his windows for him! Dunk him in the fjord!

A MAN *(in the crowd)*: Blast your horn, Evensen! Honk, honk!

The sound of the horn; whistles and wild shrieks. The DOCTOR *and his family move toward the exit,* HORSTER *clearing the way for them.*

THE WHOLE CROWD *(howling after them)*: Enemy! Enemy! Enemy of the people!

BILLING *(organizing his notes)*: Ye gods, I wouldn't drink toddy at the Stockmann's tonight!

The crowd surges toward the exit; the noise diffuses outside; from the street the cry continues: "Enemy! Enemy of the people!"

ACT V

DR. STOCKMANN's *study. Bookcases and cabinets filled with various medicines line the walls. In the back wall is a door to the hall; in the foreground, left, the door to the living room. At the right, opposite, are two windows, with all their panes shattered. In the middle of the room is the* DOCTOR's *desk, covered with books and papers. The room is in disorder. It is morning.* DR. STOCKMANN, *in a dressing gown, slippers, and a smoking cap, is bent down, raking under one of the cabinets with an umbrella; after some effort, he sweeps out a stone.*

DR. STOCKMANN (*calling through the open living-room door*): Katherine, I found another one.

MRS. STOCKMANN (*from the living room*): Oh, I'm sure you'll find a lot more yet.

DR. STOCKMANN (*adding the stone to a pile of others on the table*): I'm going to preserve these stones as holy relics. Eilif and Morten have got to see them every day; and when they're grown, they'll inherit them from me. (*Raking under a bookcase.*) Hasn't— what the hell's her name—the maid—hasn't she gone for the glazier yet?

MRS. STOCKMANN (*enters*): Of course, but he said he didn't know if he could come today.

DR. STOCKMANN: More likely he doesn't dare.

MRS. STOCKMANN: Yes, Randina thought he was afraid of what the neighbors might say. (*Speaking into the living room.*) What do you want, Randina? Oh yes. (*Goes out and comes back immediately.*) Here's a letter for you, Thomas.

DR. STOCKMANN: Let me see. (*Opens it and reads.*) Of course.

MRS. STOCKMANN: Who's it from?

DR. STOCKMANN: The landlord. He's giving us notice.

MRS. STOCKMANN: Is that true! He's such a decent man—

DR. STOCKMANN (*reading on in the letter*): He doesn't dare not to, he says. It pains him to do it, but he doesn't dare not to—in fairness to his fellow townspeople—a matter of public opinion— not independent—can't affront certain powerful men—

MRS. STOCKMANN: You see, Thomas.

DR. STOCKMANN: Yes, yes, I see very well. They're cowards, all of them here in town. Nobody dares do anything, in fairness to all the others. *(Hurls the letter on the table.)* But that's nothing to us, Katherine. We're off for the New World now—

MRS. STOCKMANN: But, Thomas, is that really the right solution, to emigrate?

DR. STOCKMANN: Maybe I ought to stay here, where they've pilloried me as an enemy of the people, branded me, smashed in my windows! And look at this, Katherine; they even tore my black trousers.

MRS. STOCKMANN: Oh, no—and they're the best you have!

DR. STOCKMANN: One should never wear his best trousers when he goes out fighting for truth and freedom. It's not that I'm so concerned about the trousers, you understand; you can always mend them for me. But what grates is that mob setting on me bodily as if they were my equals—by God, that's the thing I can't bear!

MRS. STOCKMANN: Yes, they've abused you dreadfully in this town, Thomas. But do we have to leave the country entirely because of *that*?

DR. STOCKMANN: Don't you think the common herd is just as arrogant in other towns as well? Why, of course—it's all one and the same. Ahh, shoot! Let the mongrels yap; they're not the worst. The worst of it is that everyone the country over is a slave to party. But *that's* not the reason—it's probably no better in the free United States; I'm sure they have a plague of solid majorities and liberal public opinions and all the other bedevilments. But the scale there is so immense, you see. They might kill you, but they don't go in for slow torture; they don't lock a free soul in the jaws of a vise, the way they do here at home. And, if need be, there's space to get away. *(Pacing the floor.)* If I only knew of some primeval forest, or a little South Sea island at a bargain price—

MRS. STOCKMANN: But, Thomas, think of the boys.

DR. STOCKMANN *(stopping in his tracks)*: You are remarkable, Katherine! Would you rather they grew up in a society like ours? You saw yourself last night that half the population are raging maniacs; and if the other half haven't lost their reason, it's because they're such muttonheads they haven't any reason to lose.

MRS. STOCKMANN: Yes, but dear, you're so intemperate in your speech.

DR. STOCKMANN: Look! Isn't it true, what I'm saying? Don't they turn every idea upside down? Don't they scramble right and wrong completely? Don't they call everything a lie that I know for the truth? But the height of insanity is that here you've got all these full-grown liberals going around in a bloc and deluding themselves and the others that they're independent thinkers! Did you ever hear the like of it, Katherine?

MRS. STOCKMANN: Yes, yes, it's all wrong of course, but—

PETRA *enters from the living room.*

MRS. STOCKMANN: You're back from school already?

PETRA: Yes. I got my notice.

MRS. STOCKMANN: Your notice.

DR. STOCKMANN: You, too!

PETRA: Mrs. Busk gave me my notice, so I thought it better to leave at once.

DR. STOCKMANN: You did the right thing!

MRS. STOCKMANN: Who would have thought Mrs. Busk would prove such a poor human being!

PETRA: Oh, Mother, she really isn't so bad. It was plain to see how miserable she felt. but she said she didn't dare not to. So I got fired.

DR. STOCKMANN (*laughs and rubs his hands*): She didn't dare not to, either. Oh, that's charming.

MRS. STOCKMANN: Well, after that awful row last night—

PETRA: It was more than just that. Father, listen now!

DR. STOCKMANN: What?

PETRA: Mrs. Busk showed me no less than three letters she'd gotten this morning.

DR. STOCKMANN: Anonymous, of course?

PETRA: Yes.

DR. STOCKMANN: Because they don't *dare* sign their names, Katherine.

PETRA: And two of them stated that a gentleman who's often visited this household had declared in the club last night that I had extremely free ideas on various matters—

DR. STOCKMANN: And that you didn't deny, I hope.

PETRA: No, you know that. Mrs. Busk has some pretty liberal ideas herself, when it's just the two of us talking. But with this all coming out about me, she didn't dare keep me on.

MRS. STOCKMANN: And to think—it was one of our regular visitors! You see, Thomas, there's what you get for your hospitality.

DR. STOCKMANN: We won't go on living in a pigsty like this. Katherine, get packed as soon as you can. Let's get out of here, the quicker the better.

MRS. STOCKMANN: Be quiet—I think there's someone in the hall. Have a look, Petra.

PETRA *(opening the door)*: Oh, is it you, Captain Horster? Please, come in.

HORSTER *(from the hall)*: Good morning. I thought I ought to stop by and see how things stand.

DR. STOCKMANN *(shaking his hand)*: Thanks. That certainly is kind of you.

MRS. STOCKMANN: And thank you, Captain Horster, for helping us through last night.

PETRA: But how did you ever make it home again?

HORSTER: Oh, no problem. I can handle myself pretty well; and they're mostly a lot of hot air, those people.

DR. STOCKMANN: Yes, isn't it astounding, this bestial cowardice? Come here, and I'll show you something. See, here are all the stones they rained in on us. Just look at them! I swear, there aren't more than two respectable paving blocks in the whole pile; the rest are nothing but gravel—only pebbles. And yet they stood out there, bellowing, and swore they'd hammer me to a pulp. But action—action—no, you don't see much of that in this town!

HORSTER: I'd say this time that was lucky for you, Doctor.

DR. STOCKMANN: Definitely. But it's irritating, all the same; because if it ever comes to a serious fight to save this country, you'll see how public opinion is all for ducking the issue, and how the solid majority runs for cover like a flock of sheep. That's what's so pathetic when you think of it; it makes me heartsick— Damn it all, no—this is sheer stupidity; they've labeled me an enemy of the people, so I better act like one.

MRS. STOCKMANN: You never could be that, Thomas.

DR. STOCKMANN: Don't count on it, Katherine. To be called some ugly name hurts like a stabbing pain in the lung. And that damnable label—I can't shake it off; its fixed itself here in the pit of my stomach, where it sits and rankles and corrodes like acid. And there's no magnesia to work against that.

PETRA: Oh, Father, you should just laugh at them.

HORSTER: People will come around in their thinking, Doctor.

MRS. STOCKMANN: As sure as you're standing here, they will.

DR. STOCKMANN: Yes, maybe after it's too late. Well, they've got it coming! Let them stew in their own mess and rue the day they drove a patriot into exile. When are you sailing, Captain Horster?

HORSTER: Hm—as a matter of fact, that's why I stopped by to talk to you—

DR. STOCKMANN: Oh, has something gone wrong with the ship?

HORSTER: No. But it looks like I won't sail with her.

PETRA: You haven't been fired, have you?

HORSTER (*smiles*): Yes, exactly.

PETRA: You, too.

MRS. STOCKMANN: See there, Thomas.

DR. STOCKMANN: And all this for the truth! Oh, if only I could have foreseen—

HORSTER: Now, don't go worrying about me; I'll find a post with some shipping firm out of town.

DR. STOCKMANN: And there we have Mr. Vik—a merchant, a man of wealth, independent in every way—! What a disgrace!

HORSTER: He's quite fair-minded otherwise. He said himself he'd gladly have retained me if he dared to—

DR. STOCKMANN: But he didn't dare? No, naturally!

HORSTER: It's not so easy, he was telling me, when you belong to a party—

DR. STOCKMANN: There's a true word from the merchant prince. A political party—it's like a sausage grinder; it grinds all the heads up together into one mash, and then it turns them out, link by link, into fatheads and meatheads!

MRS. STOCKMANN: Thomas, really!

PETRA (*to* HORSTER): If you just hadn't seen us home, things might not have gone like this.

HORSTER: I don't regret it.

PETRA (*extending her hand to him*): Thank you!

HORSTER *(to the* DOCTOR*)*: So, what I wanted to say was, if you're still serious about leaving, then I've thought of another plan—

DR. STOCKMANN: Excellent. If we can only clear out of here fast—

MRS. STOCKMANN: Shh! Didn't someone knock?

PETRA: It's Uncle, I'll bet.

DR. STOCKMANN: Aha! *(Calls.)* Come in!

MRS. STOCKMANN: Thomas dear, you must promise me—

The MAYOR *enters from the hall.*

MAYOR STOCKMANN *(in the doorway)*: Oh, you're occupied. Well, then I'd better—

DR. STOCKMANN: No, no, come right in.

MAYOR STOCKMANN: But I wanted to speak to you alone.

MRS. STOCKMANN: We'll go into the living room for a time.

HORSTER: And I'll come by again later.

DR. STOCKMANN: No, you go in with them, Captain Horster. I need to hear something more about—

HORSTER: Oh yes, I'll wait then.

He accompanies MRS. STOCKMANN *and* PETRA *into the living room. The* MAYOR *says nothing, but glances at the windows.*

DR. STOCKMANN: Maybe you find it a bit drafty here today? Put your hat on.

MAYOR STOCKMANN: Thank you, if I may. *(Does so.)* I think I caught cold last night. I was freezing out there—

DR. STOCKMANN: Really? It seemed more on the warm side to me.

MAYOR STOCKMANN: I regret that it wasn't within my power to curb those excesses last evening.

DR. STOCKMANN: Do you have anything else in particular to say to me?

MAYOR STOCKMANN *(taking out a large envelope)*: I have this document for you from the board of directors.

DR. STOCKMANN: It's my notice?

MAYOR STOCKMANN: Yes, effective today. *(Places the envelope on the table.)* This pains us deeply, but—to be quite candid—we didn't dare not to, in view of public opinion.

DR. STOCKMANN *(smiles)*: Didn't dare? Seems as though I've already heard those words today.

MAYOR STOCKMANN: I suggest that you face your positon clearly.

After this, you mustn't count on any practice whatsoever here in town.

DR. STOCKMANN: To hell with the practice! But how can you be so sure?

MAYOR STOCKMANN: The Home Owners Council is circulating a resolution, soliciting all responsible citizens to dispense with your services. And I venture to say that not one single householder will risk refusing to sign. Quite simply, they wouldn't dare.

DR. STOCKMANN: I don't doubt it. But what of it?

MAYOR STOCKMANN: If I could give you some advice, it would be that you leave this area for a while—

DR. STOCKMANN: Yes, I've been half thinking of just that.

MAYOR STOCKMANN: Good. Then, after you've had some six months, more or less, to reconsider things, if on mature reflection you find yourself capable of a few words of apology, acknowledging your mistakes—

DR. STOCKMANN: Then maybe I could get my job back you mean?

MAYOR STOCKMANN: Perhaps. It's not at all unlikely.

DR. STOCKMANN: Yes, but public opinion? You could hardly dare, in that regard.

MAYOR STOCKMANN: Opinion tends to go from one extreme to another. And to be quite honest, it's especially important to us to get a signed statement to that effect from you.

DR. STOCKMANN: Yes, wouldn't you lick your chinchoppers for that! But, damnation, don't you remember what I already said about that kind of foxy game?

MAYOR STOCKMANN: Your position was much more favorable then. You could imagine then that you had the whole town in back of you—

DR. STOCKMANN: Yes, and I feel now as if the whole town's on my back— *(Flaring up.)* But even if the devil and his grandmother were riding me—never! Never, you hear me!

MAYOR STOCKMANN: A family provider can't go around risking everythng the way you do. You can't risk it, Thomas!

DR. STOCKMANN: Can't risk! There's just one single thing in this world a free man can't risk; and do you know what that is?

MAYOR STOCKMANN: No.

DR. STOCKMANN: Of course not. But *I'll* tell you. A free man can't risk befouling himself like a savage. He doesn't dare sink to the point that he'd like to spit in his own face.

MAYOR STOCKMANN: This all sounds highly plausible; and if there weren't another prior explanation for your stubborn arrogance—but then of course, there is—

DR. STOCKMANN: What do you mean by *that*?

MAYOR STOCKMANN: You understand perfectly well. But as your brother and as a man of some discernment, let me advise you not to build too smugly on prospects that might very well never materialize.

DR. STOCKMANN: What in the world are you driving at?

MAYOR STOCKMANN: Are you actually trying to make me believe you're ignorant of the terms of Morten Kiil's will?

DR. STOCKMANN: I know that the little he has is going to a home for destitute craftsmen. But how does that apply to me?

MAYOR STOCKMANN: First of all, the amount under discussion is far from little. Morten Kiil is a rather wealthy man.

DR. STOCKMANN: I hadn't the slightest idea—!

MAYOR STOCKMANN: Hm—really? And you hadn't any idea, either, that a considerable part of his fortune will pass to your children, with you and your wife enjoying the interest for life. He hasn't told you that?

DR. STOCKMANN: Not one blessed word of it! Quite the contrary, he goes on fuming endlessly about the outrageously high taxes he pays. But how do you know this for sure, Peter?

MAYOR STOCKMANN: I have it from a totally reliable source.

DR. STOCKMANN: But, my Lord, then Katherine's provided for— and the children too! I really must tell her— *(Shouts.)* Katherine, Katherine!

MAYOR STOCKMANN *(restraining him)*: Shh, don't say anything yet!

MRS. STOCKMANN *(opening the door)*: What is it?

DR. STOCKMANN: Nothing, dear. Go back inside.

MRS. STOCKMANN *shuts the door.*

DR. STOCKMANN *(pacing the floor)*: Provided for! Just imagine— every one of them, provided for. And for life! What a blissful feeling, to know you're secure!

MAYOR STOCKMANN: Yes, but that's precisely what you aren't. Morten Kiil can revise his will any time he pleases.

DR. STOCKMANN: But, my dear Peter, he won't do that. The Badger's enraptured by the way I've gone after you and your smart friends.

MAYOR STOCKMANN *(starts and looks penetratingly at him)*: Aha, that puts a new light on things.

DR. STOCKMANN: What things?

MAYOR STOCKMANN: So this whole business has been a collusion. These reckless, violent assaults you've aimed, in the name of truth, at our leading citizens were—

DR. STOCKMANN: Yes—were what?

MAYOR STOCKMANN: They were nothing more than a calculated payment for a piece of that vindictive old man's estate.

DR. STOCKMANN *(nearly speechless)*: Peter—you're the cheapest trash I've known in all my days.

MAYOR STOCKMANN: Between us, everything is through. Your dismissal is irrevocable—for now we've got a weapon against you. *(He goes.)*

DR. STOCKMANN: Why, that scum—aaah! *(Shouts.)* Katherine! Scour the floors where he's been! Have her come in with a pail—that girl—whozzis, damn it—the one with the smudgy nose—

MRS. STOCKMANN *(in the living-room doorway)*: Shh, Thomas. Shh!

PETRA *(also in the doorway)*: Father, Grandpa's here and wonders if he can speak to you alone.

DR. STOCKMANN: Yes, of course he can. *(By the door.)* Come in.

MORTEN KIIL *enters. The* DOCTOR *closes the door after him.*

DR. STOCKMANN: Well, what is it? Have a seat.

MORTEN KIIL: Won't sit. *(Looking about.)* You've made it very attractive here today, Stockmann.

DR. STOCKMANN: Yes, don't you think so?

MORTEN KIIL: Really attractive. And fresh air, too. Today you've got enough of that oxygen you talked about yesterday. You must have a marvelous conscience today, I imagine.

DR. STOCKMANN: Yes, I have.

MORTEN KIIL: I can imagine. *(Tapping his chest.)* But do you know what *I* have here?

DR. STOCKMANN: Well, I'm hoping a marvelous conscience, too.

MORTEN KIIL: Pah! No, it's something better than that. *(He takes out a thick wallet, opens it, and displays a sheaf of papers.)*

DR. STOCKMANN *(stares at him, amazed)*: Shares in the baths.

MORTEN KIIL: They weren't hard to get today.

DR. STOCKMANN: And you were out buying—?

MORTEN KIIL: As many as I could afford.

DR. STOCKMANN: But, my dear Father-in-law—with everything at the baths in jeopardy!

MORTEN KIIL: If you go back to acting like a reasonable man, you'll soon get the baths on their feet again.

DR. STOCKMANN: You can see yourself, I'm doing all I can; but the people are crazy in this town.

MORTEN KIIL: You said yesterday that the worst pollution came from my tannery. But now if that *is* true, then my grandfather and my father before me and I myself over numbers of years have been poisoning this town right along, like three angels of death. You think I can rest with that disgrace on my head?

DR. STOCKMANN: I'm afraid you'll have to learn how.

MORTEN KIIL: No thanks. I want my good name and reputation. People call me the Badger, I've heard. A badger's a kind of pig, isn't it? They're not going to be right about that. Never. I want to live and die a clean human being.

DR. STOCKMANN: And how are you going to do that?

MORTEN KIIL: You'll make me clean, Stockmann.

DR. STOCKMANN: I!

MORTEN KIIL: Do you know where I got the money to buy these shares? No, you couldn't know that, but now I'll tell you. It's the money Katherine and Petra and the boys will be inheriting from me someday. Yes, because, despite everything, I've laid a little aside, you see.

DR. STOCKMANN *(flaring up)*: So you went out and spent Katherine's money for *those*!

MORTEN KIIL: Yes, now the money's completely bound up in the baths. And now I'll see if you're really so ranting, raging mad after all, Stockmann. Any more about bugs and such coming down from my tannery, it'll be exactly the same as cutting great strips out of Katherine's skin, and Petra's, and the boys'. But no normal man would do that—he'd *have* to be mad.

DR. STOCKMANN (*pacing back and forth*): Yes, but I *am* a madman; I *am* a madman!

MORTEN KIIL: But you're not so utterly out of your senses as to flay your wife and children.

DR. STOCKMANN (*stopping in front of him*): Why couldn't you talk with me before you went out and bought all that worthless paper?

MORTEN KIIL: When a thing's been done, it's best to hang on.

DR. STOCKMANN (*paces the room restlessly*): If only I weren't so certain in this—! But I'm perfectly sure I'm right.

MORTEN KIIL (*weighing the wallet in his hand*): If you keep on with this foolishness, then these aren't going to be worth much, will they? (*He replaces the wallet in his pocket.*)

DR. STOCKMANN: Damn it, science should be able to provide some counter-agent, some kind of germicide—

MORTEN KIIL: You mean something to kill those little animals?

DR. STOCKMANN: Yes, or else make them harmless.

MORTEN KIIL: Couldn't you try rat poison?

DR. STOCKMANN: Oh, that's nonsense! But—everyone says this is all just imagination. Well, why not? Let them have what they want! Stupid, mean little mongrels—didn't they brand me enemy of the people? And weren't they spoiling to tear the clothes off my back?

MORTEN KIIL: And all the windows they broke for you.

DR. STOCKMANN: And I do have family obligations! I must talk this over with Katherine; she's very shrewd in these things.

MORTEN KIIL: Good. You pay attention to a sensible woman's advice.

DR. STOCKMANN (*turning on him*): And you, too—how could you make such a mess of it! Gambling with Katherine's money; tormenting me with this horrible dilemma! When I look at you, I could be seeing the devil himself—!

MORTEN KIIL: I think I'd better be going. But by two o'clock I want your answer: yes—or no. If it's no, the stock gets willed to charity—and right this very day.

DR. STOCKMANN: And what does Katherine get then?

MORTEN KIIL: Not a crumb.

The hall door is opened. HOVSTAD *and* ASLAKSEN *come into view, standing outside.*

MORTEN KIIL: Well, will you look at *them*?

DR. STOCKMANN (*staring at them*): What—! You still dare to come around here?

HOVSTAD: Of course we do.

ASLAKSEN: You see, we've something to talk with you about.

MORTEN KIIL (*in a whisper*): Yes or no—by two o'clock.

ASLAKSEN (*glancing at* HOVSTAD): Aha!

MORTEN KIIL *leaves.*

DR. STOCKMANN: Well now, what do you want? Cut it short.

HOVSTAD: I can easily realize your bitterness toward us for the posture we took at last night's meeting—

DR. STOCKMANN: You call that a posture! Yes, that was a lovely posture! I call it spinelessness, like a bent old woman—holy God!

HOVSTAD: Call it what you will, we couldn't do otherwise.

DR. STOCKMANN: You didn't *dare*, you mean. Isn't that right?

HOVSTAD: Yes, if you like.

ASLAKSEN: But why didn't you pass us the word beforehand? Just the least little hint to Hovstad or me.

DR. STOCKMANN: A hint? What about?

ASLAKSEN: The reason why.

DR. STOCKMANN: I simply don't understand you.

ASLAKSEN (*nods confidentially*): Oh, yes, you do, Dr. Stockmann.

HOVSTAD: Let's not make a mystery out of it any longer.

DR. STOCKMANN (*looking from one to the other*): What in sweet blazes *is* this—!

ASLAKSEN: May I ask—hasn't your father-in-law been combing the town to buy up stock in the baths?

DR. STOCKMANN: Yes, he's bought a few shares today; but—?

ASLAKSEN: It would have been more clever if you'd gotten someone else to do it—someone less closely related.

HOVSTAD: And you shouldn't have moved under your own name. No one had to know the attack on the baths came from you. You should have brought me in on it, Doctor.

DR. STOCKMANN (*stares blankly in front of him; a light seems to dawn on him, and he says as if thunderstruck*): It's unbelievable! Do these things happen?

ASLAKSEN (*smiles*): Why, of course they do. But they only happen when you use finesse, if you follow me.

HOVSTAD: And they go better when a few others are involved. The risk is less for the individual when the responsibility is shared.

DR. STOCKMANN *(regaining his composure)*: In short, gentlemen, what is it you want?

ASLAKSEN: Mr. Hovstad can best—

HOVSTAD: No, Aslaksen, you explain.

ASLAKSEN: Well, it's this—that now that we know how it all fits together, we thought we might venture to put the *People's Courier* at your disposal.

DR. STOCKMANN: Ah, so now you'll venture? But public opinion? Aren't you afraid there'll be a storm raised against us?

HOVSTAD: We're prepared to ride out the storm.

ASLAKSEN: And you should be prepared for a quick reversal in position, Doctor. As soon as your attack has served its purpose—

DR. STOCKMANN: You mean as soon as my father-in-law and I have cornered all the stock at a dirt-cheap price—?

HOVSTAD: I suppose it's mostly for scientific purposes that you want control of the baths.

DR. STOCKMANN: Naturally. It was for scientific purposes that I got the old Badger in with me on this. So we'll tinker a bit with the water pipes and dig around a little on the beach, and it won't cost the town half a crown. That ought to do it, don't you think? Hm?

HOVSTAD: I think so—as long as you've got the *Courier* with you.

ASLAKSEN: The press is a power in a free society, Doctor.

DR. STOCKMANN: How true. And so's public opinion. Mr. Aslaksen, I assume you'll take care of the Home Owners Council?

ASLAKSEN: The Home Owners Council and the Temperance Union both. You can count on that.

DR. STOCKMANN: But, gentlemen—it embarrasses me to mention it, but—*your* compensation—?

HOVSTAD: Preferably, of course, we'd like to help you for nothing, as you can imagine. But the *Courier's* on shaky legs these days; it's not doing too well; and to shut the paper down now when there's so much to work for in the larger political scene strikes me as insupportable.

DR. STOCKMANN: Clearly. That would be a hard blow for a friend of the people like you. *(In an outburst.)* But *I'm* an enemy of the people *(Lunges about the room.)* Where do I have my stick? Where in hell is that stick?

HOVSTAD: What's this?

ASLAKSEN: You're not going to—?

DR. STOCKMANN *(stops)*: And what if I didn't give you one iota of my shares? We tycoons aren't so free with our money, don't forget.

HOVSTAD: And don't *you* forget that this matter of shares can be posed in two different lights.

DR. STOCKMANN: Yes, you're just the man for that. If I don't bail out the *Courier*, you'll put a vile construction on it all. You'll hound me down—set upon me—try to choke me off like a dog chokes a hare!

HOVSTAD: That's the law of nature. Every animal has to struggle for survival.

ASLAKSEN: We take our food where we can find it, you know.

DR. STOCKMANN: Then see if you can find yours in the gutter! *(Striding about the room.)* Because now we're going to learn, by God, who's the strongest animal among the three of us! *(Finds his umbrella and flourishes it.)* Hi, look out—!

HOVSTAD: Don't hit us!

ASLAKSEN: Watch out with that umbrella!

DR. STOCKMANN: Out of the window with you, Hovstad.

HOVSTAD *(by the hall door)*: Have you lost your mind?

DR. STOCKMANN: Out of the window, Aslaksen! I said, jump! Don't be the last to go.

ASLAKSEN *(running around the desk)*: Moderation, Doctor! I'm out of condition—I'm not up to this— *(Shrieks.)* Help! Help!

MRS. STOCKMANN, PETRA, *and* HORSTER *enter from the living room.*

MRS. STOCKMANN: My heavens, Thomas, what's going on in here?

DR. STOCKMANN *(swinging his umbrella)*: Jump, I'm telling you! Into the gutter!

HOVSTAD: This is unprovoked assault! Captain Horster, I'm calling you for a witness. *(He scurries out down the hall.)*

ASLAKSEN *(confused)*: If I just knew the layout here— *(Sneaks out through the living-room door.)*

MRS. STOCKMANN *(holding onto the* DOCTOR*)*: Now you control yourself, Thomas!

DR. STOCKMANN (*flings the umbrella away*): Damn, they got out of it after all!

MRS. STOCKMANN: But what did they want you for?

DR. STOCKMANN: You can hear about it later. I have other things to think about now. (*Goes to the desk and writes on a visiting card.*) See, Katherine. What's written here?

MRS. STOCKMANN: "No," repeated three times. Why is that?

DR. STOCKMANN: You can hear about that later, too. (*Holding the card out.*) Here, Petra, tell Smudgy-face to run over to the Badger's with this, quick as she can. Hurry!

PETRA *leaves with the card by the hall door.*

Well, if I haven't had visits today from all the devil's envoys, I don't know what. But now I'll sharpen my pen into a stiletto and skewer them; I'll dip it in venom and gall; I'll sling my inkstand right at their skulls!

MRS. STOCKMANN: Yes, but we're leaving here, Thomas.

PETRA *returns.*

DR. STOCKMANN: Well?

PETRA: It's on its way.

DR. STOCKMANN: Good. Leaving, you say? The hell we are! We're staying here where we are, Katherine!

PETRA: We're staying?

MRS. STOCKMANN: In this town?

DR. STOCKMANN: Exactly. This is the battleground; here's where the fighting will be; and here's where I'm going to win! As soon as I've got my trousers patched, I'm setting out to look for a house. We'll need a roof over our heads by winter.

HORSTER: You can share mine.

DR. STOCKMANN: I can?

HORSTER: Yes, perfectly well. There's room enough, and I'm scarcely ever home.

MRS. STOCKMANN: Oh, how kind of you, Horster.

PETRA: Thank you!

DR. STOCKMANN (*shaking his hand*): Many, many thanks! So that worry is over. Now I can make a serious start right today. Oh, Katherine, it's endless, the number of things that need looking into here! And it's lucky I have so much time now to spend—

yes, because, I meant to tell you, I got my notice from the baths—

MRS. STOCKMANN *(sighing)*: Ah me, I've been expecting it.

DR. STOCKMANN: And then they want to take my practice away, too. Well, let them! I'll keep the poor people at least—the ones who can't pay at all; and, Lord knows, they're the ones that need me the most. But, by thunder, they'll have to hear me out. I'll preach to them in season and out of season, as someone once said.

MRS. STOCKMANN: But, dear, I think you've seen how much good preaching does.

DR. STOCKMANN: You really are preposterous, Katherine. Should I let myself be whipped from the field by public opinion and the solid majority and other such barbarities? No, thank you! Besides, what I want is so simple and clear and basic. I just want to hammer into the heads of these mongrels that the so-called liberals are the most insidious enemies of free men—that party programs have a way of smothering every new, germinal truth— that acting out of expediency turns morality and justice into a hollow mockery, until it finally becomes monstrous to go on living. Captain Horster, don't you think I could get people to recognize that?

HORSTER: Most likely. I don't understand much about such things.

DR. STOCKMANN: Don't you see—let me explain! The party leaders have to be eradicated—because a party leader's just like a wolf, an insatiable wolf that needs so and so many smaller animals to feed off per annum, if he's going to survive. Look at Hovstad and Aslaksen! How many lesser creatures haven't they swallowed up—or they maul and mutilate them till they can't be more than home owners and subscribers to the *Courier!* *(Sitting on the edge of the desk.)* Ah, come here, Katherine—look at that sunlight, how glorious, the way it streams in today. And how wonderful and fresh the spring air is.

MRS. STOCKMANN: Yes, if we only could live on sunlight and spring air, Thomas.

DR. STOCKMANN: Well, you'll have to skimp and save a bit here and there—it'll turn out. That's my least concern. No, what's worse is that I don't know any man who's free-spirited enough to carry my work on after me.

PETRA: Oh, don't think of that, Father; you've lots of time. Why, look—the boys, already.

EILIF *and* MORTEN *come in from the living room.*

MRS. STOCKMANN: Did you get let out early?

MORTEN: No. We had a fight with some others at recess—

EILIF: That isn't true; it was the others that fought us.

MORTEN: Yes, and so Mr. Rørland said we'd better stay home for a few days.

DR. STOCKMANN *(snapping his fingers and jumping down off the desk)*: I've got it! So help me, I've got it! You'll never set foot in school again.

THE BOYS: No more school?

MRS. STOCKMANN: But, Thomas—

DR. STOCKMANN: I said, never! I'll teach you myself—by that, I mean, you won't learn a blessed fact—

THE BOYS: Hurray!

DR. STOCKMANN: But I'll make you into free-spirited and accomplished men. Listen, you have to help me, Petra.

PETRA: Yes, of course I will.

DR. STOCKMANN: And the school—that'll be held in the room where they assailed me as an enemy of the people. But we have to be more. I need at least twelve boys to begin with.

MRS. STOCKMANN: You'll never get them from this town.

DR. STOCKMANN: Let's see about that. *(To the* BOYS*)* Don't you know any boys off the street—regular little punks—

MORTEN: Sure, I know lots of them!

DR. STOCKMANN: So, that's fine. Bring around a few samples. I want to experiment with mongrels for a change. There might be some fantastic minds out there.

MORTEN: But what'll we do when we've become free-spirited and accomplished men?

DR. STOCKMANN: You'll drive all the wolves into the Far West, boys!

EILIF *looks somewhat dubious;* MORTEN *jumps about and cheers.*

MRS. STOCKMANN: Ah, just so those wolves aren't hunting you anymore, Thomas.

DR. STOCKMANN: Are you utterly mad, Katherine! Hunt *me* down! Now, when I'm the strongest man in town!

MRS. STOCKMANN: The strongest—now?

DR. STOCKMANN: Yes, I might go further and say that now I'm one of the strongest men in the whole world.

MORTEN: You mean it?

DR. STOCKMANN *(lowering his voice)*: Shh, don't talk about it yet—but I've made a great discovery.

MRS. STOCKMANN: What, again?

DR. STOCKMANN: Yes, why not! *(Gathers them around him and speaks confidentially.)* And the essence of it, you see, is that the strongest man in the world is the one who stands most alone.

MRS. STOCKMANN: *(smiling and shaking her head)*: Oh, Thomas, Thomas—!

PETRA *(buoyantly, gripping his hands)*: Father!

AUGUST STRINDBERG

The Stronger

A Play in One Scene

Characters

MRS. X., *a married actress*
MISS Y., *an unmarried actress*
A WAITRESS

A corner of a café for ladies. Two wrought iron tables; a sofa upholstered with red shag; several chairs. MISS Y. *is seated at one of the tables. Before her is a half-empty bottle of ale. She is reading an illustrated periodical, which she later exchanges for others on the table.* MRS. X. *enters. She is dressed in winter apparel and wears a hat and cloak. She carries a Japanese shopping bag or basket, of exquisite design, on her arm.*

MRS. X.: How do you do, Amelie dear! You are sitting here all by yourself on Christmas Eve—like some poor bachelor. . . .

MISS Y. *looks up from the magazine, gives* MRS. X. *a nod, and resumes her reading.*

MRS. X.: You know it hurts me to see you sitting here—alone—alone in a café, and, of all times, on Christmas Eve. It makes me feel as bad as when I once saw a wedding party in a restaurant in Paris. The bride sat reading a comic paper, while the bridegroom was playing billiards with the wedding guests. Ugh, I thought to myself, with a beginning like that, what will the marriage be like—and how will it end? *He,* playing billiards on their wedding night—And *she* reading a comic paper, you mean to say? . . . Ah, but there is a certain difference, don't you think?

The WAITRESS *enters with a cup of chocolate which she places before* MRS. X. *Then she leaves.*

MRS. X.: Do you know what, Amelie! I believe you would have been better off if you had married him. . . . You remember that I urged you from the very first to forgive him. You remember that? You could have been his wife now, and had a home of your own. . . . Do you recall how happy you were last Christmas when you spent the holidays with your fiancé's parents out in the country? How you sang the praises of domestic life and literally longed to get away from the theatre?—Yes, Amelie dear, a home is the best after all—next to the theatre. And children, you know. . . . Well, but you wouldn't understand that!

MISS Y. *expresses disdain.*

MRS. X. *(sips a few teaspoonfuls of her chocolate. Then she opens her shopping bag and brings out some Christmas presents.):* Here—let me show you what I have bought for my little ones. *(She shows her a doll.)* Look at this one! This is for Lisa. . . . Do you see how she rolls her eyes and turns her head! Do you? Do you see?—And here is a popgun for Maja. . . . *(She loads the toy gun and pops it at* MISS Y.*)*

MISS Y. *makes a gesture of fright.*

MRS. X.: Did I frighten you? You didn't think I was going to shoot you, did you? Did you?—Upon my soul, I really think you did! If *you* had wanted to shoot *me*, I wouldn't have been surprised. After all, I have stood in your way—and I realize that you can never forget that . . . even though I was entirely blameless. You still believe that I schemed to have you dismissed from the Grand Theatre—don't you? But I didn't! You may think whatever you like, but I had nothing to do with it! I realize, however, that no matter what I say, you will still believe I was responsible for it! *(She takes out a pair of embroidered bedroom slippers from the bag.)* And these are for my better half. I embroidered them myself—with tulips. You understand, I hate tulips, but my husband has to have tulips on everything. . . .

MISS Y. *looks up from her magazine with an expression of irony mixed with curiosity.*

MRS. X. *(places a hand inside each slipper)*: See what tiny feet Bob has! See? And I wish you could see how elegantly he walks! You never saw him in slippers, did you?

MISS Y. *laughs aloud*

MRS. X.: Look, let me show you! *(She makes the slippers walk on the table.)*

MISS Y. *gives another loud laugh.*

MRS. X.: And when he gets angry, he stamps his foot, like this: "Damnation! These stupid maids who never can learn to make coffee! And look at this! The idiots don't even know how to trim a lamp wick!" And when there is a draft from the floor and his feet are cold: "Heavens! It's freezing cold, and the incorrigible fools let the fire go out in the grate!" *(She rubs the sole of one slipper against the top of the other.)*

MISS Y. *gives a shriek of laughter.*

MRS. X.: And when he comes home, he goes hunting for his slippers which Marie has put under the chiffonier. . . . Oh, but it's a shame to sit and make fun of my own husband like this. After all, he is so nice. He is a good little husband. . . . You should have had a husband like him, Amelie!—What are you laughing at, if I may ask? What is it? What's the matter?—And the best of it is that he is faithful to me—yes, that I know. He has told me so himself . . . Why the sneering grin? He told me that Frédérique tried to seduce him while I was on a tour in Norway. . . . Can you imagine such impudence! *(There is a silence.)* I would have torn her eyes out! That's what I'd have done, if she had come near him while I was at home! *(Again there is silence.)* I was lucky enough to hear about it from Bob himself before being told by some gossip. . . . *(Silence.)* But Frédérique was not the only one, let me tell you! I can't understand it, but women seem to be absolutely crazy about my husband. They must think he has something to say about the engaging of the artists, because he is on the board of administration. . . . I would not be surprised if you, too, had used your wiles on him! I never did trust you too much. . . . But I know now that he could not be interested in you—and it seemed to me you always acted as if you bore some sort of grudge against him. . . . *(There is a silence and they regard each other with some embarrassment.* MRS. X.

continues.) Why don't you come home to us this evening, Amelie, just to show that you have no hard feelings—at least not against me. . . . I can't explain just why—but I think it is so unpleasant to be bad friends—with you especially. Perhaps it is because I stood in your way that time *(In a slower tempo.)* . . . or . . . *I can't imagine . . . what the reason could have been— really . . . (There is a silence.)*

MISS Y. *gazes fixedly and curiously at* MRS. X.

MRS. X. *(pensively)*: Our relationship was such a strange one. . . . The first time I saw you, I was frightened of you. I was so frightened that I didn't dare let you out of my sight. No matter when or where I went—I always found myself next to you. . . . I didn't have the courage to be your enemy, and so I became your friend. But whenever you came to our home, it always led to discord. I noticed that my husband could not bear the sight of you and it made me feel ill at ease—as when a garment does not fit. I did everything I could to persuade him to show you some friendliness, but it was no use—not until you announced your engagement! Then suddenly a violent friendship blossomed between you two! At the time it appeared as if only then you dared to show your true feelings—when it was safe for you to do so! And then—what happened afterwards? . . . I didn't feel any jealousy—and that seems strange to me now! And I can remember the scene at the christening, when you were the godmother, and I had to coax him to kiss you. When he did, you were so abashed and confused—and quite frankly, I didn't notice it at the time, didn't give it a thought. I never thought of it until—until this very moment. . . . *(She rises violently, impassioned.)* Why don't you say something? You haven't uttered one single word all this time! You have let me sit here, talking on and on! You have been sitting there, drawing out of me all these thoughts that have been lying like raw silk in the cocoon— thoughts . . . yes, even suspicions. . . . Let me see! Why did you break off your engagement? Why did you never come to our home again after that? Why won't you come to our home tonight?

MISS Y. *seems to be about to break her silence.*

MRS. X.: Don't speak! You needn't say a word! Now I understand everything! It was because of this—and that—and that! That's it exactly. Now the accounts are balanced! Now I know the answer!—For shame! I won't sit at the same table with you! *(She moves her things to the other table.)* That is why I had to embroider tulips on his slippers—because you liked tulips.... That's why we—*(She throws the slippers on the floor.)*—why we had to spend the summers at Lake Mälar—because you didn't like the open sea; that's why my son was named Eskil—because that was your father's name; that's the reason I had to wear your colors, read your authors, eat your favorite dishes, drink what you liked—your chocolate, for instance.... That is why ... Oh, my God—it's frightening to think of it—horrible! Everything, everything came to me from you, even your passions! Your soul crept into mine, like a worm into an apple, worming its way, boring and boring, until nothing was left but the rind and a speck of black dust inside. I tried to get away from you, but I couldn't! You charmed me, bewitched me like a snake, with your black eyes.... Every time I lifted my wings to escape, I felt myself being dragged down again: I lay in the water with bound feet—and the harder I fought to keep afloat, the further down I went—down, down, until I sank to the bottom, where you lay in wait like a giant crab to seize me with your claws—and there is where I am now.

Ugh! How I detest you, hate you, hate you! But you—all you do is to sit there silent, cold and impassive! You don't care whether it's new moon or full moon, Christmas or New Year—whether people around you are happy or unhappy! You have neither the capacity to hate nor to love; you are as cold-blooded as a stork watching a rathole; you are incapable of scenting your prey and pursuing it—but you know how to hide in holes and corners and exhaust your prey. Here you sit—I suppose you know that people call this corner the rat trap, in your honor—scanning the newspapers in the hope that you may read about someone who has had bad luck or been struck by misfortune, or about someone who has been dismissed from the theatre.... Here you sit, lurking for victims, figuring out your chances like a pilot in a shipwreck. Here you receive your tributes! Poor Amelie! You know, in spite of everything, I feel sorry for you, because I am aware that you are miserable—miserable like some wounded beast!—and made spiteful and vicious because of having been wounded! I find it hard to be angry with you, despite feeling that I ought to be—but, after all, you are the weaker one. . . . As for the episode with Bob—well, I shan't let that bother me. . . . It hasn't really harmed me! And if *you* got me into the habit of drinking chocolate, or if someone else did, matters little . . . *(She takes a spoonful of chocolate; then, common-sense-like.)* Besides, chocolate is a healthful beverage. And if you have taught me how to dress—*tant mieux!* My husband has become all the more fond of me as a result! That is one thing I have gained, and that you lost. As a matter of fact, judging from what I have seen, I think you have already lost him! But no doubt it was your intention that I should leave him—as you did—and which you now regret. But, you see, that's just what I don't intend to do! We must not be one-sided or selfish, you know. But why should I take only what someone else doesn't want? All said and done, perhaps I am at this moment really the stronger. . . . You never received anything from *me*—while *you gave* something to me! And now I have had the same experience as the proverbial thief had: When *you* woke up, *I* possessed what *you* had lost! And why was it that everything you touched became sterile and empty? Your tulips and your passions proved insufficient to keep a man's love—while I was able to keep it. Your authors could not teach you the art of living—as I have learned it. Nor did you bear a little Eskil—even if your father bore that name. . . . And why are you forever silent, your lips eternally sealed? I confess I used to think it a sign of strength—but perhaps it is only because you have nothing to say! Perhaps it is for lack of thoughts! *(She rises and picks up the slippers from the floor.)* Now I am going home—and I take the tulips with me. Your tulips! You found it hard to learn from others—you found it hard to bend, to humble yourself—and so you broke like a dry reed—and I survived! I thank you, Amelie, for all that you have taught me! And thank you for teaching my husband how to love! Now I am going home—to love him! *(She leaves.)*

ANTON CHEKHOV

A Marriage Proposal

Characters
LOMOV
CHUBUKOV
NATALIA

Chubukov's mansion—the living room. LOMOV *enters, formally dressed in evening jacket, white gloves, top hat. He is nervous from the start.*

CHUBUKOV *(Rising)*: Well, look who's here! Ivan Vassilevitch! *(Shakes his hand warmly)* What a surprise, old man! How are you?

LOMOV: Oh, not too bad. And you?

CHUBUKOV: Oh, we manage, we manage. Do sit down, please. You know, you've been neglecting your neighbours, my dear fellow. It's been ages. Say, why the formal dress? Tails, gloves, and so forth. Where's the funeral, my boy? Where are you headed?

LOMOV: Oh, nowhere. I mean, here; just to see you, my dear Stepan Stepanovitch.

CHUBUKOV: Then why the full dress, old boy? It's not New Year's, and so forth.

LOMOV: Well, you see, it's like this. I have come here, my dear Stepan Stepanovitch, to bother you with a request. More than once, or twice, or more than that, it has been my privilege to apply to you for assistance in things, and you've always, well, responded. I mean, well, you have. Yes. Excuse me, I'm getting all mixed up. May I have a glass of water, my dear Stepan Stepanovitch? *(Drinks)*

CHUBUKOV *(Aside)*: Wants to borrow some money. Not a chance! *(Aloud)* What can I do for you my dear friend?

LOMOV: Well, you see, my dear Stepanitch . . . Excuse me, I mean Stepan my Dearovitch . . . No, I mean, I get all confused, as you can see. To make a long story short, you're the only one who can help me. Of course, I don't deserve it, and there's no reason why I should expect you to, and all that.

CHUBUKOV: Stop beating around the bush! Out with it!

LOMOV: In just a minute. I mean, now, right now. The truth is, I have come to ask the hand . . . I mean, your daughter, Natalia Stepanovna, I, I want to marry her!

CHUBUKOV *(Overjoyed)*: Great heavens! Ivan Vassilevitch! Say it again!

LOMOV: I have come humbly to ask for the hand . . .

CHUBUKOV *(Interrupting)*: You're a prince! I'm overwhelmed, delighted, and so forth. Yes, indeed, and all that! *(Hugs and kisses LOMOV)* This is just what I've been hoping for. It's my fondest dream come true. *(Sheds a tear)* And, you know, I've always looked upon you, my boy, as if you were my own son. May God grant to both of you His Mercy and His Love, and so forth. Oh, I have been wishing for this . . . But why am I being so idiotic? It's just that I'm off my rocker with joy, my boy! Completely off my rocker! Oh, with all my soul I'm . . . I'll go get Natalia, and so forth.

LOMOV *(Deeply moved)*: Dear Stepan Stepanovitch, do you think she'll agree?

CHUBUKOV: Why, of course, old friend. Great heavens! As if she wouldn't! Why she's crazy for you! Good God! Like a love-sick cat, and so forth. Be right back. *(Leaves)*

LOMOV: God, it's cold. I'm gooseflesh all over, as if I had to take a test. But the main thing is, to make up my mind, and keep it that way. I mean, if I take time out to think, or if I hesitate, or talk about it, or have ideals, or wait for real love, well, I'll just never get married! Brrrr, it's cold! Natalia Stepanovna is an excellent housekeeper. She's not too bad looking. She's had a good education. What more could I ask? Nothing. I'm so nervous, my ears are buzzing. *(Drinks)* Besides, I've just got to get married. I'm thirty-five already. It's sort of a critical age. I've got to settle down and lead a regular life. I mean, I'm always getting palpitations, and I'm nervous, and I get upset so easy. Look, my lips are quivering, and my eyebrow's twitching. The worst thing is the night. Sleeping. I get into bed, doze off, and, suddenly, something inside me jumps. First my head snaps, and then my shoulder blade, and I roll out of bed like a lunatic and try to walk it off. Then I try to go back to sleep, but, as soon as I do, something jumps again! Twenty times a night, sometimes . . .

NATALIA STEPANOVNA *enters*

NATALIA: Oh, it's only you. All Papa said was: 'Go inside, there's a merchant come to collect his goods.' How do you do, Ivan Vassilevitch?

LOMOV: How do you do, dear Natalia Stepanovna?

NATALIA: Excuse my apron, and not being dressed. We're shelling peas. You haven't been around lately. Oh, do sit down. *(They do)* Would you like some lunch?

LOMOV: No thanks, I had some.

NATALIA: Well, then smoke if you want. *(He doesn't)* The weather's nice today . . . but yesterday, it was so wet the workmen couldn't get a thing done. Have you got much hay in? I felt so greedy I had a whole field done, but now I'm not sure I was right. With the rain it could rot, couldn't it? I should have waited. But why are you so dressed up? Is there a dance or something? Of course, I must say you look splendid, but . . . Well, tell me, why are you so dressed up?

LOMOV *(Excited)*: Well, you see, my dear Natalia Stepanovna, the truth is, I made up my mind to ask you to . . . well, to, listen to me. Of course, it'll probably surprise you and even maybe make you angry, but . . . *(Aside)* God it's cold in here!

NATALIA: Why, what do you mean? *(A pause)* Well?

LOMOV: I'll try to get it over with. I mean, you know, my dear Natalia Stepanovna that I've known, since childhood, even, known, and had the privilege of knowing, your family. My late aunt, and her husband, who, as you know, left me my estate, they always had the greatest respect for your father, and your late mother. The Lomovs and the Chubukovs have always been very friendly, you might even say affectionate. And, of course, you know, our land borders on each other's. My Oxen Meadows touch your birch grove . . .

NATALIA: I hate to interrupt you, my dear Ivan Vassilevitch, but you said: 'my Oxen Meadows.' Do you really think they're yours?

LOMOV: Why of course they're mine.

NATALIA: What do you mean? The Oxen Meadows are ours, not yours!

LOMOV: Oh, no, my dear Natalia Stepanovna, they're mine.

NATALIA: Well, this is the first I've heard about it! Where did you get that idea?

LOMOV: Where? Why, I mean the Oxen Meadows that are wedged between your birches and the marsh.

NATALIA: Yes, of course, they're ours.

LOMOV: Oh, no, you're wrong, my dear Natalia Stepanovna, they're mine.

NATALIA: Now, come, Ivan Vassilevitch! How long have they been yours?

LOMOV: How long? Why, as long as I can remember!

NATALIA: Well, really, you can't expect me to believe that!

LOMOV: But, you can see for yourself in the deed, my dear Natalia Stepanovna. Of course, there was once a dispute about them, but everyone knows they're mine now. There's nothing to argue about. There was a time when my aunt's grandmother let your father's grandfather's peasants use the land, but they were supposed to bake bricks for her in return. Naturally, after a few years they began to act as if they owned it, but the real truth is . . .

NATALIA: That has nothing to do with the case! Both my grandfather and my great-grandfather said that their land went as far as the marsh, which means that the Meadows are ours! There's nothing whatever to argue about. It's foolish.

LOMOV: But I can show you the deed, Natalia Stepanovna.

NATALIA: You're just making fun of me . . . Great heavens! Here we have the land for hundreds of years, and suddenly you try to tell us it isn't ours. What's wrong with you, Ivan Vassilevitch? Those meadows aren't even fifteen acres, and they're not worth three hundred rubles, but I just can't stand unfairness! I just can't stand unfairness!

LOMOV: But, you must listen to me. Your father's grandfather's peasants, as I've already tried to tell you, they were supposed to bake bricks for my aunt's grandmother. And my aunt's grandmother, why, she wanted to be nice to them . . .

NATALIA: It's just nonsense, this whole business about aunts and grandfathers and grandmothers. The Meadows are ours! That's all there is to it!

LOMOV: They're mine!

NATALIA: Ours! You can go on talking for two days, and you can put on fifteen evening coats and twenty pairs of gloves, but I tell you they're ours, ours, ours!

LOMOV: Natalia Stepanovna, I don't want the Meadows! I'm just acting on principle. If you want, I'll give them to you.

NATALIA: I'll give them to *you*! Because they're ours! And that's all there is to it! And if I may say so, your behaviour, my dear Ivan Vassilevitch, is very strange. Until now, we've always considered you a good neighbour, even a friend. After all, last year we lent you our threshing machine, even though it meant putting off our own threshing until November. And here you are treating us like a pack of gypsies. Giving me my own land, indeed! Really! Why that's not being a good neighbour. It's sheer impudence, that's what it is . . .

LOMOV: Oh, so you think I'm just a land-grabber? My dear lady, I've never grabbed anybody's land in my whole life, and no-one's going to accuse me of doing it now! *(Quickly walks over to the pitcher and drinks some more water)* The Oxen Meadows are mine!

NATALIA: That's a lie. They're ours!

LOMOV: Mine!

NATALIA: A lie! I'll prove it. I'll send my mowers out there today!

LOMOV: What?

NATALIA: My mowers will mow it today!

LOMOV: I'll kick them out!

NATALIA: You just dare!

LOMOV *(Clutching his heart)*: The Oxen Meadows are mine! Do you understand? Mine!

NATALIA: Please don't shout! You can shout all you want in your own house, but here I must ask you to control yourself.

LOMOV: If my heart wasn't palpitating the way it is, if my insides weren't jumping like mad, I wouldn't talk to you so calmly. *(Yelling)* The Oxen Meadows are mine!

NATALIA: Ours!

LOMOV: Mine!

NATALIA: Ours!

LOMOV: Mine!

Enter CHUBUKOV

CHUBUKOV: What's going on? Why all the shouting?

NATALIA: Papa, will you please inform this gentleman who owns the Oxen Meadows, he or we?

CHUBUKOV *(To* LOMOV*)*: Why, they're ours, old fellow.

LOMOV: But how can they be yours, my dear Stepan Stepanovitch? Be fair. Perhaps my aunt's grandmother did let your grandfather's peasants work the land, and maybe they did get so used to it that they acted as if it was their own, but . . .

CHUBUKOV: Oh, no, no . . . my dear boy. You forget something. The reason the peasants didn't pay your aunt's grandmother, and so forth, was that the land was disputed, even then. Since then it's been settled. Why, everyone knows it's ours.

LOMOV: I can prove it's mine.

CHUBUKOV: You can't prove a thing, old boy.

LOMOV: Yes I can!

CHUBUKOV: My dear lad, why yell like that? Yelling doesn't prove a thing. Look, I'm not after anything of yours, just as I don't intend to give up anything of mine. Why should I? Besides, if you're going to keep arguing about it, I'd just as soon give the land to the peasants, so there!

LOMOV: There nothing! Where do you get the right to give away someone else's property?

CHUBUKOV: I certainly ought to know if I have the right or not. And you had better realize it, because, my dear young man, I am not used to being spoken to in that tone of voice, and so forth. Besides which, my dear young man, I am twice as old as you are, and I ask you to speak to me without getting yourself into such a tizzy, and so forth!

LOMOV: Do you think I'm a fool? First you call my property yours, and then you expect me to keep calm and polite! Good neighbours don't act like that, my dear Stepan Stepanovitch. You're no neighbour, you're a land grabber!

CHUBUKOV: What was that? What did you say?

NATALIA: Papa, send the mowers out to the meadows at once!

CHUBUKOV: What did you say, sir?

NATALIA: The Oxen Meadows are ours, and we'll never give them up, never, never, never, never!

LOMOV: We'll see about that. I'll go to court. I'll show you!

CHUBUKOV: Go to court? Well, go to court, and so forth! I know you, just waiting for a chance to go to court, and so forth. You pettifogging shyster, you! All of your family is like that. The whole bunch of them!

LOMOV: You leave my family out of this! The Lomovs have always been honourable, upstanding people, and not a one of them was ever tried for embezzlement, like your grandfather was.

CHUBUKOV: The Lomovs are a pack of lunatics, the whole bunch of them!

NATALIA: The whole bunch!

CHUBUKOV: Your grandfather was a drunkard, and what about your other aunt, the one who ran away with the architect? And so forth.

NATALIA: And so forth!

LOMOV: Your mother was a hunch back! *(Clutches at his heart)* Oh, I've got a stitch in my side . . . My head's whirling . . . Help! Water!

CHUBUKOV: Your father was a rum-soaked gambler.

NATALIA: And your aunt was queen of the scandalmongers!

LOMOV: My left foot's paralyzed. You're a plotter . . . Oh, my heart. It's an open secret that in the last elections you brib . . . I'm seeing stars! Where's my hat?

NATALIA: It's a low-mean, spiteful . . .

CHUBUKOV: And you're a two-faced, malicious schemer!

LOMOV: Here's my hat . . . Oh, my heart . . . Where's the door? How do I get out of here? . . . Oh, I think I'm going to die . . . My foot's numb. *(Goes)*

CHUBUKOV *(Following him)*: And don't you ever set foot in my house again!

NATALIA: Go to court, indeed! We'll see about that!

LOMOV *staggers out.*

CHUBUKOV: The devil with him! *(Gets a drink, walks back and forth excited)*

NATALIA: What a rascal! How can you trust your neighbours after an incident like that?

CHUBUKOV: The villain! The scarecrow!

NATALIA: He's a monster! First he tries to steal our land, and then he has the nerve to yell at you.

CHUBUKOV: Yes, and that turnip, that stupid rooster, has the gall to make a proposal. Some proposal!

NATALIA: What proposal?

CHUBUKOV: Why, he came to propose to you.

NATALIA: To propose? To me? Why didn't you tell me before?

CHUBUKOV: So he gets all dressed up in his formal clothes. That stuffed sausage, that dried up cabbage!

NATALIA: To propose to me? Ohhhh! *(Falls into a chair and starts wailing)* Bring him back! Back! Go get him! Bring him back! Ohhhh!

CHUBUKOV: Bring who back?

NATALIA: Hurry up, hurry up! I'm sick. Get him! *(Complete hysterics)*

CHUBUKOV: What for? *(To her)* What's the matter with you? *(Clutches his head)* Oh, what a fool I am! I'll shoot myself! I'll hang myself! I ruined her chances!

NATALIA: I'm dying. Get him!

CHUBUKOV: All right, all right, right away! Only don't yell! *(He runs out)*

NATALIA: What are they doing to me? Get him! Bring him back! Bring him back!

A pause. CHUBUKOV *runs in.*

CHUBUKOV: He's coming, and so forth, the snake. Oof! You talk to him. I'm not in the mood.

NATALIA *(Wailing)*: Bring him back! Bring him back!

CHUBUKOV *(Yelling)*: I told you, he's coming! Oh Lord, what agony to be the father of a grown-up daughter. I'll cut my throat some day, I swear I will. *(To her)* We cursed him, we insulted him, abused him, kicked him out, and now . . . because you, you . . .

NATALIA: Me? It was all your fault!

CHUBUKOV: My fault? What do you mean my fau . . ? (LOMOV *appears in the doorway)* Talk to him yourself! *(Goes out.* LOMOV *enters, exhausted)*

LOMOV: What palpitations! My heart! And my foot's absolutely asleep. Something keeps giving me a stitch in the side . . .

NATALIA: You must forgive us, Ivan Vassilevitch. We all got too excited. I remember now. The Oxen Meadows are yours.

LOMOV: My heart's beating something awful. My Meadows. My eyebrows, they're both twitching!

NATALIA: Yes, the Meadows are all yours, yes, yours. Do sit down. *(They sit)* We were wrong, of course.

LOMOV: I argued on principle. My land isn't worth so much to me, but the principle . . .

NATALIA: Oh, yes, of course, the principle, that's what counts. But let's change the subject.

LOMOV: Besides, I have evidence. You see, my aunt's grandmother let your father's grandfather's peasants use the land . . .

NATALIA: Yes, yes, yes, but forget all that. *(Aside)* I wish I knew how to get him going. *(Aloud)* Are you going to start hunting soon?

LOMOV: After the harvest I'll try for grouse. But oh, my dear Natalia Stepanovna, have you heard about the bad luck I've had? You know my dog, Guess? He's gone lame.

NATALIA: What a pity. Why?

LOMOV: I don't know. He must have twisted his leg, or got in a fight, or something. *(Sighs)* My best dog, to say nothing of the cost. I paid Mironov 125 rubles for him.

NATALIA: That was too high, Ivan Vassilevitch.

LOMOV: I think it was quite cheap. He's a first class dog.

NATALIA: Why Papa only paid 85 rubles for Squeezer, and he's much better than Guess.

LOMOV: Squeezer better than Guess! What an idea! *(Laughs)* Squeezer better than Guess!

NATALIA: Of course he's better. He may still be too young but on points and pedigree, he's a better dog even than any Volchanetsky owns.

LOMOV: Excuse me, Natalia Stepanovna, but you're forgetting he's overshot, and overshot dogs are bad hunters.

NATALIA: Oh, so he's overshot, is he? Well, this is the first time I've heard about it.

LOMOV: Believe me, his lower jaw is shorter than his upper.

NATALIA: You've measured them?

LOMOV: Yes, He's all right for pointing, but if you want him to retrieve . . .

NATALIA: In the first place, our Squeezer is a thoroughbred, the son of Harness and Chisel, while your mutt doesn't even have a pedigree. He's as old and worn out as a pedlar's horse.

LOMOV: He may be old, but I wouldn't take five Squeezers for him. How can you argue? Guess is a dog, Squeezer's a laugh. Anyone you can name has a dog like Squeezer hanging around somewhere. They're under every bush. If he only cost twenty-five rubles you got cheated.

NATALIA: The devil is in you today, Ivan Vassilevitch! You want to contradict everything. First you pretend the Oxen Meadows are yours, and now you say Guess is better than Squeezer. People should say what they really mean, and you know Squeezer is a hundred times better than Guess. Why say he isn't?

LOMOV: So, you think I'm a fool or a blind man,—Natalia Stepanovna! Once and for all, Squeezer is overshot!

NATALIA: He is not!

LOMOV: He is so!

NATALIA: He is not!

LOMOV: Why shout, my dear lady?

NATALIA: Why talk such nonsense? It's terrible. Your Guess is old enough to be buried, and you compare him with Squeezer!

LOMOV: I'm sorry, I can't go on. My heart . . . it's palpitating!

NATALIA: I've always noticed that the hunters who argue most don't know a thing.

LOMOV: Please! Be quiet a moment. My heart's falling apart . . . (Shouts) Shut up!

NATALIA: I'm not going to shut up until you admit that Squeezer's a hundred times better than Guess.

LOMOV: A hundred times worse! His head . . . My eyes . . . shoulder . . .

NATALIA: Guess is half-dead already!

LOMOV (Weeping): Shut up! My heart's exploding!

NATALIA: I won't shut up!

CHUBUKOV comes in.

CHUBUKOV: What's the trouble now?

NATALIA: Papa, will you please tell us which is the better dog, his Guess or our Squeezer?

LOMOV: Stepan Stepanovitch, I implore you to tell me just one thing; Is your Squeezer overshot or not? Yes or no?

CHUBUKOV: Well what if he is? He's still the best dog in the neighbourhood, and so forth.

LOMOV: Oh, but isn't my dog, Guess, better? Really?

CHUBUKOV: Don't get yourself so fraught up, old man. Of course, your dog has his good points—thoroughbred, firm on his feet, well sprung ribs, and so forth. But, my dear fellow, you've got to admit he has two defects; he's old and he's short in the muzzle.

LOMOV: Short in the muzzle? Oh, my heart! Let's look at the facts! On the Marusinsky hunt my dog ran neck and neck with the Count's, while Squeezer was a mile behind them . . .

CHUBUKOV: That's because the Count's groom hit him with a whip.

LOMOV: And he was right, too! We were fox hunting; what was your dog chasing sheep for?

CHUBUKOV: That's a lie! Look, I'm going to lose my temper . . . *(Controlling himself)* my dear friend, so let's stop arguing, for that reason alone. You're only arguing because we're all jealous of somebody else's dog. Who can help it? As soon as you realize some dog is better than yours, in this case our dog, you start in with this and that, and the next thing you know—pure jealousy! I remember the whole business.

LOMOV: I remember too!

CHUBUKOV *(Mimicking)*: 'I remember too!' What do you remember?

LOMOV: My heart . . . my foot's asleep . . . I can't . . .

NATALIA *(Mimicking)*: 'My heart . . . my foot's asleep.' What kind of a hunter are you? You should be hunting cockroaches in the kitchen, not foxes. 'My heart!'

CHUBUKOV: Yes, what kind of a hunter are you anyway? You should be sitting at home with your palpitations, not tracking down animals. You don't hunt anyhow. You just go out to argue with people and interfere with their dogs, and so forth. For God's sake, let's change the subject before I lose my temper. Anyway, you're just not a hunter.

LOMOV: But you, you're a hunter? Ha! You only go hunting to get in good with the count, and to plot, and intrigue, and scheme . . . Oh, my heart! You're a schemer, that's what!

CHUBUKOV: What's that? Me a schemer? *(Shouting)* Shut up!

LOMOV: A schemer!

CHUBUKOV: You infant! You puppy!

LOMOV: You old rat! You Jesuit!

CHUBUKOV: You shut up, or I'll shoot you down like a partridge! You idiot!

LOMOV: Everyone knows that—oh, my heart—that your wife used to beat you . . . Oh, my feet . . . my head . . . I'm seeing stars . . . I'm going to faint! *(He drops into an armchair)* Quick, a doctor! *(Faints)*

CHUBUKOV *(Going on, oblivious)*: Baby! Weakling! Idiot! I'm getting sick. *(Drinks water)* Me! I'm sick!

NATALIA: What kind of a hunter are you? You can't even sit on a horse! *(To her father)* Papa, what's the matter with him? Look, papa! *(Screaming)* Ivan Vassilevitch! He's dead.

CHUBUKOV: I'm choking, I can't breathe . . . Give me air.

NATALIA: He's dead! *(Pulling LOMOV's sleeve)* Ivan Vassilevitch! Ivan Vassilevitch! What have you done to me? He's dead! *(She falls into an armchair. Screaming hysterically)* A doctor! A doctor! A doctor!

CHUBUKOV: Ohhhh . . . What's the matter? What happened?

NATALIA *(Wailing)*: He's dead! He's dead!

CHUBUKOV: Who's dead *(Looks at LOMOV)* My God, he is! Quick! Water! A doctor! *(Puts glass to LOMOV's lips)* Here, drink this! Can't drink it—he must be dead, and so forth . . . Oh what a miserable life! Why don't I shoot myself! I should have cut my throat long ago! What am I waiting for? Give me a knife! Give me a pistol! *(LOMOV stirs)* Look, he's coming to. Here, drink some water. That's it.

LOMOV: I'm seeing stars . . . misty . . . Where am I?

CHUBUKOV: Just you hurry up and get married, and then the devil with you! She accepts. *(Puts LOMOV's hand in NATALIA's)* She accepts and so forth! I give you my blessing, and so forth! Only leave me in peace!

LOMOV *(Getting up)*: Huh? What? Who?

CHUBUKOV: She accepts! Well? Kiss her, damn you!

NATALIA: He's alive! Yes, yes, I accept.

CHUBUKOV: Kiss each other!

LOMOV: Huh? Kiss? Kiss who? *(They kiss)* That's nice. I mean, excuse me, what happened? Oh, now I get it . . . my heart . . . those stars . . . I'm very happy, Natalia Stepanovna. *(Kisses her hand)* My foot's asleep.

NATALIA: I . . . I'm happy too.

CHUBUKOV: What a load off my shoulders! Whew!

NATALIA: Well, now maybe you'll admit that Squeezer is better than Guess?

LOMOV: Worse!

NATALIA: Better!

CHUBUKOV: What a way to enter matrimonial bliss! Let's have some champagne!

LOMOV: He's worse!

NATALIA: Better! Better, better, better, better!

CHUBUKOV *(Trying to shout her down)*: Champagne! Bring some champagne! Champagne! Champagne!

WILLIAM BUTLER YEATS

Purgatory

Characters
A BOY
AN OLD MAN

A ruined house and a bare tree in the background.

BOY: Half-door, hall door,
　　Hither and thither day and night,
　　Hill or hollow, shouldering this pack,
　　Hearing you talk.
OLD MAN:　　　　　Study that house.
　　I think about its jokes and stories;
　　I try to remember what the butler
　　Said to the drunken gamekeeper
　　In mid-October, but I cannot.
　　If I cannot, none living can.
　　Where are the jokes and stories of a house,
　　Its threshold gone to patch a pig-sty?
BOY: So you have come this path before?
OLD MAN: The moonlight falls upon the path
　　The shadow of a cloud upon the house,
　　And that's symbolical; study that tree,
　　What is it like?
BOY:　　　　　A silly old man.
OLD MAN: It's like—no matter what it's like.
　　I saw it a year ago stripped bare as now,
　　So I chose a better trade.
　　I saw it fifty years ago
　　Before the thunderbolt had riven it,

Green leaves, ripe leaves, leaves thick as butter,
Fat, greasy life. Stand there and look,
Because there is somebody in that house.

The BOY *puts down pack and stands in the doorway.*

BOY: There's nobody here.
OLD MAN: There's somebody there.
BOY: The floor is gone, the windows gone,
   And where there should be roof there's sky,
   And here's a bit of an egg-shell thrown
   Out of a jackdaw's nest.
OLD MAN: But there are some
   That do not care what's gone, what's left:
   The souls in Purgatory that come back
   To habitations and familiar spots.
BOY: Your wits are out again.
OLD MAN: Re-live
   Their transgressions, and that not once
   But many times; they know at last
   The consequence of those transgressions
   Whether upon others or upon themselves;
   Upon others, others may bring help,
   For when the consequence is at an end
   The dream must end; if upon themselves,
   There is no help but in themselves
   And in the mercy of God.
BOY: I have had enough!
   Talk to the jackdaws, if talk you must.
OLD MAN: Stop! Sit there upon that stone.
   That is the house where I was born.
BOY: The big old house that was burnt down?
OLD MAN: My mother that was your grand-dam owned it,
   This scenery and this countryside,
   Kennel and stable, horse and hound—
   She had a horse at the Curragh, and there met
   My father, a groom in a training stable,
   Looked at him and married him.
   Her mother never spoke to her again,
   And she did right.

BOY: What's right and wrong?
 My grand-dad got the girl and the money.
OLD MAN: Looked at him and married him,
 And he squandered everything she had.
 She never knew the worst, because
 She died in giving birth to me,
 But now she knows it all, being dead.
 Great people lived and died in this house;
 Magistrates, colonels, members of Parliament,
 Captains and Governors, and long ago
 Men that had fought at Aughrim and the Boyne.
 Some that had gone on Government work
 To London or to India came home to die,
 Or came from London every spring
 To look at the may-blossom in the park.
 They had loved the trees that he cut down
 To pay what he had lost at cards
 Or spent on horses, drink, and women;
 Had loved the house, had loved all
 The intricate passages of the house,
 But he killed the house; to kill a house
 Where great men grew up, married, died,
 I here declare a capital offence.
BOY: My God, but you had luck! Grand clothes,
 And maybe a grand horse to ride.
OLD MAN: That he might keep me upon his level
 He never sent me to school, but some
 Half-loved me for my half of her:
 A gamekeeper's wife taught me to read,
 A Catholic curate taught me Latin.
 There were old books and books made fine
 By eighteenth-century French binding, books
 Modern and ancient, books by the ton.
BOY: What education have you given me?
OLD MAN: I gave the education that befits
 A bastard that a pedlar got
 Upon a tinker's daughter in a ditch.
 When I had come to sixteen years old
 My father burned down the house when drunk.

BOY: But that is my age, sixteen years old,
   At the Puck Fair.
OLD MAN: And everything was burnt;
   Books, library, all were burnt.
BOY: Is what I have heard upon the road the truth,
   That you killed him in the burning house?
OLD MAN: There's nobody here but our two selves?
BOY: Nobody, Father.
OLD MAN: I stuck him with a knife,
   That knife that cuts my dinner now,
   And after that I left him in the fire.
   They dragged him out, sombody saw
   The knife-wound but could not be certain
   Because the body was all black and charred.
   Then some that were his drunken friends
   Swore they would put me upon trial,
   Spoke of quarrels, a threat I had made.
   The gamekeeper gave me some old clothes,
   I ran away, worked here and there
   Till I became a pedlar on the roads,
   No good trade, but good enough
   Because I am my father's son,
   Because of what I did or may do.
   Listen to the hoof-beats! Listen, listen!
BOY: I cannot hear a sound.
OLD MAN: Beat! Beat!
   This night is the anniversary
   Of my mother's wedding night,
   Or of the night wherein I was begotten.
   My father is riding from the public-house,
   A whiskey-bottle under his arm. (*A window is lit showing a
      young girl.*)
   Look at the window; she stands there
   Listening, the servants are all in bed,
   She is alone, he has stayed late
   Bragging and drinking in the public-house.
BOY: There's nothing but an empty gap in the wall.
   You have made it up. No, you are mad!
   You are getting madder every day.

OLD MAN: It's louder now because he rides
  Upon a gravelled avenue
  All grass to-day. The hoof-beat stops,
  He has gone to the other side of the house,
  Gone to the stable, put the horse up.
  She has gone down to open the door.
  This night she is no better than her man
  And does not mind that he is half drunk,
  She is mad about him. They mount the stairs.
  She brings him into her own chamber.
  And that is the marriage-chamber now.
  The window is dimly lit again.

  Do not let him touch you! It is not true
  That drunken men cannot beget,
  And if he touch he must beget
  And you must bear his murderer.
  Deaf! Both deaf! If I should throw
  A stick or a stone they would not hear;
  And that's a proof my wits are out.
  But there's a problem: she must live
  Through everything in exact detail,
  Driven to it by remorse, and yet
  Can she renew the sexual act
  And find no pleasure in it, and if not,
  If pleasure and remorse must both be there,
  Which is the greater?
                     I lack schooling.
  Go fetch Tertullian; he and I
  Will ravel all that problem out
  Whilst those two lie upon the mattress
  Begetting me.
                Come back! Come back!
  And so you thought to slip away,
  My bag of money between your fingers,
  And that I could not talk and see!
  You have been rummaging in the pack. *(The light in the
    window has faded out.)*
BOY: You never gave me my right share.

OLD MAN: And had I given it, young as you are,
　You would have spent it upon drink.
BOY: What if I did? I had a right
　To get it and spend it as I chose.
OLD MAN: Give me that bag and no more words.
BOY: I will not.
OLD MAN:　　　　I will break your fingers.

*They struggle for the bag. In the struggle it drops, scattering the
money. The* OLD MAN *staggers but does not fall. They stand
looking at each other. The window is lit up. A man is seen pouring
whiskey into a glass.*

BOY: What if I killed you? You killed my grand-dad,
　Because you were young and he was old.
　Now I am young and you are old.
OLD MAN *(staring at window)*: Better-looking, those sixteen
　years—
BOY: What are you muttering?
OLD MAN:　　　　　　　　Younger—and yet
　She should have known he was not her kind.
BOY: What are you saying? Out with it! *(Old Man points to
　window.)*
　My God! The window is lit up
　And somebody stands there, although
　The floorboards are all burnt away.
OLD MAN: The window is lit up because my father
　Has come to find a glass for his whiskey.
　He leans there like some tired beast.
BOY: A dead, living, murdered man!
OLD MAN: "Then the bride-sleep fell upon Adam":
　Where did I read those words?
　　　　　　　　　　　　And yet
　There's nothing leaning in the window
　But the impression upon my mother's mind;
　Being dead she is alone in her remorse.
BOY: A body that was a bundle of old bones
　Before I was born. Horrible! Horrible! *(He covers his eyes.)*
OLD MAN: That beast there would know nothing, being nothing,
　If I should kill a man under the window

He would not even turn his head. *(He stabs the* BOY.*)*
My father and my son on the same jack-knife!
That finishes—there—there—there— *(He stabs again and*
  again. The window grows dark.)
"Hush-a-bye baby, thy father's a knight,
Thy mother a lady, lovely and bright."
No, that is something that I read in a book,
And if I sing it must be to my mother,
And I lack rhyme *(The stage has grown dark except where the*
  tree stands in white light.)
                              Study that tree.
It stands there like a purified soul,
All cold, sweet, glistening light.
Dear mother, the window is dark again,
But you are in the light because
I finished all that consequence.
I killed that lad because had he grown up
He would have struck a woman's fancy,
Begot, and passed pollution on.
I am a wretched foul old man
And therefore harmless. When I have stuck
This old jack-knife into a sod
And pulled it out all bright again,
And picked up all the money that he dropped,
I'll to a distant place, and there
Tell my old jokes among new men. *(He cleans the knife and*
  begins to pick up money.)
Hoof-beats! Dear God,
How quickly it returns—beat—beat—!

Her mind cannot hold up that dream.
Twice a murderer and all for nothing,
And she must animate that dead night
Not once but many times!
                              O God,
Release my mother's soul from its dream!
Mankind can do no more. Appease
The misery of the living and the remorse of the dead.

JOHN MILLINGTON SYNGE

Riders to the Sea

———

Characters

MAURYA, *an old woman*
BARTLEY, *her son*
CATHLEEN, *her daughter*
NORA, *a younger daughter*
MEN AND WOMEN

Scene *An island off the West of Ireland*

Cottage kitchen, with nets, oilskins, spinning-wheel, some new boards standing by the wall, etc. CATHLEEN, *a girl of about twenty, finishes kneading cake, and puts it down in the pot-oven by the fire; then wipes her hands, and begins to spin at the wheel.* NORA, *a young girl, puts her head in at the door.*

NORA *(in a low voice)*: Where is she?

CATHLEEN: She's lying down, God help her, and maybe sleeping, if she's able.

NORA *comes in softly, and takes a bundle from under her shawl.*

CATHLEEN *(spinning the wheel rapidly)*: What is it you have?

NORA: The young priest is after bringing them. It's a shirt and a plain stocking were got off a drowned man in Donegal.

CATHLEEN *stops her wheel with a sudden movement, and leans out to listen.*

NORA: We're to find out if it's Michael's they are, some time herself will be down looking by the sea.

CATHLEEN: How would they be Michael's, Nora? How would he go the length of that way to the far north?

NORA: The young priest says he's known the like of it. 'If it's

Michael's they are,' says he, 'you can tell herself he's got a clean burial, by the grace of God; and if they're not his, let no one say a word about them, for she'll be getting her death,' says he, 'with crying and lamenting.'

The door which NORA *half closed is blown open by a gust of wind.*

CATHLEEN *(looking out anxiously)*: Did you ask him would he stop Bartley going this day with the horses to the Galway fair?

NORA: 'I won't stop him,' says he; 'but let you not be afraid. Herself does be saying prayers half through the night, and the Almighty God won't leave her destitute,' says he, 'with no son living.'

CATHLEEN: Is the sea bad by the white rocks, Nora?

NORA: Middling bad, God help us. There's a great roaring in the west, and it's worse it'll be getting when the tide's turned to the wind. *(She goes over to the table with the bundle.)* Shall I open it now?

CATHLEEN: Maybe she'd wake up on us, and come in before we'd done *(coming to the table)*. It's a long time we'll be, and the two of us crying.

NORA *(goes to the inner door and listens)*: She's moving about on the bed. She'll be coming in a minute.

CATHLEEN: Give me the ladder, and I'll put them up in the turf-loft, the way she won't know of them at all, and maybe when the tide turns she'll be going down to see would he be floating from the east.

They put the ladder against the gable of the chimney; CATHLEEN *goes up a few steps and hides the bundle in the turf-loft.* MAURYA *comes from the inner room.*

MAURYA *(looking up at* CATHLEEN *and speaking querulously)*: Isn't it turf enough you have for this day and evening?

CATHLEEN: There's a cake baking at the fire for a short space *(throwing down the turf)*, and Bartley will want it when the tide turns if he goes to Connemara.

NORA *picks up the turf and puts it round the pot-oven.*

MAURYA *(sitting down on a stool at the fire)*: He won't go this day with the wind rising from the south and west. He won't go this day, for the young priest will stop him surely.

NORA: He'll not stop him, mother; and I heard Eamon Simon and Stephen Pheety and Colum Shawn saying he would go.

MAURYA: Where is he itself?

NORA: He went down to see would there be another boat sailing in the week, and I'm thinking it won't be long till he's here now, for the tide's turning at the green head, and the hooker's tacking from the east.

CATHLEEN: I hear some one passing the big stones.

NORA (*looking out*): He's coming now, and he in a hurry.

BARTLEY (*comes in and looks round the room. Speaking sadly and quietly*): Where is the bit of new rope, Cathleen, was bought in Connemara?

CATHLEEN (*coming down*): Give it to him, Nora; it's on a nail by the white boards. I hung it up this morning, for the pig with the black feet was eating it.

NORA (*giving him a rope*): Is that it, Bartley?

MAURYA: You'd do right to leave that rope, Bartley, hanging by the boards (BARTLEY *takes the rope*). It will be wanting in this place, I'm telling you, if Michael is washed up tomorrow morning or the next morning, or any morning in the week; for it's a deep grave we'll make him, by the grace of God.

BARTLEY (*beginning to work with the rope*): I've no halter the way I can ride down on the mare, and I must go now quickly. This is the one boat going for two weeks or beyond it, and the fair will be a good fair for horses, I heard them saying below.

MAURYA: It's a hard thing they'll be saying below if the body is washed up and there's no man in it to make the coffin, and I after giving a big price for the finest white boards you'd find in Connemara.

She looks round at the boards.

BARTLEY: How would it be washed up, and we after looking each day for nine days, and a strong wind blowing a while back from the west and south?

MAURYA: If it isn't found itself, that wind is raising the sea, and there was a star up against the moon, and it rising in the night. If it was a hundred horses, or a thousand horses, you had itself, what is the price of a thousand horses against a son where there is one son only?

BARTLEY (*working at the halter, to* CATHLEEN): Let you go down each day, and see the sheep aren't jumping in on the rye, and if the jobber comes you can sell the pig with the black feet if there is a good price going.

MAURYA: How would the like of her get a good price for a pig?

BARTLEY (*to* CATHLEEN): If the west wind holds with the last bit of the moon let you and Nora get up weed enough for another cock for the kelp. It's hard set we'll be from this day with no one in it but one man to work.

MAURYA: It's hard set we'll be surely the day you're drowned with the rest. What way will I live and the girls with me, and I an old woman looking for the grave?

BARTLEY *lays down the halter, takes off his old coat, and puts on a newer one of the same flannel.*

BARTLEY (*to* NORA): Is she coming to the pier?

NORA (*looking out*): She's passing the green head and letting fall her sails.

BARTLEY (*getting his purse and tobacco*): I'll have half an hour to go down, and you'll see me coming again in two days, or in three days, or maybe in four days if the wind is bad.

MAURYA (*turning round to the fire, and putting her shawl over her head*): Isn't it a hard and cruel man won't hear a word from an old woman, and she holding him from the sea?

CATHLEEN: It's the life of a young man to be going on the sea, and who would listen to an old woman with one thing and she saying it over?

BARTLEY (*taking the halter*): I must go now quickly. I'll ride down on the red mare, and the grey pony 'ill run behind me. . . . The blessing of God on you.

He goes out.

MAURYA (*crying out as he is in the door*): He's gone now, God spare us, and we'll not see him again. He's gone now, and when the black night is falling I'll have no son left me in the world.

CATHLEEN: Why wouldn't you give him your blessing and he looking round in the door? Isn't it sorrow enough is on every one in this house without you sending him out with an unlucky word behind him, and a hard word in his ear?

MAURYA *takes up the tongs and begins raking the fire aimlessly without looking round.*

NORA *(turning towards her)*: You're taking away the turf from the cake.

CATHLEEN *(crying out)*: The Son of God forgive us, Nora, we're after forgetting his bit of bread. *(She comes over to the fire.)*

NORA: And it's destroyed he'll be going till dark night, and he after eating nothing since the sun went up.

CATHLEEN *(turning the cake out of the oven)*: It's destroyed he'll be, surely. There's no sense left on any person in a house where an old woman will be talking for ever.

MAURYA *sways herself on her stool.*

CATHLEEN *(cutting off some of the bread and rolling it in a cloth; to* MAURYA*)*: Let you go down now to the spring well and give him this and he passing. You'll see him then and the dark word will be broken, and you can say 'God speed you,' the way he'll be easy in his mind.

MAURYA *(taking the bread)*: Will I be in it as soon as himself?

CATHLEEN: If you go now quickly.

MAURYA *(standing up unsteadily)*: It's hard set I am to walk.

CATHLEEN *(looking at her anxiously)*: Give her the stick, Nora, or maybe she'll slip on the big stones.

NORA: What stick?

CATHLEEN: The stick Michael brought from Connemara.

MAURYA *(taking a stick* NORA *gives her)*. In the big world the old people do be leaving things after them for their sons and children, but in this place it is the young men do be leaving things behind for them that do be old.

She goes out slowly. NORA *goes over to the ladder.*

CATHLEEN: Wait, Nora, maybe she'd turn back quickly. She's that sorry, God help her, you wouldn't know the thing she'd do.

NORA: Is she gone round by the bush?

CATHLEEN *(looking out)*: She's gone now. Throw it down quickly, for the Lord knows when she'll be out of it again.

NORA *(getting the bundle from the loft)*: The young priest said he'd be passing tomorrow, and we might go down and speak to him below if it's Michael's they are surely.

CATHLEEN *(taking the bundle)*: Did he say what way they were found?

NORA *(coming down)*: 'There were two men,' says he, 'and they rowing round with poteen before the cocks crowed, and the oar of one of them caught the body, and they passing the black cliffs of the north.'

CATHLEEN *(trying to open the bundle)*: Give me a knife, Nora; the string's perished with salt water, and there's a black knot on it you wouldn't loosen in a week.

NORA *(giving her a knife)*: I've heard tell it was a long way to Donegal.

CATHLEEN *(cutting the string)*: It is surely. There was a man in here a while ago—the man sold us that knife—and he said if you set off walking from the rocks beyond, it would be in seven days you'd be in Donegal.

NORA: And what time would a man take, and he floating?

CATHLEEN *opens the bundle and takes out a bit of a shirt and a stocking. They look at them eagerly.*

CATHLEEN *(in a low voice)*: The Lord spare us, Nora! isn't it a queer hard thing to say if it's his they are surely?

NORA: I'll get his shirt off the hook the way we can put the one flannel on the other. *(She looks through some clothes hanging in the corner.)* It's not with them, Cathleen, and where will it be?

CATHLEEN: I'm thinking Bartley put it on him in the morning, for his own shirt was heavy with the salt in it. *(Pointing to the corner.)* There's a bit of a sleeve was of the same stuff. Give me that and it will do.

NORA *brings it to her and they compare the flannel.*

CATHLEEN: It's the same stuff, Nora; but if it is itself, aren't there great rolls of it in the shops of Galway, and isn't it many another man may have a shirt of it as well as Michael himself?

NORA *(who has taken up the stocking and counted the stitches, crying out)*: It's Michael, Cathleen, it's Michael; God spare his soul, and what will herself say when she hears this story, and Bartley on the sea?

CATHLEEN *(taking the stocking)*: It's a plain stocking.

NORA: It's the second one of the third pair I knitted, and I put up three-score stitches, and I dropped four of them.

CATHLEEN *(counts the stitches)*: It's that number is in it *(crying out)*. Ah, Nora, isn't it a bitter thing to think of him floating that way to the far north, and no one to keen him but the black hags that do be flying on the sea?

NORA *(swinging herself half round, and throwing out her arms on the clothes)*: And isn't it a pitiful thing when there is nothing left of a man who was a great rower and fisher but a bit of an old shirt and a plain stocking?

CATHLEEN *(after an instant)*: Tell me is herself coming, Nora? I hear a little sound on the path.

NORA *(looking out)*: She is, Cathleen. She's coming up to the door.

CATHLEEN: Put these things away before she'll come in. Maybe it's easier she'll be after giving her blessing to Bartley, and we won't let on we've heard anything the time he's on the sea.

NORA *(helping CATHLEEN to close the bundle)*: We'll put them here in the corner.

They put them into a hole in the chimney corner. CATHLEEN *goes back to the spinning-wheel.*

NORA: Will she see it was crying I was?

CATHLEEN: Keep your back to the door the way the light'll not be on you.

NORA *sits down at the chimney corner, with her back to the door.* MAURYA *comes in very slowly, without looking at the girls, and goes over to her stool at the other side of the fire. The cloth with the bread is still in her hand. The girls look at each other, and* NORA *points to the bundle of bread.*

CATHLEEN *(after spinning for a moment)*: You didn't give him his bit of bread?

MAURYA *begins to keen softly, without turning round.*

CATHLEEN: Did you see him riding down?

MAURYA *goes on keening.*

CATHLEEN *(a little impatiently)*: God forgive you; isn't it a better thing to raise your voice and tell what you seen, than to be making lamentation for a thing that's done? Did you see Bartley, I'm saying to you?

MAURYA (*with a weak voice*): My heart's broken from this day.

CATHLEEN (*as before*): Did you see Bartley?

MAURYA: I seen the fearfulest thing.

CATHLEEN (*leaves her wheel and looks out*): God forgive you; he's riding the mare now over the green head, and the grey pony behind him.

MAURYA (*Starts, so that her shawl falls back from her head and shows her white tossed hair. With a frightened voice*): The grey pony behind him. . . .

CATHLEEN (*coming to the fire*): What is it ails you at all?

MAURYA (*speaking very slowly*): I've seen the fearfulest thing any person has seen since the day Bride Dara seen the dead man with the child in his arms.

CATHLEEN *and* NORA: Uah.

They crouch down in front of the old woman at the fire.

NORA: Tell us what it is you seen.

MAURYA: I went down to the spring well, and I stood there saying a prayer to myself. Then Bartley came along, and he riding on the red mare with the grey pony behind him (*she puts up her hands, as if to hide something from her eyes*). The Son of God spare us, Nora!

CATHLEEN: What is it you seen?

MAURYA: I seen Michael himself.

CATHLEEN (*speaking softly*): You did not, mother. It wasn't Michael you seen, for his body is after being found in the far north, and he's got a clean burial, by the grace of God.

MAURYA (*a little defiantly*): I'm after seeing him this day, and he riding and galloping. Bartley came first on the red mare, and I tried to say 'God speed you,' but something choked the words in my throat. He went by quickly; and 'the blessing of God on you,' says he, and I could say nothing. I looked up then, and I crying, at the grey pony, and there was Michael upon it—with fine clothes on him, and new shoes on his feet.

CATHLEEN (*begins to keen*): It's destroyed we are from this day. It's destroyed, surely.

NORA: Didn't the young priest say the Almighty God won't leave her destitute with no son living?

MAURYA (*in a low voice, but clearly*): It's little the like of him knows of the sea. . . . Bartley will be lost now, and let you call in Eamon and make me a good coffin out of the white boards, for I won't live after them. I've had a husband, and a husband's father, and six sons in this house—six fine men, though it was a hard birth I had with every one of them and they coming to the world—and some of them were found and some of them were not found, but they're gone now the lot of them. . . . There were Stephan and Shawn were lost in the great wind, and found after in the Bay of Gregory of the Golden Mouth, and carried up the two of them on one plank, and in by that door.

She pauses for a moment, the girls start as if they heard something through the door that is half open behind them.

NORA *(in a whisper)*: Did you hear that, Cathleen? Did you hear a noise in the north-east?

CATHLEEN *(in a whisper)*: There's someone after crying out by the seashore.

MAURYA *(continues without hearing anything)*: There was Sheamus and his father, and his own father again, were lost in a dark night, and not a stick or sign was seen of them when the sun went up. There was Patch after was drowned out of a curagh that turned over. I was sitting here with Bartley, and he a baby lying on my two knees, and I seen two women, and three women, and four women coming in, and they crossing themselves and not saying a word. I looked out then, and there were men coming after them, and they holding a thing in the half of a red sail, and water dripping out of it—it was a dry day, Nora— and leaving a track to the door.

She pauses again with her hand stretched out towards the door. It opens softly and old women begin to come in, crossing themselves on the threshold, and kneeling down in front of the stage with red petticoats over their heads.

MAURYA *(half in a dream, to* CATHLEEN*)*: Is it Patch, or Michael, or what is it at all?

CATHLEEN: Michael is after being found in the far north, and when he is found there how could he be here in this place?

MAURYA: There does be a power of young men floating round in the sea, and what way would they know if it was Michael they had, or another man like him, for when a man is nine days in the sea, and the wind blowing, it's hard set his own mother would be to say what man was in it.

CATHLEEN: It's Michael, God spare him, for they're after sending us a bit of his clothes from the far north.

She reaches out and hands MAURYA *the clothes that belonged to Michael.* MAURYA *stands up slowly, and takes them in her hands.* NORA *looks out.*

NORA: They're carrying a thing among them, and there's water dripping out of it and leaving a track by the big stones.

CATHLEEN (*in a whisper to the women who have come in*): Is it Bartley it is?

ONE OF THE WOMEN: It is, surely, God rest his soul.

Two younger women come in and pull out the table. Then men carry in the body of BARTLEY, *laid on a plank, with a bit of a sail over it, and lay it on the table.*

CATHLEEN (*to the women as they are doing so*): What way was he drowned?

ONE OF THE WOMEN: The grey pony knocked him over into the sea, and he was washed out where there is a great surf on the white rocks.

MAURYA *has gone over and knelt down at the head of the table. The women are keening softly and swaying themselves with a slow movement.* CATHLEEN *and* NORA *kneel at the other end of the table. The men kneel near the door.*

MAURYA (*raising her head and speaking as if she did not see the people around her*): They're all gone now, and there isn't anything more the sea can do to me. . . . I'll have no call now to be up crying and praying when the wind breaks from the south, and you can hear the surf is in the east, and the surf is in the west, making a great stir with the two noises, and they hitting one on the other. I'll have no call now to be going down and getting Holy Water in the dark nights after Samhain, and I won't care what way the sea is when the other women will be keening. (*To* NORA.) Give me the Holy Water, Nora; there's a small sup still on the dresser.

NORA *gives it to her.*

MAURYA (*drops Michael's clothes across* BARTLEY's *feet, and sprin-*

kles the Holy Water over him): It isn't that I haven't prayed for you, Bartley, to the Almighty God. It isn't that I haven't said prayers in the dark night till you wouldn't know what I'd be saying; but it's a great rest I'll have now, and it's time, surely. It's a great rest I'll have now, and great sleeping in the long nights after Samhain, if it's only a bit of wet flour we do have to eat, and maybe a fish that would be stinking.

She kneels down again, crossing herself, and saying prayers under her breath.

CATHLEEN *(to an old man)*: Maybe yourself and Eamon would make a coffin when the sun rises. We have fine white boards herself bought, God help her, thinking Michael would be found, and I have a new cake you can eat while you'll be working.

THE OLD MAN *(looking at the boards)*: Are there nails with them?

CATHLEEN: There are not, Colum; we didn't think of the nails.

ANOTHER MAN: It's a great wonder she wouldn't think of the nails, and all the coffins she's seen made already.

CATHLEEN: It's getting old she is, and broken.

MAURYA *stands up again very slowly and spreads out the pieces of Michael's clothes beside the body, sprinkling them with the last of the Holy Water.*

NORA *(in a whisper to CATHLEEN)*: She's quiet now and easy; but the day Michael was drowned you could hear her crying out from this to the spring well. It's fonder she was of Michael, and would anyone have thought that?

CATHLEEN *(slowly and clearly)*: An old woman will be soon tired with anything she will do, and isn't it nine days herself is after crying and keening, and making great sorrow in the house?

MAURYA *(puts the empty cup mouth downwards on the table, and lays her hands together on Bartley's feet)*: They're all together this time, and the end is come. May the Almighty God have mercy on Bartley's soul, and on Michael's soul, and on the souls of Sheamus and Patch, and Stephen and Shawn *(bending her head);* and may He have mercy on my soul, Nora, and on the soul of every one is left living in the world.

She pauses, and the keen rises a little more loudly from the women, then sinks away.

MAURYA *(continuing)*: Michael has a clean burial in the far north, by the grace of Almighty God. Bartley will have a fine coffin out of the white boards, and a deep grave surely. What more can we want than that? No man at all can be living for ever, and we must be satisfied.

She kneels down again and the curtain falls slowly.

SUSAN GLASPELL

Trifles

⟶

Characters

GEORGE HENDERSON, *county attorney*
HENRY PETERS, *sheriff*
LEWIS HALE, *a neighboring farmer*
MRS. PETERS
MRS. HALE

Scene   *The kitchen in the now abandoned farmhouse of John Wright, a gloomy kitchen, and left without having been put in order—unwashed pans under the sink, a loaf of bread outside the breadbox, a dish towel on the table—other signs of incompleted work. At the rear the outer door opens and the* SHERIFF *comes in followed by the* COUNTY ATTORNEY *and* HALE. *The* SHERIFF *and* HALE *are men in middle life, the* COUNTY ATTORNEY *is a young man; all are much bundled up and go at once to the stove. They are followed by two women—the Sheriff's wife first; she is a slight wiry woman, a thin nervous face.* MRS. HALE *is larger and would ordinarily be called more comfortable looking, but she is disturbed now and looks fearfully about as she enters. The women have come in slowly, and stand close together near the door.*

COUNTY ATTORNEY (*rubbing his hands*): This feels good. Come up to the fire, ladies.

MRS. PETERS (*after taking a step forward*): I'm not—cold.

SHERIFF (*unbuttoning his overcoat and stepping away from the stove as if to mark the beginning of official business*): Now, Mr. Hale, before we move things about, you explain to Mr. Henderson just what you saw when you came here yesterday morning.

COUNTY ATTORNEY: By the way, has anything been moved? Are things just as you left them yesterday?

SHERIFF (*looking about*): It's just the same. When it dropped below zero last night I thought I'd better send Frank out this morning to make a fire for us—no use getting pneumonia with a big case on, but I told him not to touch anything except the stove—and you know Frank.

COUNTY ATTORNEY: Somebody should have been left here yesterday.

SHERIFF: Oh—yesterday. When I had to send Frank to Morris Center for that man who went crazy—I want you to know I had my hands full yesterday, I knew you could get back from Omaha by today and as long as I went over everything here myself—

COUNTY ATTORNEY: Well, Mr. Hale, tell just what happened when you came here yesterday morning.

HALE: Harry and I had started to town with a load of potatoes. We came along the road from my place and as I got here I said, "I'm going to see if I can't get John Wright to go in with me on a party telephone." I spoke to Wright about it once before and he put me off, saying folks talked too much anyway, and all he asked was peace and quiet—I guess you know about how much he talked himself; but I thought maybe if I went to the house and talked about it before his wife, though I said to Harry that I didn't know as what his wife wanted made such difference to John—

COUNTY ATTORNEY: Let's talk about that later, Mr. Hale. I do want to talk about that, but tell now just what happened when you got to the house.

HALE: I didn't hear or see anything; I knocked at the door, and still it was all quiet inside. I knew they must be up, it was past eight o'clock. So I knocked again, and I thought I heard somebody say, "Come in." I wasn't sure, I'm not sure yet, but I opened the door—this door (*indicating the door by which the two women are still standing*) and there in that rocker—(*pointing to it*) sat Mrs. Wright.

They all look at the rocker.

COUNTY ATTORNEY: What—was she doing?

HALE: She was rockin' back and forth. She had her apron in her hand and was kind of—pleating it.

COUNTY ATTORNEY: And how did she—look?

HALE: Well, she looked queer.

COUNTY ATTORNEY: How do you mean—queer?

HALE: Well, as if she didn't know what she was going to do next. And kind of done up.

COUNTY ATTORNEY: How did she seem to feel about your coming?

HALE: Why, I don't think she minded—one way or other. She didn't pay much attention. I said, "How do, Mrs. Wright, it's cold, ain't it?" And she said, "Is it?"—and went on kind of pleating at her apron. Well, I was surprised; she didn't ask me to come up to the stove, or to set down, but just sat there, not even looking at me, so I said, "I want to see John." And then she—laughed. I guess you would call it a laugh. I thought of Harry and the team outside, so I said a little sharp: "Can't I see John?" "No," she says, kind o' dull like. "Ain't he home?" says I. "Yes," says she, "he's home." "Then why can't I see him?" I asked her, out of patience. " 'Cause he's dead," says she. "*Dead?*" says I. She just nodded her head, not getting a bit excited, but rockin' back and forth. "Why—where is he?" says I, not knowing what to say. She just pointed upstairs—like that *(himself pointing to the room above)*. I got up, with the idea of going up there. I walked from there to here—then I says, "Why, what did he die of?" "He died of a rope round his neck," says she, and just went on pleatin' at her apron. Well, I went out and called Harry. I thought I might—need help. We went upstairs and there he was lyin'—

COUNTY ATTORNEY: I think I'd rather have you go into that upstairs, where you can point it all out. Just go on now with the rest of the story.

HALE: Well, my first thought was to get that rope off. It looked . . . *(stops, his face twitches)* . . . but Harry, he went up to him, and he said, "No, he's dead all right, and we'd better not touch anything." So we went back down stairs. She was still sitting that same way. "Has anybody been notified?" I asked. "No," says she, unconcerned. "Who did this, Mrs. Wright?" said Harry. He said it businesslike—and she stopped pleatin' of her apron. "I don't know," she says. "You don't *know?*" says Harry. "No," says she. "Weren't you sleepin' in the bed with him?" says Harry. "Yes," says she, "but I was on the inside." "Somebody slipped a rope round his neck and strangled him and you didn't wake up?" says Harry. "I didn't wake up," she said after him. We must 'a looked as if we didn't see how that could be, for after a minute she said, "I sleep sound." Harry was going to ask her more questions but I said maybe we ought to let her tell her story first to the coroner, or the sheriff, so Harry went fast as he could to Rivers' place, where there's a telephone.

COUNTY ATTORNEY: And what did Mrs. Wright do when she knew that you had gone for the coroner?

HALE: She moved from that chair to this one over here *(pointing to a small chair in the corner)* and just sat there with her hands held together and looking down. I got a feeling that I ought to make some conversation, so I said I had come in to see if John wanted to put in a telephone, and at that she started to laugh, and then she stopped and looked at me—scared. *(The* COUNTY ATTORNEY, *who has had his notebook out, makes a note.)* I dunno, maybe it wasn't scared. I wouldn't like to say it was. Soon Harry got back, and then Dr. Lloyd came, and you, Mr. Peters, and so I guess that's all I know that you don't.

COUNTY ATTORNEY *(looking around)*: I guess we'll go upstairs first—and then out to the barn and around there. *(to the* SHERIFF) You're convinced that there was nothing important here—nothing that would point to any motive.

SHERIFF: Nothing here but kitchen things.

The COUNTY ATTORNEY, *after again looking around the kitchen, opens the door of a cupboard closet. He gets up on a chair and looks on a shelf. Pulls his hand away, sticky.*

COUNTY ATTORNEY: Here's a nice mess.

The women draw nearer.

MRS. PETERS *(to the other woman)*: Oh, her fruit; it did freeze. *(to the* COUNTY ATTORNEY) She worried about that when it turned so cold. She said the fire'd go out and her jars would break.

SHERIFF: Well, can you beat the women! Held for murder and worryin' about her preserves.

COUNTY ATTORNEY: I guess before we're through she may have something more serious than preserves to worry about.

HALE: Well, women are used to worrying over trifles.

The two women move a little closer together.

COUNTY ATTORNEY *(with the gallantry of a young politician)*: And yet, for all their worries, what would we do without the ladies? *(The women do not unbend. He goes to the sink, takes a dipperful of water from the pail and pouring it into a basin, washes his hands. Starts to wipe them on the roller towel, turns it for a cleaner place.)* Dirty towels! *(kicks his foot against the pans under the sink)* Not much of a housekeeper, would you say ladies?

MRS. HALE *(stiffly)*: There's a great deal of work to be done on a farm.

COUNTY ATTORNEY: To be sure. And yet *(with a little bow to her)* I know there are some Dickson county farmhouses which do not have such roller towels.

He gives it a pull to expose its full length again.

MRS. HALE: Those towels get dirty awful quick. Men's hands aren't always as clean as they might be.

COUNTY ATTORNEY: Ah, loyal to your sex, I see. But you and Mrs. Wright were neighbors. I suppose you were friends, too.

MRS. HALE *(shaking her head)*: I've not seen much of her of late years. I've not been in this house—it's more than a year.

COUNTY ATTORNEY: And why was that? You didn't like her?

MRS. HALE: I liked her all well enough. Farmers' wives have their hands full, Mr. Henderson. And then—

COUNTY ATTORNEY: Yes—?

MRS. HALE *(looking about)*: It never seemed a very cheerful place.

COUNTY ATTORNEY: No—it's not cheerful. I shouldn't say she had the homemaking instinct.

MRS. HALE: Well, I don't know as Wright had, either.

COUNTY ATTORNEY: You mean that they didn't get on very well?

MRS. HALE: No, I don't mean anything. But I don't think a place'd be any cheerfuller for John Wright's being in it.

COUNTY ATTORNEY: I'd like to talk more of that a little later. I want to get the lay of things upstairs now.

He goes to the left, where three steps lead to a stair door.

SHERIFF: I suppose anything Mrs. Peters does'll be all right. She was to take in some clothes for her, you know, and a few little things. We left in such a hurry yesterday.

COUNTY ATTORNEY: Yes, but I would like to see what you take, Mrs. Peters, and keep an eye out for anything that might be of use to us.

MRS. PETERS: Yes, Mr. Henderson.

The women listen to the men's steps on the stairs, then look about the kitchen.

MRS. HALE: I'd hate to have men coming into my kitchen, snooping around and criticising.

She arranges the pans under sink which the COUNTY ATTORNEY *had shoved out of place.*

MRS. PETERS: Of course it's no more than their duty.

MRS. HALE: Duty's all right, but I guess that deputy sheriff that came out to make the fire might have got a little of this on. *(gives the roller towel a pull)* Wish I'd thought of that sooner. Seems mean to talk about her for not having things slicked up when she had to come away in such a hurry.

MRS. PETERS *(who has gone to a small table in the left rear corner of the room, and lifted one end of a towel that covers a pan)*: She had bread set.

Stands still.

MRS. HALE *(eyes fixed on a loaf of bread beside the breadbox, which is on a low shelf at the other side of the room. Moves slowly toward it.)*: She was going to put this in there. *(Picks up loaf, then abruptly drops it. In a manner of returning to familiar things.)* It's a shame about her fruit. I wonder if it's all gone. *(Gets up on the chair and looks.)* I think there's some here that's all right, Mrs. Peters. Yes—here; *(holding it toward the window)* this is cherries, too. *(looking again)* I declare I believe that's the only one. *(Gets down, bottle in her hand. Goes to the sink and wipes it off on the outside.)* She'll feel awful bad after all her hard work in the hot weather. I remember the afternoon I put up my cherries last summer.

She puts the bottle on the big kitchen table, center of the room. With a sigh, is about to sit down in the rocking-chair. Before she is seated realizes what chair it is; with a slow look at it, steps back. The chair which she has touched rocks back and forth.

MRS. PETERS: Well, I must get those things from the front room closet. *(She goes to the door at the right, but after looking into the other room, steps back.)* You coming with me, Mrs. Hale? You could help me carry them.

They go in the other room; reappear, MRS. PETERS *carrying a dress and skirt,* MRS. HALE *following with a pair of shoes.*

MRS. PETERS: My, it's cold in there.

She puts the clothes on the big table, and hurries to the stove.

MRS. HALE *(examining her skirt)*: Wright was close. I think maybe that's why she kept so much to herself. She didn't even belong to the Ladies Aid. I suppose she felt she couldn't do her part, and then you don't enjoy things when you feel shabby. She used to wear pretty clothes and be lively, when she was Minnie Foster, one of the town girls singing in the choir. But that—oh, that was thirty years ago. This all you was to take in?

MRS. PETERS: She said she wanted an apron. Funny thing to want, for there isn't much to get you dirty in jail, goodness knows. But I suppose just to make her feel more natural. She said they was in the top drawer in this cupboard. Yes, here. And then her little shawl that always hung behind the door. *(opens stair door and looks)* Yes, here it is.

Quickly shuts door leading upstairs.

MRS. HALE *(abruptly moving toward her)*: Mrs. Peters?

MRS. PETERS: Yes, Mrs. Hale?

MRS. HALE: Do you think she did it?

MRS. PETERS *(in a frightened voice)*: Oh, I don't know.

MRS. HALE: Well, I don't think she did. Asking for an apron and her little shawl. Worrying about her fruit.

MRS. PETERS *(Starts to speak, glances up, where footsteps are heard in the room above. In a low voice.)*: Mr. Peters says it looks bad for her. Mr. Henderson is awful sarcastic in a speech and he'll make fun of her sayin' she didn't wake up.

MRS. HALE: Well, I guess John Wright didn't wake when they was slipping that rope under his neck.

MRS. PETERS: No, it's strange. It must have been done awful crafty and still. They say it was such a—funny way to kill a man, rigging it all up like that.

MRS. HALE: That's just what Mr. Hale said. There was a gun in the house. He says that's what he can't understand.

MRS. PETERS: Mr. Henderson said coming out that what was needed for the case was a motive; something to show anger, or—sudden feeling.

MRS. HALE (*who is standing by the table*): Well, I don't see any signs of anger around here. (*She puts her hand on the dish towel which lies on the table, stands looking down at table, one half of which is clean, the other half messy.*) It's wiped to here. (*Makes a move as if to finish work, then turns and looks at loaf of bread outside the breadbox. Drops towel. In that voice of coming back to familiar things.*) Wonder how they are finding things upstairs. I hope she had it a little more red-up[†] up there. You know, it seems kind of *sneaking.* Locking her up in town and then coming out here and trying to get her own house to turn against her!

MRS. PETERS: But Mrs. Hale, the law is the law.

MRS. HALE: I s'pose 'tis. (*unbuttoning her coat*) Better loosen up your things, Mrs. Peters. You won't feel them when you go out.

Mrs. Peters takes off her fur tippet, goes to hang it on hook at back of room, stands looking at the under part of the small corner table.

MRS. PETERS: She was piecing a quilt.

She brings the large sewing basket and they look at the bright pieces.

MRS. HALE: It's log cabin pattern. Pretty, isn't it? I wonder if she was goin' to quilt it or just knot it?

Footsteps have been heard coming down the stairs. The SHERIFF *enters followed by* HALE *and the* COUNTY ATTORNEY.

[†]**red-up** (*slang*) *prettified, like a woman who touches up her face with rouge.*

SHERIFF: They wonder if she was going to quilt it or just knot it!

The men laugh; the women look abashed.

COUNTY ATTORNEY *(rubbing his hands over the stove)*: Frank's fire didn't do much up there, did it? Well, let's go out to the barn and get that cleared up.

The men go outside.

MRS. HALE *(resentfully)*: I don't know as there's anything so strange, our takin' up our time with little things while we're waiting for them to get the evidence. *(She sits down at the big table smoothing out a block with decision.)* I don't see as it's anything to laugh about.

MRS. PETERS *(apologetically)*: Of course they've got awful important things on their minds.

Pulls up a chair and joins Mrs. Hale at the table.

MRS. HALE *(examining another block)*: Mrs. Peters, look at this one. Here, this is the one she was working on, and look at the sewing! All the rest of it has been so nice and even. And look at this! It's all over the place! Why, it looks as if she didn't know what she was about!

After she has said this they look at each other, then start to glance back at the door. After an instant MRS. HALE *has pulled at a knot and ripped the sewing.*

MRS. PETERS: Oh, what are you doing, Mrs. Hale?

MRS. HALE *(mildly)*: Just pulling out a stitch or two that's not sewed very good. *(threading a needle)* Bad sewing always made me fidgety.

MRS. PETERS *(nervously)*: I don't think we ought to touch things.

MRS. HALE: I'll just finish up this end. *(suddenly stopping and leaning forward)* Mrs. Peters?

MRS. PETERS: Yes, Mrs. Hale?

MRS. HALE: What do you suppose she was so nervous about?

MRS. PETERS: Oh—I don't know. I don't know as she was nervous. I sometimes sew awful queer when I'm just tired. *(MRS. HALE starts to say something, looks at MRS. PETERS, then goes on sewing.)* Well, I must get these things wrapped up. They may be through sooner than we think. *(putting apron and other things together)* I wonder where I can find a piece of paper, and string.

MRS. HALE: In that cupboard, maybe.

MRS. PETERS *(looking in cupboard)*: Why, here's a birdcage. *(holds it up)* Did she have a bird, Mrs. Hale?

MRS. HALE: Why, I don't know whether she did or not—I've not been here for so long. There was a man around last year selling canaries cheap, but I don't know as she took one; maybe she did. She used to sing real pretty herself.

MRS. PETERS *(glancing around)*: Seems funny to think of a bird here. But she must have had one, or why would she have a cage? I wonder what happened to it.

MRS. HALE: I s'pose maybe the cat got it.

MRS. PETERS: No, she didn't have a cat. She's got that feeling some people have about cats—being afraid of them. My cat got in her room and she was real upset and asked me to take it out.

MRS. HALE: My sister Bessie was like that. Queer, ain't it?

MRS. PETERS *(examining the cage)*: Why, look at this door. It's broke. One hinge is pulled apart.

MRS. HALE *(looking too)*: Looks as if someone must have been rough with it.

MRS. PETERS: Why, yes.

She brings the cage forward and puts it on the table.

MRS. HALE: I wish if they're going to find any evidence they'd be about it. I don't like this place.

MRS. PETERS: But I'm awful glad you came with me, Mrs. Hale. It would be lonesome for me sitting here alone.

MRS. HALE: It would, wouldn't it? *(dropping her sewing)* But I tell you what I do wish, Mrs. Peters. I wish I had come over sometimes when *she* was here. I— *(looking around the room)*— wish I had.

MRS. PETERS: But of course you were awful busy, Mrs. Hale— your house and your children.

MRS. HALE: I could've come. I stayed away because it weren't cheerful—and that's why I ought to have come. I—I've never liked this place. Maybe because it's down in a hollow and you don't see the road. I dunno what it is but it's a lonesome place

and always was. I wish I had come over to see Minnie Foster
sometimes. I can see now—

Shakes her head.

MRS. PETERS: Well, you mustn't reproach yourself, Mrs. Hale.
Somehow we just don't see how it is with other folks until—
something comes up.

MRS. HALE: Not having children makes less work—but it makes a
quiet house, and Wright out to work all day, and no company
when he did come in. Did you know John Wright, Mrs. Peters?

MRS. PETERS: Not to know him; I've seen him in town. They say
he was a good man.

MRS. HALE: Yes—good; he didn't drink, and kept his word as well
as most, I guess, and paid his debts. But he was a hard man,
Mrs. Peters. Just to pass the time of day with him—*(shivers)*
Like a raw wind that gets to the bone. *(pauses, her eye falling
on the cage)* I should think she would 'a wanted a bird. But
what do you suppose went with it?

MRS. PETERS: I don't know, unless it got sick and died.

*She reaches over and swings the broken door, swings it again. Both
women watch it.*

MRS. HALE: You weren't raised round here, were you? *(Mrs. Peters shakes her head.)* You didn't know—her?

MRS. PETERS: Not till they brought her yesterday.

MRS. HALE: She—come to think of it, she was kind of like a bird
herself—real sweet and pretty, but kind of timid and—fluttery.
How—she—did—change. *(silence; then as if struck by a happy
thought and relieved to get back to everday things)* Tell you
what, Mrs. Peters, why don't you take the quilt in with you? It
might take up her mind.

MRS. PETERS: Why, I think that's a real nice idea, Mrs. Hale. There
couldn't possibly be any objection to it, could there? Now, just
what would I take? I wonder if her patches are in here—and her
things.

They look in the sewing basket.

MRS. HALE: Here's some red. I expect this has got sewing things
in it. *(Brings out a fancy box.)* What a pretty box. Looks like
something somebody would give you. Maybe her scissors are in

here. (*Opens box. Suddenly puts her hand to her nose.*) Why—
(MRS. PETERS *bends nearer, then turns her face away.*) There's
something wrapped up in this piece of silk.

MRS. PETERS: Why, this isn't her scissors.

MRS. HALE (*lifting the silk*): Oh, Mrs. Peters—it's—

MRS. PETERS *bends closer.*

MRS. PETERS: It's the bird.

MRS. HALE (*jumping up*): But, Mrs. Peters—look at it! Its neck!
Look at its neck! It's all—other side *to.*

MRS. PETERS: Somebody—wrung—its—neck.

*Their eyes meet. A look of growing comprehension, of horror.
Steps are heard outside.* MRS. HALE *slips box under quilt pieces,
and sinks into her chair. Enter* SHERIFF *and* COUNTY ATTORNEY.
MRS. PETERS *rises.*

COUNTY ATTORNEY (*as one turning from serious things to little
pleasantries*): Well, ladies, have you decided whether she was
going to quilt it or knot it?

MRS. PETERS: We think she was going to—knot it.

COUNTY ATTORNEY: Well, that's interesting, I'm sure. (*seeing the
bridcage*) Has the bird flown?

MRS. HALE (*putting more quilt pieces over the box*): We think
the—cat got it.

COUNTY ATTORNEY (*preoccupied*): Is there a cat?

MRS. HALE *glances in a quick covert way at* MRS. PETERS.

MRS. PETERS: Well, not *now.* They're superstitious, you know.
They leave.

COUNTY ATTORNEY (*to* SHERIFF PETERS, *continuing an interrupted
conversation*): No sign at all of anyone having come from the
outside. Their own rope. Now let's go up again and go over it
piece by piece. (*They start upstairs.*) It would have to have
been someone who knew just the—

MRS. PETERS *sits down. The two women sit there not looking at
one another, but as if peering into something and at the same time
holding back. When they talk now it is in the manner of feeling
their way over strange ground, as if afraid of what they are saying,
but as if they can not help saying it.*

MRS. HALE: She liked the bird. She was going to bury it in that
pretty box.

MRS. PETERS *(in a whisper)*: When I was a girl—my kitten—there was a boy took a hatchet, and before my eyes—and before I could get there—*(covers her face an instant)* If they hadn't held me back I would have—*(catches herself, looks upstairs where steps are heard, falters weakly)*—hurt him.

MRS. HALE *(with a slow look around her)*: I wonder how it would seem never to have had any children around. *(pause)* No, Wright wouldn't like the bird—a thing that sang. She used to sing. He killed that, too.

MRS. PETERS *(moving uneasily)*: We don't know who killed the bird.

MRS. HALE: I knew John Wright.

MRS. PETERS: It was an awful thing was done in this house that night, Mrs. Hale. Killing a man while he slept, slipping a rope around his neck that choked the life out of him.

MRS. HALE: His neck. Choked the life out of him.

Her hand goes out and rests on the birdcage.

MRS. PETERS *(with rising voice)*: We don't know who killed him. We don't know.

MRS. HALE *(her own feeling not interrupted)*: If there'd been years and years of nothing, then a bird to sing to you, it would be awful—still, after the bird was still.

MRS. PETERS *(something within her speaking)*: I know what stillness is. When we homesteaded in Dakota, and my first baby died—after he was two years old, and me with no other then—

MRS. HALE *(moving)*: How soon do you suppose they'll be through, looking for the evidence?

MRS. PETERS: I know what stillness is. *(pulling herself back)* The law has got to punish crime, Mrs. Hale.

MRS. HALE *(not as if answering that)*: I wish you'd seen Minnie Foster when she wore a white dress with blue ribbons and stood up there in the choir and sang. *(a look around the room)* Oh, I *wish* I'd come over here once in a while! That was a crime! That was a crime! Who's going to punish that?

MRS. PETERS *(looking upstairs)*: We mustn't—take on.

MRS. HALE: I might have known she needed help! I know how things can be—for women. I tell you, it's queer, Mrs. Peters. We live close together and we live far apart. We all go through the same things—it's all just a different kind of the same thing. *(brushes her eyes; noticing the bottle of fruit, reaches out for it)* If I was you I wouldn't tell her her fruit was gone. Tell her it *ain't*. Tell her it's all right. Take this in to prove it to her. She— she may never know whether it was broke or not.

MRS. PETERS *(Takes the bottle, looks about for something to wrap it in; takes petticoat from the clothes brought from the other room, very nervously begins winding this around the bottle. In a false voice.)*: My, it's a good thing the men couldn't hear us. Wouldn't they just laugh! Getting all stirred up over a little thing like a—dead canary. As if that could have anything to do with— with—wouldn't they *laugh*!

The men are heard coming down stairs.

MRS. HALE *(under her breath)*: Maybe they would—maybe they wouldn't.

COUNTY ATTORNEY: No, Peters, it's all perfectly clear except a reason for doing it. But you know juries when it comes to women. If there was some definite thing. Something to show— something to make a story about—a thing that would connect up with this strange way of doing it—

The women's eyes meet for an instant. Enter HALE *from outer door.*

HALE: Well, I've got the team around. Pretty cold out there.

COUNTY ATTORNEY: I'm going to stay here a while by myself. *(to the* SHERIFF*)* You can send Frank out for me, can't you? I want to go over everything. I'm not satisfied that we can't do better.

SHERIFF: Do you want to see what Mrs. Peters is going to take in?

The COUNTY ATTORNEY *goes to the table, picks up the apron, laughs.*

COUNTY ATTORNEY: Oh, I guess they're not very dangerous things the ladies have picked out. *(Moves a few things about, disturbing the quilt pieces which cover the box. Steps back.)* No, Mrs. Peters doesn't need supervising. For that matter, a sheriff's wife is married to the law. Ever think of it that way, Mrs. Peters?

MRS. PETERS: Not—just that way.

SHERIFF *(chuckling)*: Married to the law. *(moves toward the other room)* I just want you to come in here a minute, George. We ought to take a look at these windows.

COUNTY ATTORNEY *(scoffingly)*: Oh, windows!

SHERIFF: We'll be right out, Mr. Hale.

HALE *goes outside. The* SHERIFF *follows the* COUNTY ATTORNEY *into the other room. Then* MRS. HALE *rises, hands tight together, looking intensely at* MRS. PETERS, *whose eyes make a slow turn, finally meeting* MRS. HALE's. *A moment* MRS. HALE *holds her, then her own eyes point the way to where the box is concealed. Suddenly* MRS. PETERS *throws back quilt pieces and tries to put the box in the bag she is wearing. It is too big. She opens box, starts to take bird out, cannot touch it, goes to pieces, stands there helpless. Sound of a knob turning in the other room.* MRS. HALE *snatches the box and puts it in the pocket of her big coat. Enter* COUNTY ATTORNEY *and* SHERIFF.

COUNTY ATTORNEY *(facetiously)*: Well, Henry, at least we found out that she was not going to quilt it. She was going to—what is it you call it, ladies?

MRS. HALE *(her hand against her pocket)*: We call it—knot it, Mr. Henderson.

TENNESSEE WILLIAMS

The Glass Menagerie

⎯⎯⎯

Nobody, not even the rain, has such small hands.

—E. E. CUMMINGS

Characters

AMANDA WINGFIELD, *the mother. A little woman of great but confused vitality clinging frantically to another time and place. Her characterization must be carefully created, not copied from type. She is not paranoiac, but her life is paranoia. There is much to admire in* AMANDA, *and as much to love and pity as there is to laugh at. Certainly she has endurance and a kind of heroism, and though her foolishness makes her unwittingly cruel at times, there is tenderness in her slight person.*

LAURA WINGFIELD, *her daughter.* AMANDA, *having failed to establish contact with reality, continues to live vitally in her illusions, but* LAURA's *situation is even greater. A childhood illness has left her crippled, one leg slightly shorter than the other, and held in a brace. This defect need not be more than suggested on the stage. Stemming from this,* LAURA's *separation increases till she is like a piece of her own glass collection, too exquisitely fragile to move from the shelf.*

TOM WINGFIELD, *her son. And the narrator of the play. A poet with a job in a warehouse. His nature is not remorseless, but to escape from a trap he has to act without pity.*

JIM O'CONNOR, *the gentleman caller. A nice, ordinary, young man.*

Scene *An alley in St. Louis.*

Part I *Preparation for a Gentleman Caller.*

Part II *The Gentleman Calls.*

Time *Now and the Past.*

Scene I

The Wingfield apartment is in the rear of the building, one of those vast hive-like conglomerations of cellular living-units that flower as warty growths in overcrowded urban centers of lower middle-class population and are symptomatic of the impulse of this largest and fundamentally enslaved section of American society to avoid fluidity and differentiation and to exist and function as one inter-fused mass of automatism.

The apartment faces an alley and is entered by a fire-escape, a structure whose name is a touch of accidental poetic truth, for all of these huge buildings are always burning with the slow and implacable fires of human desperation. The fire-escape is included in the set—that is, the landing of it and steps descending from it.

The scene is memory and is therefore nonrealistic. Memory takes a lot of poetic license. It omits some details; others are exaggerated, according to the emotional value of the articles it touches, for memory is seated predominantly in the heart. The interior is therefore rather dim and poetic.

At the rise of the curtain, the audience is faced with the dark, grim rear wall of the Wingfield tenement. This building, which runs parallel to the footlights, is flanked on both sides by dark, narrow alleys which run into murky canyons of tangled clotheslines, garbage cans and the sinister latticework of neighboring fire-escapes. It is up and down these side alleys that exterior entrances and exits are made, during the play. At the end of TOM's *opening commentary, the dark tenement wall slowly reveals (by means of a transparency) the interior of the ground floor Wingfield apartment.*

Downstage is the living room, which also serves as a sleeping room for LAURA, *the sofa unfolding to make her bed. Upstage, center, and divided by a wide arch or second proscenium with transparent faded portieres (or second curtain), is the dining room. In an old-fashioned what-not in the living room are seen scores of transparent glass animals. A blown-up photograph of the father hangs on the wall of the living room, facing the audience, to the left of the archway. It is the face of a very handsome young man in a doughboy's First World War cap. He is gallantly smiling, ineluctably smiling, as if to say, "I will be smiling forever."*

The audience hears and sees the opening scene in the dining room through both the transparent fourth wall of the building and the transparent gauze portieres of the dining-room arch. It is during this revealing scene that the fourth wall slowly ascends, out of sight. This transparent exterior wall is not brought down again until the very end of the play, during TOM's *final speech.*

The narrator is an undisguised convention of the play. He takes whatever license with dramatic convention as is convenient to his purposes.

TOM *enters dressed as a merchant sailor from the alley, stage left, and strolls across the front of the stage to the fire-escape. There he stops and lights a cigarette. He addresses the audience.*

TOM: Yes, I have tricks in my pocket, I have things up my sleeve. But I am the opposite of a stage magician. He gives you illusion that has the appearance of truth. I give you truth in the pleasant disguise of illusion. To begin with, I turn back time. I reverse it to that quaint period, the thirties, when the huge middle class of America was matriculating in a school for the blind. Their eyes had failed them, or they had failed their eyes, and so they were having their fingers pressed forcibly down on the fiery Braille alphabet of a dissolving economy. In Spain there was revolution. Here there was only shouting and confusion. In Spain there was Guernica. Here there were disturbances of labor, sometimes pretty violent, in otherwise peaceful cities such as Chicago, Cleveland, Saint Louis. . . . This is the social background of the play.

(Music.)

The play is memory. Being a memory play, it is dimly lighted, it is sentimental, it is not realistic. In memory everything seems to happen to music. That explains the fiddle in the wings. I am the narrator of the play, and also a character in it. The other characters are my mother, Amanda, my sister, Laura, and a gentleman caller who appears in the final scenes. He is the most realistic character in the play, being an emissary from a world of reality that we were somehow set apart from. But since I have a poet's weakness for symbols, I am using this character also as a symbol; he is the long delayed but always expected something that we live for. There is a fifth character in the play who doesn't appear except in this larger-than-life photograph over the mantel. This is our father who left us a long time ago. He was a telephone man who fell in love with long distances; he gave up his job with the telephone company and skipped the light fantastic out of town ... The last we heard of him was a picture post-card from Mazatlan, on the Pacific coast of Mexico, containing a message of two words—"Hello—Good-bye!" and an address. I think the rest of the play will explain itself. ...

AMANDA's *voice becomes audible through the portieres.*

(Legend On Screen: "Où Sont Les Neiges.")[†]

He divides the portieres and enters the upstage area.

    AMANDA *and* LAURA *are seated at a drop-leaf table. Eating is indicated by gestures without food or utensils.* AMANDA *faces the audience.* TOM *and* LAURA *are seated in profile.*

    The interior has lit up softly and through the scrim we see AMANDA *and* LAURA *seated at the table in the upstage area.*

AMANDA *(calling):* Tom?

TOM: Yes, Mother.

AMANDA: We can't say grace until you come to the table!

TOM: Coming, Mother. *(He bows slightly and withdraws, reappearing a few moments later in his place at the table.)*

AMANDA *(to her son):* Honey, don't *push* with your *fingers*. If you have to push with something, the thing to push with is a crust of bread. And chew—chew! Animals have sections in their stom-

---

[†]("**Legend ... Neiges.**") "*Where are the snows (of yesteryear)?*" *A slide bearing this line by the French poet François Villon is to be projected on a stage wall.*

achs which enable them to digest food without mastication, but human beings are supposed to chew their food before they swallow it down. Eat food leisurely, son, and really enjoy it. A well-cooked meal has lots of delicate flavors that have to be held in the mouth for appreciation. So chew your food and give your salivary glands a chance to function!

TOM *deliberately lays his imaginary fork down and pushes his chair back from the table.*

TOM: I haven't enjoyed one bite of this dinner because of your constant directions on how to eat it. It's you that makes me rush through meals with your hawk-like attention to every bite I take. Sickening—spoils my appetite—all this discussion of animals' secretion—salivary glands—mastication!

AMANDA *(lightly)*: Temperament like a Metropolitan star! *(He rises and crosses downstage.)* You're not excused from the table.

TOM: I am getting a cigarette.

AMANDA: You smoke too much.

LAURA *rises.*

LAURA: I'll bring in the blanc mange.

He remains standing with his cigarette by the portieres during the following.

AMANDA *(rising)*: No, sister, no, sister—you be the lady this time and I'll be the darky.

LAURA: I'm already up.

AMANDA: Resume your seat, little sister—I want you to stay fresh and pretty—for gentlemen callers!

LAURA: I'm not expecting any gentlemen callers.

AMANDA *(Crossing out to kitchenette. Airily.)*: Sometimes they come when they are least expected! Why, I remember one Sunday afternoon in Blue Mountain—*(Enters kitchenette.)*

TOM: I know what's coming!

LAURA: Yes. But let her tell it.

TOM: Again?

LAURA: She loves to tell it.

AMANDA *returns with bowl of dessert.*

AMANDA: One Sunday afternoon in Blue Mountain—your mother

received—*seventeen*—gentlemen callers! Why, sometimes there weren't chairs enough to accommodate them all. We had to send the nigger over to bring in folding chairs from the parish house.

TOM *(remaining at portieres)*: How did you entertain those gentlemen callers?

AMANDA: I understood the art of conversation!

TOM: I bet you could talk.

AMANDA: Girls in those days *knew* how to talk, I can tell you.

TOM: Yes?

(Image: Amanda As A Girl On A Porch Greeting Callers.)

AMANDA: They knew how to entertain their gentlemen callers. It wasn't enough for a girl to be possessed of a pretty face and a graceful figure—although I wasn't slighted in either respect. She also needed to have a nimble wit and a tongue to meet all occasions.

TOM: What did you talk about?

AMANDA: Things of importance going on in the world! Never anything coarse or common or vulgar. *(She addresses Tom as though he were seated in the vacant chair at the table though he remains by portieres. He plays this scene as though he held the book.)* My callers were gentlemen—all! Among my callers were some of the most prominent young planters of the Mississippi Delta—planters and sons of planters!

TOM *motions for music and a spot of light on* AMANDA. *Her eyes lift, her face glows, her voice becomes rich and elegiac.*

(Screen Legend: "Où Sont Les Neiges.")

There was a young Champ Laughlin who later became vice-president of the Delta Planters Bank. Hadley Stevenson who was drowned in Moon Lake and left his widow one hundred and fifty thousand in Government Bonds. There were the Cutrere brothers, Wesley and Bates. Bates was one of my bright particular beaux! He got in a quarrel with that wild Wainright boy. They shot it out on the floor of Moon Lake Casino. Bates was shot through the stomach. Died in the ambulance on his way to Memphis. His widow was also well-provided for, came into eight or ten thousand acres, that's all. She married him on the rebound—never loved her—carried my picture on him the night he died! And there was that boy that every girl in the Delta had set her cap for! That beautiful, brilliant young Fitzhugh boy from Green County!

TOM: What did he leave his widow?

AMANDA: He never married! Gracious, you talk as though all of my old admirers had turned up their toes to the daisies!

TOM: Isn't this the first you mentioned that still survives?

AMANDA: That Fitzhugh boy went North and made a fortune— came to be known as the Wolf of Wall Street! He had the Midas touch, whatever he touched turned to gold! And I could have been Mrs. Duncan J. Fitzhugh, mind you! But—I picked your *father*!

LAURA *(rising)*: Mother, let me clear the table.

AMANDA: No dear, you go in front and study your typewriter chart. Or practice your shorthand a little. Stay fresh and pretty— It's almost time for our gentlemen callers to start arriving. *(She flounces girlishly toward the kitchenette.)* How many do you suppose we're going to entertain this afternoon?

TOM *throws down the paper and jumps up with a groan.*

LAURA *(alone in the dining room)*: I don't believe we're going to receive any, Mother.

AMANDA *(reappearing, airily)*: What? No one—not one? You must be joking! *(*LAURA *nervously echoes her laugh. She slips in a fugitive manner through the half-open portieres and draws them gently behind her. A shaft of very clear light is thrown on her face against the faded tapestry of the curtains.)* (**Music: "The Glass Menagerie" Under Faintly.**) *(Lightly.)* Not one gentleman caller? It can't be true! There must be a flood, there must have been a tornado!

LAURA: It isn't a flood, it's not a tornado, Mother. I'm just not popular like you were in Blue Mountain.... *(*TOM *utters another groan.* LAURA *glances at him with a faint, apologetic smile. Her voice catching a little.)* Mother's afraid I'm going to be an old maid.

(The Scene Dims Out With "Glass Menagerie" Music.)

Scene II

"Laura, Haven't You Ever Liked Some Boy?"

On the dark stage the screen is lighted with the image of blue
roses.

Gradually LAURA's figure becomes apparent and the screen goes
out.

The music subsides.

LAURA is seated in the delicate ivory chair at the small clawfoot
table.

She wears a dress of soft violet material for a kimono—her hair
tied back from her forehead with a ribbon.

She is washing and polishing her collection of glass.

AMANDA appears on the fire-escape steps. At the sound of her
ascent, LAURA catches her breath, thrusts the bowl of ornaments
away and seats herself stiffly before the diagram of the typewriter
keyboard as though it held her spellbound. Something has happened to AMANDA. It is written in her face as she climbs to the
landing: a look that is grim and hopeless and a little absurd.

She has on one of those cheap or imitation velvety-looking cloth
coats with imitation fur collar. Her hat is five or six years old, one
of those dreadful cloche hats that were worn in the late twenties,
and she is clasping an enormous black patent-leather pocketbook
with nickel clasp and initials. This is her fulldress outfit, the one
she usually wears to the D.A.R.

Before entering she looks through the door.

She purses her lips, opens her eyes wide, rolls them upward and
shakes her head.

Then she slowly lets herself in the door. Seeing her mother's
expression LAURA touches her lips with a nervous gesture.

LAURA: Hello, Mother, I was—*(She makes a nervous gesture toward the chart on the wall.* AMANDA *leans against the shut door
and stares at* LAURA *with a martyred look.)*

AMANDA: Deception? Deception? *(She slowly removes her hat and
gloves, continuing the swift suffering stare. She lets the hat and
gloves fall on the floor—a bit of acting.)*

LAURA *(shakily)*: How was the D.A.R. meeting? *(*AMANDA *slowly
opens her purse and removes a dainty white handkerchief which*

363

she shakes out delicately and delicately touches to her lips and nostrils.) Didn't you go the D.A.R. meeting, Mother?

AMANDA *(faintly, almost inaudibly)*: —No.—No. *(then more forcibly)* I did not have the strength—to go the D.A.R. In fact, I did not have the courage! I wanted to find a hole in the ground and hide myself in it forever! *(She crosses slowly to the wall and removes the diagram of the typewriter keyboard. She holds it in front of her for a second, staring at it sweetly and sorrowfully—then bites her lips and tears it in two pieces.)*

LAURA *(faintly)*: Why did you do that, Mother? *(AMANDA repeats the same procedure with the chart of the Gregg Alphabet.)* Why are you—

AMANDA: Why? Why? How old are you, Laura?

LAURA: Mother, you know my age.

AMANDA: I thought that you were an adult; it seems that I was mistaken. *(She crosses slowly to the sofa and sinks down and stares at LAURA.)*

LAURA: Please don't stare at me, Mother.

AMANDA *closes her eyes and lowers her head. Count ten.*

AMANDA: What are we going to do, what is going to become of us, what is the future?

Count ten.

LAURA: Has something happened, Mother? *(AMANDA draws a long breath and takes out the handkerchief again. Dabbing process.)* Mother, has—something happened?

AMANDA: I'll be all right in a minute. I'm just bewildered—*(count five)*—by life. . . .

LAURA: Mother, I wish that you would tell me what's happened.

AMANDA: As you know, I was supposed to be inducted into my office at the D.A.R. this afternoon. *(Image: A Swarm of Typewriters.)* But I stopped off at Rubicam's Business College to speak to your teachers about your having a cold and ask them what progress they thought you were making down there.

LAURA: Oh. . . .

AMANDA: I went to the typing instructor and introduced myself as your mother. She didn't know who you were. Wingfield, she said. We don't have any such student enrolled at the school! I assured her she did, that you had been going to classes since early in January. "I wonder," she said, "if you could be talking about that terribly shy little girl who dropped out of school after only a few days' attendance?" "No," I said, "Laura, my daughter, has been going to school every day for the past six weeks." "Excuse me," she said. She took the attendance book out and there was your name, unmistakably printed, and all the dates you were absent until they decided that you had dropped out of school. I still said, "No, there must have been some mistake! There must have been some mix-up in the records." And she said, "No—I remember her perfectly now. Her hand shook so that she couldn't hit the right keys! The first time we gave a speed-test, she broke down completely—was sick at the stomach and almost had to be carried into the wash-room! After that morning she never showed up any more. We phoned the house but never got any answer"—while I was working at Famous and Barr, I suppose, demonstrating those—Oh! I felt so weak I could barely keep on my feet. I had to sit down while they got me a glass of water! Fifty dollars' tuition, all of our plans—my hopes and ambitions for you—just gone up the spout, just gone up the spout like that. (LAURA *draws a long breath and gets awkwardly to her feet. She crosses to the victrola and winds it up.*) What are you doing?

LAURA: Oh! (*She releases the handle and returns to her seat.*)

AMANDA: Laura, where have you been going when you've gone out pretending that you were going to business college?

LAURA: I've just been going out walking.

AMANDA: That's not true.

LAURA: It is. I just went walking.

AMANDA: Walking? Walking? In winter? Deliberately courting pneumonia in that light coat? Where did you walk to, Laura?

LAURA: It was the lesser of two evils, Mother. (*Image: Winter Scene In Park.*) I couldn't go back up. I—threw up—on the floor!

AMANDA: From half past seven till after five every day you mean to tell me you walked around in the park, because you wanted to make me think that you were still going to Rubicam's Business College?

LAURA: It wasn't as bad as it sounds. I went inside places to get warmed up.

AMANDA: Inside where?

LAURA: I went in the art museum and the bird-houses at the Zoo. I visited the penguins every day! Sometimes I did without lunch and went to the movies. Lately I've been spending most of my afternoons in the Jewel-box, that big glass house where they raise the tropical flowers.

AMANDA: You did all this to deceive me, just for the deception? *(LAURA looks down.)* Why?

LAURA: Mother, when you're disappointed, you get that awful suffering look on your face, like the picture of Jesus' mother in the museum!

AMANDA: Hush!

LAURA: I couldn't face it.

Pause. A whisper of strings.

(Legend: "The Crust Of Humility.")

AMANDA *(hopelessly fingering the huge pocketbook)*: So what are we going to do the rest of our lives? Stay home and watch the parades go by? Amuse ourselves with the glass menagerie, darling? Eternally play those worn-out phonograph records your father left as a painful reminder of him? We won't have a business career—we've given that up because it gave us nervous indigestion! *(Laughs wearily.)* What is there left but dependency all our lives? I know so well what becomes of unmarried women who aren't prepared to occupy a position. I've seen such pitiful cases in the South—barely tolerated spinsters living upon the grudging patronage of sister's husband or brother's wife— stuck away in some little mouse-trap of a room—encouraged by one in-law to visit another—little birdlike women without any nest—eating the crust of humility all their life! Is that the future that we've mapped out for ourselves? I swear it's the only alternative I can think of! It isn't a very pleasant alternative, is it? Of course—some girls *do marry*. *(LAURA twists her hands nervously.)* Haven't you ever liked some boy?

LAURA: Yes I liked one once. *(rises)* I came across his picture a while ago.

AMANDA *(with some interest)*: He gave you his picture?

LAURA: No, it's in the year-book.

AMANDA *(disappointed)*: Oh—a high-school boy.

(Screen Image: Jim As A High-School Hero Bearing A Silver Cup.)

LAURA: Yes. His name was Jim. *(LAURA lifts the heavy annual from the clawfoot table.)* Here he is in *The Pirates of Penzance*.

AMANDA *(absently)*: The what?

LAURA: The operetta the senior class put on. He had a wonderful voice and we sat across the aisle from each other Mondays, Wednesdays and Fridays in the Aud. Here he is with the silver cup for debating! See his grin?

AMANDA *(absently)*: He must have had a jolly disposition.

LAURA: He used to call me—Blue Roses.

(Image: Blue Roses.)

AMANDA: Why did he call you such a name as that?

LAURA: When I had that attack of pleurosis—he asked me what was the matter when I came back. I said pleurosis—he thought that I said Blue Roses! So that's what he always called me after that. Whenever he saw me, he'd holler, "Hello, Blue Roses!" I didn't care for the girl that he went out with. Emily Meisenbach. Emily was the best-dressed girl at Soldan. She never struck me, though, as being sincere . . . It says in the Personal Section— they're engaged. That's—six years ago! They must be married by now.

AMANDA: Girls that aren't cut out for business careers usually wind up married to some nice man. *(Gets up with a spark of revival.)* Sister, that's what you'll do!

LAURA *utters a startled, doubtful laugh. She reaches quickly for a piece of glass.*

LAURA: But, Mother—

AMANDA: Yes? *(crossing to photograph)*

LAURA *(in a tone of frightened apology)*: I'm—crippled!

(Image: Screen.)

AMANDA: Nonsense! Laura, I've told you never, never to use that word. Why, you're not crippled, you just have a little defect— hardly noticeable, even! When people have some slight disadvantage like that, they cultivate other things to make up for it— develop charm—and vivacity—and—*charm*! That's all you have to do! *(She turns again to the photograph.)* One thing your father had *plenty of*—was *charm*!

TOM *motions to the fiddle in the wings.*

(The Scene Fades Out With Music.)

SCENE III

(Legend On The Screen: "After The Fiasco—")

TOM *speaks from the fire-escape landing.*

TOM: After the fiasco at Rubicam's Business College, the idea of getting a gentleman caller for Laura began to play a more important part in Mother's calculations. It became an obsession. Like some archetype of the universal unconscious, the image of the gentleman caller haunted our small apartment. . . . *(Image: Young Man At Door With Flowers.)* An evening at home rarely passed without some allusion to this image, this spectre, this hope. . . . Even when he wasn't mentioned, his presence hung in Mother's preoccupied look and in my sister's frightened, apologetic manner—hung like a sentence passed upon the Wingfields! Mother was a woman of action as well as words. She began to take logical steps in the planned direction. Late that winter and in the early spring—realizing that extra money would be needed to properly feather the nest and plume the bird—she conducted a vigorous campaign on the telephone, roping in subscribers to one of those magazines for matrons called *The Home-maker's Companion,* the type of journal that features the serialized sublimations of ladies of letters who think in terms of delicate cup-like breasts, slim, tapering waists, rich, creamy thighs, eyes like wood-smoke in autumn, fingers that soothe and caress like strains of music, bodies as powerful as Etruscan sculpture.

(Screen Image: Glamour Magazine Cover.)

AMANDA *enters with phone on long extension cord. She is spotted in the dim stage.*

AMANDA: Ida Scott? This is Amanda Wingfield! We *missed* you at the D.A.R. last Monday! I said to myself: She's probably suffering with that sinus condition! How is that sinus condition? Horrors! Heaven have mercy!—You're a Christian martyr, yes, that's what you are, a Christian martyr! Well, I just now happened to notice that your subscription to the *Companion's* about to expire! Yes, it expires with the next issue, honey!—just when that wonderful new serial by Bessie Mae Hopper is getting off to such an exciting start. Oh, honey, it's something that you can't miss! You remember how *Gone With the Wind* took everybody by storm? You simply couldn't go out if you hadn't read it. All everybody *talked* was Scarlett O'Hara. Well, this is a book that critics already compare to *Gone With the Wind*. It's the *Gone With the Wind* of the post-World War generation!— What?—Burning?—Oh, honey, don't let them burn, go take a look in the oven and I'll hold the wire! Heavens—I think she's hung up!

(Dim Out)

(Legend On Screen: "You Think I'm In Love With Continental Shoemakers?")

Before the stage is lighted, the violent voices of TOM *and* AMANDA *are heard. They are quarreling behind the portieres. In front of them stands* LAURA *with clenched hands and panicky expression.*

A clear pool of light on her figure throughout this scene.

TOM: What in Christ's name am I—
AMANDA *(shrilly)*: Don't you use that—
TOM: Supposed to do!
AMANDA: Expression! Not in my—
TOM: Ohhh!
AMANDA: Presence! Have you gone out of your senses?
TOM: I have, that's true, *driven* out!
AMANDA: What is the matter with you, you—big—big—IDIOT!
TOM: Look—I've got *no thing,* no single thing—
AMANDA: Lower your voice!
TOM: In my life here that I can call my OWN! Everything is—
AMANDA: Stop that shouting!
TOM: Yesterday you confiscated my books! You had the nerve to—

AMANDA: I took that horrible novel back to the library—yes! That hideous book by that insane Mr. Lawrence. (TOM *laughs wildly.*) I cannot control the output of diseased minds or people who cater to them— (TOM *laughs still more wildly.*) BUT I WON'T ALLOW SUCH FILTH BROUGHT INTO MY HOUSE! No, no, no, no, no!

TOM: House, house! Who pays rent on it, who makes a slave of himself to—

AMANDA (*fairly screeching*): Don't you DARE to—

TOM: No, No, I mustn't say things! *I've* got to just—

AMANDA: Let me tell you—

TOM: I don't want to hear any more! (*He tears the portieres open. The upstage area is lit with a turgid smoky red glow.*)

AMANDA's *hair is in metal curlers and she wears a very old bathrobe, much too large for her slight figure, a relic of the faithless Mr. Wingfield.*

An upright typewriter and a wild disarray of manuscripts are on the drop-leaf table. The quarrel was probably precipitated by AMANDA's *interruption of his creative labor. A chair is lying overthrown on the floor.*

Their gesticulating shadows are cast on the ceiling by the fiery glow.

AMANDA: You *will* hear more, you—

TOM: No, I won't hear more, I'm going out!

AMANDA: You come right back in—

TOM: Out, out out! Because I'm—

AMANDA: Come back here, Tom Wingfield! I'm not through talking to you!

TOM: Oh, go—

LAURA (*desperately*): Tom!

AMANDA: You're going to listen, and no more insolence from you! I'm at the end of my patience! (*He comes back toward her.*)

TOM: What do you think I'm at? Aren't I supposed to have any patience to reach the end of, Mother? I know, I know. It seems unimportant to you, what I'm *doing*—what I *want* to do—having a little *difference* between them! You don't think that—

AMANDA: I think you've been doing things that you're ashamed of. That's why you act like this. I don't believe that you go every night to the movies. Nobody goes to the movies night after night. Nobody in their right minds goes to the movies as often as you pretend to. People don't go to the movies at nearly midnight, and movies don't let out at two A.M. Come in stumbling. Muttering to yourself like a maniac! You get three hours sleep and then go to work. Oh, I can picture the way you're doing down there. Moping, doping, because you're in no condition.

TOM *(wildly)*: No, I'm in no condition!

AMANDA: What right have you got to jeopardize your job? Jeopardize the security of us all? How do you think we'd manage if you were—

TOM: Listen! You think I'm crazy *about* the *warehouse?* *(He bends fiercely toward her slight figure.)* You think I'm in love with the Continental Shoemakers? You think I want to spend fifty-five *years* down there in that—*celotex interior!* with—*fluorescent—tubes!* Look! I'd rather somebody picked up a crowbar and battered out my brains—than go back mornings! I *go!* Every time you come in yelling that God damn *"Rise and Shine!"* *"Rise and Shine!"* I say to myself How *lucky dead* people are!" But I get up. I *go!* For sixty-five dollars a month I give up all that I dream of doing and being *ever!* And you say self—*self's* all I ever think of. Why, listen, if self is what I thought of, Mother, I'd be where he is—GONE! *(pointing to father's picture)* As far as the system of transportation reaches! *(He starts past her. She grabs his arm.)* Don't grab at me, Mother!

AMANDA: Where are you going?

TOM: I'm going to the *movies!*

AMANDA: I don't believe that lie!

TOM *(Crouching toward her, overtowering her tiny figure. She backs away, gasping)*: I'm going to opium dens! Yes, opium dens, dens of vice and criminals' hang-outs, Mother. I've joined the Hogan gang, I'm a hired assassin, I carry a tommy-gun in a violin case! I run a string of cat-houses in the Valley! They call me Killer, Killer Wingfield, I'm leading a double-life, a simple, honest warehouse worker by day, by night a dynamic *czar* of the *underworld, Mother.* I go to gambling casinos, I spin away fortunes on the roulette table! I wear a patch over one eye and a false mustache, sometimes I put on green whiskers. On those occasions they call me—*El Diablo!* Oh, I could tell you things to make you sleepless! My enemies plan to dynamite this place. They're going to blow us all sky-high some night! I'll be glad, very happy, and so will you! You'll go up, up on a broomstick, over Blue Mountain with seventeen gentlemen callers! You ugly—babbling old—*witch*.... (*He goes through a series of violent, clumsy movements, seizing his overcoat, lunging to the door, pulling it fiercely open. The women watch him, aghast. His arm catches in the sleeve of the coat as he struggles to pull it on. For a moment he is pinioned by the bulky garment. With an outraged groan he tears the coat off again, splitting the shoulders of it, and hurls it across the room. It strikes against the shelf of Laura's glass collection, there is a tinkle of shattering glass. Laura cries out as if wounded.*)

(Music Legend: "The Glass Menagerie.")

LAURA (*shrilly*): My glass!—menagerie.... *She covers her face and turns away.*)

But AMANDA *is still stunned and stupefied by the "ugly witch" so that she barely notices this occurrence. Now she recovers her speech.*

AMANDA (*in an awful voice*): I won't speak to you—until you apologize! *She crosses through portieres and draws them together behind her.* TOM *is left with* LAURA. LAURA *clings weakly to the mantel with her face averted.* TOM *stares at her stupidly for a moment. Then he crosses to shelf. Drops awkwardly to his knees to collect the fallen glass, glancing at* LAURA *as if he would speak but couldn't.*)

"The Glass Menagerie" steals in as

(The Scene Dims Out.)

SCENE IV

The interior is dark. Faint in the alley.
A deep-voiced bell in a church is tolling the hour of five as the scene commences.

TOM *appears at the top of the alley. After each solemn boom of the bell in the tower, he shakes a little noise-maker or rattle as if to express the tiny spasm of man in contrast to the sustained power and dignity of the Almighty. This and the unsteadiness of his advance make it evident that he has been drinking.*

As he climbs the few steps to the fire-escape landing light steals up inside. LAURA *appears in night-dress, observing* TOM's *empty bed in the front room.*

TOM *fishes in his pockets for the door-key, removing a motley assortment of articles in the search, including a perfect shower of movie-ticket stubs and an empty bottle. At last he finds the key, but just as he is about to insert it, it slips from his fingers. He strikes a match and crouches below the door.*

TOM *(bitterly)*: One crack—and it falls through!

LAURA *opens the door.*

LAURA: Tom! Tom, what are you doing?

TOM: Looking for a door-key.

LAURA: Where have you been all this time?

TOM: I have been to the movies.

LAURA: All this time at the movies?

TOM: There was a very long program. There was a Garbo picture and a Mickey Mouse and a travelogue and a newsreel and a preview of coming attractions. And there was an organ solo and a collection for the milk-fund—simultaneously—which ended up in a terrible fight between a fat lady and an usher!

LAURA *(innocently)*: Did you have to stay through everything?

TOM: Of course! And, oh, I forgot! There was a big stage show! The headliner on this stage show was Malvolio the Magician. He performed wonderful tricks, many of them, such as pouring water back and forth between pitchers. First it turned to wine and then it turned to beer and then it turned to whiskey. I know it was whiskey it finally turned into because he needed somebody to come up out of the audience to help him, and I came up— both shows! It was Kentucky Straight Bourbon. A very generous fellow, he gave souvenirs. *(He pulls from his back pocket a shimmering rainbow-colored scarf.)* He gave me this. This is his magic scarf. You can have it, Laura. You wave it over a canary cage and you get a bowl of gold-fish. You wave it over the gold-fish bowl and they fly away canaries. . . . But the wonderfullest trick of all was the coffin trick. We nailed him into a coffin and he got out of the coffin without removing one nail. *(He has come inside.)* There is a trick that would come in handy for me—get me out of this 2 by 4 situation! *(flops onto bed and starts removing shoes)*

LAURA: Tom—Shhh!

TOM: What you shushing me for?

LAURA: You'll wake up Mother.

TOM: Goody, goody! Pay 'er back for all those "Rise an' Shines." *(lies down, groaning)* You know it don't take much intelligence to get yourself into a nailed-up coffin, Laura. But who in hell ever got himself out of one without removing one nail?

As if in answer, the father's grinning photograph lights up.

(Scene Dims Out.)

Immediately following: The church bell is heard striking six. At the sixth stroke the alarm clock goes off in AMANDA's *room, and after a few moments we hear her calling: "Rise and Shine! Rise and Shine! Laura, go tell your brother to rise and shine!"*

TOM *(sitting up slowly)*: I'll rise—but I won't shine.

The light increases.

AMANDA: Laura, tell your brother his coffee is ready.

LAURA *slips into front room.*

LAURA: Tom! it's nearly seven. Don't make Mother nervous. *(He stares at her stupidly. Beseechingly.)* Tom, speak to Mother this morning. Make up with her, apologize, speak to her!

TOM: She won't to me. It's her that started not speaking.

LAURA: If you just say you're sorry she'll start speaking.

TOM: Her not speaking—is that such a tragedy?

LAURA: Please—please!

AMANDA *(calling from kitchenette)*: Laura, are you going to do what I asked you to do, or do I have to get dressed and go out myself?

LAURA: Going, going—soon as I get on my coat! *(She pulls on a shapeless felt hat with nervous, jerky movement, pleadingly glancing at* TOM. *Rushes awkwardly for coat. The coat is one* of AMANDA's *inaccurately made-over, the sleeves too short for* LAURA.) Butter and what else?

AMANDA *(entering upstage):* Just butter. Tell them to charge it.

LAURA: Mother, they make such faces when I do that.

AMANDA: Sticks and stones may break my bones, but the expression on Mr. Garfinkel's face won't harm us! Tell your brother his coffee is getting cold.

LAURA *(at door):* Do what I asked you, will you, will you, Tom?

He looks sullenly away.

AMANDA: Laura, go now or just don't go at all!

LAURA *(rushing out):* Going—going! *(A second later she cries out.* TOM *springs up and crosses to the door.* AMANDA *rushes anxiously in.* TOM *opens the door.)*

TOM: Laura?

LAURA: I'm all right. I slipped, but I'm all right.

AMANDA *(peering anxiously after her):* If anyone breaks a leg on those fire-escape steps, the landlord ought to be sued for every cent he possesses! *(She shuts door. Remembers she isn't speaking and returns to other room.)*

As TOM *enters listlessly for his coffee, she turns her back to him and stands rigidly facing the window on the gloomy gray vault of the areaway. Its light on her face with its aged but childish features is cruelly sharp, satirical as a Daumier print.*

(Music Under: "Ave Maria.")

TOM *glances sheepishly but sullenly at her averted figure and slumps at the table. The coffee is scalding hot; he sips it and gasps and spits it back in the cup. At his gasp,* AMANDA *catches her breath and half turns. Then catches herself and turns back to window.*

TOM *blows on his coffee, glancing sidewise at his mother. She clears her throat.* TOM *clears his. He starts to rise. Sinks back down again, scratches his head, clears his throat again.* AMANDA *coughs.* TOM *raises his cup in both hands to blow on it, his eyes staring over the rim of it at his mother for several moments. Then he slowly sets the cup down and awkwardly and hestitantly rises from the chair.*

TOM *(hoarsely):* Mother. I—I apologize. Mother. *(AMANDA *draws a quick, shuddering breath. Her face works grotesquely. She*

375

breaks into childlike tears.) I'm sorry for what I said, for everything that I said, I didn't mean it.

AMANDA *(sobbingly)*: My devotion has made me a witch and so I make myself hateful to my children!

TOM: No, you *don't*.

AMANDA: I worry so much, don't sleep, it makes me nervous!

TOM *(gently)*: I understand that.

AMANDA: I've had to put up a solitary battle all these years. But you're my right-hand bower! Don't fall down, don't fail!

TOM *(gently)*: I try, Mother.

AMANDA *(with great enthusiasm)*: Try and you will SUCCEED! *(The notion makes her breathless.)* Why, you—you're just *full* of natural endowments! Both of my children—they're *unusual* children! Don't you think I know it? I'm so—*proud!* Happy and—feel I've—so much to be thankful for but—Promise me one thing, son!

TOM: What, Mother?

AMANDA: Promise, son, you'll—never be a drunkard!

TOM *(turns to her grinning)*: I will never be a drunkard, Mother.

AMANDA: That's what frightened me so, that you'd be drinking! Eat a bowl of Purina!

TOM: Just coffee, Mother.

AMANDA: Shredded wheat biscuit?

TOM: No. No, Mother, just coffee.

AMANDA: You can't put in a day's work on an empty stomach. You've got ten minutes—don't gulp! Drinking too-hot liquids makes cancer of the stomach. . . . Put cream in.

TOM: No, thank you.

AMANDA: To cool it.

TOM: No! No, thank you, I want it black.

AMANDA: I know, but it's not good for you. We have to do all that we can to build ourselves up. In these trying times we live in, all that we have to cling to is—each other. . . . That's why it's so important to—Tom, I—I sent out your sister so I could discuss something with you. If you hadn't spoken I would have spoken to you. *(Sits down.)*

TOM *(gently)*: What is it, Mother, that you want to discuss?

AMANDA: Laura!

TOM *puts his cup down slowly.*

(Legend On Screen: "Laura.")

(Music: "The Glass Menagerie.")

TOM: —Oh.—Laura . . .

AMANDA *(touching his sleeve)*: You know how Laura is. So quiet but—still water runs deep! She notices things and I think she—broods about them. (TOM *looks up.*) A few days ago I came in and she was crying.

TOM: What about?

AMANDA: You.

TOM: Me?

AMANDA: She has an idea that you're not happy here.

TOM: What gave her that idea?

AMANDA: What gives her any idea? However, you do act strangely. I—I'm not criticizing, understand *that!* I know your ambitions do not lie in the warehouse, that like everybody in the whole wide world—you've had to—make sacrifices, but—Tom—Tom—life's not easy, it calls for—Spartan endurance! There's so many things in my heart that I cannot describe to you! I've never told you but I—*loved* your father. . . .

TOM *(gently)*: I know that, Mother.

AMANDA: And you—when I see you taking after his ways! Staying out late—and—well, you *had* been drinking the night you were in that—terrifying condition! Laura says that you hate the apartment and that you go out nights to get away from it! Is that true, Tom?

TOM: No. You say there's so much in your heart that you can't describe to me. That's true of me, too. There's so much in my heart that I can't describe to *you!* So let's respect each other's—

AMANDA: But, why—*why,* Tom—are you always so *restless?* Where do you go to, nights?

TOM: I—go to the movies.

AMANDA: Why do you go to the movies so much, Tom?

TOM: I go to the movies because—I like adventure. Adventure is something I don't have much of at work, so I go to the movies.

AMANDA: But, Tom, you go to the movies *entirely* too *much!*

TOM: I like a lot of adventure.

AMANDA *looks baffled, then hurt. As the familiar inquisition resumes he becomes hard and impatient again.* AMANDA *slips back into her querulous attitude toward him.*

(Image On Screen: Sailing Vessel With Jolly Roger.)

AMANDA: Most young men find adventure in their careers.

TOM: Then most young men are not employed in a warehouse.

AMANDA: The world is full of young men employed in warehouses and offices and factories.

TOM: Do all of them find adventure in their careers?

AMANDA: They do or they do without it! Not everybody has a craze for adventure.

TOM: Man is by instinct a lover, a hunter, a fighter, and none of those instincts are given much play at the warehouse!

AMANDA: Man is by instinct! Don't quote instinct to me! Instinct is something that people have got away from! It belongs to animals! Christian adults don't want it!

TOM: What do Christian adults want, then, Mother?

AMANDA: Superior things! Things of the mind and the spirit! Only animals have to satisfy instincts! Surely your aims are somewhat higher than theirs! Than monkeys—pigs—

TOM: I reckon they're not.

AMANDA: You're joking. However, that isn't what I wanted to discuss.

TOM *(rising)*: I haven't much time.

AMANDA *(pushing his shoulders)*: Sit down.

TOM: You want me to punch in red at the warehouse, Mother?

AMANDA: You have five minutes. I want to talk about Laura.

(Legend: "Plans And Provisions.")

TOM: All right! What about Laura?

AMANDA: We have to be making plans and provisions for her. She's older than you, two years, and nothing has happened. She just drifts along doing nothing. It frightens me terribly how she just drifts along.

TOM: I guess she's the type that people call home girls.

AMANDA: There's no such type, and if there is, it's a pity! That is unless the home is hers, with a husband!

TOM: What?

AMANDA: Oh, I can see the handwriting on the wall as plain as I see the nose in front of my face! It's terrifying! More and more you remind me of your father! He was out all hours without explanation—Then *left! Goodbye!* And me with the bag to hold. I saw that letter you got from the Merchant Marine. I know what you're dreaming of. I'm not standing here blindfolded. Very well, then. Then *do* it! But not till there's somebody to take your place.

TOM: What do you mean?

AMANDA: I mean that as soon as Laura has got somebody to take care of her, married, a home of her own, independent—why, then you'll be free to go wherever you please, on land, on sea, whichever way the wind blows! But until that time you've got to look out for your sister. I don't say me because I'm old and don't matter! I say for your sister because she's young and dependent. I put her in business college—a dismal failure! Frightened her so it made her sick to her stomach. I took her over to the Young People's League at the church. Another fiasco. She spoke to nobody, nobody spoke to her. Now all she does is fool with those pieces of glass and play those worn-out records. What kind of a life is that for a girl to lead!

TOM: What can I do about it?

AMANDA: Overcome selfishness! Self, self, self is all that you ever think of! (TOM *springs up and crosses to get his coat. It is ugly and bulky. He pulls on a cap with earmuffs.*) Where is your muffler? Put your wool muffler on! (*He snatches it angrily from the closet and tosses it around his neck and pulls both ends tight.*) Tom! I haven't said what I had in mind to ask you.

TOM: I'm too late to—

AMANDA (*Catching his arms—very importunately. Then shyly*): Down at the warehouse, aren't there some—nice young men?

TOM: No!

AMANDA: There *must* be—*some* . . .

TOM: Mother—

Gesture.

AMANDA: Find out one that's clean-living—doesn't drink and—ask him out for sister!

TOM: What?

AMANDA: For *sister!* To *meet!* Get *acquainted!*

TOM (*stamping to door*): Oh, my *go-osh!*

AMANDA: Will you? (*He opens door. Imploringly.*) Will you?
(*He starts down.*) Will you? *Will* you, dear?

TOM (*calling back*): YES!

AMANDA *closes the door hesitantly and with a troubled but faintly
hopeful expression.*

(Screen Image: Glamour Magazine Cover.)

Spot AMANDA *at phone.*

AMANDA: Ella Cartwright? This is Amanda Wingfield! How are
you, honey? How is that kidney condition? (*count five*) *Horrors!* (*count five*) You're a Christian martyr, yes, honey, that's
what you are, a Christian martyr! Well, I just happened to notice
in my little red book that your subscription to the *Companion*
has just run out! I knew that you wouldn't want to miss out on
the wonderful serial starting in this new issue. It's by Bessie Mae
Hopper, the first thing she's written since *Honeymoon for Three.*
Wasn't that a strange and interesting story? Well, this one is
even lovelier, I believe. It has a sophisticated society background.
It's all about the horsey set on Long Island!

(Fade Out.)

SCENE V

(Legend On Screen: "Annunciation.") *Fade with music.*

*It is early dusk of a spring evening. Supper has just been finished
in the Wingfield apartment.* AMANDA *and* LAURA *in light colored
dresses are removing dishes from the table, in the upstage area,
which is shadowy, their movements formalized almost as a dance
or ritual, their moving forms as pale and silent as moths.*

TOM, *in white shirt and trousers, rises from the table and crosses
toward the fire-escape.*

AMANDA (*as he passes her*): Son, will you do me a favor?

TOM: What?

AMANDA: Comb your hair! You look so pretty when your hair is combed! (TOM *slouches on sofa with evening paper. Enormous caption "Franco Triumphs."*) There is only one respect in which I would like you to emulate your father.

TOM: What respect is that?

AMANDA: The care he always took of his appearance. He never allowed himself to look untidy. (*He throws down the paper and crosses to fire-escape.*) Where are you going?

TOM: I'm going out to smoke.

AMANDA: You smoke too much. A pack a day at fifteen cents a pack. How much would that amount to in a month? Thirty times fifteen is how much, Tom? Figure it out and you will be astounded at what you could save. Enough to give you a night-school course in accounting at Washington U! Just think what a wonderful thing that would be for you, son!

TOM *is unmoved by the thought.*

TOM: I'd rather smoke. (*He steps out on landing, letting the screen door slam.*)

AMANDA (*sharply*): I know! That's the tragedy of it. . . . (*Alone, she turns to look at her husband's picture.*)

(Dance Music: "All The World Is Waiting For The Sunrise.")

TOM (*to the audience*): Across the alley from us was the Paradise Dance Hall. On evenings in spring the windows and doors were open and the music came outdoors. Sometimes the lights were turned out except for a large glass sphere that hung from the ceiling. It would turn slowly about and filter the dusk with delicate rainbow colors. Then the orchestra played a waltz or a tango, something that had a slow and sensuous rhythm. Couples would come outside, to the relative privacy of the alley. You could see them kissing behind ash-pits and telephone poles. This was the compensation for lives that passed like mine, without any change or adventure. Adventure and change were imminent in this year. They were waiting around the corner for all these kids. Suspended in the mist over Berchtesgaden, caught in the folds of Chamberlain's umbrella—In Spain there was Guernica! But here there was only hot swing music and liquor, dance halls, bars, and movies, and sex that hung in the gloom like a chandelier and flooded the world with brief, deceptive rainbows. . . . All the world was waiting for bombardments!

AMANDA *turns from the picture and comes outside.*

AMANDA *(sighing)*: A fire-escape landing's a poor excuse for a porch. *(She spreads a newspaper on a step and sits down, gracefully and demurely as if she were settling into a swing on a Mississippi veranda.)* What are you looking at?

TOM: The moon.

AMANDA: Is there a moon this evening?

TOM: It's rising over Garfinkel's Delicatessen.

AMANDA: So it is! A little silver slipper of a moon. Have you made a wish on it yet?

TOM: Um-hum.

AMANDA: What did you wish for?

TOM: That's a secret.

AMANDA: A secret, huh? Well, I won't tell mine either. I will be just as mysterious as you.

TOM: I bet I can guess what yours is.

AMANDA: Is my head so transparent?

TOM: You're not a sphinx.

AMANDA: No, I don't have secrets. I'll tell you what I wished for on the moon. Success and happiness for my precious children! I wish for that whenever there's a moon, and when there isn't a moon, I wish for it, too.

TOM: I thought perhaps you wished for a gentleman caller.

AMANDA: Why do you say that?

TOM: Don't you remember asking me to fetch one?

AMANDA: I remember suggesting that it would be nice for your sister if you brought home some nice young man from the warehouse. I think I've made that suggestion more than once.

TOM: Yes, you have made it repeatedly.

AMANDA: Well?

TOM: We are going to have one.

AMANDA: What?

TOM: A gentleman caller!

(The Annunciation Is Celebrated With Music.)

AMANDA *rises.*

(Image On Screen: Caller With Bouquet.)

AMANDA: You mean you have asked some nice young man to come over?

TOM: Yep. I've asked him to dinner.

AMANDA: You really did?

TOM: I did!

AMANDA: You did, and did he—*accept?*

TOM: He did!

AMANDA: Well, well—well, well! That's—lovely!

TOM: I thought that you would be pleased.

AMANDA: It's definite, then?

TOM: Very definite.

AMANDA: Soon?

TOM: Very soon.

AMANDA: For heaven's sake, stop putting on and tell me some things, will you?

TOM: What things do you want me to tell you?

AMANDA: Naturally I would like to know when he's *coming!*

TOM: He's coming tomorrow.

AMANDA: *Tomorrow?*

TOM: Yep. Tomorrow.

AMANDA: But, Tom!

TOM: Yes, Mother?

AMANDA: Tomorrow gives me no time!

TOM: Time for what?

AMANDA: Preparations! Why didn't you phone me at once, as soon as you asked him, the minute that he accepted? Then, don't you see, I could have been getting ready!

TOM: You don't have to make any fuss.

AMANDA: Oh, Tom, Tom, Tom, of course I have to make a fuss! I want things nice, not sloppy! Not thrown together. I'll certainly have to do some fast thinking, won't I?

TOM: I don't see why you have to think at all.

AMANDA: You just don't know. We can't have a gentleman caller in a pig-sty! All my wedding silver has to be polished, the monogrammed table linen ought to be laundered! The windows have to be washed and fresh curtains put up. And how about clothes? We have to *wear* something, don't we?

TOM: Mother, this boy is no one to make a fuss over!

AMANDA: Do you realize he's the first young man we've introduced to your sister? It's terrible, dreadful, disgraceful that poor little sister has never received a single gentleman caller! Tom, come inside! *(She opens the screen door.)*

TOM: What for?

AMANDA: I want to ask you some things.

TOM: If you're going to make such a fuss, I'll call it off, I'll tell him not to come.

AMANDA: You certainly won't do anything of the kind. Nothing offends people worse than broken engagements. It simply means I'll have to work like a Turk! We won't be brilliant, but we'll pass inspection. Come on inside. (TOM *follows, groaning.)* Sit down.

TOM: Any particular place you would like me to sit?

AMANDA: Thank heavens I've got that new sofa! I'm also making payments on a floor lamp I'll have sent out! And put the chintz covers on, they'll brighten things up! Of course I'd hoped to have these walls re-papered. . . . What is the young man's name?

TOM: His name is O'Connor.

AMANDA: That, of course, means fish—tomorrow is Friday! I'll have that salmon loaf—with Durkee's dressing! What does he do? He works at the warehouse?

TOM: Of course! How else would I—

AMANDA: Tom, he—doesn't drink?

TOM: Why do you ask me that?

AMANDA: Your father *did!*

TOM: Don't get started on that!

AMANDA: He *does* drink, then?

TOM: Not that I know of!

AMANDA: Make sure, be certain! The last thing I want for my daughter's a boy who drinks!

TOM: Aren't you being a little premature? Mr. O'Connor has not yet appeared on the scene!

AMANDA: But will tomorrow. To meet your sister, and what do I know about his character? Nothing! Old maids are better off than wives of drunkards!

TOM: Oh, my God!

AMANDA: Be still!

TOM *(leaning forward to whisper)*: Lots of fellows meet girls whom they don't marry!

AMANDA: Oh, talk sensibly, Tom—and don't be sarcastic! *(She has gotten a hairbrush.)*

TOM: What are you doing?

AMANDA: I'm brushing that cow-lick down! What is this young man's position at the warehouse?

TOM *(submitting grimly to the brush and the interrogation)*: This young man's position is that of a shipping clerk, Mother.

AMANDA: Sounds to me like a fairly responsible job, the sort of a job *you* would be in if you just had more *get-up*. What is his salary? Have you got any idea?

TOM: I would judge it to be approximately eighty-five dollars a month.

AMANDA: Well—not princely, but—

TOM: Twenty more than I make.

AMANDA: Yes, how well I know! But for a family man, eight-five dollars a month is not much more than you can just get by on. . . .

TOM: Yes, but Mr. O'Connor is not a family man.

AMANDA: He might be, mightn't he? Some time in the future?

TOM: I see. Plans and provisions.

AMANDA: You are the only young man that I know of who ignores the fact that the future becomes the present, the present the past, and the past turns into everlasting regret if you don't plan for it!

TOM: I will think that over and see what I can make of it.

AMANDA: Don't be supercilious with your mother! Tell me some more about this—what do you call him?

TOM: James D. O'Connor. The D. is for Delaney.

AMANDA: Irish on *both* sides! *Gracious!* And doesn't drink?

TOM: Shall I call him up and ask him right this minute?

AMANDA: The only way to find out about those things is to make discreet inquiries at the proper moment. When I was a girl in Blue Mountain and it was suspected that a young man drank, the girl whose attentions he had been receiving, if any girl *was,* would sometimes speak to the minister of his church, or rather her father would if her father was living, and sort of feel him out on the young man's character. That is the way such things are discreetly handled to keep a young woman from making a tragic mistake!

TOM: Then how did you happen to make a tragic mistake?

AMANDA: That innocent look of your father's had everyone fooled! He *smiled*—the world was *enchanted!* No girl can do worse than put herself at the mercy of a handsome appearance! I hope that Mr. O'Connor is not too good-looking.

TOM: No, he's not too good-looking. He's covered with freckles and hasn't too much of a nose.

AMANDA: He's not right-down homely, though?

TOM: Not right-down homely. Just medium homely, I'd say.

AMANDA: Character's what to look for in a man.

TOM: That's what I've always said, Mother.

AMANDA: You've never said anything of the kind and I suspect you would never give it a thought.

TOM: Don't be suspicious of me.

AMANDA: At least I hope he's the type that's up and coming.

TOM: I think he really goes in for self-improvement.

AMANDA: What reason have you to think so?

TOM: He goes to night school.

AMANDA (*beaming*): Splendid! What does he do, I mean study?

TOM: Radio engineering and public speaking!

AMANDA: Then he has visions of being advanced in the world! Any young man who studies public speaking is aiming to have an executive job some day! And radio engineering? A thing for the future! Both of these facts are very illuminating. Those are the sort of things that a mother should know concerning any young man who comes to call on her daughter. Seriously or—not.

TOM: One little warning. He doesn't know about Laura. I didn't let on that we had dark ulterior motives. I just said, why don't you come have dinner with us? He said okay and that was the whole conversation.

AMANDA: I bet it was! You're eloquent as an oyster. However, he'll know about Laura when he gets here. When he sees how lovely and sweet and pretty she is, he'll thank his lucky stars he was asked to dinner.

TOM: Mother, you mustn't expect too much of Laura.

AMANDA: What do you mean?

TOM: Laura seems all those things to you and me because she's ours and we love her. We don't even notice she's crippled any more.

AMANDA: Don't say crippled! You know that I never allow that word to be used!

TOM: But face facts, Mother. She is and—that's not all—

AMANDA: What do you mean "not all"?

TOM: Laura is very different from other girls.

AMANDA: I think the difference is all to her advantage.

TOM: Not quite all—in the eyes of others—strangers—she's terribly shy and lives in a world of her own and those things make her seem a little peculiar to people outside the house.

AMANDA: Don't say peculiar.

TOM: Face the facts. She is.

(The Dance-hall Music Changes To A Tango That Has A Minor And Somewhat Ominous Tone.)

AMANDA: In what way is she peculiar—may I ask?

TOM *(gently)*: She lives in a world of her own—a world of—little glass ornaments, Mother. . . . *(Gets up.* AMANDA *remains holding brush, looking at him, troubled.)* She plays old phonograph records and—that's about all—*(He glances at himself in the mirror and crosses to door.)*

AMANDA *(sharply)*: Where are you going?

TOM: I'm going to the movies. *(out screen door)*

AMANDA: Not to the movies, every night to the movies! *(follows quickly to screen door)* I don't believe you always go to the movies! *(He is gone.* AMANDA *looks worriedly after him for a moment. Then vitality and optimism return and she turns from the door. Crossing to portieres.)* Laura! Laura! *(*LAURA *answers from kitchenette.)*

LAURA: Yes, Mother.

AMANDA: Let those dishes go and come in front! *(*LAURA *appears with dish towel. Gaily.)* Laura, come here and make a wish on the moon!

LAURA *(entering)*: Moon—moon?

AMANDA: A little silver slipper of a moon. Look over your left shoulder, Laura, and make a wish! *(*LAURA *looks faintly puzzled* *as if called out of sleep.* AMANDA *seizes her shoulders and turns her at an angle by the door.)* Now! Now, darling, *wish!*

LAURA: What shall I wish for, Mother?

AMANDA *(her voice trembling and her eyes suddenly filling with tears)*: Happiness! Good Fortune!

The violin rises and the stage dims out.

SCENE VI

(Image: High-School Hero.)

TOM: And so the following evening I brought Jim home to dinner. I had known Jim slightly in high school. In high school Jim was a hero. He had tremendous Irish good nature and vitality with the scrubbed and polished look of white chinaware. He seemed to move in a continual spotlight. He was a star in basketball, captain of the debating club, president of the senior class and the glee club and he sang the male lead in the annual light operas. He was always running or bounding, never just walking. He seemed always at the point of defeating the law of gravity. He was shooting with such velocity through his adolescence that you would logically expect him to arrive at nothing short of the White House by the time he was thirty. But Jim apparently ran into more interference after his graduation from Soldan. His speed had definitely slowed. Six years after he left high school he was holding a job that wasn't much better than mine.

(Image: Clerk.)

He was the only one at the warehouse with whom I was on friendly terms. I was valuable to him as someone who could remember his former glory, who had seen him win basketball games and the silver cup in debating. He knew of my secret practice of retiring to a cabinet of the washroom to work on poems when business was slack in the warehouse. He called me Shakespeare. And while the other boys in the warehouse regarded me with suspicious hostility, Jim took a humorous attitude toward me. Gradually his attitude affected the others, their hostility wore off and they also began to smile at me as people smile at an oddly fashioned dog who trots across their path at some distance.

I knew that Jim and Laura had known each other at Soldan, and I had heard Laura speak admiringly of his voice. I didn't know if Jim remembered her or not. In high school Laura had been as unobtrusive as Jim had been astonishing. If he did remember Laura, it was not as my sister, for when I asked him to dinner, he grinned and said, "You know, Shakespeare, I never thought of you as having folks!"

He was about to discover that I did. . . .

(Light Up Stage.)

(Legend On Screen: "The Accent Of A Coming Foot.")

Friday evening. It is about five o'clock of a late spring evening which comes "scattering poems in the sky."

A delicate lemony light is in the Wingfield apartment.

AMANDA *has worked like a Turk in preparation for the gentleman caller. The results are astonishing. The new floor lamp with its rose-silk shade is in place, a colored paper lantern conceals the broken light fixture in the ceiling, new billowing white curtains are at the windows, chintz covers are on chairs and sofa, a pair of new sofa pillows make their initial appearance.*

Open boxes and tissue paper are scattered on the floor.

LAURA *stands in the middle with lifted arms while* AMANDA *crouches before her, adjusting the hem of the new dress, devout and ritualistic. The dress is colored and designed by memory. The arrangement of Laura's hair is changed; it is softer and more becoming. A fragile, unearthly prettiness has come out in* LAURA: *she is like a piece of translucent glass touched by light, given a momentary radiance, not actual, not lasting.*

AMANDA *(impatiently)*: Why are you trembling?

LAURA: Mother, you've made me so nervous!

AMANDA: How have I made you nervous?

LAURA: By all this fuss! You make it seem so important!

AMANDA: I don't understand you, Laura. You couldn't be satisfied with just sitting home, and yet whenever I try to arrange something for you, you seem to resist it. *(She gets up.)* Now take a look at yourself. No, wait! Wait just a moment—I have an idea!

LAURA: What is it now?

AMANDA *produces two powder puffs which she wraps in handkerchiefs and stuffs in* LAURA's *bosom.*

LAURA: Mother, what are you doing?

AMANDA: They call them "Gay Deceivers"!

LAURA: I won't wear them!

AMANDA: You will!

LAURA: Why should I?

AMANDA: Because, to be painfully honest, your chest is flat.

LAURA: You make it seem like we were setting a trap.

AMANDA: All pretty girls are a trap, a pretty trap, and men expect them to be. (*Legend: "A Pretty Trap."*) Now look at yourself, young lady. This is the prettiest you will ever be! I've got to fix myself now! You're going to be surprised by your mother's appearance! (*She crosses through portieres, humming gaily.*)

LAURA *moves slowly to the long mirror and stares solemnly at herself.*

A wind blows the white curtains inward in a slow, graceful motion and with a faint, sorrowful sighing.

AMANDA (*offstage*): It isn't dark enough yet. (*She turns slowly before the mirror with a troubled look.*)

(Legend On Screen: "This Is My Sister: Celebrate Her With Strings!" Music.)

AMANDA (*laughing off*): I'm going to show you something. I'm going to make a spectacular appearance!

LAURA: What is it, Mother?

AMANDA: Possess your soul in patience—you will see! Something I've resurrected from that old trunk! Styles haven't changed so terribly much after all. . . . (*She parts the portieres.*) Now just look at your mother! (*She wears a girlish frock of yellowed voile with a blue silk sash. She carries a bunch of jonquils—the legend of her youth is nearly revived. Feverishly.*) This is the dress in which I led the cotillion. Won the cakewalk twice at Sunset Hill, wore one spring to the Governor's ball in Jackson! See how I sashayed around the ballroom, Laura? (*She raises her skirt and does a mincing step around the room.*) I wore it on Sundays for my gentlemen callers! I had it on the day I met your father—I had malaria fever all that spring. The change of climate from East Tennessee to the Delta—weakened resistance—I had a little temperature all the time—not enough to be serious—just enough to make me restless and giddy! Invitations poured in— parties all over the Delta!—"Stay in bed," said Mother, "you have fever!"—but I just wouldn't.—I took quinine but kept on going, going!—Evenings, dances!—Afternoons, long, long rides! Picnics—lovely!—So lovely, that country in May.—All lacy with dogwood, literally flooded with jonquils!—That was the spring I had the craze for jonquils. Jonquils became an absolute obsession. Mother said, "Honey, there's no more room for jonquils." And still I kept bringing in more jonquils. Whenever, wherever I saw them, I'd say, "Stop! Stop! I see jonquils." I made the young men help me gather the jonquils! It was a joke, Amanda and her jonquils! Finally there were no more vases to hold them, every available space was filled with jonquils. No vases to hold them? All right, I'll hold them myself! And then I—*(She stops in front of the picture.) (Music)* met your father! Malaria fever and jonquils and then—this—boy.... *(She switches on the rose-colored lamp.)* I hope they get here before it starts to rain. *(She crosses upstage and places the jonquils in bowl on table.)* I gave your brother a little extra change so he and Mr. O'Connor could take the service car home.

LAURA *(with altered look)*: What did you say his name was?
AMANDA: O'Connor.
LAURA: What is his first name?
AMANDA: I don't remember. Oh, yes, I do. It was—Jim!

Laura sways slightly and catches hold of a chair.

(Legend On Screen: "Not Jim!")

LAURA *(faintly)*: Not—Jim!
AMANDA: Yes, that was it, it was Jim! I've never known a Jim that wasn't nice!

(Music: Ominous.)

LAURA: Are you sure his name is Jim O'Connor?
AMANDA: Yes. Why?
LAURA: Is he the one that Tom used to know in high school?

AMANDA: He didn't say so. I think he just got to know him at the warehouse.

LAURA: There was a Jim O'Connor we both knew in high school— *(Then, with effort.)* If that is the one that Tom is bringing to dinner—you'll have to excuse me, I won't come to the table.

AMANDA: What sort of nonsense is this?

LAURA: You asked me once if I'd ever liked a boy. Don't you remember I showed you this boy's picture?

AMANDA: You mean the boy you showed me in the year book?

LAURA: Yes, that boy.

AMANDA: Laura, Laura, were you in love with that boy?

LAURA: I don't know, Mother. All I know is I couldn't sit at the table if it was him!

AMANDA: It won't be him! It isn't the least bit likely. But whether it is or not, you will come to the table. You will not be excused.

LAURA: I'll have to be, Mother.

AMANDA: I don't intend to humor your silliness, Laura. I've had too much from you and your brother, both! So just sit down and compose yourself till they come. Tom has forgotten his key so you'll have to let them in, when they arrive.

LAURA *(panicky)*: Oh, Mother—*you* answer the door!

AMANDA *(lightly)*: I'll be in the kitchen—busy!

LAURA: Oh, Mother, please answer the door, don't make me do it!

AMANDA *(crossing into kitchenette)*: I've got to fix the dressing for the salmon. Fuss, fuss—silliness!—over a gentleman caller!

Door swings, shut. LAURA is left alone.

(Legend: "Terror!")

She utters a low moan and turns off the lamp—sits stiffly on the edge of the sofa, knotting her fingers together.

(Legend On Screen: "The Opening Of A Door!")

TOM *and* JIM *appear on the fire-escape steps and climb to landing. Hearing their approach, LAURA rises with a panicky gesture. She retreats to the portieres.*

The doorbell. Laura catches her breath and touches her throat. Low drums.

AMANDA *(calling)*: Laura, sweetheart! The door!

LAURA *stares at it without moving.*

JIM: I think we just beat the rain.

TOM: Uh-huh. *(He rings again, nervously.* JIM *whistles and fishes for a cigarette.)*

AMANDA *(very, very gaily)*: Laura, that is your brother and Mr. O'Connor! Will you let them in, darling?

LAURA *crosses toward kitchenette door.*

LAURA *(breathlessly)*: Mother—you go to the door!

AMANDA *steps out of kitchenette and stares furiously at Laura. She points imperiously at the door.*

LAURA: Please, please!

AMANDA *(in a fierce whisper)*: What is the matter with you, you silly thing?

LAURA *(desperately)*: Please, you answer it, *please!*

AMANDA: I told you I wasn't going to humor you, Laura. Why have you chosen this moment to lose your mind?

LAURA: Please, please, please, you go!

AMANDA: You'll have to go to the door because I can't!

LAURA *(despairingly)*: I can't either!

AMANDA: Why?

LAURA: I'm *sick!*

AMANDA: I'm sick too—of your nonsense! Why can't you and your brother be normal people? Fantastic whims and behavior! *(TOM gives a long ring.)* Preposterous goings on! Can you give me one reason—*(calls out lyrically)* COMING! JUST ONE SECOND!—why should you be afraid to open a door? Now you answer it, Laura!

LAURA: Oh, oh, oh . . . *(She returns through the portieres. Darts to the victrola and winds it frantically and turns it on.)*

AMANDA: Laura Wingfield, you march right to that door!

LAURA: Yes—yes, Mother!

A faraway, scratchy rendition of "Dardanella" softens the air and gives her strength to move through it. She slips to the door and draws it cautiously open. TOM *enters with the caller,* JIM O'CONNOR.

TOM: Laura, this is Jim. Jim, this is my sister, Laura.

JIM *(stepping inside)*: I didn't know that Shakespeare had a sister!

LAURA *(retreating stiff and trembling from the door)*: How—how do you do?

JIM *(heartily extending his hand)*: Okay!

LAURA *touches it hesitantly with hers.*

JIM: Your hand's *cold*, Laura!

LAURA: Yes, well—I've been playing the victrola. . . .

JIM: Must have been playing classical music on it! You ought to play a little hot swing music to warm you up!

LAURA: Excuse me—I haven't finished playing the victrola. . . .

She turns awkwardly and hurries into the front room. She pauses a second by the victrola. Then catches her breath and darts through the portieres like a frightened deer.

JIM *(grinning)*: What was the matter?

TOM: Oh—with Laura? Laura is—terribly shy.

JIM: Shy, huh? It's unusual to meet a shy girl nowadays. I don't believe you ever mentioned you had a sister.

TOM: Well, now you know. I have one. Here is the *Post Dispatch*. You want a piece of it?

JIM: Uh-huh.

TOM: What piece? The comics?

JIM: Sports! *(glances at it)* Ole Dizzy Dean is on his bad behavior.

TOM *(disinterest)*: Yeah? *(lights cigarette and crosses back to fire-escape door)*

JIM: Where are *you* going?

TOM: I'm going out on the terrace.

JIM *(goes after him)*: You know, Shakespeare—I'm going to sell you a bill of goods!

TOM: What goods?

JIM: A course I'm taking.

TOM: Huh?

JIM: In public speaking! You and me, we're not the warehouse type.

TOM: Thanks—that's good news. But what has public speaking got to do with it?

JIM: It fits you for—executive positions!

TOM: Awww.

JIM: I tell you it's done a helluva lot for me.

(Image: Executive At Desk.)

TOM: In what respect?

JIM: In every! Ask yourself what is the difference between you an' me and men in the office down front? Brains?—No!—Ability?—No! Then what? Just one little thing—

TOM: What is that one little thing?

JIM: Primarily it amounts to—social poise! Being able to square up to people and hold your own on any social level!

AMANDA *(offstage)*: Tom?

TOM: Yes, Mother?

AMANDA: Is that you and Mr. O'Connor?

TOM: Yes, Mother.

AMANDA: Well, you just make yourselves comfortable in there.

TOM: Yes, Mother.

AMANDA: Ask Mr. O'Connor if he would like to wash his hands.

JIM: Aw—no—thank you—I took care of that at the warehouse. Tom—

TOM: Yes?

JIM: Mr. Mendoza was speaking to me about you.

TOM: Favorably?

JIM: What do you think?

TOM: Well—

JIM: You're going to be out of a job if you don't wake up.

TOM: I am waking up—

JIM: You show no signs.

TOM: The signs are interior.

(Image On Screen: The Sailing Vessel With Jolly Roger Again.)

TOM: I'm planning to change. *(He leans over the rail speaking with quiet exhilaration. The incandescent marquees and signs of the first-run movie houses light his face from across the alley. He looks like a voyager.)* I'm right at the point of committing myself to a future that doesn't include the warehouse and Mr. Mendoza or even a night-school course in public speaking.

JIM: What are you gassing about?

TOM: I'm tired of the movies.

JIM: Movies!

TOM: Yes, movies! Look at them—*(a wave toward the marvels of Grand Avenue)* All of those glamorous people—having adventures—hogging it all, gobbling the whole thing up! You know what happens? People go to the *movies* instead of *moving!* Hollywood characters are supposed to have all the adventures for everybody in America, while everybody in America sits in a dark room and watches them have them! Yes, until there's a war. That's when adventure becomes available to the masses! *Everyone's* dish, not only Gable's! Then the people in the dark room come out of the dark room to have some adventures themselves—Goody, goody—It's our turn now, to go to the South Sea Island—to make a safari—to be exotic, far-off—But I'm not patient. I don't want to wait till then. I'm tired of the *movies* and I am *about* to *move!*

JIM *(incredulously)*: Move?

TOM: Yes.

JIM: When?

TOM: Soon!

JIM: Where? Where?

Theme three music seems to answer the question, while TOM *thinks it over. He searches among his pockets.*

TOM: I'm starting to boil inside. I know I seem dreamy, but inside—well, I'm boiling! Whenever I pick up a shoe, I shudder a little thinking how short life is and what I am doing!—Whatever that means. I know it doesn't mean shoes—except as something to wear on a traveler's feet! *(finds paper)* Look—

JIM: What?

TOM: I'm a member.

JIM *(reading)*: The Union of Merchant Seamen.

TOM: I paid my dues this month, instead of the light bill.

JIM: You will regret it when they turn the lights off.

TOM: I won't be here.

JIM: How about your mother?

TOM: I'm like my father. The bastard son of a bastard! See how he grins? And he's been absent going on sixteen years!

JIM: You're just talking, you drip. How does your mother feel about it?

TOM: Shhh—Here comes Mother! Mother is not acquainted with my plans!

AMANDA *(enters portieres)*: Where are you all?

TOM: On the terrace, Mother.

They start inside. She advances to them. TOM *is distinctly shocked at her appearance. Even* JIM *blinks a little. He is making his first contact with girlish Southern vivacity and in spite of the night-school course in public speaking is somewhat thrown off the beam by the unexpected outlay of social charm.*

Certain responses are attempted by JIM *but are swept aside by* AMANDA'*s gay laughter and chatter.* TOM *is embarrassed but after the first shock* JIM *reacts very warmly. Grins and chuckles, is altogether won over.*

(Image: Amanda As A Girl.)

AMANDA *(coyly smiling, shaking her girlish ringlets)*: Well, well, well, so this is Mr. O'Connor. Introductions entirely unnecessary. I've heard so much about you from my boy. I finally said to him, Tom—good gracious!—why don't you bring this paragon to supper? I'd like to meet this nice young man at the warehouse!—Instead of just hearing him sing your praises so much! I don't know why my son is so stand-offish—that's not Southern behavior! Let's sit down and—I think we could stand a little more air in here! Tom, leave the door open. I felt a nice fresh breeze a moment ago. Where has it gone? Mmm, so warm already! And not quite summer, even. We're going to burn up when summer really gets started. However, we're having—we're having a very light supper. I think light things are better fo' this time of year. The same as light clothes are. Light clothes an' light food are what warm weather calls fo'. You know our blood gets so thick during th' winter—it takes a while fo' us to *adjust* ou'selves!—when the season changes . . . It's come so quick this year. I wasn't prepared. All of a sudden—heavens! Already summer!—I ran to the trunk an' pulled out this light dress—Terribly old! Historical almost! But feels so good—so good an' co-ol, y'know. . . .

TOM: Mother—

AMANDA: Yes, honey?

TOM: How about—supper?

AMANDA: Honey, you go ask Sister if supper is ready! You know that Sister is in full charge of supper! Tell her you hungry boys are waiting for it. *(To* JIM.*)* Have you met Laura?

JIM: She—

AMANDA: Let you in? Oh, good, you've met already! It's rare for a girl as sweet an' pretty as Laura to be domestic! But Laura is, thank heavens, not only pretty but also very domestic. I'm not at all. I never was a bit. I never could make a thing but angel-food cake. Well, in the South we had so many servants. Gone, gone, gone. All vestiges of gracious living! Gone completely! I wasn't prepared for what the future brought me. All of my gentlemen callers were sons of planters and so of course I assumed that I would be married to one and raise my family on a large piece of land with plenty of servants. But man proposes— and woman accepts the proposal!—To vary that old, old saying a little bit—I married no planter! I married a man who worked for the telephone company!— that gallantly smiling gentleman over there! *(points to the picture)* A telephone man who—fell in love with long-distance!—Now he travels and I don't even know where!—But what am I going on for about my—tribulations? Tell me yours—I hope you don't have any! Tom?

TOM *(returning)*: Yes, Mother?

AMANDA: Is supper nearly ready?

TOM: It looks to me like supper is on the table.

AMANDA: Let me look—*(She rises prettily and looks through portieres.)* Oh, lovely—But where is Sister?

TOM: Laura is not feeling well and she says that she thinks she'd better not come to the table.

AMANDA: What?—Nonsense!—Laura? Oh, Laura!

LAURA *(offstage, faintly)*: Yes, Mother.

AMANDA: You really must come to the table. We won't be seated until you come to the table! Come in, Mr. O'Connor. You sit over there and I'll—Laura? Laura Wingfield! You're keeping us waiting, honey! We can't say grace until you come to the table!

The back door is pushed weakly open and LAURA *comes in. She is obviously quite faint, her lips trembling, her eyes wide and staring. She moves unsteadily toward the table.*

(Legend: "Terror!")

Outside a summer storm is coming abruptly. The white curtains billow inward at the windows and there is a sorrowful murmur and deep blue dusk.

LAURA *suddenly stumbles—She catches at a chair with a faint moan.*

TOM: Laura!

AMANDA: Laura! *(There is a clap of thunder.)* (**Legend: "Ah!"**) *(despairingly)* Why, Laura, you *are* sick, darling! Tom, help your sister into the living room, dear! Sit in the living room, Laura—rest on the sofa. Well! *(to the gentleman caller)* Standing over the hot stove made her ill!—I told her that it was just too warm this evening, but—*(*TOM *comes back in.* LAURA *is on the sofa.)* Is Laura all right now?

TOM: Yes.

AMANDA: What *is* that? Rain? A nice cool rain has come up! *(She gives the gentleman caller a frightened look.)* I think we may—have grace—now . . . *(*TOM *looks at her stupidly.)* Tom, honey—you say grace!

TOM: Oh . . . "For these and all thy mercies—" *(They bow their heads,* AMANDA *stealing a nervous glance at Jim. In the living room* LAURA, *stretched on the sofa, clenches her hand to her lips, to hold back a shuddering sob.)* God's Holy Name be praised—

(The Scene Dims Out.)

SCENE VII

A Souvenir.

Half an hour later. Dinner is just being finished in the upstage area which is concealed by the drawn portieres.

As the curtain rises LAURA *is still huddled upon the sofa, her feet drawn under her, her head resting on a pale blue pillow, her eyes wide and mysteriously watchful. The new floor lamp with its shade of rose-colored silk gives a soft, becoming light to her face, bringing out the fragile, unearthly prettiness which usually escapes attention. There is a steady murmur of rain, but it is slackening and stops soon after the scene begins; the air outside becomes pale and luminous as the moon breaks out.*

A moment after the curtain rises, the lights in both rooms flicker and go out.

JIM: Hey, there, Mr. Light Bulb!

AMANDA *laughs nervously.*

(Legend: "Suspension Of A Public Service.")

AMANDA: Where was Moses when the lights went out? Ha-ha. Do you know the answer to that one, Mr. O'Connor?

JIM: No, Ma'am, what's the answer?

AMANDA: In the dark! *(JIM laughs appreciatively.)* Everybody sit still. I'll light the candles. Isn't it lucky we have them on the table? Where's a match? Which of you gentlemen can provide a match?

JIM: Here.

AMANDA: Thank you, sir.

JIM: Not at all, Ma'am!

AMANDA: I guess the fuse has burnt out. Mr. O'Connor, can you tell a burnt-out fuse? I know I can't and Tom is a total loss when it comes to mechanics. *(Sound: Getting Up: Voices Recede A Little To Kitchenette.)* Oh, be careful you don't bump into something. We don't want our gentleman caller to break his neck. Now wouldn't that be a fine howdy-do?

JIM: Ha-ha! Where is the fuse-box?

AMANDA: Right here next to the stove. Can you see anthing?

JIM: Just a minute.

AMANDA: Isn't electricity a mysterious thing? Wasn't it Benjamin Franklin who tied a key to a kite? We live in such a mysterious universe, don't we? Some people say that science clears up all the mysteries for us. In my opinion it only creates more! Have you found it yet?

JIM: No, Ma'am. All these fuses look okay to me.

AMANDA: Tom!

TOM: Yes, Mother?

AMANDA: That light bill I gave you several days ago. The one I told you we got the notices about?

TOM: Oh.—Yeah.

(Legend: "Ha!")

AMANDA: You didn't neglect to pay it by any chance?

TOM: Why, I—

AMANDA: Didn't! I might have known it!

JIM: Shakespeare probably wrote a poem on that light bill, Mrs. Wingfield.

AMANDA: I might have known better than to trust him with it! There's such a high price for negligence in this world!

JIM: Maybe the poem will win a ten-dollar prize.

AMANDA: We'll just have to spend the remainder of the evening in the nineteenth century, before Mr. Edison made the Mazda lamp!

JIM: Candlelight is my favorite kind of light.

AMANDA: That shows you're romantic! But that's no excuse for Tom. Well, we got through dinner. Very considerate of them to let us get through dinner before they plunged us into everlasting darkness, wasn't it, Mr. O'Connor?

JIM: Ha-ha!

AMANDA: Tom, as a penalty for your carelessness you can help me with the dishes.

JIM: Let me give you a hand.

AMANDA: Indeed you will not!

JIM: I ought to be good for something.

AMANDA: Good for something? *(Her tone is rhapsodic.) You?* Why, Mr. O'Connor, nobody, *nobody's* given me this much entertainment in years—as you have!

JIM: Aw, now, Mrs. Wingfield!

AMANDA: I'm not exaggerating, not one bit! But Sister is all by her lonesome. You go keep her company in the parlor! I'll give you this lovely old candelabrum that used to be on the altar at the church of the Heavenly Rest. It was melted a little out of shape when the church burnt down. Lightning struck it one spring. Gypsy Jones was holding a revival at the time and he intimated that the church was destroyed because the Episcopalians gave card parties.

JIM: Ha-ha.

AMANDA: And how about coaxing Sister to drink a little wine? I think it would be good for her! Can you carry both at once?

JIM: Sure. I'm Superman!

AMANDA: Now, Thomas, get into this apron!

The door of kitchenette swings closed on AMANDA's *gay laughter; the flickering light approaches the portieres.*

LAURA *sits up nervously as he enters. Her speech at first is low and breathless from the almost intolerable strain of being alone with a stranger.*

(The Legend: "I Don't Suppose You Remember Me At All!")

In her first speeches in this scene, before JIM's *warmth overcomes her paralyzing shyness,* LAURA's *voice is thin and breathless as though she has run up a steep flight of stairs.*

JIM's *attitude is gently humorous. In playing this scene it should be stressed that while the incident is apparently unimportant, it is to* LAURA *the climax of her secret life.*

JIM: Hello, there, Laura.

LAURA *(faintly)*: Hello. *(She clears her throat.)*

JIM: How are you feeling now? Better?

LAURA: Yes. Yes, thank you.

JIM: This is for you. A little dandelion wine. *(He extends it toward her with extravagant gallantry.)*

LAURA: Thank you.

JIM: Drink it—but don't get drunk! *(He laughs heartily.* LAURA *takes the glass uncertainly; laughs shyly.)* Where shall I set the candles?

LAURA: Oh—oh, anywhere . . .

JIM: How about here on the floor? Any objections?

LAURA: No.

JIM: I'll spread a newspaper under to catch the drippings. I like to sit on the floor. Mind if I do?

LAURA: Oh, no.

JIM: Give me a pillow?

LAURA: What?

JIM: A pillow!

LAURA: Oh . . . *(hands him one quickly)*

JIM: How about you? Don't you like to sit on the floor?

LAURA: Oh—yes.

JIM: Why don't you, then?

LAURA: I—will.

JIM: Take a pillow! *(LAURA does. Sits on the other side of the candelabrum.* JIM *crosses his legs and smiles engagingly at her.)* I can't hardly see you sitting way over there.

LAURA: I can—see you.

JIM: I know, but that's not fair, I'm in the limelight. *(LAURA moves her pillow closer.)* Good! Now I can see you! Comfortable?

LAURA: Yes.

JIM: So am I. Comfortable as a cow. Will you have some gum?

LAURA: No, thank you.

JIM: I think that I will indulge, with your permission. *(musingly unwraps it and holds it up.)* Think of the fortune made by the guy that invented the first piece of chewing gum. Amazing, huh? The Wrigley Building is one of the sights of Chicago.—I saw it summer before last when I went up to the Century of Progress. Did you take in the Century of Progress?

LAURA: No, I didn't.

JIM: Well, it was quite a wonderful exposition. What impressed me most was the Hall of Science. Gives you an idea of what the future will be in America, even more wonderful than the present time is! *(Pause. Smiling at her.)* Your brother tells me you're shy. Is that right, Laura?

LAURA: I—don't know.

JIM: I judge you to be an old-fashioned type of girl. Well, I think that's a pretty good type to be. Hope you don't think I'm being too personal—do you?

LAURA *(hastily, out of embarrassment)*: I believe I *will* take a piece of gum, if you—don't mind. *(Clearing her throat.)* Mr. O'Connor, have you—kept up with your singing?

JIM: Singing? Me?

LAURA: Yes. I remember what a beautiful voice you had.

JIM: When did you hear me sing?

(Voice Offstage In The Pause.)

VOICE *(offstage)*:   O blow, ye winds, heigh-ho,
               A-roving I will go!
               I'm off to my love
               With a boxing glove—
               Ten thousand miles away!

JIM: You say you've heard me sing?

LAURA: Oh, yes! Yes, very often . . . I—don't suppose you remember me—at all?

JIM (*smiling doubtfully*): You know I have an idea I've seen you before. I had that idea soon as you opened the door. It seemed almost like I was about to remember your name. But the name that I started to call you—wasn't a name! And so I stopped myself before I said it.

LAURA: Wasn't it—Blue Roses?

JIM (*springs up, grinning*): Blue Roses! My gosh, yes—Blue Roses! That's what I had on my tongue when you opened the door! Isn't it funny what tricks your memory plays? I didn't connect you with the high school somehow or other. But that's where it was; it was high school. I didn't even know you were Shakespeare's sister! Gosh, I'm sorry.

LAURA: I didn't expect you to. You—barely knew me!

JIM: But we did have a speaking acquaintance, huh?

LAURA: Yes, we—spoke to each other.

JIM: When did you recognize me?

LAURA: Oh, right away!

JIM: Soon as I came in the door?

LAURA: When I heard your name I thought it was probably you. I knew that Tom used to know you a little in high school. So when you came in the door—Well, then I was—sure.

JIM: Why didn't you *say* something, then?

LAURA (*breathlessly*): I didn't know what to say, I was—too surprised!

JIM: For goodness' sakes! You know, this sure is funny!

LAURA: Yes! Yes, isn't it, though . . .

JIM: Didn't we have a class in something together?

LAURA: Yes, we did.

JIM: What class was that?

LAURA: It was—singing—Chorus!

JIM: Aw!

LAURA: I sat across the aisle from you in the Aud.

JIM: Aw.

LAURA: Mondays, Wednesdays and Fridays.

JIM: Now I remember—you always came in late.

LAURA: Yes, it was so hard for me, getting upstairs. I had that brace on my leg—it clumped so loud!

JIM: I never heard any clumping.

LAURA: *(wincing at the recollection)*. To me it sounded like—thunder!

JIM: Well, well, well. I never even noticed.

LAURA: And everybody was seated before I came in. I had to walk in front of all those people. My seat was in the back row. I had to go clumping all the way up the aisle with everyone watching!

JIM: You shouldn't have been self-conscious.

LAURA: I know, but I was. It was always such a relief when the singing started.

JIM: Aw, yes, I've placed you now! I used to call you Blue Roses. How was it that I got started calling you that?

LAURA: I was out of school a little while with pleurosis. When I came back you asked me what was the matter. I said I had pleurosis—you thought I said Blue Roses. That's what you always called me after that!

JIM: I hope you didn't mind.

LAURA: Oh, no—I liked it. You see, I wasn't acquainted with many—people. . . .

JIM: As I remember you sort of stuck by yourself.

LAURA: I—I—never had much luck at—making friends.

JIM: I don't see why you wouldn't.

LAURA: Well, I—started out badly.

JIM: You mean being—

LAURA: Yes, it sort of—stood between me—

JIM: You shouldn't have let it!

LAURA: I know, but it did, and—

JIM: You were shy with people!

LAURA: I tried not to be but never could—

JIM: Overcome it?

LAURA: No, I—I never could!

JIM: I guess being shy is something you have to work out of kind of gradually.

LAURA *(sorrowfully)*: Yes—I guess it—

JIM: Takes time!

LAURA: Yes—

JIM: People are not so dreadful when you know them. That's what you have to remember! And everybody has problems, not just you, but practically everybody has got some problems. You think of yourself as having the only problems, as being the only one who is disappointed. But just look around you and you will see lots of people as disappointed as you are. For instance, I hoped when I was going to high school that I would be further along at this time, six years later, than I am now—You remember that wonderful write-up I had in *The Torch?*

LAURA: Yes! *(She rises and crosses to table.)*

JIM: It said I was bound to succeed in anything I went into! *(*LAURA* returns with the annual.)* Holy Jeez! *The Torch!* (He accepts it reverently. They smile across it with mutual wonder. *LAURA* crouches beside him and they begin to turn through it. *LAURA*'s shyness is dissolving in his warmth.)*

LAURA: Here you are in *Pirates of Penzance!*

JIM *(wistfully)*: I sang the baritone lead in that operetta.

LAURA *(rapidly)*: So—*beautifully!*

JIM *(protesting)*: Aw—

LAURA: Yes, yes—beautifully—beautifully!

JIM: You heard me?

LAURA: All three times!

JIM: No!

LAURA: Yes!

JIM: All three performances?

LAURA *(looking down)*: Yes.

JIM: Why?

LAURA: I—wanted to ask you to—autograph my program.

JIM: Why didn't you ask me to?

LAURA: You were always surrounded by your own friends so much that I never had a chance to.

JIM: You should have just—

LAURA: Well, I—thought you might think I was—

JIM: Thought I might think you was—what?

LAURA: Oh—

JIM *(with reflective relish)*: I was beleaguered by females in those days.

LAURA: You were terribly popular!

JIM: Yeah—

LAURA: You had such a—friendly way—

JIM: I was spoiled in high school.

LAURA: Everybody—liked you!

JIM: Including you?

LAURA: I—yes, I—I did, too— *(She gently closes the book in her lap.)*

JIM: Well, well, well!—Give me that program, Laura. *(She hands it to him. He signs it with a flourish.)* There are you—better late than never!

LAURA: Oh, I—what a—surprise!

JIM: My signature isn't worth very much right now. But some day—maybe—it will increase in value! Being disappointed is one thing and being discouraged is something else. I am disappointed but I'm not discouraged. I'm twenty-three years old. How old are you?

LAURA: I'll be twenty-four in June.

JIM: That's not old age!

LAURA: No, but—

JIM: You finished high school?

LAURA *(with difficulty)*: I didn't go back.

JIM: You mean you dropped out?

LAURA: I made bad grades in my final examinations. *(She rises and replaces the book and the program. Her voice strained.)* How is—Emily Meisenbach getting along?

JIM: Oh, that kraut-head!

LAURA: Why do you call her that?

JIM: That's what she was.

LAURA: You're not still—going with her?

JIM: I never see her.

LAURA: It said in the Personal Section that you were—engaged!

JIM: I know, but I wasn't impressed by that—propaganda!

LAURA: It wasn't—the truth?

JIM: Only in Emily's optimistic opinion!

LAURA: Oh—

(Legend: "What Have You Done Since High School?")

JIM *lights a cigarette and leans indolently back on his elbows smiling at* LAURA *with a warmth and charm which light her inwardly with altar candles. She remains by the table and turns in her hands a piece of glass to cover her tumult.*

JIM *(after several reflective puffs on a cigarette)*: What have you done since high school? *(She seems not to hear him.)* Huh?

(LAURA *looks up.*) I said what have you done since high school, Laura?

LAURA: Nothing much.

JIM: You must have been doing something these six long years.

LAURA: Yes.

JIM: Well, then, such as what?

LAURA: I took a business course at business college—

JIM: How did that work out?

LAURA: Well, not very—well—I had to drop out, it gave me—indigestion—

JIM *laughs gently.*

JIM: What are you doing now?

LAURA: I don't do anything—much. Oh, please don't think I sit around doing nothing! My glass collection takes up a good deal of my time. Glass is something you have to take good care of.

JIM: What did you say—about glass?

LAURA: Collection I said—I have one— *(She clears her throat and turns away again, acutely shy).*

JIM *(abruptly)*: You know what I judge to be the trouble with you? Inferiority complex! Know what that is? That's what they call it when someone low-rates himself! I understand it because I had it, too. Although my case was not so aggravated as yours seems to be. I had it until I took up public speaking, developed my voice, and learned that I had an aptitude for science. Before that time I never thought of myself as being outstanding in any way whatsoever! Now I've never made a regular study of it, but I have a friend who says I can analyze people better than doctors that make a profession of it. I don't claim that to be necessarily true, but I can sure guess a person's psychology, Laura! *(takes out his gum)* Excuse me, Laura. I always take it out when the flavor is gone. I'll use this scrap of paper to wrap it in. I know how it is to get it stuck on a shoe. Yep—that's what I judge to be your principal trouble. A lack of confidence in yourself as a person. You don't have the proper amount of faith in yourself. I'm basing that fact on a number of your remarks and also on certain observations I've made. For instance that clumping you thought was so awful in high school. You say that you even dreaded to walk into class. You see what you did? You dropped out of school, you gave up an education because of a clump, which as far as I know was practically non-existent! A little physical defect is what you have. Hardly noticeable even! Magnified thousands of times by imagination! You know what my strong advice to you is? Think of yourself as *superior* in some way!

LAURA: In what way would I think?

JIM: Why, man alive, Laura! Just look about you a little. What do you see? A world full of common people! All of 'em born and all of 'em going to die! Which of them has one-tenth of your good points! Or mine! Or anyone else's, as far as that goes—Gosh! Everybody excels in some one thing. Some in many! *(unconsciously glances at himself in the mirror)* All you've got to do is discover in *what*! Take me, for instance. *(He adjusts his tie at the mirror.)* My interest happens to lie in electro-dynamics. I'm taking a course in radio engineering at night school, Laura, on top of a fairly responsible job at the warehouse. I'm taking that course and studying public speaking.

LAURA: Ohhhh.

JIM: Because I believe in the future of television! *(turning back to her)* I wish to be ready to go up right along with it. Therefore I'm planning to get in on the ground floor. In fact, I've already made the right connections and all that remains is for the industry itself to get under way! Full steam— *(His eyes are starry.)* Knowledge—Zzzzzp! *Money*—Zzzzzp!—*Power*! That's the cycle democracy is built on! *(His attitude is convincingly dynamic.* LAURA *stares at him, even her shyness eclipsed in her absolute wonder. He suddenly grins.)* I guess you think I think a lot of myself!

LAURA: No—o-o-o, I—

JIM: Now how about you? Isn't there something you take more interest in than anything else?

LAURA: Well, I do—as I said—have my—glass collection—

A peal of girlish laughter from the kitchen.

JIM: I'm not right sure I know what you're talking about. What kind of glass is it?

LAURA: Little articles of it, they're ornaments mostly! Most of them are little animals made out of glass, the tiniest little animals in the world. Mother calls them a glass menagerie! Here's an example of one, if you'd like to see it! This one is one of the oldest. It's nearly thirteen. *(He stretches out his hand.)* (**Music: "The Glass Menagerie."**) Oh, be careful—if you breathe, it breaks!

JIM: I'd better not take it. I'm pretty clumsy with things.

LAURA: Go on, I trust you with him! *(places it in his palm)* There now—you're holding him gently! Hold him over the light, he loves the light! You see how the light shines through him?

JIM: It sure does shine!

LAURA: I shouldn't be partial, but he is my favorite one.

JIM: What kind of a thing is this one supposed to be?

LAURA: Haven't you noticed the single horn on his forehead?

JIM: A unicorn, huh?

LAURA: Mmm-hmmm!

JIM: Unicorns, aren't they extinct in the modern world?

LAURA: I know!

JIM: Poor little fellow, he must feel sort of lonesome.

LAURA *(smiling)*: Well, if he does he doesn't complain about it. He stays on a shelf with some horses that don't have horns and all of them seem to get along nicely together.

JIM: How do you know?

LAURA *(lightly)*: I haven't heard any arguments among them!

JIM *(grinning)*: No arguments, huh? Well, that's a pretty good sign! Where shall I set him?

LAURA: Put him on the table. They all like a change of scenery once in a while!

JIM *(stretching)*: Well, well, well, well—Look how big my shadow is when I stretch!

LAURA: Oh, oh, yes—it stretches across the ceiling!

JIM *(crossing to door)*: I think it's stopped raining. *(opens fire-escape door)* Where does the music come from?

LAURA: From the Paradise Dance Hall across the alley.

JIM: How about cutting the rug a little, Miss Wingfield?

LAURA: Oh, I—

JIM: Or is your program filled up? Let me have a look at it. *(grasps imaginary card)* Why, every dance is taken! I'll just have to scratch some out. (**Waltz Music: *"La Golondrina."***) Ahhh, a waltz! *(He executes some sweeping turns by himself, then holds his arms toward* LAURA.*)*

LAURA *(breathlessly)*: I—can't dance!

JIM: There you go, that inferiority stuff!

LAURA: I've never danced in my life!

JIM: Come on, try!

LAURA: Oh, but I'd step on you!

JIM: I'm not made out of glass.

LAURA: How—how—how do we start?

JIM: Just leave it to me. You hold your arms out a little.

LAURA: Like this?

JIM: A little bit higher. Right. Now don't tighten up, that's the main thing about it—relax.

LAURA *(laughing breathlessly)*: It's hard not to.

JIM: Okay.

LAURA: I'm afraid you can't budge me.

JIM: What do you bet I can't? *(He swings her into motion.)*

LAURA: Goodness, yes, you can!

JIM: Let yourself go, now, Laura, just let yourself go.

LAURA: I'm—

JIM: Come on!

LAURA: Trying?

JIM: Not so stiff—Easy does it!

LAURA: I know but I'm—

JIM: Loosen th' backbone! There now, that's a lot better.

LAURA: Am I?

JIM: Lots, lots better! *(He moves her about the room in a clumsy waltz.)*

LAURA: Oh, my!

JIM: Ha-ha!

LAURA: Goodness, yes you can!

JIM: Ha-ha-ha! *(They suddenly bump into the table. Jim stops.)* What did we hit on?

LAURA: Table.

JIM: Did something fall off it? I think—

LAURA: Yes.

JIM: I hope that it wasn't the little glass horse with the horn!

LAURA: Yes.

JIM: Aw, aw, aw. Is it broken?

LAURA: Now it is just like all the other horses.

JIM: It's lost its—

LAURA: Horn! It doesn't matter. Maybe it's a blessing in disguise.

JIM: You'll never forgive me. I bet that that was your favorite piece of glass.

LAURA: I don't have favorites much. It's no tragedy, Freckles. Glass breaks so easily. No matter how careful you are. The traffic jars the shelves and things fall off them.

JIM: Still I'm awfully sorry that I was the cause.

LAURA *(smiling)*: I'll just imagine he had an operation. The horn was removed to make him feel less—freakish! *(They both laugh.)* Now he will feel more at home with the other horses, the ones that don't have horns . . .

JIM: Ha-ha, that's very funny! *(suddenly serious)* I'm glad to see that you have a sense of humor. You know—you're—well—very different! Surprisingly different from anyone else I know! *(His voice becomes soft and hesitant with a genuine feeling.)* Do you mind me telling you that? *(LAURA is abashed beyond speech.)* You make me feel sort of—I don't know how to put it! I'm usually pretty good at expressing things, but—This is something that I don't know how to say! *(LAURA touches her throat and clears it—turns the broken unicorn in her hands.)* *(even softer)* Has anyone ever told you that you were pretty? **(Pause: Music.)** *(LAURA looks up slowly, with wonder, and shakes her head.)* Well, you are! In a very different way from anyone else. And all the nicer because of the difference, too. *(His voice becomes low and husky. LAURA turns away, nearly faint with the novelty of her emotions.)* I wish you were my sister. I'd teach you to have some confidence in yourself. The different people are not like other people, but being different is nothing to be ashamed of. Because other people are not such wonderful people. They're one hundred times one thousand. You're one times one! They walk all over the earth. You just stay here. They're common as—weeds, but—you—well, you're—*Blue Roses!*

(Image On Screen: Blue Roses.)

(Music Changes.)

LAURA: But blue is wrong for—roses . . .

JIM: It's right for you—You're—pretty!

LAURA: In what respect am I pretty?

JIM: In all respects—believe me! Your eyes—your hair—are pretty! Your hands are pretty! *(He catches hold of her hand.)* You think I'm making this up because I'm invited to dinner and have to be nice. Oh, I could do that! I could put on an act for you, Laura, and say lots of things without being very sincere. But this time I am. I'm talking to you sincerely. I happened to notice you had this inferiority complex that keeps you from feeling comfortable with people. Somebody needs to build your confidence up and make you proud instead of shy and turning away and—blushing—Somebody ought to—ought to—*kiss* you, Laura! *(His hand slips slowly up her arm to her shoulder.)* **(Music Swells Tumultuously.)** *(He suddenly turns her about and kisses her on the lips. When he releases her* LAURA *sinks on the sofa with a bright, dazed look.* JIM *backs away and fishes in his pocket for a cigarette.)* **(Legend On Screen: "Souvenir.")** Stumble-john! *(He lights the cigarette, avoiding her look. There is a peal of girlish laughter from* AMANDA *in the kitchen.* LAURA *slowly raises and opens her hand. It still contains the little broken glass animal. She looks at it with a tender, bewildered expression.)* Stumble-john! I shouldn't have done that—That was way off the beam. You don't smoke, do you? *(She looks up, smiling, not hearing the question. He sits beside her a little gingerly. She looks at him speechlessly—waiting. He coughs decorously and moves a little farther aside as he considers the situation and senses her feelings, dimly, with perturbation. Gently.)* Would you—care for a—mint? *(She doesn't seem to hear him but her look grows brighter even.)* Peppermint—Life Saver? My pocket's a regular drug store—wherever I go ... *(He pops a mint in his mouth. Then gulps and decides to make a clean breast of it. He speaks slowly and gingerly.)* Laura, you know, if I had a sister like you, I'd do the same thing as Tom, I'd bring out fellows—introduce her to them. The right type of boys of a type to—appreciate her. Only—well—he made a mistake about me. Maybe I've got no call to be saying this. That may not have been the idea in having me over. But what if it was? There's nothing wrong about that. The only trouble is that in my case—I'm not in a situation to—do the right thing. I can't take down your number and say I'll phone. I can't call up next week and—ask for a date. I thought I had better explain the situation in case you misunderstood it and—hurt your feelings. . . . (*Pause. Slowly, very slowly,* LAURA's *look changes, her eyes returning slowly from his to the ornament in her palm.*)

AMANDA *utters another gay laugh in the kitchen.*

LAURA (*faintly*): You—won't—call again?

JIM: No, Laura, I can't. (*He rises from the sofa.*) As I was just explaining, I've—got strings on me, Laura, I've—been going steady! I go out all the time with a girl named Betty. She's a home-girl like you, and Catholic, and Irish, and in a great many ways we—get along fine. I met her last summer on a moonlight boat trip up the river to Alton, on the *Majestic*. Well—right away from the start it was—love! (***Legend: Love!***) (LAURA *sways slightly forward and grips the arm of the sofa. He fails to notice, now enrapt in his own comfortable being.*) Being in love has made a new man of me! (*Leaning stiffly forward, clutching the arm of the sofa,* LAURA *struggles visibly with her storm. But* JIM *is oblivious, she is a long way off.*) The power of love is really pretty tremendous! Love is something that—changes the whole world, Laura! (*The storm abates a little and* LAURA *leans back. He notices her again.*) It happened that Betty's aunt took sick, she got a wire and had to go to Centralia. So Tom—when he asked me to dinner—I naturally just accepted the invitation, not knowing that you—that he—that I—(*He stops awkwardly.*) Huh—I'm a stumble-john! (*He flops back on the sofa. The holy candles in the altar of* LAURA's *face have been snuffed out! There is a look of almost infinite desolation. Jim glances at her uneasily.*) I wish that you would—say something. (*She bites her lip which was trembling and then bravely smiles. She opens her hand again on the broken glass ornament. Then she gently takes his hand and raises it level with her own. She carefully places the unicorn in the palm of his hand, then pushes his fingers closed upon it.*) What are you—doing that for? You want me to have him?—Laura? (*She nods.*) What for?

LAURA: A—souvenir . . .

She rises unsteadily and crouches beside the victrola to wind it up.

(Legend On Screen: "Things Have A Way Of Turning Out So Badly.")

(Or Image: "Gentleman Caller Waving Good-bye!—Gaily.")

At this moment AMANDA *rushes brightly back in the front room. She bears a pitcher of fruit punch in an old-fashioned cut-glass pitcher and a plate of macaroons. The plate has a gold border and poppies painted on it.*

AMANDA: Well, well, well! Isn't the air delightful after the shower? I've made you children a little liquid refreshment. *(turns gaily to the gentleman caller)* Jim, do you know that song about lemonade?

> "Lemonade, lemonade
> Made in the shade and stirred with a spade—
> Good enough for any old maid!"

JIM *(uneasily)*: Ha-ha! No—I never heard it.

AMANDA: Why, Laura! You look so serious!

JIM: We were having a serious conversation.

AMANDA: Good! Now you're better acquainted!

JIM *(uncertainly)*: Ha-ha! Yes.

AMANDA: You modern young people are much more serious-minded than my generation. I was so gay as a girl!

JIM: You haven't changed, Mrs. Wingfield.

AMANDA: Tonight I'm rejuvenated! The gaiety of the occasion, Mr. O'Connor! *(She tosses her head with a peal of laughter. Spills lemonade.)* Oooo! I'm baptizing myself!

JIM: Here—let me—.

AMANDA *(setting the pitcher down)*: There now. I discovered we had some maraschino cherries. I dumped them in, juice and all!

JIM: You shouldn't have gone to that trouble. Mrs. Wingfield.

AMANDA: Trouble, trouble? Why it was loads of fun! Didn't you hear me cutting up in the kitchen? I bet your ears were burning! I told Tom how outdone with him I was for keeping you to himself so long a time! He should have brought you over much, much sooner! Well, now that you've found your way, I want you to be a very frequent caller! Not just occasional but all the time. Oh, we're going to have a lot of gay times together! I see them coming! Mmm, just breathe that air! So fresh, and the moon's so pretty! I'll skip back out—I know where my place is when young folks are having a—serious conversation!

JIM: Oh, don't go out, Mrs. Wingfield. The fact of the matter is I've got to be going.

AMANDA: Going now? You're joking! Why, it's only the shank of the evening, Mr. O'Connor!

JIM: Well, you know how it is.

AMANDA: You mean you're a young workingman and have to keep working-men's hours. We'll let you off early tonight. But only on the condition that next time you stay later. What's the best night for you? Isn't Saturday night the best night for you workingmen?

JIM: I have a couple of time-clocks to punch, Mrs. Wingfield. One at morning, another at night!

AMANDA: My, but you *are* ambitious! You work at night, too?

JIM: No, Ma'am, not work but—Betty! *(He crosses deliberately to pick up his hat. The band at the Paradise Dance Hall goes into a tender waltz.)*

AMANDA: Betty? Betty? Who's—Betty! *(There is an ominous cracking sound in the sky.)*

JIM: Oh, just a girl. The girl I go steady with! *(He smiles charmingly. The sky falls.)*

(Legend: "The Sky Falls.")

AMANDA *(a long-drawn exhalation)*: Ohhhh . . . Is it a serious romance, Mr. O'Connor?

JIM: We're going to be married the second Sunday in June.

AMANDA: Ohhhh—how nice! Tom didn't mention that you were engaged to be married.

JIM: The cat's not out of the bag at the warehouse yet. You know how they are. They call you Romeo and stuff like that. *(He stops at the oval mirror to put on his hat. He carefully shapes the brim and the crown to give a discreetly dashing effect.)* It's been a wonderful evening, Mrs. Wingfield. I guess this is what they mean by Southern hospitality.

AMANDA: It really wasn't anything at all.

JIM: I hope it don't seem like I'm rushing off. But I promised Betty I'd pick her up at the Wabash depot, an' by the time I get my jalopy down there her train'll be in. Some women are pretty upset if you keep 'em waiting.

AMANDA: Yes, I know—The tyranny of women! *(extends her hand)* Goodbye, Mr. O'Connor. I wish you luck—and happiness—and success! All three of them, and so does Laura!—Don't you, Laura?

LAURA: Yes!

JIM *(taking her hand)*: Goodbye, Laura. I'm certainly going to treasure that souvenir. And don't you forget the good advice I gave you. *(raises his voice to a cheery shout)* So long, Shakespeare! Thanks again, ladies—Good night!

He grins and ducks jauntily out.

Still bravely grimacing, AMANDA *closes the door on the gentleman caller. Then she turns back to the room with a puzzled expression. She and* LAURA *don't dare to face each other.* LAURA *crouches beside the victrola to wind it.*

AMANDA *(faintly)*: Things have a way of turning out so badly. I don't believe that I would play the victrola. Well, well—well— Our gentleman caller was engaged to be married! Tom!

TOM *(from back)*: Yes, Mother?

AMANDA: Come in here a minute. I want to tell you something awfully funny.

TOM *(enters with macaroon and a glass of the lemonade)*: Has the gentleman caller gotten away already?

AMANDA: The gentleman caller has made an early departure. What a wonderful joke you played on us!

TOM: How do you mean?

AMANDA: You didn't mention that he was engaged to be married.

TOM: Jim? Engaged?

AMANDA: That's what he just informed us.

TOM: I'll be jiggered! I didn't know about that.

AMANDA: That seems very peculiar.

TOM: What's peculiar about it?

AMANDA: Didn't you call him your best friend down at the warehouse?

TOM: He is, but how did I know?

AMANDA: It seems extremely peculiar that you wouldn't know your best friend was going to be married!

TOM: The warehouse is where I work, not where I know things about people!

AMANDA: You don't know things anywhere! You live in a dream; you manufacture illusions! *(He crosses to door.)* Where are you going?

TOM: I'm going to the movies.

AMANDA: That's right, now that you've had us make such fools of ourselves. The effort, the preparations, all the expense! The new floor lamp, the rug, the clothes for Laura! All for what? To entertain some other girl's fiancé! Go to the movies, go! Don't think about us, a mother deserted, an unmarried sister who's crippled and has no job! Don't let anything interfere with your selfish pleasure! Just go, go, go—to the movies!

TOM: All right, I will! The more you shout about my selfishness to me the quicker I'll go, and I won't go to the movies!

AMANDA: Go, then! Then go to the moon—you selfish dreamer!

TOM *smashes his glass on the floor. He plunges out on the fire-escape, slamming the door.* LAURA *screams—cut by door.*

Dance-hall music up. TOM *goes to the rail and grips it desperately, lifting his face in the chill white moonlight penetrating the narrow abyss of the alley.*

(Legend On Screen: "And So Good-bye . . .")

TOM's *closing speech is timed with the interior pantomime. The interior scene is played as though viewed through sound-proof glass.* AMANDA *appears to be making a comforting speech to* LAURA *who is huddled upon the sofa. Now that we cannot hear the mother's speech, her silliness is gone and she has dignity and tragic beauty.* LAURA's *dark hair hides her face until at the end of the speech she lifts it to smile at her mother.* AMANDA's *gestures are slow and graceful, almost dancelike, as she comforts the daughter. At the end of her speech she glances a moment at the father's picture—then withdraws through the portieres. At close of* TOM's *speech,* LAURA *blows out the candles, ending the play.*

TOM: I didn't go to the moon, I went much further—for time is the longest distance between two places—Not long after that I was fired for writing a poem on the lid of a shoe-box. I left Saint Louis. I descended the steps of this fire-escape for a last time and followed, from then on, in my father's footsteps, attempting to find in motion what was lost in space—I traveled around a great deal. The cities swept about me like dead leaves, leaves that were brightly colored but torn away from the branches. I would have stopped, but was pursued by something. It always came upon me unawares, taking me altogether by surprise. Perhaps it was a familiar bit of music. Perhaps it was only a piece of transparent glass. Perhaps I am walking along a street at night, in some strange city, before I have found companions. I pass the lighted window of a shop where perfume is sold. The window is filled with pieces of colored glass, tiny transparent bottles in delicate colors, like bits of a shattered rainbow. Then all at once my sister touches my shoulder. I turn around and look into her eyes . . . Oh, Laura, Laura, I tried to leave you behind me, but I am more faithful than I intended to be! I reach for a cigarette, I cross the street, I run into the movies or a bar, I buy a drink, I speak to the nearest stanger—anything that can blow your candles out! (LAURA *bends over the candles.*)—for nowadays the world is lit by lightning! Blow out your candles, Laura—and so goodbye . . .

She blows the candles out.

(The Scene Dissolves.)

EUGÈNE IONESCO

The Gap

An English translation by Rosette Lamont

Characters

THE FRIEND
THE ACADEMICIAN
THE ACADEMICIAN'S WIFE

Set *A rich bourgeois living room with artistic pretensions. One or two sofas, a number of armchairs, among which, a green, Régence style one, right in the middle of the room. The walls are covered with framed diplomas. One can make out, written in heavy script at the top of a particularly large one, "Doctor Honoris causa." This is followed by an almost illegible Latin inscription. Another equally impressive diploma states: "Doctorat honoris causa," again followed by a long, illegible text. There is an abundance of smaller diplomas, each of which bears a clearly written "doctorate."*

A door to the right of the audience.

As the curtain rises, one can see THE ACADEMICIAN'S WIFE *dressed in a rather crumpled robe. She has obviously just gotten out of bed, and has not had time to dress.* THE FRIEND *faces her. He is well dressed: hat, umbrella in hand, stiff collar, black jacket and striped trousers, shiny black shoes.*

THE WIFE: Dear friend, tell me all.

THE FRIEND: I don't know what to say.

THE WIFE: I know.

THE FRIEND: I heard the news last night. I did not want to call you. At the same time I couldn't wait any longer. Please forgive me for coming so early with such terrible news.

THE WIFE: He didn't make it! How terrible! We were still hoping. . . .

THE FRIEND: It's hard. I know. He still had a chance. Not much of one. We had to expect it.

THE WIFE: I didn't expect it. He was always so successful. He could always manage somehow, at the last moment.

THE FRIEND: In that state of exhaustion. You shouldn't have let him!

THE WIFE: What can we do, what can we do! . . . How awful!

THE FRIEND: Come on, dear friend, be brave. That's life.

THE WIFE: I feel faint: I'm going to faint. *(She falls in one of the armchairs.)*

THE FRIEND *(holding her, gently slapping her cheeks and hands)*: I shouldn't have blurted it out like that. I'm sorry.

THE WIFE: No, you were right to do so. I had to find out somehow or other.

THE FRIEND: I should have prepared you, carefully.

THE WIFE: I've got to be strong. I can't help thinking of him, the wretched man. I hope they won't put it in the papers. Can we count on the journalists' discretion?

THE FRIEND: Close your door. Don't answer the telephone. It will still get around. You could go to the country. In a couple of months, when you are better, you'll come back, you'll go on with your life. People forget such things.

THE WIFE: People won't forget so fast. That's all they were waiting for. Some friends will feel sorry, but the others, the others. . . .

THE ACADEMICIAN *comes in, fully dressed: uniform, chest covered with decorations, his sword on his side.*

THE ACADEMICIAN: Up so early, my dear? *(to* THE FRIEND*)* You've come early too. What's happening? Do you have the final results?

THE WIFE: What a disgrace!

THE FRIEND: You mustn't crush him like this, dear friend. *(to* THE ACADEMICIAN*)* You have failed.

THE ACADEMICIAN: Are you quite sure?

THE FRIEND: You should never have tried to pass the baccalaureate examination.

THE ACADEMICIAN: They failed me. The rats! How dare they do this to me!

THE FRIEND: The marks were posted late in the evening.

THE ACADEMICIAN: Perhaps it was difficult to make them out in the dark. How could you read them?

THE FRIEND: They had set up spotlights.

THE ACADEMICIAN: They're doing everything to ruin me.

THE FRIEND: I passed by in the morning: the marks were still up.

THE ACADEMICIAN: You could have bribed the concierge into pulling them down.

THE FRIEND: That's exactly what I did. Unfortunately the police were there. Your name heads the list of those who failed. Everyone's standing in line to get a look. There's an awful crush.

THE ACADEMICIAN: Who's there? The parents of the candidates?

THE FRIEND: Not only they.

THE WIFE: All your rivals, all your colleagues must be there. All those you attacked in the press for ignorance: your undergraduates, your graduate students, all those you failed when you were chairman of the board of examiners.

THE ACADEMICIAN: I am discredited! But I won't let them. There must be some mistake.

THE FRIEND: I saw the examiners. I spoke with them. They gave me your marks. Zero in mathematics.

THE ACADEMICIAN: I had no scientific training.

THE FRIEND: Zero in Greek, zero in Latin.

THE WIFE *(to her husband)*: You, a humanist, the spokesman for humanism, the author of that famous treatise "The Defense of Poesy and Humanism."

THE ACADEMICIAN: I beg your pardon, but my book concerns itself with twentieth-century humanism. *(to* THE FRIEND*)* What about composition? What grade did I get in composition?

THE FRIEND: Nine hundred. You have nine hundred points.

THE ACADEMICIAN: That's perfect. My average must be all the way up.

THE FRIEND: Unfortunately not. They're marking on the basis of two thousand. The passing grade is one thousand.

THE ACADEMICIAN: They must have changed the regulations.

THE WIFE: They didn't change them just for you. You have a frightful persecution complex.

THE ACADEMICIAN: I tell you they changed them.

THE FRIEND: They went back to the old ones, back to the time of Napoleon.

THE ACADEMICIAN: Utterly outmoded. Besides, when did they make those changes? It isn't legal. I'm chairman of the Baccalaureate Commission of the Ministry of Public Education. They didn't consult me, and they cannot make any changes without my approval. I'm going to expose them. I'm going to bring government charges against them.

THE WIFE: Darling, you don't know what you're doing. You're in your dotage. Don't you recall handing in your resignation just before taking the examination so that no one could doubt the complete objectivity of the board of examiners?

THE ACADEMICIAN: I'll take it back.

THE WIFE: You should never have taken that test. I warned you. After all, it's not as if you needed it. But you have to collect all the honors, don't you? You're never satisfied. What did you need this diploma for? Now all is lost. You have your Doctorate, your Master's, your high school diploma, your elementary school certificate, and even the first part of the baccalaureate.

THE ACADEMICIAN: There was a gap.

THE WIFE: No one suspected it.

THE ACADEMICIAN: But *I* knew it. Others might have found out. I went to the office of the Registrar and asked for a transcript of my record. They said to me: "Certainly Professor, Mr. President, Your Excellency. . . ." Then they looked up my file, and the Chief Registrar came back looking embarrassed, most embarrassed indeed. He said: "There's something peculiar, very peculiar. You have your Master's, certainly, but it's no longer valid." I asked him why, of course. He answered: "There's a gap behind your Master's. I don't know how it happened. You must have registered and been accepted at the University without having passed the second part of the baccalaureate examination."

THE FRIEND: And then?

THE WIFE: Your Master's degree is no longer valid?

THE ACADEMICIAN: No, not quite. It's suspended. "The duplicate you are asking for will be delivered to you upon completion of the baccalaureate. Of course you will pass the examination with no trouble." That's what I was told, so you see now that I had to take it.

THE FRIEND: Your husband, dear friend, wanted to fill the gap. He's a conscientious person.

THE WIFE: It's clear you don't know him as I do. That's not it at all. He wants fame, honors. He never had enough. What does one diploma more or less matter? No one notices them anyway, but he sneaks in at night, on tiptoe, into the living room, just to look at them, and count them.

THE ACADEMICIAN: What else can I do when I have insomnia?

THE FRIEND: The questions asked at the baccalaureate are usually known in advance. You were admirably situated to get this particular information. You could also have sent in a replacement to take the test for you. One of your students, perhaps. Or if you wanted to take the test without people realizing that you already knew the questions, you could have sent your maid to the black market, where one can buy them.

THE ACADEMICIAN: I don't understand how I could have failed in my composition. I filled three sheets of paper. I treated the subject fully, taking into account the historical background. I interpreted the situation accurately . . . at least plausibly. I didn't deserve a bad grade.

THE FRIEND: Do you recall the subject?

THE ACADEMICIAN: Hum . . . let's see. . . .

THE FRIEND: He doesn't even remember what he discussed.

THE ACADEMICIAN: I do . . . wait . . . hum.

THE FRIEND: The subject to be treated was the following: "Discuss the influence of Renaissance painters on novelists of the Third Republic." I have here a photostatic copy of your examination paper. Here is what you wrote.

THE ACADEMICIAN (*grabbing the photostat and reading*): "The trial of Benjamin: After Benjamin was tried and acquitted, the assessors holding a different opinion from that of the President murdered him, and condemned Benjamin to the suspension of his civic rights, imposing on him a fine of nine hundred francs. . . ."

THE FRIEND: That's where the nine hundred points come from.

THE ACADEMICIAN: "Benjamin appealed his case . . . Benjamin appealed his case. . . ." I can't make out the rest. I've always had bad handwriting. I ought to have taken a typewriter along with me.

THE WIFE: Horrible handwriting, scribbling and crossing out; ink spots didn't help you much.

THE ACADEMICIAN (goes on with his reading after having retrieved the text his wife had pulled out of his hand): "Benjamin appealed his case. Flanked by policemen dressed in zouave uniforms . . . in zouave uniforms. . . ." It's getting dark. I can't see the rest. . . . I don't have my glasses.

THE WIFE: What you've written has nothing to do with the subject.

THE FRIEND: Your wife's quite right, friend. It has nothing to do with the subject.

THE ACADEMICIAN: Yes, it has. Indirectly.

THE FRIEND: Not even indirectly.

THE ACADEMICIAN: Perhaps I chose the second question.

THE FRIEND: There was only one.

THE ACADEMICIAN: Even if there was only that one, I treated another quite adequately. I went to the end of the story. I stressed the important points, explaining the motivations of the characters, highlighting their behavior. I explained the mystery, making it plain and clear. There was even a conclusion at the end. I can't make out the rest. (to THE FRIEND) Can you read it?

THE FRIEND: It's illegible. I don't have my glasses either.

THE WIFE (taking the text): It's illegible and I have excellent eyes. You pretended to write. Mere scribbling.

THE ACADEMICIAN: That's not true. I've even provided a conclusion. It's clearly marked here in heavy print: "Conclusion or sanction . . . Conclusion or sanction. . . ." They can't get away with it. I'll have this examination rendered null and void.

THE WIFE: Since you treated the wrong subject, and treated it badly, setting down only titles, and writing nothing in between, the mark you received is justified. You'd lose your case.

THE FRIEND: You'd most certainly lose. Drop it. Take a vacation.

THE ACADEMICIAN: You're always on the side of the Others.

THE WIFE: After all, these professors know what they're doing. They haven't been granted their rank for nothing. They passed examinations, received serious training. They know the rules of composition.

THE ACADEMICIAN: Who was on the board of examiners?

THE FRIEND: For Mathematics, a movie star. For Greek, one of the Beatles. For Latin, the champion of the automobile race, and many others.

THE ACADEMICIAN: But these people aren't any more qualified than I am. And for composition?

THE FRIEND: A woman, a secretary in the editorial division of the review *Yesterday, the Day Before Yesterday, and Today.*

THE ACADEMICIAN: Now I know. This wretch gave me a poor grade out of spite because I never joined her political party. It's an act of vengeance. But I have ways and means of rendering the examination null and void. I'm going to call the President.

THE WIFE: Don't. You'll make yourself look even more ridiculous. *(to* THE FRIEND*)* Please try to restrain him. He listens to you more than to me. *(*THE FRIEND *shrugs his shoulders, unable to cope with the situation.* THE WIFE *turns to her husband, who has just lifted the receiver off the hook.)* Don't call!

THE ACADEMICIAN *(on the telephone)*: Hello, John? It is I . . . What? . . . What did you say? . . . But, listen, my dear friend . . . but, listen to me . . . Hello! Hello! *(Puts down the receiver.)*

THE FRIEND: What did he say?

THE ACADEMICIAN: He said . . . He said. . . . "I don't want to talk to you. My mummy won't let me make friends with boys at the bottom of the class." Then he hung up on me.

THE WIFE: You should have expected it. All is lost. How could you do this to me? How could you do this to me?

THE ACADEMICIAN: Think of it! I lectured at the Sorbonne, at Oxford, at American universities. Ten thousand theses have been written on my work; hundreds of critics have analyzed it. I hold an *honoris causa* doctorate from Amsterdam as well as a secret university Chair with the Duchy of Luxembourg. I received the Nobel Prize three times. The King of Sweden himself was amazed by my erudition. A doctorate *honoris causa, honoris causa* . . . and I failed the baccalaureate examination!

THE WIFE: Everyone will laugh at us!

THE ACADEMICIAN *takes off his sword and breaks it on his knee.*

THE FRIEND *(picking up the two pieces)*: I wish to preserve these in memory of our ancient glory.

THE ACADEMICIAN *meanwhile in a fit of rage is tearing down his decorations, throwing them on the floor, and stepping on them.*

THE WIFE *(trying to salvage the remains)*: Don't do this! Don't! That's all we've got left.

ARTHUR MILLER

A View from the Bridge

Characters

LOUIS	TONY
MIKE	RODOLPHO
ALFIERI	FIRST IMMIGRATION OFFICER
EDDIE	SECOND IMMIGRATION OFFICER
CATHERINE	MR. LIPARI
BEATRICE	MRS. LIPARI
MARCO	TWO "SUBMARINES"

A tenement house and the street before it.

Like the play, the set is stripped of everything but its essential elements. The main acting area is EDDIE CARBONE'S *living-dining room, furnished with a round table, a few chairs, a rocker, and a phonograph.*

This room is slightly elevated from the stage floor and is shaped in a free form designed to contain the acting space required, and that is all. At its back is an opaque wall-like shape, around whose right and left sides respectively entrances are made to an unseen kitchen and bedrooms.

Downstage, still in this room, and to the left, are two columnar shapes ending in air, and indicating the house front and entrance. Suspended over the entire front is an architectural element indicating a pediment over the columns, as well as the facing of a tenement building. Through this entrance a stairway is seen, beginning at floor level of the living-dining room, then curving upstage and around the back to the second-floor landing overhead.

Downstage center is the street. At the right, against the proscenium are a desk and chair belonging to MR. ALFIERI, *whose office this is, and a coat hook or rack. Near the office, but separated from it, is a low iron railing such as might form a barrier on a street to guard a basement stair. Later in the play a coin telephone will appear against the proscenium at the left.*

The intention is to make concrete the ancient element of this tale through the unmitigated forms of the commonest life of the big-city present, the one playing against the other to form a new world on the stage.

As the curtain rises, LOUIS *and* MIKE, *longshoremen, are pitching coins against the building at left.*

A distant foghorn blows.

Enter ALFIERI, *a lawyer in his fifties, turning gray, portly, good-humored, and thoughtful. The two pitchers nod to him as he passes; he crosses the stage to his desk and removes his hat and coat, hangs them, then turns to the audience.)*

ALFIERI: I am smiling because they nod so uneasily to me.
That's because I am a lawyer, and in this neighborhood a lawyer's like a priest—
They only think of us when disaster comes. So we're unlucky.
Good evening. Welcome to the theater.
My name is Alfieri. I'll come directly to the point, even though I am a lawyer. I am getting on. And I share the weakness of so many of my profession—I believe I have had some amazingly interesting cases.
When one is still young the more improbable vagaries of life only make one impatient. One looks for logic.
But when one is old, facts become precious; in facts I find all the poetry, all the wonder, all the amazement of spring. And spring is especially beautiful after fifty-five. I love what happened, instead of what might or ought to have happened.
My wife has warned me, so have my friends: they tell me the people in this neighborhood lack elegance, glamour. After all, who have I dealt with in my life? Longshoremen and their wives and fathers and grandfathers—compensation cases, evictions, family squabbles—the petty troubles of the poor— and yet . . .

When the tide is right,
And the wind blows the sea air against these houses,

I sit here in my office,
Thinking it is all so timeless here.
I think of Sicily, from where these people came,
The Roman rocks of Calabria,
Siracusa on the cliff, where Carthaginian and Greek
Fought such bloody fights. I think of Hannibal,
Who slew the fathers of these people; Caesar,
Whipping them on in Latin.

Which is all, of course, ridiculous.
Al Capone learned his trade on these pavements,
And Frankie Yale was cut in half
On the corner of Union Street and President,
Where so many were so justly shot,
By unjust men.

It's different now, of course.
I no longer keep a pistol in my filing cabinet;
We are quite American, quite civilized—
Now we settle for half. And I like it better.

And yet, when the tide is right,
And the green smell of the sea
Floats through my window,
I must look up at the circling pigeons of the poor,
And I see falcons there,
The hunting eagles of the olden time,
Fierce above Italian forests. . . .

This is Red Hook, a slum that faces the bay,
Seaward from Brooklyn Bridge.

Enter EDDIE *along the street. He joins the penny-pitchers.*

Once in every few years there is a case,
And as the parties tell me what the trouble is,
I see cobwebs tearing, Adriatic ruins rebuilding themselves;
   Calabria;
The eyes of the plaintiff seem suddenly carved,
His voice booming toward me over many fallen stones.

This one's name was Eddie Carbone,
A longshoreman working the docks
From Brooklyn Bridge to the breakwater. . . .

EDDIE *picks up pennies*

EDDIE: Well, I'll see ya, fellas.

LOUIS: You workin' tomorrow?

EDDIE: Yeah, there's another day yet on that ship. See ya, Louis. (EDDIE *goes into the house, climbs the stairs, as light rises in the apartment.* EDDIE *is forty, a husky, slightly overweight long-shoreman.*)

CATHERINE, *his niece, is discovered standing at the window of the apartment, waving down at* LOUIS, *who now sees her and waves back up. She is seventeen and is now holding dishes in her hand, preparatory to laying out the dinner on the table.* EDDIE *enters, and she immediately proceeds to lay the table. The lights go out on* ALFIERI *and the street.*

CATHERINE (*she has a suppressed excitement on her*): Hi, Eddie.

EDDIE (*with a trace of wryness*): What's the shoes for?

CATHERINE: I didn't go outside with them.

EDDIE (*removing his zipper jacket and hat*): Do me a favour, heh?

CATHERINE: Why can't I wear them in the house?

EDDIE: Take them off, will you please? You're beautiful enough without the shoes.

CATHERINE: I'm only trying them out.

EDDIE: When I'm home I'm not in the movies,
I don't wanna see young girls
Walking around in spike-heel shoes.

CATHERINE: Oh, brother.

Enter BEATRICE, EDDIE'S *wife; she is his age.*

BEATRICE: You find out anything?

EDDIE (*sitting in a rocker*): The ship came in. They probably get off anytime now.

BEATRICE (*softly clapping her hands together, half in prayer, half in joy*): Oh, boy. You find Tony?

EDDIE (*preoccupied*): Yeah, I talked to him. They're gonna let the crew off tonight. So they'll be here any time, he says.

CATHERINE: Boy, they must be shakin'.

EDDIE: Naa, they'll get off all right. They got regular seamen papers; they walk off with the crew. *(to* BEATRICE*)* I just hope they know where they're going to sleep, heh?

BEATRICE: I told them in the letter we got no room.

CATHERINE: You didn't meet them, though, heh? You didn't see them?

EDDIE: They're still on board. I only met Tony on the pier. What are you all hopped up about?

CATHERINE: I'm not hopped up.

BEATRICE *(in an ameliorative tone)*: It's something new in the house, she's excited.

EDDIE *(to* CATHERINE*)*: 'Cause they ain't comin' here for parties, they're only comin' here to work.

CATHERINE *(blushing, even enjoying his ribbing)*: Who's lookin' for parties?

EDDIE: Why don't you wear them nice shoes you got? *(He indicates her shoes.)* Those are for an actress. Go ahead.

CATHERINE: Don't tell nothin' till I come back. *(She hurries out, kicking off her shoes.)*

EDDIE *(as* BEATRICE *comes toward him)*: Why do you let her wear stuff like that? That ain't her type. *(*BEATRICE *bends and kisses his cheek.)* What's that for?

BEATRICE: For bein' so nice about it.

EDDIE: As long as they know we got nothin', B.; that's all I'm worried about.

BEATRICE: They're gonna pay for everything; I told them in the letter.

EDDIE: Because this ain't gonna end up with you on the floor, like when your mother's house burned down.

BEATRICE: Eddie, I told them in the letter we got no room.

CATHERINE *enters in low-heeled shoes.*

EDDIE: Because as soon as you see a relative I turn around you're on the floor.

BEATRICE *(half amused, half serious)*: All right, stop it already. You want a beer? The sauce is gotta cook a little more.

EDDIE *(to* BEATRICE*)*: No, it's too cold. *(to* CATHERINE*)* You do your lessons today, Garbo?

CATHERINE: Yeah; I'm way ahead anyway. I just gotta practice from now on.

BEATRICE: She could take it down almost as fast as you could talk already. She's terrific. Read something to her later, you'll be surprised.

EDDIE: That's the way, Katie. You're gonna be all right, kid, you'll see.

CATHERINE *(proudly)*: I could get a job right now, Eddie. I'm not even afraid.

EDDIE: You got time. Wait'll you're eighteen. We'll look up the ads—find a nice company, or maybe a lawyer's office or somethin' like that.

CATHERINE: Oh, boy! I could go to work now, my teacher said.

EDDIE: Be eighteen first. I want you to have a little more head on your shoulders. You're still dizzy yet. *(to* BEATRICE.*)* Where's the kids? They still outside?

BEATRICE: I put them with my mother for tonight. They'd never go to sleep otherwise. So what kinda cargo you have today?

EDDIE: Coffee. It was nice.

BEATRICE: I thought all day I smelled coffee here!

EDDIE: Yeah, Brazil. That's one time, boy, to be a longshoreman is a pleasure. The whole ship smelled from coffee. It was like flowers. We'll bust a bag tomorrow; I'll bring you some. Well, let's eat, heh?

BEATRICE: Two minutes. I want the sauce to cook a little more.

EDDIE *goes to a bowl of grapes.*

CATHERINE: How come he's not married, Beatrice, if he's so old? The younger one.

BEATRICE *(to* EDDIE*)*: Twenty-five is old!

EDDIE *(to* CATHERINE*)*: Is that all you got on your mind?

CATHERINE *(wryly)*: What else should I have on my mind?

EDDIE: There's plenty a things.

CATHERINE: Like what?

EDDIE: What the hell are you askin' me? I shoulda been struck by lightning when I promised your mother I would take care of you.

CATHERINE: You and me both.

EDDIE *(laughing)*: Boy, God bless you, you got a tongue in your mouth like the Devil's wife. You oughta be on the television.

CATHERINE: Oh, I wish!

EDDIE: You wish! You'd be scared to death.

CATHERINE: Yeah? Try me.

EDDIE: Listen, by the way, Garbo, what'd I tell you about wavin' from the window?

CATHERINE: I was wavin' to Louis!

EDDIE: Listen, I could tell you things about Louis which you wouldn't wave to him no more.

CATHERINE (to BEATRICE, *who is grinning*): Boy, I wish I could find one guy that he couldn't tell me things about!

EDDIE (*going to her, cupping her cheek*): Now look, Catherine, don't joke with me.

I'm responsible for you, kid.

I promised your mother on her deathbed.

So don't joke with me. I mean it.

I don't like the sound of them high heels on the sidewalk,

I don't like that clack, clack, clack,

I don't like the looks they're givin' you.

BEATRICE: How can she help it if they look at her?

EDDIE: She don't walk right. (*to* CATHERINE) Don't walk so wavy like that.

BEATRICE *goes out into the kitchen.*

CATHERINE: Who's walkin' wavy?

EDDIE: Now don't aggravate me, Katie, you are walkin' wavy!

CATHERINE: Those guys look at all the girls, you know that.

EDDIE: They got mothers and fathers. You gotta be more careful.

BEATRICE *enters with a tureen.*

CATHERINE: Oh, Jesus! (*She goes out into the kitchen.*)

EDDIE (*calling after her*): Hey, lay off the language, heh?

BEATRICE (*alone with him, loading the plates—she is riding lightly over a slightly sore issue*): What do you want from her all the time?

EDDIE: Boy, she grew up! Your sister should see her now. I'm tellin' you, it's like a miracle—one day she's a baby; you turn around and she's— (*enter* CATHERINE *with knives and forks*) Y'know? When she sets a table she looks like a Madonna. (BEATRICE *wipes a strand of hair off* CATHERINE's *face. To* CATHERINE.) You're the Madonna type. That's why you shouldn't be flashy, Kate. For you it ain't beautiful. You're more the Madonna type. And anyway, it ain't nice in an office. They don't go for that in an office. *(He sits at the table.)*

BEATRICE *(sitting to eat)*: Sit down, Katie-baby. (CATHERINE *sits. They eat.)*

EDDIE: Geez, how quiet it is here without the kids!

CATHERINE: What happens? How they gonna find the house here?

EDDIE: Tony'll take them from the ship and bring them here.

BEATRICE: That Tony must be makin' a nice dollar off this.

EDDIE: Naa, the syndicate's takin' the heavy cream.

CATHERINE: What happens when the ship pulls out and they ain't on it, though?

EDDIE: Don't worry; captain's pieced-off.

CATHERINE: Even the captain?

EDDIE: Why, the captain don't have to live? Captain gets a piece, maybe one of the mates, a piece for the guy in Italy who fixed the papers for them— *(to* BEATRICE*)* They're gonna have to work six months for that syndicate before they keep a dime for theirselfs; they know that, I hope.

BEATRICE: Yeah, but Tony'll fix jobs for them, won't he?

EDDIE: Sure, as long as they owe him money he'll fix jobs; it's after the pay-off—they're gonna have to scramble like the rest of us. I just hope they know that.

BEATRICE: Oh, they must know. Boy, they must've been starvin' there. To go through all this just to make a couple of dollars. I'm tellin' ya, it could make you cry.

EDDIE: By the way, what are you going to tell the people in the house? If somebody asks what they're doin' here?

BEATRICE: Well, I'll tell 'em—Well, who's gonna ask? They probably know anyway.

EDDIE: What do you mean, they know? Listen, Beatrice, the Immigration Bureau's got stool pigeons all over the neighborhood.

BEATRICE: Yeah, but not in this house—?

EDDIE: How do you know, not in this house? Listen, both a yiz. If anybody asks you, they're your cousins visitin' here from Philadelphia.

CATHERINE: Yeah, but what would they know about Philadelphia? I mean if somebody asks them—

EDDIE: Well—they don't talk much, that's all. But don't get confidential with nobody, you hear me? Because there's a lotta guys do anything for a couple of dollars, and the Immigration pays good for that kinda news.

CATHERINE: I could teach them about Philadelphia.

EDDIE: Do me a favor, baby, will ya? Don't teach them, and don't mix in with them. Because with that blabbermouth the less you know the better off we're all gonna be. They're gonna work, and they're gonna come home here and go to sleep, and I don't want you payin' no attention to them. This is a serious business; this is the United States Government. So you don't know they're alive. I mean don't get dizzy with your friends about it. It's nobody's business. *(slight pause)* Where's the salt?

Pause.

CATHERINE: It's gettin' dark.

EDDIE: Yeah, gonna snow tomorrow, I think.

Pause.

BEATRICE *(She is frightened.)*: Geez, remember that Vinny Bolzano years ago? Remember him?

EDDIE: That funny? I was just thinkin' about him before.

CATHERINE: Who's he?

BEATRICE: You were a baby then. But there was a kid, Vinny, about sixteen. Lived over there on Sackett Street. And he snitched on somebody to the Immigration. He had five brothers, and the old man. And they grabbed him in the kitchen, and they pulled him down three flights, his head was bouncin' like a coconut—we lived in the next house. And they spit on him in the street, his own father and his brothers. It was so terrible.

CATHERINE: So what happened to him?

BEATRICE: He went away, I think. *(to EDDIE.)* Did you ever see him again?

EDDIE: Him? Naa, you'll never see him no more. A guy do a thing like that—how could he show his face again? There's too much salt in here.

BEATRICE: So what'd you put salt for?

EDDIE *lays the spoon down, leaves the table.*

EDDIE: Geez, I'm gettin' nervous, y'know?

BEATRICE: What's the difference; they'll only sleep here; you won't hardly see them. Go ahead, eat. *(He looks at her, disturbed.)* What could I do? They're my cousins. *(He returns to her and clasps her face admiringly as the lights fade on them and rise on Alfieri.)*

ALFIERI: I only know that they had two children;
He was as good a man as he had to be
In a life that was hard and even.
He worked on the piers when there was work,
He brought home his pay, and he lived.
And toward ten o'clock of that night,
After they had eaten, the cousins came.

While he is speaking EDDIE *goes to the window and looks out.* CATHERINE *and* BEATRICE *clear the dishes.* EDDIE *sits down and reads the paper. Enter* TONY, *escorting* MARCO *and* RODOLPHO, *each with a valise.* TONY *halts, indicates the house. They stand for a moment, looking at it.*

MARCO *(He is a square-built peasant of thirty-two, suspicious and quiet-voiced.)*: Thank you.

TONY: You're on your own now. Just be careful, that's all. Ground floor.

MARCO: Thank you.

TONY: I'll see you on the pier tomorrow. You'll go to work.

MARCO *nods,* TONY *continues on, walking down the street.* RODOLPHO *is in his early twenties, an eager boy, one moment a gamin, the next a brooding adult. His hair is startlingly blond.*

RODOLPHO: This will be the first house I ever walked into in America!

MARCO: Sssh! Come. *(They mount the stoop.)*

RODOLPHO: Imagine! She said they were poor!

MARCO: Ssh!

They pass between the columns. Light rises inside the apartment. EDDIE, CATHERINE, BEATRICE *hear and raise their heads toward the door.* MARCO *knocks.* BEATRICE *and* CATHERINE *look to* EDDIE, *who rises and goes and opens the door. Enter* MARCO *and* RODOLPHO, *removing their caps.*

EDDIE: You Marco?

MARCO *nods, looks to the women, and fixes on* BEATRICE.

MARCO: Are you my cousin?

BEATRICE *(touching her chest with her hand)*: Beatrice. This is my husband, Eddie. *(All nod.)* Catherine, my sister Nancy's daughter. *(The brothers nod.)*

MARCO *(indicating* RODOLPHO*)*: My brother, Rodolpho. *(*RO-DOLPHO *nods.* MARCO *comes with a certain formal stiffness to* EDDIE.*)* I want to tell you now, Eddie—when you say go, we will go.

EDDIE: Oh, no—

MARCO: I see it's a small house, but soon, maybe, we can have our own house.

EDDIE: You're welcome, Marco, we got plenty of room here. Katie, give them supper, heh?

CATHERINE: Come here, sit down. I'll get you some soup.

They go to the table.

MARCO: We ate on the ship. Thank you. *(to* EDDIE*)* Thank you.

BEATRICE: Get some coffee. We'll all have coffee. Come sit down.

CATHERINE: How come he's so dark and you're so light, Rodolpho?

RODOLPHO: I don't know. A thousand years ago, they say, the Danes invaded Sicily. *(He laughs.)*

CATHERINE *(to* BEATRICE*)*: He's practically blond!

EDDIE: How's the coffee doin'?

CATHERINE *(brought up short)*: I'm gettin' it. *(She hurries out.)*

EDDIE: Yiz have a nice trip?

MARCO: The ocean is always rough in the winter. But we are good sailors.

EDDIE: No trouble gettin' here?

MARCO: No. The man brought us. Very nice man.

RODOLPHO: He says we start to work tomorrow. Is he honest?

EDDIE: No. But as long as you owe them money they'll get you plenty of work. *(to* MARCO*)* Yiz ever work on the piers in Italy?

MARCO: Piers? Ts! No.

RODOLPHO *(smiling at the smallness of his town)*: In our town there are no piers,
Only the beach, and little fishing boats.

BEATRICE: So what kinda work did yiz do?

MARCO *(shrugging shyly, even embarrassed)*: Whatever there is, anything.

RODOLPHO: Sometimes they build a house,

Or if they fix the bridge—
Marco is a mason,
And I bring him the cement.

He laughs.

In harvest time we work in the fields—
If there is work. Anything.
EDDIE: Still bad there, heh?
MARCO: Bad, yes.
RODOLPHO: It's terrible.
We stand around all day in the piazza,
Listening to the fountain like birds.

He laughs.

Everybody waits only for the train.
BEATRICE: What's on the train?
RODOLPHO: Nothing. But if there are many passengers
And you're lucky you make a few lire
To push the taxi up the hill.

Enter CATHERINE, *who sits, listens.*

BEATRICE: You gotta push a taxi?
RODOLPHO *(with a laugh)*: Oh, sure! It's a feature in our town.
The horses in our town are skinnier than goats.
So if there are too many passengers
We help to push the carriages up to the hotel.

He laughs again.

In our town the horses are only for the show.
CATHERINE: Why don't they have automobile taxis?
RODOLPHO: There is one—we push that too.

They laugh.

Everything in our town, you gotta push.
BEATRICE *(to* EDDIE, *sorrowfully)*: How do you like that—
EDDIE *(to* MARCO*)*: So what're you wanna do, you gonna stay here
in this country or you wanna go back?
MARCO *(surprised)*: Go back?
EDDIE: Well, you're married, ain't you?
MARCO: Yes. I have three children.
BEATRICE: Three! I thought only one.

MARCO: Oh, no. I have three now.

Four years, five years, six years.

BEATRICE: Ah, I bet they're cryin' for you already, heh?

MARCO: What can I do?

The older one is sick in his chest;

My wife—she feeds them from her own mouth.

I tell you the truth,

If I stay there they will never grow up.

They eat the sunshine.

BEATRICE: My God. So how long you want to stay?

MARCO: With your permission, we will stay maybe a—

EDDIE: She don't mean in this house, she means in the country.

MARCO: Oh. Maybe four, five, six years, I think.

RODOLPHO (*smiling*): He trusts his wife.

BEATRICE: Yeah, but maybe you'll get enough, You'll be able to go back quicker.

MARCO: I hope. I don't know. (*to* EDDIE) I understand it's not so good here either.

EDDIE: Oh, you guys'll be all right—till you pay them off, anyway. After that, you'll have to scramble, that's all. But you'll make better here than you could there.

RODOLPHO: How much? We hear all kinds of figures. How much can a man make? We work hard, We'll work all day, all night . . .

EDDIE (*He is coming more and more to address* MARCO *only.*): On the average a whole year? Maybe—well, it's hard to say, see. Sometimes we lay off, there's no ships three-four weeks.

MARCO: Three, four weeks! Ts!

EDDIE: But I think you could probably—Thirty, forty a week over the whole twelve months of the year.

MARCO: Dollars.

EDDIE: Sure dollars.

MARCO (*looking happily at* RODOLPHO): If we can stay here a few months, Beatrice—

BEATRICE: Listen, you're welcome, Marco—

MARCO: Because I could send them a little more if I stay here—

BEATRICE: As long as you want; we got plenty a room—

MARCO (*his eyes showing tears*): My wife—my wife . . . I want to send right away maybe twenty dollars.

EDDIE: You could send them something next week already.

MARCO *(near tears)*: Eduardo—

EDDIE: Don't thank me. Listen, what the hell, it's no skin off me. *(to* CATHERINE.*)* What happened to the coffee?

CATHERINE: I got it on. *(to* RODOLPHO*)* You married too? No.

RODOLPHO: Oh, no.

BEATRICE: I told you he—

CATHERINE *(to her)*: I know, I just thought maybe he got married recently.

RODOLPHO: I have no money to get married. I have a nice face, but no money. *(He laughs.)*

CATHERINE *(to* BEATRICE*)*: He's a real blond!

BEATRICE *(to* RODOLPHO*)*: You want to stay here too, heh? For good?

RODOLPHO: Me? Yes, forever! Me, I want to be an American.
And then I want to go back to Italy
When I am rich. And I will buy a motorcycle. *(He smiles.)*

CATHERINE: A motorcycle!

RODOLPHO: With a motorcycle in Italy you will never starve any more.

BEATRICE: I'll get you coffee. *(She exits.)*

EDDIE: What're you do with a motorcycle?

MARCO: He dreams, he dreams.

RODOLPHO: Why? Messages! The rich people in the hotel
Always need someone who will carry a message.
But quickly, and with a great noise.
With a blue motorcycle I would station myself
In the courtyard of the hotel,
And in a little while I would have messages.

MARCO: When you have no wife you have dreams.

EDDIE: Why can't you just walk, or take a trolley or sump'm?

Enter BEATRICE *with coffee.*

RODOLPHO: Oh, no, the machine, the machine is necessary.
A man comes into a great hotel and says,
"I am a messenger." Who is this man?
He disappears walking, there is no noise, nothing—
Maybe he will never come back,
Maybe he will never deliver the message.

But a man who rides up on a great machine,
This man is responsible, this man exists.
He will be given messages.
I am also a singer, though.

EDDIE: You mean a regular—?

RODOLPHO: Oh, yes. One night last year
Andreola got sick. Baritone.
And I took his place in the garden of the hotel.
Three arias I sang without a mistake;
Thousand-lire notes they threw from the tables,
Money was falling like a storm in the treasury;
It was magnificent.
We lived six months on that night, eh, Marco?

MARCO *nods doubtfully.*

MARCO: Two months.

BEATRICE: Can't you get a job in that place?

RODOLPHO: Andreola got better.
He's a baritone, very strong; otherwise I—

MARCO *(to* BEATRICE*)*: He sang too loud.

RODOLPHO: Why too loud!

MARCO: Too loud. The guests in that hotel are all Englishmen.
They don't like too loud.

RODOLPHO: Then why did they throw so much money?

MARCO: They pay for your courage. *(to* EDDIE*)* The English like
courage, but once is enough.

RODOLPHO *(to all but* MARCO*)*: I never heard anybody say it was
too loud.

CATHERINE: Did you ever hear of jazz?

RODOLPHO: Oh, sure! I sing jazz.

CATHERINE: You could sing jazz?

RODOLPHO: Oh, I sing Napolidan, jazz, bel canto—
I sing "Paper Doll"; you like "Paper Doll"?

CATHERINE: Oh, sure, I'm crazy for "Paper Doll." Go ahead,
sing it.

RODOLPHO *(he takes his stance, and with a high tenor voice)*:

"I'll tell you boys it's tough to be alone,
And it's tough to love a doll that's not your own.
I'm through with all of them,

I'll never fall again,
Hey, boy, what you gonna do—

I'm goin' to buy a paper doll that I can call my own,
A doll that other fellows cannot steal,
And then the flirty, flirty guys
With their flirty, flirty eyes
Will have to flirt with dollies that are real.
When I come home at night she will be waiting.
She'll be the truest doll in all this world—"

EDDIE *(he has been slowly moving in agitation)*: Hey, kid—hey, wait a minute—

CATHERINE *(enthralled)*: Leave him finish. It's beautiful! *(to BEATRICE)* He's terrific! It's terrific, Rodolpho!

EDDIE: Look, kid; you don't want to be picked up, do ya?

MARCO: No-no!

EDDIE *(indicating the rest of the building)*: Because we never had no singers here—and all of a sudden there's a singer in the house, y'know what I mean?

MARCO: Yes, yes. You will be quiet, Rodolpho.

EDDIE *(flushed)*: They got guys all over the place, Marco. I mean.

MARCO: Yes. He will be quiet. *(to RODOLPHO)* Quiet.

EDDIE *(with iron control, even a smile)*: You got the shoes again, Garbo?

CATHERINE: I figured for tonight—

EDDIE: Do me a favor, will you? *(He indicates the bedroom.)* Go ahead.

Embarrassed now, angered, CATHERINE *goes out into the bedroom.* BEATRICE *watches her go and gets up, and, in passing, gives* EDDIE *a cold look, restrained only by the strangers, and goes to the table to pour coffee.*

EDDIE *(to MARCO, but directed as much to BEATRICE)*: All actresses they want to be around here. *(He goes to draw a shade down.)*

RODOLPHO *(happy about it)*: In Italy too! All the girls.

EDDIE *(sizing up RODOLPHO—there is a concealed suspicion)*: Yeah, heh?

RODOLPHO: Yes! *(He laughs, indicating CATHERINE with his head—her bedroom.)* Especially when they are so beautiful!

CATHERINE *emerges from the bedroom in low-heeled shoes, comes to the table.* RODOLPHO *is lifting a cup.*

CATHERINE: You like sugar?

RODOLPHO: Sugar? Yes! I like sugar very much!

EDDIE *is downstage, watching, as she pours a spoonful of sugar into* RODOLPHO's *cup.* EDDIE *turns and draws a shade, his face puffed with trouble, and the room dies. Light rises on* ALFIERI.)

ALFIERI: Who can ever know what will be discovered?

Sunlight rises on the street and house.

Eddie Carbone had never expected to have a destiny.

EDDIE *comes slowly, ambling, down the stairs into the street.*

A man works, raises his family, goes bowling,
Eats, gets old, and then he dies.
Now, as the weeks passed, there was a future,
There was a trouble that would not go away.

BEATRICE *appears with a shopping bag. Seeing her,* EDDIE *meets her at the stoop.*

EDDIE: It's after four.

BEATRICE: Well, it's a long show at the Paramount.

EDDIE: They must've seen every picture in Brooklyn by now.
He's supposed to stay in the house when he ain't workin'.
He ain't supposed to go advertising himself.

BEATRICE: So what am I gonna do?

EDDIE: Last night they went to the park. You know that? Louis seen them in the park.

BEATRICE: She's goin' on eighteen, what's so terrible?

EDDIE: I'm responsible for her.

BEATRICE: I just wish once in a while you'd be responsible for me, you know that?

EDDIE: What're you beefin'?

BEATRICE: You don't know why I'm beefin'? *(He turns away, making as though to scan the street, his jaws clamped.)* What's eatin' you? You're gonna bust your teeth, you grind them so much in bed, you know that? It's like a factory all night. *(He doesn't answer, looks peeved.)* What's the matter, Eddie?

EDDIE: It's all right with you? You don't mind this?

BEATRICE: Well what you want, keep her in the house a little baby all her life? What do you want, Eddie?

EDDIE: That's what I brung her up for? For that character?

BEATRICE: Why? He's a nice fella. Hard-workin', he's a good-lookin'

EDDIE: That's good-lookin'?

BEATRICE: He's handsome, for God's sake.

EDDIE: He gives me the heeby-jeebies. I don't like his whole way.

BEATRICE *(smiling)*: You're jealous, that's all.

EDDIE: Of *him*? Boy, you don't think much of me.

BEATRICE *(going to him)*: What are you worried about? She knows how to take care of herself.

EDDIE: She don't know nothin'. He's got her rollin'; you see the way she looks at him? The house could burn down she wouldn't know.

BEATRICE: Well, she's got a boy-friend finally, so she's excited. So?

EDDIE: He sings on the ships, didja know that?

BEATRICE *(mystified)*: What do you mean, he sings?

EDDIE: He sings. Right on the deck, all of a sudden—a whole song. They're callin' him Paper Doll, now. Canary. He's like a weird. Soon as he comes onto the pier it's a regular free show.

BEATRICE: Well, he's a kid; he don't know how to behave himself yet.

EDDIE: And with that wacky hair; he's like a chorus girl or sump'm.

BEATRICE: So he's blond, so—

EDDIE *(not looking at her)*: I just hope that's his regular hair, that's all I hope.

BEATRICE *(alarmed)*: You crazy or sump'm?

EDDIE *(only glancing at her)*: What's so crazy? You know what I heard them call him on Friday? I was on line for my check, somebody calls out, "Blondie!" I turn around, they're callin' *him*! Blondie now!

BEATRICE: You never seen a blond guy in your life? What about Whitey Balso?

EDDIE: Sure, but Whitey don't sing; he don't do like that on the ships—

BEATRICE: Well, maybe that's the way they do in Italy.

EDDIE: Then why don't his brother sing? Marco goes around like a man; nobody kids Marco. *(He shifts, with a glance at her.)* I don't like him, B. And I'm tellin' you now, I'm not gonna stand for it. For that character I didn't bring her up.

BEATRICE: All right—well, go tell her, then.

EDDIE: How am I gonna tell her? She won't listen to me, she can't even see me. I come home, she's in a dream. Look how thin she got, she could walk through a wall—

BEATRICE: All right, listen—

EDDIE: It's eatin' me out, B. I can't stand to look at his face. And what happened to the stenography? She don't practice no more, does she?

BEATRICE: All right, listen. I want you to lay off, you hear me? Don't work yourself up. You hear? This is her business.

EDDIE: B., he's takin' her for a ride!

BEATRICE: All right, that's her ride. It's time already; let her be somebody else's Madonna now. Come on, come in the house, you got your own to worry about. *(She glances around.)* She ain't gonna come any quicker if you stand on the street, Eddie. It ain't nice.

EDDIE: I'll be up right away. I want to take a walk. *(He walks away.)*

BEATRICE: Come on, look at the kids for once.

EDDIE: I'll be up right away. Go ahead.

BEATRICE *(with a shielded tone)*: Don't stand around, please. It ain't nice. I mean it.

She goes into the house. He reaches the upstage right extremity, stares at nothing for a moment; then, seeing someone coming, he goes to the railing downstage and sits, as LOUIS *and* MIKE *enter and join him.*

LOUIS: Wanna go bowlin' tonite?

EDDIE: I'm too tired. Goin' to sleep.

LOUIS: How's your two submarines?

EDDIE: They're okay.

LOUIS: I see they're gettin' work allatime.

EDDIE: Oh yeah, they're doin' all right.

MIKE: That's what we oughta do. We oughta leave the country and come in under the water. Then we get work.

EDDIE: You ain't kiddin'.

LOUIS: Well, what the hell. Y'know?

EDDIE: Sure.

LOUIS: Believe me, Eddie, you got a lotta credit comin' to you.

EDDIE: Aah, they don't bother me, don't cost me nutt'n.

MIKE: That older one, boy, he's a regular bull. I seen him the other day liftin' coffee bags over the Matson Line. They leave him alone he woulda load the whole ship by himself.

EDDIE: Yeah, he's a strong guy, that guy. My Frankie takes after him, I think. Their father was a regular giant, supposed to be.

LOUIS: Yeah, you could see. He's a regular slave.

MIKE: That blond one, though—(EDDIE *looks at him.*) He's got a sense of humor.

EDDIE *(searchingly)*: Yeah. He's funny—

MIKE *(laughing through his speech)*: Well, he ain't ezackly funny, but he's always like makin' remarks, like, y'know? He comes around, everybody's laughin'.

EDDIE *(uncomfortably)*: Yeah, well—he's got a sense of humor.

MIKE: Yeah, I mean, he's always makin' like remarks, like, y'know? (LOUIS *is quietly laughing with him.*)

EDDIE: Yeah, I know. But he's a kid yet, y'know? He—he's just a kid, that's all.

MIKE: I know. You take one look at him—everybody's happy. I worked one day with him last week over the Moore-Mac-Cormack, I'm tellin' you they was all hysterical.

EDDIE: Why? What'd he do?

MIKE: I don't know—he was just humorous. You never can remember what he says, y'know? But it's the way he says it. I mean he gives you a look sometimes and you start laughin'!

EDDIE: Yeah. *(troubled)* He's got a sense of humor.

MIKE *(laughing)*: Yeah.

LOUIS: Well, we'll see ya, Eddie.

EDDIE: Take it easy.

LOUIS: Yeah. See ya.

MIKE: If you wanna come bowlin' later we're goin' Flatbush Avenue.

They go. EDDIE, *in troubled thought, stares after them; they arrive at the left extremity, and their laughter, untroubled and friendly, rises as they see* RODOLPHO, *who is entering with* CATHERINE *on his arm. The longshoremen exit.* RODOLPHO *waves a greeting to them.*

CATHERINE: Hey, Eddie, what a picture we saw! Did we laugh!

EDDIE *(he can't help smiling at sight of her)*: Where'd you go?

CATHERINE: Paramount. It was with those two guys, y'know? That—

EDDIE: Brooklyn Paramount?

CATHERINE *(with an edge of anger, embarrassed before RODOLPHO)*: Sure the Brooklyn Paramount. I told you we wasn't goin' to New York.

EDDIE *(retreating before the threat of her anger)*: All right, I only asked you. *(to RODOLPHO)* I just don't want her hangin' around Times Square, see; it's full of tramps over there.

RODOLPHO: I would like to go to Broadway once, Eddie.
I would like to walk with her once
Where the theaters are, and the opera;
Since I was a boy I see pictures of those lights—

EDDIE *(his little patience waning)*: I want to talk to her a minute, Rodolpho; go upstairs, will you?

RODOLPHO: Eddie, we only walk together in the streets,
She teaches me—

CATHERINE: You know what he can't get over?
That there's no fountains in Brooklyn!

EDDIE *(smiling unwillingly, to RODOLPHO)*: Fountains?

RODOLPHO *smiles at his own naïveté.*

CATHERINE: In Italy, he says, every town's got fountains,
And they meet there. And you know what?
They got oranges on the trees where he comes from,
And lemons. Imagine? On the trees?
I mean it's interesting. But he's crazy for New York!

RODOLPHO *(attempting familiarity)*: Eddie, why can't we go once to Broadway?

EDDIE: Look, I gotta tell her something—

RODOLPHO *nods, goes to the stoop.*

RODOLPHO: Maybe you can come too. I want to see all those lights . . .

He sees no response in EDDIE'S *face. He glances at* CATHERINE *and goes into the house.*

CATHERINE: Why don't you talk to him, Eddie? He blesses you, and you don't talk to him hardly.

EDDIE *(enveloping her with his eyes)*: I bless you, and you don't talk to me. *(He tries to smile.)*

CATHERINE: I don't talk to you? *(She hits his arm.)* What do you mean!

EDDIE: I don't see you no more. I come home you're runnin' around someplace—

CATHERINE *takes his arm, and they walk a little.*

CATHERINE: Well, he wants to see everything, that's all, so we go. You mad at me?

EDDIE: No. *(He is smiling sadly, almost moony.)* It's just I used to come home, you was always there. Now, I turn around, you're a big girl. I don't know how to talk to you.

CATHERINE: Why!

EDDIE: I don't know, you're runnin', you're runnin', Katie. I don't think you listening any more to me.

CATHERINE: Ah, Eddie, sure I am. What's the matter? You don't like him?

Slight pause.

EDDIE: *You* like him, Katie?

CATHERINE *(with a blush, but holding her ground)*: Yeah. I like him.

EDDIE *(his smile goes)*: You like him.

CATHERINE *(looking down)*: Yeah. *(Now she looks at him for the consequences, smiling but tense. He looks at her like a lost boy.)* What're you got against him? I don't understand. He only blesses you.

EDDIE: He don't bless me, Katie.

CATHERINE: He does! You're like a father to him!

EDDIE: Katie.

CATHERINE: What, Eddie?

EDDIE: You gonna marry him?

CATHERINE: I don't know. We just been—goin' around, that's all.

EDDIE: He don't respect you, Katie.

CATHERINE: Why!

EDDIE: Katie, if you wasn't an orphan, wouldn't he ask your father permission before he run around with you like this?

CATHERINE: Oh, well, he didn't think you'd mind.

EDDIE: He knows I mind, but it don't bother him if I mind, don't you see that?

CATHERINE: No, Eddie, he's got all kinds of respect for me. And you too! We walk across the street, he takes my arm—he almost bows to me! You got him all wrong, Eddie; I mean it, you—

EDDIE: Katie, he's only bowin' to his passport.

CATHERINE: His passport!

EDDIE: That's right. He marries you he's got the right to be an American citizen. That's what's goin' on here. *(She is puzzled and surprised.)* You understand what I'm tellin' you? The guy is lookin' for his break, that's all he's lookin' for.

CATHERINE *(pained)*: Oh, no, Eddie, I don't think so.

EDDIE: You don't think so! Katie, you're gonna make me cry here. Is that a workin' man? What does he do with his first money? A snappy new jacket he buys, records, a pointy pair new shoes, and his brother's kids are starvin' with tuberculosis over there? That's a hit-and-run guy, baby; he's got bright lights in his head, Broadway—them guys don't think of nobody but theirself! You marry him and the next time you see him it'll be for the divorce!

CATHERINE: Eddie, he never said a word about his papers or—

EDDIE: You mean he's supposed to tell you that?

CATHERINE: I don't think he's even thinking about it.

EDDIE: What's better for him to think about? He could be picked up any day here and he's back pushin' taxis up the hill!

CATHERINE: No, I don't believe it.

EDDIE *(grabbing her hand)*: Katie, don't break my heart, listen to me—

CATHERINE: I don't want to hear it. Lemme go.

EDDIE *(holding her)*: Katie, listen—

CATHERINE: He loves me!

EDDIE *(with deep alarm)*: Don't say that, for God's sake! This is the oldest racket in the country.

CATHERINE *(desperately, as though he had made his imprint)*: I don't believe it!

EDDIE: They been pullin' this since the immigration law was put in! They grab a green kid that don't know nothin' and they—

CATHERINE: I don't believe it and I wish to hell you'd stop it!

She rushes, sobbing, into the house.

EDDIE: Katie!

He starts in after her, but halts as though realizing he has no force over her. From within, music is heard now, radio jazz. He glances up and down the street, then moves off, his chest beginning to rise and fall in anger. Light rises on ALFIERI, *seated behind his desk.*

ALFIERI: It was at this time that he first came to me.
    I had represented his father in an accident case
      some years before,
    And I was acquainted with the family in a casual way.
    I remember him now as he walked through my doorway—
    His eyes were like tunnels;
    My first thought was that he had committed a crime,

EDDIE *enters, sits beside the desk, cap in hand, looking out.*
    But soon I saw it was only a passion
    That had moved into his body, like a stranger.

ALFIERI *pauses, looks down at his desk, then to* EDDIE, *as though he were continuing a conversation with him.*
    I don't quite understand what I can do for you. Is there a question of law somewhere?

EDDIE: That's what I want to ask you.

ALFIERI: Because there's nothing illegal about a girl falling in love with an immigrant.

EDDIE: Yeah, but what about if the only reason for it is to get his papers?

ALFIERI: First of all, you don't know that—

EDDIE: I see it in his eyes; he's laughin' at her and he's laughin' at me.

ALFIERI: Eddie, I'm a lawyer; I can only deal in what's provable. You understand that, don't you? Can you prove that?

EDDIE: I know what's in his mind, Mr. Alfieri!

ALFIERI: Eddie, even if you could prove that—

EDDIE: Listen—Will you listen to me a minute? My father always said you was a smart man. I want you to listen to me.

ALFIERI: I'm only a lawyer, Eddie—

EDDIE: Will you listen a minute? I'm talkin' about the law. Lemme just bring out what I mean. A man, which he comes into the country illegal, don't it stand to reason he's gonna take every penny and put it in the sock? Because they don't know from one day to the nother, right?

ALFIERI: All right.

EDDIE: He's spendin'. Records he buys now. Shoes. Jackets. Y'understand me? This guy ain't worried. This guy is *here*. So it must be that he's got it all laid out in his mind already—he's stayin'. Right?

ALFIERI: Well? What about it?

EDDIE: All right. (*He glances over his shoulder as though for intruders, then back to* ALFIERI, *then down to the floor.*) I'm talkin' to you confidential, ain't I?

ALFIERI: Certainly.

EDDIE: I mean it don't go no place but here. Because I don't like to say this about anybody. Even to my wife I didn't exactly say this.

ALFIERI: What is it?

EDDIE (*he takes a breath*): The guy ain't right, Mr. Alfieri.

ALFIERI: What do you mean?

EDDIE (*glancing over his shoulder again*): I mean he ain't right.

ALFIERI: I don't get you.

EDDIE (*he shifts to another position in the chair*): Dja ever get a look at him?

ALFIERI: Not that I know of, no.

EDDIE: He's a blond guy. Like—platinum. You know what I mean?

ALFIERI: No.

EDDIE: I mean if you close the paper fast—you could blow him over.

ALFIERI: Well, that doesn't mean—

EDDIE: Wait a minute, I'm tellin' you sump'm. He sings, see. Which is—I mean it's all right, but sometimes he hits a note, see. I turn around. I mean—high. You know what I mean?

ALFIERI: Well, that's a tenor.

EDDIE: I know a tenor, Mr. Alfieri. This ain't no tenor. I mean if you came in the house and you didn't know who was singin', you wouldn't be lookin' for him, you'd be lookin' for her.

ALFIERI: Yes, but that's not—

EDDIE: I'm tellin' you sump'm, wait a minute; please, Mr. Alfieri. I'm tryin' to bring out my thoughts here. Couple a nights ago my niece brings out a dress, which it's too small for her because she shot up like a light this last year. He takes the dress, lays it on the table, he cuts it up; one-two-three, he makes a new dress. I mean he looked so sweet there, like an angel—you could kiss him he was so sweet.

ALFIERI: Now, look, Eddie—

EDDIE: Mr. Alfieri, they're laughin' at him on the piers. I'm ashamed. Paper Doll, they call him. Blondie now. His brother thinks it's because he's got a sense of humor, see—which he's got—but that ain't what they're laughin'. Which they're not goin' to come out with it because they know he's my relative, which they have to see me if they make a crack, y'know? But I know what they're laughin' at, and when I think of that guy layin' his hands on her I could—I mean it's eatin' me out, Mr. Alfieri, because I struggled for that girl. And now he comes in my house—

ALFIERI: Eddie, look. I have my own children, I understand you. But the law is very specific. The law does not—

EDDIE (*with a fuller flow of indignation*): You mean to tell me that there's no law that a guy which he ain't right can go to work and marry a girl and—?

ALFIERI: You have no recourse in the law, Eddie.

EDDIE: Yeah, but if he ain't right, Mr. Alfieri, you mean to tell me—

ALFIERI: There is nothing you can do, Eddie, believe me.

EDDIE: Nothin'.

ALFIERI: Nothing at all. There's only one legal question here.

EDDIE: What?

ALFIERI: The manner in which they entered the country. But I don't think you want to do anything about that, do you?

EDDIE: You mean—?

ALFIERI: Well, they entered illegally.

EDDIE: Oh, Jesus, no, I wouldn't do nothin' about that. I mean—

ALFIERI: All right, then, let me talk now, eh?

EDDIE: Mr. Alfieri, I can't believe what you tell me. I mean there must be some kinda law which—

453

ALFIERI: Eddie, I want you to listen to me.

Pause.

> You know, sometimes God mixes up the people.
> We all love somebody, the wife, the kids—
> Every man's got somebody that he loves, heh?
> But sometimes—there's too much. You know?
> There's too much, and it goes where it mustn't.
> A man works hard, he brings up a child,
> Sometimes it's a niece, sometimes even a daughter,
> And he never realizes it, but through the years—
> There is too much love for the daughter,
> There is too much love for the niece.
> Do you understand what I'm saying to you?

EDDIE *(sardonically)*: What do you mean, I shouldn't look out for her good?

ALFIERI: Yes, but these things have to end, Eddie, that's all.

> The child has to grow up and go away,
> And the man has to learn how to forget.
> Because after all, Eddie—
> What other way can it end?

Pause.

> Let her go. That's my advice. You did your job,
> Now it's her life; wish her luck,
> And let her go.

Pause.

> Will you do that? Because there's no law, Eddie;
> Make up your mind to it; the law is not interested in this.

EDDIE: You mean to tell me, even if he's a punk? If he's—

ALFIERI: There's nothing you can do.

EDDIE *sits almost grinding his jaws. He stands, wipes one eye.*

EDDIE: Well, all right, thanks. Thanks very much.

ALFIERI: What are you going to do?

EDDIE *(with a helpless but ironic gesture)*: What can I do? I'm a patsy, what can a patsy do? I worked like a dog twenty years so a punk could have her, so that's what I done. I mean, in the worst times, in the worst, when there wasn't a ship comin' in the harbor, I didn't stand around lookin' for relief—I hustled.

454

When there was empty piers in Brooklyn I went to Hoboken, Staten Island, the West Side, Jersey, all over—because I made a promise. I took out of my own kids' mouths to give to her. I took out of my mouth. I walked hungry plenty days in this city! *(It begins to break through.)* And now I gotta sit in my own house and look at a son-of-a-bitch punk like that!—which he came out of nowhere! I give him my house to sleep! I take the blankets off my bed for him, and he takes and puts his dirty filthy hands on her like a goddam thief!

ALFIERI: But Eddie, she's a woman now—

EDDIE: He's stealin' from me!

ALFIERI: She wants to get married, Eddie. She can't marry you, can she?

EDDIE *(furiously)*: What're you talkin' about, marry me! I don't know what the hell you're talkin' about!

Pause.

ALFIERI: I gave you my advice, Eddie. That's it.

EDDIE *gathers himself. A pause.*

EDDIE: Well, thanks. Thanks very much. It just—it's breakin' my heart, y'know. I—

ALFIERI: I understand. Put it out of your mind. Can you do that?

EDDIE: I'm—*(He feels the threat of sobs, and with a helpless wave.)* I'll see you around. *(He goes out.)*

ALFIERI: There are times when you want to spread an alarm,
But nothing has happened. I knew, I knew then and there—
I could have finished the whole story that afternoon.
It wasn't as though there were a mystery to unravel.
I could see every step coming, step after step,
Like a dark figure walking down a hall toward a certain door.
I knew where he was heading for;
I knew where he was going to end.
And I sat here many afternoons,
Asking myself why, being an intelligent man,
I was so powerless to stop it.
I even went to a certain old lady in the neighborhood,
A very wise old woman, and I told her,
And she only nodded, and said,
"Pray for him."

And so I—*(he sits)*—waited here.

As the light goes out on ALFIERI *it rises in the apartment, where all are finishing dinner. There is silence, but for the clink of a dish. Now* CATHERINE *looks up.*

CATHERINE: You know where they went?

BEATRICE: Where?

CATHERINE: They went to Africa once. On a fishing boat. *(*EDDIE *glances at her.)* It's true, Eddie.

EDDIE: I didn't say nothin'. *(He finishes his coffee and leaves the table.)*

CATHERINE: And I was never even in Staten Island.

EDDIE *(sitting with a paper in his rocker)*: You didn't miss nothin'. *(Pause.* CATHERINE *takes dishes out;* BEATRICE *and* RODOLPHO *stack the others.)* How long that take you, Marco—to get to Africa?

MARCO: Oh—two days. We go all over.

RODOLPHO: Once we went to Yugoslavia.

EDDIE *(to* MARCO*)*: They pay all right on them boats?

MARCO: If they catch fish they pay all right.

RODOLPHO: They're family boats, though. And nobody in our family owned one. So we only worked when one of the families was sick.

CATHERINE *re-enters.*

BEATRICE: Y'know, Marco, what I don't understand—there's an ocean full of fish and yiz are all starvin'.

EDDIE: They gotta have boats, nets, you need money.

BEATRICE: Yeah, but couldn't they like fish from the beach? You see them down Coney Island—

MARCO: Sardines.

EDDIE: Sure. How you gonna catch sardines on a hook?

BEATRICE: Oh, I didn't know they're sardines. *(to* CATHERINE*)* They're sardines!

CATHERINE: Yeah, they follow them all over the ocean—Africa, Greece, Yugoslavia . . .

BEATRICE *(to* EDDIE*)*: It's funny, y'know? You never think of it, that sardines are swimming in the ocean!

CATHERINE: I know. It's like oranges and lemons on a tree. *(to* EDDIE*)* I mean you ever think of oranges and lemons on a tree?

EDDIE: Yeah, I know. It's funny. *(to* MARCO*)* I heard that they paint the oranges to make them look orange.

MARCO: Paint?

EDDIE: Yeah, I heard that they grow like green—

MARCO: No, in Italy the oranges are orange.

RODOLPHO: Lemons are green.

EDDIE *(resenting his instruction)*: I know lemons are green, for Christ's sake, you see them in the store they're green sometimes. I said oranges they paint, I didn't say nothin' about lemons.

BEATRICE *(diverting their attention)*: Your wife is gettin' the money all right, Marco?

MARCO: Oh, yes. She bought medicine for my boy.

BEATRICE: That's wonderful. You feel better, heh?

MARCO: Oh, yes! But I'm lonesome.

BEATRICE: I just hope you ain't gonna do like some of them around here. They're here twenty-five years, some men, and they didn't get enough together to go back twice.

MARCO: Oh, I know. We have many families in our town, the children never saw the father. But I will go home. Three, four years, I think.

BEATRICE: Maybe you should keep more here, no? Because maybe she thinks it comes so easy you'll never get ahead of yourself.

MARCO: Oh, no, she saves. I send everything. My wife is very lonesome. *(He smiles shyly.)*

BEATRICE: She must be nice. She pretty? I bet, heh?

MARCO *(blushing)*: No, but she understands everything.

RODOLPHO: Oh, he's got a clever wife!

EDDIE: I betcha there's plenty surprises sometimes when those guys get back there, heh?

MARCO: Surprises?

EDDIE: I mean, you know—they count the kids and there's a couple extra than when they left?

MARCO: No—no. The women wait, Eddie. Most. Most. Very few surprises.

RODOLPHO: It's more strict in our town. *(*EDDIE *looks at him now.)* It's not so free.

EDDIE: It ain't so free here either, Rodolpho, like you think. I seen greenhorns sometimes get in trouble that way—they think just because a girl don't go around with a shawl over her head that

457

she ain't strict, y'know? Girl don't have to wear black dress to be strict. Know what I mean?

RODOLPHO: Well, I always have respect—

EDDIE: I know, but in your town you wouldn't just drag off some girl without permission, I mean. *(He turns.)* You know what I mean, Marco? It ain't that much different here.

MARCO *(cautiously)*: Yes.

EDDIE *(to RODOLPHO)*: I mean I seen some a yiz get the wrong idea sometimes. I mean it might be a little more free here but it's just as strict.

RODOLPHO: I have respect for her, Eddie. I do anything wrong?

EDDIE: Look, kid, I ain't her father, I'm only her uncle—

MARCO: No, Eddie, if he does wrong you must tell him. What does he do wrong?

EDDIE: Well, Marco, till he came here she was never out on the street twelve o'clock at night.

MARCO *(to RODOLPHO)*: You come home early now.

CATHERINE: Well, the movie ended late.

EDDIE: I'm just sayin—he thinks you always stayed out like that. I mean he don't understand, honey, see?

MARCO: You come home early now, Rodolpho.

RODOLPHO *(embarrassed)*: All right, sure.

EDDIE: It's not only for her, Marco. *(to CATHERINE)* I mean it, kid, he's gettin' careless. The more he runs around like that the more chance he's takin'. *(to RODOLPHO)* I mean suppose you get hit by a car or sump'm, where's your papers, who are you? Know what I mean?

RODOLPHO: But I can't stay in the house all the time, I—

BEATRICE: Listen, he's gotta go out sometime—

EDDIE: Well, listen, it depends, Beatrice. If he's here to work, then he should work; if he's here for a good time, then he could fool around! *(to MARCO)* But I understood, Marco, that you was both comin' to make a livin' for your family. You understand me, don't you, Marco?

MARCO *(he sees it nearly in the open now, and.with reserve)*: I beg your pardon, Eddie.

EDDIE: I mean that's what I understood in the first place, see?

MARCO: Yes. That's why we came.

EDDIE: Well, that's all I'm askin'.

There is a pause, an awkwardness. Now CATHERINE *gets up and puts a record on the phonograph. Music.*

CATHERINE *(flushed with revolt)*: You wanna dance, Rodolpho?

RODOLPHO *(in deference to* EDDIE*)*: No, I—I'm tired.

CATHERINE: Ah, come on. He plays a beautiful piano, that guy. Come. *(She has taken his hand, and he stiffly rises, feeling* EDDIE*'s eyes on his back, and they dance.)*

EDDIE *(to* CATHERINE*)*: What's that, a new record?

CATHERINE: It's the same one. We bought it the other day.

BEATRICE *(to* EDDIE*)*: They only bought three records. *(She watches them dance;* EDDIE *turns his head away.* MARCO *just sits there, waiting. Now* BEATRICE *turns to* EDDIE*.)* Must be nice to go all over in one of them fishin' boats. I would like that myself. See all them other countries?

EDDIE: Yeah.

BEATRICE *(to* MARCO*)*: But the women don't go along, I bet.

MARCO: No, not on the boats. Hard work.

BEATRICE: What're you got, a regular kitchen and everything?

MARCO: Yes, we eat very good on the boats—especially when Rodolpho comes along; everybody gets fat.

BEATRICE: Oh, he cooks?

MARCO: Sure, very good cook. Rice, pasta, fish, everything.

EDDIE: He's a cook too! *(He looks at* RODOLPHO*.)* He sings, he cooks . . .

RODOLPHO *smiles thankfully.*

BEATRICE: Well, it's good; he could always make a living.

EDDIE: It's wonderful. He sings, he cooks, he could make dresses . . .

CATHERINE: They get some high pay, them guys. The head chefs in all the big hotels are men. You read about them.

EDDIE: That's what I'm sayin'.

CATHERINE *and* RODOLPHO *continue dancing.*

CATHERINE: Yeah, well, I mean.

EDDIE *(to* BEATRICE*)*: He's lucky, believe me. *(A slight pause; he looks away, then back to* BEATRICE*.)* That's why the waterfront is no place for him. I mean, like me—I can't cook, I can't sing, I can't make dresses, so I'm on the waterfront. But if I could cook, if I could sing, if I could make dresses, I wouldn't be on the waterfront. *(They are all regarding him now; he senses he is exposing the issue, but he is driven on.)* I would be someplace else. I would be like in a dress store. *(He suddenly gets up and pulls his pants up over his belly.)* What do you say, Marco, we go to the bouts next Saturday night? You never seen a fight, did you?

MARCO *(uneasily)*: Only in the moving pictures.

EDDIE: I'll treat yiz. What do you say, Danish? You wanna come along? I'll buy the tickets.

RODOLPHO: Sure. I like to go.

CATHERINE *(nervously happy now)*: I'll make some coffee, all right?

EDDIE: Go ahead, make some! *(He draws her near him.)* Make it nice and strong. *(Mystified, she smiles and goes out. He is weirdly elated; he is rubbing his fists into his palms.)* You wait, Marco, you see some real fights here. You ever do any boxing?

MARCO: No, I never.

EDDIE *(to RODOLPHO)*: Betcha you done some, heh?

RODOLPHO: No.

EDDIE: Well, get up, come on, I'll teach you.

BEATRICE: What's he got to learn that for?

EDDIE: Ya can't tell, one a these days somebody's liable to step on his foot, or sump'm. Come on, Rodolpho, I show you a couple a passes.

BEATRICE *(unwillingly, carefully)*: Go ahead, Rodolpho. He's a good boxer; he could teach you.

RODOLPHO *(embarrassed)*: Well, I don't know how to—

EDDIE: Just put your hands up. Like this, see? That's right. That's very good, keep your left up, because you lead with the left, see? like this. *(He gently moves his left into RODOLPHO's face.)* See? Now what you gotta do is you gotta block me, so when I come in like that you— *(RODOLPHO parries his left.)* Hey, that's very good! *(RODOLPHO laughs.)* All right, now come into me. Come on.

RODOLPHO: I don't want to hit you, Eddie.

EDDIE: Don't pity me, come on. Throw it; I'll show you how to block it. *(RODOLPHO jabs at him, laughing.)* 'At's it. Come on, again. For the jaw, right here. *(RODOLPHO jabs with more assurance.)* Very good!

BEATRICE *(to* MARCO*)*: He's very good!

EDDIE: Sure, he's great! Come on, kid, put sump'm behind it; you can't hurt me. *(*RODOLPHO, *more seriously, jabs at* EDDIE*'s jaw and grazes it.)* Attaboy. Now I'm gonna hit you, so block me, see?

CATHERINE *comes from the kitchen, watches.*

CATHERINE *(with beginning alarm)*: What are they doin'?

They are lightly boxing now.

BEATRICE *(She senses only the comradeship in it now.)*: He's teachin' him; he's very good!

EDDIE: Sure, he's terrific! Look at him go! *(*RODOLPHO *lands a blow.)* 'At's it! Now watch out, here I come, Danish! *(He feints with his left hand and lands with his right. It mildly staggers* RODOLPHO.*)*

CATHERINE *(rushing to* RODOLPHO*)*: Eddie!

EDDIE: Why? I didn't hurt him. *(going to help the dizzy* RODOLPHO*)* Did I hurt you, kid?

RODOLPHO: No, no, he didn't hurt me. *(to* EDDIE, *with a certain gleam and a smile)* I was only surprised.

BEATRICE: That's enough, Eddie; he did pretty good, though.

EDDIE: Yeah. *(He rubs his fists together.)* He could be very good, Marco. I'll teach him again.

MARCO *nods at him dubiously.*

RODOLPHO *(as a new song comes on the radio, his voice betraying a new note of command)*: Dance, Catherine. Come.

RODOLPHO *takes her in his arms. They dance.* EDDIE, *in thought, sits in his chair, and* MARCO *rises and comes downstage to a chair and looks down at it.* BEATRICE *and* EDDIE *watch him.*

MARCO: Can you lift this chair?

EDDIE: What do you mean?

MARCO: From here. *(He gets on one knee with one hand behind his back, and grasps the bottom of one of the chair legs but does not raise it.)*

EDDIE: Sure, why not? *(He comes to the chair, kneels, grasps the leg, raises the chair one inch, but it leans over to the floor.)* Gee, that's hard, I never knew that. *(He tries again, and again fails.)* It's on an angle, that's why, heh?

MARCO: Here. *(He kneels, grasps, and with strain slowly raises the chair higher and higher, getting to his feet now.)*

And RODOLPHO *and* CATHERINE *have stopped dancing as* MARCO *raises the chair over his head.*

He is face to face with EDDIE, *a strained tension gripping his eyes and jaw, his neck stiff, the chair raised like a weapon—and he transforms what might appear like a glare of warning into a smile of triumph, and* EDDIE's *grin vanishes as he absorbs the look; as the lights go down.*

The stage remains dark for a moment. Ships' horns are heard. Light rises on ALFIERI *at his desk. He is discovered in dejection, his face bent to the desk, on which his arms rest. Now he looks up and front.*

ALFIERI: On the twenty-third of that December
A case of Scotch whisky slipped from a net
While being unloaded—as a case of Scotch whisky
Is inclined to do on the twenty-third of December
On Pier Forty-one. There was no snow, but it was cold.
His wife was out shopping.
Marco was still at work.
The boy had not been hired that day;
Catherine told me later that this was the first time
They had been alone together in the house.

Light is rising on CATHERINE, *who is ironing in the apartment. Music is playing.* RODOLPHO *is in* EDDIE's *rocker, his head leaning back. A piano jazz cadenza begins. Luxuriously he turns his head to her and smiles, and she smiles at him, then continues ironing. He comes to the table and sits beside her.*

CATHERINE: You hungry?

RODOLPHO: Not for anything to eat. *(He leans his chin on the back of his hand on the table, watching her iron.)* I have nearly three hundred dollars. *(He looks up at her.)* Catherine?

CATHERINE: I heard you.

RODOLPHO *reaches out and takes her hand and kisses it, then lets it go. She resumes ironing. He rests his head again on the back of his hand.*

RODOLPHO: You don't like to talk about it any more?

CATHERINE: Sure, I don't mind talkin' about it.

RODOLPHO: What worries you, Catherine?

CATHERINE *continues ironing. He now reaches out and takes her hand off the iron, and she sits back in her chair, not looking directly at him.*

CATHERINE: I been wantin' to ask you about something. Could I?

RODOLPHO: All the answers are in my eyes, Catherine. But you don't look in my eyes lately. You're full of secrets. *(She looks at him. He presses her hand against his cheek. She seems withdrawn.)* What is the question?

CATHERINE: Suppose I wanted to live in Italy.

RODOLPHO *(smiling at the incongruity)*: You going to marry somebody rich?

CATHERINE: No, I mean live there—you and me.

RODOLPHO *(his smile is vanishing)*: When?

CATHERINE: Well—when we get married.

RODOLPHO *(astonished)*: You want to be an Italian?

CATHERINE: No, but I could live there without being Italian. Americans live there.

RODOLPHO: Forever?

CATHERINE: Yeah.

RODOLPHO: You're fooling.

CATHERINE: No, I mean it.

RODOLPHO: Where do you get such an idea?

CATHERINE: Well, you're always saying it's so beautiful there, with the mountains and the ocean and all the—

RODOLPHO: You're fooling me.

CATHERINE: I mean it.

RODOLPHO: Catherine, if I ever brought you home
With no money, no business, nothing,
They would call the priest and the doctor
And they would say Rodolpho is crazy.

CATHERINE: I know, but I think we would be happier there.

RODOLPHO: Happier! What would you eat? You can't cook the view!

CATHERINE: Maybe you could be a singer, like in Rome or—

RODOLPHO: Rome! Rome is full of singers.

CATHERINE: Well, I could work then.

RODOLPHO: Where?

CATHERINE: God, there must be jobs somewhere!

RODOLPHO: There's nothing! Nothing, nothing,
    Nothing. Now tell me what you're talking about.
    How can I bring you from a rich country
    To suffer in a poor country?
    What are you talking about?

She searches for words.

    I would be a criminal stealing your face;
    In two years you would have an old, hungry face.
    When my brother's babies cry they give them water,
    Water that boiled a bone.
    Don't you believe that?

CATHERINE *(quietly)*: I'm afraid of Eddie here.

A slight pause.

RODOLPHO: We wouldn't live here.
    Once I am a citizen I could work anywhere,
    And I would find better jobs,
    And we would have a house, Catherine.
    If I were not afraid to be arrested
    I would start to be something wonderful here!

CATHERINE *(steeling herself)*: Tell me something. I mean just tell
    me, Rodolpho. Would you still want to do it if it turned out we
    had to go live in Italy? I mean just if it turned out that way.

RODOLPHO: This is your question or his question?

CATHERINE: I would like to know, Rodolpho. I mean it.

RODOLPHO: To go there with nothing?

CATHERINE: Yeah.

RODOLPHO: No. *(She looks at him wide-eyed.)* No.

CATHERINE: You wouldn't?

RODOLPHO: No; I will not marry you to live in Italy.
    I want you to be my wife
    And I want to be a citizen.
    Tell him that, or I will. Yes.

He moves about angrily.

    And tell him also, and tell yourself, please,
    That I am not a beggar,
    And you are not a horse, a gift,
    A favor for a poor immigrant.

CATHERINE: Well, don't get mad!
RODOLPHO: I am furious!
　Do you think I am so desperate?
　My brother is desperate, not me.
　You think I would carry on my back
　The rest of my life a woman I didn't love
　Just to be an American? It's so wonderful?
　You think we have no tall buildings in Italy?
　Electric lights? No wide streets? No flags?
　No automobiles? Only work we don't have.
　I want to be an American so I can work,
　That is the only wonder here—work!
　How can you insult me, Catherine?
CATHERINE: I didn't mean that—
RODOLPHO: My heart dies to look at you.
　Why are you so afraid of him?
CATHERINE *(near tears)*: I don't know!

RODOLPHO *turns her to him.*

RODOLPHO: Do you trust me, Catherine? You?
CATHERINE: It's only that I—
　He was good to me, Rodolpho.
　You don't know him; he was always the sweetest guy to me.
　Good. He razzes me all the time,
　But he don't mean it. I know.
　I would—just feel ashamed if I made him sad.
　'Cause I always dreamt that when I got married
　He would be happy at the wedding, and laughin'.
　And now he's—mad all the time, and nasty.

She is weeping.

　Tell him you'd live in Italy—just tell him,
　And maybe he would start to trust you a little, see?
　Because I want him to be happy; I mean—
　I like him, Rodolpho—and I can't stand it!

She weeps, and he holds her.

RODOLPHO: Catherine—oh, little girl—
CATHERINE: I love you, Rodolpho, I love you.
RODOLPHO: I think that's what you have to tell him, eh?
　Can't you tell him?

CATHERINE: I'm ascared, I'm so scared.

RODOLPHO: Ssssh. Listen, now. Tonight when he comes home
  We will both sit down after supper
  And we will tell him—you and I.

He sees her fear rising.

  But you must believe me yourself, Catherine.
  It's true—you have very much to give me;
  A whole country! Sure, I hold America when I hold you.
  But if you were not my love,
  If every day I did not smile so many times
  When I think of you,
  I could never kiss you, not for a hundred Americas.
  Tonight I'll tell him,
  And you will not be frightened any more, eh?
  And then in two, three months I'll have enough,
  We will go to the church, and we'll come back to our own—

He breaks off, seeing the conquered longing in her eyes, her smile.

  Catherine—

CATHERINE: Now. There's nobody here.

RODOLPHO: Oh, my little girl. Oh God!

CATHERINE *(kissing his face)*: Now!

He turns her upstage. They walk embraced, her head on his shoulder, and he sings to her softly. They go into a bedroom.

  A pause. Ships' horns sound in the distance. EDDIE *enters on the street. He is unsteady, drunk. He mounts the stairs. The sounds continue. He enters the apartment, looks around, takes out a bottle from one pocket, puts it on the table; then another bottle from another pocket; and a third from an inside pocket. He sees the iron, goes over to it and touches it, pulls his hand quickly back, turns toward upstage.*

EDDIE: Beatrice? *(He goes to the open kitchen door and looks in. He turns to a bedroom door.)* Beatrice? *(He starts for this door; it opens, and* CATHERINE *is standing there; under his gaze she adjusts her dress.)*

CATHERINE: You got home early.

EDDIE *(trying to unravel what he senses)*: Knocked off for Christmas early. *(She goes past him to the ironing board. Indicating the iron.)* You start a fire that way.

CATHERINE: I only left it for a minute.

RODOLPHO *appears in the bedroom doorway.* EDDIE *sees him, and his arm jerks slightly in shock.* RODOLPHO *nods to him testingly.* EDDIE *looks to* CATHERINE, *who is looking down at the ironing as she works.*

RODOLPHO: Beatrice went to buy shoes for the children.

EDDIE: Pack it up. Go ahead. Get your stuff and get outa here. *(*CATHERINE *puts down the iron and walks toward the bedroom, and* EDDIE *grabs her arm.)* Where you goin?

CATHERINE: Don't bother me, Eddie. I'm goin' with him.

EDDIE: You goin' with him. You goin' with him, heh? *(He grabs her face in the vise of his two hands.) You goin' with him!*

He kisses her on the mouth as she pulls at his arms; he will not let go, keeps his face pressed against hers. RODOLPHO *comes to them now.*

RODOLPHO *(tentatively at first)*: Eddie! No, Eddie! *(He now pulls full force on* EDDIE's *arms to break his grip.)* Don't! No!

CATHERINE *breaks free, and* EDDIE *is spun around by* RODOLPHO's *force, to face him.*

EDDIE: You want something?

RODOLPHO: She'll be my wife.

EDDIE: But what're you gonna be? That's what I wanna know! What're you gonna be!

RODOLPHO *(with tears of rage)*: Don't say that to me!

RODOLPHO *flies at him in attack.* EDDIE *pins his arms, laughing, and suddenly kisses him.*

CATHERINE: Eddie! Let go, ya hear me! I'll kill you! Leggo of him!

She tears at EDDIE's *face, and* EDDIE *releases* RODOLPHO *and stands there, tears rolling down his face as he laughs mockingly at* RODOLPHO. *She is staring at him in horror, her breasts heaving.* RODOLPHO *is rigid; they are like animals that have torn at each other and broken up without a decision, each waiting for the other's mood.*

EDDIE: I give you till tomorrow, kid. Get outa here. Alone. You hear me? Alone.

CATHERINE: I'm goin' with him, Eddie.

EDDIE (*indicating* RODOLPHO *with his head*): Not with that. (*He sits, still panting for breath, and they watch him helplessly as he leans his head back on the chair and, striving to catch his breath, closes his eyes.*) Don't make me do nuttin', Catherine.

The lights go down on EDDIE'*s apartment and rise on* ALFIERI.

ALFIERI: On December twenty-seventh I saw him next.
  I normally go home well before six,
  But that day I sat around,
  Looking out my window at the bay,
  And when I saw him walking through my doorway
  I knew why I had waited.
  And if I seem to tell this like a dream,
  It was that way. Several moments arrived
  In the course of the two talks we had
  When it occurred to me how—almost transfixed
  I had come to feel. I had lost my strength somewhere.

EDDIE *enters, removing his cap, sits in the chair, looks thoughtfully out.*

  I looked in his eyes more than I listened—
  In fact, I can hardly remember the conversation.
  But I will never forget how dark the room became
  When he looked at me; his eyes were like tunnels.
  I kept wanting to call the police,
  But nothing had happened.
  Nothing at all had really happened.

He breaks off and looks down at the desk. Then he turns to EDDIE.

  So in other words, he won't leave?

EDDIE: My wife is talkin' about renting a room upstairs for them. An old lady on the top floor is got an empty room.

ALFIERI: What does Marco say?

EDDIE: He just sits there. Marco don't say much.

ALFIERI: I guess they didn't tell him, heh? What happened?

EDDIE: I don't know; Marco don't say much.

ALFIERI: What does your wife say?

EDDIE (*unwilling to pursue this*): Nobody's talkin' much in the house. So what about that?

ALFIERI: But you didn't prove anything about him.

EDDIE: Mr. Alfieri, I'm tellin' you—

ALFIERI: You're not telling me anything, Eddie;
  It sounds like he just wasn't strong enough to break your grip.
EDDIE: I'm tellin' you I know—he ain't right.
  Somebody that don't want it can break it.
  Even a mouse, if you catch a teeny mouse
  And you hold it in your hand, that mouse
  Can give you the right kind of fight,
  And he didn't give me the right kind of fight.
  I know it, Mr. Alfieri, the guy ain't right.
ALFIERI: What did you do that for, Eddie?
EDDIE: To show her what he is! So she would see, once and for
  all! Her mother'll turn over in the grave! *(He gathers himself
  almost peremptorily.)* So what do I gotta do now? Tell me what
  to do.
ALFIERI: She actually said she's marrying him?
EDDIE: She told me, yeah. So what do I do?

A slight pause.

ALFIERI: This is my last word, Eddie,
  Take it or not, that's your business.
  Morally and legally you have no rights;
  You cannot stop it; she is a free agent.
EDDIE *(angering)*: Didn't you hear what I told you?
ALFIERI *(with a tougher tone)*: I heard what you told me,
  And I'm telling you what the answer is. I'm not only telling you
    now, I'm warning you—
  The law is nature.
  The law is only a word for what has a right to happen.
  When the law is wrong it's because it's unnatural,
  But in this case it is natural,
  And a river will drown you
  If you buck it now.
  Let her go. And bless her.

*As he speaks, a phone begins to glow on the opposite side of the
stage, a faint, lonely blue.* EDDIE *stands up, jaws clenched.*

  Somebody had to come for her, Eddie, sooner or later.

EDDIE *starts to turn to go, and* ALFIERI *rises with new anxiety.*

  You won't have a friend in the world, Eddie!
  Even those who understand will turn against you,

Even the ones who feel the same will despise you!

EDDIE *moves off quickly.*

Put it out of your mind! Eddie!

The light goes out on ALFIERI. EDDIE *has at the same time appeared beside the phone, and he lifts it.*

EDDIE: I want to report something. Illegal immigrants. Two of them. That's right. Four-forty-one Saxon Street, Brooklyn, yeah. Ground floor. Heh? *(with greater difficulty)* I'm just around the neighborhood, that's all. Heh?

Evidently he is being questioned further, and he slowly hangs up. He comes out of the booth just as LOUIS *and* MIKE *come down the street. They are privately laughing at some private joke.*

LOUIS: Go bowlin', Eddie?

EDDIE: No, I'm due home.

LOUIS: Well, take it easy.

EDDIE: I'll see yiz.

They leave him, and he watches them go. They resume their evidently amusing conversation. He glances about, then goes up into the house, and, as he enters, the lights go on in the apartment. BEATRICE *is seated, sewing a pair of child's pants.*

BEATRICE: Where you been so late?

EDDIE: I took a walk, I told you. *(He gets out of his zipper jacket, picks up a paper that is lying in a chair, prepares to sit.)* Kids sleepin'?

BEATRICE: Yeah, they're all sleepin'.

Pause. EDDIE *looks out the window.*

EDDIE: Where's Marco?

BEATRICE: They decided to move upstairs with Mrs. Dondero.

EDDIE *(turning to her)*: They're up there now?

BEATRICE: They moved all their stuff. Catherine decided. It's better, Eddie, they'll be outa your way. They're happy and we'll be happy.

EDDIE: Catherine's up there too?

BEATRICE: She just went up to bring pillow cases. She'll be down right away.

EDDIE *(nodding)*: Well, they're better off up there; the whole house knows they were here anyway, so there's nothin' to hide no more.

BEATRICE: That's what I figured. And besides, with the other ones up there maybe it'll look like they're just boarders too, or sump'm. You want eat?

EDDIE: What other ones?

BEATRICE: The two guys she rented the other room to. She's rentin' two rooms. She bought beds and everything: I told you.

EDDIE: When'd you tell me?

BEATRICE: I don't know; I think we were talkin' about it last week, even. She is startin' like a little boarding house up there. Only she's got no pillow cases yet.

EDDIE: I didn't hear nothin' about no boarding house.

BEATRICE: Sure, I loaned her my big fryin' pan beginning of the week. I told you. *(She smiles and goes to him.)* You gotta come to yourself, kid; you're in another world all the time. *(He is silent, peering; she touches his head.)* I wanna tell you, Eddie; it was my fault, and I'm sorry. No kiddin'. I shoulda put them up there in the first place.

EDDIE: Dja ever see these guys?

BEATRICE: I see them on the stairs every couple a days. They're kinda young guys. You look terrible, y'know?

EDDIE: They longshoremen?

BEATRICE: I don't know; they never said only hello, and she don't say nothin', so I don't ask, but they look like nice guys. (EDDIE, *silent, stares.)* What's the matter? I thought you would like it.

EDDIE: I'm just wonderin'—where they come from? She's got no sign outside; she don't know nobody. How's she find boarders all of a sudden?

BEATRICE: What's the difference? She—

EDDIE: The difference is they could be cops, that's all.

BEATRICE: Oh, no, I don't think so.

EDDIE: It's all right with me, I don't care. Except for this kinda work they don't wear badges, y'know. I mean you gotta face it, they could be cops. And Rodolpho'll start to shoot his mouth off up there, and they got him.

BEATRICE: I don't think so. You want some coffee?

EDDIE: No. I don't want nothin'.

BEATRICE: You gettin' sick or sump'm?

EDDIE: Me—no, I'm all right. *(mystified)* When did you tell me she had boarders?

BEATRICE: Couple a times.

EDDIE: Geez, I don't even remember. I thought she had the one room. *(He touches his forehead, alarmed.)*

BEATRICE: Sure, we was all talkin' about it last week. I loaned her my big fryin' pan. I told you.

EDDIE: I must be dizzy or sump'm.

BEATRICE: I think you'll come to yourself now, Eddie. I mean it, we shoulda put them up there in the first place. You can never bring strangers in a house. *(Pause. They are seated.)* You know what?

EDDIE: What?

BEATRICE: Why don't you tell her you'll go to her it's all right— Katie? Give her a break. A wedding should be happy.

EDDIE: I don't care. Let her do what she wants to do.

BEATRICE: Why don't you tell her you'll go to the wedding? It's terrible, there wouldn't be no father there. She's broken-hearted.

EDDIE: They made up the date already?

BEATRICE: She wants him to have like six, seven hundred. I told her, I says, "If you start off with a little bit you never gonna get ahead of yourself," I says. So they're gonna wait yet. I think maybe the end of the summer. But if you would tell them you'll be at the wedding—I mean, it would be nice, they would both be happy. I mean live and let live, Eddie, I mean?

EDDIE *(as though he doesn't care)*: All right, I'll go to the wedding. *(CATHERINE is descending the stairs from above.)*

BEATRICE *(darting a glance toward the sound)*: You want me to tell her?

EDDIE *(He thinks, then turns to her with a certain deliberativeness.)*: If you want, go ahead.

CATHERINE *enters, sees him, and starts for the bedroom door.*

BEATRICE: Come here, Katie. *(CATHERINE looks doubtfully at her.)* Come here, honey. *(CATHERINE comes to her, and BEATRICE puts an arm around her. EDDIE looks off.)* He's gonna come to the wedding.

CATHERINE: What do I care if he comes? *(She starts upstage, but BEATRICE holds her.)*

BEATRICE: Ah, Katie, don't be that way. I want you to make up with him; come on over here. You're his baby! *(She tries to draw* CATHERINE *near* EDDIE.*)*

CATHERINE: I got nothin' to make up with him, he's got somethin' to make up with me.

EDDIE: Leave her alone, Beatrice, she knows what she wants to do. *(Now, however, he turns for a second to* CATHERINE.*)* But if I was you I would watch out for those boarders up there.

BEATRICE: He's worried maybe they're cops.

CATHERINE: Oh, no, they ain't cops. Mr. Lipari from the butcher store—they're his nephews; they just come over last week.

EDDIE *(coming alive)*: They're submarines?

CATHERINE: Yeah, they come from around Bari. They ain't cops.

She walks to her bedroom. EDDIE *tries to keep silent, and when he speaks it has an unwilling sharpness of anxiety.*

EDDIE: Catherine. *(She turns to him. He is getting to his feet in a high but subdued terror.)* You think that's a good idea?

CATHERINE: What?

EDDIE: How do you know what enemies Lipari's got? Which they would love to stab him in the back? I mean you never do that, Catherine, put in two strange pairs like that together. They track one, they'll catch 'em all. I ain't tryin' to advise you, kid, but that ain't smart. Anybody tell you that. I mean you just takin' a double chance, y'understand?

CATHERINE: Well, what'll I do with them?

EDDIE: What do you mean? The neighborhood's full of rooms. Can't you stand to live a couple a blocks away from him? He's got a big family, Lipari—these guys get picked up he's liable to blame you or me, and we got his whole family on our head. That's no joke, kid. They got a temper, that family.

CATHERINE: Well, maybe tomorrow I'll find some other place—

EDDIE: Kid, I'm not tellin' you nothin' no more because I'm just an ignorant jerk. I know that; but if I was you I would get them outa this house tonight, see?

CATHERINE: How'm I gonna find a place tonight?

EDDIE *(his temper rising)*: Catherine, don't mix yourself with somebody else's family, Catherine.

Two men in overcoats and felt hats appear on the street, start into the house.

EDDIE: You want to do yourself a favor? Go up and get them out of the house, kid.

CATHERINE: Yeah, but they been in the house so long already—

EDDIE: You think I'm always tryin' to fool you or sump'm? What's the matter with you? Don't you believe I could think of your good? *(He is breaking into tears.)* Didn't I work like a horse keepin' you? You think I got no feelin's? I never told you nothin' in my life that wasn't for your good. Nothin'! And look at the way you talk to me! Like I was an enemy! Like I—*(There is a knock on the door. His head swerves. They all stand motionless. Another knock. EDDIE firmly draws CATHERINE to him. And, in a whisper, pointing upstage.)* Go out the back up the fire escape; get them out over the back fence.

FIRST OFFICER *(in the hall)*: Open up in there! immigration!

EDDIE: Go, go. Hurry up! *(He suddenly pushes her upstage, and she stands a moment, staring at him in a realized horror.)* Well what're you lookin' at?

FIRST OFFICER: Open up!

EDDIE: Who's that there?

FIRST OFFICER: Immigration. Open up.

With a sob of fury and that glance, CATHERINE *streaks into a bedroom.* EDDIE *looks at* BEATRICE, *who sinks into a chair, turning her face from him.*

EDDIE: All right, take it easy, take it easy. *(He goes and opens the door. The officers step inside.)* What's all this?

FIRST OFFICER: Where are they?

EDDIE: Where's who?

FIRST OFFICER: Come on, come on, where are they?

EDDIE: Who? We got nobody here. *(The FIRST OFFICER opens the door and exits into a bedroom. SECOND OFFICER goes and opens the other bedroom door and exits through it. BEATRICE now turns her head to look at EDDIE. He goes to her, reaches for her, and involuntarily she withdraws herself. Then, pugnaciously, furious.)* What's the matter with you?

The FIRST OFFICER enters from the bedroom, calls quietly into the other bedroom.

FIRST OFFICER: Dominick?

Enter SECOND OFFICER *from bedroom.*

SECOND OFFICER: Maybe it's a different apartment.

FIRST OFFICER: There's only two more floors up there. I'll take the front, you go up the fire escape. I'll let you in. Watch your step up there.

SECOND OFFICER: Okay, right, Charley. *(He re-enters the bedroom. The* FIRST OFFICER *goes to the apartment door, turns to* EDDIE.*)*

FIRST OFFICER: This is Four-forty-one, isn't it?

EDDIE: That's right.

The officer goes out into the hall, closing the door, and climbs up out of sight. BEATRICE *slowly sits at the table.* EDDIE *goes to the closed door and listens. Knocking is heard from above, voices.* EDDIE *turns to* BEATRICE. *She looks at him now and sees his terror, and, weakened with fear, she leans her head on the table.*

BEATRICE: Oh, Jesus, Eddie.

EDDIE: What's the matter with *you?* *(He starts toward her, but she swiftly rises, pressing her palms against her face, and walks away from him.)*

BEATRICE: Oh, my God, my God.

EDDIE: What're you, accusin' me?

BEATRICE *(her final thrust is to turn toward him instead of running from him)*: My God, what did you do!

Many steps on the outer stair draw his attention. We see the FIRST OFFICER *descending with* MARCO, *behind him* RODOLPHO, *and* CATHERINE *and two strange men, followed by* SECOND OFFICER. BEATRICE *hurries and opens the door.*

CATHERINE *(as they appear on the stairs)*: What do yiz want from them? They work, that's all. They're boarders upstairs, they work on the piers.

BEATRICE *(now appearing in the hall, to* FIRST OFFICER*)*: Ah, mister, what do you want from them? Who do they hurt?

CATHERINE *(pointing to* RODOLPHO*)*: They ain't no submarines; he was born in Philadelphia.

FIRST OFFICER: Step aside, lady.

CATHERINE: What do you mean? You can't just come in a house and—

FIRST OFFICER: All right, take it easy. *(to* RODOLPHO*)* What street were you born in Philadelphia?

CATHERINE: What do you mean, what street? Could you tell me what street you were born?

FIRST OFFICER: Sure. Four blocks away, One-eleven Union Street. Let's go, fellas.

CATHERINE *(fending him off* RODOLPHO*)*: No, you can't! Now, get outa here!

FIRST OFFICER *(moving her into the apartment)*: Look, girlie, if they're all right they'll be back tomorrow. If they're illegal they go back where they came from. If you want, get yourself a lawyer, although I'm tellin' you now you're wasting your money. *(He goes back to the group in the hall.)* Let's get them in the car, Dom. *(to the men)* Andiamo, andiamo, let's go.

The men start out toward the street—but MARCO *hangs back, letting them pass.*

BEATRICE: Who're they hurtin', for God's sake? What do you want from them? They're starvin' over there, what do you want!

MARCO *suddenly breaks from the group and dashes into the room and faces* EDDIE, *and* BEATRICE *and the* FIRST OFFICER *rush in as* MARCO *spits into* EDDIE's *face.* CATHERINE *has arrived at the door and sees it.* EDDIE, *with an angered cry, lunges for* MARCO.

EDDIE: Oh, you mother's—!

The FIRST OFFICER *quickly intercedes and pushes* EDDIE *from* MARCO, *who stands there accusingly.*

FIRST OFFICER *(pushing* EDDIE *from* MARCO*)*: Cut it out!

EDDIE *(over the* FIRST OFFICER's *shoulder to* MARCO*)*: I'll kill you for that, you son of a bitch!

FIRST OFFICER: Hey! *(He shakes* EDDIE.*)* Stay in here now, don't come down, don't bother him. You hear me? Don't come down, fella.

For an instant there is silence. Then the FIRST OFFICER *turns and takes* MARCO's *arm and then gives a last, informative look at* EDDIE; *and as he and* MARCO *are going out into the hall* EDDIE *erupts.*

EDDIE: I don't forget that, Marco! You hear what I'm sayin'?

Out in the hall, the FIRST OFFICER *and* MARCO *go down the stairs.*

CATHERINE *rushes out of the room and past them toward* RODOLPHO, *who, with the* SECOND OFFICER *and the two strange men, is emerging into the street. Now, in the street,* LOUIS, MIKE, *and several neighbors, including the butcher,* LIPARI, *a stout, intense, middle-aged man are gathering around the stoop.*

EDDIE *follows* CATHERINE *and calls down after* MARCO. BEATRICE *watches him from within the room, her hands clasped together in fear and prayer.*

EDDIE: That's the thanks I get? Which I took the blanket off my bed for yiz? *(He hurries down the stairs, shouting.* BEATRICE *descends behind him, ineffectually trying to hold him back.)* You gonna apologize to me, Marco! *Marco!*

EDDIE *appears on the stoop and sees the little crowd looking up at him, and falls silent, expectant.* LIPARI, *the butcher, walks over to the two strange men, and he kisses them. His wife, keening, goes and kisses their hands.*

FIRST OFFICER: All right, lady, let them go. Get in the car, fellas, it's right over there.

The SECOND OFFICER *begins moving off with the two strange men and* RODOLPHO. CATHERINE *rushes to the* FIRST OFFICER, *who is drawing* MARCO *off now.*

CATHERINE: He was born in Philadelphia! What do you want from him?

FIRST OFFICER: Step aside, lady, come on now—

MARCO *(suddenly, taking advantage of the* FIRST OFFICER'*s being occupied with* CATHERINE, *freeing himself and pointing up at* EDDIE*)*: That one! I accuse that one!

FIRST OFFICER *(grabbing him and moving him quickly off)*: Come on!

MARCO *(as he is taken off, pointing back and up the stoop at* EDDIE*)*: That one! He killed my children! That one stole the food from my children!

MARCO *is gone. The crowd has turned to* EDDIE.

EDDIE: He's crazy. I give them the blankets off my bed. Six months I kept them like my own brothers! *(*LIPARI, *the butcher, turns and starts off with his wife behind him.)* Lipari! *(*EDDIE *comes down and reaches* LIPARI *and turns him about.)* For Christ's sake, I kept them, I give them the blankets off my bed! *(LIPARI turns away in disgust and anger and walks off with his keening wife. The crowd is now moving away. EDDIE calls.)* Louis! *(LOUIS barely turns, then walks away with MIKE.)* LOUIS! *(Only BEATRICE is left on the stoop—and CATHERINE now returns, blank-eyed, from offstage and the car. EDDIE turns to CATHERINE.)* He's gonna take that back. He's gonna take that back or I'll kill him! *(He faces all the buildings, the street down which the crowd has vanished.)* You hear me? I'll kill him!

Blackout. There is a pause in darkness before the lights rise. On the left—opposite where the desk stands—is a backless wooden bench. Seated on it are RODOLPHO and MARCO. There are two wooden chairs. It is a room in the jail. CATHERINE and ALFIERI are seated on the chairs.

ALFIERI: I'm waiting, Marco. What do you say? *(MARCO glances at him, then shrugs.)* That's not enough; I want an answer from you.

RODOLPHO: Marco never hurt anybody.

ALFIERI: I can bail you out until your hearing comes up.
But I'm not going to do it—you understand me?—
Unless I have your promise. You're an honorable man,
I will believe your promise. Now what do you say?

MARCO: In my country he would be dead now.
He would not live this long.

ALFIERI: All right, Rodolpho, you come with me now. *(He rises.)*

RODOLPHO: No! Please, mister. Marco—
Promise the man. Please, I want you to watch the wedding.
How can I be married and you're in here?
Please, you're not going to do anything; you know you're not—

MARCO *is silent.*

CATHERINE: Marco, don't you understand? He can't bail you out if you're gonna do something bad. To hell with Eddie. Nobody is gonna talk to him again if he lives to a hundred. Everybody knows you spit in his face, that's enough, isn't it? Give me the satisfaction—I want you at the wedding. You got a wife and kids, Marco—you could be workin' till the hearing comes up, instead of layin' around here. You're just giving him satisfaction layin' here.

MARCO (*after a slight pause, to* ALFIERI): How long you say before the hearing?

ALFIERI: I'll try to stretch it out, but it wouldn't be more than five or six weeks.

CATHERINE: So you could make a couple of dollars in the meantime, y'see?

MARCO (*to* ALFIERI): I have no chance?

ALFIERI: No, Marco. You're going back. The hearing is a formality, that's all.

MARCO: But him? There is a chance, eh?

ALFIERI: When she marries him he can start to become an American. They permit that, if the wife is born here.

MARCO (*looking at* RODOLPHO): Well—we did something. (*He lays a palm on* RODOLPHO's *cheek, then lowers his hand.*)

RODOLPHO: Marco, tell the man.

MARCO: What will I tell him? (*He looks at* ALFIERI.) He knows such a promise is dishonorable.

ALFIERI: To promise not to kill is not dishonorable.

MARCO: No?

ALFIERI: No.

MARCO (*gesturing with his head—this is a new idea*): Then what is done with such a man?

ALFIERI: Nothing. If he obeys the law, he lives. That's all.

MARCO: The law? All the law is not in a book.

ALFIERI: Yes. In a book. There is no other law.

MARCO (*his anger rising*): He degraded my brother—my blood. He robbed my children, he mocks my work. I work to come here, mister!

ALFIERI: I know, Marco—

MARCO: There is no law for that? Where is the law for that?

ALFIERI: There is none.

MARCO (*shaking his head*): I don't understand this country. (*Pause. He stands staring his fury.*)

ALFIERI: Well? What is your answer? You have five or six weeks you could work. Or else you sit here. What do you say to me?

MARCO *lowers his eyes. It almost seems he is ashamed.*

MARCO: All right.

ALFIERI: You won't touch him. This is your promise.

Slight pause.

MARCO: Maybe he wants to apologize to me.

ALFIERI (*taking one of his hands*): This is not God, Marco. You hear? Only God makes justice.

MARCO *withdraws his hand and covers it with the other.*

MARCO: All right.

ALFIERI: Is your uncle going to the wedding?

CATHERINE: No. But he wouldn't do nothin' anyway. He just keeps talkin' so people will think he's in the right, that's all. He talks. I'll take them to the church, and they could wait for me there.

ALFIERI: Why, where are you going?

CATHERINE: Well, I gotta get Beatrice.

ALFIERI: I'd rather you didn't go home.

CATHERINE: Oh, no, for my wedding I gotta get Beatrice. Don't worry, he just talks big, he ain't gonna do nothin', Mr. Alfieri. I could go home.

ALFIERI (*nodding, not with assurance*): All right, then—let's go. (MARCO *rises.* RODOLPHO *suddenly embraces him.* MARCO *pats him on the back, his mind engrossed.* RODOLPHO *goes to* CATHERINE, *kisses her hand. She pulls his head to her shoulder, and they go out.* MARCO *faces* ALFIERI.) Only God, Marco.

MARCO *turns and walks out.* ALFIERI, *with a certain processional tread, leaves the stage. The lights dim out.*

Light rises in the apartment. EDDIE *is alone in the rocker, rocking back and forth in little surges. Pause. Now* BEATRICE *emerges from a bedroom, then* CATHERINE. *Both are in their best clothes, wearing hats.*

BEATRICE (*with fear*): I'll be back in about an hour, Eddie. All right?

EDDIE: What, have I been talkin' to myself?

BEATRICE: Eddie, for God's sake, it's her wedding.

EDDIE: Didn't you hear what I told you? You walk out that door to that wedding you ain't comin' back here, Beatrice.

BEATRICE: Why? What do you want?

EDDIE: I want my respect. Didn't you ever hear of that? From my wife?

CATHERINE: It's after three; we're supposed to be there already, Beatrice. The priest won't wait.

BEATRICE: Eddie. It's her wedding. There'll be nobody there from her family. For my sister let me go. I'm goin' for my sister.

EDDIE: Look, I been arguin' with you all day already, Beatrice, and I said what I'm gonna say. He's gonna come here and apologize to me or nobody from this house is goin' into that church today. Now if that's more to you than I am, then go. But don't come back. You be on my side or on their side, that's all.

CATHERINE *(suddenly)*: Who the hell do you think you are?

BEATRICE: Sssh!

CATHERINE: You got no more right to tell nobody nothin'! Nobody! The rest of your life, nobody!

BEATRICE: Shut up, Katie!

CATHERINE *(pulling BEATRICE by the arm)*: You're gonna come with me!

BEATRICE: I can't, Katie, I can't—

CATHERINE: How can you listen to him? This rat!

EDDIE *gets up.*

BEATRICE *(to CATHERINE, in terror at sight of his face)*: Go, go— I'm not goin'—

CATHERINE: What're you scared of? He's a rat! He belongs in the sewer! In the garbage he belongs! *(She is addressing him.)* He's a rat from under the piers! He bites people when they sleep! He comes when nobody's lookin' and he poisons decent people!

EDDIE *rushes at her with his hand raised, and BEATRICE struggles with him. RODOLPHO appears, hurrying along the street, and runs up the stairs.*

BEATRICE *(screaming)*: Get out of here, Katie! *(to EDDIE)* Please, Eddie, Eddie, please!

EDDIE *(trying to free himself of BEATRICE)*: Don't bother me!

RODOLPHO *enters the apartment. A pause.*

EDDIE: Get outa here.

RODOLPHO: Marco is coming, Eddie. *(Pause. BEATRICE raises her hands.)* He's praying in the church. You understand?

Pause.

BEATRICE *(in terror)*: Eddie. Eddie, get out.

EDDIE: What do you mean, get out?

BEATRICE: Eddie, you got kids, go 'way, go 'way from here! Get outa the house!

EDDIE: Me get outa the house? *Me* get outa the house?
What did I do that I gotta get outa the house?
That I wanted a girl not to turn into a tramp?
That I made a promise and I kept my promise
She should be sump'm in her life?

CATHERINE *goes trembling to him.*

CATHERINE: Eddie—

EDDIE: What do *you* want?

CATHERINE: Please, Eddie, go away. He's comin' for you.

EDDIE: What do you care? What do you care he's comin' for me?

CATHERINE *(weeping, she embraces him)*: I never meant to do nothin' bad to you in my life, Eddie!

EDDIE *(with tears in his eyes)*: Then who meant somethin' bad? How'd it get bad?

CATHERINE: I don't know, I don't know!

EDDIE *(pointing to* RODOLPHO *with the new confidence of the embrace)*: They made it bad! This one and his brother made it bad which they came like thieves to rob, to rob!

He grabs her arm and swings her behind him so that he is between her and RODOLPHO, *who is alone at the door.*

You go tell him to come and come quick.
You go tell him I'm waitin' here for him to apologize
For what he said to me in front of the neighborhood!
Now get goin'!

RODOLPHO *(starting around* EDDIE *toward* CATHERINE*)*: Come, Catherine, we—

EDDIE *(nearly throwing* RODOLPHO *out the door)*: Get away from her!

RODOLPHO *(starting back in)*: Catherine!

EDDIE *(turning on* CATHERINE*)*: Tell him to get out! *(She stands paralyzed before him.)* Katie! I'll do somethin' if he don't get outa here!

BEATRICE *(rushing to him, her open hands pressed together before him as though in prayer)*: Eddie, it's her husband, it's her husband! Let her go, it's her husband!

CATHERINE, *moaning, breaks for the door, and she and* RODOLPHO *start down the stairs;* EDDIE *lunges and catches her; he holds her, and she weeps up into his face. And he kisses her on the lips.*

EDDIE *(like a lover, out of his madness)*: It's me, ain't it?
BEATRICE *(hitting his body)*: Eddie! God, Eddie!
EDDIE: Katie, it's me, ain't it? You know it's me!
CATHERINE: Please, please, Eddie, lemme go. Heh? Please?

She moves to go. MARCO *appears on the street.*

EDDIE *(to* RODOLPHO*)*: Punk! Tell her what you are! You know what you are, you punk!
CATHERINE *(pulling* RODOLPHO *out the doorway)*: Come on!

EDDIE *rushes after them to the doorway.*

EDDIE: Make him tell you what he is! Tell her, punk! *(He is on the stairway, calling down.)* Why don't he answer me! Punk, answer me! *(He rushes down the stairs,* BEATRICE *after him.)*
BEATRICE: Eddie, come back!

(Outside, RODOLPHO *sees* MARCO *and cries out, "No, Marco. Marco, go away, go away!" But* MARCO *nears the stoop, looking up at the descending* EDDIE*.)*

EDDIE *(emerging from the house)*: Punk, what are you gonna do with a girl! I'm waitin' for your answer, punk. Where's your— answer!

He sees MARCO. *Two other neighbors appear on the street, stand and watch.* BEATRICE *now comes in front of him.*

BEATRICE: Go in the house, Eddie!
EDDIE *(pushing her aside, coming out challengingly on the stoop, and glaring down at* MARCO*)*: What do you mean, go in the house? Maybe he came to apologize to me. *(to the people)* Which I took the blankets off my bed for them;
Which I brought up a girl, she wasn't even my daughter,
And I took from my own kids to give to her—
And they took her like you take from a stable,
Like you go in and rob from your own family!
And never a word to me!
And now accusations in the bargain?
Makin' my name like a dirty rag?

He faces MARCO *now, and moves toward him.*

You gonna take that back?

BEATRICE: Eddie! Eddie!

EDDIE: I want my good name, Marco! You took my name!

BEATRICE *rushes past him to* MARCO *and tries to push him away.*

BEATRICE: Go, go!

MARCO: Animal! You go on your knees to me!

He strikes EDDIE *powerfully on the side of the head.* EDDIE *falls back and draws a knife.* MARCO *springs to a position of defense, both men circling each other.* EDDIE *lunges, and* MIKE, LOUIS, *and all the neighbors move in to stop them, and they fight up the steps of the stoop, and there is a wild scream—*BEATRICE's*—and they all spread out, some of them running off.*

MARCO *is standing over* EDDIE, *who is on his knees, a bleeding knife in his hands.* EDDIE *falls forward on his hands and knees, and he crawls a yard to* CATHERINE. *She raises her face away—but she does not move as he reaches over and grasps her leg, and, looking up at her, he seems puzzled, questioning, betrayed.*

EDDIE: Catherine—why—?

He falls forward and dies. CATHERINE *covers her face and weeps. She sinks down beside the weeping* BEATRICE. *The lights fade, and* ALFIERI *is illuminated in his office.*

ALFIERI: Most of the time now we settle for half,
    And I like it better.
    And yet, when the tide is right
    And the green smell of the sea
    Floats in through my window,
    The waves of this bay
    Are the waves against Siracusa,
    And I see a face that suddenly seems carved;
    The eyes look like tunnels
    Leading back toward some ancestral beach
    Where all of us once lived.

    And I wonder at those times
    How much of all of us

Really lives there yet,
And when we will truly have moved on,
On and away from that dark place,
That world that has fallen to stones?

This is the end of the story. Good night.

LORRAINE HANSBERRY

A Raisin in the Sun

Characters

RUTH YOUNGER

TRAVIS YOUNGER

WALTER LEE YOUNGER (BROTHER)

BENEATHA YOUNGER

LENA YOUNGER (MAMA)

JOSEPH ASAGAI

GEORGE MURCHISON

MRS. JOHNSON

KARL LINDNER

BOBO

MOVING MEN

The action of the play is set in Chicago's Southside, sometime between World War II and the present.

Act I

Scene I *Friday morning.*
Scene II *The following morning.*

Act II

Scene I *Later, the same day.*
Scene II *Friday night, a few weeks later.*
Scene III *Moving day, one week later.*

Act III

An hour later.

ACT I

SCENE I

The YOUNGER *living room would be a comfortable and well-ordered room if it were not for a number of indestructible contradictions to this state of being. Its furnishings are typical and un-*

distinguished and their primary feature now is that they have clearly had to accommodate the living of too many people for too many years—and they are tired. Still, we can see that at some time, a time probably no longer remembered by the family (except perhaps for MAMA*), the furnishings of this room were actually selected with care and love and even hope—and brought to this apartment and arranged with taste and pride.*

That was a long time ago. Now the once loved pattern of the couch upholstery has to fight to show itself from under acres of crocheted doilies and couch covers which have themselves finally come to be more important than the upholstery. And here a table or a chair has been moved to disguise the worn places in the carpet; but the carpet has fought back by showing its weariness, with depressing uniformity, elsewhere on its surface.

Weariness has, in fact, won in this room. Everything has been polished, washed, sat on, used, scrubbed too often. All pretenses but living itself have long since vanished from the very atmosphere of this room.

Moreover, a section of this room, for it is not really a room unto itself, though the landlord's lease would make it seem so, slopes backward to provide a small kitchen area, where the family prepares the meals that are eaten in the living room proper, which must also serve as dining room. The single window that has been provided for these "two" rooms is located in this kitchen area. The sole natural light the family may enjoy in the course of a day is only that which fights it way through this little window.

At left, a door leads to a bedroom which is shared by MAMA *and her daughter,* BENEATHA*. At right, opposite, is a second room (which in the beginning of the life of this apartment was probably the breakfast room) which serves as a bedroom for* WALTER *and his wife,* RUTH*.*

Time *Sometime between World War II and the present.*

Place *Chicago's Southside.*

At rise *It is morning dark in the living room.* TRAVIS *is asleep on the make-down bed at center. An alarm clock sounds from within the bedroom at right, and presently* RUTH *enters from that room and closes the door behind her. She crosses sleepily toward* *the window. As she passes her sleeping son she reaches down and shakes him a little. At the window she raises the shade and a dusky Southside morning light comes in feebly. She fills a pot with water and puts it on to boil. She calls to the boy, between yawns, in a slightly muffled voice.*

RUTH *is about thirty. We can see that she was a pretty girl, even exceptionally so, but now it is apparent that life has been little that she expected, and disappointment has already begun to hang in her face. In a few years, before thirty-five even, she will be known among her people as a "settled woman."*

She crosses to her son and gives him a good, final, rousing shake.

RUTH: Come on now, boy, it's seven thirty! *(Her son sits up at last, in a stupor of sleepiness.)* I say hurry up, Travis! You ain't the only person in the world got to use a bathroom! *(The child, a sturdy, handsome little boy of ten or eleven, drags himself out of the bed and almost blindly takes his towels and "today's clothes" from drawers and a closet and goes out to the bathroom, which is in an outside hall and which is shared by another family or families on the same floor.* RUTH *crosses to the bedroom door at right and opens it and calls in to her husband.)* Walter Lee! . . . It's after seven thirty! Lemme see you do some waking up in there now! *(She waits.)* You better get up from there, man! It's after seven thirty I tell you. *(She waits again.)* All right, you just go ahead and lay there and next thing you know Travis be finished and Mr. Johnson'll be in there and you'll be fussing and cussing round here like a madman! And be late too! *(She waits, at the end of patience.)* Walter Lee— it's time for you to GET UP!

She waits another second and then starts to go into the bedroom, but is apparently satisfied that her husband has begun to get up. She stops, pulls the door to, and returns to the kitchen area. She wipes her face with a moist cloth and runs her fingers through her sleep-disheveled hair in a vain effort and ties an apron around her housecoat. The bedroom door at right opens and her husband stands in the doorway in his pajamas, which are rumpled and mismated. He is a lean, intense young man in his middle thirties, inclined to quick nervous movements and erratic speech habits— and always in his voice there is a quality of indictment.

WALTER: Is he out yet?

RUTH: What you mean *out*? He ain't hardly got in there good yet.

WALTER *(wandering in, still more oriented to sleep than to a new day)*: Well, what was you doing all that yelling for if I can't even get in there yet? *(Stopping and thinking.)* Check coming today?

RUTH: They *said* Saturday and this is just Friday and I hopes to God you ain't going to get up here first thing this morning and start talking to me 'bout no money—'cause I 'bout don't want to hear it.

WALTER: Something the matter with you this morning?

RUTH: No—I'm just sleepy as the devil. What kind of eggs you want?

WALTER: Not scrambled. *(RUTH starts to scramble eggs.)* Paper come? *(RUTH points impatiently to the rolled up Tribune on the table, and he gets it and spreads it out and vaguely reads the front page.)* Set off another bomb yesterday.

RUTH *(maximum indifference)*: Did they?

WALTER *(looking up)*: What's the matter with you?

RUTH: Ain't nothing the matter with me. And don't keep asking me that this morning.

WALTER: Ain't nobody bothering you. *(reading the news of the day absently again)* Say Colonel McCormick is sick.

RUTH *(affecting tea-party interest)*: Is he now? Poor thing.

WALTER *(sighing and looking at his watch)*: Oh, me. *(He waits.)* Now what is that boy doing in that bathroom all this time? He just going to have to start getting up earlier. I can't be being late to work on account of him fooling around in there.

RUTH *(turning on him)*: Oh, no he ain't going to be getting up no earlier no such thing! It ain't his fault that he can't get to bed no earlier nights 'cause he got a bunch of crazy good-for-nothing clowns sitting up running their mouths in what is supposed to be his bedroom after ten o'clock at night . . .

WALTER: That's what you mad about, ain't it? The things I want to talk about with my friends just couldn't be important in your mind, could they?

He rises and finds a cigarette in her handbag on the table and crosses to the little window and looks out, smoking and deeply enjoying this first one.

RUTH (*almost matter of factly, a complaint too automatic to deserve emphasis*): Why you always got to smoke before you eat in the morning?

WALTER (*at the window*): Just look at 'em down there . . . Running and racing to work . . . (*He turns and faces his wife and watches her a moment at the stove, and then, suddenly*) You look young this morning, baby.

RUTH (*indifferently*): Yeah?

WALTER: Just for a second—stirring them eggs. Just for a second it was—you looked real young again. (*He reaches for her; she crosses away. Then, drily*) It's gone now—you look like yourself again!

RUTH: Man, if you don't shut up and leave me alone.

WALTER (*looking out to the street again*): First thing a man ought to learn in life is not to make love to no colored woman first thing in the morning. You all some eeeevil people at eight o'clock in the morning.

TRAVIS *appears in the hall doorway, almost fully dressed and quite wide awake now, his towels and pajamas across his shoulders. He opens the door and signals for his father to make the bathroom in a hurry.*)

TRAVIS (*watching the bathroom*): Daddy, come on!

WALTER *gets his bathroom utensils and flies out to the bathroom.*

RUTH: Sit down and have your breakfast, Travis.

TRAVIS: Mama, this is Friday. (*gleefully*) Check coming tomorrow, huh?

RUTH: You get your mind off money and eat your breakfast.

TRAVIS (*eating*): This is the morning we supposed to bring the fifty cents to school.

RUTH: Well, I ain't got no fifty cents this morning.

TRAVIS: Teacher say we have to.

RUTH: I don't care what teacher say. I ain't got it. Eat your breakfast, Travis.

TRAVIS: I *am* eating.

RUTH: Hush up now and just eat!

490

The boy gives her an exasperated look for her lack of understanding, and eats grudgingly.

TRAVIS: You think Grandmama would have it?

RUTH: No! And I want you to stop asking your grandmother for money, you hear me?

TRAVIS *(outraged)*: Gaaaleee! I don't ask her, she just gimme it sometimes!

RUTH: Travis Willard Younger—I got too much on me this morning to be—

TRAVIS: Mabe Daddy—

RUTH: *Travis!*

The boy hushes abruptly. They are both quiet and tense for several seconds.

TRAVIS *(presently)*: Could I maybe go carry some groceries in front of the supermarket for a little while after school then?

RUTH: Just hush, I said. *(Travis jabs his spoon into his cereal bowl viciously, and rests his head in anger upon his fists.)* If you through eating, you can get over there and make your bed.

The boy obeys stiffly and crosses the room, almost mechanically, to the bed and more or less folds the bedding into a heap, then angrily gets his books and cap.

TRAVIS *(sulking and standing apart from her unnaturally)*: I'm gone.

RUTH *(looking up from the stove to inspect him automatically)*: Come here. *(He crosses to her and she studies his head.)* If you don't take this comb and fix this here head, you better! *(TRAVIS puts down his books with a great sigh of oppression, and crosses to the mirror. His mother mutters under her breath about his "slubbornness.")* 'Bout to march out of here with that head looking just like chickens slept in it! I just don't know where you get your stubborn ways . . . And get your jacket, too. Looks chilly out this morning.

TRAVIS *(with conspicuously brushed hair and jacket)*: I'm gone.

RUTH: Get carfare and milk money—*(waving one finger)*—and not a single penny for no caps, you hear me?

TRAVIS *(with sullen politeness)*: Yes'm.

He turns in outrage to leave. His mother watches after him as in his frustration he approaches the door almost comically. When she speaks to him, her voice has become a very gentle tease.

RUTH (*mocking, as she thinks he would say it*): Oh, Mama makes me so mad sometimes, I don't know what to do! (*She waits and continues to his back as he stands stock-still in front of the door.*) I wouldn't kiss that woman good-bye for nothing in this world this morning! (*The boy finally turns around and rolls his eyes at her, knowing the mood has changed and he is vindicated; he does not, however, move toward her yet.*) Not for nothing in this world! (*She finally laughs aloud at him and holds out her arms to him and we see that it is a way between them, very old and practiced. He crosses to her and allows her to embrace him warmly but keeps his face fixed with masculine rigidity. She holds him back from her presently and looks at him and runs her fingers over the features of his face. With utter gentleness—*) Now—whose little old angry man are you?

TRAVIS (*the masculinity and gruffness start to fade at last.*): Aw gaalee—Mama . . .

RUTH (*mimicking*): Aw—gaaaaalleeeee, Mama! (*She pushes him, with rough playfulness and finality, toward the door.*) Get on out of here or you going to be late.

TRAVIS (*in the face of love, new aggressiveness*): Mama, could I *please* go carry groceries?

RUTH: Honey, it's starting to get so cold evenings.

WALTER (*coming in from the bathroom and drawing a make-believe gun from a make-believe holster and shooting at his son*): What is it he wants to do?

RUTH: Go carry groceries after school at the supermarket.

WALTER: Well, let him go . . .

TRAVIS (*quickly, to the ally*): I *have* to—she won't gimme the fifty cents . . .

WALTER (*to his wife only*): Why not?

RUTH (*simply, and with flavor*): 'Cause we don't have it.

WALTER (*to RUTH only*): What you tell the boy things like that for? (*Reaching down into his pants with a rather important gesture*) Here, son—

(*He hands the boy the coin, but his eyes are directed to his wife's. TRAVIS takes the money happily.*)

TRAVIS: Thanks, Daddy.

He starts out. RUTH *watches both of them with murder in her eyes.*
WALTER *stands and stares back at her with defiance, and suddenly
reaches into his pocket again on an afterthought.*

WALTER *(without even looking at his son, still staring hard at his
wife)*: In fact, here's another fifty cents . . . Buy yourself some
fruit today—or take a taxicab to school or something!

TRAVIS: Whoopee—

*He leaps up and clasps his father around the middle with his legs,
and they face each other in mutual appreciation; slowly* WALTER
LEE *peeks around the boy to catch the violent rays from his wife's
eyes and draws his head back as if shot.*

WALTER: You better get down now—and get to school, man.

TRAVIS *(at the door)*: O.K. Good-bye. *(He exits.)*

WALTER *(after him, pointing with pride)*: That's *my* boy. *(She
looks at him in disgust and turns back to her work.)* You know
what I was thinking 'bout in the bathroom this morning?

RUTH: No.

WALTER: How come you always try to be so pleasant!

RUTH: What is there to be pleasant 'bout!

WALTER: You want to know what I was thinking 'bout in the
bathroom or not!

RUTH: I know what you thinking 'bout.

WALTER *(ignoring her)*: 'Bout what me and Willy Harris was talking about last night.

RUTH *(immediately—a refrain)*: Willy Harris is a good-for-nothing
loudmouth.

WALTER: Anybody who talks to me has got to be a good-for-
nothing loudmouth, ain't he? And what you know about who
is just a good-for-nothing loudmouth? Charlie Atkins was just
a "good-for-nothing loudmouth" too, wasn't he! When he
wanted me to go in the dry-cleaning business with him. And
now—he's grossing a hundred thousand a year. A hundred thousand dollars a year! You still call *him* a loudmouth!

RUTH *(bitterly)*: Oh, Walter Lee . . .

She folds her head on her arms over the table.

WALTER *(rising and coming to her and standing over her)*: You
tired, ain't you? Tired of everything. Me, the boy, the way we

live—this beat-up hole—everything. Ain't you? *(She doesn't look up, doesn't answer.)* So tired—moaning and groaning all the time, but you wouldn't do nothing to help, would you? You couldn't be on my side that long for nothing, could you?

RUTH: Walter, please leave me alone.

WALTER: A man needs a woman to back him up . . .

RUTH: Walter—

WALTER: Mama would listen to you. You know she listen to you more than she do me and Bennie. She think more of you. All you have to do is just sit down with her when you drinking your coffee one morning and talking 'bout things like you do and— *(He sits down beside her and demonstrates graphically what he thinks her methods and tone should be.)*—you just sip your coffee, see, and say easy like that you been thinking 'bout that deal Walter Lee is so interested in, 'bout the store and all, and sip some more coffee, like what you saying ain't really that important to you—And the next thing you know, she be listening good and asking you questions and when I come home—I can tell her the details. This ain't no fly-by-night proposition, baby. I mean we figured it out, me and Willy and Bobo.

RUTH *(with a frown)*: Bobo?

WALTER: Yeah. You see, this little liquor store we got in mind cost seventy-five thousand and we figured the initial investment on the place be 'bout thirty thousand, see. That be ten thousand each. Course, there's a couple of hundred you got to pay so's you don't spend your life just waiting for them clowns to let your license get approved—

RUTH: You mean graft?

WALTER *(frowning impatiently)*: Don't call it that. See there, that just goes to show you what women understand about the world. Baby, don't *nothing* happen for you in this world 'less you pay *somebody* off!

RUTH: Walter, leave me alone! *(She raises her head and stares at him vigorously—then says, more quietly.)* Eat your eggs, they gonna be cold.

WALTER *(straightening up from her and looking off)*: That's it. There you are. Man say to his woman: I got me a dream. His woman say: Eat your eggs. *(Sadly, but gaining in power.)* Man say: I got to take hold of this here world, baby! And a woman

will say: Eat your eggs and go to work. *(Passionately now.)*
Man say: I got to change my life, I'm choking to death, baby!
And his woman say—*(in utter anguish as he brings his fists down on his thighs)*—Your eggs is getting cold!

RUTH *(softly)*: Walter, that ain't none of our money.

WALTER *(not listening at all or even looking at her)*: This morning, I was lookin' in the mirror and thinking about it . . . I'm thirty-five years old; I been married eleven years and I got a boy who sleeps in the living room—*(very, very quietly)*—and all I got to give him is stories about how rich white people live . . .

RUTH: Eat your eggs, Walter.

WALTER *(slams the table and jumps up)*: —DAMN MY EGGS— DAMN ALL THE EGGS THAT EVER WAS!

RUTH: Then go to work.

WALTER *(looking up at her)*: See—I'm trying to talk to you 'bout myself—*(shaking his head with the repetition)*—and all you can say is eat them eggs and go to work.

RUTH *(wearily)*: Honey, you never say nothing new. I listen to you every day, every night and every morning, and you never say nothing new. *(shrugging)* So you would rather *be* Mr. Arnold than be his chauffeur. So—I would *rather* be living in Buckingham Palace.

WALTER: That is just what is wrong with the colored woman in this world . . . Don't understand about building their men up and making 'em feel like they somebody. Like they can do something.

RUTH *(drily, but to hurt)*: There *are* colored men who do things.

WALTER: No thanks to the colored woman.

RUTH: Well, being a colored woman, I guess I can't help myself none.

She rises and gets the ironing board and sets it up and attacks a huge pile of rough-dried clothes, sprinkling them in preparation for the ironing and then rolling them into tight fat balls.

WALTER *(mumbling)*: We one group of men tied to a race of women with small minds!

His sister BENEATHA enters. She is about twenty, as slim and intense as her brother. She is not as pretty as her sister-in-law, but her lean, almost intellectual face has a handsomeness of its own. She wears a bright-red flannel nightie, and her thick hair stands wildly about her head. Her speech is a mixture of many things; it is different from the rest of the family's insofar as education has permeated her sense of English—and perhaps the Midwest rather than the South has finally—at last—won out in her inflection; but not altogether, because over all of it is a soft slurring and transformed use of vowels which is the decided influence of the Southside. She passes through the room without looking at either RUTH *or* WALTER *and goes to the outside door and looks, a little blindly, out to the bathroom. She sees that it has been lost to the Johnsons. She closes the door with a sleepy vengeance and crosses to the table and sits down a little defeated.*

BENEATHA: I am going to start timing those people.

WALTER: You should get up earlier.

BENEATHA *(Her face in her hands. She is still fighting the urge to go back to bed.):* Really—would you suggest dawn? Where's the paper?

WALTER *(pushing the paper across the table to her as he studies her almost clinically, as though he has never seen her before):* You a horrible-looking chick at this hour.

BENEATHA *(drily):* Good morning, everybody.

WALTER *(senselessly):* How is school coming?

BENEATHA *(in the same spirit):* Lovely. Lovely. And you know, biology is the greatest. *(looking up at him)* I dissected something that looked just like you yesterday.

WALTER: I just wondered if you've made up your mind and everything.

BENEATHA *(gaining in sharpness and impatience):* And what did I answer yesterday morning—and the day before that?

RUTH *(from the ironing board, like someone disinterested and old):* Don't be so nasty, Bennie.

BENEATHA *(still to her brother):* And the day before that and the day before that!

WALTER *(defensively):* I'm interested in you. Something wrong with that? Ain't many girls who decide—

WALTER *and* BENEATHA *(in unison):* —"to be a doctor." *(silence)*

WALTER: Have we figured out yet just exactly how much medical school is going to cost?

RUTH: Walter Lee, why don't you leave the girl alone and get out of here to work?

BENEATHA *(exits to the bathroom and bangs on the door)*: Come on out of there, please! *(She comes back into the room.)*

WALTER *(looking at his sister intently)*: You know the check is coming tomorrow.

BENEATHA *(turning on him with a sharpness all her own)*: That money belongs to Mama, Walter, and it's for her to decide how she wants to use it. I don't care if she wants to buy a house or a rocket ship or just nail it up somewhere and look at it. It's hers. Not ours—*hers.*

WALTER *(bitterly)*: Now ain't that fine! You just got your mother's interest at heart, ain't you, girl? You such a nice girl—but if Mama got that money she can always take a few thousand and help you through school too—can't she?

BENEATHA: I have never asked anyone around here to do anything for me!

WALTER: No! And the line between asking and just accepting when the time comes is big and wide—ain't it!

BENEATHA *(with fury)*: What do you want from me, Brother—that I quit school or just drop dead, which!

WALTER: I don't want nothing but for you to stop acting holy 'round here. Me and Ruth done made some sacrifices for you— why can't you do something for the family?

RUTH: Walter, don't be dragging me in it.

WALTER: You are in it—Don't you get up and go work in some-body's kitchen for the last three years to help put clothes on her back?

RUTH: Oh, Walter—that's not fair . . .

WALTER: It ain't that nobody expects you to get on your knees and say thank you, Brother; thank you, Ruth; thank you, Mama—and thank you, Travis, for wearing the same pair of shoes for two semesters—

BENEATHA *(dropping to her knees)*: Well—I *do*—all right?—thank everybody! And forgive me for ever wanting to be anything at all! *(pursuing him on her knees across the floor)* FORGIVE ME, FORGIVE ME, FORGIVE ME!

RUTH: Please stop it! Your mama'll hear you.

WALTER: Who the hell told you you had to be a doctor? If you so crazy 'bout messing 'round with sick people—then go be a nurse like other women—or just get married and be quiet . . .

BENEATHA: Well—you finally got it said . . . It took you three years but you finally got it said. Walter, give up; leave me alone—it's Mama's money.

WALTER: *He was my father, too!*

BENEATHA: So what? He was mine, too—and Travis' grand-father—but the insurance money belongs to Mama. Picking on me is not going to make her give it to you to invest in any liquor stores—*(underbreath, dropping into a chair)*—and I for one say, God bless Mama for that!

WALTER *(to* RUTH*)*: See—did you hear? Did you hear!

RUTH: Honey, please go to work.

WALTER: Nobody in this house is ever going to understand me.

BENEATHA: Because you're a nut.

WALTER: Who's a nut?

BENEATHA: You—you are a nut. Thee is mad, boy.

WALTER *(looking at his wife and his sister from the door, very sadly)*: The world's most backward race of people, and that's a fact.

BENEATHA *(turning slowly in her chair)*: And then there are all those prophets who would lead us out of the wilderness—*(*WALTER *slams out of the house.)*—into the swamps!

RUTH: Bennie, why you always gotta be pickin' on your brother? Can't you be a little sweeter sometimes? *(Door opens.* WALTER *walks in. He fumbles with his cap, starts to speak, clears throat, looks everywhere but at* RUTH. *Finally:)*

WALTER *(to* RUTH*)*: I need some money for carfare.

RUTH *(looks at him, then warms; teasing, but tenderly)*: Fifty cents? *(She goes to her bag and gets money.)* Here—take a taxi!

WALTER *exits.* MAMA *enters. She is a woman in her early sixties, full-bodied and strong. She is one of those women of a certain grace and beauty who wear it so unobtrusively that it takes a while to notice. Her dark-brown face is surrounded by the total whiteness of her hair, and, being a woman who has adjusted to many things in life and overcome many more, her face is full of strength. She has, we can see, wit and faith of a kind that keep her eyes lit and full of interest and expectancy. She is, in a word, a beautiful woman. Her bearing is perhaps most like the noble bearing of the women of the Hereros of Southwest Africa—rather as if she imagines that as she walks she still bears a basket or a vessel upon her head. Her speech, on the other hand, is as careless as her carriage is precise—she is inclined to slur everything—but her voice is perhaps not so much quiet as simply soft.*

MAMA: Who that 'round here slamming doors at this hour?

She crosses through the room, goes to the window, opens it, and brings in a feeble little plant growing doggedly in a small pot on the window sill. She feels the dirt and puts it back out.

RUTH: That was Walter Lee. He and Bennie was at it again.

MAMA: My children and they tempers. Lord, if this little old plant don't get more sun than it's been getting it ain't never going to see spring again. *(She turns from the window.)* What's the matter with you this morning, Ruth? You looks right peaked. You aiming to iron all them things? Leave some for me. I'll get to 'em this afternoon. Bennie honey, it's too drafty for you to be sitting 'round half dressed. Where's your robe?

BENEATHA: In the cleaners.

MAMA: Well, go get mine and put it on.

BENEATHA: I'm not cold, Mama, honest.

MAMA: I know—but you so thin . . .

BENEATHA *(irritably)*: Mama, I'm not cold.

MAMA *(seeing the make-down bed as TRAVIS has left it)*: Lord have mercy, look at that poor bed. Bless his heart—he tries, don't he?

She moves to the bed TRAVIS has sloppily made up.

RUTH: No—he don't half try at all 'cause he knows you going to come along behind him and fix everything. That's just how come he don't know how to do nothing right now—you done spoiled that boy so.

MAMA *(folding bedding)*: Well—he's a little boy. Ain't supposed to know 'bout housekeeping. My baby, that's what he is. What you fix for his breakfast this morning?

RUTH *(angrily)*: I feed my son, Lena!

MAMA: I ain't meddling—*(underbreath; busy-bodyish)* I just noticed all last week he had cold cereal, and when it starts getting this chilly in the fall a child ought to have some hot grits or something when he goes out in the cold—

RUTH *(furious)*: I gave him hot oats—is that all right!

MAMA: I ain't meddling. *(pause)* Put a lot of nice butter on it? (RUTH *shoots her an angry look and does not reply.*) He likes lots of butter.

RUTH *(exasperated)*: Lena—

MAMA *(To BENEATHA. MAMA is inclined to wander conversationally sometimes.)*: What was you and your brother fussing 'bout this morning?

BENEATHA: It's not important, Mama.

She gets up and goes to look out at the bathroom, which is apparently free, and she picks up her towels and rushes out.

MAMA: What was they fighting about?

RUTH: Now you know as well as I do.

MAMA *(shaking her head)*: Brother still worrying hisself sick about that money?

RUTH: You know he is.

MAMA: You had breakfast?

RUTH: Some coffee.

MAMA: Girl, you better start eating and looking after yourself better. You almost thin as Travis.

RUTH: Lena—

MAMA: Un-hunh?

RUTH: What are you going to do with it?

MAMA: Now don't you start, child. It's too early in the morning to be talking about money. It ain't Christian.

RUTH: It's just that he got his heart set on that store—

MAMA: You mean that liquor store that Willy Harris want him to invest in?

RUTH: Yes—

MAMA: We ain't no business people, Ruth. We just plain working folks.

RUTH: Ain't nobody business people till they go into business. Walter Lee say colored people ain't never going to start getting ahead till they start gambling on some different kinds of things in the world—investments and things.

MAMA: What done got into you, girl? Walter Lee done finally sold you on investing.

RUTH: No. Mama, something is happening between Walter and me. I don't know what it is—but he needs something—something I can't give him any more. He needs this chance, Lena.

MAMA *(frowning deeply)*: But liquor, honey—

RUTH: Well—like Walter say—I spec people going to always be drinking themselves some liquor.

MAMA: Well—whether they drinks it or not ain't none of my business. But whether I go into business selling it to 'em *is,* and I don't want that on my ledger this late in life. *(stopping suddenly and studying her daughter-in-law)* Ruth Younger, what's the matter with you today? You look like you could fall over right there.

RUTH: I'm tired.

MAMA: Then you better stay home from work today.

RUTH: I can't stay home. She'd be calling up the agency and screaming at them, "My girl didn't come in today—send me somebody! My girl didn't come in!" Oh, she just have a fit . . .

MAMA: Well, let her have it. I'll just call her up and say you got the flu—

RUTH *(laughing)*: Why the flu?

MAMA: 'Cause it sounds respectable to 'em. Something white people get, too. They know 'bout the flu. Otherwise they think you been cut up or something when you tell 'em you sick.

RUTH: I got to go in. We need the money.

MAMA: Somebody would of thought my children done all but starved to death the way they talk about money here late. Child, we got a great big old check coming tomorrow.

RUTH *(sincerely, but also self-righteously)*: Now that's your money. It ain't got nothing to do with me. We all feel like that— Walter and Bennie and me—even Travis.

MAMA *(thoughtfully, and suddenly very far away)*: Ten thousand dollars—

RUTH: Sure is wonderful.

MAMA: Ten thousand dollars.

RUTH: You know what you should do, Miss Lena? You should take yourself a trip somewhere. To Europe or South America or someplace—

MAMA (*throwing up her hands at the thought*): Oh, child!

RUTH: I'm serious. Just pack up and leave! Go on away and enjoy yourself some. Forget about the family and have yourself a ball for once in your life—

MAMA (*drily*): You sound like I'm just about ready to die. Who'd go with me? What I look like wandering 'round Europe by myself?

RUTH: Shoot—these here rich white women do it all the time. They don't think nothing of packing up they suitcases and piling on one of them big steamships and—swoosh!—they gone, child.

MAMA: Something always told me I wasn't no rich white woman.

RUTH: Well—what are you going to do with it then?

MAMA: I ain't rightly decided. (*Thinking. She speaks now with emphasis.*) Some of it got to be put away for Beneatha and her schoolin'—and ain't nothing going to touch that part of it. Nothing. (*She waits several seconds, trying to make up her mind about something, and looks at* RUTH *a little tentatively before going on.*) Been thinking that we maybe could meet the notes on a little old two-story somewhere, with a yard where Travis could play in the summertime, if we use part of the insurance for a down payment and everybody kind of pitch in. I could maybe take on a little day work again, few days a week—

RUTH (*studying her mother-in-law furtively and concentrating on her ironing, anxious to encourage without seeming to*): Well, Lord knows, we've put enough rent into this here rat trap to pay for four houses by now . . .

MAMA (*looking up at the words "rat trap" and then looking around and leaning back and sighing—in a suddenly reflective mood—*): "Rat trap"—yes, that's all it is. (*smiling*) I remember just as well the day me and Big Walter moved in here. Hadn't been married but two weeks and wasn't planning on living here no more than a year. (*She shakes her head at the dissolved dream.*) We was going to set away, little by little, don't you know, and buy a little place out in Morgan Park. We had even picked out the house. (*chuckling a little*) Looks right dumpy today. But Lord, child, you should know all the dreams I had 'bout buying that house and fixing it up and making me a little garden in the back— (*She waits and stops smiling.*) And didn't none of it happen. (*dropping her hands in a futile gesture*)

RUTH *(keeps her head down, ironing)*: Yes, life can be a barrel of disappointments, sometimes.

MAMA: Honey, Big Walter would come in here some nights back then and slump down on that couch there and just look at the rug, and look at me and look at the rug and then back at me—and I'd know he was down then . . . really down. *(After a second very long and thoughtful pause; she is seeing back to times that only she can see.)* And then, Lord, when I lost that baby—little Claude—I almost thought I was going to lose Big Walter too. Oh, that man grieved hisself! He was one man to love his children.

RUTH: Ain't nothin' can tear at you like losin' your baby.

MAMA: I guess that's how come that man finally worked hisself to death like he done. Like he was fighting his own war with this here world that took his baby from him.

RUTH: He sure was a fine man, all right. I always liked Mr. Younger.

MAMA: Crazy 'bout his children! God knows there was plenty wrong with Walter Younger—hard-headed, mean, kind of wild with women—plenty wrong with him. But he sure loved his children. Always wanted them to have something—be something. That's where Brother gets all these notions, I reckon. Big Walter used to say, he'd get right wet in the eyes sometimes, lean his head back with the water standing in his eyes and say, "Seem like God didn't see fit to give the black man nothing but dreams—but He did give us children to make them dreams seem worth while." *(She smiles.)* He could talk like that, don't you know.

RUTH: Yes, he sure could. He was a good man, Mr. Younger.

MAMA: Yes, a fine man—just couldn't never catch up with his dreams, that's all.

BENEATHA *comes in, brushing her hair and looking up to the ceiling, where the sound of a vacuum cleaner has started up.*

BENEATHA: What could be so dirty on that woman's rugs that she has to vacuum them every single day?

RUTH: I wish certain young women 'round here who I could name would take inspiration about certain rugs in a certain apartment I could also mention.

BENEATHA (*shrugging*): How much cleaning can a house need, for Christ's sakes.

MAMA (*not liking the Lord's name used thus*): Bennie!

RUTH: Just listen to her—just listen!

BENEATHA: Oh God!

MAMA: If you use the Lord's name just one more time—

BENEATHA (*a bit of a whine*): Oh, Mama—

RUTH: Fresh—just fresh as salt, this girl!

BENEATHA (*drily*): Well—if the salt loses its savor—

MAMA: Now that will do. I just ain't going to have you 'round here reciting the scriptures in vain—you hear me?

BENEATHA: How did I manage to get on everybody's wrong side by just walking into a room?

RUTH: If you weren't so fresh—

BENEATHA: Ruth, I'm twenty years old.

MAMA: What time you be home from school today?

BENEATHA: Kind of late. (*with enthusiasm*) Madeline is going to start my guitar lessons today.

(MAMA *and* RUTH *look up with the same expression.*)

MAMA: Your *what* kind of lessons?

BENEATHA: Guitar.

RUTH: Oh, Father!

MAMA: How come you done taken it in your mind to learn to play the guitar?

BENEATHA: I just want to, that's all.

MAMA (*smiling*): Lord, child, don't you know what to get tired of this now—like you got tired of that little do with yourself? How long it going to be before you play-acting group you joined last year? (*looking at* RUTH) And what was it the year before that?

RUTH: The horseback-riding club for which she bought that fifty-five-dollar riding habit that's been hanging in the closet ever since!

MAMA (*to* BENEATHA): Why you got to flit so from one thing to another, baby?

BENEATHA (*sharply*): I just want to learn to play the guitar. Is there anything wrong with that?

MAMA: Ain't nobody trying to stop you. I just wonders sometimes why you has to flit so from one thing to another all the time.

You ain't never done nothing with all that camera equipment you brought home—

BENEATHA: I don't flit! I—I experiment with different forms of expression—

RUTH: Like riding a horse?

BENEATHA: —People have to express themselves one way or another.

MAMA: What is it you want to express?

BENEATHA *(angrily)*: Me! (MAMA *and* RUTH *look at each other and burst into raucous laughter.*) Don't worry—I don't expect you to understand.

MAMA *(to change the subject)*: Who you going out with tomorrow night?

BENEATHA *(with displeasure)*: George Murchison again.

MAMA *(pleased)*: Oh—you getting a little sweet on him?

RUTH: You ask me, this child ain't sweet on nobody but herself— *(underbreath)* Express herself!

(They laugh.)

BENEATHA: Oh—I like George all right, Mama. I mean I like him enough to go out with him and stuff, but—

RUTH *(for devilment)*: What does *and stuff* mean?

BENEATHA: Mind your own business.

MAMA: Stop picking at her now, Ruth. *(She chuckles—then a suspicious sudden look at her daughter as she turns in her chair for emphasis.)* What DOES it mean?

BENEATHA *(wearily)*: Oh, I just mean I couldn't ever really be serious about George. He's—he's so shallow.

RUTH: Shallow—what do you mean he's shallow? He's *Rich!*

MAMA: Hush, Ruth.

BENEATHA: I know he's rich. He knows he's rich, too.

RUTH: Well—what other qualities a man got to have to satisfy you, little girl?

BENEATHA: You wouldn't even begin to understand. Anybody who married Walter could not possibly understand.

MAMA *(outraged)*: What kind of way is that to talk about your brother?

BENEATHA: Brother is a flip—let's face it.

MAMA *(to RUTH, helplessly)*: What's a flip?

RUTH *(glad to add kindling)*: She's saying he's crazy.

BENEATHA: Not crazy. Brother isn't really crazy yet—he—he's an elaborate neurotic.

MAMA: Hush your mouth!

BENEATHA: As for George. Well. George looks good—he's got a beautiful car and he takes me to nice places and, as my sister-in-law says, he is probably the richest boy I will ever get to know and I even like him sometimes—but if the Youngers are sitting around waiting to see if their little Bennie is going to tie up the family with the Murchisons, they are wasting their time.

RUTH: You mean you wouldn't marry George Murchison if he asked you someday? That pretty, rich thing? Honey, I knew you was odd—

BENEATHA: No I would not marry him if all I felt for him was what I feel now. Besides, George's family wouldn't really like it.

MAMA: Why not?

BENEATHA: Oh, Mama—The Murchisons are honest-to-God-real-*live*-rich colored people, and the only people in the world who are more snobbish than rich white people are rich colored people. I thought everybody knew that. I've met Mrs. Murchison. She's a scene!

MAMA: You must not dislike people 'cause they well off, honey.

BENEATHA: Why not? It makes just as much sense as disliking people 'cause they are poor, and lots of people do that.

RUTH *(A wisdom-of-the-ages manner. To* MAMA.*)*: Well, she'll get over some of this—

BENEATHA: Get over it? What are you talking about, Ruth? Listen, I'm going to be a doctor. I'm not worried about who I'm going to marry yet—if I ever get married.

MAMA *and* RUTH: *If!*

MAMA: Now, Bennie—

BENEATHA: Oh, I probably will . . . but first I'm going to be a doctor, and George, for one, still thinks that's pretty funny. I couldn't be bothered with that. I am going to be a doctor and everybody around here better understand that!

MAMA *(kindly)*: 'Course you going to be a doctor, honey, God willing.

BENEATHA *(drily)*: God hasn't got a thing to do with it.

MAMA: Beneatha—that just wasn't necessary.

BENEATHA: Well—neither is God. I get sick of hearing about God.

MAMA: Beneatha!

BENEATHA: I mean it! I'm just tired of hearing about God all the time. What has He got to do with anything? Does he pay tuition?

MAMA: You 'bout to get your fresh little jaw slapped!

RUTH: That's just what she needs, all right!

BENEATHA: Why? Why can't I say what I want to around here, like everybody else?

MAMA: It don't sound nice for a young girl to say things like that— you wasn't brought up that way. Me and your father went to trouble to get you and Brother to church every Sunday.

BENEATHA: Mama, you don't understand. It's all a matter of ideas, and God is just one idea I don't accept. It's not important. I am not going out and be immoral or commit crimes because I don't believe in God. I don't even think about it. It's just that I get tired of Him getting credit for all the things the human race achieves through its own stubborn effort. There simply is no blasted God—there is only man and it is *he* who makes miracles!

MAMA *absorbs this speech, studies her daughter and rises slowly and crosses to* BENEATHA *and slaps her powerfully across the face. After, there is only silence and the daughter drops her eyes from her mother's face, and* MAMA *is very tall before her.*

MAMA: Now—you say after me, in my mother's house there is still God. (*There is a long pause and* BENEATHA *stares at the floor wordlessly.* MAMA *repeats the phrase with precision and cool emotion.*) In my mother's house there is still God.

BENEATHA: In my mother's house there is still God. (*a long pause*)

MAMA (*walking away from* BENEATHA, *too disturbed for triumphant posture. Stopping and turning back to her daughter.*): There are some ideas we ain't going to have in this house. Not as long as I am at the head of this family.

BENEATHA: Yes, ma'am. (MAMA *walks out of the room.*)

RUTH (*almost gently, with profound understanding*): You think you a woman, Bennie—but you still a little girl. What you did was childish—so you got treated like a child.

BENEATHA: I see. (*quietly*) I also see that everybody thinks it's all

right for Mama to be a tyrant. But all the tyranny in the world
will never put a God in the heavens! *(She picks up her books
and goes out. Pause.)*

RUTH *(goes to* MAMA's *door)*: She said she was sorry.

MAMA *(coming out, going to her plant)*: They frightens me, Ruth.
My children.

RUTH: You got good children, Lena. They just a little off sometimes—but they're good.

MAMA: No—there's something come down between me and them
that don't let us understand each other and I don't know what
it is. One done almost lost his mind thinking 'bout money all
the time and the other done commence to talk about things I
can't seem to understand in no form or fashion. What is it that's
changing, Ruth?

RUTH *(soothingly, older than her years)*: Now . . . you taking it all
too seriously. You just got strong-willed children and it takes a
strong woman like you to keep 'em in hand.

MAMA *(looking at her plant and sprinkling a little water on it)*:
They spirited all right, my children. Got to admit they got
spirit—Bennie and Walter. Like this little old plant that ain't
never had enough sunshine or nothing—and look at it . . .

She has her back to RUTH, *who has had to stop ironing and lean
against something and put the back of her hand to her forehead.*

RUTH *(trying to keep* MAMA *from noticing)*: You . . . sure . . . loves
that little old thing, don't you? . . .

MAMA: Well, I always wanted me a garden like I used to see sometimes at the back of the houses down home. This plant is close
as I ever got to having one. *(She looks out of the window as
she replaces the plant.)* Lord, ain't nothing as dreary as the view
from this window on a dreary day, is there? Why ain't you
singing this morning, Ruth? Sing that "No Ways Tired." That
song always lifts me up so—*(She turns at last to see that* RUTH
has slipped quietly to the floor, in a state of semiconsciousness.)
Ruth! Ruth honey—what's the matter with you . . . Ruth!

It is the following morning; a Saturday morning, and house clean-ing is in progress at the YOUNGERS. *Furniture has been shoved hither and yon and* MAMA *is giving the kitchen-area walls a wash-ing down.* BENEATHA, *in dungarees, with a handkerchief tied around her face, is spraying insecticide into the cracks in the walls. As they work, the radio is on and a Southside disk-jockey program is inappropriately filling the house with a rather exotic saxophone blues.* TRAVIS, *the sole idle one, is leaning on his arms, looking out of the window.*

TRAVIS: Grandmama, that stuff Bennie is using smells awful. Can I go downstairs, please?

MAMA: Did you get all them chores done already? I ain't seen you doing much.

TRAVIS: Yes'm—finished early. Where did Mama go this morning?

MAMA *(looking at* BENEATHA*)*: She had to go on a little errand.

The phone rings. BENEATHA *runs to answer it and reaches it before* WALTER, *who has entered from bedroom.*

TRAVIS: Where?

MAMA: To tend to her business.

BENEATHA: Haylo . . . *(disappointed)* Yes, he is. *(She tosses the phone to* WALTER, *who barely catches it.)* It's Willie Harris again.

WALTER *(as privately as possible under* MAMA's *gaze)*: Hello, Wil-lie. Did you get the papers from the lawyer? . . . No, not yet. I told you the mailman doesn't get here till ten-thirty . . . No, I'll come there . . . Yeah! Right away. *(He hangs up and goes for his coat.)*

BENEATHA: Brother, where did Ruth go?

WALTER *(as he exits)*: How should I know!

TRAVIS: Aw come on, Grandma. Can I go outside?

MAMA: Oh, I guess so. You stay right in front of the house, though, and keep a good lookout for the postman.

TRAVIS: Yes'm. *(He darts into bedroom for stickball and bat, reenters, and sees* BENEATHA *on her knees spraying under sofa with behind upraised. He edges closer to the target, takes aim, and lets her have it. She screams.)* Leave them poor little cockroaches alone, they ain't bothering you none! (*He runs as she swings the spraygun at him viciously and playfully.*) Grandma! Grandma!

MAMA: Look out there, girl, before you be spilling some of that stuff on that child!

TRAVIS (*safely behind the bastion of* MAMA): That's right—look out, now! (*He exits.*)

BENEATHA (*drily*): I can't imagine that it would hurt him—it has never hurt the roaches.

MAMA: Well, little boys' hides ain't as tough as Southside roaches. You better get over there behind the bureau. I seen one marching out of there like Napoleon yesterday.

BENEATHA: There's really only one way to get rid of them, Mama—

MAMA: How?

BENEATHA: Set fire to this building! Mama, where did Ruth go?

MAMA (*looking at her with meaning*): To the doctor, I think.

BENEATHA: The doctor? What's the matter? (*They exchange glances.*) You don't think—

MAMA (*with her sense of drama*): Now I ain't saying what I think. But I ain't never been wrong 'bout a woman neither. (*The phone rings.*)

BENEATHA (*at the phone*): Hay-lo . . . (*pause, and a moment of recognition.*) Well—when did you get back! . . . And how was it? . . . Of course I've missed you—in my way . . . This morning? No . . . house cleaning and all that and Mama hates it if I let people come over when the house is like this . . . You *have?* Well, that's different . . . What is it—Oh, what the hell, come on over . . . Right, see you then. *Arrivederci. (She hangs up.)*

MAMA (*who has listened vigorously, as is her habit*): Who is that you inviting over here with this house looking like this? You ain't got the pride you was born with!

BENEATHA: Asagai doesn't care how houses look Mama—he's an intellectual.

MAMA: *Who?*

BENEATHA: Asagai—Joseph Asagai. He's an African boy I met on campus. He's been studying in Canada all summer.

MAMA: What's his name?

BENEATHA: Asagai, Joseph. Ah-sah-guy . . . He's from Nigeria.

MAMA: Oh, that's the little country that was founded by slaves way back . . .

BENEATHA: No, Mama—that's Liberia.

MAMA: I don't think I never met no African before.

BENEATHA: Well, do me a favor and don't ask him a whole lot of ignorant questions about Africans. I mean, do they wear clothes and all that—

MAMA: Well, now, I guess if you think we so ignorant 'round here maybe you shouldn't bring your friends here—

BENEATHA: It's just that people ask such crazy things. All anyone seems to know about when it comes to Africa is Tarzan—

MAMA *(indignantly)*: Why should I know anything about Africa?

BENEATHA: Why do you give money at church for the missionary work?

MAMA: Well, that's to help save people.

BENEATHA: You mean save them from *heathenism*—

MAMA *(innocently)*: Yes.

BENEATHA: I'm afraid they need more salvation from the British and the French.

RUTH *comes in forlornly and pulls off her coat with dejection. They both turn to look at her.*

RUTH *(dispiritedly)*: Well, I guess from all the happy faces—everybody knows.

BENEATHA: You pregnant?

MAMA: Lord have mercy, I sure hope it's a little old girl. Travis ought to have a sister.

BENEATHA *and* RUTH *give her a hopeless look for this grandmotherly enthusiasm.*

BENEATHA: How far along are you?

RUTH: Two months.

BENEATHA: Did you mean to? I mean did you plan it or was it an accident?

MAMA: What do you know about planning or not planning?

BENEATHA: Oh, Mama.

RUTH *(wearily)*: She's twenty years old, Lena.

BENEATHA: Did you plan it, Ruth?

RUTH: Mind your own business.

BENEATHA: It is my business—where is he going to live, on the roof? *(There is silence following the remark as the three women react to the sense of it.)* Gee—I didn't mean that, Ruth, honest. Gee, I don't feel like that at all. I—I think it is wonderful.

RUTH *(dully)*: Wonderful.

BENEATHA: Yes—really.

MAMA *(looking at RUTH, worried)*: Doctor say everything going to be all right?

RUTH *(far away)*: Yes—she says everything is going to be fine . . .

MAMA *(immediately suspicious)*: "She"—What doctor you went to?

RUTH *folds over, near hysteria.*

MAMA *(worriedly hovering over RUTH)*: Ruth honey—what's the matter with you—you sick?

RUTH *has her fists clenched on her thighs and is fighting hard to suppress a scream that seems to be rising in her.*

BENEATHA: What's the matter with her, Mama?

MAMA *(working her fingers in RUTH's shoulders to relax her)*: She be all right. Women gets right depressed sometimes when they get her way. *(speaking softly, expertly, rapidly)* Now you just relax. That's right . . . just lean back, don't think 'bout nothing at all . . . nothing at all—

RUTH: I'm all right . . .

The glassy-eyed look melts and then she collapses into a fit of heavy sobbing. The bell rings.

BENEATHA: Oh, my God—that must be Asagai.

MAMA *(to RUTH)*: Come on now, honey. You need to lie down and rest awhile . . . then have some nice hot food.

They exit, RUTH's weight on her mother-in-law. BENEATHA, herself profoundly disturbed, opens the door to admit a rather dramatic-looking young man with a large package.

ASAGAI: Hello, Alaiyo—

BENEATHA *(holding the door open and regarding him with pleasure)*: Hello . . . *(long pause)* Well—come in. And please excuse everything. My mother was very upset about my letting anyone come here with the place like this.

ASAGAI *(coming into the room)*: You look disturbed too . . . Is something wrong?

BENEATHA: *(still at the door, absently)*: Yes . . . we've all got acute ghetto-itus. *(She smiles and comes toward him, finding a cigarette and sitting.)* So—sit down! No! Wait! *(She whips the spraygun off sofa where she had left it and puts the cushions back. At last perches on arm of sofa. He sits.)* So, how was Canada?

ASAGAI *(a sophisticate)*: Canadian.

BENEATHA *(looking at him)*: Asagai, I'm very glad you are back.

ASAGAI *(looking back at her in turn)*: Are you really?

BENEATHA: Yes—very.

ASAGAI: Why?—you were quite glad when I went away. What happened?

BENEATHA: You went away.

ASAGAI: Ahhhhhhhh.

BENEATHA: Before—you wanted to be so serious before there was time.

ASAGAI: How much time must there be before one knows what one feels?

BENEATHA *(Stalling this particular conversation. Her hands pressed together, in a deliberately childish gesture.)*: What did you bring me?

ASAGAI *(handing her the package)*: Open it and see.

BENEATHA *(eagerly opening the package and drawing out some records and the colorful robes of a Nigerian woman)*: Oh, Asagai! . . . You got them for me! . . . How beautiful . . . and the records too! *(She lifts out the robes and runs to the mirror with them and holds the drapery up in front of herself.)*

ASAGAI *(coming to her at the mirror)*: I shall have to teach you how to drape it properly. *(He flings the material about her for the moment and stands back to look at her.)* Ah—Oh-pay-gay-day, oh-gbah-mu-shay. *(a Yoruba exclamation for admiration)* You wear it well . . . very well . . . mutilated hair and all.

BENEATHA *(turning suddenly)*: My hair—what's wrong with my hair?

ASAGAI *(shrugging)*: Were you born with it like that?

BENEATHA *(reaching up to touch it)*: No . . . of course not. *(She looks back to the mirror, disturbed.)*

ASAGAI *(smiling)*: How then?

BENEATHA: You know perfectly well how ... as crinkly as yours ... that's how.

ASAGAI: And it is ugly to you that way?

BENEATHA *(quickly)*: Oh, no—not ugly ... *(more slowly, apologetically)* But it's so hard to manage when it's, well—raw.

ASAGAI: And so to accommodate that—you mutilate it every week?

BENEATHA: It's not mutilation!

ASAGAI *(laughing aloud at her seriousness)*: Oh ... please! I am only teasing you because you are so very serious about these things. *(He stands back from her and folds his arms across his chest as he watches her pulling at her hair and frowning in the mirror.)* Do you remember the first time you met me at school? ... *(He laughs.)* You came up to me and you said— and I thought you were the most serious little thing I had ever seen—you said: *(He imitates her.)* "Mr. Asagai—I want very much to talk with you. About Africa. You see, Mr. Asagai, I am looking for my *identity!*" *(He laughs.)*

BENEATHA *(turning to him, not laughing)*: Yes—. *(Her face is quizzical, profoundly disturbed.)*

ASAGAI *(still teasing and reaching out and taking her face in his hands and turning her profile to him)*: Well ... it is true that this is not so much a profile of a Hollywood queen as perhaps a queen of the Nile— *(a mock dismissal of the importance of the question)* But what does it matter? Assimilationism is so popular in your country.

BENEATHA *(wheeling, passionately, sharply)*: I am not an assimilationist!

ASAGAI *(the protest hangs in the room for a moment and* ASAGAI *studies her, his laughter fading)*: Such a serious one. *(There is a pause.)* So—you like the robes? You must take excellent care of them—they are from my sister's personal wardrobe.

BENEATHA *(with incredulity)*: You—you sent all the way home— for me?

ASAGAI *(with charm)*: For you—I would do much more ... Well, that is what I came for. I must go.

BENEATHA: Will you call me Monday?

ASAGAI: Yes ... We have a great deal to talk about. I mean about identity and time and all that.

BENEATHA: Time?

ASAGAI: Yes. About how much time one needs to know what one feels.

BENEATHA: You see! You never understood that there is more than one kind of feeling which can exist between a man and a woman—or, at least, there should be.

ASAGAI *(shaking his head negatively but gently)*: No. Between a man and a woman there need be only one kind of feeling. I have that for you . . . Now even . . . right this moment . . .

BENEATHA: I know—and by itself—it won't do. I can find that anywhere.

ASAGAI: For a woman it should be enough.

BENEATHA: I know—because that's what it says in all the novels that men write. But it isn't. Go ahead and laugh—but I'm not interested in being someone's little episode in America or—*(with feminine vengeance)*—one of them! (ASAGAI *has burst into laughter again.)* That's funny as hell, huh!

ASAGAI: It's just that every American girl I have known has said that to me. White—black—in this you are all the same. And the same speech, too!

BENEATHA *(angrily)*: Yuk, yuk, yuk!

ASAGAI: It's how you can be sure that the world's most liberated women are not liberated at all. You all talk about it too much!

MAMA *enters and is immediately all social charm because of the presence of a guest.*

BENEATHA: Oh—Mama—this is Mr. Asagai.

MAMA: How do you do?

ASAGAI *(total politeness to an elder)*: How do you do, Mrs. Younger. Please forgive me for coming at such an outrageous hour on a Saturday.

MAMA: Well, you are quite welcome. I just hope you understand that our house don't always look like this. *(chatterish)* You must come again. I would love to hear all about—*(not sure of the name)*—your country. I think it's so sad the way our American Negroes don't know nothing about Africa 'cept Tarzan and all that. And all that money they pour into these churches when they ought to be helping you people over there drive out them French and Englishmen done taken away your land.

The mother flashes a slightly superior look at her daughter upon completion of the recitation.

ASAGAI *(taken aback by this sudden and acutely unrelated expression of sympathy)*: Yes . . . yes . . .

MAMA *(smiling at him suddenly and relaxing and looking him over)*: How many miles is it from here to where you come from?

ASAGAI: Many thousands.

MAMA *(looking at him as she would* WALTER*)*: I bet you don't half look after yourself, being away from your mama either. I spec you better come 'round here from time to time to get yourself some decent home-cooked meals . . .

ASAGAI *(moved)*: Thank you. Thank you very much. *(They are all quiet, then—)* Well . . . I must go. I will call you Monday, Alaiyo.

MAMA: What's that he call you?

ASAGAI: Oh—"Alaiyo." I hope you don't mind. It is what you would call a nickname, I think. It is a Yoruba word. I am a Yoruba.

MAMA *(looking at* BENEATHA*)*: I—I thought he was from—*(uncertain)*

ASAGAI *(understanding)*: Nigeria is my country. Yoruba is my tribal origin—

BENEATHA: You didn't tell us what Alaiyo means . . . for all I know, you might be calling me Little Idiot or something . . .

ASAGAI: Well . . . let me see . . . I do not know how just to explain it . . . The sense of a thing can be so different when it changes languages.

BENEATHA: You're evading.

ASAGAI: No—really it is difficult . . . *(thinking)* It means . . . it means One for Whom Bread—Food—Is Not Enough. *(He looks at her.)* Is that all right?

BENEATHA *(understanding, softly)*: Thank you.

MAMA *(looking from one to the other and not understanding any of it)*: Well . . . that's nice . . . You must come see us again— Mr.——

ASAGAI: Ah-sah-guy . . .

MAMA: Yes . . . Do come again.

ASAGAI: Good-bye. *(He exits.)*

MAMA *(after him)*: Lord, that's a pretty thing just went out here! *(insinuatingly, to her daughter)* Yes, I guess I see why we done commence to get so interested in Africa 'round here. Missionaries my aunt Jenny! *(She exits.)*

BENEATHA: Oh, Mama! . . .

She picks up the Nigerian dress and holds it up to her in front of the mirror again. She sets the headdress on haphazardly and then notices her hair again and clutches at it and then replaces the headdress and frowns at herself. Then she starts to wriggle in front of the mirror as she thinks a Nigerian woman might. TRAVIS *enters and stands regarding her.*

TRAVIS: What's the matter girl, you cracking up?

BENEATHA: Shut up.

She pulls the headdress off and looks at herself in the mirror and clutches at her hair again and squinches her eyes as if trying to imagine something. Then, suddenly, she gets her raincoat and kerchief and hurriedly prepares for going out.

MAMA *(coming back into the room)*: She's resting now. Travis, baby, run next door and ask Miss Johnson to please let me have a little kitchen cleanser. This here can is empty as Jacob's kettle.

TRAVIS: I just came in.

MAMA: Do as you told. *(He exits and she looks at her daughter.)* Where you going?

BENEATHA *(halting at the door)*: To become a queen of the Nile!

She exits in a breathless blaze of glory. RUTH *appears in the bedroom doorway.*

MAMA: Who told you to get up?

RUTH: Ain't nothing wrong with me to be lying in no bed for. Where did Bennie go?

MAMA *(drumming her fingers)*: Far as I could make out—to Egypt. *(RUTH just looks at her.)* What time is it getting to?

RUTH: Ten twenty. And the mailman going to ring that bell this morning just like he done every morning for the last umpteen years.

TRAVIS *comes in with the cleanser can.*

TRAVIS: She say to tell you that she don't have much.

MAMA *(angrily)*: Lord, some people I could name sure is tight-fisted! *(directing her grandson)* Mark two cans of cleanser down on the list there. If she that hard up for kitchen cleanser, I sure don't want to forget to get her none!

RUTH: Lena—maybe the woman is just short on cleanser—

MAMA *(not listening)*: —Much baking powder as she done borrowed from me all these years, she could of done gone into the baking business!

The bell sounds suddenly and sharply and all three are stunned—serious and silent—mid-speech. In spite of all the other conversations and distractions of the morning, this is what they have been waiting for, even TRAVIS, *who looks helplessly from his mother to his grandmother.* RUTH *is the first to come to life again.*

RUTH *(to* TRAVIS*)*: Get down them steps, boy! *(*TRAVIS *snaps to life and flies out to get the mail.)*

MAMA *(her eyes wide, her hand to her breast)*: You mean it done really come?

RUTH *(excited)*: Oh, Miss Lena!

MAMA *(collecting herself)*: Well . . . I don't know what we all so excited about 'round here for. We known it was coming for months.

RUTH: That's a whole lot different from having it come and being able to hold it in your hands . . . a piece of paper worth ten thousand dollars . . . *(*TRAVIS *bursts back into the room. He holds the envelope high above his head, like a little dancer, his face is radiant and he is breathless. He moves to his grandmother with sudden slow ceremony and puts the envelope into her hands. She accepts it, and then merely holds it and looks at it.)* Come on! Open it . . . Lord have mercy, I wish Walter Lee was here!

TRAVIS: Open it, Grandmama!

MAMA *(staring at it)*: Now you all be quiet. It's just a check.

RUTH: Open it . . .

MAMA *(still staring at it)*: Now don't act silly . . . We ain't never been no people to act silly 'bout no money—

RUTH *(swiftly)*: We ain't never had none before—OPEN IT!

MAMA *finally makes a good strong tear and pulls out the thin blue slice of paper and inspects it closely. The boy and his mother study it raptly over* MAMA's *shoulders.*

MAMA: *Travis! (She is counting off with doubt.)* Is that the right number of zeros?

TRAVIS: Yes'm . . . ten thousand dollars. Gaalee, Grandmama, you rich.

MAMA *(She holds the check away from her, still looking at it. Slowly her face sobers into a mask of unhappiness.)*: Ten thousand dollars. *(She hands it to* RUTH.*)* Put it away somewhere, Ruth. *(She does not look at* RUTH; *her eyes seem to be seeing something somewhere very far off.)* Ten thousand dollars they give you. Ten thousand dollars.

TRAVIS *(to his mother, sincerely)*: What's the matter with Grandmama—don't she want to be rich?

RUTH *(distractedly)*: You go on out and play now, baby. *(*TRAVIS *exits.* MAMA *starts wiping dishes absently, humming intently to herself.* RUTH *turns to her, with kind exasperation.)* You've gone and got yourself upset.

MAMA *(not looking at her)*: I spec if it wasn't for you all . . . I would just put that money away or give it to the church or something.

RUTH: Now what kind of talk is that. Mr. Younger would just be plain mad if he could hear you talking foolish like that.

MAMA *(stopping and staring off)*: Yes . . . he sure would. *(sighing)* We got enough to do with that money, all right. *(She halts then, and turns and looks at her daughter-in-law hard;* RUTH *avoids her eyes and* MAMA *wipes her hands with finality and starts to speak firmly to* RUTH.*)* Where did you go today, girl?

RUTH: To the doctor.

MAMA *(impatiently)*: Now, Ruth . . . you know better than that. Old Doctor Jones is strange enough in his way but there ain't nothing 'bout him make somebody slip and call him "she"—like you done this morning.

RUTH: Well, that's what happened—my tongue slipped.

MAMA: You went to see that woman, didn't you?

RUTH *(defensively, giving herself away)*: What woman you talking about?

MAMA *(angrily)*: That woman who—(WALTER *enters in great excitement.*)

WALTER: Did it come?

MAMA *(quietly)*: Can't you give people a Christian greeting before you start asking about money?

WALTER *(to RUTH)*: Did it come? (RUTH *unfolds the check and lays it quietly before him, watching him intently with thoughts of her own.* WALTER *sits down and grasps it close and counts off the zeros.*) Ten thousand dollars—(*He turns suddenly, frantically to his mother and draws some papers out of his breast pocket.*) Mama—look. Old Willy Harris put everything on paper—

MAMA: Son—I think you ought to talk to your wife . . . I'll go on out and leave you alone if you want—

WALTER: I can talk to her later—Mama, look—

MAMA: Son—

WALTER: WILL SOMEBODY PLEASE LISTEN TO ME TODAY!

MAMA *(quietly)*: I don't 'low no yellin' in this house, Walter Lee, and you know it—(WALTER *stares at them in frustration and starts to speak several times.*) And there ain't going to be no investing in no liquor stores.

WALTER: But, Mama, you ain't even looked at it.

MAMA: I don't aim to have to speak on that again. *(a long pause)*

WALTER: You ain't looked at it and you don't aim to have to speak on that again? You ain't even looked at it and *you* have decided—(*crumpling his papers*) Well, *you* tell that to my boy tonight when you put him to sleep on the living-room couch . . . *(turning to* MAMA *and speaking directly to her)* Yeah—and tell it to my wife, Mama, tomorrow when she has to go out of here to look after somebody else's kids. And tell it to *me*, Mama, every time we need a new pair of curtains and I have to watch *you* go and work in somebody's kitchen. Yeah, you tell me then! (WALTER *starts out.*)

RUTH: Where you going?

WALTER: I'm going out!

RUTH: Where?

WALTER: Just out of this house somewhere—

RUTH *(getting her coat)*: I'll come too.

WALTER: I don't want you to come!

RUTH: I got something to talk to you about, Walter.

WALTER: That's too bad.

MAMA *(still quietly)*: Walter Lee— *(She waits and he finally turns and looks at her.)* Sit down.

WALTER: I'm a grown man, Mama.

MAMA: Ain't nobody said you wasn't grown. But you still in my house and my presence. And as long as you are—you'll talk to your wife civil. Now sit down.

RUTH *(suddenly)*: Oh, let him go on out and drink himself to death! He makes me sick to my stomach! *(She flings her coat against him and exits to bedroom.)*

WALTER *(violently flinging the coat after her)*: And you turn mine too, baby! *(The door slams behind her.)* That was my biggest mistake—

MAMA *(still quietly)*: Walter, what is the matter with you?

WALTER: Matter with me? Ain't nothing the matter with *me!*

MAMA: Yes there is. Something eating you up like a crazy man. Something more than me not giving you this money. The past few years I been watching it happen to you. You get all nervous acting and kind of wild in the eyes— *(WALTER jumps up impatiently at her words.)* I said sit there now, I'm talking to you!

WALTER: Mama—I don't need no nagging at me today.

MAMA: Seem like you getting to a place where you always tied up in some kind of knot about something. But if anybody ask you 'bout it you just yell at 'em and bust out the house and go out and drink somewheres. Walter Lee, people can't live with that. Ruth's a good, patient girl in her way—but you getting to be too much. Boy, don't make the mistake of driving that girl away from you.

WALTER: Why—what she do for me?

MAMA: She loves you.

WALTER: Mama—I'm going out. I want to go off somewhere and be by myself for a while.

MAMA: I'm sorry 'bout your liquor store, son. It just wasn't the thing for us to do. That's what I want to tell you about—

WALTER: I got to go out, Mama— *(He rises.)*

MAMA: It's dangerous, son.

WALTER: What's dangerous?

MAMA: When a man goes outside his home to look for peace.

WALTER *(beseechingly)*: Then why can't there never be no peace in this house then?

MAMA: You done found it in some other house?

WALTER: No—there ain't no woman! Why do women always think there's a woman somewhere when a man gets restless. *(picks up the check)* Do you know what this money means to me? Do you know what this money can do for us? *(puts it back)* Mama—Mama—I want so many things . . .

MAMA: Yes, son—

WALTER: I want so many things that they are driving me kind of crazy . . . Mama—look at me.

MAMA: I'm looking at you. You a good-looking boy. You got a job, a nice wife, a fine boy and—

WALTER: A job. *(looks at her)* Mama, a job? I open and close car doors all day long. I drive a man around in his limousine and I say, "Yes, sir; no, sir; very good, sir; shall I take the Drive, sir?" Mama, that ain't no kind of job . . . that ain't nothing at all. *(very quietly)* Mama, I don't know if I can make you understand.

MAMA: Understand what, baby?

WALTER *(quietly)*: Sometimes it's like I can see the future stretched out in front of me—just plain as day. The future, Mama. Hanging over there at the edge of my days. Just waiting for me—a big, looming blank space—full of *nothing*. Just waiting for *me*. But it don't have to be. *(Pause. Kneeling beside her chair.)* Mama—sometimes when I'm downtown and I pass them cool, quiet-looking restaurants where them white boys are sitting back and talking 'bout things . . . sitting there turning deals worth millions of dollars . . . sometimes I see guys don't look much older than me—

MAMA: Son—how come you talk so much 'bout money?

WALTER *(with immense passion)*: Because it is life, Mama!

MAMA *(quietly)*: Oh—*(very quietly)* So now it's life. Money is life. Once upon a time freedom used to be life—now it's money. I guess the world really do change . . .

WALTER: No—it was always money, Mama. We just didn't know about it.

MAMA: No . . . something has changed. *(She looks at him.)* You something new, boy. In my time we was worried about not being lynched and getting to the North if we could and how to stay alive and still have a pinch of dignity too . . . Now here come you and Beneatha—talking 'bout things we never even thought about hardly, me and your daddy. You ain't satisfied or proud of nothing we done. I mean that you had a home; that we kept you out of trouble till you was grown; that you don't have to ride to work on the back of nobody's streetcar—You my children—but how different we done become.

WALTER (*A long beat. He pats her hand and gets up*): You just don't understand, Mama, you just don't understand.

MAMA: Son—do you know your wife is expecting another baby? (WALTER *stands, stunned, and absorbs what his mother has said.*) That's what she wanted to talk to you about. (WALTER *sinks down into a chair.*) This ain't for me to be telling—but you ought to know. (*She waits.*) I think Ruth is thinking 'bout getting rid of that child.

WALTER (*slowly understanding*): —No—no—Ruth wouldn't do that.

MAMA: When the world gets ugly enough—a woman will do anything for her family. *The part that's already living.*

WALTER: You don't know Ruth, Mama, if you think she would do that.

RUTH *opens the bedroom door and stands there a little limp.*

RUTH (*beaten*): Yes I would too, Walter. (*Pause.*) I gave her a five-dollar down payment.

There is total silence as the man stares at his wife and the mother stares at her son.

MAMA (*presently*): Well—(*tightly*) Well—son, I'm waiting to hear you say something . . . (*She waits.*) I'm waiting to hear how you be your father's son. Be the man he was . . . (*Pause. The silence shouts.*) Your wife say she going to destroy your child. And I'm waiting to hear you talk like him and say we a people who give children life, not who destroys them—(*She rises.*) I'm waiting to see you stand up and look like your daddy and say we done give up one baby to poverty and that we ain't going to give up nary another one . . . I'm waiting.

WALTER: Ruth—*(He can say nothing.)*

MAMA: If you a son of mine, tell her! *(WALTER picks up his keys and his coat and walks out. She continues, bitterly.)* You . . . you are a disgrace to your father's memory. Somebody get me my hat!

ACT II

SCENE I

Time   *Later the same day.*

At rise   RUTH *is ironing again. She has the radio going. Presently* BENEATHA'*s bedroom door opens and* RUTH'*s mouth falls and she puts down the iron in fascination.*

RUTH: What have we got on tonight!

BENEATHA *(emerging grandly from the doorway so that we can see her thoroughly robed in the costume Asagai brought)*: You are looking at what a well-dressed Nigerian woman wears—*(She parades for* RUTH, *her hair completely hidden by the headdress; she is coquettishly fanning herself with an ornate oriental fan, mistakenly more like Butterfly than any Nigerian that ever was.)* Isn't it beautiful? *(She promenades to the radio and, with an arrogant flourish, turns off the good loud blues that is playing.)* Enough of this assimilationist junk! *(*RUTH *follows her with her eyes as she goes to the phonograph and puts on a record and turns and waits ceremoniously for the music to come up. Then, with a shout—)* OCOMOGOSIAY!

RUTH *jumps. The music comes up, a lovely Nigerian melody.* BENEATHA *listens, enraptured, her eyes far away—"back to the past." She begins to dance.* RUTH *is dumfounded.*

RUTH: What kind of dance is that?

BENEATHA: A folk dance.

RUTH *(Pearl Bailey)*: What kind of folks do that, honey?

BENEATHA: It's from Nigeria. It's a dance of welcome.

RUTH: Who you welcoming?

BENEATHA: The men back to the village.

RUTH: Where they been?

BENEATHA: How should I know—out hunting or something. Anyway, they are coming back now . . .

RUTH: Well, that's good.

BENEATHA *(with the record)*:

>Alundi, alundi
>Alundi alunya
>Jop pu a jeepua
>Ang gu soooooooooo
>
>Ai yai yae . . .
>Ayehaye—alundi . . .

WALTER *comes in during this performance; he has obviously been drinking. He leans against the door heavily and watches his sister, at first with distaste. Then his eyes look off—"back to the past"— as he lifts both his fists to the roof, screaming.*

WALTER: YEAH . . . AND ETHIOPIA STRETCH FORTH HER HANDS AGAIN! . . .

RUTH *(drily, looking at him)*: Yes—and Africa sure is claiming her own tonight. *(She gives them both up and starts ironing again.)*

WALTER *(all in a drunken, dramatic shout)*: Shut up! . . . I'm digging them drums . . . them drums move me! . . . *(He makes his weaving way to his wife's face and leans in close to her.)* In my heart of hearts—*(He thumps his chest.)*—I am much warrior!

RUTH *(without even looking up)*: In your heart of hearts you are much drunkard.

WALTER *(coming away from her and starting to wander around the room, shouting)*: Me and Jomo . . . *(Intently, in his sister's face. She has stopped dancing to watch him in this unknown mood.)* That's my man, Kenyatta. *(shouting and thumping his chest)* FLAMING SPEAR! HOT DAMN! *(He is suddenly in possession of an imaginary spear and actively spearing enemies all over the room.)* OCOMOGOSIAY . . .

BENEATHA *(to encourage* WALTER, *thoroughly caught up with this side of him)*: OCOMOGOSIAY, FLAMING SPEAR!

WALTER: THE LION IS WAKING . . . OWIMOWEH! *(He pulls his shirt open and leaps up on the table and gestures with his spear.)*

BENEATHA: OWIMOWEH!

WALTER (*On the table, very far gone, his eyes pure glass sheets. He sees what we cannot, that he is a leader of his people, a great chief, a descendant of Chaka, and that the hour to march has come.*): Listen, my black brothers—

BENEATHA: OCOMOGOSIAY!

WALTER: —Do you hear the waters rushing against the shores of the coastlands—

BENEATHA: OCOMOGOSIAY!

WALTER: —Do you hear the screeching of the cocks in yonder hills beyond where the chiefs meet in council for the coming of the mighty war—

BENEATHA: OCOMOGOSIAY!

And now the lighting shifts subtly to suggest the world of WALTER'S *imagination, and the mood shifts from pure comedy. It is the inner* WALTER *speaking: the Southside chauffeur has assumed an unexpected majesty.*

WALTER: —Do you hear the beating of the wings of the birds flying low over the mountains and the low places of our land—

BENEATHA: OCOMOGOSIAY!

WALTER: Do you hear the singing of the women, singing the war songs of our fathers to the babies in the great houses? Singing the sweet war songs! (*The doorbell rings.*) OH, DO YOU HEAR, MY *BLACK* BROTHERS!

BENEATHA (*completely gone*): We hear you, Flaming Spear—

RUTH *shuts off the phonograph and opens the door.* GEORGE MURCHISON *enters.*

WALTER: Telling us to prepare for the GREATNESS OF THE TIME! (*Lights back to normal. He turns and sees* GEORGE.) Black Brother! (*He extends his hand for the fraternal clasp.*)

GEORGE: Black Brother, hell!

RUTH (*having had enough, and embarrassed for the family*): Beneatha, you got company—what's the matter with you? Walter Lee Younger, get down off that table and stop acting like a fool . . .

WALTER *comes down off the table suddenly and makes a quick exit to the bathroom.*

RUTH: He's had a little to drink . . . I don't know what her excuse is.

GEORGE *(to* BENEATHA*)*: Look honey, we're going *to* the theatre — we're not going to be *in* it . . . so go change, huh?

BENEATHA *looks at him and slowly, ceremoniously, lifts her hands and pulls off the headdress. Her hair is close-cropped and unstraightened.* GEORGE *freezes mid-sentence and* RUTH'S *eyes all but fall out of her head.*

GEORGE: What in the name of —

RUTH *(touching* BENEATHA'S *hair)*: Girl, you done lost your natural mind!? Look at your head!

GEORGE: What have you done to your head — I mean your hair?

BENEATHA: Nothing — except cut it off.

RUTH: Now that's the truth — it's what ain't been done to it! You expect this boy to go out with you with your head all nappy like that?

BENEATHA *(looking at* GEORGE*)*: That's up to George. If he's ashamed of his heritage —

GEORGE: Oh, don't be so proud of yourself, Bennie — just because you look eccentric.

BENEATHA: How can something that's natural be eccentric?

GEORGE: That's what being eccentric means — being natural. Get dressed.

BENEATHA: I don't like that, George.

RUTH: Why must you and your brother make an argument out of everything people say?

BENEATHA: Because I hate assimilationist Negroes!

RUTH: Will somebody please tell me what assimila-whoever means!

GEORGE: Oh, it's just a college girl's way of calling people Uncle Toms — but that isn't what it means at all.

RUTH: Well, what does it mean?

BENEATHA *(cutting* GEORGE *off and staring at him as she replies to* RUTH*)*: It means someone who is willing to give up his own culture and submerge himself completely in the dominant, and in this case *oppressive* culture!

GEORGE: Oh, dear, dear, dear! Here we go! A lecture on the African past! On our Great West African Heritage! In one second we will hear all about the great Ashanti empires; the great Songhay civilizations; and the great sculpture of Bénin—and then some poetry in the Bantu—and the whole monologue will end with the word *heritage!* *(nastily)* Let's face it, baby, your heritage is nothing but a bunch of raggedy-assed spirituals and some grass huts!

BENEATHA: GRASS HUTS! *(RUTH crosses to her and forcibly pushes her toward the bedroom.)* See there . . . you are standing there in your splendid ignorance talking about people who were the first to smelt iron on the face of the earth! *(RUTH is pushing her through the door.)* The Ashanti were performing surgical operations when the English—(RUTH *pulls the door to, with* BENEATHA *on the other side, and smiles graciously at* GEORGE. BENEATHA *opens the door and shouts the end of the sentence defiantly at* GEORGE.)—were still tatooing themselves with blue dragons! *(She goes back inside.)*

RUTH: Have a seat, George. *(They both sit.* RUTH *folds her hands rather primly on her lap, determined to demonstrate the civilization of the family.)* Warm, ain't it? I mean for September. *(pause)* Just like they always say about Chicago weather: If it's too hot or cold for you, just wait a minute and it'll change. *(She smiles happily at this cliché of clichés.)* Everybody say it's got to do with them bombs and things they keep setting off. *(pause)* Would you like a nice cold beer?

GEORGE: No, thank you. I don't care for beer. *(He looks at his watch.)* I hope she hurries up.

RUTH: What time is the show?

GEORGE: It's an eight-thirty curtain. That's just Chicago, though. In New York standard curtain time is eight forty. *(He is rather proud of this knowledge.)*

RUTH *(properly appreciating it)*: You get to New York a lot?

GEORGE *(offhand)*: Few times a year.

RUTH: Oh—that's nice. I've never been to New York. *(WALTER enters. We feel he has relieved himself, but the edge of unreality is still with him.)*

WALTER: New York ain't got nothing Chicago ain't. Just a bunch of hustling people all squeezed up together—being "Eastern." *(He turns his face into a screw of displeasure.)*

GEORGE: Oh—you've been?

WALTER: *Plenty* of times.

RUTH *(shocked at the lie)*: Walter Lee Younger!

WALTER *(staring her down)*: Plenty! *(pause)* What we got to drink in this house? Why don't you offer this man some refreshment. *(to* GEORGE*)* They don't know how to entertain people in this house, man.

GEORGE: Thank you—I don't really care for anything.

WALTER *(feeling his head; sobriety coming)*: Where's Mama?

RUTH: She ain't come back yet.

WALTER *(looking* MURCHISON *over from head to toe, scrutinizing his carefully casual tweed sports jacket over cashmere V-neck sweater over soft eyelet shirt and tie, and soft slacks, finished off with white buckskin shoes)*: Why all you college boys wear them faggoty-looking white shoes?

RUTH: Walter Lee!

GEORGE MURCHISON *ignores the remark.*

WALTER *(to* RUTH*)*: Well, they look crazy as hell—white shoes, cold as it is.

RUTH *(crushed)*: You have to excuse him—

WALTER: No he don't! Excuse me for what? What you always excusing me for! I'll excuse myself when I needs to be excused! *(a pause)* They look as funny as them black knee socks Beneatha wears out of here all the time.

RUTH: It's the college *style,* Walter.

WALTER: Style, hell. She looks like she got burnt legs or something!

RUTH: Oh, Walter—

WALTER *(an irritable mimic)*: Oh, Walter! Oh, Walter! *(to* MUR-CHISON*)* How's your old man making out? I understand you all going to buy that big hotel on the Drive? *(He finds a beer in the refrigerator, wanders over to* MURCHISON, *sipping and wiping his lips with the back of his hand, and straddling a chair backwards to talk to the other man.)* Shrewd move. Your old man is all right, man. *(tapping his head and half winking for emphasis)* I mean he knows how to operate. I mean he thinks *big,* you know what I mean, I mean for a *home,* you know? But I think he's kind of running out of ideas now. I'd like to talk to him. Listen, man, I got some plans that could turn this city upside down. I mean think like he does. *Big.* Invest big, gamble big, hell, lose *big* if you have to, you know what I mean. It's hard to find a man on this whole Southside who understands my kind of thinking—you dig? *(He scrutinizes* MURCHISON *again, drinks his beer, squints his eyes and leans in close, confidential, man to man.)* Me and you ought to sit down and talk sometimes, man. Man, I got me some ideas . . .

MURCHISON *(with boredom)*: Yeah—sometimes we'll have to do that, Walter.

WALTER *(understanding the indifference, and offended)*: Yeah—well, when you get the time, man. I know you a busy little boy.

RUTH: Walter, please—

WALTER *(bitterly, hurt)*: I know ain't nothing in this world as busy as you colored college boys with your fraternity pins and white shoes . . .

RUTH *(covering her face with humiliation)*: Oh, Walter Lee—

WALTER: I see you all all the time—with the books tucked under your arms—going to your *(British A—a mimic)* "clahsses." And for what! What the hell you learning over there? Filling up your heads—*(counting off on his fingers)*—with the sociology and the psychology—but they teaching you how to be a man? How to take over and run the world? They teaching you how to run a rubber plantation or a steel mill? Naw—just to talk proper and read books and wear them faggoty-looking white shoes . . .

GEORGE *(looking at him with distaste, a little above it all)*: You're all wacked up with bitterness, man.

WALTER *(intently, almost quietly, between the teeth, glaring at the boy)*: And you—ain't you bitter, man? Ain't you just about had it yet? Don't you see no stars gleaming that you can't reach out and grab? You happy?—You contented son-of-a-bitch—you happy? You got it made? Bitter? Man, I'm a volcano. Bitter? Here I am a giant—surrounded by ants! Ants who can't even understand what it is the giant is talking about.

RUTH *(passionately and suddenly)*: Oh, Walter—ain't you with nobody!

WALTER *(violently)*: No! 'Cause ain't nobody with me! Not even my own mother!

RUTH: Walter, that's a terrible thing to say!

BENEATHA *enters, dressed for the evening in a cocktail dress and earrings, hair natural.*

GEORGE: Well—hey—*(crosses to* BENEATHA; *thoughful, with emphasis, since this is a reversal)* You look great!

WALTER *(seeing his sister's hair for the first time)*: What's the matter with your head?

BENEATHA *(tired of the jokes now)*: I cut it off, Brother.

WALTER *(coming close to inspect it and walking around her)*: Well, I'll be damned. So that's what they mean by the African bush . . .

BENEATHA: Ha ha. Let's go, George.

GEORGE *(looking at her)*: You know something? I like it. It's sharp. I mean it really is. *(helps her into her wrap)*

RUTH: Yes—I think so, too. *(She goes to the mirror and starts to clutch at her hair.)*

WALTER: Oh no! You leave yours alone, baby. You might turn out to have a pin-shaped head or something!

BENEATHA: See you all later.

RUTH: Have a nice time.

GEORGE: Thanks. Good night. *(Half out the door, he reopens it. To* WALTER.*)* Good night, Prometheus!

BENEATHA *and* GEORGE *exit.*

WALTER *(to* RUTH*)*: Who is Prometheus?

RUTH: I don't know. Don't worry about it.

WALTER *(in fury, pointing after* GEORGE*)*: See there—they get to a point where they can't insult you man to man—they got to go talk about something ain't nobody never heard of!

RUTH: How do you know it was an insult? *(to humor him)* Maybe Prometheus is a nice fellow.

WALTER: Prometheus! I bet there ain't even no such thing! I bet that simple-minded clown—

RUTH: Walter—*(She stops what she is doing and looks at him.)*

WALTER *(yelling)*: Don't start!

RUTH: Start what?

WALTER: Your nagging! Where was I? Who was I with? How much money did I spend?

RUTH *(plaintively)*: Walter Lee—why don't we just try to talk about it . . .

WALTER *(not listening)*: I been out talking with people who understand me. People who care about the things I got on my mind.

RUTH *(wearily)*: I guess that means people like Willy Harris.

WALTER: Yes, people like Willy Harris.

RUTH *(with a sudden flash of impatience)*: Why don't you all just hurry up and go into the banking business and stop talking about it!

WALTER: Why? You want to know why? 'Cause we all tied up in a race of people that don't know how to do nothing but moan, pray and have babies! *(The line is too bitter even for him and he looks at her and sits down.)*

RUTH: Oh, Walter . . . *(softly)* Honey, why can't you stop fighting me?

WALTER *(without thinking)*: Who's fighting you! Who even cares about you? *(This line begins the retardation of his mood.)*

RUTH: Well—*(She waits a long time, and then with resignation starts to put away her things.)* I guess I might as well go on to bed . . . *(more or less to herself)* I don't know where we lost it . . . but we have . . . *(then, to him)* I—I'm sorry about this new baby, Walter. I guess maybe I better go on and do what I started . . . I guess I just didn't realize how bad things was with us . . . I guess I just didn't really realize—*(She starts out to the bedroom and stops.)* You want some hot milk?

WALTER: Hot milk?

RUTH: Yes—hot milk.

WALTER: Why hot milk?

RUTH: 'Cause after all that liquor you come home with you ought to have something hot in your stomach.

WALTER: I don't want no milk.

RUTH: You want some coffee then?

WALTER: No, I don't want no coffee. I don't want nothing hot to drink. *(almost plaintively)* Why you always trying to give me something to eat?

RUTH *(standing and looking at him helplessly)*: What *else* can I give you, Walter Lee Younger?

She stands and looks at him and presently turns to go out again. He lifts his head and watches her going away from him in a new mood which began to emerge when he asked her "Who cares about you?"

WALTER: It's been rough, ain't it, baby? *(She hears and stops but does not turn around and he continues to her back.)* I guess between two people there ain't never as much understood as folks generally thinks there is. I mean like between me and you — *(She turns to face him.)* How we gets to the place where we scared to talk softness to each other. *(He waits, thinking hard himself.)* Why you think it got to be like that? *(He is thoughtful, almost as a child would be.)* Ruth, what is it gets into people ought to be close?

RUTH: I don't know, honey. I think about it a lot.

WALTER: On account of you and me, you mean? The way things are with us. The way something done come down between us.

RUTH: There ain't so much between us, Walter . . . Not when you come to me and try to talk to me. Try to be with me . . . a little even.

WALTER *(total honesty)*: Sometimes . . . sometimes . . . I don't even know how to try.

RUTH: Walter —

WALTER: Yes?

RUTH *(coming to him, gently and with misgiving, but coming to him)*: Honey . . . life don't have to be like this. I mean sometimes people can do things so that things are better . . . You remember how we used to talk when Travis was born . . . about the way we were going to live . . . the kind of house . . . *(She is stroking his head.)* Well, it's all starting to slip away from us . . .

He turns her to him and they look at each other and kiss, tenderly and hungrily. The door opens and MAMA *enters —* WALTER *breaks away and jumps up. A beat.)*

WALTER: Mama, where have you been?

MAMA: My — them steps is longer than they used to be. Whew! *(She sits down and ignores him.)* How you feeling this evening, Ruth?

RUTH *shrugs, disturbed at having been interrupted and watching her husband knowingly.*

WALTER: Mama, where have you been all day?

MAMA (*still ignoring him and leaning on the table and changing to more comfortable shoes*): Where's Travis?

RUTH: I let him go out earlier and he ain't come back yet. Boy, is he going to get it!

WALTER: Mama!

MAMA (*as if she has heard him for the first time*): Yes, son?

WALTER: Where did you go this afternoon?

MAMA: I went downtown to tend to some business that I had to tend to.

WALTER: What kind of business?

MAMA: You know better than to question me like a child, Brother.

WALTER (*rising and bending over the table*): Where were you, Mama? (*bringing his fists down and shouting*) Mama, you didn't go do something with that insurance money, something crazy?

The front door opens slowly, interrupting him, and TRAVIS *peeks his head in, less than hopefully.*

TRAVIS (*to his mother*): Mama, I—

RUTH: "Mama I" nothing! You're going to get it, boy! Get on in that bedroom and get yourself ready!

TRAVIS: But I—

MAMA: Why don't you all never let the child explain hisself.

RUTH: Keep out of it now, Lena.

MAMA *clamps her lips together, and* RUTH *advances toward her son menacingly.*

RUTH: A thousand times I have told you not to go off like that—

MAMA (*holding out her arms to her grandson*): Well—at least let me tell him something. I want him to be the first one to hear ... Come here, Travis. (*The boy obeys, gladly.*) Travis—(*She takes him by the shoulder and looks into his face.*)—you know that money we got in the mail this morning?

TRAVIS: Yes'm—

MAMA: Well—what you think your grandmama gone and done with that money?

TRAVIS: I don't know, Grandmama.

MAMA (*putting her finger on his nose for emphasis*): She went out and she bought you a house! (*The explosion comes from* WALTER *at the end of the revelation and he jumps up and turns away from all of them in a fury.* MAMA *continues, to* TRAVIS.) You glad about the house? It's going to be yours when you get to be a man.

TRAVIS: Yeah—I always wanted to live in a house.

MAMA: All right, gimme some sugar then—(TRAVIS *puts his arms around her neck as she watches her son over the boy's shoulder. Then, to* TRAVIS, *after the embrace.)* Now when you say your prayers tonight, you thank God and your grandfather—'cause it was him who give you the house—in his way.

RUTH *(taking the boy from* MAMA *and pushing him toward the bedroom)*: Now you get out of here and get ready for your beating.

TRAVIS: Aw, Mama—

RUTH: Get on in there—*(closing the door behind him and turning radiantly to her mother-in-law)* So you went and did it!

MAMA *(quietly, looking at her son with pain)*: Yes, I did.

RUTH *(raising both arms classically)*: PRAISE GOD! *(Looks at* WALTER *a moment, who says nothing. She crosses rapidly to her husband.)* Please, honey—let me be glad . . . you be glad too. *(She has laid her hands on his shoulders, but he shakes himself free of her roughly, without turning to face her.)* Oh, Walter . . . a home . . . *a home. (She comes back to* MAMA.) Well—where is it? How big is it? How much it going to cost?

MAMA: Well—

RUTH: When we moving?

MAMA *(smiling at her)*: First of the month.

RUTH *(throwing back her head with jubilance)*: *Praise God!*

MAMA *(tentatively, still looking at her son's back turned against her and* RUTH*)*: It's—it's a nice house too . . . *(She cannot help speaking directly to him. An imploring quality in her voice, her manner, makes her almost like a girl now.)* Three bedrooms—nice big one for you and Ruth . . . Me and Beneatha still have to share our room, but Travis have one of his own—and *(with difficulty)* I figure if the—new baby—is a boy, we could get one of them double-decker outfits. . . And there's a yard with a little patch of dirt where I could maybe get to grow me a few flowers . . . And a nice big basement . . .

RUTH: Walter honey, be glad—

MAMA *(still to his back, fingering things on the table)*: 'Course I don't want to make it sound fancier than it is . . . It's just a plain little old house—but it's made good and solid—and it will be *ours*. Walter Lee—it makes a difference in a man when he can walk on floors that belong to *him* . . .

RUTH: Where is it?

MAMA *(frightened at this telling)*: Well—well—it's out there in Clybourne Park—

RUTH's *radiance fades abruptly, and* WALTER *finally turns slowly to face his mother with incredulity and hostility.*

RUTH: Where?

MAMA *(matter-of-factly)*: Four o six Clybourne Street, Clybourne Park.

RUTH: Clybourne Park? Mama, there ain't no colored people living in Clybourne Park.

MAMA *(almost idiotically)*: Well, I guess there's going to be some now.

WALTER *(bitterly)*: So that's the peace and comfort you went out and bought for us today!

MAMA *(raising her eyes to meet his finally)*: Son—I just tried to find the nicest place for the least amount of money for my family.

RUTH *(trying to recover from the shock)*: Well—well—'course I ain't one never been 'fraid of no crackers, mind you—but—well, wasn't there no other houses nowhere?

MAMA: Them houses they put up for colored in them areas way out all seem to cost twice as much as other houses. I did the best I could.

RUTH *(Struck senseless with the news, in its various degrees of goodness and trouble, she sits a moment, her fists propping her chin in thought, and then she starts to rise, bringing her fists down with vigor, the radiance spreading from cheek to cheek again.)*: Well—well!—All I can say is—if this is my time in life— MY TIME—to say good-bye—*(and she builds with momentum as she starts to circle the room with an exuberant, almost tearfully happy release)*—to these Goddamned cracking walls!—*(She pounds the walls.)*—and these marching roaches!—*(She wipes at an imaginary army of marching roaches.)*—and this cramped little closet which ain't now or never was no kitchen! . . . then I say it loud and good, HALLELUJAH! AND GOOD-BYE MIS-

ERY... I DON'T NEVER WANT TO SEE YOUR UGLY FACE AGAIN! *(She laughs joyously, having practically destroyed the apartment, and flings her arms up and lets them come down happily, slowly, reflectively, over her abdomen, aware for the first time perhaps that the life therein pulses with happiness and not despair.)* Lena?

MAMA *(moved, watching her happiness)*: Yes, honey?

RUTH *(looking off)*: Is there—is there a whole lot of sunlight?

MAMA *(understanding)*: Yes, child, there's a whole lot of sunlight. *(long pause)*

RUTH *(collecting herself and going to the door of the room* TRAVIS *is in)*: Well—I guess I better see 'bout Travis. *(to* MAMA*)* Lord, I sure don't feel like whipping nobody today! *(She exits.)*

MAMA *(The mother and son are left alone now and the mother waits a long time, considering deeply, before she speaks.)*: Son—you—you—understand what I done, don't you? *(*WALTER *is silent and sullen.)* I—I just seen my family falling apart today . . . just falling to pieces in front of my eyes . . . We couldn't of gone on like we was today. We was going backwards 'stead of forwards—talking 'bout killing babies and wishing each other was dead . . . When it gets like that in life—you just got to do something different, push on out and do something bigger . . . *(She waits.)* I wish you say something, son . . . I wish you'd say how deep inside you think I done the right thing—

WALTER *(crossing slowly to his bedroom door and finally turning there and speaking measuredly)*: What you need me to say you done right for? *You* the head of this family. You run our lives like you want to. It was your money and you did what you wanted with it. So what you need for me to say it was all right for? *(bitterly, to hurt her as deeply as he knows is possible)* So you butchered up a dream of mine—you—who always talking 'bout your children's dreams . . .

MAMA: Walter Lee—

He just closes the door behind him. MAMA *sits alone, thinking heavily.*

Scene II

Time *Friday night. A few weeks later.*

At rise *Packing crates mark the intention of the family to move.* BENEATHA *and* GEORGE *come in, presumably from an evening out again.*

GEORGE: O.K. . . . O.K., whatever you say . . . *(They both sit on the couch. He tries to kiss her. She moves away.)* Look, we've had a nice evening; let's not spoil it, huh? . . .

He again turns her head and tries to nuzzle in and she turns away from him, not with distaste but with momentary lack of interest; in a mood to pursue what they were talking about.

BENEATHA: I'm *trying* to talk to you.

GEORGE: We always talk.

BENEATHA: Yes—and I love to talk.

GEORGE *(exasperated, rising)*: I know it and I don't mind it sometimes . . . I want you to cut it out, see—The moody stuff, I mean. I don't like it. You're a nice-looking girl . . . all over. That's all you need, honey, forget the atmosphere. Guys aren't going to go for the atmosphere—they're going to go for what they see. Be glad for that. Drop the Garbo routine. It doesn't go with you. As for myself, I want a nice—*(groping)*—simple *(thoughtfully)*—sophisticated girl . . . not a poet—O.K.? *(He starts to kiss her, she rebuffs him again and he jumps up.)*

BENEATHA: Why are you angry, George?

GEORGE: Because this is stupid! I don't go out with you to discuss the nature of "quiet desperation" or to hear all about your thoughts—because the world will go on thinking what it thinks regardless—

BENEATHA: Then why read books? Why go to school?

GEORGE *(with artificial patience, counting on his fingers)*: It's simple. You read books—to learn facts—to get grades—to pass the course—to get a degree. That's all—it has nothing to do with thoughts. *(a long pause)*

BENEATHA: I see. *(He starts to sit.)* Good night, George.

GEORGE *looks at her a little oddly, and starts to exit. He meets* MAMA *coming in.*

538

GEORGE: Oh—hello, Mrs. Younger.

MAMA: Hello, George, how you feeling?

GEORGE: Fine—fine, how are you?

MAMA: Oh, a little tired. You know them steps can get you after a day's work. You all have a nice time tonight?

GEORGE: Yes—a fine time. A fine time.

MAMA: Well, good night.

GEORGE: Good night. *(He exits.* MAMA *closes the door behind her.)* Hello, honey. What you sitting like that for?

BENEATHA: I'm just sitting.

MAMA: Didn't you have a nice time?

BENEATHA: No.

MAMA: No? What's the matter?

BENEATHA: Mama, George is a fool—honest. *(She rises.)*

MAMA *(Hustling around unloading the packages she has entered with. She stops.)*: Is he, baby?

BENEATHA: Yes.

BENEATHA *makes up* TRAVIS' *bed as she talks.*

MAMA: You sure?

BENEATHA: Yes.

MAMA: Well—I guess you better not waste your time with no fools.

BENEATHA *looks up at her mother, watching her put groceries in the refrigerator. Finally she gathers up her things and starts into the bedroom. At the door she stops and looks back at her mother.*

BENEATHA: Mama—

MAMA: Yes, baby—

BENEATHA: Thank you.

MAMA: For what?

BENEATHA: For understanding me this time.

She exits quickly and the mother stands, smiling a little, looking at the place where BENEATHA *just stood.* RUTH *enters.*

RUTH: Now don't you fool with any of this stuff, Lena—

MAMA: Oh, I just thought I'd sort a few things out. Is Brother here?

RUTH: Yes.

MAMA *(with concern)*: Is he—

RUTH *(reading her eyes)*: Yes.

MAMA *is silent and someone knocks on the door.* MAMA *and* RUTH *exchange weary and knowing glances and* RUTH *opens it to admit the neighbor,* MRS. JOHNSON,[†] *who is a rather squeaky wide-eyed lady of no particular age, with a newspaper under her arm.*

MAMA *(changing her expression to acute delight and a ringing cheerful greeting)*: Oh—hello there, Johnson.

JOHNSON *(This is a woman who decided long ago to be enthusiastic about EVERYTHING in life and she is inclined to wave her wrist vigorously at the height of her exclamatory comments.)*: Hello there, yourself! H'you this evening, Ruth?

RUTH *(not much of a deceptive type)*: Fine, Mis' Johnson, h'you?

JOHNSON: Fine. *(reaching out quickly, playfully, and patting* RUTH'S *stomach)* Ain't you starting to poke out none yet! *(She mugs with delight at the over-familiar remark and her eyes dart around looking at the crates and packing preparation;* MAMA'S *face is a cold sheet of endurance.)* Oh, ain't we getting ready round here, though! Yessir! Lookathere! I'm telling you the Youngers is really getting ready to "move on up a little higher!"—Bless God!

MAMA *(a little drily, doubting the total sincerity of the Blesser)*: Bless God.

JOHNSON: He's good, ain't He?

MAMA: Oh yes, He's good.

JOHNSON: I mean sometimes He works in mysterious ways . . . but He works, don't He!

MAMA *(the same)*: Yes, He does.

JOHNSON: I'm just sooooooo happy for y'all. And this here child— *(about* RUTH*)* looks like she could just pop open with happiness, don't she. Where's all the rest of the family?

MAMA: Bennie's gone to bed—

JOHNSON: Ain't no . . . *(The implication is pregnancy.)* sickness done hit you—I hope . . . ?

MAMA: No—she just tired. She was out this evening.

JOHNSON *(All is a coo, an emphatic coo)*: Aw—ain't that lovely. She still going out with the little Murchison boy?

MAMA *(drily)*: Ummmm huh.

[†]This character and the scene of her visit were cut from the original production and early editions of the play.

JOHNSON: That's lovely. You sure got lovely children, Younger. Me and Isaiah talks all the time 'bout what fine children you was blessed with. We sure do.

MAMA: Ruth, give Mis' Johnson a piece of sweet potato pie and some milk.

JOHNSON: Oh honey, I can't stay hardly a minute—I just dropped in to see if there was anything I could do. *(accepting the food easily)* I guess y'all seen the news what's all over the colored paper this week . . .

MAMA: No—didn't get mine yet this week.

JOHNSON *(lifting her head and blinking with the spirit of catastrophe)*: You mean you ain't read 'bout them colored people that was bombed out their place out there?

RUTH *straightens with concern and takes the paper and reads it.*
JOHNSON *notices her and feeds commentary.*

JOHNSON: Ain't it something how bad these here white folks is getting here in Chicago! Lord, getting so you think you right down in Mississippi! *(with a tremendous and rather insincere sense of melodrama)* 'Course I thinks it's wonderful how our folks keeps on pushing out. You hear some of these Negroes round here talking 'bout how they don't go where they ain't wanted and all that—but not me, honey! *(This is a lie.)* Wilhemenia Othella Johnson goes anywhere, any time she feels like it! *(with head movement for emphasis)* Yes I do! Why if we left it up to these here crackers, the poor niggers wouldn't have nothing—*(She clasps her hand over her mouth.)* Oh, I always forgets you don't 'low that word in your house.

MAMA *(quietly, looking at her)*: No—I don't 'low it.

JOHNSON *(vigorously again)*: Me neither! I was just telling Isaiah yesterday when he come using it in front of me—I said, "Isaiah, it's just like Mis' Younger says all the time—"

MAMA: Don't you want some more pie?

JOHNSON: No—no thank you; this was lovely. I got to get on over home and have my midnight coffee. I hear some people say it don't let them sleep but I finds I can't close my eyes right lessen I done had that laaaast cup of coffee . . . *(She waits. A beat. Undaunted.)* My Goodnight coffee, I calls it!

MAMA *(with much eye-rolling and communication between herself and* RUTH*)*: Ruth, why don't you give Mis' Johnson some coffee?

RUTH *gives* MAMA *an unpleasant look for her kindness.*

JOHNSON *(accepting the coffee)*: Where's Brother tonight?

MAMA: He's lying down.

JOHNSON: MMmmmmm, he sure gets his beauty rest, don't he? Good-looking man. Sure is a good-looking man! *(reaching out to pat* RUTH*'s stomach again)* I guess that's how come we keep on having babies around here. *(She winks at* MAMA.*)* One thing 'bout Brother, he always know how to have a *good* time. And soooooo ambitious! I bet it was his idea y'all moving out to Clybourne Park. Lord—I bet this time next month y'all's names will have been in the papers plenty—*(holding up her hands to mark off each word of the headline she can see in front of her)* "NEGROES INVADE CLYBOURNE PARK—BOMBED!"

MAMA *(She and* RUTH *look at the woman in amazement.)*: We ain't exactly moving out there to get bombed.

JOHNSON: Oh, honey—you know I'm praying to God every day that don't nothing like that happen! But you have to think of life like it is—and these here Chicago peckerwoods is some baaaad peckerwoods.

MAMA *(wearily)*: We done thought about all that Mis' Johnson.

BENEATHA *comes out of the bedroom in her robe and passes through to the bathroom.* MRS. JOHNSON *turns.*

JOHNSON: Hello there, Bennie!

BENEATHA *(crisply)*: Hello, Mrs. Johnson.

JOHNSON: How is school?

BENEATHA *(crisply)*: Fine, thank you. *(She goes out.)*

JOHNSON *(insulted)*: Getting so she don't have much to say to nobody.

MAMA: The child was on her way to the bathroom.

JOHNSON: I know—but sometimes she act like ain't got time to pass the time of day with nobody ain't been to college. Oh—I ain't criticizing her none. It's just—you know how some of our young people gets when they get a little education. *(*MAMA *and* RUTH *say nothing, just look at her.)* Yes—well. Well, I guess I better get on home. *(unmoving)* 'Course I can understand how she must be proud and everything—being the only one in the family to make something of herself. I know just being a chauffeur ain't never satisfied Brother none. He shouldn't feel like that, though. Ain't nothing wrong with being a chauffeur.

MAMA: There's plenty wrong with it.

JOHNSON: What?

MAMA: Plenty. My husband always said being any kind of a servant wasn't a fit thing for a man to have to be. He always said a man's hands was made to make things, or to turn the earth with—not to drive nobody's car for 'em—or—*(She looks at her own hands.)* carry they slop jars. And my boy is just like him—he wasn't meant to wait on nobody.

JOHNSON *(rising, somewhat offended)*: Mmmmmmmmmm. The Youngers is too much for me! *(She looks around.)* You sure one proud-acting bunch of colored folks. Well—I always thinks like Booker T. Washington said that time—"Education has spoiled many a good plow hand"—

MAMA: Is that what old Booker T. said?

JOHNSON: He sure did.

MAMA: Well, it sounds just like him. The fool.

JOHNSON *(indignantly)*: Well—he was one of our great men.

MAMA: Who said so?

JOHNSON *(nonplussed)*: You know, me and you ain't never agreed about some things, Lena Younger. I guess I better be going—

RUTH *(quickly)*: Good night.

JOHNSON: Good night. Oh—*(thrusting it at her)* You can keep the paper! *(with a trill)* 'Night.

MAMA: Good night, Mis' Johnson. *(MRS. JOHNSON exits.)*

RUTH: If ignorance was gold . . .

MAMA: Shush. Don't talk about folks behind their backs.

RUTH: You do.

MAMA: I'm old and corrupted. *(BENEATHA enters.)* You was rude to Mis' Johnson, Beneatha, and I don't like it at all.

BENEATHA *(at her door)*: Mama, if there are two things we, as a people, have got to overcome, one is the Klu Klux Klan—and the other is Mrs. Johnson. *(She exits.)*

MAMA: Smart aleck. *(The phone rings.)*

RUTH: I'll get it.

MAMA: Lord, ain't this a popular place tonight.

RUTH *(at the phone)*: Hello—Just a minute. *(goes to door)* Wal-

ter, it's Mrs. Arnold. *(Waits. Goes back to the phone. Tense.)*
Hello. Yes, this is his wife speaking . . . He's lying down now.
Yes . . . well, he'll be in tomorrow. He's been very sick. Yes—I
know we should have called, but we were so sure he'd be able
to come in today. Yes—yes, I'm very sorry. Yes . . . Thank you
very much. *(She hangs up.* WALTER *is standing in the doorway
of the bedroom behind her.)* That was Mrs. Arnold.

WALTER *(indifferently)*: Was it?

RUTH: She said if you don't come in tomorrow that they are getting
a new man . . .

WALTER: Ain't that sad—ain't that crying sad.

RUTH: She said Mr. Arnold has had to take a cab for three days . . .
Walter, you ain't been to work for three days! *(This is a revelation to her.)* Where you been, Walter Lee Younger! *(*WALTER
looks at her and starts to laugh.) You're going to lose your job.

WALTER: That's right . . . *(He turns on the radio.)*

RUTH: Oh, Walter, and with your mother working like a dog every
day—

A steamy, deep blues pours into the room.

WALTER: That's sad too—Everything is sad.

MAMA: What you been doing for these three days, son?

WALTER: Mama—you don't know all the things a man what got
leisure can find to do in this city . . . What's this—Friday night?
Well—Wednesday I borrowed Willy Harris' car and I went for
a drive . . . just me and myself and I drove and drove . . . Way
out . . . way past South Chicago, and I parked the car and I sat
and looked at the steel mills all day long. I just sat in the car
and looked at them big black chimneys for hours. Then I drove
back and I went to the Green Hat. *(pause)* And Thursday—
Thursday I borrowed the car again and I got in it and I pointed
it the other way and I drove the other way—for hours—way,
way up to Wisconsin, and I looked at the farms. I just drove
and looked at the farms. Then I drove back and I went to the
Green Hat. *(pause)* And today—today I didn't get the car. Today I just walked. All over the Southside. And I looked at the
Negroes and they looked at me and finally I just sat down on
the curb at Thirty-ninth and South Parkway and I just sat there
and watched the Negroes go by. And then I went to the Green

Hat. You all sad? You all depressed? And you know where I am going right now—

RUTH *goes out quietly.*

MAMA: Oh, Big Walter, is this the harvest of our days?

WALTER: You know what I like about the Green Hat? I like this little cat they got there who blows a sax . . . He blows. He talks to me. He ain't but 'bout five feet tall and he's got a conked head and his eyes is always closed and he's all music—

MAMA *(rising and getting some papers out of her handbag)*: Walter—

WALTER: And there's this other guy who plays the piano . . . and they got a sound. I mean they can work on some music . . . They got the best little combo in the world in the Green Hat . . . You can just sit there and drink and listen to them three men play and you realize that don't nothing matter worth a damn, but just being there—

MAMA: I've helped do it to you, haven't I, son? Walter I been wrong.

WALTER: Naw—you ain't never been wrong about nothing, Mama.

MAMA: Listen to me, now. I say I been wrong, son. That I been doing to you what the rest of the world been doing to you. *(She turns off the radio.)* Walter—*(She stops and he looks up slowly at her and she meets his eyes pleadingly.)* What you ain't never understood is that I ain't got nothing, don't own nothing, ain't never really wanted nothing that wasn't for you. There ain't nothing as precious to me . . . There ain't nothing worth holding on to, money, dreams, nothing else—if it means—if it means it's going to destroy my boy. *(She takes an envelope out of her handbag and puts it in front of him and he watches her without speaking or moving.)* I paid the man thirty-five hundred dollars down on the house. That leaves sixty-five hundred dollars. Monday morning I want you to take this money and take three thousand dollars and put it in a savings account for Beneatha's medical schooling. The rest you put in a checking account—with your name on it. And from now on any penny that come out of it or that go in it is for you to look after. For you to decide. *(She drops her hands a little helplessly.)* It ain't much, but it's

all I got in the world and I'm putting it in your hands. I'm telling
you to be the head of this family from now on like you supposed
to be.

WALTER *(stares at the money)*: You trust me like that, Mama?

MAMA: I ain't never stop trusting you. Like I ain't never stop loving
you.

She goes out, and WALTER *sits looking at the money on the table.
Finally, in a decisive gesture, he gets up, and, in mingled joy and
desperation, picks up the money. At the same moment,* TRAVIS
enters for bed.

TRAVIS: What's the matter, Daddy? You drunk?

WALTER *(sweetly, more sweetly than we have ever known him)*:
No, Daddy ain't drunk. Daddy ain't going to never be drunk
again . . .

TRAVIS: Well, good night, Daddy.

The FATHER *has come from behind the couch and leans over,
embracing his son.*

WALTER: Son, I feel like talking to you tonight.

TRAVIS: About what?

WALTER: Oh, about a lot of things. About you and what kind of
man you going to be when you grow up . . . Son—son, what do
you want to be when you grow up?

TRAVIS: A bus driver.

WALTER *(laughing a little)*: A what? Man, that ain't nothing to
want to be!

TRAVIS: Why not?

WALTER: 'Cause, man—it ain't big enough—you know what I
mean.

TRAVIS: I don't know then. I can't make up my mind. Sometimes
Mama asks me that too. And sometimes when I tell her I just
want to be like you—she says she don't want me to be like that
and sometimes she says she does . . .

WALTER *(gathering him up in his arms)*: You know what, Travis?
In seven years you going to be seventeen years old. And things
is going to be very different with us in seven years, Travis . . .
One day when you are seventeen I'll come home—home from
my office downtown somewhere—

TRAVIS: You don't work in no office, Daddy.

WALTER: No—but after tonight. After what your daddy gonna do tonight, there's going to be offices—a whole lot of offices . . .

TRAVIS: What you gonna do tonight, Daddy?

WALTER: You wouldn't understand yet, son, but your daddy's gonna make a transaction . . . a business transaction that's going to change our lives . . . That's how come one day when you 'bout seventeen years old I'll come home and I'll be pretty tired, you know what I mean, after a day of conferences and secretaries getting things wrong the way they do . . . 'cause an executive's life is hell, man—*(The more he talks the farther away he gets.)* And I'll pull the car up on the driveway . . . just a plain black Chrysler, I think, with white walls—no—black tires. More elegant. Rich people don't have to be flashy . . . though I'll have to get something a little sportier for Ruth—maybe a Cadillac convertible to do her shopping in . . . And I'll come up the steps to the house and the gardener will be clipping away at the hedges and he'll say, "Good evening, Mr. Younger." And I'll say, "Hello, Jefferson, how are you this evening?" And I'll go inside and Ruth will come downstairs and meet me at the door and we'll kiss each other and she'll take my arm and we'll go up to your room to see you sitting on the floor with the catalogues of all the great schools in America around you . . . All the great schools in the world! And—and I'll say, all right son—it's your seventeenth birthday, what is it you've decided? . . . Just tell me where you want to go to school and you'll *go.* Just tell me, what it is you want to be—and you'll *be* it . . . Whatever you want to be—Yessir! *(He holds his arms open for* TRAVIS.*)* You just name it, son . . . *(*TRAVIS *leaps into them.)* and I hand you the world!

WALTER's *voice has risen in pitch and hysterical promise and on the last line he lifts* TRAVIS *high.*

Blackout

Scene III

Time *Saturday, moving day, one week later.*

Before the curtain rises, RUTH's *voice, a strident, dramatic church alto, cuts through the silence.*

*It is, in the darkness, a triumphant surge, a penetrating state-
ment of expectation: "Oh, Lord, I don't feel no ways tired! Children, oh, glory hallelujah!"*

As the curtain rises we see that RUTH *is alone in the living room,
finishing up the family's packing. It is moving day. She is nailing
crates and tying cartons.* BENEATHA *enters, carrying a guitar case,
and watches her exuberant sister-in-law.*

RUTH: Hey!

BENEATHA *(putting away the case)*: Hi.

RUTH *(pointing at a package)*: Honey—look in that package there
and see what I found on sale this morning at the South Center.
(RUTH *gets up and moves to the package and draws out some
curtains.)* Lookahere—hand-turned hems!

BENEATHA: How do you know the window size out there?

RUTH *(who hadn't thought of that)*: Oh—Well, they bound to fit
something in the whole house. Anyhow, they was too good a
bargain to pass up. (RUTH *slaps her head, suddenly remembering something.)*: Oh, Bennie—I meant to put a special note on
that carton over there. That's your mama's good china and she
wants 'em to be very careful with it.

BENEATHA: I'll do it.

BENEATHA *finds a piece of paper and starts to draw large letters
on it.*

RUTH: You know what I'm going to do soon as I get in that new
house?

BENEATHA: What?

RUTH: Honey—I'm going to run me a tub of water up to here . . .
(with her fingers practically up to her nostrils) And I'm going
to get in it—and I am going to sit . . . and sit . . . and sit in that
hot water and the first person who knocks to tell *me* to hurry
up and come out—

BENEATHA: Gets shot at sunrise.

RUTH *(laughing happily)*: You said it, sister! *(noticing how large*
BENEATHA *is absent-mindedly making the note)* Honey, they
ain't going to read that from no airplane.

BENEATHA *(laughing herself)*: I guess I always think things have
more emphasis if they are big, somehow.

RUTH *(looking up at her and smiling)*: You and your brother seem to have that as a philosophy of life. Lord, that man—done changed so 'round here. You know—you know what we did last night? Me and Walter Lee?

BENEATHA: What?

RUTH (*smiling to herself*): We went to the movies. (*looking at* BENEATHA *to see if she understands*) We went to the movies. You know the last time me and Walter went to the movies together?

BENEATHA: No.

RUTH: Me neither. That's how long it been. (*smiling again*) But we went last night. The picture wasn't much good, but that didn't seem to matter. We went—and we held hands.

BENEATHA: Oh, Lord!

RUTH: We held hands—and you know what?

BENEATHA: What?

RUTH: When we come out of the show it was late and dark and all the stores and things was closed up . . . and it was kind of chilly and there wasn't many people on the streets . . . and we was still holding hands, me and Walter.

BENEATHA: You're killing me.

WALTER *enters with a large package. His happiness is deep in him; he cannot keep still with his new-found exuberance. He is singing and wiggling and snapping his fingers. He puts his package in a corner and puts a phonograph record, which he has brought in with him, on the record player. As the music, soulful and sensuous, comes up he dances over to* RUTH *and tries to get her to dance with him. She gives in at last to his raunchiness and in a fit of giggling allows herself to be drawn into his mood. They dip and she melts into his arms in a classic, body-melding "slow drag."*

BENEATHA (*regarding them a long time as they dance, then drawing in her breath for a deeply exaggerated comment which she does not particularly mean*): Talk about—olddddddddddd-fashioneddddddd—Negroes!

WALTER (*stopping momentarily*): What kind of Negroes? (*He says this in fun. He is not angry with her today, nor with anyone. He starts to dance with his wife again.*)

BENEATHA: Old-fashioned.

WALTER (*as he dances with* RUTH): You know, when these *New*

Negroes have their convention—*(pointing at his sister)*—that is
going to be the chairman of the Committee on Unending Agitation. *(He goes on dancing, then stops.)* Race, race, race! ...
Girl, I do believe you are the first person in the history of the
entire human race to successfully brainwash yourself. (BENEA-
THA *breaks up and he goes on dancing. He stops again, enjoying
his tease.)* Damn, even the N double A C P takes a holiday
sometimes! (BENEATHA *and* RUTH *laugh. He dances with* RUTH
*some more and starts to laugh and stops and pantomimes some-
one over an operating table.)* I can just see that chick someday
looking down at some poor cat on an operating table and before
she starts to slice him, she says ... *(pulling his sleeves back
maliciously)* "By the way, what are your views on civil rights
down there? ..." *(He laughs at her again and starts to dance
happily. The bell sounds.)*

BENEATHA: Sticks and stones may break my bones but ... words
will never hurt me!

BENEATHA *goes to the door and opens it as* WALTER *and* RUTH *go
on with the clowning.* BENEATHA *is somewhat surprised to see a
quiet-looking middle-aged white man in a business suit holding his
hat and a briefcase in his hand and consulting a small piece of
paper.*

MAN: Uh—how do you do, miss. I am looking for a Mrs.—*(He
looks at the slip of paper.)* Mrs. Lena Younger? *(He stops short,
struck dumb at the sight of the oblivious* WALTER *and* RUTH.)

BENEATHA *(smoothing her hair with slight embarrassment)*: Oh—
yes, that's my mother. Excuse me. *(She closes the door and turns
to quiet the other two.)* Ruth! Brother! *(Enunciating precisely
but soundlessly: "There's a white man at the door!" They stop
dancing,* RUTH *cuts off the phonograph,* BENEATHA *opens the
door. The man casts a curious quick glance at all of them.)* Uh—
come in please.

MAN *(coming in)*: Thank you.

BENEATHA: My mother isn't here just now. Is it business?

MAN: Yes ... well, of a sort.

WALTER *(freely, the Man of the House)*: Have a seat. I'm Mrs.
Younger's son. I look after most of her business matters.

RUTH *and* BENEATHA *exchange amused glances.*

MAN *(regarding* WALTER, *and sitting)*: Well—My name is Karl Lindner . . .

WALTER *(stretching out his hand)*: Walter Younger. This is my wife—(RUTH *nods politely.)*—and my sister.

LINDNER: How do you do.

WALTER *(amiably, as he sits himself easily on a chair, leaning forward on his knees with interest and looking expectantly into the newcomer's face)*: What can we do for you, Mr. Lindner!

LINDNER *(some minor shuffling of the hat and briefcase on his knees)*: Well—I am a representative of the Clybourne Park Improvement Association—

WALTER *(pointing)*: Why don't you sit your things on the floor?

LINDNER: Oh—yes. Thank you. *(He slides the briefcase and hat under the chair.)* And as I was saying—I am from the Clybourne Park Improvement Association and we have had it brought to our attention at the last meeting that you people—or at least your mother—has bought a piece of residential property at— *(He digs for the slip of paper again.)*—four o six Clybourne Street . . .

WALTER: That's right. Care for something to drink? Ruth, get Mr. Lindner a beer.

LINDNER *(upset for some reason)*: Oh—no, really. I mean thank you very much, but no thank you.

RUTH *(innocently)*: Some coffee?

LINDNER: Thank you, nothing at all.

BENEATHA *is watching the man carefully.*

LINDNER: Well, I don't know how much you folks know about our organization. *(He is a gentle man; thoughtful and somewhat labored in his manner.)* It is one of these community organizations set up to look after—oh, you know, things like block upkeep and special projects and we also have what we call our New Neighbors Orientation Committee . . .

BENEATHA *(drily)*: Yes—and what do they do?

LINDNER *(turning a little to her and then returning the main force to* WALTER*)*: Well—it's what you might call a sort of welcoming committee, I guess. I mean they, we—I'm the chairman of the committee—go around and see the new people who move into the neighborhood and sort of give them the lowdown on the way we do things out in Clybourne Park.

BENEATHA *(with appreciation of the two meanings, which escape* RUTH *and* WALTER*)*: Un-huh.

LINDNER: And we also have the category of what the association calls—*(He looks elsewhere.)*—uh—special community problems . . .

BENEATHA: Yes—and what are some of those?

WALTER: Girl, let the man talk.

LINDNER *(with understated relief)*: Thank you. I would sort of like to explain this thing in my own way. I mean I want to explain to you in a certain way.

WALTER: Go ahead.

LINDNER: Yes. Well. I'm going to try to get right to the point. I'm sure we'll all appreciate that in the long run.

BENEATHA: Yes.

WALTER: Be still now!

LINDNER: Well—

RUTH *(still innocently)*: Would you like another chair—you don't look comfortable.

LINDNER *(more frustrated than annoyed)*: No, thank you very much. Please. Well—to get right to the point I—*(A great breath, and he is off at last.)* I am sure you people must be aware of some of the incidents which have happened in various parts of the city when colored people have moved into certain areas— *(BENEATHA exhales heavily and starts tossing a piece of fruit up and down in the air.)* Well—because we have what I think is going to be a unique type of organization in American community life—not only do we deplore that kind of thing—but we are trying to do something about it. *(BENEATHA stops tossing and turns with a new and quizzical interest to the man.)* We feel—*(gaining confidence in his mission because of the interest in the faces of the people he is talking to)*—we feel that most of the trouble in this world, when you come right down to it—*(He hits his knee for emphasis.)*—most of the trouble exists because people just don't sit down and talk to each other.

RUTH *(nodding as she might in church, pleased with the remark)*: You can say that again, mister.

LINDNER (*more encouraged by such affirmation*): That we don't try hard enough in this world to understand the other fellow's problem. The other guy's point of view.

RUTH: Now that's right.

BENEATHA *and* WALTER *merely watch and listen with genuine interest.*

LINDNER: Yes—that's the way we feel out in Clybourne Park. And that's why I was elected to come here this afternoon and talk to you people. Friendly like, you know, the way people should talk to each other and see if we couldn't find some way to work this thing out. As I say, the whole business is a matter of *caring* about the other fellow. Anybody can see that you are a nice family of folks, hard working and honest I'm sure. (BENEATHA *frowns slightly, quizzically, her head tilted regarding him.*) Today everybody knows what it means to be on the outside of *something.* And of course, there is always somebody who is out to take advantage of people who don't always understand.

WALTER: What do you mean?

LINDNER: Well—you see our community is made up of people who've worked hard as the dickens for years to build up that little community. They're not rich and fancy people; just hard-working, honest people who don't really have much but those little homes and a dream of the kind of community they want to raise their children in. Now, I don't say we are perfect and there is a lot wrong in some of the things they want. But you've got to admit that a man, right or wrong, has the right to want to have the neighborhood he lives in a certain kind of way. And at the moment the overwhelming majority of our people out there feel that people get along better, take more of a common interest in the life of the community, when they share a common background. I want you to believe me when I tell you that race prejudice simply doesn't enter into it. It is a matter of the people of Clybourne Park believing, rightly or wrongly, as I say, that for the happiness of all concerned that our Negro families are happier when they live in their *own* communities.

BENEATHA (*with a grand and bitter gesture*): This, friends, is the Welcoming Committee!

WALTER *(dumfounded, looking at* LINDNER*)*: Is this what you came marching all the way over here to tell us?

LINDNER: Well, now we've been having a fine conversation. I hope you'll hear me all the way through.

WALTER *(tightly)*: Go ahead, man.

LINDNER: You see—in the face of all the things I have said, we are prepared to make your family a very generous offer . . .

BENEATHA: Thirty pieces and not a coin less!

WALTER: Yeah?

LINDNER *(putting on his glasses and drawing a form out of the briefcase)*: Our association is prepared, through the collective effort of our people, to buy the house from you at a financial gain to your family.

RUTH: Lord have mercy, ain't this the living gall!

WALTER: All right, you through?

LINDNER: Well, I want to give you the exact terms of the financial arrangement—

WALTER: We don't want to hear no exact terms of no arrangements. I want to know if you got any more to tell us 'bout getting together?

LINDNER *(taking off his glasses)*: Well—I don't suppose that you feel . . .

WALTER: Never mind how I feel—you got any more to say 'bout how people ought to sit down and talk to each other? . . . Get out of my house, man. *(He turns his back and walks to the door.)*

LINDNER *(looking around at the hostile faces and reaching and assembling his hat and briefcase)*: Well—I don't understand why you people are reacting this way. What do you think you are going to gain by moving into a neighborhood where you just aren't wanted and where some elements—well—people can get awful worked up when they feel that their whole way of life and everything they've ever worked for is threatened.

WALTER: Get out.

LINDNER *(at the door, holding a small card)*: Well—I'm sorry it went like this.

WALTER: Get out.

LINDNER *(almost sadly regarding* WALTER*)*: You just can't force people to change their hearts, son.

He turns and puts his card on a table and exits. WALTER *pushes the door to with stinging hatred, and stands looking at it.* RUTH *just sits and* BENEATHA *just stands. They say nothing.* MAMA *and* TRAVIS *enter.*

MAMA: Well—this all the packing got done since I left out of here this morning. I testify before God that my children got all the energy of the *dead!* What time the moving men due?

BENEATHA: Four o'clock. You had a caller, Mama. *(She is smiling, teasingly.)*

MAMA: Sure enough—who?

BENEATHA *(her arms folded saucily)*: The Welcoming Committee.

WALTER *and* RUTH *giggle.*

MAMA *(innocently)*: Who?

BENEATHA: The Welcoming Committee. They said they're sure going to be glad to see you when you get there.

WALTER *(devilishly)*: Yeah, they said they can't hardly wait to see your face.

Laughter.

MAMA *(sensing their facetiousness)*: What's the matter with you all?

WALTER: Ain't nothing the matter with us. We just telling you 'bout the gentleman who came to see you this afternoon. From the Clybourne Park Improvement Association.

MAMA: What he want?

RUTH *(in the same mood as* BENEATHA *and* WALTER*)*: To welcome you, honey.

WALTER: He said they can't hardly wait. He said the one thing they don't have, that they just *dying* to have out there is a fine family of fine colored people! *(to* RUTH *and* BENEATHA*)* Ain't that right!

RUTH *(mockingly)*: Yeah! He left his card—

BENEATHA *(handling card to* MAMA*)*: In case.

MAMA *reads and throws it on the floor—understanding and looking off as she draws her chair up to the table on which she has put her plant and some sticks and some cord.*

MAMA: Father, give us strength. *(knowingly—and without fun)* Did he threaten us?

BENEATHA: Oh—Mama—they don't do it like that any more. He talked Brotherhood. He said everybody ought to learn how to sit down and hate each other with good Christian fellowship.

She and WALTER *shake hands to ridicule the remark.*

MAMA *(sadly)*: Lord, protect us . . .

RUTH: You should hear the money those folks raised to buy the house from us. All we paid and then some.

BENEATHA: What they think we going to do—eat 'em?

RUTH: No, honey, marry 'em.

MAMA *(shaking her head)*: Lord, Lord, Lord . . .

RUTH: Well—that's the way the crackers crumble. *(a beat)* Joke.

BENEATHA *(laughingly noticing what her mother is doing)*: Mama, what are you doing?

MAMA: Fixing my plant so it won't get hurt none on the way . . .

BENEATHA: Mama, you going to take *that* to the new house?

MAMA: Un-huh—

BENEATHA: That raggedy-looking old thing?

MAMA *(stopping and looking at her)*: It expresses ME!

RUTH *(with delight, to* BENEATHA*)*: So there, Miss Thing!

WALTER *comes to* MAMA *suddenly and bends down behind her and squeezes her in his arms with all his strength. She is overwhelmed by the suddenness of it and, though delighted, her manner is like that of* RUTH *and* TRAVIS.

MAMA: Look out now, boy! You make me mess up my thing here!

WALTER *(his face lit, he slips down on his knees beside her, his arms still about her)*: Mama . . . you know what it means to climb up in the chariot?

MAMA *(gruffly, very happy)*: Get on away from me now . . .

RUTH *(near the gift-wrapped package, trying to catch* WALTER's *eye)*: Psst—

WALTER: What the old song say, Mama . . .

RUTH: Walter—Now? *(She is pointing at the package.)*

WALTER *(speaking the lines, sweetly, playfully, in his mother's face)*:

> *I got wings . . . you got wings . . .*
> *All God's Children got wings . . .*

MAMA: Boy—get out of my face and do some work . . .

WALTER:

> *When I get to heaven gonna put on my wings,*
> *Gonna fly all over God's heaven . . .*

BENEATHA *(teasingly, from across the room)*: Everybody talking 'bout heaven ain't going there!

WALTER *(to RUTH, who is carrying the box across to them)*: I don't know, you think we ought to give her that . . . Seems to me she ain't been very appreciative around here.

MAMA *(eying the box, which is obviously a gift*: What is that?

WALTER *(taking it from RUTH and putting it on the table in front of MAMA)*: Well—what you all think? Should we give it to her?

RUTH: Oh—she was pretty good today.

MAMA: I'll good you— *(She turns her eyes to the box again.)*

BENEATHA: Open it, Mama. *(She stands up, looks at it, turns and looks at all of them, and then presses her hands together and does not open the package.)*

WALTER *(sweetly)*: Open it, Mama. It's for you. *(MAMA looks in his eyes. It is the first present in her life without its being Christmas. Slowly she opens her package and lifts out, one by one, a brand-new sparkling set of gardening tools. WALTER continues, prodding.)* Ruth made up the note—read it . . .

MAMA *(picking up the card and adjusting her glasses)*: "To our own Mrs. Miniver—Love from Brother, Ruth and Beneatha." Ain't that lovely . . .

TRAVIS *(tugging at his father's sleeve)*: Daddy, can I give her mine now?

WALTER: All right, son. *(TRAVIS flies to get his gift.)*

MAMA: Now I don't have to use my knives and forks no more . . .

WALTER: Travis didn't want to go in with the rest of us, Mama. He got his own. *(somewhat amused)* We don't know what it is . . .

TRAVIS *(racing back in the room with a large hatbox and putting it in front of his grandmother)*: Here!

MAMA: Lord have mercy, baby. You done gone and bought your grandmother a hat?

TRAVIS *(very proud)*: Open it! *(She does and lifts out an elaborate, but very elaborate, wide gardening hat, and all the adults break up at the sight of it.)*

RUTH: Travis, honey, what is that?

TRAVIS *(who thinks it is beautiful and appropriate)*: It's a garden-ing hat! Like the ladies always have on in the magazines when they work in their gardens.

BENEATHA *(giggling fiercely)*: Travis—we were trying to make Mama Mrs. Miniver—not Scarlett O'Hara!

MAMA *(indignantly)*: What's the matter with you all! This here is a beautiful hat! *(absurdly)* I always wanted me one just like it! *(She pops it on her head to prove it to her grandson, and the hat is ludicrous and considerably oversized.)*

RUTH: Hot dog! Go, Mama!

WALTER *(doubled over with laughter)*: I'm sorry, Mama—but you look like you ready to go out and chop you some cotton sure enough!

They all laugh except MAMA, *out of deference to* TRAVIS' *feelings.*

MAMA *(gathering the boy up to her)*: Bless your heart—this is the prettiest hat I ever owned—*(*WALTER, RUTH *and* BENEATHA *chime in—noisily, festively and insincerely congratulating* TRAVIS *on his gift.)* What are we all standing around here for? We ain't finished packin' yet. Bennie, you ain't packed one book. *(The bell rings.)*

BENEATHA: That couldn't be the movers . . . it's not hardly two good yet—

BENEATHA *goes into her room.* MAMA *starts for the door.*

WALTER *(turning, stiffening)*: Wait—wait—I'll get it. *(He stands and looks at the door.)*

MAMA: You expecting company, son?

WALTER *(just looking at the door)*: Yeah—yeah . . .

MAMA *looks at* RUTH, *and they exchange innocent and unfrightened glances.*

MAMA *(not understanding)*: Well, let them in, son.

BENEATHA *(from her room)*: We need some more string.

MAMA: Travis—you run to the hardware and get me some string cord.

MAMA *goes out and* WALTER *turns and looks at* RUTH. TRAVIS *goes to a dish for money.*

RUTH: Why don't you answer the door, man?

WALTER *(suddenly bounding across the floor to embrace her)*: 'Cause sometimes it hard to let the future begin! *(Stooping down in her face.)*

> I got wings! You got wings!
> All God's children got wings!

He crosses to the door and throws it open. Standing there is a very slight little man in a not too prosperous business suit and with haunted frightened eyes and a hat pulled down tightly, brim up, around his forehead. TRAVIS *passes between the men and exits.* WALTER *leans deep in the man's face, still in his jubilance.*

> When I get to heaven gonna put on my wings,
> Gonna fly all over God's heaven . . .

(The little man just stares at him.)

> Heaven—

(Suddenly he stops and looks past the little man into the empty hallway.) Where's Willy, man?

BOBO: He ain't with me.

WALTER *(not disturbed)*: Oh—come on in. You know my wife.

BOBO *(dumbly, taking off his hat)*: Yes—h'you, Miss Ruth.

RUTH *(quietly, a mood apart from her husband already, seeing* BOBO*)*: Hello, Bobo.

WALTER: You right on time today . . . Right on time. That's the way! *(He slaps* BOBO *on his back.)* Sit down . . . lemme hear.

RUTH *stands stiffly and quietly in back of them, as though somehow she senses death, her eyes fixed on her husband.*

BOBO *(his frightened eyes on the floor, his hat in his hands)*: Could I please get a drink of water, before I tell you about it, Walter Lee?

WALTER *does not take his eyes off the man.* RUTH *goes blindly to the tap and gets a glass of water and brings it to* BOBO.

WALTER: There ain't nothing wrong, is there?

BOBO: Lemme tell you—

WALTER: Man—didn't nothing go wrong?

BOBO: Lemme tell you—Walter Lee. *(looking at* RUTH *and talking to her more than to* WALTER*)* You know how it was. I got to tell you how it was. I mean first I got to tell you how it was all the way . . . I mean about the money I put in, Walter Lee . . .

WALTER *(with taut agitation now)*: What about the money you put in?

BOBO: Well—it wasn't much as we told you—me and Willy—*(He stops.)* I'm sorry, Walter. I got a bad feeling about it. I got a real bad feeling about it . . .

WALTER: Man, what you telling me about all this for? . . . Tell me what happened in Springfield . . .

BOBO: Springfield.

RUTH *(like a dead woman)*: What was supposed to happen in Springfield?

BOBO *(to her)*: This deal that me and Walter went into with Willy—Me and Willy was going to go down to Springfield and spread some money 'round so's we wouldn't have to wait so long for the liquor license . . . That's what we were going to do. Everybody said that was the way you had to do, you understand, Miss Ruth?

WALTER: Man—what happened down there?

BOBO *(a pitiful man, near tears)*: I'm trying to tell you, Walter.

WALTER *(screaming at him suddenly)*: THEN TELL ME GOD-DAMNIT . . . WHAT'S THE MATTER WITH YOU?

BOBO: Man . . . I didn't go to no Springfield, yesterday.

WALTER *(halted, life hanging in the moment)*: Why not?

BOBO *(the long way, the hard way to tell)*: 'Cause I didn't have no reasons to . . .

WALTER: Man, what are you talking about!

BOBO: I'm talking about the fact that when I got to the train station yesterday morning—eight o'clock like we planned . . . Man—*Willy didn't never show up.*

WALTER: Why . . . where was he . . . where is he?

BOBO: That's what I'm trying to tell you . . . I don't know . . . I waited six hours . . . I called his house . . . and I waited . . . six hours . . . I waited in that train station six hours . . . *(breaking into tears)* That was all the extra money I had in the world . . . *(looking up at* WALTER *with the tears running down his face)* Man, Willy is gone.

WALTER: Gone, what you mean Willy is gone? Gone where? You mean he went by himself. You mean he went off to Springfield by himself—to take care of getting the license—*(turns and looks anxiously at* RUTH*)* You mean maybe he didn't want too many people in on the business down there? *(looks to* RUTH *again, as before)* You know Willy got his own ways. *(looks back to* BOBO*)* Maybe you was late yesterday and he just went on down there without you. Maybe—maybe—he's been callin' you at home tryin' to tell you what happened or something. Maybe— maybe—he just got sick. He's somewhere—he's got to be some- where. We just got to find him—me and you got to find him. *(grabs* BOBO *senselessly by the collar and starts to shake him)* We got to!

BOBO *(in sudden angry, frightened agony)*: What's the matter with you, Walter! *When a cat take off with your money he don't leave you no road maps!*

WALTER *(turning madly, as though he is looking for* WILLY *in the very room)*: Willy! . . . Willy . . . don't do it . . . Please don't do it . . . Man, not with that money . . . Man, please, not with that money . . . Oh, God . . . Don't let it be true . . . *(He is wander- ing around, crying out for* WILLY *and looking for him or perhaps for help from God.)* Man . . . I trusted you . . . Man, I put my life in your hands . . . *(He starts to crumple down on the floor as* RUTH *just covers her face in horror.* MAMA *opens the door and comes into the room with* BENEATHA *behind her.)* Man . . . *(He starts to pound the floor with his fists, sobbing wildly.)* THAT MONEY IS MADE OUT OF MY FATHER'S FLESH—

BOBO *(standing over him helplessly)*: I'm sorry, Walter . . . *(Only* WALTER's *sobs reply.* BOBO *puts on his hat.)* I had my life staked on this deal, too . . . *(He exits.)*

MAMA *(to* WALTER*)*: Son— *(She goes to him, bends down to him, talks to his bent head.)* Son . . . Is it gone? Son, I gave you sixty- five hundred dollars. Is it gone? All of it? Beneatha's money too?

WALTER *(lifting his head slowly)*: Mama . . . I never . . . went to the bank at all . . .

MAMA *(not wanting to believe him)*: You mean . . . your sister's school money . . . you used that too . . . Walter? . . .

WALTER: Yessss! All of it . . . It's all gone . . .

There is total silence. RUTH *stands with her face covered with her hands;* BENEATHA *leans forlornly against a wall, fingering a piece of red ribbon from the mother's gift.* MAMA *stops and looks at her son without recognition and then, quite without thinking about it, starts to beat him senselessly in the face.* BENEATHA *goes to them and stops it.*

BENEATHA: Mama!

MAMA *stops and looks at both of her children and rises slowly and wanders vaguely, aimlessly away from them.*

MAMA: I seen ... him ... night after night ... come in ... and look at that rug ... and then look at me ... the red showing in his eyes ... the veins moving in his head ... I seen him grow thin and old before he was forty ... working and working and working like somebody's old horse ... killing himself ... and you—you give it all away in a day— *(She raises her arms to strike him again.)*

BENEATHA: Mama—

MAMA: Oh, God ... *(She looks up to Him.)* Look down here— and show me the strength.

BENEATHA: Mama—

MAMA *(folding over)*: Strength ...

BENEATHA *(plaintively)*: Mama ...

MAMA: Strength!

ACT III

An hour later.

At curtain, there is a sullen light of gloom in the living room, gray light not unlike that which began the first scene of Act One. At left we can see WALTER *within his room, alone with himself. He is stretched out on the bed, his shirt out and open, his arms under his head. He does not smoke, he does not cry out, he merely lies there, looking up at the ceiling, much as if he were alone in the world.*

In the living room BENEATHA *sits at the table, still surrounded by the now almost ominous packing crates. She sits looking off. We feel that this is a mood struck perhaps an hour before, and it lingers now, full of the empty sound of profound disappointment. We see on a line from her brother's bedroom the sameness of their attitudes. Presently the bell rings and* BENEATHA *rises without am-*

bition or interest in answering. It is ASAGAI, *smiling broadly, striding into the room with energy and happy expectation and conversation.*

ASAGAI: I came over . . . I had some free time. I thought I might help with the packing. Ah, I like the look of packing crates! A household in preparation for a journey! It depresses some people . . . but for me . . . it is another feeling. Something full of the flow of life, do you understand? Movement, progress . . . It makes me think of Africa.

BENEATHA: Africa!

ASAGAI: What kind of a mood is this? Have I told you how deeply you move me?

BENEATHA: He gave away the money, Asagai . . .

ASAGAI: Who gave away what money?

BENEATHA: The insurance money. My brother gave it away.

ASAGAI: Gave it away?

BENEATHA: He made an investment! With a man even Travis wouldn't have trusted with his most worn-out marbles.

ASAGAI: And it's gone?

BENEATHA: Gone!

ASAGAI: I'm very sorry . . . And you, now?

BENEATHA: Me? . . . Me? . . . Me, I'm nothing . . . Me. When I was very small . . . we used to take our sleds out in the wintertime and the only hills we had were the ice-covered stone steps of some houses down the street. And we used to fill them in with snow and make them smooth and slide down them all day . . . and it was very dangerous, you know . . . far too steep . . . and sure enough one day a kid named Rufus came down too fast and hit the sidewalk and we saw his face just split open right there in front of us . . . And I remember standing there looking at his bloody open face thinking that was the end of Rufus. But the ambulance came and they took him to the hospital and they fixed the broken bones and they sewed it all up . . . and the next time I saw Rufus he just had a little line down the middle of his face . . . I never got over that . . .

ASAGAI: What?

BENEATHA: That that was what one person could do for another, fix him up — sew up the problem, make him all right again. That was the most marvelous thing in the world . . . I wanted to do that. I always thought it was the one concrete thing in the world that a human being could do. Fix up the sick, you know—and make them whole again. This was truly being God . . .

ASAGAI: You wanted to be God?

BENEATHA: No—I wanted to cure. It used to be so important to me. I wanted to cure. It used to matter. I used to care. I mean about people and how their bodies hurt . . .

ASAGAI: And you've stopped caring?

BENEATHA: Yes—I think so.

ASAGAI: Why?

BENEATHA *(bitterly)*: Because it doesn't seem deep enough, close enough to what ails mankind! It was a child's way of seeing things—or an idealist's.

ASAGAI: Children see things very well sometimes—and idealists even better.

BENEATHA: I know that's what you think. Because you are still where I left off. You with all your talk and dreams about Africa! You still think you can patch up the world. Cure the Great Sore of Colonialism—*(loftily, mocking it)* with the Penicillin of Independence—!

ASAGAI: Yes!

BENEATHA: Independence *and then what?* What about all the crooks and thieves and just plain idiots who will come into power and steal and plunder the same as before—only now they will be black and do it in the name of the new Independence— WHAT ABOUT THEM?!

ASAGAI: That will be the problem for another time. First we must get there.

BENEATHA: And where does it end?

ASAGAI: End? Who even spoke of an end? To life? To living?

BENEATHA: An end to misery! To stupidity! Don't you see there isn't any real progress, Asagai, there is only one large circle that we march in, around and around, each of us with our own little picture in front of us—our own little mirage that we think is the future.

ASAGAI: That is the mistake.

BENEATHA: What?

ASAGAI: What you just said—about the circle. It isn't a circle—it is simply a long line—as in geometry, you know, one that reaches into infinity. And because we cannot see the end—we also cannot see how it changes. And it is very odd but those who see the changes—who dream, who will not give up—are called idealists . . . and those who see only the circle—we call *them* the "realists"!

BENEATHA: Asagai, while I was sleeping in that bed in there, people went out and took the future right out of my hands! And nobody asked me, nobody consulted me—they just went out and changed my life!

ASAGAI: Was it your money?

BENEATHA: What?

ASAGAI: Was it your money he gave away?

BENEATHA: It belonged to all of us.

ASAGAI: But did you earn it? Would you have had it at all if your father had not died?

BENEATHA: No.

ASAGAI: Then isn't there something wrong in a house—in a world—where all dreams, good or bad, must depend on the death of a man? I never thought to see *you* like this, Alaiyo. You! Your brother made a mistake and you are grateful to him so that now you can give up the ailing human race on account of it! You talk about what good is struggle, what good is anything! Where are we all going and why are we bothering!

BENEATHA: AND YOU CANNOT ANSWER IT!

ASAGAI (*shouting over her*): *I LIVE THE ANSWER!* (*pause*) In my village at home it is the exceptional man who can even read a newspaper . . . or who ever sees a book at all. I will go home and much of what I will have to say will seem strange to the people of my village. But I will teach and work and things will happen, slowly and swiftly. At times it will seem that nothing changes at all . . . and then again the sudden dramatic events which make history leap into the future. And then quiet again. Retrogression even. Guns, murder, revolution. And I even will have moments when I wonder if the quiet was not better than all that death and hatred. But I will look about my village at the illiteracy and disease and ignorance and I will not wonder long. And perhaps . . . perhaps I will be a great man . . . I mean perhaps I will hold on to the substance of truth and find my way always with the right course . . . and perhaps for it I will be butchered in my bed some night by the servants of empire . . .

BENEATHA: *The martyr!*

ASAGAI *(He smiles)*: . . . or perhaps I shall live to be a very old man, respected and esteemed in my new nation . . . And perhaps I shall hold office and this is what I'm trying to tell you, Alaiyo: Perhaps the things I believe now for my country will be wrong and outmoded, and I will not understand and do terrible things to have things my way or merely to keep my power. Don't you see that there will be young men and women—not British soldiers then, but my own black countrymen—to step out of the shadows some evening and slit my then useless throat? Don't you see they have always been there . . . that they always will be. And that such a thing as my own death will be an advance? They who might kill me even . . . actually replenish all that I was.

BENEATHA: Oh, Asagai, I know all that.

ASAGAI: Good! Then stop moaning and groaning and tell me what you plan to do.

BENEATHA: Do?

ASAGAI: I have a bit of a suggestion.

BENEATHA: What?

ASAGAI *(rather quietly for him)*: That when it is all over—that you come home with me—

BENEATHA *(staring at him and crossing away with exasperation)*: Oh—Asagai—at this moment you decide to be romantic!

ASAGAI *(quickly understanding the misunderstanding)*: My dear, young creature of the New World—I do not mean across the city—I mean across the ocean: home—to Africa.

BENEATHA *(slowly understanding and turning to him with murmured amazement)*: To Africa?

ASAGAI: Yes! . . . *(smiling and lifting his arms playfully)* Three hundred years later the African Prince rose up out of the seas and swept the maiden back across the middle passage over which her ancestors had come—

BENEATHA *(unable to play)*: To—to Nigeria?

ASAGAI: Nigeria. Home. *(coming to her with genuine romantic flippancy)* I will show you our mountains and our stars; and give you cool drinks from gourds and teach you the old songs

and the ways of our people — and, in time, we will pretend that —
(very softly) — you have only been away for a day. Say that you'll
come — *(He swings her around and takes her full in his arms in
a kiss which proceeds to passion.)*

BENEATHA *(pulling away suddenly)*: You're getting me all mixed
up —

ASAGAI: Why?

BENEATHA: Too many things — too many things have happened
today. I must sit down and think. I don't know what I feel about
anything right this minute. *(She promptly sits down and props
her chin on her fist.)*

ASAGAI *(charmed)*: All right, I shall leave you. No — don't get up.
(touching her, gently, sweetly) Just sit awhile and think ...
Never be afraid to sit awhile and think. *(He goes to door and
looks at her.)* How often I have looked at you and said, "Ah —
so this is what the New World hath finally wrought ..."

He exits. BENEATHA *sits on alone. Presently* WALTER *enters from
his room and starts to rummage through things, feverishly looking
for something. She looks up and turns in her seat.*

BENEATHA *(hissingly)*: Yes — just look at what the New World
hath wrought! ... Just look! *(She gestures with bitter disgust.)* There he is! *Monsieur le petit bourgeois noir* — himself!
There he is — Symbol of a Rising Class! Entrepreneur! Titan of
the system! *(*WALTER *ignores her completely and continues
frantically and destructively looking for something and hurling
things to floor and tearing things out of their place in his
search.* BENEATHA *ignores the eccentricity of his actions and
goes on with the monologue of insult.)* Did you dream of
yachts on Lake Michigan, Brother? Did you see yourself on
that Great Day sitting down at the Conference Table, surrounded by all the mighty bald-headed men in America? All
halted, waiting, breathless, waiting for your pronouncements
on industry? Waiting for you — Chairman of the Board! *(*WAL-
TER *finds what he is looking for — a small piece of white paper — and pushes it in his pocket and puts on his coat and
rushes out without ever having looked at her. She shouts after
him.)* I look at you and I see the final triumph of stupidity in
the world!

The door slams and she returns to just sitting again. RUTH *comes quickly out of* MAMA's *room.*

RUTH: Who was that?

BENEATHA: Your husband.

RUTH: Where did he go?

BENEATHA: Who knows—maybe he has an appointment at U.S. Steel.

RUTH (*anxiously, with frightened eyes*): You didn't say nothing bad to him, did you?

BENEATHA: Bad? Say anything bad to him? No—I told him he was a sweet boy and full of dreams and everything is strictly peachy keen, as the ofay kids say!

MAMA *enters from her bedroom. She is lost, vague, trying to catch hold, to make some sense of her former command of the world, but it still eludes her. A sense of waste overwhelms her gait; a measure of apology rides on her shoulders. She goes to her plant, which has remained on the table, looks at it, picks it up and takes it to the window sill and sits it outside, and she stands and looks at it a long moment. Then she closes the window, straightens her body with effort and turns around to her children.*

MAMA: Well—ain't it a mess in here, though? (*a false cheerfulness, a beginning of something*) I guess we all better stop moping around and get some work done. All this unpacking and everything we got to do. (RUTH *raises her head slowly in response to the sense of the line; and* BENEATHA *in similar manner turns very slowly to look at her mother.*) One of you all better call the moving people and tell 'em not to come.

RUTH: Tell 'em not to come?

MAMA: Of course, baby. Ain't no need in 'em coming all the way here and having to go back. They charges for that too. (*She sits down, fingers to her brow, thinking.*) Lord, ever since I was a little girl, I always remembers people saying, "Lena—Lena Eggleston, you aims too high all the time. You needs to slow down and see life a little more like it is. Just slow down some." That's what they always used to say down home—"Lord, that Lena Eggleston is a high-minded thing. She'll get her due one day!"

RUTH: No, Lena . . .

MAMA: Me and Big Walter just didn't never learn right.

RUTH: Lena, no! We gotta go. Bennie—tell her . . . *(She rises and crosses to* BENEATHA *with her arms outstretched.* BENEATHA *doesn't respond.)* Tell her we can still move . . . the notes ain't but a hundred and twenty-five a month. We got four grown people in this house—we can work . . .

MAMA *(to herself)*: Just aimed too high all the time—

RUTH *(turning and going to* MAMA *fast—the words pouring out with urgency and desperation)*: Lena—I'll work . . . I'll work twenty hours a day in all the kitchens in Chicago . . . I'll strap my baby on my back if I have to and scrub all the floors in America and wash all the sheets in America if I have to—but we got to MOVE! We got to get OUT OF HERE!!

MAMA *reaches out absently and pats* RUTH*'s hand.*

MAMA: No—I sees things differently now. Been thinking 'bout some of the things we could do to fix this place up some. I seen a second-hand bureau over on Maxwell Street just the other day that could fit right there. *(She points to where the new furniture might go.* RUTH *wanders away from her.)* Would need some new handles on it and then a little varnish and it look like something brand-new. And—we can put up them new curtains in the kitchen . . . Why this place be looking fine. Cheer us all up so that we forget trouble ever come . . . *(to* RUTH*)* And you could get some nice screens to put up in your room round the baby's bassinet . . . *(She looks at both of them, pleadingly.)* Sometimes you just got to know when to give up some things . . . and hold on to what you got . . .

WALTER *enters from the outside, looking spent and leaning against the door, his coat hanging from him.*

MAMA: Where you been, son?

WALTER *(breathing hard)*: Made a call.

MAMA: To who, son?

WALTER: To The Man. *(He heads for his room.)*

MAMA: What man, baby?

WALTER *(stops in the door)*: The Man, Mama. Don't you know who The Man is?

RUTH: Walter Lee?

WALTER: *The Man.* Like the guys in the streets say—The Man. Captain Boss—Mistuh Charley . . . Old Cap'n Please Mr. Bossman . . .

BENEATHA *(suddenly)*: Lindner!

WALTER: That's right! That's good. I told him to come right over.

BENEATHA *(fiercely, understanding)*: For what? What do you want to see him for!

WALTER *(looking at his sister)*: We going to do business with him.

MAMA: What you talking 'bout, son?

WALTER: Talking 'bout life, Mama. You all always telling me to see life like it is. Well—I laid in there on my back today . . . and I figured it out. Life just like it is. Who gets and who don't get. *(He sits down with his coat on and laughs.)* Mama, you know it's all divided up. Life is. Sure enough. Between the takers and the "tooken." *(He laughs.)* I've figured it out finally. *(He looks around at them.)* Yeah. Some of us always getting "tooken." *(He laughs.)* People like Willy Harris, they don't never get "tooken." And you know why the rest of us do? 'Cause we all mixed up. Mixed up bad. We get to looking 'round for the right and the wrong; and we worry about it and cry about it and stay up nights trying to figure out 'bout the wrong and the right of things all the time . . . And all the time, man, them takers is out there operating, just taking and taking. Willy Harris? Shoot— Willy Harris don't even count. He don't even count in the big scheme of things. But I'll say one thing for old Willy Harris . . . he's taught me something. He's taught me to keep my eye on what counts in this world. Yeah—*(shouting out a little.)* Thanks, Willy!

RUTH: What did you call that man for, Walter Lee?

WALTER: Called him to tell him to come on over to the show. Gonna put on a show for the man. Just what he wants to see. You see, Mama, the man came here today and he told us that them people out there where you want us to move—well they so upset they willing to pay us *not* to move! *(He laughs again.)* And—and oh, Mama—you would of been proud of the way me and Ruth and Bennie acted. We told him to get out . . . Lord have mercy! We told the man to get out! Oh, we was some proud folks this afternoon, yeah. *(He lights a cigarette.)* We were still full of that old-time stuff . . .

RUTH (*coming toward him slowly*): You talking 'bout taking them people's money to keep us from moving in that house?

WALTER: I ain't just talking 'bout it, baby—I'm telling you that's what's going to happen!

BENEATHA: Oh, God! Where is the bottom! Where is the real honest-to-God bottom so he can't go any farther!

WALTER: See—that's the old stuff. You and that boy that was here today. You all want everybody to carry a flag and a spear and sing some marching songs, huh? You wanna spend your life looking into things and trying to find the right and the wrong part, huh? Yeah. You know what's going to happen to that boy someday—he'll find himself sitting in a dungeon, locked in forever—and the takers will have the key! Forget it, baby! There ain't no causes—there ain't nothing but taking in this world, and he who takes most is smartest—and it don't make a damn bit of difference *how*.

MAMA: You making something inside me cry, son. Some awful pain inside me.

WALTER: Don't cry, Mama. Understand. That white man is going to walk in that door able to write checks for more money than we ever had. It's important to him and I'm going to help him . . . I'm going to put on the show, Mama.

MAMA: Son—I come from five generations of people who was slaves and sharecroppers—but ain't nobody in my family never let nobody pay 'em no money that was a way of telling us we wasn't fit to walk the earth. We ain't never been that poor. (*raising her eyes and looking at him*) We ain't never been that—dead inside.

BENEATHA: Well—we are dead now. All the talk about dreams and sunlight that goes on in this house. It's all dead now.

WALTER: What's the matter with you all! I didn't make this world! It was give to me this way! Hell, yes, I want me some yachts someday! Yes, I want to hang some real pearls 'round my wife's neck. Ain't she supposed to wear no pearls? Somebody tell me—tell me, who decides which women is suppose to wear pearls in this world. I tell you I am a *man*—and I think my wife should wear some pearls in this world!

This last line hangs a good while and WALTER *begins to move about*

the room. The word "Man" has penetrated his consciousness; he
mumbles it to himself repeatedly between strange agitated pauses
as he moves about.

MAMA: Baby, how you going to feel on the inside?

WALTER: Fine! . . . Going to feel fine . . . a man . . .

MAMA: You won't have nothing left then, Walter Lee.

WALTER *(coming to her)*: I'm going to feel fine, Mama. I'm going
   to look that son-of-a-bitch in the eyes and say—*(He falters.)*—
   and say, "All right, Mr. Lindner—*(He falters even more.)*—
   that's *your* neighborhood out there! You got the right to keep
   it like you want! You got the right to have it like you want! Just
   write the check and—the house is yours." And—and I am going
   to say—*(His voice almost breaks.)* "And you—you people just
   put the money in my hand and you won't have to live next to
   this bunch of stinking niggers! . . ." *(He straightens up and
   moves away from his mother, walking around the room.)* And
   maybe—maybe I'll just get down on my black knees . . . *(He
   does so; RUTH and BENNIE and MAMA watch him in frozen horror.)* "Captain, Mistuh, Bossman—*(groveling and grinning and
   wringing his hands in profoundly anguished imitation of the
   slow-witted movie stereotype.)* A-hee-hee-hee! Oh, yassuh boss!
   Yasssssuh! Great white!—*(Voice breaking, he forces himself to
   go on.)*—Father, just gi' ussen de money, fo' God's sake, and
   we's—we's ain't gwine come out deh and dirty up yo' white
   folks neighborhood . . ." *(He breaks down completely.)* And
   I'll feel fine! Fine! FINE! *(He gets up and goes into the bedroom.)*

BENEATHA: That is not a man. That is nothing but a toothless rat.

MAMA: Yes—death done come in this here house. *(She is nodding,
   slowly, reflectively.)* Done come walking in my house on the
   lips of my children. You what supposed to be my beginning
   again. You—what supposed to be my harvest. *(to* BENEATHA*)*
   You—you mourning your brother?

BENEATHA: He's no brother of mine.

MAMA: What you say?

BENEATHA: I said that that individual in that room is no brother
   of mine.

MAMA: That's what I thought you said. You feeling like you better than he is today? (BENEATHA *does not answer.*) Yes? What you tell him a minute ago? That he wasn't a man? Yes? You give him up for me? You done wrote his epitaph too—like the rest of the world? Well, who give you the privilege?

BENEATHA: Be on my side for once! You saw what he just did, Mama! You saw him—down on his knees. Wasn't it you who taught me to despise any man who would do that? Do what he's going to do?

MAMA: Yes—I taught you that. Me and your daddy. But I thought I taught you something else too . . . I thought I taught you to love him.

BENEATHA: Love him? There is nothing left to love.

MAMA: There is *always* something left to love. And if you ain't learned that, you ain't learned nothing. (*Looking at her.*) Have you cried for that boy today? I don't mean for yourself and for the family 'cause we lost the money. I mean for him: what he been through and what it done to him. Child, when do you think is the time to love somebody the most? When they done good and made things easy for everybody? Well, then, you ain't through learning—because that ain't the time at all. It's when he's at his lowest and can't believe in hisself 'cause the world done whipped him so! When you starts measuring somebody, measure him right, child, measure him right. Make sure you done taken into account what hills and valleys he come through before he got to wherever he is.

TRAVIS *bursts into the room at the end of the speech, leaving the door open.*

TRAVIS: Grandmama—the moving men are downstairs! The truck just pulled up.

MAMA (*turning and looking at him*): Are they, baby? They downstairs?

She sighs and sits. LINDNER *appears in the doorway. He peers in and knocks lightly, to gain attention, and comes in. All turn to look at him.*

LINDNER (*hat and briefcase in hand*): Uh—hello . . .

RUTH *crosses mechanically to the bedroom door and opens it and lets it swing open freely and slowly as the lights come up on*

WALTER *within, still in his coat, sitting at the far corner of the room. He looks up and out though the room to* LINDNER.

RUTH: He's here. *(A long minute passes and* WALTER *slowly gets up.)*

LINDNER *(coming to the table with efficiency, putting his briefcase on the table and starting to unfold papers and unscrew fountain pens)*: Well, I certainly was glad to hear from you people. *(WAL-TER has begun the trek out of the room, slowly and awkwardly, rather like a small boy, passing the back of his sleeve across his mouth from time to time.)* Life can really be so much simpler than people let it be most of the time. Well—with whom do I negotiate? You, Mrs. Younger, or your son here? *(MAMA sits with her hands folded on her lap and her eyes closed as* WALTER *advances.* TRAVIS *goes closer to* LINDNER *and looks at the papers curiously.)* Just some official papers, sonny.

RUTH: Travis, you go downstairs—

MAMA *(opening her eyes and looking into* WALTER'*s)*: No. Travis, you stay right here. And you make him understand what you doing, Walter Lee. You teach him good. Like Willy Harris taught you. You show where our five generations done come to. *(WALTER looks from her to the boy, who grins at him innocently.)* Go ahead, son—*(She folds her hands and closes her eyes.)* Go ahead.

WALTER *(at last crosses to* LINDNER, *who is reviewing the contract:* Well, Mr. Lindner. *(BENEATHA turns away.)* We called you— *(There is a profound, simple groping quality in his speech.)*— because, well, me and my family *(He looks around and shifts from one foot to the other.)* Well—we are very plain people . . .

LINDNER: Yes—

WALTER: I mean—I have worked as a chauffeur most of my life— and my wife here, she does domestic work in people's kitchens. So does my mother. I mean—we are plain people . . .

LINDNER: Yes, Mr. Younger—

WALTER *(really like a small boy, looking down at his shoes and then up at the man)*: And—uh—well, my father, well, he was a laborer most of his life . . .

LINDNER *(absolutely confused)*: Uh, yes—yes, I understand. *(He turns back to the contract.)*

WALTER *(a beat, staring at him)*: And my father—*(with sudden intensity)* My father almost *beat a man to death* once because this man called him a bad name or something, you know what I mean?

LINDNER *(looking up, frozen)*: No, no, I'm afraid I don't—

WALTER *(A beat. The tension hangs; then* WALTER *steps back from it.)*: Yeah. Well—what I mean is that we come from people who had a lot of *pride.* I mean—we are very proud people. And that's my sister over there and she's going to be a doctor—and we are very proud—

LINDNER: Well—I am sure that is very nice, but—

WALTER: What I am telling you is that we called you over here to tell you that we are very proud and that this—*(signaling to* TRAVIS) Travis, come here. *(*TRAVIS *crosses and* WALTER *draws him before him facing the man.)* This is my son, and he makes the sixth generation our family in this country. And we have all thought about your offer—

LINDNER: Well, good . . . good—

WALTER: And we have decided to move into our house because my father—my father—he earned it for us brick by brick. *(*MAMA *has her eyes closed and is rocking back and forth as though she were in church, with her head nodding the Amen yes.)* We don't want to make no trouble for nobody or fight no causes, and we will try to be good neighbors. And that's *all* we got to say about that. *(He looks the man absolutely in the eyes.)* We don't want your money. *(He turns and walks away.)*

LINDNER: *(looking around at all of them)*: I take it then—that you have decided to occupy . . .

BENEATHA: That's what the man said.

LINDNER *(to* MAMA *in her reverie)*: Then I would like to appeal to you, Mrs. Younger. You are older and wiser and understand things better I am sure . . .

MAMA: I am afraid you don't understand. My son said we was going to move and there ain't nothing left for me to say. *(briskly)* You know how these young folks is nowadays, mister. Can't do a thing with 'em! *(As he opens his mouth, she rises.)* Goodbye.

LINDNER *(folding up his materials)*: Well—if you are that final about it . . . there is nothing left for me to say. *(He finishes, almost ignored by the family, who are concentrating on* WALTER

LEE. *At the door* LINDNER *halts and looks around.)* I sure hope you people know what you're getting into. *(He shakes his head and exits.)*

RUTH *(looking around and coming to life)*: Well, for God's sake— if the moving men are here—LET'S GET THE HELL OUT OF HERE!

MAMA *(into action)*: Ain't it the truth! Look at all this here mess. Ruth, put Travis' good jacket on him ... Walter Lee, fix your tie and tuck your shirt in, you look like somebody's hoodlum! Lord have mercy, where is my plant? *(She flies to get it amid the general bustling of the family, who are deliberately trying to ignore the nobility of the past moment.)* You all start on down ... Travis child, don't go empty-handed ... Ruth, where did I put that box with my skillets in it? I want to be in charge of it myself ... I'm going to make us the biggest dinner we ever ate tonight ... Beneatha, what's the matter with them stockings? Pull them things up, girl ...

The family starts to file out as two moving men appear and begin to carry out the heavier pieces of furniture, bumping into the family as they move about.

BENEATHA: Mama, Asagai asked me to marry him today and go to Africa—

MAMA *(in the middle of her getting-ready activity)*: He did? You ain't old enough to marry nobody—*(seeing the moving men lifting one of her chairs precariously)* Darling, that ain't no bale of cotton, please handle it so we can sit in it again! I had that chair twenty-five years ...

The movers sigh with exasperation and go on with their work.

BENEATHA *(girlishly and unreasonably trying to pursue the conversation)*: To go to Africa, Mama—be a doctor in Africa ...

MAMA *(distracted)*: Yes, baby—

WALTER: *Africa!* What he want you to go to Africa for?

BENEATHA: To practice there ...

WALTER: Girl, if you don't get all them silly ideas out your head! You better marry yourself a man with some loot ...

BENEATHA *(angrily, precisely as in the first scene of the play)*: What have you got to do with who I marry!

WALTER: Plenty. Now I think George Murchison—

BENEATHA: *George Murchison!* I wouldn't marry him if he was Adam and I was Eve!

WALTER *and* BENEATHA *go out yelling at each other vigorously and the anger is loud and real till their voices diminish.* RUTH *stands at the door and turns to* MAMA *and smiles knowingly.*

MAMA *(fixing her hat at last)*: Yeah—they something all right, my children . . .

RUTH: Yeah—they're something. Let's go, Lena.

MAMA *(stalling, starting to look around at the house)*: Yes—I'm coming. Ruth—

RUTH: Yes?

MAMA *(quietly, woman to woman)*: He finally come into his manhood today, didn't he? Kind of like a rainbow after the rain . . .

RUTH *(biting her lip lest her own pride explode in front of* MAMA*)*: Yes, Lena.

WALTER'S *voice calls for them raucously.*

WALTER *(off stage)*: Y'all come on! These people charges by the hour, you know!

MAMA *(waving* RUTH *out vaguely)*: All right, honey—go on down. I be down directly.

RUTH *hesitates, then exits.* MAMA *stands, at last alone in the living room, her plant on the table before her as the lights start to come down. She looks around at all the walls and ceilings and suddenly, despite herself, while the children call below, a great heaving thing rises in her and she puts her fist to her mouth to stifle it, takes a final desperate look, pulls her coat about her, pats her hat and goes out. The lights dim down. The door opens and she comes back in, grabs her plant, and goes out for the last time.*

SAM SHEPARD

True West

Characters

AUSTIN, *early thirties, light blue sports shirt, light tan cardigan sweater, clean blue jeans, white tennis shoes*

LEE, *his older brother, early forties, filthy white t-shirt, tattered brown overcoat covered with dust, dark blue baggy suit pants from the Salvation Army, pink suede belt, pointed black forties dress shoes scuffed up, holes in the soles, no socks, no hat, long pronounced sideburns, "Gene Vincent" hairdo, two days' growth of beard, bad teeth*

SAUL KIMMER, *late forties, Hollywood producer, pink and white flower print sports shirt, white sports coat with matching polyester slacks, black and white loafers*

MOM, *early sixties, mother of the brothers, small woman, conservative white skirt and matching jacket, red shoulder bag, two pieces of matching red luggage*

Scene *All nine scenes take place on the same set; a kitchen and adjoining alcove of an older home in a Southern California suburb, about 40 miles east of Los Angeles. The kitchen takes up most of the playing area to stage left. The kitchen consists of a sink, upstage center, surrounded by counter space, a wall telephone, cupboards, and a small window just above it bordered by neat yellow curtains. Stage left of sink is a stove. Stage right, a refrigerator. The alcove adjoins the kitchen to stage right. There is no wall division or door to the alcove. It is open and easily accessible from the kitchen and defined only by the objects in it: a small round glass breakfast table mounted on white iron legs, two matching white iron chairs set across from each other. The two exterior walls of the alcove which prescribe a corner in the upstage right are composed of* many small windows, beginning from a solid wall about three feet high and extending to the ceiling. The windows look out to bushes and citrus trees. The alcove is filled with all sorts of house plants in various pots, mostly Boston ferns hanging in planters at different levels. The floor of the alcove is composed of green synthetic grass.

All entrances and exits are made stage left from the kitchen. There is no door. The actors simply go off and come onto the playing area.

Note on set and costume The set should be constructed realistically with no attempt to distort its dimensions, shapes, objects, or colors. No objects should be introduced which might draw special attention to themselves other than the props demanded by the script. If a stylistic "concept" is grafted onto the set design it will only serve to confuse the evolution of the characters' situation, which is the most important focus of the play.

Likewise, the costumes should be exactly representative of who the characters are and not added onto for the sake of making a point to the audience.

Note on sound The Coyote of Southern California has a distinct yapping, dog-like bark, similar to a Hyena. This yapping grows more intense and maniacal as the pack grows in numbers, which is usually the case when they lure and kill pets from suburban yards. The sense of growing frenzy in the pack should be felt in the background, particularly in Scenes 7 and 8. In any case, these Coyotes never make the long, mournful, solitary howl of the Hollywood stereotype.

The sound of Crickets can speak for itself.

These sounds should also be treated realistically even though they sometimes grow in volume and numbers.

ACT I

Scene I

Night. Sound of crickets in dark. Candlelight appears in alcove, illuminating AUSTIN, seated at glass table hunched over a writing notebook, pen in hand, cigarette burning in ashtray, cup of coffee, typewriter on table, stacks of paper, candle burning on table.

Soft moonlight fills kitchen illuminating LEE, *beer in hand, six-pack on counter behind him. He's leaning against the sink, mildly drunk; takes a slug of beer.*

LEE: So, Mom took off for Alaska, huh?

AUSTIN: Yeah.

LEE: Sorta' left you in charge.

AUSTIN: Well, she knew I was coming down here so she offered me the place.

LEE: You keepin' the plants watered?

AUSTIN: Yeah.

LEE: Keepin' the sink clean? She don't like even a single tea leaf in the sink ya' know.

AUSTIN *(trying to concentrate on writing)*: Yeah, I know. *(pause)*

LEE: She gonna' be up there a long time?

AUSTIN: I don't know.

LEE: Kinda' nice for you, huh? Whole place to yourself.

AUSTIN: Yeah, it's great.

LEE: Ya' got crickets anyway. Tons a' crickets out there. *(looks around kitchen)* Ya' got groceries? Coffee?

AUSTIN *(looking up from writing)*: What?

LEE: You got coffee?

AUSTIN: Yeah.

LEE: At's good. *(short pause)* Real coffee? From the bean?

AUSTIN: Yeah. You want some?

LEE: Naw. I brought some uh— *(motions to beer)*

AUSTIN: Help yourself to whatever's— *(motions to refrigerator)*

LEE: I will. Don't worry about me. I'm not the one to worry about. I mean I can uh— *(pause)* You always work by candlelight?

AUSTIN No—uh—Not always.

LEE: Just sometimes?

AUSTIN *(puts pen down, rubs his eyes)*: Yeah. Sometimes it's soothing.

LEE: Isn't that what the old guys did?

AUSTIN: What old guys?

LEE: The Forefathers. You know.

AUSTIN: Forefathers?

LEE: Isn't that what they did? Candlelight burning into the night? Cabins in the wilderness.

AUSTIN *(rubs hand through his hair)*: I suppose.

LEE: I'm not botherin' you am I? I mean I don't wanna break into yer uh—concentration or nothin'.

AUSTIN: No, it's all right.

LEE: That's good. I mean I realize that yer line a' work demands a lota' concentration.

AUSTIN: It's okay.

LEE: You probably think that I'm not fully able to comprehend somethin' like that, huh?

AUSTIN: Like what?

LEE: That stuff yer doin'. That art. You know. Whatever you call it.

AUSTIN: It's just a little research.

LEE: You may not know it but I did a little art myself once.

AUSTIN: You did?

LEE: Yeah! I did some a' that. I fooled around with it. No future in it.

AUSTIN: What'd you do?

LEE: Never mind what I did! Just never mind about that. *(pause)* It was ahead of its time.

Pause.

AUSTIN: So, you went out to see the old man, huh?

LEE: Yeah, I seen him.

AUSTIN: How's he doing?

LEE: Same. He's doin' just about the same.

AUSTIN: I was down there too, you know.

LEE: What d'ya' want, an award? You want some kinda medal? You were down there. He told me all about you.

AUSTIN: What'd he say?

LEE: He told me. Don't worry.

Pause.

AUSTIN: Well—

LEE: You don't have to say nothin'.

AUSTIN: I wasn't.

LEE: Yeah, you were gonna' make somethin' up. Somethin' brilliant.

Pause.

AUSTIN: You going to be down here very long, Lee?

LEE: Might be. Depends on a few things.

AUSTIN: You got some friends down here?

LEE *(laughs)*: I know a few people. Yeah.

AUSTIN: Well, you can stay here as long as I'm here.

LEE: I don't need your permission do I?

AUSTIN: No.

LEE: I mean she's my mother too, right?

AUSTIN: Right.

LEE: She might've just as easily asked me to take care of her place as you.

AUSTIN: That's right.

LEE: I mean I know how to water plants.

Long pause.

AUSTIN: So you don't know how long you'll be staying then?

LEE: Depends mostly on houses, ya' know.

AUSTIN: Houses?

LEE: Yeah. Houses. Electric devices. Stuff like that. I gotta' make a little tour first.

Short pause.

AUSTIN: Lee, why don't you just try another neighborhood, all right?

LEE *(laughs)*: What'sa' matter with this neighborhood? This is a great neighborhood. Lush. Good class a' people. Not many dogs.

AUSTIN: Well, our uh—Our mother just happens to live here. That's all.

LEE: Nobody's gonna' know. All they know is somethin's missing. That's all. She'll never even hear about it. Nobody's gonna' know.

AUSTIN: You're going to get picked up if you start walking around here at night.

LEE: Me? I'm gonna' git picked up? What about you? You stick out like a sore thumb. Look at you. You think yer regular lookin'?

AUSTIN: I've got too much to deal with here to be worrying about—

LEE: Yer not gonna' have to worry about me! I've been doin' all right without you. I haven't been anywhere near you for five years! Now isn't that true?

AUSTIN: Yeah.

LEE: So you don't have to worry about me. I'm a free agent.

AUSTIN: All right.

LEE: Now all I wanna' do is borrow yer car.

AUSTIN: No!

LEE: Just fer a day. One day.

AUSTIN: No!

LEE: I won't take it outside a twenty mile radius. I promise ya'. You can check the speedometer.

AUSTIN: You're not borrowing my car! That's all there is to it.

Pause.

LEE: Then I'll just take the damn thing.

AUSTIN: Lee, look—I don't want any trouble, all right?

LEE: That's a dumb line. That is a dumb fuckin' line. You git paid fer dreamin' up a line like that?

AUSTIN: Look, I can give you some money if you need money.

LEE *suddenly lunges at* AUSTIN, *grabs him violently by the shirt and shakes him with tremendous power.*

LEE: Don't you say that to me! Don't you ever say that to me! *(Just as suddenly he turns him loose, pushes him away and backs off.)* You may be able to git away with that with the Old Man. Git him tanked up for a week! Buy him off with yer Hollywood blood money, but not me! I can git my own money my own way. Big money!

AUSTIN: I was just making an offer.

LEE: Yeah, well keep it to yourself!

Long pause.

Those are the most monotonous fuckin' crickets I ever heard in my life.

AUSTIN: I kinda' like the sound.

LEE: Yeah. Supposed to be able to tell the temperature by the number a' pulses. You believe that?

AUSTIN: The temperature?

LEE: Yeah. The air. How hot it is.

AUSTIN: How do you do that?

LEE: I don't know. Some woman told me that. She was a Botanist. So I believed her.

AUSTIN: Where'd you meet her?

LEE: What?

AUSTIN: The woman Botanist?

LEE: I met her on the desert. I been spendin' a lota' time on the desert.

AUSTIN: What were you doing out there?

LEE *(pause, stares in space)*: I forgit. Had me a Pit Bull there for a while but I lost him.

AUSTIN: Pit Bull?

LEE: Fightin' dog. Damn I made some good money off that little dog. Real good money.

Pause.

AUSTIN: You could come up north with me, you know.

LEE: What's up there?

AUSTIN: My family.

LEE: Oh, that's right, you got the wife and kiddies now don't ya'. The house, the car, the whole slam. That's right.

AUSTIN: You could spend a couple days. See how you like it. I've got an extra room.

LEE: Too cold up there.

Pause.

AUSTIN: You want to sleep for a while?

LEE *(pause, stares at* AUSTIN*)*: I don't sleep.

(Lights to black.)

SCENE II

Morning. AUSTIN *is watering plants with a vaporizer,* LEE *sits at glass table in alcove drinking beer.*

LEE: I never realized the old lady was so security-minded.

AUSTIN: How do you mean?

LEE: Made a little tour this morning. She's got locks on everything. Locks and double-locks and chain locks and—What's she got that's so valuable?

AUSTIN: Antiques I guess. I don't know.

LEE: Antiques? Brought everything with her from the old place, huh. Just the same crap we always had around. Plates and spoons.

AUSTIN: I guess they have personal value to her.

LEE: Personal value. Yeah. Just a lota' junk. Most of it's phony anyway. Idaho decals. Now who in the hell wants to eat offa' plate with the State of Idaho starin' ya' in the face? Every time ya' take a bite ya' get to see a little bit more.

AUSTIN: Well it must mean something to her or she wouldn't save it.

LEE: Yeah, well personally I don't wann' be invaded by Idaho when I'm eatin'. When I'm eatin' I'm home. Ya' know what I'm sayin'? I'm not driftin', I'm home. I don't need my thoughts swept off to Idaho. I don't need that!

Pause.

AUSTIN: Did you go out last night?

LEE: Why?

AUSTIN: I thought I heard you go out.

LEE: Yeah, I went out. What about it?

AUSTIN: Just wondered.

LEE: Damn coyotes kept me awake.

AUSTIN: Oh yeah, I heard them. They must've killed somebody's dog or something.

LEE: Yappin' their fool heads off. They don't yap like that on the desert. They howl. These are city coyotes here.

AUSTIN: Well, you don't sleep anyway do you?

Pause, LEE *stares at him.*

LEE: You're pretty smart, aren't ya?

AUSTIN: How do you mean?

LEE: I mean you never had any more on the ball than I did. But here you are gettin' invited into prominent people's houses. Sittin' around talkin' like you know somethin'.

AUSTIN: They're not so prominent.

LEE: They're a helluva' lot more prominent than the houses I get invited into.

AUSTIN: Well you invite yourself.

LEE: That's right. I do. In fact I probably got a wider range a' choices than you do, come to think of it.

AUSTIN: I wouldn't doubt it.

LEE: In fact I been inside some pretty classy places in my time. And I never even went to any Ivy League school either.

AUSTIN: You want some breakfast or something?

LEE: Breakfast?

AUSTIN: Yeah. Don't you eat breakfast?

LEE: Look, don't worry about me pal. I can take care a' myself. You just go ahead as though I wasn't even here, all right?

AUSTIN *goes into kitchen, makes coffee.*

AUSTIN: Where'd you walk to last night?

Pause.

LEE: I went up in the foothills there. Up in the San Gabriels. Heat was drivin' me crazy.

AUSTIN: Well, wasn't it hot out on the desert?

LEE: Different kinda' heat. Out there it's clean. Cools off at night. There's a nice little breeze.

AUSTIN: Where were you, the Mojave?

LEE: Yeah. The Mojave. That's right.

AUSTIN: I haven't been out there in years.

LEE: Out past Needles there.

AUSTIN: Oh yeah.

LEE: Up here it's different. This country's real different.

AUSTIN: Well, it's been built up.

LEE: Built up? Wiped out is more like it. I don't even hardly recognize it.

AUSTIN: Yeah. Foothills are the same though, aren't they?

LEE: Pretty much. It's funny goin' up in there. The smells and everything. Used to catch snakes up there, remember?

AUSTIN: You caught snakes.

LEE: Yeah. And you'd pretend you were Geronimo or some damn thing. You used to go right out to lunch.

AUSTIN: I enjoyed my imagination.

LEE: That what you call it? Looks like yer still enjoyin' it.

AUSTIN: So you just wandered around up there, huh?

LEE: Yeah. With a purpose.

AUSTIN: See any houses?

Pause.

LEE: Couple. Couple a' real nice ones. One of 'em didn't even have a dog. Walked right up and stuck my head in the window. Not a peep. Just a sweet kinda' suburban silence.

AUSTIN: What kind of a place was it?

LEE: Like a paradise. Kinda' place that sorta' kills ya' inside. Warm yellow lights. Mexican tile all around. Copper pots hangin' over the stove. Ya' know like they got in the magazines. Blonde people movin' in and outa' the rooms, talkin' to each other. (*Pause.*) Kinda' place you wish you sorta' grew up in, ya' know.

AUSTIN: That's the kind of place you wish you'd grown up in?

LEE: Yeah, why not?

AUSTIN: I thought you hated that kind of stuff.

LEE: Yeah, well you never knew too much about me did ya'?

Pause.

AUSTIN: Why'd you go out to the desert in the first place?

LEE: I was on my way to see the old man.

AUSTIN: You mean you just passed through there?

LEE: Yeah. That's right. Three months of passin' through.

AUSTIN: Three months?

LEE: Somethin' like that. Maybe more. Why?

AUSTIN: You lived on the Mojave for three months?

LEE: Yeah. What'sa' matter with that?

AUSTIN: By yourself?

LEE: Mostly. Had a couple a' visitors. Had that dog for a while.

AUSTIN: Didn't you miss people?

LEE (*laughs*): People?

AUSTIN: Yeah. I mean I go crazy if I have to spend three nights in a motel by myself.

LEE: Yer not in a motel now.

AUSTIN: No, I know. But sometimes I have to stay in motels.

LEE: Well, they got people in motels don't they?

AUSTIN: Strangers.

LEE: Yer friendly aren't ya'? Aren't you the friendly type?

Pause.

AUSTIN: I'm going to have somebody coming by here later, Lee.

LEE: Ah! Lady friend?

AUSTIN: No, a producer.

LEE: Aha! What's he produce?

AUSTIN: Film. Movies. You know.

LEE: Oh, movies. Motion Pictures! A Big Wig huh?

AUSTIN: Yeah.

LEE: What's he comin' by here for?

AUSTIN: We have to talk about a project.

LEE: Whadya' mean, "a project"? What's "a project"?

AUSTIN: A script.

LEE: Oh. That's what yer doin' with all these papers?

AUSTIN: Yeah.

LEE: Well, what's the project about?

AUSTIN: We're uh—it's a period piece.

LEE: What's "a period piece"?

AUSTIN: Look, it doesn't matter. The main thing is we need to discuss this alone. I mean—

LEE: Oh, I get it. You want me outa' the picture.

AUSTIN: Not exactly. I just need to be alone with him for a couple of hours. So we can talk.

LEE: Yer afraid I'll embarrass ya' huh?

AUSTIN: I'm not afraid you'll embarrass me!

LEE: Well, I tell ya' what—Why don't you just gimme the keys to yer car and I'll be back here around six o'clock or so. That give ya' enough time?

AUSTIN: I'm not loaning you my car, Lee.

LEE: You want me to just git lost huh? Take a hike? Is that it? Pound the pavement for a few hours while you bullshit yer way into a million bucks.

AUSTIN: Look, it's going to be hard enough for me to face this character on my own without—

LEE: You don't know this guy?

AUSTIN: No I don't know—He's a producer. I mean I've been meeting with him for months but you never get to know a producer.

LEE: Yer tryin' to hustle him? Is that it?

AUSTIN: I'm not trying to hustle him! I'm trying to work out a deal! It's not easy.

LEE: What kinda' deal?

AUSTIN: Convince him it's a worthwhile story.

LEE: He's not convinced? How come he's comin' over here if he's not convinced? I'll convince him for ya'.

AUSTIN: You don't understand the way things work down here.

LEE: How do things work down here?

Pause.

AUSTIN: Look, if I loan you my car will you have it back here by six?

LEE: On the button. With a full tank a' gas.

AUSTIN *(digging in his pocket for keys)*: Forget about the gas.

LEE: Hey, these days gas is gold, old buddy.

AUSTIN *hands the keys to* LEE.

You remember that car I used to loan you?

AUSTIN: Yeah.

LEE: Forty Ford. Flathead.

AUSTIN: Yeah.

LEE: Sucker hauled ass didn't it?

AUSTIN: Lee, it's not that I don't want to loan you my car—

LEE: You are loanin' me yer car.

LEE *gives* AUSTIN *a pat on the shoulder, pause.*

AUSTIN: I know. I just wish—

LEE: What? You wish what?

AUSTIN: I don't know. I wish I wasn't—I wish I didn't have to be doing business down here. I'd like to spend some time with you.

LEE: I thought it was "Art" you were doin'.

LEE *moves across kitchen toward exit, tosses keys in his hand.*

AUSTIN: Try to get it back here by six, okay?

LEE: No sweat. Hey, ya' know, if that uh—story of yours doesn't go over with the guy—tell him I got a couple a' "projects" he might be interested in. Real commercial. Full a' suspense. True-to-life stuff.

LEE *exits,* AUSTIN *stares after* LEE *then turns, goes to papers at table, leafs through pages, lights fade to black.*

SCENE III

Afternoon. Alcove, SAUL KIMMER *and* AUSTIN *seated across from each other at table.*

SAUL: Well, to tell you the truth, Austin, I have never felt so confident about a project in quite a long time.

AUSTIN: Well, that's good to hear, Saul.

SAUL: I am absolutely convinced we can get this thing off the ground. I mean we'll have to make a sale to television and that means getting a major star. Somebody bankable. But I think we can do it. I really do.

AUSTIN: Don't you think we need a first draft before we approach a star?

SAUL: No, no, not at all. I don't think it's necessary. Maybe a brief synopsis. I don't want you to touch the typewriter until we have some seed money.

AUSTIN: That's fine with me.

SAUL: I mean it's a great story. Just the story alone. You've really managed to capture something this time.

AUSTIN: I'm glad you like it, Saul.

LEE *enters abruptly into kitchen carrying a stolen television set, short pause.*

LEE: Aw shit, I'm sorry about that. I am really sorry, Austin.

AUSTIN *(standing)*: That's all right.

LEE *(moving toward them)*: I mean I thought it was way past six already. You said to have it back here by six.

AUSTIN: We were just finishing up. *(to SAUL)* This is my, uh— brother, Lee.

SAUL *(standing)*: Oh, I'm very happy to meet you.

LEE *sets T.V. on sink counter, shakes hands with SAUL.*

LEE: I can't tell ya' how happy I am to meet you sir.

SAUL: Saul Kimmer.

LEE: Mr. Kipper.

SAUL: Kimmer.

AUSTIN: Lee's been living out on the desert and he just uh—

SAUL: Oh, that's terrific! *(to LEE)* Palm Springs?

LEE: Yeah. Yeah, right. Right around in that area. Near uh—Bob Hope Drive there.

SAUL: Oh I love it out there. I just love it. The air is wonderful.

LEE: Yeah. Sure is. Healthy.

SAUL: And the golf. I don't know if you play golf, but the golf is just about the best.

LEE: I play a lota' golf.

SAUL: Is that right?

LEE: Yeah. In fact I was hoping I'd run into somebody out here who played a little golf. I've been lookin' for a partner.

SAUL: Well, I uh—

AUSTIN: Lee's just down for a visit while our mother's in Alaska.

SAUL: Oh, your mother's in Alaska?

AUSTIN: Yes. She went up there on a little vacation. This is her place.

SAUL: I see. Well isn't that something. Alaska.

LEE: What kinda' handicap do ya' have, Mr. Kimmer?

SAUL: Oh I'm just a Sunday duffer really. You know.

LEE: That's good 'cause I haven't swung a club in months.

SAUL: Well we ought to get together sometime and have a little game. Austin, do you play?

SAUL *mimes a Johnny Carson golf swing for* AUSTIN.

AUSTIN: No. I don't uh—I've watched it on T.V.

LEE *(to* SAUL*)*: How 'bout tomorrow morning? Bright and early. We could get out there and put in eighteen holes before breakfast.

SAUL: Well, I've got uh—I have several appointments—

LEE: No, I mean real early. Crack a'dawn. While the dew's still thick on the fairway.

SAUL: Sounds really great.

LEE: Austin could be our caddie.

SAUL: Now that's an idea. *(laughs)*

AUSTIN: I don't know the first thing about golf.

LEE: There's nothin' to it. Isn't that right, Saul? He'd pick it up in fifteen minutes.

SAUL: Sure. Doesn't take long. 'Course you have to play for years to find your true form. *(chuckles)*

LEE *(to* AUSTIN*)*: We'll give ya' a quick run-down on the club faces. The irons, the woods. Show ya' a couple pointers on the basic swing. Might even let ya' hit the ball a couple times. Whadya' think, Saul?

SAUL: Why not. I think it'd be great. I haven't had any exercise in weeks.

LEE: 'At's the spirit! We'll have a little orange juice right afterwards.

Pause.

SAUL: Orange juice?

LEE: Yeah! Vitamin C! Nothin' like a shot a' orange juice after a round a' golf. Hot shower. Snappin' towels at each others' privates. Real sense a' fraternity.

SAUL *(smiles at* AUSTIN*)*: Well, you make it sound very inviting, I must say. It really does sound great.

LEE: Then it's a date.

SAUL: Well, I'll call the country club and see if I can arrange something.

LEE: Great! Boy, I sure am sorry that I busted in on ya' all in the middle of yer meeting.

SAUL: Oh that's quite all right. We were just about finished anyway.

LEE: I can wait out in the other room if you want.

SAUL: No really—

LEE: Just got Austin's color T.V. back from the shop. I can watch a little amateur boxing now.

LEE *and* AUSTIN *exchange looks.*

SAUL: Oh—Yes.

LEE: You don't fool around in Television, do you, Saul?

SAUL: Uh—I have in the past. Produced some T.V. Specials. Network stuff. But it's mainly features now.

LEE: That's where the big money is, huh?

SAUL: Yes. That's right.

AUSTIN: Why don't I call you tomorrow, Saul, and we'll get together. We can have lunch or something.

SAUL: That'd be terrific.

LEE: Right after the golf.

Pause.

SAUL: What?

LEE: You can have lunch right after the golf.

SAUL: Oh, right.

LEE: Austin was tellin' me that yer interested in stories.

SAUL: Well, we develop certain projects that we feel have commercial potential.

LEE: What kinda' stuff do ya' go in for?

SAUL: Oh, the usual. You know. Good love interest. Lots of action. *(chuckles at* AUSTIN*)*

LEE: Westerns?

SAUL: Sometimes.

AUSTIN: I'll give you a ring, Saul.

AUSTIN *tries to move* SAUL *across the kitchen but* LEE *blocks their way.*

LEE: I got a Western that'd knock yer lights out.

SAUL: Oh really?

LEE: Yeah. Contemporary Western. Based on a true story. 'Course I'm not a writer like my brother here. I'm not a man of the pen.

SAUL: Well—

LEE: I mean I can tell ya' a story off the tongue but I can't put it down on paper. That don't make any difference though does it?

SAUL: No, not really.

LEE: I mean plenty a' guys have stories don't they? True-life stories. Musta' been a lota' movies made from real life.

SAUL: Yes. I suppose so.

LEE: I haven't seen a good Western since "Lonely Are the Brave." You remember that movie?

SAUL: No, I'm afraid I—

LEE: Kirk Douglas. Helluva' movie. You remember that movie, Austin?

AUSTIN: Yes.

LEE *(to* SAUL*)*: The man dies for the love of a horse.

SAUL: Is that right?

LEE: Yeah. Ya' hear the horse screamin' at the end of it. Rain's comin' down. Horse is screamin'. Then there's a shot. BLAM! Just a single shot like that. Then nothin' but the sound of rain. And Kirk Douglas is ridin' in the ambulance. Ridin' away from the scene of the accident. And when he hears that shot he knows that his horse has died. He knows. And you see his eyes. And his eyes die. Right inside his face. And then his eyes close. And you know that he's died too. You know that Kirk Douglas has died from the death of his horse.

SAUL *(eyes* AUSTIN *nervously)*: Well, it sounds like a great movie. I'm sorry I missed it.

LEE: Yeah, you shouldn't a' missed that one.

SAUL: I'll have to try to catch it some time. Arrange a screening or something. Well, Austin, I'll have to hit the freeway before rush hour.

AUSTIN *(ushers him toward exit)*: It's good seeing you, Saul.

AUSTIN *and* SAUL *shake hands.*

LEE: So ya' think there's room for a real Western these days? A true-to-life Western?

SAUL: Well, I don't see why not. Why don't you uh—tell the story to Austin and have him write a little outline.

LEE: You'd take a look at it then?

SAUL: Yes. Sure. I'll give it a read-through. Always eager for new material. *(smiles at* AUSTIN*)*

LEE: That's great! You'd really read it then huh?

SAUL: It would just be my opinion of course.

LEE: That's all I want. Just an opinion. I happen to think it has a lota' possibilities.

SAUL: Well, it was great meeting you and I'll—

SAUL *and* LEE *shake.*

LEE: I'll call you tomorrow about the golf.

SAUL: Oh. Yes, right.

LEE: Austin's got your number, right?

SAUL: Yes.

LEE: So long, Saul. *(gives* SAUL *a pat on the back)*

SAUL *exits,* AUSTIN *turns to* LEE, *looks at T.V. then back to* LEE.

AUSTIN: Give me the keys.

AUSTIN *extends his hand toward* LEE, LEE *doesn't move, just stares at* AUSTIN, *smiles, lights to black.*

Scene IV

Night. Coyotes in distance, fade, sound of typewriter in dark, crickets, candlelight in alcove, dim light in kitchen, lights reveal AUSTIN *at glass table typing,* LEE *sits across from him, foot on table, drinking beer and whiskey, the T.V. is still on sink counter,* AUSTIN *types for a while, then stops.*

LEE: All right, now read it back to me.

AUSTIN: I'm not reading it back to you, Lee. You can read it when we're finished. I can't spend all night on this.

LEE: You got better things to do?

AUSTIN: Let's just go ahead. Now what happens when he leaves Texas?

LEE: Is he ready to leave Texas yet? I didn't know we were that far along. He's not ready to leave Texas.

AUSTIN: He's right at the border.

LEE *(sitting up)*: No, see this is one a' the crucial parts. Right here. *(taps paper with beer can)* We can't rush through this. He's not right at the border. He's a good fifty miles from the border. A lot can happen in fifty miles.

AUSTIN: It's only an outline. We're not writing an entire script now.

LEE: Well ya' can't leave things out even if it is an outline. It's one a' the most important parts. Ya' can't go leavin' it out.

AUSTIN: Okay, okay. Let's just—get it done.

LEE: All right. Now. He's in the truck and he's got his horse trailer and his horse.

AUSTIN: We've already established that.

LEE: And he sees this other guy comin' up behind him in another truck. And that truck is pullin' a gooseneck.

AUSTIN: What's a gooseneck?

LEE: Cattle trailer. You know the kind with a gooseneck, goes right down in the bed a' the pick-up.

AUSTIN: Oh. All right. *(types)*

LEE: It's important.

AUSTIN: Okay. I got it.

LEE: All these details are important.

(AUSTIN *types as they talk.*)

AUSTIN: I've got it.

LEE: And this other guy's got his horse all saddled up in the back a' the gooseneck.

AUSTIN: Right.

LEE: So both these guys have got their horses right along with 'em, see.

AUSTIN: I understand.

LEE: Then this first guy suddenly realizes two things.

AUSTIN: The guy in front?

LEE: Right. The guy in front realizes two things almost at the same time. Simultaneous.

AUSTIN: What were the two things?

LEE: Number one, he realizes that the guy behind him is the husband of the woman he's been—

LEE *makes gesture of screwing by pumping his arm.*

AUSTIN *(sees LEE's gesture)*: Oh. Yeah.

LEE: And number two, he realizes he's in the middle of Tornado Country.

AUSTIN: What's "Tornado Country"?

LEE: Panhandle.

AUSTIN: Panhandle?

LEE: Sweetwater. Around in that area. Nothin'. Nowhere. And number three—

AUSTIN: I thought there was only two.

LEE: There's three. There's a third unforeseen realization.

AUSTIN: And what's that?

LEE: That he's runnin' outa' gas.

AUSTIN *(stops typing)*: Come on, Lee.

AUSTIN *gets up, moves to kitchen, gets a glass of water.*

LEE: Whadya' mean, "come on"? That's what it is. Write it down! He's runnin' outa' gas.

AUSTIN: It's too—

LEE: What? It's too what? It's too real! That's what ya' mean isn't it? It's too much like real life!

AUSTIN: It's not like real life! It's not enough like real life. Things don't happen like that.

LEE: What! Men don't fuck other men's women?

AUSTIN: Yes. But they don't end up chasing each other across the Panhandle. Through "Tornado Country."

LEE: They do in this movie!

AUSTIN: And they don't have horses conveniently along with them when they run out of gas! And they don't run out of gas either!

LEE: These guys run outa' gas! This is my story and one a' these guys runs outa' gas!

AUSTIN: It's just a dumb excuse to get them into a chase scene. It's contrived.

LEE: It is a chase scene! It's already a chase scene. They been chasin' each other fer days.

AUSTIN: So now they're supposed to abandon their trucks, climb on their horses and chase each other into the mountains?

LEE *(standing suddenly)*: There aren't any mountains in the Panhandle! It's flat!

LEE *turns violently toward windows in alcove and throws beer can at them.*

LEE: Gooddamn these crickets! *(yells at crickets)* Shut up out there! *(pause, turns back toward table)* This place is like a fuckin' rest home here. How're you supposed to think!

AUSTIN: You wanna' take a break?

LEE: No, I don't wanna' take a break! I wanna get this done! This is my last chance to get this done.

AUSTIN *(moves back into alcove)*: All right. Take it easy.

LEE: I'm gonna be leavin' this area. I don't have time to mess around here.

AUSTIN: Where are you going?

LEE: Never mind where I'm goin'! That's got nothin' to do with you. I just gotta' get this done. I'm not like you. Hangin' around bein' a parasite offa' other fools. I gotta' do this thing and get out.

Pause.

AUSTIN: A parasite? Me?

LEE: Yeah, you!

AUSTIN: After you break into people's houses and take their televisions?

LEE: They don't need their televisions! I'm doin' them a service.

AUSTIN: Give me back my keys, Lee.

LEE: Not until you write this thing! You're gonna' write this outline thing for me or that car's gonna' wind up in Arizona with a different paint job.

AUSTIN: You think you can force me to write this? I was doing you a favor.

LEE: Git off yer high horse will ya'! Favor! Big favor. Handin' down favors from the mountain top.

AUSTIN: Let's just write it, okay? Let's sit down and not get upset and see if we can just get through this.

AUSTIN *sits at typewriter.*

Long pause.

LEE: Yer not gonna' even show it to him, are ya'?

AUSTIN: What?

LEE: This outline. You got no intention of showin' it to him. Yer just doin' this 'cause yer afraid a' me.

AUSTIN: You can show it to him yourself.

LEE: I will, boy! I'm gonna' read it to him on the golf course.

AUSTIN: And I'm not afraid of you either.

LEE: Then how come yer doin' it?

AUSTIN *(pause)*: So I can get my keys back.

Pause as LEE *takes keys out of his pocket slowly and throws them on table, long pause,* AUSTIN *stares at keys.*

LEE: There. Now you got yer keys back.

AUSTIN *looks up at* LEE *but doesn't take keys.*

LEE: Go ahead. There's yer keys.

AUSTIN *slowly takes keys off table and puts them back in his own pocket.*

Now what're you gonna' do? Kick me out?

AUSTIN: I'm not going to kick you out, Lee.

LEE: You couldn't kick me out, boy.

AUSTIN: I know.

LEE: So you can't even consider that one. *(pause)* You could call the police. That'd be the obvious thing.

AUSTIN: You're my brother.

LEE: That don't mean a thing. You go down to the L.A. Police Department there and ask them what kinda' people kill each other the most. What do you think they'd say?

AUSTIN: Who said anything about killing?

LEE: Family people. Brothers. Brothers-in-law. Cousins. Real American-type people. They kill each other in the heat mostly. In the Smog-Alerts. In the Brush Fire Season. Right about this time a' year.

AUSTIN: This isn't the same.

LEE: Oh no? What makes it different?

AUSTIN: We're not insane. We're not driven to acts of violence like that. Not over a dumb movie script. Now sit down.

Long pause, LEE *considers which way to go with it.*

LEE: Maybe not. *(He sits back down at table across from* AUSTIN.*)* Maybe you're right. Maybe we're too intelligent, huh? *(pause)* We got our heads on our shoulders. One of us has even got a Ivy League diploma. Now that means somethin' don't it? Doesn't that mean somethin'?

AUSTIN: Look, I'll write this thing for you, Lee. I don't mind writing it. I just don't want to get all worked up about it. It's not worth it. Now, come on. Let's just get through it, okay?

LEE: Nah. I think there's easier money. Lotsa' places I could pick up thousands. Maybe millions. I don't need this shit. I could go up to Sacramento Valley and steal me a diesel. Ten thousand a week dismantling one a' those suckers. Ten thousand a week!

LEE *opens another beer, puts his foot back up on table.*

AUSTIN: No, really, look, I'll write it out for you. I think it's a great idea.

LEE: Nah, you got yer own work to do. I don't wanna' interfere with yer life.

AUSTIN: I mean it'd be really fantastic if you could sell this. Turn it into a movie. I mean it.

Pause.

LEE: Ya' think so huh?

AUSTIN: Absolutely. You could really turn your life around, you know. Change things.

LEE: I could get me a house maybe.

AUSTIN: Sure you could get a house. You could get a whole ranch if you wanted to.

LEE *(laughs)*: A ranch? I could get a ranch?

AUSTIN: 'Course you could. You know what a screenplay sells for these days?

LEE: No. What's it sell for?

AUSTIN: A lot. A whole lot of money.

LEE: Thousands?

AUSTIN: Yeah. Thousands.

LEE: Millions?

AUSTIN: Well—

LEE: We could get the old man outa' hock then.

AUSTIN: Maybe.

LEE: Maybe? Whadya' mean, maybe?

AUSTIN: I mean it might take more than money.

LEE: You were just tellin' me it'd change my whole life around. Why wouldn't it change his?

AUSTIN: He's different.

LEE: Oh, he's of a different ilk huh?

AUSTIN: He's not gonna change. Let's leave the old man out of it.

LEE: That's right. He's not gonna' change but I will. I'll just turn myself right inside out. I could be just like you then, huh? Sittin' around dreamin' stuff up. Gettin' paid to dream. Ridin' back and forth on the freeway just dreamin' my fool head off.

AUSTIN: It's not all that easy.

LEE: It's not, huh?

AUSTIN: No. There's a lot of work involved.

LEE: What's the toughest part? Deciding whether to jog or play tennis?

Long pause.

AUSTIN: Well, look. You can stay here—do whatever you want to. Borrow the car. Come in and out. Doesn't matter to me. It's not my house. I'll help you write this thing or—not. Just let me know what you want. You tell me.

LEE: Oh. So now suddenly you're at my service. Is that it?

AUSTIN: What do you want to do Lee?

Long pause, LEE *stares at him then turns and dreams at windows.*

LEE: I tell ya' what I'd do if I still had that dog. Ya' wanna' know what I'd do?

AUSTIN: What?

LEE: Head out to Ventura. Cook up a little match. God that little dog could bear down. Lota' money in dog fightin'. Big money.

Pause.

AUSTIN: Why don't we try to see this through, Lee. Just for the hell of it. Maybe you've really got something here. What do you think?

Pause, LEE *considers.*

LEE: Maybe so. No harm in tryin' I guess. You think it's such a hot idea. Besides, I always wondered what'd be like to be you.

AUSTIN: You did?

LEE: Yeah, sure. I used to picture you walking' around some campus with yer arms fulla' books. Blonds chasin' after ya'.

AUSTIN: Blondes? That's funny.

LEE: What's funny about it?

AUSTIN: Because I always used to picture you somewhere.

LEE: Where'd you picture me?

AUSTIN: Oh, I don't know. Different places. Adventures. You were always on some adventure.

LEE: Yeah.

AUSTIN: And I used to say to myself, "Lee's got the right idea. He's out there in the world and here I am. What am I doing?"

LEE: Well you were settin' yourself up for somethin'.

AUSTIN: I guess.

LEE: We better get started on this thing then.

AUSTIN: Okay.

AUSTIN *sits up at typewriter, puts new paper in.*

LEE: Oh. Can I get the keys back before I forget?

AUSTIN *hesitates.*

You said I could borrow the car if I wanted, right? Isn't that what you said?

AUSTIN: Yeah. Right.

AUSTIN *takes keys out of his pocket, sets them on table,* LEE *takes keys slowly, plays with them in his hand.*

LEE: I could get a ranch, huh?

AUSTIN: Yeah. We have to write it first though.

LEE: Okay. Let's write it.

Lights start dimming slowly to end of scene as AUSTIN *types,* LEE *speaks.*

So they take off after each other straight into an endless black prairie. The sun is just comin' down and they can feel the night on their backs. What they don't know is that each one of 'em is afraid, see. Each one separately thinks that he's the only one that's afraid. And they keep ridin' like that straight into the night. Not knowing. And the one who's chasin' doesn't know where the other one is taking him. And the one who's being chased doesn't know where he's going.

Lights to black, typing stops in the dark, crickets fade.

ACT II

SCENE V

Morning. LEE *at the table in alcove with a set of golf clubs in a fancy leather bag,* AUSTIN *at sink washing a few dishes.*

AUSTIN: He really liked it, huh?

LEE: He wouldn't a' gave me these clubs if he didn't like it.

AUSTIN: He gave you the clubs?

LEE: Yeah. I told ya' he gave me the clubs. The bag too.

AUSTIN: I thought he just loaned them to you.

LEE: He said it was part a' the advance. A little gift like. Gesture of his good faith.

AUSTIN: He's giving you an advance?

LEE: Now what's so amazing about that? I told ya' it was a good story. You even said it was a good story.

AUSTIN: Well that is really incredible Lee. You know how many guys spend their whole lives down here trying to break into this business? Just trying to get in the door?

LEE *(pulling clubs out of bag, testing them)*: I got no idea. How many?

Pause.

AUSTIN: How much of an advance is he giving you?

LEE: Plenty. We were talkin' big money out there. Ninth hole is where I sealed the deal.

AUSTIN: He made a firm commitment?

LEE: Absolutely.

AUSTIN: Well, I know Saul and he doesn't fool around when he says he likes something.

LEE: I thought you said you didn't know him.

AUSTIN: Well, I'm familiar with his tastes.

LEE: I let him get two up on me goin' into the back nine. He was sure he had me cold. You shoulda' seen his face when I pulled out the old pitching wedge and plopped it pin-high, two feet from the cup. He 'bout shit his pants. "Where'd a guy like you ever learn how to play golf like that?" he says.

LEE *laughs,* AUSTIN *stares at him.*

602

AUSTIN: 'Course there's no contract yet. Nothing's final until it's on paper.

LEE: It's final, all right. There's no way he's gonna' back out of it now. We gambled for it.

AUSTIN: Saul, gambled?

LEE: Yeah, sure. I mean he liked the outline already so he wasn't risking that much. I just guaranteed it with my short game.

Pause.

AUSTIN: Well, we should celebrate or something. I think Mom left a bottle of champagne in the refrigerator. We should have a little toast.

AUSTIN *gets glasses from cupboard, goes to refrigerator, pulls out bottle of champagne.*

LEE: You shouldn't oughta' take her champagne, Austin. She's gonna' miss that.

AUSTIN: Oh, she's not going to mind. She'd be glad we put it to good use. I'll get her another bottle. Besides, it's perfect for the occasion.

Pause.

LEE: Yer gonna' get a nice fee fer writin' the script a' course. Straight fee.

AUSTIN *stops, stares at* LEE, *puts glasses and bottle on table, pause.*

AUSTIN: I'm writing the script?

LEE: That's what he said. Said we couldn't hire a better screen-writer in the whole town.

AUSTIN: But I'm already working on a script. I've got my own project. I don't have time to write two scripts.

LEE: No, he said he was gonna' drop that other one.

Pause.

AUSTIN: What? You mean mine? He's going to drop mine and do yours instead?

LEE *(smiles)*: Now look Austin, it's jest beginner's luck ya' know. I mean I sank a fifty foot putt for this deal. No hard feelings.

AUSTIN *goes to phone on wall, grabs it, starts dialing.*

He's not gonna' be in, Austin. Told me he wouldn't be in 'till late this afternoon.

AUSTIN *(stays on phone, dialing, listens)*: I can't believe this. I just can't believe it. Are you sure he said that? Why would he drop mine?

LEE: That's what he told me.

AUSTIN: He can't do that without telling me first. Without talking to me at least. He wouldn't just make a decision like that without talking to me!

LEE: Well I was kinda' surprised myself. But he was real enthusiastic about my story.

AUSTIN *hangs up phone violently, paces.*

AUSTIN: What'd he say! Tell me everything he said!

LEE: I been tellin' ya'! He said he liked the story a whole lot. It was the first authentic Western to come along in a decade.

AUSTIN: He liked that story! Your story?

LEE: Yeah! What's so surprising about that?

AUSTIN: It's stupid! It's the dumbest story I ever heard in my life.

LEE: Hey, hold on! That's my story yer talkin' about!

AUSTIN: It's a bullshit story! It's idiotic. Two lamebrains chasing each other across Texas! Are you kidding? Who do you think's going to go see a film like that?

LEE: It's not a film! It's a movie. There's a big difference. That's somethin' Saul told me.

AUSTIN: Oh he did, huh?

LEE: Yeah, he said, "In this business we make movies, American movies. Leave the films to the French."

AUSTIN: So you got real intimate with old Saul huh? He started pouring forth his vast knowledge of Cinema.

LEE: I think he liked me a lot, to tell ya' the truth. I think he felt I was somebody he could confide in.

AUSTIN: What'd you do, beat him up or something?

LEE *(stands fast)*: Hey, I've about had it with the insults buddy! You think yer the only one in the brain department here? Yer the only one that can sit around and cook things up? There's other people got ideas too, ya' know!

AUSTIN: You must've done something. Threatened him or something. Now what'd you do Lee?

LEE: I convinced him!

LEE *makes sudden menacing lunge toward* AUSTIN, *wielding golf club above his head, stops himself, frozen moment, long pause,* LEE *lowers club.*

AUSTIN: Oh, Jesus. You didn't hurt him did you?

Long silence, LEE *sits back down at table.*

    Lee! Did you hurt him?

LEE: I didn't do nothin' to him! He liked my story. Pure and simple. He said it was the best story he's come across in a long, long time.

AUSTIN: That's what he told me about my story! That's the same thing he said to me.

LEE: Well, he musta' been lyin'. He musta' been lyin' to one of us anyway.

AUSTIN: You can't come into this town and start pushing people around. They're gonna' put you away!

LEE: I never pushed anybody around! I beat him fair and square. *(pause)* They can't touch me anyway. They can't put a finger on me. I'm gone. I can come in through the window and go out through the door. They never knew what hit 'em. You, yer stuck. Yer the one that's stuck. Not me. So don't be warnin' me what to do in this town.

Pause, AUSTIN *crosses to table, sits at typewriter, rests.*

AUSTIN: Lee, come on, level with me will you? It doesn't make any sense that suddenly he'd throw my idea out the window. I've been talking to him for months. I've got too much at stake. Everything's riding on this project.

LEE: What's yer idea?

AUSTIN: It's just a simple love story.

LEE: What kinda' love story?

AUSTIN *(stands, crosses into kitchen)*: I'm not telling you!

LEE: Ha! 'Fraid I'll steal it huh? Competition's gettin' kinda' close to home isn't it?

AUSTIN: Where did Saul say he was going?

LEE: He was gonna' take my story to a couple studios.

AUSTIN: That's *my* outline you know! I wrote that outline! You've got no right to be peddling it around.

LEE: You weren't ready to take credit for it last night.

AUSTIN: Give me my keys!

LEE: What?

AUSTIN: The keys! I want my keys back!

LEE: Where you goin'?

AUSTIN: Just give me my keys! I gotta' take a drive. I gotta' get out of here for a while.

LEE: Where you gonna' go, Austin?

AUSTIN *(pause)*: I might just drive out to the desert for a while. I gotta' think.

LEE: You can think here just as good. This is the perfect setup for thinkin'. We got some writin' to do here, boy. Now let's just have us a little toast. Relax. We're partners now.

LEE *pops the cork of the champagne bottle, pours two drinks as the lights fade to black.*

SCENE VI

Afternoon. LEE *and* SAUL *in kitchen,* AUSTIN *in alcove.*

LEE: Now you tell him. You tell him, Mr. Kipper.

SAUL: Kimmer.

LEE: Kimmer. You tell him what you told me. He don't believe me.

AUSTIN: I don't want to hear it.

SAUL: It's really not a big issue, Austin. I was simply amazed by your brother's story and—

AUSTIN: Amazed? You lost a bet! You gambled with my material!

SAUL: That's really beside the point, Austin. I'm ready to go all the way with your brother's story. I think it has a great deal of merit.

AUSTIN: I don't want to hear about it, okay? Go tell it to the executives! Tell it to somebody who's going to turn it into a package deal or something. A T.V. series. Don't tell it to me.

SAUL: But I want to continue with your project too, Austin. It's not as though we can't do both. We're big enough for that aren't we?

AUSTIN: "We"? *I* can't do both! I don't know about "we."

LEE *(to* SAUL*)*: See, what'd I tell ya'. He's totally unsympathetic.

SAUL: Austin, there's no point in our going to another screenwriter for this. It just doesn't make sense. You're brothers. You know each other. There's a familiarity with the material that just wouldn't be possible otherwise.

AUSTIN: There's no familiarity with the material! None! I don't know what "Tornado Country" is. I don't know what a "gooseneck" is. And I don't want to know! *(pointing to* LEE*)* He's a hustler! He's a bigger hustler than you are! If you can't see that, then—

LEE *(to* AUSTIN*)*: Hey, now hold on. I didn't have to bring this bone back to you, boy. I persuaded Saul here that you were the right man for the job. You don't have to go throwin' up favors in my face.

AUSTIN: Favors! I'm the one who wrote the fuckin' outline! You can't even spell.

SAUL *(to* AUSTIN*)*: Your brother told me about the situation with your father.

Pause.

AUSTIN: What? *(looks at* LEE*)*

SAUL: That's right. Now we have a clear-cut deal here, Austin. We have big studio money standing behind this thing. Just on the basis of your outline.

AUSTIN *(to* SAUL*)*: What'd he tell you about my father?

SAUL: Well—that he's destitute. He needs money.

LEE: That's right. He does.

AUSTIN *shakes his head, stares at them both.*

AUSTIN *(to* LEE*)*: And this little assignment is supposed to go toward the old man? A charity project? Is that what this is? Did you cook this up on the ninth green too?

SAUL: It's a big slice, Austin.

AUSTIN *(to* LEE*)*: I gave him money! I already gave him money. You know that. He drank it all up!

LEE: This is a different deal here.

SAUL: We can set up a trust for your father. A large sum of money. It can be doled out to him in parcels so he can't misuse it.

AUSTIN: Yeah, and who'd doing the doling?

SAUL: Your brother volunteered.

AUSTIN *laughs.*

LEE: That's right. I'll make sure he uses it for groceries.

AUSTIN *(to* SAUL*)*: I'm not doing this script! I'm not writing this crap for you or anybody else. You can't blackmail me into it. You can't threaten me into it. There's no way I'm doing it. So just give it up. Both of you.

Long pause.

SAUL: Well, that's it then. I mean this is an easy three hundred grand. Just for a first draft. It's incredible, Austin. We've got three different studios all trying to cut each other's throats to get this material. In one morning. That's how hot it is.

AUSTIN: Yeah, well you can afford to give me a percentage on the outline then. And you better get the genius here an agent before he gets burned.

LEE: Saul's gonna' be my agent. Isn't that right, Saul?

SAUL: That's right. *(to* AUSTIN*)* Your brother has really got something, Austin. I've been around too long not to recognize it. Raw talent.

AUSTIN: He's got a lota' balls is what he's got. He's taking you right down the river.

SAUL: Three hundred thousand, Austin. Just for a first draft. Now you've never been offered that kind of money before.

AUSTIN: I'm not writing it.

Pause.

SAUL: I see. Well—

LEE: We'll just go to another writer then. Right, Saul? Just hire us somebody with some enthusiasm. Somebody who can recognize the value of a good story.

SAUL: I'm sorry about this, Austin.

AUSTIN: Yeah.

SAUL: I mean I was hoping we could continue both things but now I don't see how it's possible.

AUSTIN: So you're dropping my idea altogether. Is that it? Just trade horses in midstream? After all these months of meetings.

SAUL: I wish there was another way.

AUSTIN: I've got everything riding on this, Saul. You know that. It's my only shot. If this falls through—

SAUL: I have to go with what my instincts tell me—

AUSTIN: Your instincts!

SAUL: My gut reaction.

AUSTIN: You lost! That's your gut reaction. You lost a gamble. Now you're trying to tell me you like his story? How could you possibly fall for that story? It's as phony as Hoppalong Cassidy. What do you see in it? I'm curious.

SAUL: It has the ring of truth, Austin.

AUSTIN *(laughs)*: Truth?

LEE: It is true.

SAUL: Something about the real West.

AUSTIN: Why? Because it's got horses? Because it's got grown men acting like little boys?

SAUL: Something about the land. Your brother is speaking from experience.

AUSTIN: So am I!

SAUL: But nobody's interested in love these days, Austin. Let's face it.

LEE: That's right.

AUSTIN *(to SAUL)*: He's been camped out on the desert for three months. Talking to cactus. What's he know about what people wanna' see on the screen! I drive on the freeway every day. I swallow the smog. I watch the news in color. I shop in the Safeway. I'm the one who's in touch! Not him!

SAUL: I have to go now, Austin.

SAUL *starts to leave.*

AUSTIN: There's no such thing as the West anymore! It's a dead issue! It's dried up, Saul, and so are you.

SAUL *stops and turns to* AUSTIN.

SAUL: Maybe you're right. But I have to take the gamble, don't I?

AUSTIN: You're a fool to do this, Saul.

SAUL: I've always gone on my hunches. Always. And I've never been wrong. *(to* LEE*)* I'll talk to you tomorrow, Lee.

LEE: All right, Mr. Kimmer.

SAUL: Maybe we could have some lunch.

LEE: Fine with me. *(smiles at* AUSTIN*)*

SAUL: I'll give you a ring.

SAUL *exits, lights to black as brothers look at each other from a distance.*

Scene VII

Night. Coyotes, crickets, sound of typewriter in dark, candlelight up on LEE *at typewriter struggling to type with one finger system,* AUSTIN *sits sprawled out on kitchen floor with whiskey bottle, drunk.*

AUSTIN *(singing, from floor)*

> "Red sails in the sunset
> Way out on the blue
> Please carry my loved one
> Home safely to me
>
> Red sails in the sunset—"

LEE *(slams fist on table)*: Hey! Knock it off will ya'! I'm tryin' to concentrate here.

AUSTIN *(laughs)*: You're tryin' to concentrate?

LEE: Yeah. That's right.

AUSTIN: Now you're tryin' to concentrate.

LEE: Between you, the coyotes and the crickets a thought don't have much of a chance.

AUSTIN: "Between me, the coyotes and the crickets." What a great title.

LEE: I don't need a title! I need a thought.

AUSTIN *(laughs)*: A thought! Here's a thought for ya'—

LEE: I'm not askin' fer yer thoughts! I got my own. I can do this thing on my own.

AUSTIN: You're going to write an entire script on your own?

LEE: That's right.

Pause.

AUSTIN: Here's a thought. Saul Kimmer—

LEE: Shut up will ya'!

AUSTIN: He thinks we're the same person.

LEE: Don't get cute.

AUSTIN: He does! He's lost his mind. Poor old Saul. *(giggles)* Thinks we're one and the same.

LEE: Why don't you ease up on that champagne?

AUSTIN *(holding up bottle)*: This isn't champagne anymore. We went through the champagne a long time ago. This is serious stuff. The days of champagne are long gone.

LEE: Well, go outside and drink it.

AUSTIN: I'm enjoying your company, Lee. For the first time since your arrival I am finally enjoying your company. And now you want me to go outside and drink alone?

LEE: That's right.

LEE *reads through paper in typewriter, makes an erasure.*

AUSTIN: You think you'll make more progress if you're alone? You might drive yourself crazy.

LEE: I could have this thing done in a night if I had a little silence.

AUSTIN: Well you'd still have the crickets to contend with. The coyotes. The sounds of the Police Helicopters prowling above the neighborhood. Slashing their searchlights down through the streets. Hunting for the likes of you.

LEE: I'm a screenwriter now! I'm legitimate.

AUSTIN *(laughing)*: A screenwriter!

LEE: That's right. I'm on salary. That's more'n I can say for you. I got an advance coming.

AUSTIN: This is true. This is very true. An advance. *(Pause.)* Well, maybe I oughta' go out and try my hand at your trade. Since you're doing so good at mine.

LEE: Ha!

LEE *attempts to type some more but gets the ribbon tangled up, starts trying to re-thread it as they continue talking.*

AUSTIN: Well why not? You don't think I've got what it takes to sneak into people's houses and steal their T.V.s?

LEE: You couldn't steal a toaster without losin' yer lunch.

AUSTIN *stands with a struggle, supports himself by the sink.*

AUSTIN: You don't think I could sneak into somebody's house and steal a toaster?

LEE: Go take a shower or somethin' will ya!

LEE *gets more tangled up with the typewriter ribbon, pulling it out of the machine as though it was fishing line.*

AUSTIN: You really don't think I could steal a crumby toaster? How much you wanna' bet I can't steal a toaster! How much? Go ahead! You're a gambler aren't you? Tell me how much yer willing to put on the line. Some part of your big advance? Oh, you haven't got that yet have you. I forgot.

LEE: All right. I'll bet you your car that you can't steal a toaster without gettin' busted.

AUSTIN: You already got my car!

LEE: Okay, your house then.

AUSTIN: What're you gonna' give me! I'm not talkin' about my house and my car, I'm talkin' about what are you gonna' give me. You don't have nothin' to give me.

LEE: I'll give you—shared screen credit. How 'bout that? I'll have it put in the contract that this was written by the both of us.

AUSTIN: I don't want my name on that piece of shit! I want something of value. You got anything of value? You got any tidbits from the desert? Any Rattlesnake bones? I'm not a greedy man. Any little personal treasure will suffice.

LEE: I'm gonna' just kick yer ass out in a minute.

AUSTIN: Oh, so now you're gonna' kick me out! Now I'm the intruder. I'm the one who's invading your precious privacy.

LEE: I'm trying to do some screenwriting here!!

LEE *stands, picks up typewriter, slams it down hard on table, pause, silence except for crickets.*

AUSTIN: Well, you got everything you need. You got plenty a' coffee? Groceries. You got a car. A contract. *(pause)* Might need a new typewriter ribbon but other than that you're pretty well fixed. I'll just leave ya' alone for a while.

AUSTIN *tries to steady himself to leave,* LEE *makes a move toward him.*

LEE: Where you goin'?

AUSTIN: Don't worry about me. I'm not the one to worry about.

AUSTIN *weaves toward exit, stops.*

LEE: What're you gonna' do? Just go wander out into the night?

AUSTIN: I'm gonna' make a little tour.

LEE: Why don't ya' just go to bed for Christ's sake. Yer makin' me sick.

AUSTIN: I can take care a' myself. Don't worry about me.

AUSTIN *weaves badly in another attempt to exit, he crashes to the floor,* LEE *goes to him but remains standing.*

LEE: You want me to call your wife for ya' or something?

AUSTIN *(from floor)*: My wife?

LEE: Yeah. I mean maybe she can help ya' out. Talk to ya' or somethin'.

AUSTIN *(struggles to stand again)*: She's five hundred miles away. North. North of here. Up in the North country where things are calm. I don't need any help. I'm gonna' go outside and I'm gonna' steal a toaster. I'm gonna' steal some other stuff too. I might even commit bigger crimes. Bigger than you ever dreamed of. Crimes beyond the imagination!

AUSTIN *manages to get himself vertical, tries to head for exit again.*

LEE: Just hang on a minute, Austin.

AUSTIN: Why? What for? You don't need my help, right? You got a handle on the project. Besides, I'm lookin' forward to the smell of the night. The bushes. Orange blossoms. Dust in the driveways. Rain bird sprinklers. Lights in people's houses. You're right about the lights, Lee. Everybody else is livin' the life. Indoors. Safe. This is a Paradise down here. You know that? We're living in a Paradise. We've forgotten about that.

LEE: You sound just like the old man now.

AUSTIN: Yeah, well we all sound alike when we're sloshed. We just sorta' echo each other.

LEE: Maybe if we could work on this together we could bring him back out here. Get him settled down some place.

AUSTIN *turns violently toward* LEE, *takes a swing at him, misses and crashes to the floor again,* LEE *stays standing.*

AUSTIN: I don't want him out here! I've had it with him! I went all the way out there! I went out of my way. I gave him money and all he did was play Al Jolson records and spit at me! I gave him money!

Pause.

LEE: Just help me a little with the characters, all right? You know how to do it, Austin.

AUSTIN *(on floor, laughs)*: The characters!

LEE: Yeah. You know. The way they talk and stuff. I can hear it in my head but I can't get it down on paper.

AUSTIN: What characters?

LEE: The guys. The guys in the story.

AUSTIN: Those aren't characters.

LEE: Whatever you call 'em then. I need to write somethin' out.

AUSTIN: Those are illusions of characters.

LEE: I don't give a damn what ya' call 'em! You know what I'm talkin' about!

AUSTIN: Those are fantasies of a long lost boyhood.

LEE: I gotta' write somethin' out on paper!!

Pause.

AUSTIN: What for? Saul's gonna' get you a fancy screenwriter isn't he?

LEE: I wanna' do it myself!

AUSTIN: Then do it! Yer on your own now, old buddy. You bull-dogged yer way into contention. Now you gotta' carry it through.

LEE: I will but I need some advice. Just a couple a' things. Come on, Austin. Just help me get 'em talkin' right. It won't take much.

AUSTIN: Oh, now you're having a little doubt huh? What happened? The pressure's on, boy. This is it. You gotta' come up with it now. You don't come up with a winner on your first time out they just cut your head off. They don't give you a second chance ya' know.

LEE: I got a good story! I know it's a good story. I just need a little help is all.

AUSTIN: Not from me. Not from yer little old brother. I'm retired.

LEE: You could save this thing for me, Austin. I'd give ya' half the money. I would. I only need half anyway. With this kinda' money I could be a long time down the road. I'd never bother ya' again. I promise. You'd never even see me again.

AUSTIN *(still on floor)*: You'd disappear?

LEE: I would for sure.

AUSTIN: Where would you disappear to?

LEE: That don't matter. I got plenty a' places.

AUSTIN: Nobody can disappear. The old man tried that. Look where it got him. He lost his teeth.

LEE: He never had any money.

AUSTIN: I don't mean that. I mean his teeth! His real teeth. First he lost his real teeth, then he lost his false teeth. You never knew that did ya'? He never confided in you.

LEE: Nah, I never knew that.

AUSTIN: You wanna' drink?

AUSTIN *offers bottle to* LEE, LEE *takes it, sits down on kitchen floor with* AUSTIN, *they share the bottle.*

Yeah, he lost his real teeth one at a time. Woke up every morning with another tooth lying on the mattress. Finally, he decides he's gotta' get 'em all pulled out but he doesn't have any money. Middle of Arizona with no money and no insurance and every morning another tooth is lying on the mattress. *(takes a drink)* So what does he do?

LEE: I dunno'. I never knew about that.

AUSTIN: He begs the government. G.I. Bill or some damn thing. Some pension plan he remembers in the back of his head. And they send him out the money.

LEE: They did?

They keep trading the bottle between them, taking drinks.

AUSTIN: Yeah. They send him the money but it's not enough money. Costs a lot to have all yer teeth yanked. They charge by the individual tooth, ya' know. I mean one tooth isn't equal to another tooth. Some are more expensive. Like the big ones in the back—

LEE: So what happened?

AUSTIN: So he locates a Mexican dentist in Juarez who'll do the whole thing for a song. And he takes off hitchhiking to the border.

LEE: Hitchhiking?

AUSTIN: Yeah. So how long you think it takes him to get to the border? A man his age.

LEE: I dunno.

AUSTIN: Eight days it takes him. Eight days in the rain and the sun and every day he's droppin' teeth on the blacktop and nobody'll pick him up 'cause his mouth's full a' blood.

Pause, they drink.

So finally he stumbles into the dentist. Dentist takes all his money and all his teeth. And there he is, in Mexico, with his gums sewed up and his pockets empty.

Long silence, AUSTIN *drinks.*

LEE: That's it?

AUSTIN: Then I go out to see him, see. I go out there and I take
him out for a nice Chinese dinner. But he doesn't eat. All he
wants to do is drink Martinis outa' plastic cups. And he takes
his teeth out and lays 'em on the table 'cause he can't stand the
feel of 'em. And we ask the waitress for one a' those doggie bags
to take the Chop Suey home in. So he drops his teeth in the
doggie bag along with the Chop Suey. And then we go out to
hit all the bars up and down the highway. Says he wants to
introduce me to all his buddies. And in one a' those bars, in one
a' those bars up and down the highway, he left that doggie bag
with his teeth laying in the Chop Suey.

LEE: You never found it?

AUSTIN: We went back but we never did find it. *(Pause.)* Now
that's a true story. True to life.

They drink as lights fade to black.

SCENE VIII

*Very early morning, between night and day. No crickets, coyotes
yapping feverishly in distance before light comes up, a small fire
blazes up in the dark from alcove area, sound of* LEE *smashing
typewriter with a golf club, lights coming up,* LEE *seen smashing
typewriter methodically then dropping pages of his script into a
burning bowl set on the floor of alcove, flames leap up,* AUSTIN
*has a whole bunch of stolen toasters lined up on the sink counter
along with* LEE's *stolen T.V., the toasters are of a wide variety of
models, mostly chrome,* AUSTIN *goes up and down the line of toasters, breathing on them and polishing them with a dish towel, both
men are drunk, empty whiskey bottles and beer cans litter floor of
kitchen, they share a half empty bottle on one of the chairs in the
alcove,* LEE *keeps periodically taking deliberate ax-chops at the
typewriter using a nine-iron as* AUSTIN *speaks, all of their mother's
house plants are dead and drooping.*

AUSTIN *(polishing toaster)*: There's gonna' be a general lack of
toast in the neighborhood this morning. Many, many unhappy,

bewildered breakfast faces. I guess it's best not to even think of the victims. Not to even entertain it. Is that the right psychology?

LEE *(pauses)*: What?

AUSTIN: Is that the correct criminal psychology? Not to think of the victims?

LEE: What victims?

LEE *takes another swipe at typewriter with nine-iron, adds pages to the fire.*

AUSTIN: The victims of crime. Of breaking and entering. I mean is it a prerequisite for a criminal not to have a conscience?

LEE: Ask a criminal.

Pause, LEE *stares at* AUSTIN.

What're you gonna' do with all those toasters? That's the dumbest thing I ever saw in my life.

AUSTIN: I've got hundreds of dollars worth of household appliances here. You may not realize that.

LEE: Yeah, and how many hundreds of dollars did you walk right past?

AUSTIN: It was toasters you challenged me to. Only toasters. I ignored every other temptation.

LEE: I never challenged you! That's no challenge. Anybody can steal a toaster.

LEE *smashes typewriter again.*

AUSTIN: You don't have to take it out on my typewriter ya' know. It's not the machine's fault that you can't write. It's a sin to do that to a good machine.

LEE: A sin?

AUSTIN: When you consider all the writers who never even had a machine. Who would have given an eyeball for a good typewriter. Any typewriter.

LEE *smashes typewriter again.*

AUSTIN *(polishing toasters)*: All the ones who wrote on matchbook covers. Paper bags. Toilet paper. Who had their writing destroyed by their jailers. Who persisted beyond all odds. Those writers would find it hard to understand your actions.

LEE *comes down on typewriter with one final crushing blow of the*

*nine-iron, then collapses in one of the chairs, takes a drink from
bottle, pause.*

AUSTIN *(after pause)*: Not to mention demolishing a perfectly good
golf club. What about all the struggling golfers? What about Lee
Trevino? What do you think he would've said when he was
batting balls around with broomsticks at the age of nine. Impoverished.

Pause.

LEE: What time is it anyway?

AUSTIN: No idea. Time stands still when you're havin' fun.

LEE: Is it too late to call a woman? You know any women?

AUSTIN: I'm a married man.

LEE: I mean a local woman.

AUSTIN *looks out at light through window above sink.*

AUSTIN: It's either too late or too early. You're the nature enthu-
siast. Can't you tell the time by the light in the sky? Orient
yourself around the North Star or something?

LEE: I can't tell anything.

AUSTIN: Maybe you need a little breakfast. Some toast! How 'bout
some toast?

AUSTIN *goes to cupboard, pulls out loaf of bread and starts
dropping slices into every toaster,* LEE *stays sitting, drinks, watches*
AUSTIN.

LEE: I don't need toast. I need a woman.

AUSTIN: A woman isn't the answer. Never was.

LEE: I'm not talkin' about permanent. I'm talkin' about temporary.

AUSTIN *(putting toast in toasters)*: We'll just test the merits of these
little demons. See which brands have a tendency to burn. See
which one can produce a perfectly golden piece of fluffy toast.

LEE: How much gas you got in yer car?

AUSTIN: I haven't driven my car for days now. So I haven't had
an opportunity to look at the gas gauge.

LEE: Take a guess. You think there's enough to get me to Bakersfield?

AUSTIN: Bakersfield? What's in Bakersfield?

LEE: Just never mind what's in Bakersfield! You think there's
enough goddamn gas in the car!

AUSTIN: Sure.

LEE: Sure. You could care less, right. Let me run outa' gas on the Grapevine. You could give a shit.

AUSTIN: I'd say there was enough gas to get you just about anywhere, Lee. With your determination and guts.

LEE: What the hell time is it anyway?

LEE *pulls out his wallet, starts going through dozens of small pieces of paper with phone numbers written on them, drops some on the floor, drops others in the fire.*

AUSTIN: Very early. This is the time of morning when the coyotes kill people's cocker spaniels. Did you hear them? That's what they were doing out there. Luring innocent pets away from their homes.

LEE *(searching through his papers)*: What's the area code for Bakersfield? You know?

AUSTIN: You could always call the operator.

LEE: I can't stand that voice they give ya'.

AUSTIN: What voice?

LEE: That voice that warns you that if you'd only tried harder to find the number in the phone book you wouldn't have to be calling the operator to begin with.

LEE *gets up, holding a slip of paper from his wallet, stumbles toward phone on wall, yanks receiver, starts dialing.*

AUSTIN: Well I don't understand why you'd want to talk to anybody else anyway. I mean you can talk to me. I'm your brother.

LEE *(dialing)*: I wanna' talk to a woman. I haven't heard a woman's voice in a long time.

AUSTIN: Not since the Botanist?

LEE: What?

AUSTIN: Nothing. *(starts singing as he tends toast)*

> "Red sails in the sunset
> Way out on the blue
> Please carry my loved one
> Home safely to me"

LEE: Hey, knock it off will ya'! This is long distance here.

AUSTIN: Bakersfield?

LEE: Yeah, Bakersfield. It's Kern County.

AUSTIN: Well, what County are *we* in?

LEE: You better get yourself a 7-Up, boy.

AUSTIN: One County's as good as another.

AUSTIN *hums "Red Sails" softly as* LEE *talks on phone.*

LEE *(to phone)*: Yeah, operator look—first off I wanna' know the area code for Bakersfield. Right. Bakersfield! Okay. Good. Now I wanna' know if you can help me track somebody down. *(pause)* No, no I mean a phone number. Just a phone number. Okay. *(holds a piece of paper up and reads it)* Okay, the name is Melly Ferguson. Melly. *(pause)* I dunno'. Melly. Maybe. Yeah. Maybe Melanie. Yeah. Melanie Ferguson. Okay. *(pause)* What? I can't hear ya' so good. Sounds like yer under the ocean. *(pause)* You got ten Melanie Fergusons? How could that be? Ten Melanie Fergusons in Bakersfield? Well gimme all of 'em then. *(pause)* What d'ya mean? Gimme all ten Melanie Fergusons! That's right. Just a second. *(to* AUSTIN*)* Gimme a pen.

AUSTIN: I don't have a pen.

LEE: Gimme a pencil then!

AUSTIN: I don't have a pencil.

LEE *(to phone)*: Just a second, operator. *(to* AUSTIN*)* Yer a writer and ya' don't have a pen or a pencil!

AUSTIN: I'm not a writer. You're a writer.

LEE: I'm on the phone here! Get me a pen or a pencil.

AUSTIN: I gotta' watch the toast.

LEE *(to phone)*: Hang on a second, operator.

LEE *lets the phone drop then starts pulling all the drawers in the kitchen out on the floor and dumping the contents, searching for a pencil,* AUSTIN *watches him casually.*

LEE *(crashing through drawers, throwing contents around kitchen)*: This is the last time I try to live with people, boy! I can't believe it. Here I am! Here I am again in a desperate situation! This would never happen out on the desert. I would never be in this kinda' situation out on the desert. Isn't there a pen or a pencil in this house! Who lives in this house anyway!

AUSTIN: Our mother.

LEE: How come she don't have a pen or a pencil! She's a social person isn't she? Doesn't she have to make shopping lists? She's gotta' have a pencil. *(finds pencil)* Aaha! *(He rushes back to phone, picks up receiver.)* All right operator. Operator? Hey! Operator! Goddamnit!

LEE *rips the phone off the wall and throws it down, goes back to chair and falls into it, drinks, long pause.*

AUSTIN: She hung up?

LEE: Yeah, she hung up. I knew she was gonna' hang up. I could hear it in her voice.

LEE *starts going through his slips of paper again.*

AUSTIN: Well, you're probably better off staying here with me anyway. I'll take care of you.

LEE: I don't need takin' care of! Not by you anyway.

AUSTIN: Toast is almost ready.

AUSTIN *starts buttering all the toast as it pops up.*

LEE: I don't want any toast!

Long pause.

AUSTIN: You gotta' eat something. Can't just drink. How long have we been drinking anyway?

LEE *(looking through slips of paper)*: Maybe it was Fresno. What's the area code for Fresno? How could I have lost that number! She was beautiful.

Pause.

AUSTIN: Why don't you just forget about that, Lee. Forget about the woman.

LEE: She had green eyes. You know what green eyes do to me?

AUSTIN: I know but you're not gonna' get it on with her now anyway. It's dawn already. She's in Bakersfield for Christ's sake.

Long pause, LEE *considers the situation.*

LEE: Yeah. *(Looks at windows.)* It's dawn?

AUSTIN: Let's just have some toast and—

LEE: What is this bullshit with the toast anyway! You make it sound like salvation or something. I don't want any goddamn toast! How many times I gotta' tell ya'! *(LEE gets up, crosses upstage to windows in alcove, looks out,* AUSTIN *butters toast.)*

AUSTIN: Well it is like salvation sort of. I mean the smell. I love the smell of toast. And the sun's coming up. It makes me feel like anything's possible. Ya' know?

LEE *(back to* AUSTIN, *facing windows upstage)*: So go to church why don't ya'.

AUSTIN: Like a beginning. I love beginnings.

LEE: Oh yeah. I've always been kinda' partial to endings myself.

AUSTIN: What if I come with you, Lee?

LEE *(pause as* LEE *turns toward* AUSTIN*)*: What?

AUSTIN: What if I come with you out to the desert?

LEE: Are you kiddin'?

AUSTIN: No. I'd just like to see what it's like.

LEE: You wouldn't last a day out there pal.

AUSTIN: That's what you said about the toasters. You said I couldn't steal a toaster either.

LEE: A toaster's got nothin' to do with the desert.

AUSTIN: I could make it, Lee. I'm not that helpless. I can cook.

LEE: Cook?

AUSTIN: I can.

LEE: So what! You can cook. Toast.

AUSTIN: I can make fires. I know how to get fresh water from condensation.

AUSTIN *stacks buttered toast up in a tall stack on plate.*

LEE *slams table.*

LEE: It's not somethin' you learn out of a Boy Scout handbook!

AUSTIN: Well how do you learn it then! How're you supposed to learn it!

Pause.

LEE: Ya' just learn it, that's all. Ya' learn it 'cause ya' have to learn it. You don't *have* to learn it.

AUSTIN: You could teach me.

LEE *(stands)*: What're you, crazy or somethin'? You went to college. Here, you are down here, rollin' in bucks. Floatin' up and down in elevators. And you wanna' learn how to live on the desert!

AUSTIN: I do, Lee. I really do. There's nothin' down here for me. There never was. When we were kids here it was different. There was a life here then. But now—I keep comin' down here thinkin' it's the fifties or somethin'. I keep finding myself getting off the freeway at familiar landmarks that turn out to be unfamiliar. On the way to appointments. Wandering down streets I thought

I recognized that turn out to be replicas of streets I remember. Streets I misremember. Streets I can't tell if I lived on or saw in a postcard. Fields that don't even exist anymore.

LEE: There's no point cryin' about that now.

AUSTIN: There's nothin' real down here, Lee! Least of all me!

LEE: Well I can't save you from that!

AUSTIN: You can let me come with you.

LEE: No dice, pal.

AUSTIN: You could let me come with you, Lee!

LEE: Hey, do you actually think I chose to live out in the middle a' nowhere? Do ya'? Ya' think it's some kinda' philosophical decision I took or somethin'? I'm livin' out there 'cause I can't make it here! And yer bitchin' to me about all yer success!

AUSTIN: I'd cash it all in in a second. That's the truth.

LEE *(pause, shakes his head)*: I can't believe this.

AUSTIN: Let me go with you.

LEE: Stop sayin' that will ya'! Yer worse than a dog.

AUSTIN *offers out the plate of neatly stacked toast to* LEE.

AUSTIN: You want some toast?

LEE *suddenly explodes and knocks the plate out of* AUSTIN'*s hand, toast goes flying, long frozen moment where it appears* LEE *might go all the way this time when* AUSTIN *breaks it by slowly lowering himself to his knees and begins gathering the scattered toast from the floor and stacking it back on the plate,* LEE *begins to circle* AUSTIN *in a slow, predatory way, crushing pieces of toast in his wake, no words for a while,* AUSTIN *keeps gathering toast, even the crushed pieces.*

LEE: Tell ya' what I'll do, little brother. I might just consider makin' you a deal. Little trade. (AUSTIN *continues gathering toast as* LEE *circles him through this.)* You write me up this screenplay thing just like I tell ya'. I mean you can use all yer usual tricks and stuff. Yer fancy language. Yer artistic hocus pocus. But ya' gotta' write everything like I say. Every move. Every time they run outa' gas, they run outa' gas. Every time they wanna' jump on a horse, they do just that. If they wanna' stay in Texas, by God they'll stay in Texas! *(Keeps circling.)* And you finish the whole thing up for me. Top to bottom. And you put my name on it. And I own all the rights. And every dime goes in my pocket. You do that and I'll sure enough take ya' with me to the desert. (LEE *stops, pause, looks down at* AUSTIN.) How's that sound?

Pause as AUSTIN *stands slowly holding plate of demolished toast, their faces are very close, pause.*

AUSTIN: It's a deal.

LEE *stares straight into* AUSTIN's *eyes, then he slowly takes a piece of toast off the plate, raises it to his mouth and takes a huge crushing bite never taking his eyes off* AUSTIN's. *As* LEE *crunches into the toast the lights black out.*

SCENE IX

Mid-day. No sound, blazing heat, the stage is ravaged; bottles, toasters, smashed typewriter, ripped out telephone, etc. All the debris from previous scene is now starkly visible in intense yellow light, the effect should be like a desert junkyard at high noon, the coolness of the preceding scenes is totally obliterated. AUSTIN *is seated at table in alcove, shirt open, pouring with sweat, hunched over a writing notebook, scribbling notes desperately with a ballpoint pen.* LEE *with no shirt, beer in hand, sweat pouring down his chest, is walking a slow circle around the table, picking his way through the objects, sometimes kicking them aside.*

LEE *(as he walks)*: All right, read it back to me. Read it back to me!

AUSTIN *(scribbling at top speed)*: Just a second.

LEE: Come on, come on! Just read what ya' got.

AUSTIN: I can't keep up! It's not the same as if I had a typewriter.

LEE: Just read what we got so far. Forget about the rest.

AUSTIN: All right. Let's see—okay— *(wipes sweat from his face, reads as* LEE *circles)* Luke says uh—

LEE: Luke?

AUSTIN: Yeah.

LEE: His name's Luke? All right, all right—we can change the names later. What's he say? Come on, come on.

AUSTIN: He says uh— *(reading)* "I told ya' you were a fool to follow me in here. I know this prairie like the back a' my hand."

LEE: No, no, no! That's not what I said. I never said that.

AUSTIN: That's what I wrote.

LEE: It's not what I said. I never said "like the back a' my hand." That's stupid. That's one a' those—whadya' call it? Whadya' call that?

AUSTIN: What?

LEE: Whadya' call it when somethin's been said a thousand times before. Whadya' call that?

AUSTIN: Um—a cliché?

LEE: Yeah. That's right. Cliché. That's what that is. A cliché. "The back a' my hand." That's stupid.

AUSTIN: That's what you said.

LEE: I never said that! And even if I did, that's where yer supposed to come in. That's where yer supposed to change it to somethin' better.

AUSTIN: Well how am I supposed to do that and write down what you say at the same time?

LEE: Ya' just do, that's all! You hear a stupid line you change it. That's yer job.

AUSTIN: All right. *(makes more notes)*

LEE: What're you changin' it to?

AUSTIN: I'm not changing it. I'm just trying to catch up.

LEE: Well change it! We gotta' change that, we can't leave that in there like that. ". . . the back a' my hand." That's dumb.

AUSTIN *(stops writing, sits back)*: All right.

LEE *(pacing)*: So what'll we change it to?

AUSTIN: Um—How 'bout—"I'm on intimate terms with this prairie."

LEE *(to himself considering line as he walks)*: "I'm on intimate terms with this prairie." Intimate terms, intimate terms. Intimate—that means like uh—sexual right?

AUSTIN: Well—yeah—or—

LEE: He's on sexual terms with the prairie? How dya' figure that?

AUSTIN: Well it doesn't necessarily have to mean sexual.

LEE: What's it mean then?

AUSTIN: It means uh—close—personal—

LEE: All right. How's it sound? Put it into the uh—the line there.

Read it back. Let's see how it sounds. *(to himself)* "Intimate terms."

AUSTIN *(scribbles in notebook)*: Okay. It'd go something like this: *(reads)* "I told ya' you were a fool to follow me in here. I'm on intimate terms with this prairie."

LEE: That's good. I like that. That's real good.

AUSTIN: You do?

LEE: Yeah. Don't you?

AUSTIN: Sure.

LEE: Sounds original now. "Intimate terms." That's good. Okay. Now we're cookin! That has a real ring to it.

AUSTIN *makes more notes*, LEE *walks around, pours beer on his arms and rubs it over his chest feeling good about the new progress, as he does this* MOM *enters unobtrusively down left with her luggage, she stops and stares at the scene still holding luggage as the two men continue, unaware of her presence,* AUSTIN *absorbed in his writing,* LEE *cooling himself off with beer.*

LEE *(continues)*: "He's on intimate terms with this prairie."
    Sounds real mysterious and kinda' threatening at the same time.

AUSTIN *(writing rapidly)*: Good.

LEE: Now— (LEE *turns and suddenly sees* MOM, *he stares at her for a while, she stares back,* AUSTIN *keeps writing feverishly, not noticing,* LEE *walks slowly over to* MOM *and takes a closer look, long pause.)*

LEE: Mom?

AUSTIN *looks up suddenly from his writing, sees* MOM, *stands quickly, long pause,* MOM *surveys the damage.*

AUSTIN: Mom. What're you doing back?

MOM: I'm back.

LEE: Here, lemme take those for ya.

LEE *sets beer on counter, then takes both her bags but doesn't know where to set them down in the sea of junk so he just keeps holding them.*

AUSTIN: I wasn't expecting you back so soon. I thought uh—How was Alaska?

MOM: Fine.

LEE: See any igloos?

MOM: No. Just glaciers.

AUSTIN: Cold huh?

MOM: What?

AUSTIN: It must've been cold up there?

MOM: Not really.

LEE: Musta' been colder than this here. I mean we're havin' a real scorcher here.

MOM: Oh? *(She looks at damage.)*

LEE: Yeah. Must be in the hundreds.

AUSTIN: You wanna' take your coat off, Mom?

MOM: No. *(Pause, she surveys space.)* What happened in here?

AUSTIN: Oh um—Me and Lee were just sort of celebrating and uh—

MOM: Celebrating?

AUSTIN: Yeah. Uh—Lee sold a screenplay. A story, I mean.

MOM: Lee did?

AUSTIN: Yeah.

MOM: Not you?

AUSTIN: No. Him.

MOM *(to* LEE*)*: You sold a screenplay?

LEE: Yeah. That's right. We're just sorta' finishing it up right now. That's what we're doing here.

AUSTIN: Me and Lee are going out to the desert to live.

MOM: You and Lee?

AUSTIN: Yeah. I'm taking off with Lee.

MOM *(She looks back and forth at each of them, pause.)*: You gonna go live with your father?

AUSTIN: No. We're going to a different desert Mom.

MOM: I see. Well, you'll probably wind up on the same desert sooner or later. What're all these toasters doing here?

AUSTIN: Well—we had a kind of contest.

MOM: Contest?

LEE: Yeah.

AUSTIN: Lee won.

MOM: Did you win a lot of money, Lee?

LEE: Well not yet. It's comin' in any day now.

MOM *(to* LEE*)*: What happened to your shirt?

LEE: Oh. I was sweatin' like a pig and I took it off.

AUSTIN *grabs* LEE's *shirt off the table and tosses it to him,* LEE *sets down suitcases and puts his shirt on.*

MOM: Well it's one hell of a mess in here isn't it?

AUSTIN: Yeah, I'll clean it up for you, Mom. I just didn't know you were coming back so soon.

MOM: I didn't either.

AUSTIN: What happened?

MOM: Nothing. I just started missing all my plants. *(She notices dead plants.)*

AUSTIN: Oh.

MOM: Oh, they're all dead aren't they. *(She crosses toward them, examines them closely.)* You didn't get a chance to water I guess.

AUSTIN: I was doing it and then Lee came and—

LEE: Yeah I just distracted him a whole lot here, Mom. It's not his fault.

Pause, as MOM *stares at plants.*

MOM: Oh well, one less thing to take care of I guess. *(turns toward brothers)* Oh, that reminds me—You boys will probably never guess who's in town. Try and guess.

Long pause, brothers stare at her.

AUSTIN: Whadya' mean, Mom?

MOM: Take a guess. Somebody very important has come to town. I read it, coming down on the Greyhound.

LEE: Somebody very important?

MOM: See if you can guess. You'll never guess.

AUSTIN: Mom—we're trying to uh— *(points to writing pad)*

MOM: Picasso. *(pause)* Picasso's in town. Isn't that incredible? Right now.

Pause.

AUSTIN: Picasso's dead, Mom.

MOM: No, he's not dead. He's visiting the museum. I read it on the bus. We have to go down there and see him.

AUSTIN: Mom—

MOM: This is the chance of a lifetime. Can you imagine? We could all go down and meet him. All three of us.

LEE: Uh—I don't think I'm really up fer meetin' anybody right now. I'm uh—What's his name?

MOM: Picasso! Picasso! You've never heard of Picasso? Austin, you've heard of Picasso.

AUSTIN: Mom, we're not going to have time.

MOM: It won't take long. We'll just hop in the car and go down there. An opportunity like this doesn't come along every day.

AUSTIN: We're gonna' be leavin' here, Mom!

Pause.

MOM: Oh.

LEE: Yeah.

Pause.

MOM: You're both leaving?

LEE *(looks at* AUSTIN*)*: Well we were thinkin' about that before but now I—

AUSTIN: No, we are! We're both leaving. We've got it all planned.

MOM *(to* AUSTIN*)*: Well you can't leave. You have a family.

AUSTIN: I'm leaving. I'm getting out of here.

LEE *(to* MOM*)*: I don't really think Austin's cut out for the desert, do you?

MOM: No. He's not.

AUSTIN: I'm going with you, Lee!

MOM: He's too thin.

LEE: Yeah, he'd just burn up out there.

AUSTIN *(to* LEE*)*: We just gotta' finish this screenplay and then we're gonna' take off. That's the plan. That's what you said. Come on, let's get back to work, Lee.

LEE: I can't work under these conditions here. It's too hot.

AUSTIN: Then we'll do it on the desert.

LEE: Don't be tellin' me what we're gonna' do!

MOM: Don't shout in the house.

LEE: We're just gonna' have to postpone the whole deal.

AUSTIN: I can't postpone it! It's gone past postponing! I'm doing everything you said. I'm writing down exactly what you tell me.

LEE: Yeah, but you were right all along see. It is a dumb story. "Two lamebrains chasin' each other across Texas." That's what you said, right?

AUSTIN: I never said that.

LEE *sneers in* AUSTIN's *face, then turns to* MOM.

LEE: I'm gonna' just borrow some a' your antiques, Mom. You don't mind do ya'? Just a few plates and things. Silverware.

LEE *starts going through all the cupboards in kitchen pulling out plates and stacking them on counter as* MOM *and* AUSTIN *watch.*

MOM: You don't have any utensils on the desert?

LEE: Nah, I'm fresh out.

AUSTIN *(to* LEE*)*: What're you doing?

MOM: Well some of those are very old. Bone China.

LEE: I'm tired of eatin' outa' my bare hands, ya' know. It's not civilized.

AUSTIN *(to* LEE*)*: What're you doing? We made a deal!

MOM: Couldn't you borrow the plastic ones instead? I have plenty of plastic ones.

LEE *(as he stacks plates)*: It's not the same. Plastic's not the same at all. What I need is somethin' authentic. Somethin' to keep me in touch. It's easy to get outa' touch out there. Don't worry I'll get em' back to ya'.

AUSTIN *rushes up to* LEE, *grabs him by shoulders.*

AUSTIN: You can't just drop the whole thing, Lee!

LEE *turns, pushes* AUSTIN *in the chest knocking him backwards into the alcove,* MOM *watches numbly,* LEE *returns to collecting the plates, silverware, etc.*

MOM: You boys shouldn't fight in the house. Go outside and fight.

LEE: I'm not fightin'. I'm leavin'.

MOM: There's been enough damage done already.

LEE *(his back to* AUSTIN *and* MOM, *stacking dishes on counter)*: I'm clearin' outa' here once and for all. All this town does is drive a man insane. Look what it's done to Austin there. I'm not lettin' that happen to me. Sell myself down the river. No sir. I'd rather be a hundred miles from nowhere than let that happen to me.

During this AUSTIN *has picked up the ripped-out phone from the floor and wrapped the cord tightly around both his hands, he lunges at* LEE *whose back is still to him, wraps the cord around* LEE's *neck, plants a foot in* LEE's *back and pulls back on the cord, tightening it,* LEE *chokes desperately, can't speak and can't reach* AUSTIN *with his arms.* AUSTIN *keeps applying pressure on* LEE's *back with his foot, bending him into the sink.* MOM *watches.*

AUSTIN *(tightening cord)*: You're not goin' anywhere! You're not takin' anything with you. You're not takin' my car! You're not takin' the dishes! You're not takin' anything! You're stayin' right here!

MOM: You'll have to stop fighting in the house. There's plenty of room outside to fight. You've got the whole outdoors to fight in.

LEE *tries to tear himself away, he crashes across the stage like an enraged bull dragging* AUSTIN *with him, he snorts and bellows but* AUSTIN *hangs on and manages to keep clear of* LEE's *attempts to grab him. They crash into the table, to the floor;* LEE *is face down thrashing wildly and choking,* AUSTIN *pulls cord tighter, stands with one foot planted on* LEE's *back and the cord stretched taut.*

AUSTIN *(holding cord)*: Gimme back my keys, Lee! Take the keys out! Take 'em out!

LEE *desperately tries to dig in his pockets, searching for the car keys,* MOM *moves closer.*

MOM *(calmly to* AUSTIN*)*: You're not killing him are you?

AUSTIN: I don't know. I don't know if I'm killing him. I'm stopping him. That's all. I'm just stopping him.

LEE *thrashes but* AUSTIN *is relentless.*

MOM: You oughta' let him breathe a little bit.

AUSTIN: Throw the keys out, Lee!

LEE *finally get keys out and throws them on floor but out of* AUSTIN's *reach.* AUSTIN *keeps pressure on cord, pulling* LEE's *neck back.* LEE *gets one hand to the cord but can't relieve the pressure.*

Reach me those keys would ya', Mom.

MOM *(not moving)*: Why are you doing this to him?

AUSTIN: Reach me the keys!

MOM: Not until you stop choking him.

AUSTIN: I can't stop choking him! He'll kill me if I stop choking him!

MOM: He won't kill you. He's your brother.

AUSTIN: Just get me the keys would ya'!

Pause. MOM *picks keys up off floor, hands them to* AUSTIN.

AUSTIN *(to* MOM*)*: Thanks.

MOM: Will you let him go now?

AUSTIN: I don't know. He's not gonna' let me get outa' here.

MOM: Well you can't kill him.

AUSTIN: I can kill him! I can easily kill him. Right now. Right here. All I gotta' do is just tighten up. See? *(He tightens cord, LEE thrashes wildly, AUSTIN releases pressure a little, maintaining control.)* Ya' see that?

MOM: That's a savage thing to do.

AUSTIN: Yeah well don't tell me I can't kill him because I can. I can just twist. I can just keep twisting. *(AUSTIN twists the cord tighter, LEE weakens, his breathing changes to a short rasp.)*

MOM: Austin!

AUSTIN *relieves pressure.* LEE *breathes easier but* AUSTIN *keeps him under control.*

AUSTIN *(eyes on LEE, holding cord)*: I'm goin' to the desert. There's nothing stopping me. I'm going by myself to the desert.

MOM *moving toward her luggage.*

MOM: Well, I'm going to go check into a motel. I can't stand this anymore.

AUSTIN: Don't go yet!

MOM *pauses.*

MOM: I can't stay here. This is worse than being homeless.

AUSTIN: I'll get everything fixed up for you, Mom. I promise. Just stay for a while.

MOM *(picking up luggage)*: You're going to the desert.

AUSTIN: Just wait!

LEE *thrashes,* AUSTIN *subdues him,* MOM *watches holding luggage, pause.*

MOM: It was the worst feeling being up there. In Alaska. Staring out a window. I never felt so desperate before. That's why when I saw that article on Picasso I thought—

AUSTIN: Stay here, Mom. This is where you live.

She looks around the stage.

MOM: I don't recognize it at all.

She exits with luggage. AUSTIN *makes a move toward her but* LEE *starts to struggle and* AUSTIN *subdues him again with cord, pause.*

AUSTIN *(holding cord)*: Lee? I'll make ya' a deal. You let me get outa' here. Just let me get to my car. All right, Lee? Gimme a little headstart and I'll turn you loose. Just gimme a little headstart. All right?

LEE *makes no response,* AUSTIN *slowly releases tension cord, still nothing from* LEE.

AUSTIN: Lee?

LEE *is motionless.* AUSTIN *very slowly begins to stand, still keeping a tenuous hold on the cord and his eyes riveted to* LEE *for any sign of movement.* AUSTIN *slowly drops the cord and stands. He stares down at* LEE *who appears to be dead.*

AUSTIN *(whispers)*: Lee?

Pause, AUSTIN *considers, looks toward exit, back to* LEE, *then makes a small movement as if to leave. Instantly* LEE *is on his feet and moves toward exit, blocking* AUSTIN's *escape. They square off to each other, keeping a distance between them. Pause, a single coyote heard in distance, light fade softly into moonlight, the figures of the brothers now appear to be caught in a vast desert-like landscape. They are very still but watchful for the next move, lights go slowly to black as the after-image of the brothers pulses in the dark, coyote fades.*

Writing About Drama

Reasons for Writing

Why write about drama? For many reasons. First, writing about a play encourages us to read it attentively and thus notice things we might miss during a more casual reading. Second, writing stimulates thinking. Writing is an important way to discover what you think about a play, how you feel about it, and why. Third, we may write to endorse or refute a play's values and ideas. And finally, writing gives us power over a play, enabling us to absorb it into our storehouse of knowledge and experience.

An Approach to Writing About Drama

Getting Started: Selecting a Topic   The first step in writing about a play is selecting a topic. This is sometimes done for you by your teacher, who may assign a specific writing topic. If you select your own topic, however, you should keep a few things in mind. First, make sure the topic is suited to the required length of the paper. If your essay will be less than 1,000 words long, you should probably focus on a single aspect of a play. You might choose, for example, to write about a play's dialogue, its plot and structure, its characters and conflict, its thought and theme, or its setting and staging. For instance, you might choose to write about the arrangement of the plot in Hansberry's *A Raisin in the Sun*.

Or you might focus on the characters and conflict in that play or in another, such as Sophocles' *Antigonê,* Strindberg's *The Stronger,* or Shepard's *True West.* You could discuss the handling of light and sound in Williams's *The Glass Menagerie,* the importance of ideas in Ibsen's *An Enemy of the People,* or the humor of Ionesco's *The Gap* or Molière's *The Doctor in Spite of Himself.* The important thing is to select a focus and develop your ideas about the play by keeping that focus at the heart of your analysis.

Whatever your eventual focus, choose a topic that interests you, one you are willing to invest time and effort exploring. Once you decide on your topic, think of a title that reflects its nature and focus. Deciding on a title can help clarify and focus your thinking. A clearly focused topic, moreover, can serve as a point of reference when you write and revise the paper, a reminder of your intention should you digress. In addition, a title targets the direction of your paper for a reader. Here are some possible titles for the topics suggested above: "Internal and External Conflict in *The Stronger*"; "Power and Responsibility in *An Enemy of the People*"; "Comic Action in *The Gap.*" Another way to title a paper is to use a question as your title, then make the paper an extended answer to the question. Some examples: "Who Is the Real Enemy of the People?"; "What Is Ironic About *Trifles?*"; "What Makes *The Gap* an Absurdist Play?"; "Can *A View from the Bridge* Be Considered a Tragedy?"; "What Truths About the West Are Questioned in *True West?*"

To increase your chances of finding a topic that meets the criteria of suitability, specificity, and interest, read your selected play carefully a couple of times. If the play appears in a book you own, or if you are working from a photocopy, mark the text as you read. Underline words and lines, check significant details, and write brief marginal notes. The following example shows the type of marginal annotations that can lead to the discovery of a subject or a focused aspect of a work worth exploring in writing.

This excerpt from *Antigonê* begins at the point where Antigonê has been taken into custody for violating an edict of Creon, king of Thebes. Creon's edict concerns Antigonê's brother, Polyneicês, who was killed in a battle while fighting against Thebes. Creon has forbidden Polyneicês' burial; Antigonê has buried him.

CREON *to* SENTRY: You may go.

Exit SENTRY.

    (To ANTIGONÊ*)* Tell me, tell me briefly:
    Had you heard my proclamation
       touching this matter?

> Creon can't believe that she would disobey — hence his question.

ANTIGONÊ: It was public. Could I help
    hearing it?

CREON: And yet you dared defy the law.

ANTIGONÊ: I dared.

> He sees himself as "the law."

    It was not God's proclamation. That final
      Justice
    That rules the world below makes no
      such laws.

    Your edict, King, was strong,
    But all your strength is weakness itself
      against
    The immortal unrecorded laws of God.
    They are not merely now: they were, and
      shall be,
    Operative for ever, beyond man utterly.

> Antigonê identifies conflict: God/man divine/human

    I knew I must die, even without your
      decree:
    I am only mortal. And if I must die
    Now, before it is my time to die,
    Surely this is no hardship: can anyone
    Living, as I live, with evil all about me,
    Think Death less than a friend? This
      death of mine
    Is of no importance; but if I had left my
      brother
    Lying in death unburied, I should have
      suffered.
    Now I do not.

> Is she a bit too eager to die?

             You smile at me. Ah Creon,
    Think me a fool, if you like; but it may
      well be
    That a fool convicts me of folly.

> implicit stage direction: "You smile . . ."

CHORAGOS: Like father, like daughter: both
    headstrong, deaf to reason!
  She has never learned to yield:

How important is this choral comment?

CREON: She has much to learn.
  The inflexible heart breaks first, the
    toughest iron
  Cracks first, and the wildest horses bend
    their necks
  At the pull of the smallest curb.

images: iron, horses

                Pride? In a slave?
  This girl is guilty of a double insolence.
  Breaking the given laws and boasting
    of it.
  Who is the man here,
  She or I, if this crime goes unpunished?
  Sister's child, or more than sister's child,
  Or closer yet in blood—she and her sister
  Win bitter death for this!

*conflict: man/woman
    age/youth*

(To SERVANTS.*)*

              Go, some of you.
  Arrest Ismenê. I accuse her equally.
  Bring her: you will find her sniffling in
    the house there.

Why does Creon accuse Ismenê?

  Her mind's a traitor: crimes kept in the
    dark
  Cry for light, and the guardian brain
    shudders;
  But how much worse than this
  Is brazen boasting of barefaced anarchy!

Anarchy? Is Creon a bit paranoid?

ANTIGONÊ: Creon, what more do you want
    than my death?
CREON: Nothing.
  That gives me everything.
ANTIGONÊ: Then I beg you: kill me.
  This talking is a great weariness: your
    words

Are distasteful to me, and I am sure that
    mine

She knows how to fight back.

Seem so to you. And yet they should not
    seem so:
I should have praise and honor for what I
    have done.
All these men here would praise me
Were their lips not frozen shut with fear
    of you.
(Bitterly.) Ah the good fortune of kings.
Licensed to say and do whatever they
    please!

CREON: You are alone here in that opinion.

ANTIGONÊ: No, they are with me. But they
    keep their tongues in leash.

image: dogs on a leash held in check by fear

CREON: Maybe. But you are guilty, and
    they are not.

ANTIGONÊ: There is no guilt in reverence
    for the dead.

CREON: But Eteoclês—was he not your
    brother too?

a complication: the other brother, Eteoclês

ANTIGONÊ: My brother too.

CREON: And you insult his memory?

ANTIGONÊ *(softly)*: The dead man would
    not say that I insult it.

tempo: pace picks up here with rapid-fire dialogue exchange

CREON: He would: for you honor a traitor
    as much as him.

ANTIGONÊ: His own brother, traitor or not,
    and equal in blood.

CREON: He made war on his country.
    Eteoclês defended it.

ANTIGONÊ: Nevertheless, there are honors
    due all the dead.

CREON: But not the same for the wicked as
    for the just.

buildup of intensity

ANTIGONÊ: Ah Creon, Creon,
    Which of us can say what the gods hold
    wicked?

CREON: An enemy is an enemy, even dead.
ANTIGONÊ: It is my nature to join in love,
  not hate.
CREON *(finally losing patience)*: Go join
  them then; if you must have your love.
  Find it in hell!

If you do not own your text and cannot write in the margins, you can use an alternative method of note-making—the double-entry notebook. To create a double-entry notebook, divide a page in half vertically (or open a notebook so that you face two blank pages). On one side *take* notes, summarizing the play's situation, action, and ideas. On the other side, *make* notes, responding to them. On the responding side of the notebook, record your own thinking about what you read. Ask questions; speculate; make connections.

Here is an example of a double-entry notebook for the excerpt from *Antigonê* annotated above:

DOUBLE-ENTRY NOTEBOOK

Summary and Observations

Creon's language is formal, even self-important. He sounds like, or tries to sound like, a king.

Part of Creon's anger stems from Antigonê's rebellion against *him*, against *his* law. Part derives from her seeming disregard for the law of the land more generally.

Antigonê's view seems to be that since Creon's law was a bad one, she shouldn't obey it. And even further, that she has

Responses and Reactions

Creon is unpalatable here. He's pompous and arrogant. Yet to some extent he seems justified in being angry. What's interesting here is why Creon reacts so strongly to the violation of his edict. It probably has something to do with his recent acquisition of power. He is very likely more than a little insecure in his new position. He must feel the need to assert himself and establish his authority. Suppose he ignores Antigonê's action. What will people think of a responsibility to disobey it since the gods require that family members honor their dead. She points out that her burial of her brother was necessary for her own peace of mind.

him? Won't they see him as weak?

Antigonê's point has merit. She has to do what she has to do.

Antigonê seems the more likeable of the two.

Antigonê at one point angers Creon by reminding him that he is not almighty. She attempts to put him in his place, to remind him that his rule has limits. He doesn't like that. Nor does he like her suggestion that it is better to die than to obey an unjust law or live in a corrupt society.

Antigonê enjoys pulling Creon down a peg. Her tone does sound insulting. She almost seems to enjoy thinking of herself as a martyr for a cause. Isn't she a bit theatrical here, relishing her role and the image she projects as much as, or even more than, the idea and point of view she stands up for?

Creon, of course, sees her act of rebellion and her disrespectful attitude toward him as king as the cause of societal corruption.

Doesn't Creon overreact here in seeing Antigonê's action as an example of "anarchy"? And doesn't he also overreact in assuming that Ismenê is also guilty? He assumes things without testing them.

During the course of their dialogue (more a confrontation or debate than a conversation), they insult each other. Creon calls Antigonê stubborn; Antigonê calls Creon a fool.

As in any good fight, the antagonists really do try to hurt each other.

It's an enjoyable verbal battle—for us readers.

Creon's long speech parallels and answers Antigonê's. Once the two positions have been established, we watch and listen as the dialogue speeds up as Antigonê and Creon trade arguments and insults.

Even though the dialogue is somewhat stylized and conventional, it is beautifully arranged for maximum punch and counterpunch.

Throughout this taut scene both characters seem tense and angry. They neither like nor respect each other.

The effect overall is of tension building to the point of explosion.

Drafting Your Paper—Developing and Organizing Your Ideas Once you have a tentative subject and an angle of approach, you are ready to write a rough draft. The purpose of this draft is simply to write down your ideas and to see how they can be developed and supported. Regard the rough draft as an opportunity to discover what you think about the subject and to test and refine your ideas. Don't worry about having a clearly defined thesis or main idea before beginning. Instead, use your initial draft to find a thesis and sharpen it so that it becomes clear.

In drafting the paper, consider your purpose. Are you writing to provide information and make observations about the play? Are you writing to argue for a particular way of interpreting it? Ultimately, of course, all explanations of literary works are interpretations, and all interpretations are forms of argument. That is, interpretations are attempts to persuade other readers to see the play one way rather than in other ways. When writing about a play, you will often be attempting to convince others that what you see and say about it makes sense. You will be arguing for the validity of your way of seeing, not necessarily to the exclusion of other ways, but to demonstrate that your understanding of the play is reasonable and valuable. Moreover, since readers will respond not only to your arguments themselves but also to how you present them, you will need to provide careful evidence for your ideas. Most often this evidence will come in the form of textual support—details of action, dialogue, structure, and language from the play itself. Additional evidence may come from secondary sources, that is, from books or journals in which you will find the comments of experienced readers whose observations and interpretations may influence and support your own thinking or may contradict it.

After writing the draft, try to forget it for a while—at least for a day or two, and longer, if possible. Upon returning to it, assess whether what you are saying makes sense, whether you have provided enough examples to clarify your ideas and presented sufficient evidence to make them persuasive. Read the draft critically, asking yourself what is convincing and what is not, what makes sense and what does not. Consider whether the draft centers on a single idea and stays on track. If the first draft does these things, you can begin thinking about how to tighten the paper's organization and polish its style. If, on the other hand, the draft contains frequent changes of direction and a number of different ideas, you will need to decide what to salvage and how to focus the paper more sharply.

When you have written an acceptable draft, you are then ready to view its organization. A general organizational framework would probably include an introductory section that clarifies your purpose and intention; a set of successive paragraphs that develop, explore, and explain your ideas; and a conclusion that rounds off the discussion. Within that framework, consider whether your ideas and examples have been arranged in a coherent and logical manner. Ask yourself whether the structure of your paper will be clear to readers. Consider also whether sufficient space (or perhaps too much space) has been allotted to clarifying and supporting your views. For these considerations, it may be advisable to ask someone to read your paper and make a few informal observations.

Perhaps the most important aspect of a paper's organization is that you have a clear sense of how your paper is structured. You should be able to identify each of the paper's parts and to explain how those parts are related and why you put them in the order you did. Suppose you choose to discuss the ironic dimensions of Susan Glaspell's *Trifles*. You might focus on three or four ironic details. You might discuss the ironic quality of the title, considering how the action of the play serves to undermine and reverse the literal meaning of the word *trifles*. You might decide to discuss the dialogue of the men alone, the dialogue of the two women alone, and the actions of either or both. And you might want to comment on the implied details of the murder as the women understand it to have occurred.

Whatever details you ultimately select, and however many you choose, you will need to decide on a particular order in which to discuss them. Ask yourself how the ironic aspects of the play can be related to one another. Consider what the ironic details contribute to your experience and understanding of the play overall. You will probably view some details as more important than others; you may decide to consider them in order of increasing complexity or importance. Or you may choose to subdivide and pair your examples, perhaps contrasting them. It is necessary, though, to devise an organizational plan that makes sense to you and that will seem natural and evident to your readers.

Besides deciding on the order of ideas and examples in the paper and the amount of space allotted to each, you must consider also how to move from one example to another. You will need to link the sections of your discussion so that the writing flows smoothly. Generally, you can create transitions with phrases and sentences at the beginnings of paragraphs. (Examples include such words and phrases as "first, . . . second . . ."; "on the other hand, . . ."; "in addition to . . ."; "another way in which . . .") Sometimes, however, such an explicit mark of transition from one point to another will not be necessary. In such cases, a careful ordering of the details that support your argument will be evidence enough of how one paragraph follows from, and is related to, another.

Revising Your Paper   Revision is not something that occurs only once, at the end of the writing process. Redrafting your paper to consider the ordering of paragraphs and the use of examples is itself a significant act of revision. So, too, is rereading the play and thinking about it again. Revision is a process that occurs throughout the entire span of reading and writing. It involves, essentially, reconsidering both your writing and your thinking. This reconsideration is made on three levels: conceptual, organizational, and stylistic.

Conceptual revision involves reconsidering your ideas. As you write a first or second draft, your understanding of the play and what you plan to say about it may change. While accumulating textual evidence in support of one interpretation of the work, you may discover stronger evidence for a contrasting position. When this happens, you may need to go back to the note-taking stage to explore your revised vision of the work. You will then need to make major changes in the original draft. You may end up discarding much of it and beginning again with a stronger conviction about a different approach or a revised idea. In writing about Sophocles' *Antigonê,* for example, you may have begun with a completely positive assessment of Antigonê's character, celebrating her staunch opposition to Creon's edict. But in rereading the play, you may have become uneasy with certain details that seem to run counter to this view, precipitating a change of mind about Antigonê's attitudes, motives, and character. When something like this occurs, you revise.

Organizational, or structural, revision involves asking yourself whether the arrangement of the paper's parts best presents your line of thinking. Is the organizational framework readily discernible? Does it make sense? Have you written an introduction that clarifies your topic and intention? Have you organized your supporting details in a sensible and logical manner? Does your conclusion follow logically from your discussion and bring it to a satisfying close?

Again taking *Antigonê* as an example, you might begin by identifying its general subject, the conflict between the individual and the state (or between political and religious responsibility). Then you could move toward suggesting that even though the play contains language and action that idealize Antigonê's position, it also includes other details that undermine such a romanticized conception of Antigonê. From there you would move to the body of your argument, in which you would present the details that appear supportive of Antigonê's idealized conduct and show how other details of incident and language contradict them. In your conclusion, you could reiterate your main point, relate it to some other work you've read (by Sophocles or by another writer), respond personally to the play and its meaning, and perhaps include an apt quotation that sums up your interpretation of the play.

Stylistic revision concerns smaller-scale details, such as matters of syntax, or word order; diction, or word choice; tone; imagery; and rhythm. Even though you may think about these things in early drafts, it is better to defer critical attention to them until after writing a final draft, largely because such stylistic considerations may undergo significant alteration as you rethink and reorganize your paper.

You can focus on aspects of style that may require revision by using the following questions as guidelines:

1. Are your sentences concise and clear?
2. Can you eliminate words that are not doing their job?
3. Are your tone and voice consistent? (Do you shift from a formal to an informal, even colloquial, style?)
4. Is the level of language appropriate for your audience?
5. Do your words and sentences say what you want them to?
6. Are there any grammatical errors: inconsistencies in verb tenses, problems with subject-verb agreement, run-on sentences, and the like?
7. Are there any errors in spelling and punctuation?

As a final step, proofread the paper, making sure it conforms to all of your teacher's guidelines.

Some Ways of Writing About Drama

Analysis *Analysis* involves examining the relationships among the various elements of a work. When analyzing plays, you study these elements to see what each reveals about the work overall. For example, you might analyze a play's imagery or structure to see what each contributes to its overall meaning and effect.

Analysis is not an end in itself. We analyze plays to understand better both *what* they mean and *how* they come to mean what they do. We take plays apart to reconstruct them, gaining along the way an enriched understanding of their significance and their artistry. The analytical comments in chapters one and two on Lady Gregory's *The Rising of the Moon* suggest how analysis of the elements of drama enlarges our understanding of it.

Explication A type of analysis frequently useful in explaining plays is *explication,* a careful line-by-line explanation of a passage. Explication involves the unfolding of the layers of meaning in a text. It provides a close-up look at the language of a passage with a view to explaining its meaning. To explicate is to interpret by means of careful, close reading. Because explication involves scrupulous attention to detail, it is usually reserved for specific sections or parts of plays.

Explication is particularly useful for revealing the meaning of a complex passage. The analysis of the speech from *Macbeth* that begins, "Tomorrow, and tomorrow, and tomorrow," (p. 34) provides one example. That explication is continued with the analysis of the imagery at the end of the same speech (pp. 34–35). In choosing a passage to explicate, consider those that, like Macbeth's famous speech, occur at or after a climactic moment of action. Consider also the beginnings and endings of acts and scenes, since beginnings and endings often make the strongest and most lasting impressions on reader and viewer.

Comparison and Contrast   Another useful approach in drafting a paper about a play is the comparison and contrast of elements in a single work or of a particular aspect in different works. For example, you might compare and contrast the differing perspectives on responsibility to authority in *Antigonê* and *An Enemy of the People.* Or you might compare the uses of irony in *The Gap* with its uses in *Trifles.* Possible titles for papers exploring such comparative topics include these: "The Uses and Abuses of Power in *Antigonê* and *An Enemy of the People*"; "Two Uses of Irony: Satire and Humor in *Trifles* and *The Gap.*"

Comparative analysis can sharpen your perception of the works under consideration. In looking at two works together, or at two aspects of a single work, you see what each lacks as well as what each possesses. In comparing two plays, you might notice, for example, that one is written in verse whereas the other is not; that in one the action is external whereas in the other it is internal; or that the situations, characters, imagery, or structures of the plays differ in significant and interesting ways. Such comparative observations will lead you to ask why those differences exist and why the writers developed their dramas as they did.

When writing comparative papers, keep the following guidelines in mind:

1. Compare two aspects of a play that will reward your effort. By attending carefully to a play's details, you will often find significant parallels and contrasts. Follow the leads the works provide.

2. Compare works that have a significant feature in common, such as authorship, style, subject, situation, or an aspect of technique. For example: the treatment of women in two modern plays; the effects of mistaken identity in *The Doctor in Spite of Himself* and *The Rising of the Moon;* versions of the one-act play among the works of Strindberg, Yeats, Synge, Ionesco, Glaspell, and Lady Gregory.

3. Make a point. Use comparison and contrast to support an idea, an argument, an interpretation. Your comparative analysis should lead to a conclusion, perhaps to an evaluation, not merely to a set of parallels. Your comparative and contrastive observations are important, but you must go beyond them to make connections, draw inferences, and reach conclusions, however provisional they might be.

4. Decide whether to organize your comparative discussion according to the *block* method—in which you discuss each subject separately—or according to the *alternating* method—in which you discuss the central ideas in point-by-point comparisons of specific characteristics. For example, if you are comparing speeches of two characters according to the block method, you would devote the first half of your paper to one and the second half to the other. If you use the alternating method, you consider each speech side by side, focusing on such features as their diction, imagery, implied attitude, and ideas—as these aspects reveal the characters' states of mind.

Suggestions for Writing About Drama

1. Write a paper in which you recount your experience of reading a particular play or series of plays by the same author.
2. Write a paper comparing your experience in reading a play with your experience in witnessing a live performance of it.

3. Discuss your changing perception or understanding of a particular play. Indicate how you felt about the play initially and what made you change your way of responding to it.

4. Relate the action or situation of a play to your own experience. Explain how the play is relevant to your situation, and comment on how reading and thinking about it may have helped you view your circumstances and experience more clearly.

5. Compare reading a play with watching a film of a performance or a film based on a play. For a filmed performance of a play, consider watching a VHS recording of *Macbeth*. For a film based on a play, consider the movie version of *A Raisin in the Sun*.

6. Describe and characterize a single character from any play. Present a sketch of this character by referring to the language of his or her speeches and to the playwright's use of costume and stage directions.

7. Analyze a character at the moment of making an important decision. Identify the situation, explain the reasons for the character's decision, and speculate about the possible consequences. Some possibilities: Dr. Stockmann in *An Enemy of the People*; Antigonê in *Antigonê*; Mama in *A Raisin in the Sun*; the Sergeant in *The Rising of the Moon*.

8. Explicate the opening dialogue of any play. Explain the significance of this opening section in setting the play's tone, establishing its thematic preoccupations, preparing us for what follows—or whatever you think it accomplishes.

9. Select two or three brief passages from a play, passages that appear to be significant in their implications. They may be stage directions or dialogue. Establish the connections between one passage and the others, and explain their cumulative and collective significance.

10. Explicate the closing dialogue of any play. Explain the significance of this ending, commenting on its appropriateness as a conclusion.

11. Analyze the imagery of a play. Consider how particular kinds of imagistic language serve to advance the play's theme(s) or to reveal its characters. Some possibilities: images of poison and disease in *An Enemy of the People*; political and natural

images in *Antigonê;* clothes imagery in *Macbeth;* images of dream and illusion in *The Glass Menagerie.*

12. Analyze the ironic dimensions of any play. Consider how the playwright uses irony in the plot, dialogue, and/or setting. Some possibilities: *Antigonê, Macbeth, The Doctor in Spite of Himself, An Enemy of the People, Trifles.*

13. Explain the symbolic implications of any props used in a play. Consider the dramatic functions of the objects and their symbolic resonance. Some possibilities: Laura's glass animal collection in *The Glass Menagerie;* Dr. Stockmann's lab report in *An Enemy of the People;* the dagger in *Macbeth;* the barrel and song sheets in *The Rising of the Moon.*

14. Analyze the structure of any play. Consider its major parts or sections—its acts and scenes. Explain what each contributes to the whole and how the parts fit together into a unified whole.

15. Analyze the plot of a play. Comment on the way it illustrates or deviates from the classic plot structure (see pages 26–30).

16. Analyze the setting of a play. Consider both time and place. Consider also small-scale aspects of setting, such as whether the action occurs indoors or out. Attend to the descriptive details that render the setting. Notice whether the setting changes or whether the action occurs in one place and time. What does the setting contribute to the play?

17. Analyze a character from any play. Evaluate the character, offering reasons and evidence for your view. Consider what the character does, says, does not do or say—and why. Consider also what other characters say about him or her, and how they respond in action. Consider whether the character changes during the course of the play and what that possible change (or lack thereof) may signify.

18. Discuss any two-character relationship. Consider how the characters affect each other. Explain the nature of their relationship, and speculate on its probable future.

19. Evaluate a play from the point of view of its merit or excellence—or lack thereof. Explain why you consider it to be a successful or unsuccessful play.

20. Do a comparative evaluation of the merit of any two plays.

Explain what they share, how they differ, and why one is more impressive or effective than the other.

21. Discuss the values exemplified in any play. Identify those values, relate them to your own, and comment on their significance.

22. Write a review of the performance of a play. Consider especially the aspects of staging: lighting, costumes, set design, sound effects, and so on.

23. Write a review of a play's performance concentrating on the acting. Consider how well the actors and actresses delivered their lines, how well they meshed and harmonized, and how well they communicated emotions and ideas.

24. Write a review of a film based on a play. Concentrate on the elements of drama it displays.

25. Develop an alternative ending for any play, changing the outcome in whatever way you deem appropriate. Be prepared to defend your alternative ending as a reasonable possibility. Consider why the author chose to end the play as he or she did.

26. Try your hand at writing a scene from a play. Invent a scenario, create a couple of characters, and start them talking.

27. Read a few letters or essays written by a dramatist. Consider what light they shed on your reading of his or her play or plays.

28. Read a full-scale biography of a dramatist. Write a paper explaining how the author's life is or is not reflected in his or her work.

29. Discuss how a particular playwright reflects or rebels against important social, political, moral, or cultural issues of his or her time.

30. Read a critical study of a writer's plays. Write a paper explaining how the study aided your understanding or enhanced your enjoyment of the plays.

GLOSSARY

analysis The act of examining the relationships among the various elements of a work.

antagonist A character or force against which a main character struggles.

aside Words spoken by an actor directly to the audience without being "heard" by the other actors onstage.

blank verse A line of poetry or prose in unrhymed iambic pentameter (with alternating unstressed and stressed syllables).

blocking The arrangement of actors on the stage. (Also called *grouping*.)

catastrophe The action at the end of a tragedy that initiates the denouement.

catharsis The purging of the feelings of pity and fear that, according to Aristotle, occur in the audience of tragic drama.

character An imaginary person that inhabits a literary work. Literary characters may be major or minor, flat or round, static or dynamic.

characterization The means by which playwrights present and reveal characters.

chorus A group of characters in Greek tragedy who comment on the action of a play without participating directly in its action. Their leader is the choragos.

climax The turning point of the action in the plot of the play or story. The climax represents the point of maximum tension in a play.

651

comedy   A type of drama in which the characters experience reversals of fortune, mostly for the better. In comedy things work out happily in the end. Comic drama may be either romantic—characterized by a tone of tolerance and geniality—or satiric. Satiric plays offer a darker vision of human nature, one that ridicules human folly.

comic relief   The use of a comic scene to interrupt a succession of intensely tragic dramatic moments. The comedy of a scene offering comic relief typically parallels the tragic action it interrupts.

complication   An intensification of the conflict in a play.

conflict   A struggle between opposing forces in a play, usually resolved by the end of the work.

convention   A customary feature of a play, such as the use of a chorus in Greek tragedy.

decor   The overall appearance of a play's setting, including its costumes, props, and furniture.

denouement   The resolution of the plot of a play.

deus ex machina   A god who resolves the entanglements of a play by supernatural intervention (literally, a god from the machine), or any artificial device used to resolve a play's plot.

dialogue   The conversation of characters in a play.

diction   The selection of words in a play.

dramatis personae   The characters or persons of the play.

explication   A line-by-line explanation of a written passage.

exposition   The first stage of a dramatic plot, in which necessary background information is provided.

falling action   The action following the climax, which moves toward the resolution of a play's plot.

flashback   An interruption of a work's chronology to describe or present an incident that occurred prior to the main time frame of the action.

foil   A character who contrasts and parallels the main character in a play.

foreshadowing Hints of what is to come in the action of a play.

fourth wall The imaginary wall of the box theater setting, supposedly removed to allow the audience to see the action.

genre A literary type or kind. For example, tragedy is one genre; comedy, another.

gesture The physical movement of a character during a play.

imagery The pattern of related comparisons—metaphors and similes—in the language of a play.

ironic vision A pervasiveness of irony throughout a playwright's work. (Also called an *ironic point of view*.)

irony A contrast or discrepancy between what is said and what is meant or between what happens and what is expected to happen. In *verbal irony*, characters say the opposite of what they mean. In *irony of circumstance*, or *irony of situation*, the opposite of what is expected happens. In *dramatic irony*, a character speaks in ignorance of a situation or event known to the audience or to other characters.

metaphor A comparison between essentially unlike things without a word such as *like* or *as* to initiate it.

monologue A speech by one character.

pathos A quality of a play's action that stimulates the audience to feel pity for a character.

plot The unified structure or arrangement of incidents in a play.

point of attack The point at which the playwright begins the action of the play.

props Articles or objects that appear onstage during a play.

protagonist The main character of a play.

recognition The point at which a character understands his or her situation as it really is.

resolution The sorting-out, or unraveling, of a plot at the end of a play. (Also called *denouement*.)

reversal The point at which the action of the plot turns in an unexpected direction for the protagonist.

rhetorical question A question to which an overt answer is not expected, but one that contains an implied answer.

rising action The period in a play during which incidents complicate the plot and build toward the climax.

romantic comedy A play with a gentle tone and a happy ending, intended solely for entertainment.

satire A play that criticizes human misconduct and ridicules vices, stupidities, and follies.

setting The time and place of a play's action.

simile A figure of speech involving a comparison between unlike things using *like*, *as*, or *as though* to initiate it.

soliloquy A speech in a play that represents a character's inner thoughts.

stage business The postures, gestures, movements, and facial expressions of actors and actresses onstage.

stage directions A playwright's descriptive or interpretive comments that provide information about the dialogue, setting, and action of a play.

staging The spectacle a play presents in performance, including the positions of actors and actresses onstage, the scenic background, the props and costumes, and the lighting and sound effects.

structure The design or form of a play or of a section (such as an act or a scene) of a play.

style The way a playwright chooses words, arranges them in speeches and lines of dialogue, and develops ideas and actions with description, imagery, and other literary techniques.

subject What a play is generally about; to be distinguished from plot and theme.

subplot A subsidiary or subordinate or parallel story in a play that coexists with the main plot.

symbol An object or action in a play that means more than itself; a symbol stands for something beyond itself.

tempo The pace, or rate of speed, at which a scene is acted.

theme   The idea of a play abstracted from its details of language and action, and stated as a generalization.

tone   The implied attitude of a playwright toward the subject and characters of a play.

tragedy   A type of drama in which the characters experience reversals of fortune, mostly for the worse. In tragedy, catastrophe and suffering await many of the characters, especially the hero and those related to him or her.

tragic flaw   A weakness or limitation of character resulting in the fall of the tragic hero.

tragic hero   A privileged, exalted character of high repute who, by virtue of a tragic flaw and fate, suffers a fall from glory into suffering and/or destruction.

tragicomedy   A type of play that contains elements of both tragedy and comedy.

unities   The idea established by Aristotle that a play should be limited to a specific time, place, and story. According to this idea, the events of the play's plot should occur within a twenty-four-hour period, should occur within a given geographical locale, and should tell a single story.

ABOUT THE AUTHOR

Robert DiYanni is Professor of English at Pace University, Pleasantville, where he is also Director of Interdisciplinary Studies. He received his B.A. from Rutgers and his Ph.D. from the City University of New York. He has published articles and reviews on various aspects of English and American literature and on rhetoric and composition. In addition to a pair of companion volumes to this book—*Reading Fiction* and *Reading Poetry*—Professor DiYanni has also edited a number of other textbooks, including *Literature: Reading Fiction, Poetry, Drama, and the Essay*; and *Modern American Poets: Their Voices and Visions*. He is currently working on a humanities text.